DREAMER OF
DUNE

DREAMER OF

DUNE

The Biography of Frank Herbert

Brian Herbert

TOR®

A TOM DOHERTY ASSOCIATES BOOK

NEW YORK

DREAMER OF DUNE: THE BIOGRAPHY OF FRANK HERBERT

Copyright © 2003 by Brian Herbert

Selections from the published and unpublished writings of Frank Herbert are
used with the permission of Herbert Limited Partnership.

Edited by Patrick LoBrutto

This book is printed on acid-free paper.

A Tor Book
Published by Tom Doherty Associates, LLC
175 Fifth Avenue
New York, NY 10010

www.tor.com

Tor® is a registered trademark of Tom Doherty Associates, LLC.

Library of Congress Cataloging-in-Publication Data

Herbert, Brian.
  Dreamer of Dune : the biography of Frank Herbert / Brian Herbert.—1st ed.
    p. cm.
  "A Tom Doherty Associates book."
  Includes bibliographical references (p. 537) and index.
  ISBN 0-765-30646-8 (acid-free paper)
  1. Herbert, Frank. 2. Authors, American—20th century—Biography.
3. Science fiction—Authorship. 4. Dune (Imaginary place). I. Title.

PS3558.E63 Z68   2003
813'.54—dc21
[B]
                                                          2002042951

First Edition: April 2003

Printed in the United States of America

0 9 8 7 6 5 4 3 2 1

With love and appreciation, this book is for my darling, Jan, who has given so much to me; for my mother, Beverly Stuart-Herbert, for her devotion and her sacrifices; and for my father, Frank Herbert, who did so much for my mother in her time of need. This book is also for my sister, Penny, her husband, Ron, and my brother, Bruce—and for Julie, Kim, Margaux, David, Byron, and Robert, the grandchildren of Frank and Beverly Herbert.

ACKNOWLEDGMENTS

✳

I AM grateful to many people and organizations who contributed to this biography, in particular to Audrey Alande, Susan Allison, Kevin J. Anderson, Peter Atkins, Helen Z. Ballew, Matt Bialer, Daniel and Vera Blanquie, Marcia Bromley, Charles N. Brown, California State University, Gary and Judy Blanquie, Pat and Kim Blanquie, Ron and Kathleen Blanquie, George Carlson, Barbara Castroni, Laurene Cayo, Hal and Jeanne Cook, Anna Cottle, Connie Delmore-Beals, Frank Dixon, Tom Doherty, Jennifer Duncan, Deloss (Si) Edwards, Patricia Elizabeth, Harlan Ellison, Erica M. Fitzroy, Alan Francescutti, E. J. and Morgan Gold, Frankie Goodwin-Richards, Robert Gottlieb, Lou Guzzo, Howard J. Hansen, Joanne Hansen, David Hartwell, Keith Hauer-Lowe, Beverly Herbert, Bruce Herbert, Eileen Herbert, Frank Herbert, Jr., Frank Herbert, Sr. (F.H.), Janet Herbert, Julie Herbert, Kimberly Herbert, La Rene Herbert, Louis Herbert, Margaux Herbert, Neda Herbert, Phyllis Herbert-Hart, Bart and Sheila Hrast, Darel Jenkins, Karen Jones-Wheeler, Mike and Margaret Kalton, Mary Alice Kier, King County Reference Center, Kitsap County Historical Society, Richard L. Kossen, Marie Landis-Edwards, Marguerite Landis-Forbes, Patricia Herbert Larson, Roy Larson, Hattie Mae Laxson, Lincoln High

School, Philip M. Lindsten, Pat LoBrutto, Dan Lodholm, Oak Lodholm, Sandra Macomber, Dave McCarthy, Thomas McCarthy, Byron Merritt, David Merritt, Robert Merritt, Penny Merritt, Ron Merritt, Rebecca Moesta-Anderson, Johnny Moore, James P. Morrison, Joe Muñoz, Mayme Semba Nishimura, Marilyn Niwao, Sharon O'Hara, Michael O'Leary, Oregonian Publishing Company, Ed and Jeannie Pechin, The Peninsula Historical Society, Sharon Perry, Roy Prosterman, Bill Ransom, Steve Reece, Ken and Ruth Rowntree, Violet (Peg) Rowntree, St. Joseph Hospital, Doug Sandau, *Santa Rosa Press Democrat*, Bill and Zee Scheyer, Seattle University, Theresa Shackelford, Bill Sides, Kathleen J. and Nicholas Sidjakov, Catherine Sidor, Sonoma County Library, Rosemary Stein, Paul Stevens, Stewart Intermediate School, Roscoe Stuart, Dick Swift, Clyde Taylor, Jack and Norma Vance, Helen C. Wan, Washington State Historical Society, Washington State Patrol, Phil H. Webber, Duane Wilkins, Maura Wogan.

Special appreciation is also due to Daniel J. H. Levack, who (with annotator Mark Willard) compiled a bibliography of Frank Herbert's writings, *Dune Master: A Frank Herbert Bibliography*. My mother and I provided them with assistance, as we submitted bibliographic information and the names of other people to be contacted. Their book contains summaries of published short stories and books, which aided me in analyzing the themes in the writings of my father. Other books which are useful in addressing these themes are *Frank Herbert* and *The Maker of Dune*, both by Timothy O'Reilly, and *Frank Herbert*, by William Touponce.

I have referred to the critical analyses of these writers in my father's biography, and have added my own insights to theirs. In my work I have also included an analysis of many heretofore unknown and unpublished stories and poems written by Frank Herbert. The works of Levack/Willard, O'Reilly and Touponce include very sketchy biographical information, some of which was useful to me in the assembly of this more extensive biography. Special credit is also due to Ed Naha for *The Making of Dune* (a behind-the-scenes book about the *Dune* movie) and to the army of newspaper and magazine reporters who interviewed and wrote about my illustrious father.

Lastly, I wish to thank Sister M. Jeanne of the Saint Leo Convent in Tacoma, who led twenty nuns in prayers for my mother.

CONTENTS

*

INTRODUCTION

✳

"How do we approach the study of Muad'Dib's father?"

—Frank Herbert, in *Dune*

JOSEPH CAMPBELL said the search for one's father is a major hero quest, equivalent to Telemachus seeking Odysseus. Frank Herbert was not always a heroic figure to me, for I did not get along well with him in my childhood, and only grew close to him when we were both adults. My attempt to understand him became an odyssey that went on not only during his lifetime but afterward. It continues to this day, as I learn new things about him each time I read one of his stories, and each time I speak with someone who knew him and saw a different aspect of him than I did.

He was a man of many facets, of countless passageways that ran through an intricate mind. His life was not linear. It proceeded in fifty directions at once. He was a man of surprises. My father once said to me, with a twinkle in his eye, that he had trouble using dictionaries and encyclopedias, since he so often became distracted by information on the opposite page, and this slowed him down. He had a boyish curiosity about everything, and a remarkable memory for detail. *Dune* is a reflection of this, a *magnum opus* that stands as one of the most complex, multi-layered novels ever written.

So many questions come in from fans about my father. They want to know what he was working on late in his life, what his influence was on my writing, and more about his relationship with my mother. There are even current letters addressed to him, since they see wide arrays of his books in stores and think he's alive. In a very real sense he is still with us, of course—in the magnificent literary legacy he left for his readers.

He had a fascinating, phenomenal career, and this stands out above all else: He could not have done it without my mother, who sacrificed her own career as a creative writer in order to work and support our family during difficult times. I know there can be no greater love story than that of my remarkable parents. They trapped time and kept it for themselves in brilliant little time-gems, cosmic and eternal. Frank and Beverly Herbert were significant and interesting people, rare in their abilities to leave lasting memories upon everyone coming in contact with them.

I was one of those people.

Brian Herbert
Seattle, Washington

BOOK I

CHAPTER

1

✳ Adventures in Darkest Africa ✳

FRANK HERBERT'S paternal grandfather, Otto, was born in 1864
on a boat while coming to America from Bavaria with other immi-
grants. As a young man, Otto met Mary Ellen Stanley, an illiterate
Kentucky hill-woman. By the turn of the century the couple was living
in Cairo, Illinois, with five sons.* Otto worked as a solicitor for a steam
laundry there, and subsequently on the line in a bottling works. A
restless, energetic man, he began attending meetings sponsored by the
Social Democracy of America. This was a socialist group, founded and
led by Eugene V. Debs. The SDA had a plan to colonize certain Western states, including the state of Washington, in order to dominate the
politics of those regions. Eventually they hoped to alter the moral and
economic order of the entire country. But the colonization idea was
steeped in controversy, and socialist leaders, including Debs himself,
came to feel that it was not the most efficient utilization of people and
assets on behalf of the socialist cause. Political action in the cities and
mill towns would produce better results, they thought.

Still, Burley Colony in Washington State was founded in 1898 by
"the Co-operative Brotherhood," an SDA splinter group that pushed
forward with the colonization plan. Burley Colony was on Burley

---

*The surname—Herbert—was not adopted until Otto's parents entered the United States.
The original family name has been lost.

Lagoon at the head of Henderson Bay, just north of Tacoma. This was a shallow lagoon where whales were sometimes trapped when the tide went out.

The colonists were idealistic, advocating universal brotherhood, equal pay for all jobs and equal rights for women. They had mottoes like "Make way for brotherhood, make way for man" and "Do your best and be kind." They liked to say "ours" instead of "mine," and "we" instead of "I." Each colonist received broad medical insurance.

At its zenith, Burley was headquarters for an organization having 1,200 members all over the world—only a minority of whom actually lived in the commune. There were affiliated "Temples of the Knights of Brotherhood" all over the United States, including facilities in Seattle, Tacoma, Fairhaven (Washington), Portland (Oregon), San Francisco, Reno and Chicago. Contributions came in from powerful social organizations in Chicago, New York City and Rochester.

It was a short-lived colony, an experiment in socialist utopia that would last only a decade and a half. But at its height, the colony had a large church, community hall, library, schoolhouse, post office, sawmill, shingle mill, hotel and dining hall, general store, blacksmith's shop, dairy, laundry, and many other mercantile businesses. They printed a socialist newspaper and colony currency, in the form of coupons good for purchases at commune businesses. They had factories for the preserving of catsup and pickles, and a cigar factory—the largest in Washington State. The cigar factory produced Marine Cigars, selling for three to six cents apiece. They were excellent and popular, made of fine Kentucky burley tobacco, imported to the colony. Hence the colony's name: Burley. Cigar boxes and labels were produced locally as well.

Today the town of Burley, with only a few houses, a general store, a community hall and a post office, is but a shadow of its former self. Most of the buildings, including the mills, the hotel, and the cigar factory, are long gone. Many houses, built without concrete foundations, have decayed into the ground.

In 1905, Otto and Mary, now with six sons, and Otto's younger brother, Frank, took a train from Illinois across the Great Northern route to Washington State and thence through recently opened Stampede Pass to Tacoma. From Tacoma it was a short steamboat ride across the narrows to Gig Harbor, followed by a six-mile trip by horse-drawn stage to the colony through thick virgin forests. Otto and his brother each took a small government land grant just outside of Burley and set about making themselves part of the community. With his brother's assistance, Otto built a two-story log house, and ultimately the Herberts bought property inside Burley itself—land that curved around the lagoon.

Burley, called "Circle City" by locals because of the arrangement of buildings in a half-circle around an artesian well, had undergone a dramatic economic change shortly before the arrival of the Herberts. Through an amendment to the articles of incorporation of the colony, private ownership of land and industry was permitted. The Brotherhood remained in control, with profits going in equal shares to members. But this was no longer the socialist utopia originally envisioned by its founders. It was a curious amalgam of socialism and capitalism, and would last only eight more years before falling apart entirely.

But even with the departure of the Brotherhood in 1913, a community remained, with many former co-op members staying in the area. The land of this valley was dark and fertile, excellent for farming. Other former co-op members logged, operated dairies and raised poultry. For many years Burley remained the center of intellectual and social activity for the county.

There were three Frank Herberts in my family. The first, Otto's brother, eventually gave up his land near Burley and went on the circus and vaudeville circuit as "Professor Herbert," becoming a well-known performer of strongman feats, gymnastics and daredevil acts. The next Frank Herbert, known as "F. H." in ensuing years, was Otto's third son, born in December, 1893, in Ballard County, Kentucky. F. H. in turn had a son, Frank Jr., who would become my father and one of the world's best-known authors.

In Burley, Otto, Mary and their children prospered and increased family real estate holdings. For many years Otto operated a general store, "Herbert's Store." The establishment carried, in the words of an old-timer, "everything from tires to toothpicks." It had hay, grain, cowfeed, chickenfeed, clothing, medicines, dishes, hardware and most everything else imaginable, piled high to the ceiling. It was not a "green grocery," as it sold no fresh produce. The locals grew their own vegetables and fruit, and canned them. Credit slips hung on the wall behind the cash register.

Otto's sons worked with him in the store, and when they grew up they formed "Herbert Brothers," which operated the family store, a gas station, an auto and electrical repair shop, a stage line, and a logging business.

A stern, stocky little man, Otto was the undisputed ruler of his household. He named all six of his sons, and it is said that he did so without input from Mary. The boys were raised with stern "German discipline," as my father called it later, the same sort of attention he would in turn receive from his father.

✳   ✳   ✳

At 7:30 in the morning on October 8, 1920, Frank Herbert, Jr., was born at St. Joseph Hospital in Tacoma. It was his mother's nineteenth birthday, and he would often joke in later years that he never forgot her birthday.

F. H. and his wife, Eileen, were living in Tacoma at the time of their son's birth, but at every opportunity they visited Burley and the extended family there. Fond memories were formed in this little town on a lagoon, and these halcyon times would have a lasting impact upon young Frank Herbert. At the time of Frank's birth, his father was operating an auto-bus line between Tacoma and Aberdeen to the south—an offshoot of the family's successful stage line that ran between Burley and Gig Harbor.

The business became unprofitable, however, and by 1923 F. H. was working in Tacoma as an electrical equipment salesman. A stint as an automobile salesman followed. Then he became a motorcycle patrolman for the recently created Washington State Patrol. He had the "Mount Rainier beat," from East Pierce County to the base of the mountain. He was paid $30 a week.

By 1925, family trips to Burley became easier. A modern car ferry transported them from Tacoma to Gig Harbor, and from there they drove to Burley on a fine new highway for motor vehicles.

Frank's mother, Eileen Marie (Babe) Herbert, was a McCarthy. She was one of thirteen children, most of whom were girls. "They were beautiful red-haired Irish colleens," my father would tell me many years later. Babe's grandfather, the eldest son of an eldest son, was in a direct Irish royal line of succession that could have given him Blarney Castle in County Cork, which they called "Castle McCarthy."

But under British rule, such a lineage became meaningless to Babe's great-grandfather. He was an Irish Catholic rebel, operating in County Cork and elsewhere in the mid-nineteenth century. The rebels made an attempt to overthrow British rule, but police action crushed the insurrection. The McCarthys fled their homes in Ireland, just ahead of pursuing British authorities. The family went to Canada, and then to Wisconsin in the United States, where Babe was born. Her father, John A. McCarthy, was a mining engineer.

In *The White Plague*, a novel published by my father many years later, he wrote about one of the stories his maternal grandfather, John A. McCarthy, used to tell at the dinner table. Here is the passage from the book, with actual names substituted for fictional ones:

> "All of this for seven hundred rifles!"
>
> That had been the McCarthy family plaint during the poor times. (Frank) had never lost the memory of Grampa (John's) voice regretting the flight from Ireland. It was a story told and retold until it could be called up in total recall . . . The McCarthy silver, buried to keep it from piratical English tax collectors, had been dug up to finance the purchase of seven hundred rifles for a Rising. In the aftermath of defeat, Grampa (John's) father, a price on his head, had spirited the family to (Canada) under an assumed name. They had not resumed the McCarthy name until they were safely into the United States, well away from the thieving British.

Frank Herbert's earliest memory went back to 1921, when he was around a year old. He was at his Grandmother Mary's house in Burley, and he recalled walking straight under a wooden dining room table covered with a white tablecloth.

In May 1923, at the age of two and a half, he was attacked by a vicious malamute dog, an assault that nearly blinded him and left him with a lifetime scar over his right eye, just above the lid and extending into the eyebrow. His life was saved only because the dog knocked him beyond the reach of its chain. The terrifying image of the malamute's ferocious mouth, filled with sharp teeth, remained with my father for the rest of his life, and he had difficulty overcoming an acute fear of aggressive dogs.

When Frank was five, his Uncle Ade (Adrian) McCarthy, who was a hunter, gave him a beagle puppy, which Dad took an instant liking to and named "Bub." It was not a large dog, certainly not ferocious, and his uncle told him it would help in the hunting of rabbits one day when the boy was big enough to handle a rifle.

On a Tacoma beach one day, Dad and his father were digging clams.* Bub put his face down by a hole, and a clam spat stinging saltwater in his eye. The dog yelped, and in a frenzy dug the offender out of the sand. Thereafter Bub always growled at spitting clams and dug them up for the boy. Young Frank thought it uproariously funny. For years he referred to Bub as "the dog who hated clams," and eventually wrote about him in *Chapterhouse: Dune.*

My father had an early fascination with books, and could read much of the newspaper before he was five. He learned everything around him quickly, had an excellent memory and a long attention span. His number skills came to him early, and he loved puzzles.

Everything interested him. At the age of ten, he saved enough money to buy a Kodak box camera with a flash attachment. He began taking pictures of family events that often involved hiking, sailing, or fishing. In his early teens he purchased one of the "newfangled" folding cameras, and shortly after color film was introduced in the mid-1930s he purchased a miniature camera and began developing his own film. He set up a darkroom in the basement of his parents' home. Photography would remain a lifelong love for him.

He was without question a gifted child. When a school tested his

---

*This time they were using shovels. On other occasions, young Frank dug for geoducks—large, burrowing clams—with a crowbar, which he could use to get under the creature more quickly and pop it out of the sand.

IQ, he claimed it was one hundred and ninety, well into the genius range. He would often say in later years, however, that IQ tests were not accurate in measuring intelligence. They were, in his opinion, heavily weighted toward language skills.

Frank Herbert often spoke with fondness of the extended family in which he lived as a child, of time spent at the homes of aunts, uncles and grandparents in Tacoma and Burley. His father had four brothers living in the area, and his mother had eight sisters and two brothers nearby. So young Frank had many cousins with whom he could play, and if he happened to be over at a relative's house at dinner time the aunt or uncle would phone home and say young Frank was staying for the meal, and often that he was going to spend the night.

His Irish Catholic maternal aunts, who attempted to force religion on him, became the models for the Bene Gesserit Sisterhood of *Dune*. It is no accident that the pronunciations of "Gesserit" and "Jesuit" are similar, as he envisioned his maternal aunts and the Bene Gesserit of *Dune* as female Jesuits. The attempted brainwashing by his aunts, as he later termed it, was performed over the protestations of F. H., who was an agnostic. Before giving up the fight, F. H. had many arguments with Babe over this. In the end, the boy's religious beliefs became more like those of his father's than those of any other adult he knew.

It would be impossible, perhaps, to categorize Frank Herbert's religious beliefs. He ascribed to no single organized belief system, but instead drew from many. He was attracted to Zen Buddhism in particular, as can be seen in his classic novel, *Dune*, where there are wordless truths and "Zensunni" and "Zensufi" belief systems. Though he would not study Zen in detail until he met Alan Watts in the 1960s, he was exposed to it in his childhood. For a time, he had Nisei friends, second-generation Japanese who were born and educated in the United States. Some of them held Zen Buddhist beliefs.

He also knew Coast Salish Indians, and would come to know and respect their religious beliefs. This world view would become central to his only non–science fiction novel, *Soul Catcher* (1972).

At a time before television, the children, particularly Frank, became adept at imagining adventures and frightening tales. In the evening around the fire at scout camp, everyone came to count on young Frank to come up with a scary story. Typically a boy or a counselor would call out a blood and guts idea, such as "blood in the well" or "a screaming eyeball from hell," and my father would fill in details to create a story around it. He never failed to entertain. In darkened bedrooms with his cousins, where mattresses and sleeping bags were thrown on the floor, he would do the same. His stories were filled with fright, adventure, voice alterations and sound effects, and frequently involved ghosts, the old West, and the sea.

In 1928, while still on the state patrol, F. H. moved his family to Burley, where they maintained a small subsistence farm for the production of family foodstuffs, with a cow, chickens, and pigs. Bub, "the dog who hated clams," accompanied them. They had a large vegetable garden, with corn, peas, beans, carrots, lettuce and other crops. Young Frank, now seven, had chores to do, and he accepted responsibility for them. Regularly rising in the frosty time before dawn, he milked the cow, collected eggs and fed the pigs. Sometimes the farm animals were treated as pets, and the boy named them. He stopped doing that, however, when a favored chicken ended up on the chopping block.

"Never name your dinner," his mother told him one day.

He was in the 4-H club, and participated in a number of county fairs held in Burley. In one 4-H project, he raised and canned five hundred chickens by himself.

Children in town didn't have to go to school on their birthdays. In October 1928, on the morning of his eighth birthday, Frank Herbert went downstairs to a breakfast of sourdough flapjacks and real maple syrup, favorites of his that had been prepared specially for him by his mother and paternal grandmother. After the breakfast dishes were cleared away, he climbed on top of the table and announced to his family, in a very determined tone, "I wanna be *a* author."

That morning he wrote his first short story, entitled "Adventures in Darkest Africa," which he read to his family. Crayon drawings accompanied it. A jungle tale that began with a pretty good narrative hook to get the reader's interest, it involved an interesting character who had to surmount obstacles and find his way back to camp. The jungle, though described with childish inaccuracy, was nonetheless a threatening, problem-filled environment. Young Frank had been on a number of hunting and camping trips with his father and uncles in the forests of Washington State, and this story was an extrapolation, based upon what he had learned about not getting lost in the woods. He had never been to Africa, except in imagination.

Being the son of a police officer, he had heard adventurous tales of law enforcement. These were frequent topics of conversation at the dinner table, especially when police friends came to visit. The adults told of the time Babe helped arrest a drunken soldier, and of speakeasy raids she went on with F. H. One time an arrested man committed suicide in front of F. H. There were wanted criminals, fugitive chases and police manhunts.

Such material found its way into Frank Herbert's early stories. Soon he was using soft-lead pencils to scrawl his stories on lined sheets of newsprint and in notebooks, illustrating many of them in crayon. He misspelled a number of words rather badly, and his handwriting wasn't too steady, but the tales and drawings were colorful and imaginative.

With steady work, his stories improved, and he had them piled all over his room. His mother, obsessed with keeping order in a small wood-frame house, was forever making neat piles. In a safe place, she put away stories and drawings that she particularly liked, and kept them for the rest of her life.

From an early age Frank Herbert was fastidious about his teeth, spending as much as fifteen minutes at a time brushing them. In his entire lifetime he never had one cavity, and his teeth were so perfect that dentists marveled upon seeing them.

His father, F. H., was an expert fly fisherman and a knowledgeable all-around outdoors man. Frequently he took his son on trips into the woods, out in small boats or clamming on the beaches of Henderson Bay. Young Frank especially liked to fish in Burley Creek, which was loaded with brook trout. In the fall, salmon were so plentiful that they could be caught with bare hands. There were many smokehouses in the area, some dating back to the days of Burley Colony. It was a picturesque creek, winding through a forest of cedar, alder and maple and falling across a sequence of rocky benches . . . emptying ultimately into Burley Lagoon. Often the boy went out on the salt water of Puget Sound and fished from a rowboat.

On some fishing trips with his best friend, Dan Lodholm, they rode bicycles to nearby lakes, where they fished for bass, using an unusual method taught to them by their elders. A fake mouse was secured to the fishing line, and with a short cast this mouse was plopped onto the top of a lily pad. Bass could be seen swimming under the lily pads, and when one came close, the boy would pull the line a little, toppling the mouse into the water.

Every time Frank went fishing he tossed a book in his Boy Scout pack, which he carried with him everywhere. He loved to read Rover Boys adventures, as well as the stories of H. G. Wells, Jules Verne and the science fiction of Edgar Rice Burroughs. His maternal grandfather, John McCarthy, after observing that the boy was always reading, said of him, "It's frightening. A kid that small shouldn't be so smart." The boy was not unlike Alia in *Dune*, a person having adult comprehension in a child's body, with childlike emotions.

These were formative days for my father, when the seeds of literary ideas were germinating. Throughout his career as a writer, he would continually call upon boyhood experiences.

✳ ✳ ✳

In the late 1920s, Burley was a place where gossip traveled fast. "It was a curtain-twitching town," my father would recall. "Someone looked out every time you passed a window." A colorful local, Logger Bill Nerbonne, and F. H. frequently took young Frank on hunting and camping trips. The boy's uncles, maternal and paternal, also took him hunting, particularly Uncle Ade McCarthy (one of Babe's brothers) and Uncle Marley Herbert (one of F. H.'s brothers).

One afternoon F. H. and another of young Frank's uncles, Jack Mc-Carthy, staged a convincing fight in a ditch in the middle of Burley. The whole town came to watch as the men wrestled, tore their shirts and threw fists. The fight went on for the better part of an hour, and matched any seen in Hollywood annals, with theatrics but no real injuries. Presently, F. H. and Jack put their arms around one another, tucked in their tattered shirts and walked off, saying, "That'll give 'em something to talk about."

After that, several people in town refused to speak to the Herberts or McCarthys ever again.

✳ ✳ ✳

F. H. and Babe were on-again, off-again alcoholics during my father's childhood, consuming large quantities of whiskey. When his parents were on binges, the boy was too ashamed and embarrassed to bring his friends home. So he spent much of his time away from the house, fishing, hunting and hiking. To a large degree he grew up on his own and became independent at an early age. Young Frank became something of a provider for the family, as he brought home trout, salmon, crabs, clams, rabbits and grouse for the supper table. His mother, though she had a problem with alcohol, was a wonderful cook.

Above all outdoor pursuits, Frank was a fisherman. When he didn't have to go to school he was often up before dawn, and off he would go with his fishing gear to a favored spot or to a new one he hadn't yet tried. Sometimes he took his gear to school, so that he wouldn't have to go directly home after classes. He smoked much of the salmon he caught, and took it to school for lunch, along with fruits, vegetables and hard-boiled eggs from the family farm.

The young man, despite his time spent outdoors, didn't tan readily, and his skin was pale. Some adults were concerned about his health. He had one bout with pneumonia, but overall was a tough, wiry kid, with tremendous arm and leg strength. These physical attributes made him a powerful swimmer at an early age.

In 1929, the Washington State Patrol assigned F. H. to the highway between Gig Harbor and Bremerton. A big Harley Davidson motorcycle was a common sight parked in front of the Herbert house. In those days, patrolmen wore forest-green uniforms with black pocket flaps and black trouser stripes. The hats were military-cap style, and the men wore puffy fascist trousers and high black boots. F. H. was quite a daredevil. Sometimes he turned off his motorcycle lights at night and roared up behind speeding cars, then flashed on his lights and pulled them over.

F. H. also took his son into the backcountry with camping and hunting gear on the Harley, a practice that would never be permitted today.

25

F. H. wore a Sam Browne Belt with a .38 caliber Colt "Police Positive" revolver holstered to it, and the boy sat behind him, holding onto the back of the wide belt. On one occasion they went to Sunrise Lake, up a long dirt road. They stopped to make camp, and as F. H. was setting the kickstand of his bike, he spied a blue grouse seated on a low pine bough.

With a fluid movement he drew the big Colt revolver, took aim and fired. The grouse was peppered with pine needles, but did not move. In a frenzy, F. H. emptied his revolver at the bird, missing every shot. The bird stared back at him. Frustrated, F. H. reloaded and moved closer. He fired again, but only knocked the branch out from under the bird. It flew away, eluding another hail of bullets.

Eventually F. H. became quite a marksman, moving up to captain of the patrol's drill team. A banquet was held in the state capitol at Olympia one year, at which he was slated to receive a distinguished conduct award. Frank attended, and just before his father went on, he told the master of ceremonies about the grouse. When the emcee introduced F. H., the boy took the stage and recounted the embarrassing story, breaking the audience up.

From the time when he was eight years old, young Frank went out spotlighting for deer with his paternal uncles Marley and Louis. The men had a spotlight (built at the Herbert Brothers shop) that was a swiveling car headlight hooked onto a six-volt car battery. When a deer was located, the boy flipped on the light and pointed it at the deer, causing the animal to freeze, staring into the light. Then Marley or Louis would fire their rifles. My father would recall later that there was no sport to it. They just went out and got meat for the family.

On one daylight hunting trip with Uncle Marley, Marley suddenly stopped and pointed. Frank looked, and saw a big buck with its forepaws on a tree. Marley didn't say a word or make a sound. He just passed the rifle to the boy and wagged his finger at the buck. Frank took careful aim and pulled the trigger. He hit the deer square in the chest, and it fell.

Grandpa Otto had the biggest gun in the family, an eight-gauge shotgun brought over from Germany. A muzzleloader, it had been built by an independent craftsman under the old apprenticeship system, and was such a powerful, dangerous weapon that guns of its gauge would be outlawed a decade later in the United States. One day, Grandpa Otto said Frank could fire the gun, and told him to shoot at an old rotten tree trunk. The boy understood the physics of recoil even at an early age, and was afraid to put the gun against his shoulder. So he jammed the butt of the weapon against a sapling, aimed and pulled the trigger. The roar was deafening. He blew a "hell of a big hole" in the rotten tree, and cracked the sapling with the recoil of the butt!

On other trips, Frank learned from Logger Bill that it took less energy to step over a log than on it. I, in turn, would learn this lesson from my father many years later. On one hunting trip with Logger Bill and Uncle Marley, however, an exception to the rule presented itself. Logger Bill stepped over a log onto the back of a sleeping six-point buck. The deer jumped and sent poor Logger Bill flying, with his gun coming out of his grasp.

Some of Dad's trips into the woods were with his Uncle Ade Mc-Carthy, who, along with his brother Jack, had a secret spot where they dug for crystals and loaded them into knapsacks. The men had a thriving mail-order business selling crystals for crystal radios and other uses. His uncles were also involved in oyster farming, where young Frank learned to skin dive. In these and other ventures he earned money to buy school clothes.

When he was in his teens, he converted a rifle into a shotgun for bird hunting. He remained an avid hunter throughout most of his adulthood. Late in his life, however, he would develop the opinion that hunting was one of the myths of mankind—the myth that a man could hunt for all the meat his family needed. This was linked, in his view, to the larger myth of complete self-sufficiency—that a modern family could live entirely off the land, completely independent of stores, power companies and money.

CHAPTER
2

✳ The Spanish Castle ✳

ON FRANK Herbert's ninth birthday, only three weeks before the stock market crash of October 29, 1929, Logger Bill Nerbonne gave him a superb cedar rowboat he had made himself. With oak framing and spruce oars, it was nine feet long—one foot for each of the boy's years. It rowed easily, and became a constant source of joy for the young man.

Christmas that year would be bleak for many families, as the nation reeled in the throes of economic collapse. Burley, with its many small subsistence farms, was something of an oasis from such troubles, and F. H.'s household was further insulated by the secure job he held with the state patrol.

An adventurer, Frank was in the habit of taking his tiny rowboat on long trips, too far for a child of his age. In the summer of 1930, he made a solo trip from Burley all the way up Puget Sound to the San Juan Islands . . . a round-trip distance of more than two hundred miles. He accomplished a large portion of this trip by rowing out into the shipping lanes and waiting for a tugboat pulling a barge, going in the direction he wanted to go. When the barge came near, he rowed at a furious pace and hitched himself onto it, often without being seen by the tugboat operator. Sometimes he was caught and cut loose. Other times the tugboat operators let him stay, and even slowed down so that he could hitch-on or unhitch more easily. The boy came to know the schedules and routes of the barges so well that he was a regular, if non-paying, customer. He also made shorter trips by boat to the small town of Longbranch on the Key Peninsula, around sixteen miles each way.

When he was ten, my father took his rowboat out in Puget Sound and was fishing for cutthroat trout. It was at Horsehead Bay, near Longbranch, and he lost track of time. At dusk he realized he couldn't get back in time to avoid a licking. Then he saw a fancy powerboat carrying people he knew, all of whom were whooping it up, having a merry time. Dad flagged them down, and they pulled alongside to assist. They tied his rowboat on and invited him aboard. After coming aboard, my father retied his boat properly, and saw that the adults were drunk out of their minds. Someone asked Frank to pilot the boat back to Henderson Bay, which he did easily. He knew the waters well. The only accident occurred when they reached the dock. One of the inebriates fell in the water while trying to tie up the boat.

In the spring of 1931, F. H. left his patrol duties and moved his little family to Highline, between Tacoma and Seattle. His ever-active mind was always coming up with money-making schemes, most of which didn't pan out. F. H., along with Babe and another couple, started a dance hall on old Highway 99 known as "The Spanish Castle." When construction began, my father ceremoniously turned the first spade of dirt. This was the Prohibition era and the fledgling business, a seventeen-thousand-square-foot speakeasy serving alcohol illegally, was successful from the start. Babe worked in the ticket booth, while F. H., an intelligent, mechanically inclined man, made certain the lighting and other systems operated efficiently.

F. H. worked on his own cars and maintained first-class personal shops wherever he lived. He was always coming up with inventions around the shop—tools and devices to make tasks easier. As money came in from dance-hall profits he purchased a Red Crown service station across the street, where he subsequently spent much of his time. Gasoline sold for fourteen cents a gallon. Red, white and blue banners were draped on either side of the fuel pump, and it had a glass top, so that you could check the purity of the mixture as it ran through the machine. F. H. had an auto repair shop around back. As an incentive to customers he offered free crankcase service.

29

Babe was a strong, earthy woman, though barely five feet tall. With informal training as a nurse, she even delivered babies on occasion. One story in particular says a lot about her and F. H., and about the times in which they lived. When F. H. was still on the State Patrol she went on speakeasy raids with him. While her husband and other officers raided the illegal establishments and arrested scofflaws, she waited in the backseat of the patrol car, wearing a big fur coat. "When we pulled out of there," Babe recalled years later, "I tinkled (with bottles) under my coat."

Young Frank often read past his bedtime, using a bare lightbulb on the end of an extension cord under his bedcovers, to prevent casting light under the door. The bulb often browned the sheets. He was safe from scolding, though, since now his family could afford to have their laundry done outside the house, and his mother always blamed the laundry company and their mangle.

But trouble was stirring between the dance-hall partners. During their first year of operation they got into a heated argument, in which my grandparents accused their partners of cheating them. In a huff, F. H. and Babe quit the business without compensation, then devoted their full attentions to the service station.

Over the next four decades the Spanish Castle became one of the most celebrated dance halls in the United States, visited by famous bands from all over—a situation that constantly rubbed salt into my grandparents' wounds.

Depressed when they saw what a huge mistake they had made, my grandparents began drinking more heavily than ever. This detracted from the operation of the service station, which was already struggling in the Great Depression. Soon the business went bankrupt and my grandparents lost everything. To make matters worse, Babe was pregnant. Without any source of income, F. H., Babe and Frank (now eleven) moved in with one of the McCarthy families in Tacoma. Frank—commonly called "Junior"*—shared a bedroom with two of his cousins, Thomas and Leonard McCarthy, and each night before

*For years, and ultimately into adulthood my father was referred to as "Junior" (Frank Herbert, Jr.) by family members who knew both Franks—a moniker the younger loathed.

they went to sleep regaled them with adventure stories. The boys became like brothers.

After six months, F. H. secured a job as a salesman. This enabled him to move the family to a beach home on Day Island, connected by a short bridge with the city of Tacoma. It was the spring of 1933. In May, Babe gave birth to a baby girl, Patricia Lou. After Dad's family moved to Tacoma, he visited Burley at every opportunity to see his grandparents and his old friend, Dan Lodholm.

Early one morning, just across the channel from Day Island, Frank was fishing but not doing well. It was near Fox Point on Fox Island, where much of the shoreline was densely forested. After a while he noticed a Native American man sitting on the shore, watching him intently. The man, in his late forties, motioned the boy over and showed him how to make a herring dodger, which subsequently worked very well. Over the next two years the man—Indian Henry—and my father became fast friends. Henry was a Hoh, one of the Coast Salish, and lived by himself in an old smokehouse. He semi-adopted Frank, teaching him many of the ways of his people.

This included how to catch fish with your feet, how to poach fish, and how to identify edible and medicinal plants in the forest. The Indian ate sweet red ants and found protein-rich grub worms under logs, which he also ate. The boy tasted ants and worms for the experience of it, but did not develop a taste for them! Henry also taught him how to catch a sea gull by laying a slip knot tied with fishing line on the ground and placing a piece of herring inside. When the bird stepped into the circle of line, the noose was tightened, thus securing one or both of the gull's legs. In *Soul Catcher* (1972), Frank Herbert would write of another hunting technique that he learned from Indian Henry:

Katsuk had taken the grouse from a giant hemlock near the pond. He had called it a roosting tree. The ground beneath it was white with grouse droppings. The grouse had come sleepily to the hemlock branches at dusk and Katsuk had snared one with a long pole and a string noose.

Though Indian Henry never admitted as much, his young Caucasian friend—tending toward the melodramatic—became convinced that he was a murderer who had been excommunicated from the tribe. The man hinted at something troublesome in his past, but the boy never obtained details and never felt at risk in his presence. Forty years later, Frank Herbert wrote about many of these experiences in his suspense-packed novel of Indian rage, *Soul Catcher*.

After learning how to fish in the Indian way, young Frank always brought back big bunches of fish. Finally a man who operated one of the general stores in Tacoma asked him how he did it. Naively, Frank showed him the dodger. After that, the man marketed identical dodgers, in such volume that he made a tidy sum.

To make extra money my father put a twelve-horsepower King outboard on his rowboat, and used it to tow logs back to shore, where they could be cut into firewood and sold. One day he found a 20'×20'×10' half-submerged container of fine Tennessee white oak, which he pulled in. Some of the wood was wormy, but the bulk of it was in good condition and of considerable value. By this time his family was on its economic feet again, so he got permission from his parents to barter the oak for a twenty-seven-foot sailboat that the owner didn't want, since it had a problem staying upright. By the time he was fifteen, Frank had the sailboat rebuilt and ballasted with concrete, which he poured into the hull. He took fourteen people out sailing once, including a guitarist, a clarinetist, and an accordionist. In those days, my father told me, they called an accordion a "squeeze-me-pull-me."

On sailing trips, young Frank Herbert liked to sleep out on the deck. Stars lined the roof of the sky over his head, and he memorized the names and locations of constellations and major stars. He learned to use a sextant for navigation.

When he was fourteen, he swam across the Tacoma Narrows, a mile through treacherous currents. A short while later, he and a seventeen-year-old friend, Ned Young, took a small Willits sailing canoe all the way to the fjords of the British Columbia mainland, just south of the Alaskan panhandle, a round trip of nearly two thousand miles. They turned the canoe over on beaches and slept under it. But when they got to the fjords there weren't any beaches, so an Indian woman let them sleep on the porch of her little house, and gave them breakfast.

Through learning of my father's experiences in the outdoors, I've gained an insight into the thought processes that went into his writing. His great "mainstream" novel *Soul Catcher*, about an Indian who could not accept the ways of white men, comes into clearer focus. He also wrote another Indian book, which was never published: *Circle Times*, a fictionalized but historically accurate account of the wars of the Coast Salish. My father admired the link between Native Americans and their environment, the way they lived for centuries in harmony with nature, not wreaking havoc upon it as the white man did. Frank Herbert developed a deep respect for the natural rhythms of nature. The ecology message, so prevalent in much of his writing, is one of his most important legacies.

There is also an interesting, recurrent water-and-ocean theme in his writings, from his submarine novel *The Dragon in the Sea* (1956) to the sand formations of *Dune* (1965) that resemble slow-moving waves upon a great ocean. He was a sailor, fisherman, and swimmer, and would serve in the U.S. Navy during World War II. He understood the critical importance of potable water to a backwoodsman, hiker and sailor. A tiny drop of water is the essence of all life.

One of my father's earliest short stories, "The Jonah and the Jap" (1946), concerns a seaplane that makes an emergency landing in the China Sea. In "Try to Remember!" (1961), aliens threatening Earth arrive in an immense spaceship that resembles a tiny freshwater organism with cilia. "The Mary Celeste Move" (1964) describes a phenomenon in which people abruptly leave their homes and move far away, often leaving their belongings behind—an idea based upon the mysterious sailing ship Mary Celeste, found floating in 1872 with its passengers and crew missing. "The Primitives" (1966) describes a man named Swimmer who is adept at underwater criminal activities. "The Mind Bomb" (1969) takes place in an oceanside town. "Seed Stock" (1970) concerns a world with a purple ocean, where the primary food source is a creature like a shrimp. "Songs of a Sentient Flute" (with Bill Ransom, 1979), like their collaborative novels *The Jesus Incident*

(1979) and *The Lazarus Effect* (1983), involve ocean worlds covered with vast, sentient kelp formations.

✳   ✳   ✳

As a young man, Frank Herbert was close to his grandmother, Mary Ellen Herbert. A kindly, thin woman with a long face and large round eyeglasses, she favored long dresses with flower prints, and usually wore an apron, even when away from home. Mary usually tied her gray hair in a bun, and it had a beautiful sheen from shampooing with secret ingredients. Some folks in Burley thought it was a concoction of beer and eggs, while others said it was whiskey and olive oil. Mary just laughed at all the guesses.

Though an illiterate country-woman, she was a genius with figures, and no matter how big the numbers were that anyone wanted her to add, subtract, multiply, or divide, she always got the answers right. She instilled a love of math in her favorite grandson, which he employed in his science fiction writings. She also had an incredible memory, and recalled details perfectly from decades before. Mary Herbert was, in effect, a human computer, and she became a model for the Mentats of *Dune.*

A renowned quilt maker, Grandma Herbert won so many awards at the big county fair in Burley that the fair committee finally banned her from competing. Nonetheless she continued to make quilts, and they were displayed prominently each year at the fair. Every quilt had an interesting story, something to do with the history of the Herbert family, which she related to young Frank. One year she sent a beautiful "Blue Eagle Quilt" to President Franklin Delano Roosevelt and his wife Eleanor, commemorating their wedding anniversary.

Beginning when Dad was around ten years old, he used to go over to Mary's house and read old family letters to her, which she kept in a trunk. Some of the letters were valuable, as they had eighteenth-century New England postmarks on them, even several rare Boston Post markings, so the boy handled them carefully. During moments of excitement, Grandma Herbert would lapse into Old English, a dialect spoken in her family for centuries. Sometime in the 1600s, her ancestors had immigrated to the hills of Kentucky and Tennessee, and in certain enclaves the old dialects were preserved and spoken. Upon hearing these strange words, the young Frank Herbert was fascinated. Ultimately he conducted extensive research into languages and dialects, information he used to great effect in *Dune* and other works.

My father remembered how Mary used to take out posters of his great-uncle Frank Herbert (Otto's younger brother), who had been the circus and vaudeville star Professor Herbert. She would fold open each poster carefully, saying, "This is your great-uncle Frank. You and your father were named for him."

Mary Herbert also had a red leather-bound genealogy book showing that our family was directly descended from Henry VIII, King of England, but "on the wrong side of the sheets." Henry used to frequent a public house run by a woman named Moll Golden, a place where he drank and sang. Moll had six illegitimate children, all presumably fathered by Henry. She was an exceptional singer, and it was said that she took on the name "Golden" because of her voice. Henry had his own musical talents, as he sang with her and played the lute. He may even have written the tune "Greensleeves" for her.

✳   ✳   ✳

Before the age of twelve, Frank, ever curious, read the complete works of Shakespeare and discovered the poetry of Ezra Pound. With these readings, the boy began to realize the potential of the English language. He fell in love with the sounds of words. In other literature he discovered Guy De Maupassant and Marcel Proust, and had what he called "love affairs" with them. He admired the styles of both, and was intrigued by De Maupassant's plotting techniques and Proust's powerful characterizations.

Something Ezra Pound once said remained with my father all his life, and was quoted frequently by him: "Make it new." To Dad, Pound was more than a poet. He was a nonconforming creative writer, and an ongoing inspiration.

In his early teens, Frank was for a time infatuated with the writings of Ernest Hemingway. Eventually, however, he came away with a sense that Hemingway's work was phony and filled with unnecessary brutality. Of all the writers my father read in his youth, he was perhaps most obviously influenced by Shakespeare. In *Dune*'s palaces, with their great banquet halls and dark passageways, one gets a very similar feeling to the castles in which Shakespeare's characters brooded and schemed and murdered. Treason and treachery permeate the writings of Shakespeare. When, in *Dune*, Frank Herbert wrote of "tricks within tricks within tricks" and "treachery within treachery within treachery," and "plans within plans within plans within plans," his language was reminiscent of Richard II (II, iii, 87): "Grace me no grace, nor uncle me no uncle . . ." Director David Lynch later picked up the Shakespearean mood in his 1984 movie adaptation of *Dune*.

Throughout his youth, Frank Herbert was a voracious reader, on every imaginable subject. At age eleven, he used to go alone to visit Dr. Jimmy Egan in Tacoma, their family practitioner. Frank was intrigued by his anatomy books, which the doctor let him peruse. Subsequently, Frank was able to tell his schoolmates how babies were conceived and born.

Whenever his schoolmates had a question about sex, someone invariably said, "Let's ask Herbert. He'll know."

But one little girl told her mother what was occurring. Enraged, the woman stormed over to Frank's house and confronted his mother, Babe. From the kitchen, the boy eavesdropped. The woman was so upset she could hardly speak. After getting the gist of what the woman was saying, Babe asked, calmly, "Well, did he misinform her?"

Sputtering, the woman said, "No, but . . . uh . . ."

"Then what are you complaining about?" Babe wanted to know.

It went on like this, with Babe defending her son, to the point where the woman could hardly get a word in edgewise. Exasperated, she finally gave up the effort and left.

By then, Frank was in the kitchen making a sandwich, and hardly looked up when his mother came in. Suddenly she grabbed him by the ear and whirled him around. "Explain yourself," she said.

At fourteen, Frank learned to type, and saved enough money to buy his own typewriter, a big, heavy old Remington. On it he hammered out his stories and a long, humorous poem describing Christmas and one of his father's jobs. He began copying the styles of writers he liked, such as Guy De Maupassant and Herman Melville, searching for his own style, something comfortable.

One day my father went for advice to a writer living in Tacoma who had sold a couple of novels and several short stories. The response: "Work like hell, kid."

CHAPTER

3

✳ Cub Reporter ✳

F. H. AND Babe disciplined their extremely active son erratically. At times they brought down a heavy hammer of authority on him, but on other occasions, especially when they were incapacitated by alcohol, it was exactly the opposite and they let him run free. For the most part he went wherever he pleased whenever he pleased.

As the years went by, F. H. and Babe drank more and more, to forget their business misadventures. Following a stint as a salesman, F. H. became a security guard for Northern Pacific Railroad, and after that, in 1935, a deputy sheriff for Pierce County, Washington. Many of his closest friends were on the police forces of various jurisdictions, including the State Highway Patrol where he had once worked. This did not curb the drinking.

In recalling the free-to-roam lifestyle of his childhood, my father described himself as having been a "punk kid." Perhaps he was, but if so, he retained redeeming qualities, and it was only one dimension of a complex, developing personality.

On a number of occasions, his lifestyle led him into dangerous activities, such as the long and perilous boat excursions he took, and hunting trips taken without adult supervision. Once he nearly drowned in a tricky current while swimming off a sandbar in Tacoma's Hylebos Waterway.

His school studies were always easy for him, and frequently he became bored in class. In elementary school he used to shoot spitballs at insects on the walls of the classroom, at his classmates, and at his fourth-grade teacher, Mrs. Pastor. While standing at the blackboard with her back to the class, she felt something wet hit the back of her neck.

No one told Mrs. Pastor who did it, not in so many words. But when she pulled the tiny wad of wet tissue off her neck and whirled around, all eyes turned toward the towheaded Frank, who sat in the middle of the class, near the front. She marched to his desk and plopped the spitball in front of him. A tall woman with thick glasses and her hair tied in a bun, she towered over him.

"So you're the one," she snapped, her face wrinkled in anger. "Stay after school, boy, and I'll deal with you."

I'm in for it, my father thought, as she returned to the blackboard. His mind filled with a thousand terrors, and for the rest of the day he could think of little else.

After school he sat at a little chair by her desk, looking up fearfully into the reflective glare of her glasses, searching for a way to calm her. She glared down at him, her face a glistening, explosive mask of fury.

"Why are you so mad at me?" Frank asked, his voice small and breaking.

"I'm not mad at you!" she bellowed. And she grabbed him by his shoulders and shook him violently, and shook him, and shook him, screaming all the while, "I'm not mad at you! I'm not mad at you!"

It was a bizarre scene, and years afterward, when he had time to reflect upon the event, he became aware of unconscious behavior. His teacher had been angry at him without knowing it herself. He would use this facet of psychology in his writings and in his life, with great success. He would watch what people were doing, not what they were saying.

When he was sixteen, he took the family Buick out on a date, with permission from his father. He had a girlfriend and two other couples in the car, and roared along Highway 99 outside Tacoma at more than eighty miles an hour. Presently, a state motorcycle cop pulled him over, got off his bike and walked to the driver's side.

"You!" the patrolman exclaimed, looking in the window. It was Bernie Rausch, a good friend of the family. Rausch often visited the

Herbert household at Dash Point, just north of Tacoma. He told Dad
to follow him, and with his motorcycle led the offender straight home.
While Frank waited in the car for what seemed like an eternity, Rausch
spoke at the doorway with F. H. Presently, the old man took the car
keys and told Frank to wait in the house. F. H. drove the friends home,
while Frank suffered, wondering what his punishment would be.

He didn't get a beating that time, but was grounded for two months
and prohibited from using the car. Extra chores were assigned too, and
the young man had to chop several cords of firewood.

✳　✳　✳

Frank Herbert's sister, Patricia Lou, almost thirteen years his junior,
became an increasing source of concern for him. Their parents were
on the brink of divorce, arguing constantly and drinking more than
ever. Too often she was neglected. The boy took care of her when he
could. On many occasions he bought baby food and other necessities
with his own odd-job earnings. He also purchased toys for her, or made
them of wood and whatever else he could find.

The family was living in South Tacoma at the time. He went to
nearby Stewart Intermediate School, graduating in June 1935, with a
grade point average of only 1.93. The following September, he enrolled
at Lincoln High School, only a few blocks from his home. He failed
Latin in his first semester, but on retaking the class in the spring of
1936 earned a B. Then in a subsequent attempt to take more advanced
Latin, during the spring of 1937, he dropped out of the class, receiving
no grade. The only other class he failed, also in the Spring 1937 semester, was Geometry. In other Geometry classes he received Cs each
time. In English, where he would one day write prose read by millions,
he had two Bs, a C, and a D. He received his only A in the Fall 1936
semester, in World History. His grade point average for the first two
and a half years was a meager 2.05.

When he began his senior year in the fall of 1937, he was behind in
the credits needed for graduation, so he took one extra class, and passed
everything, with slightly better than a C average. He took a journalism
class that semester, receiving a B. As part of this class, he was on the
staff of *The Lincoln News*, a high school newspaper that was run ac-

cording to professional standards by Homer Post, an ex-reporter and educational legend. The paper was a perennial national award winner.

Frank Herbert, who would later spend many years in the newspaper profession, was sixteen when he began the journalism class, and turned seventeen during it—an impressionable time of life in which to fall under the influence of a master. Earlier my father had been influenced by an ex-newspaperman living in Burley, Henry W. Stein, who regaled him with tales of life on a big-city newspaper.

Working out of the school news shack under Post's tutelage, Frank became a "general assignment news chaser," a reporter doing school and community stories. It was like a real newspaper, and he learned the importance of deadlines, how to copy-edit and how to find the most interesting angle on a story.

He often wore a blue serge suit, a light tan shirt and a tie to his classes—rather neat, though inexpensive, attire for high school. By all accounts Frank Herbert was well-liked on campus, a young man with a buoyant attitude and boundless energy. Another student remembered how blond he was, and his pink and white "peaches and cream" complexion. One day he burst in the door of the news shack and shouted, "Stop the presses! I've got a scoop!"

In the spring of 1938, Dad took two extra classes, still trying to catch up on the credits he was behind. This workload, combined with problems he was experiencing at home, proved too much for him. In May 1938, he dropped all of the classes, earning no credits for that semester. Among the classes he dropped were Journalism and Public Speaking—areas in which he would excel in later years.

In the summer, he earned extra money working for a newspaper, *The Tacoma Ledger.* He performed copyboy and other office duties, and was sent on some reporting assignments when the regular reporters were on vacation.

The following semester, in the fall of 1938, he took a normal class load, including Journalism. All that year, he excelled on the school newspaper. A number of feature stories appeared under his byline, and he wrote a regular column on page two called "Riding the Rail," in which he discussed school events, often humorously. His columns were high in political content, reflecting his knowledge of world affairs—a knowledge that was enhanced by his participation in the school debating team, where he starred. The debating experience whetted his appetite for politics, an area of interest that would remain with him for the rest of his life. He was promoted to Associate Editor of the paper.

In the 1930s there was a great deal of interest in ESP (extrasensory perception), particularly in "Rhine consciousness," the term for paranormal experiments with cards conducted by Dr. Joseph Banks Rhine of Duke University. He conducted experiments in which subjects were asked to guess what card another person was holding, when the backside was only visible to the subject. The results seemed to prove the existence of ESP.

One evening Dad was on a date with a girl named Patty, and they tried their own version of the Rhine experiments, using a standard deck of fifty-two playing cards. One by one, she held cards up, and my father guessed all of them correctly. Thinking he was tricking her, she obtained another deck of cards and took great care to mix them up and conceal them from him. Again, he guessed each card correctly. Later, under different circumstances, Dad found himself unable to repeat the astounding results.

This experience of my father's became the basis of his short story, "Encounter in a Lonely Place," published in 1973. A strong occult theme ran through a number of his most important works as well, including the *Dune* series and *Soul Catcher*.

When he was seventeen, Frank Herbert analyzed the Western fiction market by reading several boxes of books and magazines he had purchased at a used bookstore. A formula became apparent to him, and he used it to write a Western story under a pseudonym. It sold to Street and Smith for $27.50, and he was elated. Confident that he had discovered a path to instant success as a writer, he spent the money quickly. Then, in only a few weeks, he wrote two dozen more stories, all using the identical formula. Rejection letters poured in. He would not make another sale for eight years.

My father never revealed the title of that first story sale, or the pseudonym under which he wrote it. Not particularly proud of the writing, he said it was amateurish. Nonetheless, it was a sale, and he was still in high school at the time.

Displaying literary versatility and a curiosity about what lay before him on the uncharted course of life, he wrote a poem entitled "Your Life?"—published in the September 30, 1938, issue of *The Lincoln News*:

> What is the meaning of your life?
> If you live close to nature, is it hidden in—
>   A towering tree,
>   A busy worker bee,
>   A flower in bloom,
>   The sun piercing the morning's gloom?
>
> Or do you live in civilization?
> Does fancy people your imagination with thoughts of—
>   Laborers, soot and grime,
>   Youths leading lives of crime,
>   Long hours and pay day,
>   Night life in its hey-day?
>
> Are you but chaff from the Great Miller's gleaning?
> Or wherever you live does your life have a meaning?

Only two months later, his home life would fall apart entirely. He could no longer stand the suffering of his sister, now five, so again he dropped all of his classes, earning no credits toward graduation. With his parents drinking heavily and near divorce, he ran away from home, taking Patricia Lou with him. The pair caught a bus to Salem, Oregon, and sought refuge with Frank's favorite aunt, Peggy (Violet) Rowntree, and her husband, Ken Rowntree, Sr. (Peggy was one of Babe's sisters.)

Within weeks the touchy family situation improved, and Patricia moved back home. But Frank—barely eighteen—remained with his aunt and uncle, and enrolled at Salem High. Peg and Ken had a son by Ken's earlier marriage, Kenneth Jr., and they were also taking care of Jackie and Larry Sullivan, whose mother, Carmen Sullivan (one of Peggy and Babe's sisters), had died in childbirth. The boys became close, particularly Frank and Jackie, who were around the same age.

This was a much improved family situation for Frank, supported by an economically stable, loving marriage.

Dad graduated from Salem High School in 1939 with no immediate plans for college. Despite past problems the young man missed his parents and sister, and now that he was out of school he had a yearning to see new places. In the fall of that year he moved to San Pedro, California, near Los Angeles, where his parents were living. F. H. was chief of the Guard Force for Los Angeles Shipbuilding & Drydock Corporation, an important shipbuilder.

Shortly after arriving in California, "Junior" obtained a newspaper position at the *Glendale Star* as a copy editor, after lying about his age. He was just nineteen, but had a way of speaking and carrying himself that enabled him to pass himself off as a man five or six years older. He smoked a brier pipe, too, which made him look sophisticated.

At the *Star* there was an old, foul-tempered man who was also a copy editor, and the guy apparently thought that life had passed him by. He sat directly across the desk from an energetic upstart named Frank Herbert.

"I was young and he was old," my father told me later.

The old curmudgeon accused Frank of messing up the copy-editing on a story that ran in a prior edition, and Frank responded, "You're wrong. I didn't do that. I wasn't even here."

Suddenly the old man grabbed a pair of scissors from the copy desk and went after his younger counterpart, trying to stab him. Thankfully, people jumped in and grabbed the assailant and hauled him away. The fellow continued working there after he calmed down, but my father told me, "Whenever he had scissors in his hands, I stayed well clear of him!"

Another copy editor on the paper had his own style of revolt. His tactic was to refuse to bathe for two months at a time. He would not change his underwear, socks, or anything. His teeth had green film on them. People really kept their distance.

My father would accumulate many more interesting characters and stories in more than three decades in the newspaper business, a profession that for him was a window on the world . . . fascinating but low-paying. Journalism kept him on the leading edge of events, filling his hunger for political information and arming him with political data he would use in his science fiction writing.

Always impulsive, in the summer of 1940 he moved back to Salem, Oregon. For a short while he lived with the Rowntrees again, while looking for a newspaper job. He approached *The Oregon Statesman* for a position, but was told by the personnel manager that no openings were available.

After finding out who the managing editor of the paper was, the would-be journalist went to the man's house and accosted him in his front yard. The managing editor, Steve Mergler, was at first irritated, but the young man had a convincing way about him. Frank Herbert asked if he could fill in when other reporters, copy editors or photographers were on vacation. He had his own photographic equipment, and said he could even perform copyboy duties if necessary. "I can do a lot of things," he told Mergler. "I can be like a utility man on a baseball team, playing whatever position you need."

This sounded intriguing to Mergler, who had an eye for good people and appreciated an enterprising young man. So Frank, just shy of his twentieth birthday, went "on call" for the paper. He came in at all hours, did anything he was asked to do. He even worked in the advertising and subscription departments. He did everything so well, in fact, with such dedication and excellence, that it wasn't long before he was working full-time. His principal responsibilities involved photography, and, since this was the state capital, many of his assignments involved political events. One of his photographs, at a charity fund-raiser called the Salem Chest, was of U.S. Senator Douglas McKay, who would later become Secretary of the Interior. McKay took a liking to the young man, which later proved beneficial to Frank.

In Salem, Frank Herbert became enamored with airplanes and flying. He worked every angle to get into the air as a passenger, both for pleasure and on news assignments. These were small planes, single engine two-seaters.

In nearly fourteen months on *The Oregon Statesman*, Dad also reported, worked as copy editor and night editor, and wrote feature stories. In feature-writing he learned the importance of characterization, of clearly defining a person and determining what makes him tick. This, he would come to realize one day, was a central feature in any good novel.

He spent as much time as he could in the outdoors, "recharging" himself, as he described it many years later. There were ski trips with friends to nearby slopes in the Oregon Cascades, and a number of fishing trips to Elk Lake in the Three Sisters Wilderness Area. He took a canoe to Elk Lake in 1941 with a young friend, Fram Morgan. Soon afterward, Morgan joined the U.S. Marines. He was killed in the first wave at Tarawa in 1943, fighting the Japanese in the Pacific.

When my father wanted something, be it a job or a relationship, he was not to be denied. An impatient, driven man, he always found a way to get from point A to point B. While working in Salem in the spring of 1941, he met and fell in love with Flora Parkinson, a teenager. In June, they wanted to get married, and Frank thought it would be nice if they held the ceremony in his hometown, Tacoma, Washington. On impulse, they drove three hundred miles north.

At the courthouse in Tacoma, the only judge available, Judge W. A. Richmond, was conducting police court, and a number of men who had been accused of public intoxication were waiting for their cases to be heard. Undeterred, Frank, with his bride-to-be in tow, marched up to the judge and asked him in a low tone if he would marry them.

Judge Richmond appeared surprised, but he smiled and told the couple to take seats and wait. Then he hurried through a number of cases, convicting every defendant. When these matters were disposed of, he performed the wedding in front of a courtroom packed with police court spectators!

That month, Nazi Germany attacked Russia. The war in Europe was escalating. The pages of *The Oregon Statesman* were filled with news of those events and speculation about whether the United States would enter the conflict.

Another move followed, and in October 1941, the Herbert newly-weds found themselves living in San Pedro, California, near my grand-parents' apartment. Flora was pregnant. Dad went back to work for the *Glendale Star*, this time as a reporter and photographer. His love affair with flying continued, and he went on many aerial assignments

46

and personal flights, as a passenger. He took at least five thousand aerial photographs.

With U.S. involvement in World War II in December 1941, my grandfather's position as Chief of the Guard Force for Los Angeles Shipbuilding & Drydock became even more important, as it was directly related to the war effort. The yard was building a number of big Navy ships.

All over the United States, young men and women rushed to recruiting offices. Dad obtained enlistment papers from a Navy recruiter, but delayed signing them because of his family responsibilities. Of all the military branches, the Navy appealed to him most, from his love of ships and the sea.

F. H., aside from his guard duties, got together with a fire department friend to invent and patent what they called the "Dura Bomb Shovel," which was used by Los Angeles Shipbuilding & Drydock and by Douglas Aircraft. The shovel had a hollow handle (filled with sand to smother blazes) and a snow shovel–shaped bottom with a hinged lid. It was designed for fighting magnesium incendiary bomb fires, the sort expected to be used by the Japanese if they ever reached our coast. When an incendiary bomb hit, the theory went, a firefighter would rush to the scene, smother the flames with sand, scoop the bomb up and carry it away.

On February 15, 1942, Frank Herbert Jr. registered for the draft in Los Angeles County. According to his draft card, he was 5'10" and rather thin at 150 pounds. He still had the scar over his right eye and into his eyebrow, the half-inch-long mark from the malamute dog attack.

The following day, on February 16th, a baby girl, Penelope (Penny) Eileen, was born to the couple. Dad selected the mythological name Penelope from the faithful wife of Odysseus, who spurned numerous suitors during the hero's absence from Troy. The baby's middle name, Eileen, was my paternal grandmother's given name.

In July 1942, unable to wait any longer, Frank enlisted in the U.S. Navy. He gave the recruiting officer a letter of recommendation from the Supervisor of Shipbuilding at Los Angeles Shipbuilding & Drydock, a retired U.S. Navy officer.

During his physical examination for the Navy, the doctor kept looking out the window at another doctor and two pretty nurses who were waiting in a convertible, with golf clubs visible. Anxious to join them, the doctor rushed Dad through.

Frank Herbert was assigned to the huge Norfolk Naval Shipyard in Portsmouth, Virginia, where he served as a Photographer Second Class V-6 in the U.S. Naval Reserve. His mother, Babe, was extremely worried about him, and spent many nights crying.

In boot camp, Dad first encountered *The Bluejackets' Manual.* One of the entries, on swimming, went like this: "Breathing may be accomplished by swimming with the head out of water." Another entry, under the section on ships: "Q: What is the part (of the ship) known as midships? A: The middle part." And this one: "It is most important that all appliances for securing water-tightness be kept in an efficient condition." The foolishness of such passages in this bureaucratically produced manual later became the inspiration for his short story "By The Book" (1966).

He also picked up a number of mottoes on the base:

"If you can pick it up, pick it up; if you can't pick it up, paint it; if it moves, salute it."

Or: "Keep your mouth shut, your bowels open, and never volunteer."

And: "Fire at will." This one particularly amused him, because he considered it unfair to treat anyone named Will in this manner.

Despite his rating as a photographer, he did more office work than anything else, and increased his typing speed. This skill would prove beneficial to him in journalism and in his creative writing career.

He also became quite a poker player in the service, which provided him with an additional source of income. Most of his money was sent home to San Pedro for his wife and baby.

One of the fellows in Dad's outfit was going steady with a girl back home. The young man didn't drink, gamble or carouse. He sent money back to his girl, and she was supposed to bank it for their future marriage. One day he received a "Dear John" letter from her, and she requested the return of her picture. My father, ever impish, came up with a method of retaliation for his buddy. He collected fifty or sixty pictures of girlfriends from the guys in the outfit, and then dictated a letter to her, from the jilted man:

> I was disappointed to receive your letter. I'm all broken up by it. There is only one problem. I can't remember which girl you are. From this stack of pictures will you please pick out the one of you and send the rest back? Money for return postage is enclosed.

In the winter of 1942, Dad received his own "Dear John" letter from Flora, in which she told him she wanted a divorce. Devastated, he was brought to tears, and felt frustrated at having to deal with the situation from three thousand miles away. One night while on bivouac, with his mind on personal problems, he tripped over a tent tie-down and fell, hitting his head. A soft, lumpy blood clot developed on top of his skull, and he was warned by the doctor not to hit that spot again, at risk of his life—and to let the clot dissolve.

With the assistance of his uncle Ken Rowntree, he was given an early honorable discharge from the service in March 1943, less than eight months after enlisting.* He caught a military transport home to the West Coast. With a bandage on his head, he returned home to San Pedro, but discovered that Flora had disappeared, taking the baby with her.

Driving north to Bandon, Oregon, he visited the home of Flora's mother. In tears, he said to her, "All I want is my family back. Where are they?"

She wouldn't tell him, and despondent, he left. Later she confided to my half-sister, Penny, "I almost told him, but I thought it would be a mistake for them to be together."

Flora obtained custody of Penny.

Later my father would say that the letter from Flora was one of the luckiest things that ever happened to him, since it led ultimately to meeting my mother. But that remained several years off, and he would go through a painful period of adjustment.

---

*Colonel Kenneth Rowntree, Sr., was a commanding officer of Fort Worden in Port Townsend, Washington, during World War II. He also wrote an artillery handbook that was used for years as a textbook at West Point.

He moved back to his roots in the Pacific Northwest. From August 1943 to August 1945, he worked as a copy editor for the *Oregon Journal* in Portland, Oregon. This region, with its familiar landscapes and outdoor way of life, soothed his troubled spirit.

The copy desk at the *Oregon Journal* was in the shape of a half-circle. Along the outer rim of the desk, called "the rim," the copy editors sat, marking up stories that came in over the wires and stories written by staff reporters. On the other side of the desk, inside the curve, sat "the slot man," sometimes referred to as "the dealer." He dealt stories to the copy editors.

The United Press International office in the back had some tape punching machines which were in intermittent use. They were for transmitting stories to other UPI offices around the world. To send a story, it had to be typed on a special tape and held until the designated hours of transmission began. Then the tape was fed through the machine, printing the story on both the originating and receiving machines.

So, over a couple of days in odd moments, my impish father went back and cut the tape to print so that it would look like a standard UPI story. It was one of the wildest stories you ever heard.

There is an apocryphal tale about Dad, that the story he faked on the machine concerned a UFO attack on Europe in which the cities were destroyed with "green death rays." It is not difficult to imagine how this tale came about, since it circulated decades later when my father was the most famous science fiction writer in the world.

The essence of the actual story he punched out on the UPI machine was that an American flying ace was revealed to have previously been an ace for the Nazi air force, the Luftwaffe. Supposedly when he was a German flyer he was shot down over North Africa, then brought to the United States as a prisoner of war. But he had been an Austrian professor before the war, and with the assistance of academic friends in the United States he secured false identity papers and escaped from the prisoner of war camp. Subsequently he enlisted in the U.S. Air Force under this false identity.

The last line of the story read, "Any resemblance between the foregoing and anything that may have actually happened is purely coincidental."

The slot man at the time of the gag, Fred McNeil, was absolutely authoritarian, without a sense of humor. Behind him sat a copy spike—a sharp steel prong where copyboys impaled stories as they came in from the wire machines and reporters. The copyboy would come and spike a story on it—and without looking back McNeil would just grab the piece and start working on it.

Most of the people in the office knew about the gag, and Frank even had the UPI people in on it. One dull afternoon they had a machine free so that he could run his tape on it. The tape told the machine what to do, and it printed the story on standard UPI paper . . . an original and two carbons. It wasn't transmitted.

It only took a minute or so—the tape went fairly fast. Then the prankster ripped the story off, walked back to the copy desk as though coming from the john, spiked it and slid back into his seat on the rim.

Meanwhile, McNeil grabbed the story and put it down in front of him. The staff members watched him out of the corners of their eyes. It was a slack time of day with very little copy, so Frank was betting that McNeil would copy-edit it himself and not deal it, as he often did at slow times. He behaved predictably.

He sat there with his copy pencil marking the story . . . marking it . . . and saying, "My God! For God sakes!" He glanced at the clock and shouted to the wire editor (who was in on the gag), "We'd better try for a page one remake!"

McNeil was editing fast to get down to the bottom, and then he read that line. The flush started at the back of his neck and went right up over his head. He rose to his feet, balled up the paper and heaved it across the room with an angry grunt.

"If I ever find the son-of-a-bitch who did that," he shouted, "I'll kill him!"

*   *   *

In 1943, Dad hadn't been doing much fiction writing of any type, and it had been this way since 1938 when hubris had led him to believe incorrectly that he had developed a formula for writing Westerns. The war and his unsuccessful marriage further distracted him. But with the stability of the *Oregon Journal* job, he began writing again, before and after work. His efforts were rewarded, as he sold a clever two thousand word suspense yarn to *Esquire*, "Survival of the Cunning," published in the March 1945 issue. They paid him two hundred dollars—a substantial sum for a short story in those days.

Set during World War II, it described a fictional U.S. Army sergeant sent to the Alaskan arctic wilderness to locate a Japanese radio and weather station. A bad situation developed, in which the sergeant and his Eskimo guide were captured by a Japanese soldier, who had an automatic pistol. The Japanese, however, had committed the error of letting his gun warm up in the moist atmosphere of a cabin before taking it outside. Wisely, the Eskimo knew the gun would freeze up in the subzero arctic air outside, and he was able to overcome the captor.

My father had a lifelong fascination with remote regions of the Earth, from frozen locales to tropics to deserts. Desolate beauty appealed to him . . . the serenity of the wilderness. He had not journeyed to the arctic before writing the *Esquire* story, but wrote nonetheless in a convincing fashion from research, from stories that had come through newspaper offices, and from his imagination. He developed a knack for traveling in his mind, for transporting himself far away from the room in which he sat at a manual typewriter.

In August 1945, he left the *Oregon Journal* and took a position on the night rewrite desk of the *Seattle Post-Intelligencer*. This was a Hearst paper, one of a nationwide chain that maintained a steady drumbeat against Japanese Americans during the war. In large part the Hearst news organs were responsible for sentiment against American citizens of Japanese descent and their mistreatment. But now the war was ending, and more rational moods were setting in.

Frank Herbert's boyhood buddy, Dan Lodholm, was in the U.S. Coast Guard during the war. When Dan returned to the Northwest after his stint in the service, my father gave him and a number of Coast Guard war heroes a first-class tour of the *Seattle Post-Intelligencer* newspaper plant in downtown Seattle. They were suitably impressed.

Using G-I Bill financial assistance, Frank enrolled at the University of Washington in Seattle for the fall quarter of 1945. Without much regard to a major, he intended to take writing classes while still holding down his newspaper job. Soon he would fall head-over-heels for a brunette Scottish-American girl in the same creative writing class.

CHAPTER

4

✳ "But He's So Blond!" ✳

WHEN FRANK Herbert worked at the *Seattle Post-Intelligencer* in 1945 and 1946, he rented a room in the home of Mr. and Mrs. Ronald Hooper, near the Montlake Cut in Seattle. While Frank was at work one evening, the Hoopers held a piano recital at which Mr. Hooper played the piano and a well-known Russian-born artist, Jacob Elshin, sang baritone.

One of the guests was a red-haired teenager named Howard (Howie) Hansen, who was part Quileute Indian. Just before the recital began, Howie heard Hooper's wife tell someone, "We have a nice young newspaperman renting a room in the basement. His name is Frank Herbert."

The atmosphere at the recital was painfully formal, with much posturing and phony conversation. Many attendees sat with exaggerated erectness and chit-chatted, their little fingers sticking out as they held wine goblets.

Dad wandered in at around 11:00 P.M. For twenty minutes he listened to the singing (which seemed off-key to him) and noticed the hypocrisy and superficiality of the guests. I think my father must have been a little tired, or perhaps something didn't go well at work, because suddenly he dispensed with civility and announced, rather loudly, "I'd like to show you what this reminds me of."

"Oh?" Mrs. Hooper said, with a smile. "And what is it you do?"

"An ape act," Frank said. Thereupon he jumped on the sofa and began hopping from one end to the other in street shoes, curling his arms like a chimpanzee and making simian sounds.

"Hoomph! Hoomph! Hoomph!"

Everyone looked at him in stunned disbelief, except Howie, who could barely contain his laughter. Presently, Frank left the room, saying, "That's what I think of what I saw here tonight."

The next day, he was invited to move out.

So, my father lost a place to live. But he gained a lifelong friend and kindred spirit in Howie Hansen. "I was just off the reservation and pretty wild," Howie said to me later. "Maybe that's why Frank liked me." Howie, born in late 1931, was only fourteen years old when they met, but was intellectually quite mature. Frank developed the good-natured practice of calling him "H'ard" at times, and would later even autograph books to him that way.

With his stepfather's approval Howie invited Frank to live with them on a houseboat, moored near the Ballard Locks in Seattle. A short time later their new tenant showed up with a pickup truck full of items, and began unloading. He had books, skis, a microscope, footlockers, clothes and articles of furniture, piled high in the back of the truck.

When Howie's stepfather saw all of that, he exclaimed, "My God, he'll sink us!"

So Frank lost another place to live, but with the assistance of Howie arrangements were made for substitute quarters at the home of John Gerke, Jr., in the Ballard district.

Howie wanted to travel the world by ship, and tried to talk his new friend into joining the U.S. Merchant Marine with him. They would vagabond to distant, exotic parts of the world. This was tempting to my father, because he dearly loved the sea and wanted to learn everything he could about the world. But he enjoyed the newspaper business, and was planning to take writing classes soon at the University of Washington. He didn't say no, and he didn't say yes.

They often went on trips out into the countryside, and Dad always took a camera along, and a book. "He was always reading and showing me things in books," Howie recalled. Upon hearing this I thought of a boyhood description of my father when he was some fifteen years younger, at a time when he was always seen in the company of a book. He hadn't changed, and never would.

They talked about opening a camera supply store together. Frank went to Portland to contact suppliers but was delayed there when he met a girl he thought he liked. A few days later he returned to Seattle and told Howie she was a "dull-wit."

In March 1946 the *Post-Intelligencer* laid Frank Herbert off, citing obligations to returning World War II combat veterans. He had not been in combat.

In a creative writing class, English 139, he sat next to an attractive, dark-haired girl, Beverly Forbes. She had a shy way of looking at him with dark blue, half-closed eyes, and she spoke in soft tones, selecting her words carefully. Her laugh was gentle, and sometimes she broke into a girlish, nervous giggle.

Smitten, Frank told Howie, "I've just met a Scottish girl with the most beautiful black hair."

Actually she was Scottish-American, born Beverly Stuart prior to her mother's remarriage to a man named David Forbes. Like Frank she read extensively. Her interest in literature went back to her early childhood, when her maternal grandfather, Cooper Landis, introduced her to classic books. (Cooper had once been the traveling secretary of Ralph Waldo Emerson.)

Beverly told her best friend, Frankie Goodwin, about the young man she had met in writing class, Frank Herbert. Coincidentally, she was struck by his hair, as he had been with hers. "It's beautiful," she said, "the color of molten gold."

He dressed casually but neatly, typically in a black or dark turtleneck shirt, with a jacket zipped up to the center of his chest. His hair was long and neatly combed—straight back at the sides and across the top. He parted it on the left side, where my natural part is. The hair had a slight uplift on top, rising to his right.

He began a pattern of pursuit. He learned where Beverly Forbes ate lunch, and then just happened to wander by at the right moment with his own lunch. He found out where she studied in the library, and when. They discussed great books and writing, and found they shared an interest in the classics, history and poetry. They shared another interest as well, an important one: Each wanted to be a writer.

Both were working students, he at the newspaper and she as an ad writing trainee for the Clark Richards Advertising Agency in Tacoma.

They were also the only students in the class who had sold anything. Dad's "Survival of the Cunning" had been published the year before by *Esquire*, and during the course he sold another story, "The Jonah and the Jap," to *Doc Savage* magazine, published in the April 1946 issue. Like the *Esquire* story, it was set in World War II, involving characters who developed a clever means of outwitting the Japanese.

In 1946, Beverly sold a story entitled "Corner Movie Girl" to *Modern Romances* magazine, for which she received $145.00. The editor told her she liked the sincerity of the story, but thought the plot was a little weak. "Corner Movie Girl" was written as an assignment for the creative writing class she was taking, and it was read before the class and critiqued by her peers and by the instructor. Following a number of suggestions, including some from the blond young man who sat next to her, she rewrote the story.

"Corner Movie Girl" described a plain young woman who was envious of her beautiful friend for the proposals her friend constantly received from men. The plain girl dreamed of falling in love with the heir to a fortune. Subsequently she dated a rich, handsome young fellow, and they went to a fancy place to dance. But the experience left her feeling emotionally unsatisfied, and she felt cheapened for having done it. She returned to her plain, ordinary, no-frills guy, the one she really loved.

My mother's story was semi-autobiographical, as many first stories are. She had been overweight during most of her life before college, which made her feel unattractive. She never dreamed of getting a rich husband, though. Idealistic, she always intended to marry for love. Upon meeting Frank Herbert, an experienced man-about-town, she was nineteen, romantic, and somewhat naive concerning affairs of the heart.

She wrote true-confession stories of love. My father called them "sin, suffer, and repent stories." He wrote pulp adventures. She was the romantic, very feminine, and he the adventurer, strong and rugged.

Both were dreamers, but neither could have had any inkling of the remarkable life they would spend together.

Frank was having trouble with university officials. He was studying psychology, mathematics, and English (including creative writing), but wanted to select classes as if they were arrayed on a smorgasbord. He insisted upon taking a disproportionate number of psychology courses, and tried to skip introductory classes, going straight to advanced material. He already knew the preparatory stuff, he told the registrar, and didn't want to waste his time. But the bureaucrats running the school said he couldn't do as he pleased, despite straight-A grades. Besides, they said, he wasn't taking the classes necessary to qualify for a major, and everyone had to have a major.

My mother had always thought she would marry a dark-haired man like her father, while her friend Frankie expected to marry a blond. One evening, Frankie and Beverly were talking alone. "Do you like him?" Beverly inquired. "Yes," came the response. "But he's so blond!"

Beverly invited Frank to a Shakespearean play at the university, *Macbeth*. She was playing the third witch, in heavy makeup. The playhouse was at the corner of 43rd and University in Seattle, on the second floor over a dance studio. Frank went with Howie.

After the performance, Beverly's blue eyes teared up and she said to Frank, "I was just *acting* like a witch and don't want you to think I'm that kind of a person."

"Oh no," he responded. "I don't think that. I mean, I understand."

They made arrangements to go somewhere later that evening. While she changed out of her costume, Dad walked Howie to the bus stop on University Avenue. Howie recognized the symptoms he was witnessing, that his friend had "come to life." As they made their way along the sidewalk, Howie said, "Frank, you're going to marry that girl, and you're going to end your days together."

In response, my father laughed as only he could laugh. As Howie put it, he let out "a haw haw boom that filled the caverns between buildings." And Frank Herbert said, "There isn't a chance in a million, Howie. I have no intention whatsoever of getting married again."

But his young companion said again, "Frank, that's Mrs. Herbert right there. That's the future Mrs. Herbert."

"No," Dad said, shaking his head. "Once is enough, and it didn't work for me. That's it for me." His divorce from Flora had been finalized some three years before, but the trauma had remained with him.

The next day, Frank and Howie went to Kingston (on the Olympic Peninsula) by ferry and looked at an A-frame they were thinking of purchasing together. On the way back they were sitting on the beach, waiting for a ferryboat. Dad mentioned a popular song by The Ink Spots, "I Don't Want to Set the World on Fire," and said, "I don't want to set the world on fire, Howie. I just want to make the grass wave a little as I go by."*

Two weeks later, Frank called Howie and asked, "Will you stand for me (as best man) at our wedding?" Howie laughed, and consented. The wedding would be held in a few months, in June.

Frustrated with university rules concerning degree requirements, Frank Herbert decided to drop out the following June, in 1946. His wedding was scheduled for the same month.

My father had a way of springing wild plans on people. Shortly before their wedding, he found an unusual situation in which they could honeymoon and make a little money at the same time. He would be a fire watcher for the forest service atop a 5,402-foot mountain in Washington State's Snoqualmie National Forest, with permission for his young wife to accompany him. The lookout cabin—similar to the one later occupied by the beat generation icon Jack Kerouac—was perched on rugged Kelly Butte in the middle of a federal forest, thirty miles northeast of Mount Rainier. This was in the Cascade Mountain range, which divides the eastern and western portions of the state. The job would last from early summer through mid-fall 1946, and would pay $33.00 a week.

"I didn't hesitate for an instant," my mother recalled later. "When

---

*The comment was also reminiscent of the poetry of Ezra Pound, which my father read voraciously:

> And life slips by like a field mouse
> Not shaking the grass.

Frank told me about it, I just said yes." She was ready for the first adventure of their long married life, or *thought* she was.

On Sunday afternoon, June 23, 1946,* my parents were married by a minister in the front parlor of a house on Seattle's Queen Anne Hill. They exchanged simple gold wedding bands. Howie Hansen was best man,** and Frankie Goodwin the maid of honor. A reception followed in the home. Only a dozen people were in attendance, including the parents of the bride and groom.

My father did not like large weddings. Besides, he had grown independent of his extended family since achieving his majority, largely because so many of them were judgmental and he didn't care to seek their approval. On his paternal side the Herberts saw people in either white hats or black hats, with nothing in between. On his maternal side the McCarthys, devout Catholics, had expressed disapproval over his divorce from his first wife.

Up to that time Frank Herbert's life had been a paradigm of failure and instability. In addition to difficulties in school, marriage and the Navy, he had lost his job with the *Post-Intelligencer*. Contributing to his problems, his parents had not always provided a wholesome family environment for him. At last he was with a nurturing person, a potential lifelong companion, in a relationship that could enable him to fully realize his potential.

In early July 1946, the newlyweds climbed Kelly Butte and remained there until late October. Each week Dad hiked down to the nearest town of Lester for supplies, and then returned to the mountaintop, a round trip that took ten or eleven hours. Strong and barrel-chested, he was an excellent hiker and could carry a heavy pack.

The lookout cabin, a twelve-foot square, hip-roofed structure at the pinnacle of Kelly Butte, had a 360-degree view of the surrounding mountains and forests. They had no electricity or indoor plumbing, but water was plentiful, obtained from a small lake in the midst of a meadow on the butte. They had an outhouse that was in good repair,

---

*This date is based upon the marriage certificate. In the dedication to *Chapterhouse: Dune*, the date was shown incorrectly as June 20, 1946.

**For years afterward, whenever Howie said to someone, "I was best man at Frank's wedding," my father would quip, "He was the *second* best man. I was the best man!"

59

except the door didn't latch well and sometimes blew open in strong winds. The wood stove didn't draft properly, and under certain wind conditions the cabin filled with smoke.

In this excerpt from a 1,500-word piece my mother wrote about the adventure, she described her first impression of their living quarters:

> Finally we sat down on the bed (the cooler had been nailed on the north side of the cabin) and surveyed our home. Our 144 square feet of home, with 24 windows looking into the fog, and a ladder that slanted over the bed to the cupola.
>
> On the south wall across from us hung a shovel, an axe, a laundry bag, fire fighting pack, 40# of potatoes, and a washboard. So we started looking for a wash-tub. There wasn't any. We refused to think about it then. Instead we looked at the stove. We wished we hadn't. It was squat, dirty, black and looked stubborner than hell. . . .

She entitled the piece, with tongue firmly planted in cheek, "Look Out!"—a reference to the perils of honeymooning in a forest service lookout station. It formed the first chapter of what she and Dad hoped would be a collaborative book.* His contribution, two thousand words long, included the following passage:

> Oh yes, the scenery is beautiful. Our regal neighbor, Mount Rainier, looks in the window every clear day, seemingly just across the valley from us. The flowers are in bloom in the mountain meadows around us—the Indian paint brush, the lupen, the daisies, and even the mock orange. Deer pasture in the meadow, too; bear drink at our lake and the ground squirrels chase each other under our cabin. On a clear night we can even see Seattle, a mellow glow in the sky. . . .

On a Victrola hauled in by pack mule my parents listened to classical, jazz and swing music. In the evenings they read or played cards by the

---

*They never completed the book or published any part of it.

light of a kerosene lamp. They developed their own card game, a two-hand version of Hearts in which they played and drew, played and drew, so that no one knew where all the hearts were.

The young couple wrote short stories at every opportunity, sitting separately with typewriters set up on footlockers. His stories were pulp adventures and hers romances. Mom also composed an unpublished poem about what it might be like to trade places with her new husband and look back at herself:

> If I were you and you were me,
> I'd lie flat on my back and sing,
> To see you sitting where I am,
> Writing this silly thing.

She often curled up on a pillow with a good book and a red-and-white pack of Lucky Strike cigarettes that were cellophane-wrapped and bore the company slogan "LSMFT" . . . "Lucky Strike Means Fine Tobacco." Invariably she tucked a book of matches into the cellophane wrapper. She had been smoking since the age of fourteen, and had a constant, nervous need to be doing something with her hands. If she wasn't holding a cigarette, she enjoyed knitting or crocheting.

Dad found occasion to utilize his hunting skills on Kelly Butte. He hadn't brought along a rifle, but did have a .38 pistol, an Iver Johnson five-banger. Early one afternoon, near the northern boundary of the butte, he spotted a blue grouse in a clump of shrubbery. With scarcely a moment's hesitation, he drew his pistol and blew the head off the grouse, thus avenging an earlier insult committed against his father by another of that breed. The honeymooners prepared a fine meal with the fowl that evening.

One day, after transmitting the location of a fire to the dispatcher and to all other lookout towers in the area, Mom forgot and left the microphone open. Dad was preparing to make the trek into Lester, and she was going over the grocery list with him. She read the list aloud, saying, ". . . Three pounds of flour, two dozen eggs, fresh carrots, oh my God, there's a bear!" She had spotted a large black bear outside as she spoke. Subsequently they received cards and letters from fire watchers, rangers and others who had heard the broadcast and were amused by it.

On warm summer days they were in the habit of hauling mattresses outside and making love on the walkaround ramp of the lookout at sunset, with a golden glow around Mount Rainier. I was conceived on that porch.

When they saw Howie Hansen a few days later in Seattle, Dad said to him, proudly, "Just feel these muscles in my back, from carrying a pack up and down hills!"

Howie felt them. They were hard and taut, like cords.

"Do you know what we did up there?" Dad said. "We conceived a child!"

"The biggest fire in the woods was us," Mom added.

CHAPTER 5

✳ The White Witch ✳

ONE MAY afternoon in 1947 when my mother was very pregnant with me, she found herself overwhelmed by a craving for watermelon. The grocery store was only a couple of blocks away in the Queen Anne district of Seattle, so she walked there and made the purchase. On the way back, she noticed a man and woman in a car looking at her and laughing. She had been carrying the watermelon in front of her belly, and didn't realize how funny it looked.

Before dawn a few weeks later, the time came to rush her to Maynard Hospital. As my father wrote years later in a special dedication to my mother, they were in a silly, joyful mood as they entered the hospital. They laughed and giggled as they walked down the corridors, holding hands. Their ebullience drew surprised stares, since hospitals were, after all, supposed to be serious, sober places.

I was born on June 29. My parents brought me home from the hospital on Independence Day, July 4, 1947, a year to the date from the day they trekked up Kelly Butte to their honeymoon roost. As Mom walked in the door of the house with me and realized how much work she would have to do with a new baby, she thought, *This is independence?*

Like my father, I had shining, golden hair as a child. My given name, Brian, is Gaelic, meaning one who is nobly descended and honorable. Also one who is fair-spoken and wordy. My middle name, Patrick, stems from St. Patrick, credited in legend with having driven all the snakes out of Ireland. A larger design was at work as well. My parents' first child was to have an Irish Catholic name, after my father's Irish lineage on the McCarthy side. The second child was to take on a Scottish given and middle name, following my mother's Presbyterian Stuart lineage.

During the early years of his marriage to my mother, Dad worked for a number of newspapers. By late 1947 he was employed as a feature writer for the *Tacoma Times*. He had grown a beard, and when going out on assignments in the blustery northwest weather often wore a trench coat and fedora, while carrying a large Kodak Medalist camera slung over one shoulder.

In my father's lifetime there were many incidents involving his driving. He was, in fact, something of a notorious motor vehicle operator wherever he lived—mostly involving speeding incidents. In some neighborhoods, people learned to watch out for him as he raced by, and reined in their children and pets.

If someone were to ask me if he was a good driver, however, I would have to admit with all candor, "Yes. But he scared the hell out of me." He had remarkably good reactions, something inherited by my older sister, Penny, who became, among her other accomplishments, a trophy-winning jeep racer. Like my father and sister, I, too, have excellent reactions.

There are a number of stories in our family when those reactions came into play. Nothing compares, however, with the occasion in 1948 when my father was driving his mother-in-law Marguerite's big 1937 Oldsmobile. I, barely a year old, sat on the backseat with my "Nanna" Marguerite, while my mother and father sat in front. Dad claimed for years afterward that he came around the fateful turn at only forty-five miles an hour, but one of the passengers told it differently.

According to my mother, none of us were wearing seat belts, and he had the Olds going more than seventy. She'd been watching the speedometer climb, but had not said anything to him about it. It was a two-lane highway. They rounded a turn and were suddenly confronted with a flimsy two-by-four barricade in front of a bridge, with the workers sitting alongside the road having lunch. Pieces of bridge deck were missing.

Dad could either go off the road or attempt a daredevil jump over the gap. He decided in a split second to attempt a leap, similar to one he had seen performed by a circus clown at the wheel of a tiny motorized car. He floored the accelerator. The big car crashed through the barricade onto bridge decking, then went airborne for an instant before all four rubber tires smacked down on the other side.

Frank Herbert stopped the car and waved merrily to the stunned workers, then sped off.

"What fun!" Mom exclaimed. But she lit a cigarette nervously, and noticed her hands shaking. Uncharacteristically, Marguerite was quiet in the back, and admitted later she'd been terrified. It all happened so quickly she said she barely had time to grab me.

My father said at least eight solutions appeared before him when he rounded the turn and saw the barricade, in what could not have amounted to more than a tenth of a second. He compared it with a dream, in which a series of events that seemed to take a long time were in reality crammed into only a few seconds. During the emergency he weighed each option calmly and decided upon the one that worked. He said he visualized the successful leap.

It has been said that art imitates life. Years later, in his 1968 novel *The Santaroga Barrier*, he fictionalized the event:

He rounded a corner and came parallel with the river. Ahead stood the clump of willows and the long, down-sweeping curve to the bridge. Dasein . . . stepped on the throttle . . . The truck entered the curve. The road was banked nicely. The bridge came into view. There was a yellow truck parked off the road at the far side, men standing behind it drinking out of metal cups.

"Look out!" Piaget shouted.

In that instant, Dasein saw the reason for the truck—a gaping hole in the center of the bridge where the planks had been removed. That was a county work crew and they'd opened at least a ten-foot hole in the bridge.

The truck sped some forty feet during the moment it took Dasein to realize his peril.

Now, he could see a two-by-four stretched across each end of the bridge, yellow warning flags tied at their centers.

Dasein gripped the steering wheel. His mind shifted into a speed of computation he had never before experienced. The effect was to slow the external passage of time. The truck seemed to come almost to a stop while he reviewed the possibilities—

Hit the brakes?

No. Brakes and tires were old. At this speed, the truck would skid onto the bridge and into the hole.

Swerve off the road?

No. The river waited on both sides—a deep cut in the earth to swallow them.

Aim for a bridge abutment to stop the truck?

Not at this speed and without seat belts.

Hit the throttle to increase speed?

That was a possibility. There was the temporary barrier to break through, but that was only a two-by-four. The bridge rose in a slight arc up and over the river. The hole had been opened in the center. Given enough speed, the truck could leap the hole.

Dasein jammed the throttle to the floorboards. The old truck leaped ahead. There came a sharp cracking sound as they smashed through the barrier. Planks clattered beneath the wheels. There came a breathless instant of flying, a spring-crushing lurch as they landed across the hole, the "crack" of the far barrier. . . .

He hit the brakes, came to a screeching stop opposite the workmen. Time resumed its normal pace as Dasein stared out at the crew—five men, faces pale, mouths agape. . . .

Frank Herbert received only a few moving violations in the many years he drove, covering what must have amounted to millions of miles. One ticket was for failing to dim his headlights for oncoming traffic. Another involved following too closely and running into the rear of another vehicle, but that occurred on an icy street. I also remember how he backed out of driveways or narrow dead-end streets, going hell-bent-for-leather with his head out the driver's window, staring back intently or looking in the side mirror.

He learned some of his high-speed driving skills from his father, who had been a highway patrolman. When barreling down a narrow, winding road he didn't slow at the turns and instead beeped furiously. If anything was coming, it had to get out of the way! He knew how to minimize wear on automobile mechanisms, too. When driving a vehicle with a clutch, each time he had to stop on a steep hill he set the emergency brake and then released it slowly as he started out, thus putting less wear on the clutch. He never rode the clutch, and could double clutch into low gear with gear boxes that didn't have synchromesh. As a child, I always felt he was in total control, and I don't recall ever feeling at risk. In my adulthood, however, when I knew him a bit too well, I often feared for my life while riding in a car with him at the wheel.

Dad and Mom took frequent fishing trips together, while I remained with my Nanna Marguerite, who was a well-known Northwest watercolor artist. She had a large studio in her home, where she painted beach and boat scenes, and landscapes.

On one such fishing trip my parents were on a river near North Bend, Washington. During the day, Dad had been off fishing, performing his hunting and gathering role, while Mom worked around their rented cabin. When he returned with his catch, he discovered he had lost a packet containing fishing flies and hooks that had been given to him by one of his grandparents. It had sentimental as well as practical value, and he was upset.

She told him not to worry, that she would find it. He had been all over the river fishing, not staying in one place at all. Still, she led him directly to an area of unusual rocks, where she knelt over a hole, reached in and retrieved the missing gear.

"It was there that I discovered I was married to a white witch," he told me.

Another time, in her University of Washington years, her friend Frankie called to say she had lost a gold ring. Beverly told her to go back to Parrington Hall on the campus, where she would find the ring on top of a towel dispenser in the ladies' restroom. Frankie checked, and there it was.

In coming years, Dad would rely upon Mom's ability to find things for him, and upon her power to forecast events.

CHAPTER
6

✳ The Jungian Connection ✳

MOM'S MOTHER, Marguerite Forbes, gave us a piece of property on Vashon Island, near Seattle and Tacoma. When I was around a year old, Dad started construction on a small home there, with Mom helping. Unfortunately we ran out of funds. The home, half-completed, was repossessed by the bank, along with the land.

Early in 1949, Dad accepted a job with the *Santa Rosa Press Democrat* in Sonoma County, California—just north of San Francisco. This was just one of many moves we would make during my childhood. In all, we lived in twenty-three different places.

I remember how books filled our little rented house in Santa Rosa, in bookcases in the living room, in the kitchen and in my parents' bedroom. One of my earliest memories, when I was a toddler, was of my mother looking patiently up from a book on her lap as I spoke to her. She taught me that books were sacred; I was never to dog-ear pages or write on them.

My father and mother had many friends, and when they came over, Dad told stories. Heavy laughter often accompanied what he was saying. One regular visitor to our home was Bernard Zakheim, a Polish-born Jew who was a painter and sculptor. Bernard lived in Sebastopol, California, where he owned an old farmhouse with a large apple orchard. They met when Dad did a *Press Democrat* story about a terra cotta figure Bernard had cast from one of his wood carvings. The figure,

69

which I have on my desk today, was called "Angry Moses," and featured a statement of Bernard's political beliefs carved on the back of it. The men became instant friends, bonded by their interests in politics, religion, history and art.

Bernard Zakheim was one of the most famous painters and sculptors in California. A proletarian artist who identified with struggling workers, he had studied with Diego Rivera in Mexico and painted murals at Coit Memorial Tower and the University of California Medical Center in San Francisco. His creations were invariably political in nature, and he was falsely accused of being a Communist. Such a furor arose in 1934 over his work and the work of other artists at Coit Tower that authorities delayed the opening of the facility for several months. His murals at the medical center would eventually be removed, again in the midst of political controversy.

Upon looking at one of Zakheim's paintings, Dad was so moved that he wrote a poem. This is an excerpt from the unpublished piece:

> What folly to think there
> Is no place to receive this.
> No empty place for this
> Painting to be.
> Driven into the heart by the thing itself—
> We have a relationship, this
> Artist and myself.
> His hand and my eye have just met.

Dad had an ornate antique bathtub stored in the garage of our house. Several 100-pound sacks of concrete (to be used as boat ballast) were stowed in the tub, and in boxes and piles nearby were brass boat parts, ship-to-shore radio equipment and oars. These were things my father had picked up here and there, intending to build a sailboat one day to take around the world with his family. It would be a forty-five-foot ketch, he said, and he planned to write stories aboard. He had taken celestial navigation classes recently with this in mind.

Sadly this dream, like many others of Frank Herbert, would never come to pass. We would move so many times in ensuing years, with no time or money to construct a boat, that the nautical items he had saved so carefully were discarded or sold.

One symbol of our frequent moves was a waxed cardboard stencil, "F. HERBERT," with black paint smeared on it. Each time we moved, Dad used it to paint his name on our mailbox. As years went by and my father did more and more creative writing, this procedure with the stencil became increasingly important in order to make absolutely certain that the mailman did not miss our stop. Letters from agents and publishers as well as checks arrived in the mail. The mail became, to a large extent, the lifeline of our family.

My mother said we moved sometimes to elude the first wife, Flora, who chased us tirelessly for past-due child-support payments. Invariably, Flora found out where we were, and a letter from her attorney would arrive soon afterward.

One evening my mother and father went to a speech on Jungian psychology, at a Presbyterian church in Santa Rosa. The speaker, a clinical psychologist, was Irene Slattery—and as luck would have it, my parents sat in the audience next to her husband, Dr. Ralph Slattery. Ralph was the supervising clinical psychologist at Sonoma State Hospital, a sprawling sixteen-hundred-acre facility nearby. The Slatterys became our closest friends in Sonoma County.

With respect to Frank Herbert's writings, the relationship with Ralph and Irene was extremely important. Going back to his days in college only three or four years before, my father had come to realize that an understanding of human motivation was the essential component of characterization. Now, with psychologists as friends, he would gain new insights.

Dad had been interested in Carl Gustav Jung, the renowned psychologist and psychiatrist, for a number of years. Jung had known Dr. Joseph Banks Rhine, whose astounding experiments in the 1930s led Dad and a girlfriend at the time to dabble with ESP and the prediction of cards. Thinking there might be a link between ESP and what Jung referred to as "the collective unconscious" of mankind, my father subsequently studied this further in college.

Now more pieces were about to fall into place.

In the 1930s, Irene Slattery had been a personal student of Jung, at the Federal Polytechnic Institute in Zurich. She had her notes from those classes, along with papers provided by Jung, and Irene gave my father access to this information. Enthralled, he pored over everything written in English. Some of the notes and documents were in German, which Irene translated for him.

She had been in Berlin in the 1930s, where she'd seen Adolf Hitler speak before thousands of people. Hitler terrified her from the moment she first gazed upon him. He was a skillful demagogue, she said, an expert at couching twisted, angry thoughts in words that sounded convincing. He was a hero to the German people, and terribly dangerous in that position, she felt, because of the way his people followed him slavishly, without questioning him, without thinking for themselves. Irene very nearly expressed this dangerous thought to the wrong people.

Fortunately she left Germany before getting into trouble, and made her way to the United States. Years later she related her early concerns about Hitler to Frank Herbert. Her thoughts about the danger of heroes simmered in Dad's highly receptive brain, and ultimately they would form a cornerstone of the *Dune* series: Heroes are dangerous, especially when people follow them slavishly, treating them like gods.

Another cornerstone of the *Dune* series is the concept of genetically transferred memory, particularly in the Bene Gesserit sisterhood. This concept is based upon the teachings of Irene's professor, Jung, who believed in a collective unconscious produced by genetic memory.

The Slatterys were also interested in Zen Buddhism, a religious system emphasizing nonverbal interaction—understanding and saying things without words. This was my father's second exposure to Zen teachings, the first having occurred when he lived among Nisei as a child.*

Jung had been an early associate of Sigmund Freud, before breaking with Freud over, among other things, Freud's insistence upon attributing neuroses to sexual disturbances. Dad had studied Freud exten-

---

*A decade later he would also meet the Zen master Alan Watts. Zen was an ideal adjunct to the Slatterys' studies of Freud and Jung, where unconscious behavior was emphasized. In analyzing patients, the Slatterys paid close attention to mannerisms, what came to be called "body language." The Zen influence permeates the *Dune* novels.

sively, and believed in many of his hypotheses, particularly those that had to do with the subconscious motivations for human behavior.

Irene and Ralph, too, agreed with many of Freud's hypotheses. Rather than accepting the teachings of any one psychologist, however, they preferred to select from the teachings and beliefs of many, including Jung, Freud, Alfred Adler and others.

"Irene said something to me once," my father told me many years later, "and I have thought of it often. 'When you see what motivates people, you will begin to see them walking around with their intestines hanging out.' "

Now he was on a path that would lead to strong characterizations in his novels. In Santa Rosa, he began writing a novel, *Under Pressure*, about extreme psychological stress onboard a nuclear submarine during wartime. The protagonist, a crafty, world-wise Bureau of Psychology officer, had unique insights into the problems of underwater warfare. Dad's title for the book, *Under Pressure*, had double meaning: the obvious submarine reference and the underlying psychological inference, with respect to stresses exerted on the crew. (In 1955 the novel would be published in hardcover as *The Dragon in the Sea*.)

Other Frank Herbert novels were based at least in part upon the Santa Rosa experience, including *The Santaroga Barrier* (1968), about a town with a name that was a combination of two California towns—Santa Rosa and Saratoga. This novel described the mass psychology of people in the town and in the society at large, and had interesting philosophical themes, reflecting the influence of the Slatterys.

On June 26, 1951, Mom gave birth to her second child, Bruce Calvin Herbert. By prior agreement he would have a Scottish name. Mom named him after King Bruce (Robert the First).

I was a rather hyperactive child myself, and my father, when home, often lost patience with me. He was trying to write, or complete extensive research. He needed quiet, contemplative time to consider important matters. I remember him yelling at me constantly, and if I didn't do exactly as instructed, he was quick to administer corporal punishment.

At other times he enjoyed taking photographs of me, and one of the photos, of me standing at a mailbox trying to figure out how a chain beneath it could support it, was published in the *Press Democrat*. From my youthful perspective, however, there were more negative events than positive, and as years went by we would become increasingly estranged.

Unfortunately, he used Freudian methods when scolding his children. In addition to my own experiences I saw him doing this with Penny when she came to stay with us, and later with my brother as well. Virtually every mistake we made, in his opinion, was "intentional," motivated by some underlying "subconscious element." Nothing was accidental, in his view.

Frank Herbert was a man who was so observant about affairs of the world that in his writings he would accurately predict epic events—but he didn't recognize his lack of closeness to his children when they were children. In that respect, his all-seeing eye had a blind spot. This super human of awareness, this hero in so many respects who one day would become a hero to me, had an Achilles' heel. He could not handle children. Perhaps this was because he had never really been a child himself. Assuming important responsibilities from a young age, he had been more of a miniature adult, with a keenly searching mind.

His impatience with young people was perhaps his worst fault, the one that troubled me most. Children were noisy and boisterous, his *bête noire*. They clattered through the house and yard, driving him crazy when he tried to write, when he tried to think. They got into his desk and manuscript pages and smeared things around . . . much as Jules Verne's son, Michel, did to him.

Dad had an oval face, on the fleshy side, with a weak chin and long blond hair combed straight back—hair that was so light in color that it appeared thinner than it really was. His dark blue eyes had a way of flashing angrily at me when I was being scolded, and even when he smiled at me it was with a penetrating intensity that I found unnerving. Sometimes he wore eyeglasses for reading or driving: they had round lenses with mottled brown frames.

A burly, barrel-chested man, he had thick hair on his arms and chest. These features, combined with his loud and blustery ways, contributed to the "primal display" of the man from a child's perspective, making him a frightening, intimidating presence to me. Later when he grew a full beard, he would look even larger to me, and quite wild. A small mole marked the lower left side of his nose, and another mole, slightly larger, hung from the right eyebrow, a bit over the eye cavity. Near that, the dog bite scar from childhood remained over his right eye. His nose hooked down a little. A thick vein on the side of his neck and another on his temple bulged and throbbed when he was angry. During anger, his right eye looked murkier than the other, more dangerous.

Sometimes while writing in his study or working on a project in his shop, he would place a pencil in the notch over one ear, forgetting it was there afterward and walking all around the house like that. At other times he shoved his eyeglasses high on his head, into his hair, to get them out of the way while keeping them handy. He used his head to hold things. If there had been a ledge on his forehead, it might have been stocked with office supplies.

Mom often spoke of how strong he was, a natural strength, she said, from sturdy Herbert genes. He'd been a tough kid, and was even tougher now. No one pushed him around. He knew judo, a form of Japanese jujitsu that he had learned in the service. I know he had a powerful grip, because whenever he was displeased I found myself squirming in his cow-milker hands, unable to free myself. He could open any jar in an instant, and had what Mom called "asbestos skin," enabling him to touch hot pans and casserole dishes without burning himself.

His presence was overpowering, with more than a hint of police-militarism, stemming from his highway-patrolman father. When Dad questioned me, it was *with intensity*, the way the police did it. I was overpowered, mentally and physically. His commands boomed forth, and were to be followed without question.

My father often wore aviator sunglasses and military surplus clothes (especially shirts and coats), and he had other military items, including a U.S. Navy lie detector (that he would use on me later), army chests, knives, a Navy periscope, a hand-operated field generator, and an old Army sword with a green handle. As further evidence of his authority, he had handguns, rifles and shotguns, which he used for hunting and target practice.

He had a great deal of mechanical skill, in large part from the influence of his own father. Dad worked on our cars, performing a wide range of servicing and repairs. If he wasn't sure how to correct a particular mechanical problem, he would obtain the diagnoses of two or three mechanics. Then when he was certain of the answer he would perform the repairs himself. It was a technique he employed in order to survive on a limited budget, and he passed it on to Howie.

My parents rarely made any markings in books, not even in pencil. Books were considered sacred. When doing research for his freelance writing, Dad was usually careful to make notes on slips of yellow typing paper, folded vertically and kept between the pages of the books. Frequently these sheets of notepaper were the second sheets put in a typewriter under a sheet he was typing upon, done in order to protect the platen from the hard, sharp strikes of the keys. After a while, these second sheets had indentations on them from key strikes, and on these rough sheets my father made some of his notes. Undoubtedly this had to do with a pack rat aspect of his personality, from having been raised during the Depression. Nothing was ever wasted.

Late in 1952, to augment his income as a reporter, Dad took a part-time job as an early morning news announcer with KSRO, a station owned by the *Press Democrat*. It was 1350 kilocycles on the radio dial, and sometimes Mom and I listened to him. His voice was strong and clear on the air. Since Sonoma County was a prime agricultural region and nearby Petaluma was famous for chickens and eggs, much of the news concerned egg and poultry prices and production levels. He also interviewed farm advisers and other local notables and gave weather reports. If he spoke of political issues, he sometimes laced the news with commentary.

One morning Dad arrived at KSRO so early that only he and the engineer were there. The engineer was a great big guy who loved to play practical jokes on announcers. He would put pictures of naked women in with the news copy, or a wet sponge on the announcer's chair—those sorts of things. Finally Dad had endured enough of this, and decided to get even. From inside a glass-enclosed broadcast booth one morning, with the engineer sitting outside, Dad read the news over the air. Suddenly in midsentence he began mouthing words, without uttering a sound. Intermittently he would start talking again, cutting in and out.

The engineer went crazy, waving his arms wildly and pounding on the glass. Dad just waved to him innocently. After the broadcast the engineer was extremely upset, saying he would have to spend eight to ten hours tearing the transmitter apart to repair an "intermittent" in it.

"What would you give not to have to tear it apart?" Frank Herbert asked.

"Anything," the fellow said.

"Anything?"

"Yeah, sure."

"Okay," Dad said, with a smile. "I got you!" He then told the fellow what he had done, and exacted a promise from him to play no more practical jokes. The engineer kept his word.

While the Sonoma County experiences were a treasure-trove for future works, Dad didn't write much other than newspaper articles during the three years we lived there. One short story written in Santa Rosa was important, because it was his first science fiction sale. "Looking for Something" appeared in the April 1952 edition of *Startling Stories*. In this piece he described a world that was in reality an illusion created by a hypnotist.

His only other publication during our years in Sonoma County was a limited edition book published by the *Press Democrat*, also in 1952. Entitled *Survival and the Atom*, it was a collection of Dad's articles on nuclear energy, with a press run of 750 copies. This formed an early link in the chain that would ultimately make him an anti-nuclear, anti-war activist.

CHAPTER

7

﹡ The Newsman and Captain Video ﹡

MY FATHER met many famous people by doing newspaper stories on them, and a number would become lifelong friends. One was the political artist Bernard Zakheim, and later it would be the world-renowned Zen master Alan Watts. Another was the noted science fiction and fantasy author Jack Vance. Dad knew Vance's work, and late in 1952 he learned that the writer was living on a small farm not far from us, just outside of Kenwood, California. The reporter was on his way.

Vance, while the same age as Frank Herbert, was much farther along in his career at the time. He had sold many short stories to the science fiction pulps, including his well-known Magnus Ridolph tales. He was also making good money writing scripts for the *Captain Video* television show, a popular half-hour program that ran five days a week. It was sponsored by Post Toasties cereal. In the show, the hero wore a silver helmet, and whenever he flew through the air it was possible to see the wire that held him up.

Jack lived on a small farm with his wife, Norma, and drove a bright yellow Jeepster convertible. A large, scholarly man with thinning hair, Jack wore eyeglasses that had thick, round lenses. He was intense and could be gruff. But his coarse outer shell was frequently employed as a shield, preventing prying eyes from peering into his private world. The real Jack Vance, if he permitted anyone to see that far, was generous and effusive, an exceedingly nice man.

Soon the men were talking of living together in Mexico, and of joint writing projects. This was the opportunity of a lifetime for my father—to work and study with a successful writer. Jack Vance was far better off financially than we were. To save for the trip, Dad scrambled even more to augment his income. In ensuing weeks, he took every extra photography assignment he could get. He increased his hours at KSRO Radio. And, whenever he could fit it in, he worked as an assistant to Irene Slattery in her private psychiatry practice.

But his ex-wife Flora sued him, and a stipulation was entered by the court under which the plaintiff and defendant agreed to compromise the amount of past-due support payments. The required payments and attorney fees added to our financial pressures.

We had a 1950 Hillman in those days, a little four-door sedan that got excellent gas mileage. In an era of big cars and low-cost fuel, Dad predicted that most people in the world would drive economy cars one day, forced to do so by petroleum shortages and high fuel prices. "Petroleum is a finite resource," he said.

He put the Hillman up for sale to raise funds, to apply toward purchase of a Jeep station wagon with the Vances for the Mexico trip. One evening while I was riding in the backseat of the Hillman, our car was hit by another, knocking us into a ditch. The other car, a big sedan, kept going, a hit and run. I remember Dad shouting out the window and swearing, and kicking our car when it lay damaged in the ditch. The other vehicle had administered a glancing blow against the side of our car, denting the doors on that side. Fortunately, none of us were injured.

But the accident created big problems for us. Our auto insurance had lapsed for non-payment, and, since the guilty driver had disappeared, we had no hope of receiving payment from him or his insurance company. Dad didn't want to spend his Mexico money repairing the car, and now, in its damaged condition, the vehicle couldn't be sold. It ran, but rattled badly. The damaged doors didn't open, and one of the windows on that side was broken away, letting air in all the time.

Mom and Dad had taken out a loan on the Hillman from a Santa Rosa bank, but because of our credit problems, the bank had required additional guarantees. Dad had the *Press Democrat* as a co-signer on the car. After the accident he and Mom stopped sending in car payments, and instead applied all available money to their other bills and to their Mexico fund. About the time we were on the way to Mexico with the Vances in a new Jeep station wagon (paid for by the Vances), the *Press Democrat* was discovering that they owed money on a badly dented 1950 Hillman.

Several years later, when Dad got back on his feet financially, he telephoned the *Press Democrat* and, in a long, jovial conversation, made arrangements to pay them back with interest.

When my father decided to do something, he didn't allow anything to get in his way. And, while he had his lapses in paying money he owed, be it to the *Press Democrat*, his ex-wife or a variety of bill collectors, he invariably made amends later and repaid every cent.

We received a battery of typhus, typhoid, and cholera shots for the Mexico trip, and shopped for necessities we didn't expect to find in Mexico. Most of our possessions were left in storage with the Slatterys. By September, 1953, we were on the road. Eleven-year-old Penny, since she lived most of each year with her mother, did not accompany us.

The Vance's Jeep wagon was blue, with a top rack, and the men alternated driving duties. Mom kept a close accounting of our expenditures, in a ledger book. Initially I couldn't utter a word of Spanish, but I practiced on the way, and soon—at the age of six—I was speaking the language fluently.

When we arrived in Mexico, I was assailed with tropical colors and rich, earthy odors such as I had never before experienced. Tropical downpours were new to me, too. Sometimes the rain came down so hard that we had to pull the car over and wait for it to stop. I recall winding roads, green, terraced hillsides of crops rising steeply beside the highway, and a treacherous river crossing we made on a one-car ferry, where the bridge had been washed out in a flood. Once, after several hot hours of driving in the interior of the country, we came to a promontory on top of a hill, where our eyes were suddenly filled with the breathtaking blue of the Gulf of California.

Just north of Mazatlán in the State of Sinaloa, we stopped for a break at a roadside monument that marked the Tropic of Cancer. Norma placed her purse on the front fender of the car, and forgot it was there. A few miles down the road, with Jack driving, she suddenly missed it, and we made a quick "U" turn. When we arrived back at the monument, we saw the purse on the ground. It had been run over. Inside, Jack's favorite writing instrument, a fountain pen, was ruined. Since Jack did his writing by longhand, this was a serious matter, indeed. His favorite writing instrument felt right in his grip and disseminated ink perfectly. With it he had written a number of excellent stories. The pen, silver and black, now lay crushed beside a Mexican highway.

A short while later we arrived in the seaside resort city of Mazatlán, and checked into an old hotel on the southern end of the great crescent forming the bay. A massive sea wall stood across the street from our hotel, with a wonderful sandy beach there. The insects, large and black, were either flying in my face or lying dead on the beach and sea wall. I paid them little heed while Mom took care to avoid them. As Bruce and I played in the sand, she drew in her sketchbook. Later, as we sat together on the sea wall, she taught me how to draw a house in perspective, as her artistic mother Marguerite had instructed her.

The following day we set off for points farther south. Near Guadalajara in the State of Jalisco, we rented a large house in the village of Chapala, on the shore of beautiful Lake Chapala. Famous for its fishing, pleasant climate and scenery, it was the largest lake in Mexico, approximately fifty miles long and fifteen miles wide. At an elevation of five thousand feet, it had a number of small islands in its midst and four villages around the rim, including Chapala. The region had numerous farms, growing subsistence crops such as alfalfa, beans, corn and maguey.

A fishing village and artists' colony, Chapala was much favored by tourists, especially Americans. The town, while small, boasted one of the world's great beer gardens—a large tavern by the lake that had outdoor seating under a shady, striped canvas roof. On hot days, my parents and the Vances could be found there, cooling themselves in the shade. Sunsets on the lake were spectacular.

Small fishing skiffs, some with butterfly nets extended, crossed the water from early morning to late evening. Just outside town, alongside the shore, rose a massive dirt mound that locals said concealed a mysterious ancient structure. They theorized this because during heavy rains little clay figurines and pieces of pottery washed down the hillside. Recently, archaeologists had been made aware of the mound, and an excavation was planned.

Chapala was an idyllic spot in which to relax, almost too pleasant for the disciplines required of writing, too sleepy. Jack and my father would immerse themselves in their writing nonetheless.

Our two-story adobe and white stucco house, which had been converted to a duplex, stood on a hillside a block above the shores of the lake. Whenever the men were writing, usually from mid-morning to late afternoon, they enforced strict silence throughout the premises. The house had a long outside corridor where I played with my toys. Especially a little army tank.

I was in the habit of simulating war noises, and as I immersed myself in fantasy and made too much commotion Jack or Dad would bellow from one of the rooms, "*Silencio!*" ("Silence!") Or "*Callate, niño!*" ("Shut up, boy!") Dad was at his typewriter in one room clacking away, while Jack labored in another room, writing longhand passages that would subsequently be transcribed into typewritten form by Norma.

In Mexico, Jack and Dad plotted several stories together, but for a variety of reasons never completed them. Jack did go on to write and sell a solo novel based upon an idea the men developed together. The men, while fast friends, were perhaps too individualistic to write in concert. They were, each of them, assertive and dominant. Alpha males. And at the time they had divergent writing styles. Jack's imagery and skill with words were ahead of Frank Herbert's choppier abilities, although Dad was fast developing in those realms and was also learning characterization and plotting. Of key importance, he was beginning to understand the importance of "getting inside a character's head," as he liked to say later. Once a writer got sufficiently inside a character's head, my father discovered, the character behaved in a manner that was consistent with his personality. Motivations were no longer muddled, and his actions made sense to the reader. Plots fell into place.

In Chapala, Frank Herbert was hard at work on *Under Pressure*, his submarine thriller. The unfolding novel described, with great psychological insight, a submarine crew in wartime, a plot constructed with building blocks that the author had learned about human motivation. Of equal interest, the story described a world of the future where oil supplies were limited. This was not easy to envision at the time, since petroleum products were plentiful and inexpensive. For the concept, Dad recalled that oil had been of strategic importance in World War II, and he extrapolated this to another war, under much more severe conditions.

But the novel was progressing slowly, and to pay immediate bills, Dad worked primarily on short stories. They could be finished and mailed in a much shorter period of time, and if they sold, checks would appear.

The kitchen of our house was permeated with diffused tropical light, making it a cheerful room. A wooden table sat by one window, and a large basket of fruit was always on the table. I made daily trips to the outdoor market stalls with Mom or our maid, Paulina. A fine cook, the maid regularly made a seafood stew that my parents and the Vances liked.

There were flies everywhere, and, with the exception of Mom, we grew somewhat accustomed to them, even if they crawled across our plates as we were eating. We always examined our food carefully before lifting it mouthward with a fork.

Cockroaches were a great concern to us as well, and especially to my mother. Each morning we developed the habit of shaking out our clothes and shoes before putting them on. Many roaches entered through the drain in the bathtub, and if Mom or Norma saw them when they wanted to take a bath, they came out and waggled two fingers (like cockroach antennae) at one of the men. Then Dad or Jack went in and flushed the filthy creatures down the drain with hot water. Sometimes there were as many as twenty roaches at a time.

Dad wrote of this and other adventures with Mexican insects in a humorous thousand-word piece, "Life with Animalitos." (In Mexico, insects of all kinds are called "animalitos"—"little animals.") It was a first-person story, written with *Reader's Digest* in mind, since they paid well for such material. Unfortunately this yarn, like a number of others from the pen of Frank Herbert, did not find a receptive editor.

I was tutored by my mother, using schoolbooks brought from the United States. She taught me Spanish as well, and what she didn't teach me I learned from children in the streets.

By Mexican standards, the cost of living was high in Chapala, and money was running low. Short story sales weren't coming through for my father, and Jack wasn't doing much better. Jack also lost one of his steadiest sources of income, the *Captain Video* TV show. It was decided that we could get by on less in a non-tourist environment.

After two months in Chapala, we moved to another town in the state of Jalisco a few miles south, Ciudad Guzman. With a population of twenty-four thousand, it was considerably larger than Chapala. In Ciudad Guzman we rented a smaller, two-story adobe and white stucco house. It was in the midst of town, on a level street where the houses were lined up side-by-side, with small yards. Dad, recalling his farm upbringing, wanted to raise his own food and become as self-sufficient as he could. So he purchased a number of baby chickens, which he kept in an adobe-walled outdoor compound on the street side of the house.

Some of the rooms in the house had earthen floors. I remember the loamy odors of earth there, and market smells, and donkeys in the streets swatting flies from their flanks with their tails. The outdoor markets bustled with activity.

By now I was proficient in Spanish, so my parents decided to place me in Mexican public school, in the first grade. I wore a thin white peasant outfit like local children and carried my school supplies in a small canvas bag. I traveled to and from school on a unique schoolbus, an old station wagon with some of its windows broken out, including the back one. This allowed motor exhaust into the passenger compartment. I sat in the rear, probably the worst seat from the standpoint of air quality, scrunched up next to other kids.

We had been in Ciudad Guzman for only a few days when the retired Mexican Army general who ran the town asked to see Frank Herbert, in order to evaluate his application for an extended stay in Mexico. One of the local merchants took Dad in a truck to the general's beautiful three-story house, where flowers hung from wrought iron balconies. The general was very friendly. Several people were in attendance, and sweet cookies were served, which Dad liked. He ate two, realizing later that the others only took one apiece.

When Dad returned to the merchant's truck, he began to feel drunk. He told the merchant to go get their wives; they were going out to have a party. The merchant wanted no part of this, for he knew they would get into trouble. He told Dad that the cookies had been laced with the most expensive North African hashish in the world, flown in by the Mexican Air Force for the general.

Dad recalled being taken into a beautiful building and guided up a long flight of stairs to a room with a table. There the merchant and a beautiful woman filled him with six or seven cups of strong Mexican coffee. Dad came down from his hallucination, and noticed the woman was an old hag, a whorehouse madame. He left as soon as he could, and while descending the stairs noticed now that they smelled of urine, and that there was a stench of burro dung outside.

Another time, a Mexican friend gave my father a cup of tea made with "semillas" (seeds), and Dad didn't think to ask what sort of seeds they were. After consuming the delicious beverage, he learned they were morning glory seeds. Subsequently he passed out, falling into a pleasant sleep. He recalled my mother waking him up the next morning in a sunny room.

A few months later, upon returning to the United States, Dad would have a third and final experience with a hallucinatory drug. While the first two experiences were inadvert, the third, as I will explain later, was not. Through these experiences he was developing an awareness of the significance of drugs in human life, and would write about this one day in the *Dune* series. The fictional spice melange, the most important substance in the universe, was produced only on the planet Dune, and Paul Atreides's experiences with that drug mirror the author's personal experiences. Melange, in fact, would become the key to an entire political, economic, and religious structure in the Dune universe.

In Ciudad Guzman, with no money coming in, our funds soon ran dangerously low. We packed and left town for parts north. By the end of 1953 we were staying with the Vances at their farmhouse in Kenwood, California. On a small kitchen table at the rear of the house,

Mom worked with me on a scrapbook about the Mexico trip. She located a stamp pad and large rubber letters, which we used with painstaking slowness to print a story on the pages. This was one of my first writing experiences, and it was in effect a journal, albeit a brief one.

These are some of the entries:

We and the Vances got the Jeep to go to Mexico, and we went to Colton (California) in the Jeep and we stayed there for 2 days.

We went to Nogales and we went swimming.

We stayed in Guaymas for 1 night.

We stayed in Los Mochis and slept in the Jeep. Bruce and I were sweating in the hot night.

Dad played a double-reed harmonica in those days, favoring sea chanteys, Irish songs and Western tunes. He played "Greensleeves," too, which may have been written by one of our ancestors, King Henry VIII. My father's harmonica tone was sweet, with excellent tremolo effect. He could play the guitar and piano as well, with more than passable skill, and he whistled beautifully. "Worried Man Blues" and "Rhapsody in Blue" were among his favorites. He had a natural ear and was self-taught. Above all, Frank Herbert was blessed with a wonderful baritone singing voice, rich and full. My mother commented often on how much she enjoyed hearing him sing.

He was between jobs at the time, and a number of bill collectors were hot on his trail. One day, my father vowed, he would pay all the old bills in full, with interest. For the moment, however, they would have to wait.

CHAPTER
8

✳ The South Seas Dream ✳

WHILE WE stayed with the Vances in California, Dad wasn't doing much creative writing. For several years, he had been wanting to return to the Northwest, and now he had feelers out for jobs in Washington State and Oregon—either in the newspaper business or other professions that involved writing. To get by, my parents borrowed money from Mom's Aunt Ruth and Uncle Bing, who lived in nearby Sebastopol, California.

In the spring of 1954, when Dad was thirty-three years old, he obtained an important job. It was as speech writer for Guy Cordon, a U.S. Senator from Oregon who was running for re-election that year. Cordon chaired the Interior and Insular Affairs Committee, with substantial responsibilities in government land-use policy. He also sat on the powerful Senate Appropriations committee and on a number of subcommittees, including Armed Services and Atomic Energy.

Years before in Burley, Frank Herbert had been influenced by Henry W. Stein, an ex-newspaperman who spoke of the romance of life on a big-city newspaper. Stein also instilled in the boy a passionate interest in politics. Stein had been involved in state and national politics, serving as a presidential elector from the State of Washington.

Now my father jumped at the opportunity to join Cordon's staff. This would vault him into elite circles, providing his developing intellect with important insights into the mechanics of national politics—

insights that Frank Herbert could use extensively in his writing for years to come.

Initially he would work in Washington, D.C., with the Senator, but for only a six-week period between early April and the primary election in May. After that, Dad was to return to Portland, Oregon, to handle publicity and other tasks for the re-election campaign. Under those circumstances, it wasn't practical for us to accompany him to the nation's capital.

We packed at fanatical speed to move our household to Portland, and within seventy-two hours everything we owned was ready to go. Then, as always, my parents owned a lot of books, so this made up a great deal of the weight of the shipment. Dad made arrangements for men to come in and carry the items.

Two days later, with only a few suitcases, we were six hundred miles north in Portland, staying in a hotel. Cordon's previous speech writer had resigned on short notice, so Dad was needed right away. He only had one day to help Mom find an old house to rent in the city.

That evening, Mom, Bruce and I accompanied the new political staffer to Portland Airport. My parents kissed, and Mom said to Dad, "Give 'em hell, darling."

My mother would not listen to the radio until hours later, when she was certain his plane had landed safely in Washington, D.C.

A man of ethics with a perfect senatorial attendance record, Guy Cordon had been in office for a decade. Like ex-president Harry S. Truman, his close friend in the other major party, he refused to become obligated to private interests. Since Cordon was chairman of the Interior and Insular Affairs Committee, oil companies were always trying (without success) to curry favor with him. He was a "nuts and bolts" man, a technician who cared more about substance than politics. Many times he avoided publicity. My father would grow to respect him very much.

In a magazine article, Frank Herbert wrote:

Senator Cordon carries a full mane of gray hair which lends an air of dignity to a face dominated by a pair of intense, but twinkling eyes. There's something homespun and basically solid about the Senior Senator from Oregon.

My parents wrote to one another, but Mom had more time to write than he did. Her letters were more frequent and longer. One thing was common to all of their correspondence: They spoke of how much they missed one another, how much they ached to be together again.

Each evening my mother liked to read, or would knit while listening to Fulton Lewis, Jr., or Paul Harvey on the radio. The oil furnace didn't heat the house enough for her, so she liked to bundle up in an afghan and sit by a cozy fire. She read murder mysteries, historical accounts and, increasingly, books about politics. She was fascinated by biographies of American political leaders, including Eisenhower and Stevenson, and analyses of events that led to the first and second world wars.

In April and May 1954, the Army-McCarthy hearings were in full swing in Washington, D.C. Radio broadcasts began at 2:00 P.M. Portland time, and Mom listened to every moment of them.

She was a fine seamstress, and using a sewing machine borrowed from Babe, she made curtains for the house, along with her own slacks, shorts, blouses, skirts, and dresses. She also knitted sweaters for Dad.

In every way possible, she wanted to help Dad on the Cordon campaign, either with advice based upon her political researches or through other campaign-related tasks that he needed completed in Oregon. She was always volunteering to do things for him, and he very much appreciated it. She located news accounts from papers all over Oregon about Democrat Richard Neuberger, who would probably be Cordon's opponent for the senate seat after the May primaries.

Using all available information on Neuberger, my father then prepared speeches and press releases that attacked the opponent's positions on a variety of issues.

Public opinion polls came in showing Neuberger doing too well, and as panic set in on the Cordon staff, some of them discussed tactics that could only be classified as dirty politics. My father refused to participate in any of those schemes, and instead recommended a course of direct confrontation with Neuberger on the issues. Cordon followed this advice, but seemed uncomfortable campaigning. With his aversion to publicity, his accomplishments and messages did not always reach the attention of the voters. Cordon had done a great deal to promote the interests of Oregon labor, for example, by saving a Columbia River dam construction project in committee, but few people outside of the U.S. Senate ever learned about it.

Frank Herbert had taken on a formidable task, attempting to publicize a man who would not blow his own horn, a man who was widely respected by his peers in the U.S. Senate, but not well-known in his own state. In two earlier U.S. Senate elections, Cordon had won easily against weak Democratic opponents. Now, in Neuberger, he faced a former state senator and published writer who was easily recognized in Oregon. His wife, state legislator Maurine Neuberger, aided his cause with her own personal popularity, having been a champion of consumer protection issues.*

In a very real sense, Mom missed Dad so terribly that she tried to keep herself busy while he was gone. She was always asking him on the telephone and in letters when he would be home, and telling him she was keeping the home fires burning. Whenever the phone rang, she ran for it, hoping it was him, hoping he would surprise her with a call from Portland Airport. Whenever she heard footsteps on the front porch, she thought they might be his. When they spoke on the phone, I sometimes saw tears in her eyes, and as they closed she often said to him in Spanish, *"Adios, mi amor."* ("Good-bye, my love.")

Dad, who was living in a five-dollar-a-day room at the historic Mayflower Hotel, missed her just as much. As days away from her passed, he wrote in a letter home that he had been singing the words from a popular song to himself, "Sometimes I Feel Like a Motherless Child."

They counted the days remaining until my father would come home.

While in Washington, D.C., he obtained a pass through Senator Cordon's office and attended a number of the Army-McCarthy hearings. Dad sat in the Senate reserved gallery amidst much security, since five members of Congress had been wounded a short time before by Puerto Rican separatists who fired pistols from a spectators' gallery.

---

*Maurine Neuberger was also one of the first politicians to oppose the tobacco industry, and became only the third woman elected to the U.S. Senate herself.

Senator Cordon had been criticized by Neuberger for not coming out against Senator Joseph McCarthy, and this was hurting Cordon's campaign, dropping him in the polls. To counter this, Frank Herbert was sitting in on the hearings, obtaining information that Cordon might use to advantage. Cordon, former Oregon State Commander of the American Legion, was strongly pro-military, and concurred with many of McCarthy's publicly expressed positions. But troubling bits of information were reaching Cordon's ears concerning the methods of the Senator from Wisconsin.

On his maternal side, Frank Herbert was a McCarthy himself, with many relatives in Senator McCarthy's home state, including the famous red-baiter himself, who was a distant cousin. Dad referred to him as "Cousin Joe," and on one occasion they met in the nation's capital, at a cocktail party.

After initially keeping an open mind about McCarthy, Dad was appalled to learn about blacklisting methods the Senator used to prevent suspected Communists and "Communist sympathizers" from working in their chosen professions—particularly since this was often based upon scant evidence. Frank Herbert, like McCarthy, felt the leadership of the Soviet Union was psychotic enough to start a nuclear war, but believed McCarthy had gone too far in his zeal and paranoia, to the point where he was endangering essential freedoms of the people of the United States. Here my father drew the line, for he was a great believer in the Constitution of this nation—particularly in the rights of individuals. After consideration he recommended that Cordon make a strong statement against McCarthy, which Cordon did. But he didn't do it until the hearings were almost over, which Neuberger used against him.

At the hearings, Dad saw Robert F. Kennedy working as an aide to Senator McCarthy, talking in hushed tones with the Senator, doing the Senator's bidding, constantly at his side. This, when added to RFK's later position in support of federal wiretapping, branded him as a dangerous politician in my father's opinion—as a politician, who, like Senator McCarthy, would not hesitate to trample on human rights for the sake of a pet cause.

In the *Dune* series, which would begin in serial form in 1963, Dad wrote extensively about the abuses of power by leaders. These were opinions based, in large degree, upon his experiences in Washington, D.C. Another reflection of this time can be found in the short story "Committee of the Whole," which would appear in the April 1965 issue of *Galaxy*. In that story, Frank Herbert described, in highly cynical terms, the workings of a Senate committee.

Dad worked for Senator Cordon in Room 130A of the Senate Office Building. The building was commonly referred to as the "S.O.B." And Cordon's "big office," as staffers called it, was Room 333.

My father's days were long, often from early in the morning until midnight. Almost every day he had breakfast in the S.O.B. dining room, usually a poached egg on unbuttered wheat toast, a half grapefruit without sugar and two cups of black coffee. He read three newspapers with breakfast—*The Washington Post, The New York Times*, and, in great detail, *The Congressional Record*. He scanned for items of interest and read quickly—a style of research that would be beneficial to him during his long writing career.

After breakfast he liked to take a constitutional around the Capitol Building, and shortly before 8:30 A.M. he always reported to Room 130A. Dad was much more than a speech writer to the Senator. Each morning after organizing his papers, Dad went up to the third floor to consult with Robert Parkman (Senator Cordon's administrative assistant) on promotional projects for the day. Then he went back downstairs and worked on speeches, political letters and news stories about the Senator, for release to the press.

Speech writing took up most of his time and involved many rewrites. He worked on this for most of each morning and often into the early part of the afternoon. At least four lunches each week were with important people, including Secretary of the Interior Douglas McKay, a friend and supporter of Cordon. Frank Herbert knew McKay from years earlier in Salem, Oregon, when the younger man had been a reporter and McKay had been a state senator. Other lunches and important meetings were with research directors at the Defense Department (for the Army Corps of Engineers), with National Archives people, with Senator Margaret Chase Smith (whom Dad admired), and with Jack Martin, press secretary to President Eisenhower—all to obtain assistance for the Cordon campaign.

From mid-afternoon to 6:00 P.M., Dad could invariably be found in the Library of Congress, in what he called his "second office." That was Study Room 249 in the Library of Congress Annex. The little room came equipped with telephone extension 807, where he could always be reached if someone needed him right away.

Usually he took his portable Remington typewriter into that office. With piles of books and periodicals all around, he researched and wrote speeches, political letters and press releases. To add spice to the Senator's speeches, my father included familiar quotations and anecdotes of famous people, particularly American politicians with a sense of humor, such as Chauncey M. Depew. Depew, renowned as a raconteur and after-dinner speaker, wrote an autobiography, *My Memories of Eighty Years*, which Dad referred to often.

The Library of Congress, in two huge buildings by the Capitol, was the largest reference facility in the nation, with more than thirty-three million documents. As a senatorial staffer, Frank Herbert had C-9 security clearance. This permitted him access to the Legislative Reference Service, through which he could use virtually any document or book in the library. He just got on the telephone, ordered what he wanted, and presently it arrived in a cart, with blue bookmarks designating the pages that were of interest to him. Additional notes were included on material available at other government facilities, such as the National Archives. If Dad wanted any of the material, he just ordered it through the Library of Congress, and presently it was in front of him.

He had so much research to do, so much studying, that at times he felt like he was cramming for a college examination. In a moment of late-night silliness he wrote to Mom, referring to the library as "the Liberace of Congress."

Despite his schedule, remarkably, he found time to write science fiction, and that year a number of his short stories were published. One, "Pack Rat Planet" (*Astounding Science Fiction*, December 1954), was an extrapolation of his experiences in the Library of Congress. It described a huge Galactic Library built into underground chambers that took up almost the entire subsurface of the Earth. All inhabitants of the planet worked in some fashion for the library, and were referred to by the inhabitants of other planets as "pack rats," tending vast store-houses of useless information. (This was later expanded into the novel *Direct Descent*, Ace, 1980).

Dad made friends with Cordon's secretary, Dorothy Jones, and her husband, Lyle. The Joneses had lived in American Samoa, and were interested in accompanying us to Mexico on another trip. My father was becoming especially obsessed with the idea of living in American Samoa. If he could obtain a government job there, he thought it would leave him plenty of free time to write. So in his spare time he had been putting out feelers, letting people know he wanted to live there with his family.

Through Cordon, Dad met Stewart French, chief counsel of the Subcommittee on Interior and Insular Affairs. French, a powerful man in Washington, D.C., became a personal friend and invited Frank Herbert to his home on a number of occasions. French promised to help Dad obtain an appointment in American Samoa after the U.S. elections were concluded. Since U.S. territories were administered by the Department of the Interior, Dad also told Secretary of the Interior McKay of his interest. McKay said he would do what he could, again after the re-election of Cordon.

My mother was at first hesitant at the prospect of going to Samoa. She felt Dad should concentrate on the Cordon campaign and worry about future assignments afterward. Gradually, though, she came around to his way of thinking. She liked warm climates, and Portland was decidedly on the cool side much of the time.

During his stay in the nation's capital, Dad made a train trip to New York City, his first visit there. As he wandered around in the forest of buildings, staring upward, he felt like a country bumpkin. He stayed at the Biltmore Hotel on Madison Avenue, and met his literary agent, Lurton Blassingame, for the first time. Lurton was a thin man who looked like an Oxford professor. Meeting Lurton was not, however, the principal purpose of Dad's trip, which was made on behalf of the Cordon re-election committee.

On the top floor of a New York City office building, Dad tried to convince Paul Smith, board chairman of *Collier's* magazine, to run an article on Cordon. By prearrangement the article would be written by a well-known writer and former adviser to Franklin D. Roosevelt, Ray Moley, who had also promised to write several other newspaper and magazine pieces on behalf of the Senator. Smith made no commitment beyond a promise to watch for the article when it came in, whereupon he would read it himself. It would not have to go through the usual "slush pile" route of unsolicited submissions.

Frank Herbert saw the slush pile at *Collier's*, and found it disquieting. At a later writing workshop recorded by his friend Bill Ransom, Dad said the slush pile was in a large room, dominated by a long table, with big blackboards covering two walls. Mailmen came in pushing large carts full of manuscripts. These submissions were dumped on the table. College students working part-time then sorted the manuscripts, usually distributing them randomly into readers' boxes. There were messages on the blackboards, and the sorters pulled out anything that particular editors said they were looking for. Some writers were mentioned negatively, with their manuscripts tossed in a rejection sack. Envelopes that looked unprofessional were tossed directly into the rejection sack without being opened. These unfortunate writers would receive form letters, often after long delays.

When Ray Moley learned that *Collier's* wasn't offering a contract in advance, he refused to write the article. Nothing on speculation, he said. So, prompted by Cordon, Dad took on the writing chore, and set to work on it in the Library of Congress. The completed article, entitled "Undersea Riches for Everybody," was four thousand words long, a popular length at *Collier's*, and described problems of underwater oil and gas exploration on the continental shelf. It outlined Cordon's position on this issue, and, if published in time, was expected to boost the campaign.

Dad completed it in a few days and rushed it to Lurton for submission to Paul Smith. In order to make each proposal more noticeable to an editor, Lurton always submitted it in an orange folder, with an agency label bearing the story title and name of the author.

An astute judge of talent, Lurton encouraged my father and assured him, "You'll be a big name before too long." The agent became something of a father figure to Frank Herbert, and a tremendous inspiration.

He was also a no-nonsense man who said what was on his mind. Lurton's brother, Wyatt Blassingame, was an award-winning short-story writer who also offered advice and encouragement. Wyatt's work had appeared frequently in national magazines and anthologies. He had written pulp science fiction as well, with such memorable titles as "Ghouls of the Green Death" (1934) and "The Goddess of Crawling Horrors" (1937).

Lurton wanted very much to see Dad's novel completed, the psychological thriller about submarine warfare that he had begun a couple of years before in Santa Rosa. But that writing project had been derailed by the necessity of survival.

At least my father had a job, for the time being. That was not always the case during the years I lived with him.

The subjects Dad researched for Cordon were varied, and would form a basis not only for the Senator's speeches, but for the political-ecological writings of Frank Herbert in the next four decades. He researched tidelands oil, the Submerged Lands Act, the Continental Shelf Lands Act, land grants, an "oil-for-education" congressional amendment, Federal Aid to Education, issues of grazing on national forest lands, and the highly publicized Hells Canyon issue involving construction of a huge hydroelectric project on the Snake River. Sometimes Dad wrote committee reports on Senate bills for Cordon.

He also analyzed Cordon's voting record in detail, on environmental, educational, agricultural, power development, and other issues. With this information, he prepared abstracts of the Senator's comments for press releases and other purposes, slanted to show how Cordon's positions were benefiting people in the State of Oregon.

Guy Cordon, a strong influence on my father, believed in reducing government spending and in limiting the size and power of bureaucratic institutions. Between 1947 and 1951, the Senator voted to cut all federal appropriations, to cut non-defense spending, to reduce government publicity expenditures and to reduce government employee benefits. He voted to limit the President of the United States to two terms in office. Cordon also advocated state instead of federal control over offshore resources, and opposed federal construction of massive public power facilities—positions that were directly at odds with those of Neuberger.

One of Senator Cordon's most important speeches, involving what was known as the Hill Amendment, was sixteen pages long and involved wading through nearly fifty documents. Dad worked all night to complete it, and, bleary-eyed, showed up with it at Cordon's office at 9:00 one morning. He found the door to the Senator's inner office closed, which usually meant an important visitor was inside. But Cordon's secretary told Dad to go right in with the speech. Upon entering he noticed a man in a Homburg felt hat seated with his back to him. The man had his feet on Cordon's desk.

Something was *very* familiar about the hat.

Frank Herbert said, "Here's your speech, Senator," and was about to leave when he realized that the visitor was ex-president Harry S. Truman. Cordon introduced them, and they shook hands. Truman said something to the effect that he hoped it was a good speech, and Dad, flabbergasted, beat a hasty retreat. Cordon and Truman were buddies, despite being in different political parties. Both men were outspoken individualists. At the time, Truman had retired from public life and was working on his memoirs.

After reading the speech, Cordon took Dad to lunch and told him it was "a powerful piece of paper," and "one of the best damned research jobs" he had ever seen. Dad got another raise. The speech was ingenious, and in writing it my father called upon a technique he had learned in the newspaper business. Neither Cordon nor anyone on his staff had ever seen anything like it. Using what newspapermen called the "concentric circles" technique, Dad wrote the speech so that it could be cut from the end in a number of places, thus making successively shorter and shorter speeches. A variety of lengths could be chosen, and each time the length was expanded, it enlarged upon the arguments in the central theme, making it more and more convincing.

One evening late in May—so that primary voting for our neighborhood could be held in our house—Mom moved the furniture and rugs out of the front hall, living room and dining room, and scrubbed the floors. Balloting booths were moved in. Two days later on the morning of the election, a number of election officials arrived. I remember standing in the living room in a thick forest of adults who towered over me, all of whom were talking politics. At the time, I was just getting over the measles. Mom took us out to a restaurant for dinner while the heaviest election crowds were in the house.

Cordon won the Republican primary as expected, and my father returned to Portland in June. At our dinner table, he spilled forth stories of important people he had met or heard about. He spoke of a faraway place called Washington, D.C., and of distant lands he wanted to visit, such as American Samoa. He called Samoa "paradise," and showed us romantic color photographs from books and magazines of palm trees, thatched huts and sailing boats.

"We're going to live there soon," he announced.

My half-sister Penny, by Dad's first marriage, came to visit us late in the summer of 1954. Twelve years old, she wanted to spend time with her father, and despite the fact that he remained in arrears on his child-support payments, her mother assented.

That August, Dad received terrific news. *Collier's* wanted to publish his article, and were paying well for it: $1,250. Dad was elated. Through Lurton, he tried to get assurance that "Underseas Riches" would appear in time to help Cordon's re-election campaign. Dad felt strongly that the Neuberger side was engaging in a smear campaign, spreading false information about Cordon's positions on issues. Neuberger had a way of coloring the facts, of distorting them to his advantage.

In the Cordon campaign it was hoped that the article, in a popular magazine, would help set the record straight. Months went by, however, and the election occurred first. The article, while paid for by *Collier's*, was shunted aside for nearly three years, and never did appear in the magazine. Ultimately the publication folded.

The 1954 national elections were held on Tuesday, November 2nd. Oregon returns were slow coming in, since they only had one voting machine in the entire state. Consequently, the vast majority of votes had to be tabulated by hand. After polls closed in the state, Cordon held a slight lead, and it increased slowly all night long, until he was twelve thousand votes ahead. He showed surprising early strength in heavily Democratic Multnomah County. When Neuberger went to bed late that night, he thought he had lost the election. Cordon wasn't so certain. He called it a "horse race."

During the following morning and early afternoon, Cordon's lead shrank. The election was so close that the governor ordered the placement of guards on all ballot boxes, to prevent vote tampering. By 2:30 P.M., Neuberger was only eighteen hundred votes behind. Two hours later, he took the lead. The margin then increased by ones and twos and tens, and kept increasing. When all votes were tabulated, Senator Cordon carried twenty-six of thirty-six counties but still lost the election by less than four tenths of one percent, since he didn't carry the most populous counties. It was the closest U.S. Senate race in the nation and the most dramatic election in Oregon history.

Thereafter, Frank Herbert put more effort into obtaining a position in American Samoa, where he believed the slow, laid-back lifestyle would fit into the vision he had for his life. Adding to government material on the South Seas that he had shipped back from Washington, D.C., he purchased books about American Samoa and other trust territories, including a book about interesting archaeological ruins at Ponape (also known as Pohnpei, and formerly Ascension Island) in the Caroline Islands.

Dad's application for a government position went through channels to William Strand, Director of the Office of Territories. Secretary of the Interior McKay and others put in recommendations in support of it. Strand, however, had the final word. He apparently felt my father was overqualified for the position, and that he would not remain in it long before wanting to devote full time to other pursuits. Strand may have been correct in this assessment, and it may have been based upon an offhand comment made by someone who knew my father—a comment to the effect that his first love was writing. Maybe Dad told too many people about his creative interests, and word got out that he wouldn't be a good "government man."

Dad turned his attentions to his writing. He had sold more short stories in 1954 than in any previous year, along with the lucrative sale to *Collier's*. He had in mind a novel based upon his experiences working for Senator Cordon, but for the moment he was sour on politics. The unfinished submarine thriller was at hand, the novel Lurton wanted to see. Lurton also wanted more science fiction short stories.

So, with our funds dwindling once again, Dad set to work on the submarine novel.

A few days before Christmas 1954, we rented a little A-frame beach cabin in Healy Palisades, Washington. This was a tiny community between Seattle and Tacoma, in an area now known as Federal Way. The rent was low, and well it should have been. The cabin, all six hundred square feet of it, was at the bottom of a steep hill, reached by a long narrow trail. We moved in by boat, using a large open dory powered by an inboard diesel engine. This was supposed to be an interim house, a cheap place to live until Dad finished his submarine novel, *Under Pressure*. Dad set to work on the book, rising early each day and working far into the night.

My mother began to do freelance copy-editing for local stores, writing retail advertisements to bring in what money she could. Mom's work was only part-time, paying very little. To reduce family expenditures she removed frayed collars from our shirts and sewed the collars back on inside out, giving new life to old fabric. She also cut long sleeves down to short when the elbows became worn, and patched our socks and the knees of trousers.

To save money, my father regularly gave his sons what he called "butch" haircuts, using electric clippers. These were crewcuts, with our hair cut the same length all over. His haircuts turned out okay at first, but always looked funny in a few weeks when the hair grew out. I had cowlicks, and as time passed without a new trim, my head took on the shape of a large, strange flower.

The proverbial church mouse had more money than we did in those days. When we didn't have enough on hand to pay bills, Mom developed a random method of deciding which would receive priority. She threw all of them on the floor, and the ones that landed right side up were paid first. On other occasions she drew bills out of Dad's Homburg felt hat to determine which ones to pay.

For my principal chore, I was assigned to collect driftwood from the beach to heat the house. I found quite a bit, which I stacked on the porch by the front door. Dad did his own foraging for firewood, and he supplemented that by getting on as many mailing lists as he could, under a phony name. In a few weeks, junk mail was pouring in from all over the country, which Dad and Mom tossed in the wood stove in the kitchen along with the driftwood, or in a river rock fireplace in the main living area.*

Our beach cabin had one bedroom and one bath. I slept on a mattress on the floor of a tiny mezzanine overlooking the living room. Bruce's crib was set up nearby. He was three, and I was seven. Due to the absence of a wall, activities downstairs often kept me awake. Especially Dad's loud voice as he told long, convoluted "shaggy dog" stories, and his booming laughter after the punch lines. I often crawled out of bed, and in my pajamas peered through a railing at adults below. Bruce slept through anything.

A man of extremes, my father could become very angry—a side of him I saw too often. At the other end of the spectrum, he could behave like the happiest man alive. At such times his laughter was remarkable. It rolled from him in great peals. He savored each cachination, taking a couple of extra gulps of mirth at the end. When entertaining guests, my parents often had the lights down low while the fireplace blazed cheerily, giving the cabin a warm glow. A remarkable raconteur, Dad enjoyed talking far into the night.

For his desk Frank Herbert salvaged a broad slab of driftwood from the beach and mounted it on a frame constructed of plywood and two-by-fours. It was set up in the living room by a large window, so that he looked out upon the water.

One day he received an unsolicited package of peyote in the mail from a friend, along with instructions on how to take it. A note with the package said the stuff was guaranteed to cure writer's block. Mom told him not to do it, to throw the stuff away. But Dad was curious. He'd never had peyote before, and proceeded to cut up an entire blossom. With this and hot water, he made a cup of tea. The instructions

---

*The junk mail trick continued for a number of years after that, until one day Dad saw a royalty check in the fireplace with flames curling around it. He didn't get to it in time, and had to request reissuance of the check. In ensuing years he always cursed the arrival of junk mail.

said to quaff it, and Dad did so. Instantly the stuff came back up, with most of the other contents of his stomach. After cleaning up, Dad didn't feel any ill effect, and went back to writing his submarine novel at the driftwood desk.

Soon he seemed to be upon the waters of Puget Sound, with sunlight glinting off wave tops in a rhythmic pattern. He experienced sound with each beat of light—an eerie, beautiful pealing. The water was choppy, almost forming whitecaps, and sunlight glinted upon it. Suddenly he realized he was *hearing* each glint of light—the most dulcet, soothing chimes he had ever experienced in his life.

Thus when he wrote in the *Dune* series of a "vision echo," he was writing from firsthand experience, from an experience of sensory mixing.

My father discarded the rest of the peyote, and never did anything like that again. He said the regurgitation was caused by strychnine, a white fluffy material that should have been separated from the blossom's bud with a knife and thrown away.

Before we moved again in early 1955, Dad returned the driftwood desktop slab to the beach. He told my mother he had been the custodian of the wood for a short time. Years later he would say something similar to me, that none of us ever "own" land. We are merely caretakers of it, passing it along one day to other caretakers.

It is this way with the Earth, he said. We are stewards of it, not owners, and one day future generations will assume the responsibility.

102

CHAPTER
9

✳ The Family Car ✳

And always, he fought the temptation to choose a clear, safe course, warning, "That path leads ever down into stagnation."

—Frank Herbert, in *Dune*

THAT SPRING Dad received a job offer to do promotional work for the Douglas Fir Plywood Association (DFPA) in Tacoma. The position didn't pay much, but with these earnings we could afford a nicer place to live—not much of a step upward. We moved into an old ramshackle house on the tide flats of Marine View Drive, across the bay from Tacoma. The weather-beaten house, with a porch that ran around most of it, stood on a narrow stretch of land some twenty feet below road level, reached by going down two sets of steps. Part of the structure was on pilings, and below the house was an old dock.

For his study, Dad set up a desk in what had once been the living room. This afforded him a view of an industrial waterway, filled with tugboats and log booms. Each evening after work at the DFPA and every weekend I heard his portable typewriter going constantly—a rapid, machine-gun rhythm of keys.

Tacoma had long suffered a reputation for its poor air quality, known as the "Tacoma aroma." A number of pulp mills were in and around the city and the tall stack of a giant smelter across the bay was visible from our house. From the dumping of arsenic, heavy metals and other industrial wastes in the bay, the tide flats by us had a distinctive, unpleasant odor, especially when the tide was out. For the six months that we lived in that house, Bruce and I slept on thin mattresses, on a pair of toboggans set up on an unheated, enclosed porch.

Two of Frank Herbert's science fiction short stories were published that year, "Rat Race" (*Astounding Science Fiction*, July 1955) and "Occupation Force" (*Fantastic*, August 1955). Earnings from them were minimal.

These stories had been written before we moved to Marine View Drive. Now here, with every moment of spare time, he labored on his submarine novel, *Under Pressure*. He finished the 75,000-word book in April 1955, and mailed it to Lurton. It was organized into several story breaks, making it easily adaptable to serialization. When he wrote the book, he had in mind the legendary editor at *Astounding Science Fiction*, John W. Campbell. Among his other accomplishments, Campbell was a science fiction writer himself.*

Even with my father's job, we didn't have much money to spend. Flora knew where we were, and wanted her child-support money. The IRS demanded payment for back taxes, but in lieu of checks Dad sent excuses. Other bill collectors were in pursuit as well.

Dad did much of the cooking in our household, and liked to stir-fry several pounds of rice in a big wok, with a few vegetables and a minimal amount of meat. I'm sure it was good for us, with all the complex carbohydrates my father promised. But for years after I moved out I refused to eat rice. Only recently have I been able to stomach it again.

In the mid-1950s, a large new medical facility was opening in Tacoma, the Mary Bridge Children's Hospital. When Mom's freelance copywriting assignments ebbed, she took a part-time job with the facility, writing promotional literature for hospital fund-raising.

At the dinner table, my father sometimes spoke of writing and his

*Campbell's 1938 story "Who Goes There?" had been turned into a film in 1951, *The Thing*. The film had one of the most campy promotional lines of all time: "A monster so horrible it doesn't even have a name . . . *The Thing*!" It was remade by John Carpenter in 1982.

attempts to sell stories, complaining about particular editors. Sometimes as he ate, he read passages to my mother from manuscript pages stacked by his plate and asked for her opinion. She always provided honestly, and he would make pencil notations on the pages. At other times, Dad and Mom sat in the little living room, overlooking the tide flats, and he read short stories and chapters to her.

Only nine years before, in college, Beverly Herbert had dreamed of becoming a professional writer herself. With the demands of married life, this dream was fading. Reality told her there couldn't be two creative writers in one family. How could they possibly support a household?

In the midst of our pressing need for income, she told Dad not to worry, that if necessary he could leave DFPA and she would work for department stores (or wherever necessary) until his writing became successful. In this and countless other ways Beverly Herbert was totally selfless, and made an incredible sacrifice—giving my father a true gift of love. She believed in his writing ability, and always said he had more talent than she did, that she only had a flair for writing.

"Do what's in your heart, darling," she told him. "I'll be here for you."

In my mother's heart, she was sure he would become tremendously successful one day. He had such a powerful *need* to write, such a drive for it, that she knew she could never stand in his way, could never exert pressure on him to earn more money at the expense of his creative potential. He wasn't happy unless he was writing.

Aside from sacrificing a creative writing career, she was giving up a traditional home life. Mom enjoyed tinkering around the house, making a snug nest out of it, but with her career requirements there was less time for this. Still she sewed, knitted, wove, crocheted and baked pies. She made clothes for all of us and darned our socks. Essentially a homebody, she might have done well as a writer working out of the house if she'd been married to anyone else—to someone who would permit her the luxury of staying home near the typewriter. Instead she was forced out of her element into the workplace, at a time when the vast majority of women did not work away from the home.

Her faith was rewarded. Within two weeks of sending *Under Pressure* to New York, John W. Campbell made an offer to serialize it in *Astounding Science Fiction*. This was a remarkable response time for an editor. Campbell's offer was four cents a word, meaning the author would receive around $2,700 net after the deduction of Lurton's 10 percent commission. Dad accepted right away.

Campbell asked for two synopses. He planned to run the story in three installments of around twenty-five thousand words apiece, and synopses were needed to precede the second and third segments, filling the readers in on prior action. The serialization was scheduled to run from November 1955 through January 1956.

Lurton turned immediately toward selling the novel in book form. Walter I. Bradbury, managing editor of Doubleday, liked the book, and snapped it up in June 1955. This resulted in an additional $3,600 net to the author, so the book was starting to earn pretty good money for the mid-1950s. It allowed Dad to pay old debts, including some of the money owed to his ex-wife, Flora.

Doubleday was so impressed with the novel that they copy-edited it right away and scheduled it for publication in February of the following year. This was one short month following the serialization in *Astounding Science Fiction*, the earliest possible date Doubleday could publish it. The Science Fiction Book Club also picked the title up, but only paid a small amount for the rights.

Inspired by Dad's success, Mom spent every available moment writing a 64,000-word mystery novel, *Frighten the Mother*. It was dispatched to Lurton in the summer of 1955. While he liked portions of it, he felt the manuscript needed more work, and told her it was not ready for submission to publishers. Dejected, Mom set it aside. She didn't have Dad's perseverance.

In late August, Dad decided it was time to get rid of our rickety old car, a Dodge, in favor of more reliable transportation. He became aware of a most unusual set of wheels that was being advertised for sale by a funeral home in Tacoma. Terms were agreed to, and my parents purchased a used hearse for three hundred dollars. A 1940 Cadillac LaSalle, it only had nineteen thousand miles on it.

Dad wrote an unpublished 1,000-word piece about the vehicle, which he entitled, "The Invisible Car." In explanation of the title, he wrote:

> . . . Nobody looks at a hearse unless he absolutely has to. They see you, but they don't look. The eyes refuse to change focus. There's no glimmer of recognition.

Our "car" was unlike anything I had ever seen before. I hadn't even been familiar with the word "hearse," but soon learned the meaning. I don't recall being that surprised. After all, I slept on a toboggan, while other kids had beds. How was this so unusual?

Describing the hearse years later, Dad said, "It had a pre-Kettering engine, you know, before Kettering* screwed it up." He claimed the big heavy vehicle got twenty-seven miles per gallon on some stretches of road. My father was known to exaggerate on occasion, but he held firm on this. He said the Cadillac had separate hand and foot throttles, so that the hand throttle could be used as a cruise control to improve fuel efficiency.

The front compartment smelled of dust and old leather. A little electric fan sat on the dashboard, and a cracked leather seat stretched across the front—a seat that was, as Dad wrote, "as darkly blue-black as a pallbearer's suit." A pair of small glass sliding windows separated this compartment from the rear, so that anyone groaning inside a coffin could probably not be heard.

A week after acquiring the vehicle, Mom announced, "You aren't going to school here in September, Brian. Your father and I will tutor you in Mexico."

We were going to Mexico in the hearse.

Dad's American Samoa assignment hadn't materialized, so he and Mom were putting together an alternate trip to the tropics, to more familiar climes. It would be a working trip for the benefit of their writing, as on their Kelly Butte adventure and on our earlier trip to Mexico. Dad had been tinkering with a novel based upon a famous

---

*Charles F. Kettering, a General Motors research executive.

Santa Rosa murder case,* which he entitled *Storyship*. He wanted to complete it in Mexico, along with ten or fifteen short stories. Mom planned to rewrite her rejected murder mystery, *Frighten the Mother*.

The hearse, which became like a van or panel truck to our family, was black, with big rounded front fenders. It had chapel-shaped doors and pewter scrolls and candelabra on the sides of the rear compartment. Dad painted the top silver, concurring with Mom's opinion that it would reflect tropical heat better than the original black. He and Mom also painted the chapel doors bright yellow, just for fun. This would distinguish the vehicle (they thought) from a normal working hearse.

Bruce and I received a battery of shots to ward off tropical diseases. Penny, who had been staying with us recently on Marine View Drive, would not go with us.

While making preparations for the trip, Dad enjoyed driving around Tacoma in a dark suit, impersonating an undertaker. At the Cadillac dealership, where he had the car checked and tuned up, he forced the service manager to shake his hand. To his glee, he noticed the fellow then wiped his hand on his coveralls, assuming the hearse driver had been handling bodies. So Dad fiendishly maneuvered another handshake with the poor fellow, and soon afterward saw him make a beeline for the washroom.

Frank Herbert was not a patient man. In restaurants while waiting for food, he often turned into a grouchy bear. To his delight he discovered that restaurant operators were uncomfortable with a hearse parked outside, and set everything else aside to get food for the driver.

"Wouldn't you prefer take-out, sir?" one manager asked, after Dad went in and requested a table. The manager glanced nervously outside at the long vehicle, parked by the front door.

"No, thank you," Dad replied, in a halting voice. "My doctor says I need to slow down. I wouldn't want to end up . . ." He cast a sidelong glance at the hearse. "Well, you know!"

---

*The case of Joseph A. Daugherty, who stabbed his wife seven times and subsequently pled insanity, saying that this had to do with the seven sacraments of the Bible, and that Christ had put the knife in his hands to kill. Ralph Slattery was called as an expert witness, and testified that Daugherty was insane. The jury ruled otherwise, and convicted Daugherty of first-degree murder. He was executed at San Quentin in 1954.

Even fast-food drive-in restaurants accelerated when he drove up.
He and Mom liked fried chicken from one take-out place in Tacoma,
and over a couple of weeks he pulled up to the window several times
to order either two or four complete chicken dinners. It reached the
point where he noticed employees running around inside before he
even reached the window. Someone would see him pulling in, and the
order would go out for chicken.

Around this time, Dad was waiting at a stoplight in the right-hand
lane of a four-lane road, an event he described in "The Invisible Car":

> Up from behind came a hot rod packed with eight teenagers.
> They turned the corner behind me on two wheels, thundered to
> a stop in the lane at my left. I looked down, met eight pairs of
> staring eyes.
>
> "Drive carefully," I said, voice sepulcher.
>
> The light turned green.
>
> Gently, with the most delicate and sedate application of throt-
> tle, they eased across the intersection.
>
> I chose that moment to prove the Invisible Car would go from
> stop to sixty-five in nine seconds.

Just before heading for Mexico, Dad bolted a heavy steel ball on the
steering wheel of the hearse. The ball, which had been on a number of
Herbert-owned cars, resembled a trailer hitch, and was a handy thing
to hold onto. But if a driver happened to be wearing long sleeves, the
knob could become caught in the sleeve, in the opening by the button.
Thus it became commonly known as a "suicide knob." Despite my
father's vast reservoir of knowledge, this important statistical fact eluded
him for many years.

As a result, we rode to Mexico in a hearse, and the guy driving it
had a suicide knob in his grip.

Into the big heavy vehicle we loaded double-wall cardboard boxes
and trunks of our personal property, stacking them up to the bottom
of the little sliding glass windows that separated the front and rear
compartments. We took an old green Elna sewing machine, a pair of
Olympia typewriters, several boxes of typing paper, two footlockers that

had been up Kelly Butte by mule, a reel-to-reel tape recorder, tools and spare parts for the car, tape recordings of my parents' favorite music, fishing gear, camera equipment, toys, clothes . . . and maybe even a kitchen sink somewhere in the midst. Dad brought along a complete medical kit with antibiotics, hypodermics, tourniquets, and snake-bite paraphernalia, as well as several brand-new medical books, including *Cecil's Textbook of Medicine* and the *Merck Manual.*

On top of our belongings, Dad placed a layer of DFPA plywood, and above that several soft blankets. Bruce and I rode back there, with lots of room. I had my cocker spaniel Dusty with me, my best buddy, and he scrambled around happily, licking our faces. In "The Invisible Car," Dad referred to our hearse as "a traveling arena, a wrestling mat with wheels."

He installed a top rack on the hearse, where we carried a spare tire. Two gray canvas water bags were tied to the grill, draped across the front.

Since we were moving out of the rental house, arrangements had to be made for every article of personal property we owned. Items were sold or donated to charity, books were left in storage with friends, and clothing and other articles were shipped to Penny in Florence, Oregon, along with a child-support check for her mother.

On the September morning that we set out, Dad was in an incredibly good mood, singing and making witty quips about road signs. Whenever he saw a sign that read "Stop Ahead," he exclaimed, "Stop! A head in the road!"

Dad did all the driving, since Mom was afraid to drive and didn't have a license. As the days wore on, he grew tired and increasingly testy, largely because Dusty was not waiting for rest stops to do his doggy duty. Instead he picked a corner in the back, and by the second day a distinct, unpleasant aroma wafted from that vicinity. His feces and urine had soaked through the blankets, and some got around the plywood onto our things below. By the time we reached Ralph and Irene Slattery's place in Sonoma, California, Mom and Dad had endured enough of Dusty. They arranged to leave him with the Slatterys.

The hearse had a tendency to slip out of low gear, from having been driven in first gear during so many funeral processions. Dad had to hold the gear shift down at times to keep it from popping out of place. Sometimes when he wanted to keep the hearse in low gear he had Bruce or me hold the gear shift down, pressing on it so that it wouldn't slip. It was a "three on a tree" shift on the right side of the steering column.

I remember warm California and Southwest nights on the highway, with my parents' heads silhouetted against low evening light, from headlights on the road. There were flea-bitten motel rooms with no air conditioning and the windows left open. Crickets sang outside, and I smelled dry grass, cattle, fertilizers, and warm, sweltering earth.

At the border, the Mexican officers performed a cursory inspection of our belongings. Luckily they didn't remove the door panels, or they would have discovered Dad's concealed automatic pistol, which he carried for protection.

As our hearse rolled through Mexico on its journey south, peasants fell to their knees or held straw hats over their hearts. Devout Catholics, they undoubtedly thought we were carrying a poor departed soul on its final earthly journey. As soon as we left the first village in which this occurred and were on the open highway, Dad and Mom broke out laughing. They laughed so hard that tears streamed down their faces, and Dad had to pull the car over.

We didn't have much money with us, only around $3,000 in U.S. currency and traveler's checks. But prices were so low that we could live quite well, much better than in the United States. Some of the Mexican hotels in which we stayed were almost palatial, with floral-decked central patios and fine furnishings.

Dad was sure he would be able to write in Mexico to boost our monetary reserve, though years later he would refer to this belief as founded in myth. One day he would become a student of modern mythology and its correlation with individual and mass psychology. Myths were all around us, he said. The myth of owning a sailboat or a ranch, for example, or of being a great writer without having to work hard at the craft.

Or the idyllic myth he found himself seeking now, after the brief Mexican jaunt of 1953 and the failed American Samoa attempt. Frank

Herbert now envisioned himself in a remote tropical village, pounding out a literary masterpiece on a manual typewriter.

He'd sold several short stories in 1954. There were fewer short story sales in 1955, but that year he made the important novel sale, *Under Pressure*. And before leaving for Mexico, he received word from his agent that a movie producer was interested in the book.

We passed through the bustling shopping town of Toluca, just west of Mexico City, then followed a highway northwest. Our destination was the mountain village of Tlalpujahua in the state of Michoacán. This had been recommended by Mike Cunningham, an American friend with whom we had rendezvoused in the last few days. He drove ahead of us in his old wood-paneled station wagon, kicking up clouds of dust on a long dirt road leading to the village.

Near Tlalpujahua the road narrowed and jungle closed in around us. A number of houses dotted the overgrowth, in tiny carved-out clearings. Some were tin-roofed shacks while others were constructed of more sturdy adobe, with tile roofs. Many had outdoor kitchens in the form of lean-to arrangements against the houses. I smelled the acrid odor of cookfires from the burning of dry brush, grass and burro dung. Daylight faded and after dark we arrived in Tlalpujahua, where we stayed with a friend of Mike's.

Soon we rented a one-story adobe and white stucco house with a wrought-iron gate and a heavy, carved wooden door. It was set up in a U-shaped arrangement of rooms around a central outdoor courtyard. The fourteen-room home belonged to Señorita Francìsca Aguìlar, a large woman known as "Señorita Panchita." Since costs were so low, we could afford to hire a maid, a live-in cook and a gardener.

Almost every day, Dad wrote from early in the morning until early afternoon, on *Storyship* (alternate title *As Heaven Made Him*), his novel about the Santa Rosa murder case. Dealing with the legal definition of sanity and the responsibility of a criminal for his acts, the novel had both moral and political content, making it potentially pedantic.

Each day, Mom set up her own portable typewriter on the dining room table and worked on revisions to her mystery novel, *Frighten the Mother*. She didn't put in as many hours as Dad, since she spent more time than he in managing household affairs, including the household help and the children. Unfortunately, she was having trouble with the story.

When my parents' work was finished for the day they enjoyed taking walks through town together. I remember playing marbles and looking up to see them across the street holding hands and talking. They waved to me and smiled, and went on their way. They had a spot they liked to visit at sunset, where they could look across the burnt orange tile roofs of the town at a magnificent sky filled with color.

As in every other place we lived, the mail was critically important to my father. Here it was more essential than ever, since we had no telephone. Contract offers, documents and checks were expected to arrive in the mail, he told us, and for that reason all mail was to be treated with extreme care. We got to know our mailman, Jesus Chako, very well. A slender, affable man, he was always punctual. When he delivered a check one day in payment for an article Dad had written ($125 U.S.) my father said to my mother, "Jesus brings manna from Heaven!"

Unfortunately, Doubleday mailed the galley proof of *Under Pressure* to our previous address in Tacoma, and it wasn't forwarded to us in Mexico. Consequently, a duplicate galley had to be mailed to Dad. This became a matter of extreme urgency due to the publisher's schedule, so the moment Dad had the galley, he worked without sleep until it was corrected and in the mail back to New York.

Doubleday did not like the title *Under Pressure*, and asked the author for an alternate. He preferred the original title, but suggested *The Dragon in the Sea* nonetheless, which was used for the hardcover Doubleday edition. In many respects the new title was superior, for the mythology it suggested. There is an ancient Chinese legend concerning a ferocious, terrifying "dragon that lives in the sea." The Bible (Isaiah 27:1) contains a similar description: ". . . and (the Lord) shall slay the dragon that is in the sea." These passages, particularly the latter for Western readers, added subconscious depth and meaning to the title. In my father's tale, the "dragon" was a nuclear-powered subtug that transported precious oil through wartime waters, a craft that guarded the cargo against anyone who would harm it. This craft was reminiscent of mythological beasts of legend guarding a great treasure.

The mythology of such beasts was described by Sir James George

Frazer in his massive nineteenth-century magnum opus, *The Golden Bough*, one of my father's favorite and most closely studied works. Frazer described the golden fleece of the sacred ram sacrificed to Zeus, given by Phrixus to his wife's father and nailed to an oak tree, where it was guarded by a dragon that never slept. In *Beowulf*, also read by my father, a ferocious fire dragon occupied a lair under the cliffs at the edge of the sea, guarding a great treasure hoard.

This theme would later become central to Frank Herbert's *Dune*, a world in which massive, fire-breathing sandworms guarded the greatest treasure in the universe, the spice melange. As in *The Dragon in the Sea*, the treasure was beneath the surface of a planet.

Oil and melange were alike, because whoever controlled the precious limited resource controlled the known universe, as described in each novel.

✳ ✳ ✳

There were no banks in Tlalpujahua, so we banked in El Oro, seven miles away by dirt road. This was fitting, since El Oro meant "The Gold." We also did some of our shopping there, particularly for medicines, which were in short supply in Tlalpujahua.

Many times Mom went to El Oro alone on the second-class bus while Dad stayed home and wrote. The bus passengers frequently carried live chickens or turkeys onboard, and even pigs, going to or from the market. In her travel journal, my mother described what the front of the passenger compartment looked like from the inside:

> The bus was loaded, but a comparatively elegant 50 year old specimen. Above the driver's head were decals of bombers, pictures of the virgin, and a painted replica of a sway curtain on the top of the windshield (imitation of purple plush with gold fringe).

To that I would add my own memory of Mexican bus drivers, who had an unnerving habit of crossing themselves in the Catholic way, touching their forehead and each shoulder, and then pressing the accelerator pedal all the way to the floorboard, as if the fate of the bus and passengers depended solely upon the will of God and not upon the skill of the driver.

On a regular basis at our house, my parents conducted an English class for local adults. The brightest student was twenty-one-year-old Jose ("Pepe") Muñoz, who was fast becoming a close friend of our family. Pepe wore white tee shirts and stood around 5'7". A muscular man, he had long black hair and a round, Tarascan Indian face. He smiled often and easily, had a pleasant manner and a good sense of humor. Like many people in town, he was "*muy catolico*" (very Catholic). A master woodworker, he was exceedingly honest in a number of financial dealings with my parents.

I spent a good deal of my time playing marbles in the streets, and was outdoors so much that townspeople referred to me as "El Vago de los Calles" ("The Tramp of the Streets"). The friends I made were not to my mother's liking. Her journal entry of November 9, 1955, reported:

> This morning the tailor stopped Frank to tell him that the kids Brian is playing with are very *grosero** and are teaching him horrible words in Spanish which he shouts at the top of his lungs. The children described attend the government school here. . . .
>
> Went to the plaza with Frank and discovered Brian shouting Señorita Panchita has a big fat stomach (in perfect Spanish). Had a talk with him.

Initially our family was not well-accepted by the community. Dad wrote in "God's 'Helping Hand' Gave Us 5,000 *Amigos*" and "The Curate's Thumb," both unpublished first-person accounts, that the villagers were independent and inclined to form their own opinions. These were clannish, proud and fiercely nationalistic mountain people. Americans were considered a bad influence upon the local youth. Adults ignored my parents or spoke about them in whispered tones. Some children were forbidden from playing with me or with my little brother.

*Grosero: rough and course.

In October, the valve caps were stolen from our hearse tires, apparently by someone who did not fear the vengeance of God for tampering with a vehicle bearing chapel doors. A short while later the side mirrors were also taken. All of this was a surprise and a disappointment to us in view of the religious upbringing of the people.

Elsewhere in town, interesting events were occurring. It was a story my father told many times at dinner tables in ensuing years. His two unpublished versions of it ("God's 'Helping Hand' . . ." and "The Curate's Thumb") differed in minor details.

The most important man in town was the Catholic curate, Francisco Aguilar. Known as "Señor Cura," he was in his seventies. With more influence than a parish priest, his jurisdiction covered Tlalpujahua and five smaller nearby villages, including Tlalpujahuilla (little Tlalpujahua). The village mayors always visited him in his large home for approval before making important decisions. He stood 6'6", weighed 275 pounds and had a pock-rutted face, from an earlier attack of smallpox. The curate suffered from diabetes, and had to watch his diet closely. Consequently, the local physician, Dr. Gustave Iriarte, checked in on him regularly.

"Doctor Gus," as he was known affectionately, stood under five feet tall, weighed a hundred pounds and wore large eyeglasses, giving him a scholarly appearance. He had a feisty, combative nature.

While I was playing on cobblestone streets, Dad was across town. He had encountered Señor Cura on the street, and was talking with him. The curate had his hand wrapped in a dirty rag. When Dad asked him about it, he was told it was only a small scratch caused by a thorn. Frank Herbert asked to see the hand.

Slowly, grimacing with pain, the holy man unwrapped it. My father nearly gagged when he smelled the putrid odor of gangrene, an odor he had smelled two decades before and had never forgotten. The hand was swollen to nearly double its normal size, with an ugly, infected gash running between the thumb and forefinger. Dad told the curate he was in danger of losing the hand and perhaps his life from infection, and that he needed immediate medical attention. The curate's condition, my father knew, was complicated by diabetes, which created a number of potential problems. Since Dr. Gus was in Mexico City, Dad offered to drive him to El Oro to see a doctor, or even to Toluca, farther away, where better medical care was available.

The offer was declined. "God will take care of me," Señor Cura said.

Dad wondered if the curate considered the hearse an improper mode of conveyance under the circumstances, a sacrilege. In any event the elderly gentleman was adamantly opposed to getting in it. The curate also expressed an aversion toward doctors, which may in fact have been fear. Besides, he insisted, he wasn't convinced his wound was that serious. After all, it was only a little scratch from a thorn bush.

Señor Cura rewrapped his hand.

"Would you permit me to apply some medicines?" Frank Herbert asked. "I have a medical kit with antibiotics, to make you feel better."

The old man thought for a moment, then consented. Something in the manner of this Norte Americano was reassuring.

My father was taking a tremendous risk, for he could be charged with negligence and sent to Mexican prison if the curate died. But he tried not to think about that. Señor Cura was brought to our house, and at the dining room table, Dad brought out his medical books and supplies. After comparing instructions in the books, he soaked the wound in hot water with Epsom salts. This reduced the swelling. He then covered the cut with sulfa and put on a clean bandage. He also administered a shot of penicillin, after calculating the necessary cc's based upon the curate's weight.

At the curate's house, Dad gave the housekeeper two bottles of Terramycin (oxytetracyclene) antibiotic pills, telling her to make absolutely certain the old man took the pills six times a day, with plenty of water.

Dad was so worried during ensuing days that he could hardly write. The first thing every morning, he hurried over to the curate's house. There he inspected the hand, applied more sulfa and changed the bandage. After two days, the swelling diminished substantially, and the wound showed definite signs of improvement.

When Dr. Gus returned and heard what happened, he went to Señor Cura and shouted, in Spanish, "Stupid man! I've told you about infections! Señor Herbert saved your life!"

The following day, my father was amazed to see me playing marbles in the street with several boys. When I looked up and saw him, I asked,

117

"Is it true what they're saying, Dad? You saved Señor Cura's life?"

After a moment of astonishment, he broke into a broad smile and said, "Well, I did help out a little."

Soon we learned that Dr. Gus had been telling everyone in town about the heroics of my father. In the middle of the night, someone reattached the mirrors to our hearse and returned the valve caps. For the first time my brother and I were invited inside the homes of neighbors to play with their children. Quite suddenly Frank Herbert became a renowned wise man in those parts. Villagers consulted him on important matters and referred to him affectionately as "Don Pancho." We were invited to parties and picnics. Dad joined the village men's club. Just before dawn on his Saint's Day (a Roman Catholic feast day in honor of St. Francis of Paola), dozens of villagers carrying candles serenaded him from the street in front of our house with a cheerful good morning song, "Mañanita," accompanied by a mariachi band. My family stood in the doorway in robes and pajamas, smiling and waving.

In her journal, my mother wrote:

Fiesta at night with music and the upper and lower classes of town. First guests to arrive—the town's three prostitutes. Left right away. Killed whole sheep for fiesta . . . plenty of beer and *refrescos*.* Finally had to isolate more solid citizens of town in the dining room. Tequila—Aguacaliente beer—dry mutton—more Aguacaliente. Successful fiesta—Mike and Frank passed out! Pepe— official bartender—tucked two *gringos* into bed. All guests went to door of Frank's room, serenaded him. He waved, feebly.

With his background in farming and the assistance of U.S. Department of Agriculture (USDA) reference materials he'd mailed home under senatorial franking privileges while working in Washington, D.C., Dad showed Señor Cura the proper method of pruning and spraying his orange, lemon and peach trees. Word spread, and soon Dad began advising villagers on gardening and farming techniques. He

*Refrescos: cold drinks.

became, as he wrote in one of his unpublished pieces, the "unofficial farm advisor" for the region, covering all the villages in the curate's jurisdiction.

Local nuns requested my father's expert assistance at their convent, where the fruit trees were barren. Mom was quite amused by them:

> The nuns were charming—they fluttered helplessly around—told him they had complete confidence in his tree surgery—watched in fascination as he cut off excess shoots. Even hung speechless on his words on pollenization!

While he lived in Tlalpujahua, Frank Herbert translated key sections of USDA books and pamphlets into Spanish. The church mimeographed this information, stapled copies together and distributed them to farmers. The future author of an ecological masterpiece then visited farms to provide further advice, and wrote to the USDA for additional information.

Farm tracts in the region were known as *milpas*, which were jungle areas cleared by burning, then farmed for a few years and ultimately abandoned when the soil no longer contained the nutrients to sustain good crop yields. To inhibit soil erosion and control water runoff, Dad told the farmers to minimize the use of fire for land clearing, since that robbed the soil of important nutrients. He instructed them in contour plowing, terracing, water diversion systems, and in the planting of grasses, trees and shrubs. These methods were especially useful in a region of heavy tropical rains. Soils hit by deluges could not absorb water nearly as well as they did in slow rains. Soil instability caused by rains hitting inadequately planted areas had resulted in mud inundating the old village, and in continuous damage to planting areas over the years.*

Generally, Dad was in high spirits during our stay in Tlalpujahua, and my brother and I received less severe discipline from him than

---

*In ensuing years, my father would do more research, including a visit to an agricultural research station in Oregon that was studying the control of sand dunes, which are an extreme state of erosion. His understanding of the importance of grass and other plantings in inhibiting soil erosion would one day form an integral part of the ecology of *Dune*.

119

usual. I understood, as did the rest of my family, that my father did *not* like to be interrupted when he was writing. Others failed to get the message. This included our only American friend in town, Mike Cunningham. Frequently when Mike wanted to talk with Dad, he couldn't get through, since Dad was invariably in his study behind a closed door, connected to his typewriter as if it were an extension of him. When Frank Herbert was writing he was in a different universe, and no one could get through to him except my mother . . . his "moat dragon," as he liked to say.

Our gardener, Beto, despite repeated warnings, interrupted my father once too often, and my mother reported the aftermath:

Frank . . . exploded (justifiably, I believe) at Beto's interruptions when he wanted to write. Frank was in a purple pet and got me so upset I felt like crying.

In punishment for his many interruptions, the gardener was forced to prepare a sign for the study door. The sign warned anyone who came near, in Spanish, not to touch the door while the master of the house was working.

One of the worst disruptions occurred late one afternoon while Dad was in his study reading his manuscript to Mom. She emerged to take care of the problem, and found several upset people, including our friends and the household help. The center of controversy was our cook, who was accusing the maid of purchasing inferior lemons from the market.

Dad was frustrated trying to write in Mexico, and not only about the lack of quiet time in which to work. He also became sick with dysentery on a number of occasions. Following one such attack, he commented to my mother, "Maybe it's cheaper not to come to Mexico—because of work days lost through illness."

She reported other physical problems experienced by my father:

Said altitude too high for much exercise. The altitude here—almost 8,000 feet, is too much for Frank—a little exercise wears him out completely—wants to settle closer to sea level.

Late in 1955, under a contract of three hundred pesos a month from my father, Pepe Muñoz removed the gaudy chapel siding from the hearse and built plywood panels in their place. This reduced the vehicle weight by five hundred pounds, thus improving fuel efficiency. He then brush-painted the entire hearse a creamy tan color, further removing evidence of its somber past.

Dad finished his second novel, *Storyship*, and mailed it to Lurton. The agent said he liked it, particularly suspense elements and characterizations, but Doubleday turned it down. John Campbell didn't want it for *Astounding Science Fiction*, either, asserting it was more detective story than science fiction, a historically unsuccessful combination in the publishing world. Rejections followed from other publishers, some of whom thought the yarn had too many science fiction gimmicks, with an inadequately organized plot and too much preaching. He was being pedantic, having crossed the fine and dangerous line between moral instruction and entertainment.

Mom couldn't seem to overcome the problems with her own novel, primarily involving the organization of material. She found herself losing enthusiasm for it, with an increasing belief that she could never make it as a novelist.

Writing sales were supposed to finance our extended stay in Mexico, but now we were once again nearly out of money. Mom made arrangements to borrow from her Aunt Ruth and Uncle Bing, and Dad borrowed from his favorite aunt, Peg Rowntree. Just enough money came in to get us back to the Pacific Northwest.

One piece of good literary news reached us in Mexico. *The New York Times* ran an excellent review on *The Dragon in the Sea* in their book review section. This did not, however result in the instant funding we needed. A movie producer was still interested in the book, as he had been for several months, but thus far had made no offer.

My parents liked Pepe Muñoz so much that they wanted to sponsor him in the United States, bringing him into the country as a new citizen. Although Dad made repeated, glaring errors in raising his children, he could be extremely generous with friends. No idea was too wild for him. He was impulsive and childlike. The commitment to bring Pepe to the United States, so like Frank Herbert, was made on the spur of the moment, without considering details, without worrying about problems. No matter the red tape required to complete the task, and it was considerable, involving a number of delays and uncertainties in Mexico City. No matter our lack of funds and lack of prospects. No matter bald tires on the family car. We were about to drive more than three thousand miles north, on yet another adventure.

Just before we departed from Tlalpujahua in early 1956, the villagers staged a big daytime fiesta in honor of my father. In gratitude, Dad and Mom put on a big party of their own that evening, held in our courtyard. A mariachi band played from the covered walkway overlooking the garden.

A few days later we pulled out of Tlalpujahua and headed north, with Pepe sitting in the front seat between my parents. The tires on our hearse were in bad shape. We only had a little borrowed money, not enough for contingencies. Luck would have to be with us, or we wouldn't make it.

Pepe hung a silver Virgin of Carmen medal on the dashboard, a medal that had been blessed by Señor Cura. This, the curate said, would protect us on our long journey. Despite this, the tires on the hearse went flat constantly from rough road conditions, and Pepe and Dad used the jack and star wrench repeatedly. We limped from gas station to gas station, patching the beaten-up old skins and heading out again. I remember sitting in the back of the hearse as we drove along a high mountain road and looking out the window on my mother's right at a sheer drop-off. It was a long way down, at least a thousand feet.

I was only mildly concerned. The drop-off held my attention, but I was only a kid and hadn't lived long enough to really get frightened. I hadn't learned how many things could go wrong. As far as I was concerned, Dad was invincible. Nothing could overpower him. As long as he was at the wheel, we were okay. Of course I didn't know about suicide knobs on steering wheels then, how they could get caught in long shirt sleeves and cause terrible accidents. One day they would be made illegal for this reason.

Dad was a risk-taker—one of the features of his personality that made him interesting. But bald tires *and* a suicide knob on a dangerous mountain road? In a hearse? He had to be pushing his luck!

CHAPTER
10

✳ Easy Pie ✳

EARLY IN 1956, the Herbert hearse limped into Portland, Oregon, and we rented a tiny one-story house on the north side, not far from the St. Johns Bridge. Pepe Muñoz (known as Joe Muñoz now) stayed with us, and worked at a local cabinet shop as a carpenter. Money was tight. Dad and Mom set about trying to obtain "real" jobs. They were finding it too difficult to make ends meet as writers. Still, my father was on a course that would one day lead to success.

From an early stage of his writing, Frank Herbert was tuned-in to the problem of finite resources on this planet. At a time of increasing and wasteful consumer consumption in the United States, he saw, quite accurately, that it could not last forever. In *The Dragon in the Sea* he predicted the global oil shortage that would occur two decades later. One day in *Dune* he would make similar predictions about finite resources, particularly water.* In creating these novels, he asked himself

---

*Frank Herbert told me that he invented containerized shipping in *Dragon*, which was later made commercially successful by the Japanese. A number of other commercial ventures have been undertaken based upon this idea, including one by an English company, Dracon, utilizing subtugs that were very similar to the novel. Also, General Dynamics came out with a "submarine tanker," a fully contained sub designed to transport oil from the arctic under the ice to ice-free ports in Greenland or Newfoundland. And Gianfranco Germani, an Italian, recently constructed giant bladders to transport fresh water from watersheds to parched regions of the earth.

the question, "What if?" Extrapolating from conditions that existed at the time, he envisioned worlds of startling, frightening clarity.

Submariners contacted my father over the years and told him that *Dragon* accurately depicted the psychological pressures of undersea crewmen—despite the fact that the author had never served on a submarine. This ability to imagine conditions he had never experienced would serve Frank Herbert well later in the creation of *Dune*.

But Portland in 1956 was nearly a decade before *Dune*, and fifteen years before book sales would begin to take off for Frank Herbert. We were poor, a not-uncommon experience for artists and writers who are ahead of their time.

All in all, *Dragon* was doing fairly well for a first novel, although it was not earning the kind of money needed to support a family. Reviews, those few that appeared, were favorable. Based upon the book, Dad was nominated, but did not win, in the category of "Most Promising New Author" at the 1956 World Science Fiction Convention.*

No one wanted to publish his new 40,000-word novel *Storyship*, a book in which he had placed a lot of hope. For a while, *Amazing Stories* considered running a magazine serial on it, if Dad could trim it to 30,000 words. They were offering what Lurton referred to derisively as "salvage money"—only $400. Lurton was opposed to accepting this, and recommended instead *adding* 10,000 words to the length, since 50,000 words would put it into a length preferred by pocket books. The pockets would pay more as well, he said, and there would be more prestige in publishing it as a novel than in a chopped-up serial form.

Dad was in a quandary. He went over the manuscript again and decided to go against Lurton's advice. *Amazing*'s offer was a "bird in the hand," Dad felt. Besides that, he said, the story didn't seem "stretchable" to him. He told Lurton to contact *Amazing*, and a verbal agreement was reached. If the required number of words were

---

*A rumor began to circulate in the 1960s that *The Dragon in the Sea* tied with William Golding's *Lord of the Flies* for the 1955 International Fantasy Award. This was inaccurate. For many years my parents even believed *Dragon* had shared the award, and it was reported incorrectly that Frank Herbert was the only writer ever to win all three major science fiction awards, the Nebula, the Hugo, and the International Fantasy Award.

cut they promised to look at the story again, and in all likelihood would publish it.

My father set to work on the rewrite, and within a few weeks had it in the mail. *Amazing* delayed, and ultimately decided against publishing the story at all. Dad was furious, and tossed the butchered manuscript in the back of a closet. For many years, he refused to look at it again. Ultimately, it became part of his 1968 novel, *The Heaven Makers*.

Most of *Storyship* was written in Mexico, and the project's failure put a damper on future exotic trips. Thus far, neither tropical sojourn had worked out creatively, exposing the fallacy of such trips to him. He began to recognize them for the myths that they were.

Bits and pieces of the Mexican experience did find their way into Frank Herbert's writing over the years. In the short story "You Take the High Road" (*Astounding Science Fiction*, May 1958), the towns on an alien planet had cobblestone central marketplaces. A decade later, he would publish a non-fiction newspaper piece about shopping in Mexico, but most of all, Mexican scenes and descriptions appeared in unpublished stories—stories he couldn't sell for one reason or another.

In the 1950s, Dad didn't fully commit himself to science fiction. He displayed flashes of brilliance in the genre, earning accolades, but then withdrew or changed direction, turning instead to mainstream stories he hoped would sell to *Saturday Evening Post*, *The New Yorker*, *Life*, or *Reader's Digest*. Increasingly he tried to get away from science fiction, feeling it was dominated by the pulps and inane monster films. With his intellectual leanings, he didn't want to be identified with nonsensical non-literature, didn't want to have to keep explaining to people that he didn't write the trashy material known as "sci-fi," that he wrote instead a more sophisticated, thinking-man's variety.

Still, deep in his heart, he loved the elbow room afforded by science fiction. It was a field where his imagination could stretch to the limits. And this was a man of remarkable imagination. In science fiction he could write allegories filled with symbolism.

In 1956 we owed money to the IRS that we were unable to pay. After receiving his advance on *The Dragon in the Sea* the year before, Dad didn't think of setting aside funds for the payment of taxes on this income. Naively, he and Mom just took off for Mexico, thinking only of the adventures ahead of them. Any thoughts of income taxes were only vagrant, soon slipping away. There would be future story sales anyway, they reasoned, and everything would take care of itself.

Now with that myth shattered, old bill collectors and their attorneys were contacting us, demanding money. Again, Flora wanted past due child-support payments. Around the house my father kept saying we were "broke," or, even worse, "flat broke." On those rare occasions when we had people over for dinner, Dad used a code phrase with us. If there was not enough food for us to have second helpings, he would say, "FHB,NMIK"—which meant, "Family hold back, no more in kitchen." On the other hand, if we *could* have seconds, he would utter the much more blissful letters, "MIK"—"More in kitchen."

Mom found a job as a fashion advertising copywriter for a large department store in town, Olds & King. Since it was an election year, Dad accepted a speech writer position with Phil Hitchcock, who was running in the Republican primary for U.S. Senator from Oregon. Hitchcock was a professor at Lewis & Clark College in Oregon and a state senator since 1948. He had been a Republican candidate for U.S. Senator in 1954, before Guy Cordon beat him in the Republican primary. Now it was two years later, with another primary election coming up, and he was facing former Secretary of the Interior Douglas McKay for the Republican nomination. McKay had also been an Oregon state senator and governor of the state. He was a formidable opponent. Unfortunately, Hitchcock lost the May 18, 1956, primary election to McKay, so once more Frank Herbert was out of a job.

Joe Muñoz was rarely around because of his job and busy social calendar. He was dating blonde American girls, and life was good for him. He smoked little black cigarettes. Every month he sent money back to his family in Mexico.

It was a time of stress for our family, and I was not getting along with my father. A pattern of severe discipline from Dad set in—a resumption of our relationship before the last Mexico trip. Now it was worse than ever. If Dad was writing when I arrived home from school, I had to tiptoe around the house. It wasn't a very big house, so I had to be especially careful.

Sometimes I came around the house and heard music playing from inside. Dad developed the habit of writing to music, played on a large reel-to-reel tape deck in his study. With this buffer of sound between him and me, I would open the front door quietly and creep into my room, or would lie on the floor in the living room with a book, listening to the music. It was powerful, vibrant material—Brahms, Vivaldi, Beethoven, Gershwin. Even "Peter and the Wolf," which I especially enjoyed.

When *The Dragon in the Sea* was printed by Doubleday in hardcover, Dad entered my room and handed me a signed copy. A slender black volume with yellow lettering on the spine, it had a bright blue, yellow and black dust jacket and bore a $2.95 retail price. He dedicated the story to the men of the United States Submarine Service.

In reflection of the gap between us, perhaps, Dad penned this inscription to me on the flyleaf at the beginning of the book:

> To Number One Son—In hopes it will help him along
> the complicated path of understanding his father.
> Frank Herbert

After he left my room, I glanced at the first page and noted something about an Ensign Ramsey who looked like "a grown-up Tom Sawyer," but didn't read further for many years. Still, I kept his book on a little bookshelf in my room, in plain view.

Frank Herbert demanded truth in government, consumer affairs, and environmental issues. He did not tolerate evasiveness, omissions or half-truths. His blue eyes did not avert when he spoke to you. In the coming decade, in *Dune*, he would write of "Truthsayers," remarkable witches who could determine truth or falsehood from watching and listening to a person.

Dad was, by his own admission, a man obsessed with "turning over stones to see what would scurry out"—with unmasking lies. This was evident in his dealings with his children.

He had a World War II lie detector, a U.S. Navy unit. A small black box with a dial, it had ominous wires and a gray cuff that he wrapped tightly around my arm. The first time he used the machine on me, he accused me of secretly hitting my brother, and he was going to get the truth out of me. He said the lie detector always revealed falsehood, which was not, as I would learn later, exactly the case.

Admittedly I was lying about hitting my brother, and the machine indicated this, so I got a licking. After that he used the lie detector on me regularly, and on Bruce. If anything came up, such as an item missing from his desk or questions about where I had been after school, he would say, in a clipped voice, "I'm putting you on the lie detector. Let's go in the other room."

With that, he would grab my arm and lead me to the machine. On the way, I broke out in a sweat, rehearsing what I would say and how I would say it. Would he ask such and such? My mind was awhirl, full of terror.

The machine was kept in his study, and he only brought it out when I was in trouble. It was set up on a wooden table, with two straight-back chairs pulled up to it, one on each side.

He pointed to one of the chairs, and I slipped into it, shaking. Towering over me, he plugged the machine in and tapped it a couple of times for effect, ostensibly to free a sticky needle. A bare ceiling bulb threw his hulking shadow across the table.

"Roll up your left sleeve," he said, gruffly.

Shaking, I complied, and he wrapped the sensor cuff around my arm. A stream of questions and accusatory statements ensued from him, and like a prisoner undergoing the tortures of Grand Inquisitor Torquemada, perspiration poured from my brow. Dad was too smart, and phrased every query in the precise way that put me in the worst possible light. After each question, he studied the machine intently and invariably pronounced me guilty of something. According to Howie Hansen, who disapproved of the use of the device on Bruce and me, Dad had a way of rigging the machine to indicate that we were lying, even when we were telling the truth.

One day my father would write of young Paul Atreides in *Dune*—ordered to place his hand into the blackness of a box in the ordeal of the gom jabbar. Paul was commanded not to withdraw the hand no matter how much pain he felt, on penalty of death from a poison needle held at his neck—the deadly gom jabbar. Terrified, the boy complied:

Pain throbbed up his arm. Sweat stood out on his forehead . . . Without turning his head, he tried to move his eyes to see that terrible needle poised beside his neck. He sensed that he was breathing in gasps, tried to slow his breaths and couldn't . . . Pain! His world emptied of everything except that hand immersed in agony . . . His lips were so dry he had difficulty separating them.

In *Heretics of Dune*, one of the sequels to *Dune*, Frank Herbert would describe a "T-probe," a torturous memory detection device that absorbed every bit of information about a person:

He could identify where it took over his muscles and senses. It was like another person sharing his flesh, pre-empting his own reactive patterns . . . It was a hellish device! . . . It could command his body as though he had no thinking part in his own behavior . . . The whole spectrum of his senses could be copied into this T-probe and identified . . . The machine could trace those out as though it made a duplicate of him.

It was my father's gift and curse that he noticed infinitesimally small details. This enabled him to become a great writer. He had a tendency, however, to be somewhat of a nit-picker in the household. He was extremely demanding.

The Bene Gesserit of *Dune* understood nuances of meaning, subtle shiftings of voice and intonation, So it was with my father. He understood, or thought he understood, shades of meaning in every word his children uttered. He picked our sentences apart.

"What do you mean you'll *try* to do it?" he would say to me, in a voice reaching crescendo. "Don't ever use the word *try* on me! That word signifies failure, the likelihood of defeat. You'll do it, god damn it, Brian, you won't *try* to do it!" Another intolerable word to him was "can't." We didn't dare use that word or "try," because they triggered something in the man and he would fly into blind rages.

If one of the *verboten* words slipped from my mouth, I immediately wanted it back, a second chance. But there the word was, floating in the air, reaching his ears, causing his demeanor to change: a ferocious scowl on his face and loud commands from his ever-active mouth. I would cower and shake and watch for threatening movements from his beefy right hand, the hitting hand.

Of course there was an element of philosophical and moral truth in his concept, that the words "try" and "can't" were weak, indicating a person was not strong of character and was incapable of taking responsibility for his own actions. It was an important lesson of life, one I think of often to this day.

When I got to know my father many years later, I found to my surprise he was quite the opposite of what I had supposed. He was in reality a loving, caring man. But one who experienced problems with children. He was impatient around them, intolerant of youthful energies and mischief. It is true as well that Bruce and I were expected to undergo similar routines to those that Dad had experienced in his childhood.

Frank Herbert, ever the psychoanalyst, might be surprised to realize that a major component of his own behavior was mimicry, of the subconscious variety. He imitated the stern disciplinary measures taken against him by his father, F. H., who had received them in turn from his own father, Otto. It is interesting to note a curious habit that Otto had while living in Burley in the 1930s, a habit my father saw firsthand. It seems that the old man enjoyed listening to the news on the radio, and when his programs were on, no one could disturb him and no one spoke—at the risk of incurring his ire. Family members had to tiptoe around the house.

My father first learned about lie detectors from his policeman father, F. H., who said to him in the 1930s, "There are methods of determining when a suspect is telling the truth and when he is lying. Subtle things to notice . . . his gaze, the way the mouth is held, nervous ticks and mannerisms, moisture on skin surfaces . . ." He told the boy about lie detection machines and threatened to connect him to one if he didn't shape up. But he never actually brought a machine home.

The lie detector was a complete admission of failure on my father's part as a parent. He couldn't communicate with his sons, hadn't taken the time to bond with us, to learn what made us tick. Instead he tried to crush our will and spirit. There could be no deviation from the rules he prescribed. The environment around him had to be absolute serenity to keep his mind in order, so that he might create his great work.

I never saw Dad lift a finger against Penny, who came to stay with us that summer. One time he did get into a battle of wills with the tall, blonde teenager: He insisted that she eat her dessert and then rubbed it into her hair when she refused to do so. For the most part, she didn't receive the brunt of his anger, which in its most severe form became physical. I think he felt boys could (and should) take more punishment, in order to make men out of us.

Despite our chronic poverty, Mom was exceedingly proper about etiquette, a carryover from her maternal grandmother, Ada Landis. One time Penny brought a loaf of bread in its wrapper to the dinner table, and my mother hurled the loaf across the kitchen. Mom taught us the proper technique of holding silverware, and of sitting up straight as we ate. We were not to slurp drinks or soup, and bowls were always to be tipped away when we spooned the last of the soup—never toward us. "A well-mannered person is never eager to eat," she said.

Dad was around thirty-five or thirty-six at the time, and I remember a habit he had of bounding up and down the stairs of our front porch, skipping steps. From my perspective, he was an old duffer, and I couldn't believe he had that much energy. He was impatient to get wherever the staircase led, not a man to dawdle with each step.

Frank Herbert had been clean-shaven since moving to Santa Rosa in 1949 for the job with the *Press Democrat*. Seven years later now, *The Dragon in the Sea* sold to a German publisher for a small amount of money, and the publisher wanted a book jacket photograph of him. Lurton said that readers in Europe expected writers to have beards, so Dad grew it back before having the photo taken. Mom said he looked nice in it, and he took a liking to it again. At first, Bruce, Penny and I thought he looked pretty strange, but gradually we grew accustomed to the change.

In the summer of 1956, a Republican candidate for the U.S. Congress, Phil Roth, offered Dad the position of public information officer, which he accepted. Roth was running against the Democratic incumbent, Edith Green. Roth, who had been in the Civil Air Patrol during World War II, piloted his own single-engine Cessna airplane on the campaign circuit, with "Roth for Congress" painted on the sides.

After accompanying the candidate on one such trip, my father picked up a bouquet of long-stemmed red roses for Mom on the way home. He presented them to her at the front door.

"You're a sight for sore eyes!" Dad exclaimed to her.

And she responded, "Sore eye! Sore eye!"

Roth was a supporter of Indian rights, and felt the reservation system was perpetuating second-class citizenship for them. Dad concurred with this position, and contributed his own knowledge of Indian affairs to Roth's speeches. A decade and a half later, these concerns would find their way into one of Frank Herbert's greatest and most powerful stories, the mainstream novel of Indian rage, *Soul Catcher*.

Unfortunately, Roth lost in the November general election. For the third time in two years, Dad found himself on the staff of a losing Republican candidate, and he was again thrown out of work. If any of the three had won, the career of Frank Herbert might have been dramatically different—for he could have become a political appointee.

Early in December, my father made a startling announcement. He said we would no longer celebrate Christmas on Christmas Day. Instead, we would wait until Twelfth Night, January 6th, the way it was done in Mexico for children. Except in our case it would apply to the entire family. He went on to explain that the Epiphany, January 6th, was an important Christian religious holiday, representing the day the manifestation of Jesus Christ appeared before the Magi.

It got pretty tough for Bruce and me when Christmas came around and other kids played outside with new bicycles and baseball mitts and model airplanes, while we had nothing.

On Christmas Day our tree had only a few presents under it, sent by friends and relatives. Dad and Mom started shopping the day after Christmas, picking up bargains at sales. It was great for their budget, but Bruce and I thought it left something to be desired.

By December 30th, Bruce and I had raised such a ruckus about our presents that Dad agreed to let us open one gift a day between New Year's Day and January 6th. Dad and Mom selected the ones we could open first, and the best were saved for the last day.

This practice continued for three years! Finally, after vociferous protestations and monumental whining, Bruce and I were successful in eliminating it from the Herbert household for all time.

CHAPTER
11

✳ They Stopped the Moving Sands ✳

WITH THE campaign wars over and the Roth election lost, Dad felt
burned out. He'd been beating his head against political walls long
enough, and needed to get back to his writing. A number of stories
had been churning in his mind, and he wanted to get them on paper.

For a long time he had been intrigued by the effect of heroes upon
human history. A student of the flawed, tragic heroes of Greek mythology and Shakespeare, he also studied the gospels of a number of
religions. He was especially intrigued with stories of great religious
leaders—messiahs. Among his favorite nonfiction works were biographies of great leaders such as Alexander the Great, Napoleon and
Washington.

Employing his increasing understanding of psychology, he wanted
to write a novel from the perspective of a hero, venturing deep into the
character's psyche. He sought to become that character as he wrote
about him, understanding every motivation. He had faint sketches in
mind, and some of the coloration. But no canvas and no plot. So he
set the idea aside.

Another story kicking around in his head was a mainstream adventure set in Mexico, with no science fiction content. Two days after the
election loss of November 6, 1956, he was hard at work on a novelette
entitled *A Game of Authors*. He finished it in January—37,500 words—
and sent it off to his agent.

With this course change, Dad was targeting the mainstream magazine market, thinking he could earn more money with sales to slick East Coast magazines. But he hadn't done any market research—a critical error. He didn't understand what needed to be done for success. With severe space limitations, those publications were particularly finicky about length. Dad wrote each story from the seat of his pants, without considering length.

With *A Game of Authors* he was going full circle, moving away from science fiction and back to the adventures he had written in the 1940s. *Dragon* was doing relatively well, but Dad didn't feel entirely comfortable with science fiction. He hadn't intended to become a science fiction writer; it just happened. Now he was having trouble selling stories in that genre and was reappraising himself, shifting gears. Science fiction was considered a literary ghetto by many anyway, and Frank Herbert felt it might be best to get away from it.

He also had a couple of stories in mind for the men's magazine market, including *Playboy* and *Rogue*, magazines that were doing better than others financially and were paying their writers well. He even considered television script writing for a time, but Lurton discouraged him from that, telling him it was too tough to break into with his background.

A Game of Authors, a title taken from a card game, was about an American writer in Mexico, searching for a famous lost author. This was a familiar plot device in the works of Frank Herbert—a character investigating something, in the manner of a reporter. The story featured international intrigue, a *femme fatale* and a lake filled with piranhas. Unfortunately it was melodramatic, with poor use of suspense and thin characterizations. The story met the same fate as Dad's recent science fiction tales. In part this had to do with a length problem—it was too long for the extremely limited magazine markets, and around 12,500 words too short for a novel. Still, Lurton made every effort to sell it without changes. The best hope seemed to be serialization in a magazine.

Around this time, Dad wrote another mainstream story, "Paul's Friend." Set on an island in the South Pacific shortly after World War II, it was told in the first person, with an unnamed character listening to a story about a mysterious black man whose bravery in a hurricane was legendary. "Paul's Friend," while a salable length at four thousand words, did not find a publisher.

And he wrote a real gem, a wild 10,000-word story told in the first person. Bearing the improbable title "Wilfred," it described a would-be singer of inferior voice and ludicrous appearance who happened to hit the right combination of acoustics in a recording session, producing beautiful music. Sadly, "Wilfred," like Dad's other non–science fiction attempts, did not sell.

In another genre, science fiction book and magazine publishers continued to reject *Storyship*, which was only a couple of thousand words longer than *A Game of Authors*.

That spring, Universal Pictures offered four thousand dollars for the screen rights to *The Dragon in the Sea*. They presented an unfavorable contract, which gave them every conceivable right of recorded and filmed reproduction, a contract his film agent, Ned Brown, did not like at all. He wanted to hold out for a better offer. But Dad went for the bird in the hand, and said he would accept without further delay or negotiation. Reluctantly, Ned proceeded to have the contract drawn up.

While quite a bit of money for 1957, it disappeared quickly, going for old bills that had been accumulating. Dad remained confused about his writing, and was having trouble finding his literary voice. He contacted other writers for advice, to see what he might be doing wrong. Several gave him the cold shoulder—he was just another young writer to them, pestering them, taking them away from their writing.

For a time he had received advice from Lurton's brother, Wyatt, a successful short story writer—but their last contact had been a year before. One professional in Portland did offer quite a bit of advice, Tommy Thompson. A well-known screenwriter and short story writer, Thompson told Dad never to talk about a story he planned to write or that he was in the process of writing. "Just go ahead and write it," he said. "Don't waste your energy trying to explain it."

Thompson, who lived in Santa Rosa and Portland at various times, built a steam engine into an old Studebaker and ran the car on steam. It ran well, and set my father to thinking about alternative energy sources—a concept he would champion two decades later.

Referring to himself as a Jeffersonian, Frank Herbert was an admirer of the nation's second president, John Adams. These men—Jefferson, Adams and Herbert—were suspicious of the holders of power. Dad added a twist of his own, asserting that charismatic leaders were extremely dangerous. "It's one thing to make mistakes for yourself," he said, "but if you're a charismatic leader and you blunder, millions of people can follow you over the cliff."

In *The Dragon in the Sea*, the crew of the Fenian Ram followed Captain Sparrow slavishly—a perilous situation, in my father's opinion. This was a precursor to the dangerous power structure that formed around Paul Atreides, as Dad later described in the *Dune* series.

Dad missed the Puget Sound area of Washington State, where he had been born. It was his Tara and he had done his best writing there, including most of *Dragon*. It was a wild thought, perhaps, but in 1957 he felt in his gut that another move might provide the inspiration he needed.

Ever cooperative, my mother contacted retail advertising people she knew in the Seattle-Tacoma area. As luck would have it, an advertising copywriter position turned up at a large department store in Tacoma (The Bon Marche), at a slightly higher salary. She was hired, and management accepted her request for a summer employment date, after Bruce and I had completed our current school semesters.

Penny remained with her mother in Florence, Oregon—on the Pacific Coast.

Just before our departure for Washington State, a friend from the Hitchcock campaign told Dad about a U.S. Department of Agriculture research station that was, coincidentally, near Florence. It was in an area of unstable sand dunes that were being driven by wind over buildings and roads, inundating them.

By planting poverty grasses the USDA had discovered a successful method of stabilizing dunes, preventing them from traveling. It was a pilot project, and due to its success government officials were coming from all over the world to see it. Israel, Pakistan, Algeria and Chile were among the interested nations.

Dad was intrigued. He knew from his studies of history that the Sahara and other desert regions had not always been desolate. Once they had been green and fertile, sustaining great and powerful civilizations. Many of these civilizations were subsequently buried by slow-moving, relentless sand encroachment, causing more destruction than any human invader could.

Dad thought he might write a magazine article on the project. He chartered a Cessna 150 single-engine plane, with pilot, and flew to Florence. There he compiled notes and took photos. It was as advertised: the Department of Agriculture had stopped the sand.

On the way back, Dad gazed down on sand dunes that were like waves on a great sea, and he felt an emotional pull. He returned to Portland, and focused his attentions upon yet another move.

In the summer of 1957, we rented a house in Brown's Point, Washington, just north of Tacoma. One bedroom was on the main floor, on the street side, and Dad converted it to a study.

He had always wanted an antique roll-top desk, and shortly after the move he purchased a large one from a private owner who had advertised it. The desk was dark oak, with little drawers and cubbyholes, and writing boards that pulled out on the right and left sides.

In his new study, Dad placed a row of reference books along the top shelf of the desk. His Olympia portable typewriter went on a typing table by the desk. A "Singing Cowboy" rug (that Mom had crocheted from a drawing of mine) was laid on the floor, and his Mexican *serape* with silver clips went over a side chair. On the walls he hung a calendar and old maritime maps, with inaccurate but quaint cartographic impressions of the continents. He organized his musical tapes and set up his reel-to-reel tape deck and speakers so that it could fill the entire house with music. With all his preparations, we were in the house for nearly a week before he wrote a word.

Now he set to work on the magazine article, which he entitled, "They Stopped the Moving Sands." The rapid, staccato hum of his typewriter became constant background noise, a machine drone that I almost filtered out. His schedule at the time was to begin writing at midnight and work until at least 8:00 A.M. In this way he had quiet, uninterrupted time. The typewriter was my father's mistress, permitted by my mother. In this unpublished haiku poem he described what it was like at that time of night:

Typewriter clacking
In my night-encircled room-
Metal insect song.

I've never seen anyone type as fast as Dad. I hesitate to call it "touch typing," since his fingers moved so quickly over the keys that they didn't seem to touch them at all. When I interviewed Howie Hansen, my father's closest friend, he said to me:

Frank was some kind of a typist. I never saw anybody that could sit there while you're talking, as I'm talking right now, and whose fingers would be flying, and who at the end of your conversation would rip the page right out of the typewriter and hand you your finished conversation. Frank would do that. I always accused him of showing off, and he would say, "What, who me? Huh. You know me better than that." And then we'd both laugh roaringly.

Sometimes, remaining ever so quiet, I watched my father at work in his study, through the open door or from outside in the yard. When he wasn't typing, he edited pages with a pen or pencil, scribbling rapidly. He talked to himself in there, reading dialogue aloud. Not being a writer myself at the time, I had no understanding of the benefit of this technique, which makes dialogue more realistic, more flowing. Having heard that crazy people talked to themselves, I put the proverbial two and two together and decided he must be out of his mind. He was so different from other kids' fathers anyway, with his beard and Bohemian lifestyle. He didn't hold down regular jobs, didn't play catch with me in the backyard or go to baseball games with me the way normal fathers did. He didn't even allow us to have a television.

Each morning, Dad drove Mom to work at The Bon Marche department store in downtown Tacoma and then picked her up in the afternoon. Our car was a gray 1950 Studebaker that looked like some kind of a weird rolling airplane cockpit. This delivery service took him an hour and a half to two hours a day in all, and was necessary since my mother refused to drive, especially in city traffic.

She was dependent upon him for many things. Almost like a baby, so helpless without him. But he was just as dependent upon her, in other ways. She edited his manuscripts and typed the final drafts. She listened attentively and made suggestions as he read each story to her aloud. She found missing things for him, keeping his delicate emotional state balanced.

Dad was in reality completely helpless without her, but I would not realize it until many years later.

My brother and I shared an insatiable curiosity about the contents of our father's desk. I often saw Bruce in the dangerous inner sanctum of the study, and at every opportunity I was in there as well. I got into Dad's things most in the afternoons, when he was picking Mom up at work.

He had the most intriguing objects in his desk, and I spent hours at a time looking at them. He had a black and silver fountain pen, like Jack Vance's. I liked the pen very much. It felt good and substantial in my hand. In cubbyholes were piled stacks of 5 × 7 notepads with a drawing of a typewriter on top of each sheet, and the words, "FROM THE DESK OF FRANK HERBERT." In cubbyholes and drawers and on the desktop were old eyeglasses, little prisms wrapped carefully in tissue paper, fortunes from Chinese fortune cookies, pens, pencils, slide rules in a variety of shapes, political campaign buttons, typewriter ribbons wrapped in plastic bags (to keep the ribbons from drying out), little boxes and little bags and things held together with rubber bands. There were boxes of bond typing paper and stacks of inexpensive newsprint, used by my parents for first drafts and carbon copies.

My father always had a cardboard manuscript box on his desk or on the typewriter stand by it. The box, which originally came with bond typing paper in it, was slit open on one end by Dad and used to hold the completed pages. The slitted end enabled him to handle pages easily, while still keeping them organized in a box.

His portable typewriter sat on a typing table on the left side of the desk, and I never touched this machine, for the wrath it might bring down upon me. Any slip in that realm would spell BIG TROUBLE, because Dad always said the keys could be sprung if they weren't hit just right, with an even rhythm. He was extremely sensitive to the touch of his keyboard.

As letters and other paperwork came into his study, he impaled them on a copy spike on the top shelf of the desk. When in the middle of a story, he only answered the most important, earth-shaking correspondence. Everything else waited, and he developed the habit of piling up huge stacks of unanswered mail. He focused his energies upon the story in his typewriter, to the exclusion of almost everything and everyone else. When the story was finished and in the mail to his agent, he would then spend days in succession answering every letter.

His study was, in a very real sense, a sacred place in our home. I had only a faint understanding of the mysterious incantations and rituals he performed in there with his writing implements, but I knew all of his things were to be given supreme respect. So any time I was in there, I took great pains to disrupt nothing, and always listened for noises as nervously as a cat, sounds that might suggest the approach of the Lord of the Domain. I examined small areas at a time, always replacing each item exactly as I had found it.

The door of his study had a humorous sign on the outside that I never laughed about when I lived in his household. A fiendish cartoon character was depicted, with the caption: "I DON'T GET ULCERS; I GIVE THEM!"

From her job at The Bon Marche, Mom often brought home advertising layouts to work on. Many featured fashion drawings of women. On her Olympia portable typewriter, she pecked out advertising copy on newsprint, which she cut out and moved around on large sheets of paper, positioning copy and illustrations. When satisfied, she secured everything in place with rubber cement. She did well at the department store, receiving a promotion to advertising manager and then to sales promotion manager.

After a few days of working on "They Stopped the Moving Sands," Dad realized he had something bigger in front of him than a magazine article. He sat back at his desk and remembered flying over the Oregon dunes in a Cessna. Sand. A desert world. He envisioned the earth without technology to stop encroaching sand dunes, and extrapolated that idea until an entire planet had become a desert.

What sorts of characters might populate such a world, and what was their history? What religion would they follow? This last was an important question, perhaps one of the key questions he would have to answer.

Three of the world's major religions . . . Judaism, Christianity and Islam . . . came into existence and grew in desert regions. In sand, in desolation. This was the canvas he needed for the complex story he wanted to write about a hero. He selected the most fanatical of the three faiths, Islam. The story would include an Arab-like world view, and the hero would be a messiah. He envisioned a desert messiah like the Mahdi or Mohammed on horseback, with a ragtag army on horse and camelback with him, thundering across the desert. This leader would be charismatic, capable of inspiring intense loyalty among his people. A power structure would develop around him.

My father wanted a novel that would incorporate real elements from history, mixing them and casting them in a new light—always keeping in mind the saying of one of his favorite literary figures, Ezra Pound: "Make it new."

Frank Herbert knew comparatively little about the complex ecosystems of deserts but set about a thorough course of personal study. He wanted to do something futuristic in his setting, involving desert technology and advanced methods of desert warfare. Despite his mainstream leanings, he found himself changing course again and realized this had to be a science fiction novel. He needed the elbow room afforded by the genre.

This story would have a big canvas.

Dad scoured every library and book store for books about deserts, desert peoples and languages and desert religions. He learned about the behavior of sand, desert storms, water control, and dry land life forms. And he learned how people survived in the hostile, desolate environments. He read T. E. Lawrence's 1926 masterpiece about war in the desert, *Seven Pillars of Wisdom*.

His Library of Congress research skills served him well in this endeavor, for he was able to skim books and articles for the information he needed, avoiding long, time-consuming passages.

But sometimes his innate, boyish curiosity got in the way and slowed him down. While looking for one thing he would become interested

141

in another, and would spend hours learning about a topic that had little or nothing to do with the story he wanted to write.

His notes began filling file folders. The unfinished magazine article went into one of those folders: background information about the ecology of the desert planet.

The story would not occur on Earth, but the characters would be human. Readers would identify best with humans, he believed. And borrowing from the American Indian's opinion of white culture, he would describe how man inflicts himself upon his environment, usurping it and failing to live in harmony with it.

He had the science fiction bug once more, but for a respite from the rigors of novel research, he began writing short stories in that genre again and mailing them off to Lurton in New York City. This was not a total commitment to science fiction, as from time to time he would continue to make attempts at mainstream stories. . . .

Sometimes Dad kidded Mom about having a black spot on her lower back, a mark that came and went. He said it was a "Mongolian spot," indicating that she was either part Indian or part Asian. This conflicted with what Mom had been told by her family, who claimed that they had only pure "East Coast" blood in their veins.*

My parents were totally faithful to one another, and rarely argued about anything, at least not in front of the children. They were remarkably compatible. There were a few exceptions. From the first days of their marriage, Dad depended upon Mom to find things for him. She was the "white witch" of our family, he said, with mysterious methods even she could not fathom. As a natural consequence, Dad had a tendency toward carelessness about where he left personal articles—his keys, wallet, eyeglasses, books, and the like.

Sometimes his habits irritated her, because he would interrupt her in the midst of her work, or some other activity, demanding that she find something for him. If she didn't leap to his aid, he became quite upset.

---

*On her mother's side she was a Landis, descending from Swiss Mennonites. On her father's side she was a Stuart, said to be a descendant of Scottish royalty.

"I'm married to a large child," she sometimes said, in a tone of bemused resignation.

Once, to apologize for behaving poorly, Dad typed her this note:

> Forgive me, darling, if I'm rash,
> If prudence doesn't prevail—
> For I needs must be a man at times;
> I needs must be a male.

To this she typed a reply, on the same sheet of paper:

> You say you needs must be a man,
> You needs must be a male . . .
> Our romance, if you weren't a man,
> Might go a little stale.

In some respects, such as Dad's dependence upon Mom to find things, it was a symbiotic relationship, with unlike organisms living together. Another aspect of symbiosis lay in her dependence upon him to drive her everywhere she wanted to go. In 1956 she did obtain an Oregon State driver's license, passing all the tests. Then she didn't use it, and let it lapse. I hesitate to classify their relationship entirely as symbiotic, or entirely anything else, because no aspect of my parents fits neatly into descriptive niches.

They were each dependent upon the other. Where one had a short-coming, such as an inability to find things or to drive, the other filled in, and they became a complete organism. Where one needed time to write, the other worked to support the family. Frank and Beverly Herbert were inseparable.

On Thanksgiving Day, 1957, Dad and a photographer friend, Johnny Bickel, went to a wild animal sanctuary near the Green River in Washington State, called Hidden Valley Ranch. The place was run by Georges H. Westbeau and his wife, Margaret. Dad wanted to write a story on the Westbeaus for one of the slick national magazines, and he and Johnny were taking photos. The Westbeaus had a huge lioness called Little Tyke, who was internationally famous since it was a vegetarian and had never eaten meat. It had been featured in a film documentary and bestselling book, *Little Tyke*. The grounds of the compound were lovely, with a pond, rich foliage and exotic birds, including peacocks and swans.

At dinner, Georges Westbeau spoke of his famous lioness, who had died a short time before. He told of advertising for a caretaker one time, and a young couple called. Westbeau forgot to tell them about the lioness. As the couple came up the walkway, the man carrying a baby, Little Tyke appeared suddenly and bounded toward them. The woman ran away, screaming. The man followed close behind, but not before dropping the baby on the ground in the path of the lioness. Little Tyke only licked the child's face, but the couple did not get the job.

I visited Hidden Valley Ranch once with my parents, and heard another story. One of Georges Westbeau's favorite tricks was to have an uninformed visitor sit on Little Tyke's couch in the sun room of the house, a room that looked out upon the pond. At first the animal took the balance of the couch, right next to the visitor. But gradually she nudged the person more and more, until she had the whole couch and the visitor was on the floor.

Dad's feature about Hidden Valley Ranch didn't sell, but late in 1957 and early in 1958, his science fiction short stories began taking hold again. Three would be published in 1958: "Old Rambling House" (*Galaxy*, April), "You Take the High Road" (*Astounding Science Fiction*, May), and "A Matter of Traces" (*Fantastic Universe*, November).

"Old Rambling House" reflected our itinerant lifestyle and Dad's hatred of the IRS. A young couple, not unlike my mother and father, had grown tired of constantly moving. They decided to purchase a large house. Unfortunately, the house was not what they expected it to be. It transported them to another planet, where they were told that the people who sold them the house were tax collectors. The new owners were expected to fill the vacated positions.

Whenever Grandma and Grandpa Herbert came to visit and stay with us, Babe insisted on cleaning our house. She caught up on all the chores my mother didn't get around to with her busy schedule. The beds were made with fresh sheets and clean, sweet-smelling blankets. Babe even ironed the sheets.

If Grandma was a neatnik, my father was a beatnik, before the term came into vogue. He was a person leading an alternate lifestyle, without steady employment. Whenever Grandma was around, she always exuded a slight air of disapproval about her son's lack of gainful enterprise and the way he didn't live in one place for very long. She and other McCarthys, who classified people in black and white terms, saw him as something of a black sheep who didn't provide adequately for his family.

One morning Dad was surf casting on the beach near our house at Brown's Point. He heard a bang, and looked around. A strange man was lurching along the beach, coming toward him. The man had a fedora pulled down over his eyebrows, and wore a ragged tweed trench coat with the collar up so that it covered the lower part of his face, revealing only his eyes. He walked with "a terrible crazy slouch," in my father's words, and gripped a .38 caliber pistol in his right hand.

Bang! A bullet hit the sand at water's edge, well away from Dad. Then another shot rang out, and the man was getting closer.

Calmly, Frank Herbert turned away and cast his line into the surf.

Bang! Bang! Each shot rang out louder than the one before.

When the demented creature was only three feet away, Dad said, without turning, "Hi, Howie. How you been?"

They exchanged profane insults and then had a good laugh.

Dad hadn't seen Howie in a while, but he explained it this way, "I don't know why, but the first glance was enough. I knew it was Howie. *I knew it was Howie.*"

Howie put it this way: "I was trying to give him no place to go but Puget Sound. I wanted him to make a motion for the ocean."

The men then "yammered and stammered," as Howie described their playful bantering, and went back in the house.

A little shorter than my father, Howie often wore a dark blue nautical cap. He had a ruddy, square face and intelligent eyes. Of my father's many male friends, none touched his heart like this one. No matter where we moved or how far away Howie was on a maritime assignment, the men always kept in touch. One time after a separation of a few months Dad sent Howie a telegram that said, "Write, damn it, write, or we're through, by God, through!"

From a week before the Fourth of July to a week afterward, a man who lived next door to us set off firecrackers and rockets until 10:00 or 11:00 each night. Dad and Howie decided to get even. At 2:00 one morning, they set off thunderous cherry bombs in his front yard, by his bedroom window. Lights went on in the house, and the man ran outside in his underwear. He couldn't see who was creating the disturbance.

When Dad and Howie saw him outside, they split up. Dad hid behind bushes in the front yard, while Howie went in the backyard and did the same thing. Then Howie shouted, "I got him! Here he is!"

The man ran to the back, whereupon Dad set off cherry bombs in the front yard! Variations on this followed, and they kept the fellow running back and forth in confusion.

By this time I was outside in my pajamas. Seeing Howie sneaking back into our yard, I said, "Hey, that's you and Dad shooting off firecrackers, huh?"

Howie laughed.

In describing his friend, Howie said, "Frank had an infectious sense of fun." Unfortunately, my father rarely showed this side to us, his children. If we saw it at all it was as observers, not as participants.

In 1957, Avon paid $1,500 for the paperback rights to *The Dragon in the Sea*. They would publish it under yet another title, which Dad hated: *21st Century Sub*. So, in a short period of time, the same story was serialized as *Under Pressure*, printed in hardcover as *The Dragon in the Sea* and in paperback as *21st Century Sub*.

When the check for *21st Century Sub* arrived, Dad was so pleased that he wanted to take Mom out for a gourmet meal. We didn't own a vehicle that ran, so Howie loaned Dad his big gray 1949 Chrysler Windsor, a nice two-door car with white sidewalls. Dad and Howie washed and polished the car. At the restaurant, the finest in Tacoma, the valet congratulated my father on owning such a fine automobile. Dad just smiled and handed him a generous tip for the time, five dollars.

Howie and Dad spent a lot of time discussing religion, particularly the mysticism of many faiths and peoples. They drew parallels between Zen Buddhism, Hinduism, the Kabbala of Judaism, the Sufis of Islam, and American Indian beliefs. Howie, half Quileute Indian himself, was at once an intellectual giant and a spiritual man. He spoke for his ancestors and for uncounted future generations, and my father was startled by the message of the people speaking through Howie: "The Earth is dying, it is being misused by non-Indian civilizations that take and do not give."

In 1958, after being in the U.S. Merchant Marine for years, Howie returned to his Indian reservation at Lapush, Washington, in order to gather legends and songs from the remaining old folks. He had last been there in 1939, and was shocked now to see the damage to the environment. Previously the area had been a verdant primeval forest, thousands of years old, with young and middle-aged trees and old grandfather trees shading the younger ones. There had been so many trees on the reservation that to the young man they had seemed to form a tunnel, with light coming in at the ends. Now, after indiscriminate logging by big timber companies, the area was much different. Howie was saddened, and incensed.

When he visited us at Brown's Point, he had with him a book entitled *Ecology,* which had been loaned to him by an Indian friend. The book spoke of the ecological decimation of the planet Earth, and Howie combined this knowledge with what he had seen at Lapush. In a conversation with Dad, Howie told me he said angrily, "They're gonna turn this whole planet into a wasteland, just like North Africa."

"Yeah," Frank Herbert responded. "Like a big dune."

By the time Dad said this, the elements of his story were coming together. He had in mind a messianic leader in a world covered entirely with sand. Ecology would be a central theme of the story, emphasizing the delicate balances of nature.

Dad was a daily witness to conditions in Tacoma, which in the 1950s was known as one of the nation's most polluted cities, largely due to a huge smelter whose stack was visible from all over the city, a stack that belched filth into the sky. The air was "so thick you could chew it," my father liked to quip. The increasing pollution he saw all around him, in the city of his birth, contributed to his resolve that something had to be done to save the Earth. This became, perhaps, the most important message of *Dune.*

My father would write two great books tracing themselves in varying degrees to conversations with his closest friend, Howie Hansen: *Dune* (1965) and the poetically written story of Indian rage, *Soul Catcher* (1972), my father's only non–science fiction novel.

CHAPTER 12

✳ A Writer in Search of His Voice ✳

IN THE fall of 1958 Dad's writing career was not going well. We moved to Longbranch, a small town on a bay just north of Tacoma. This had been one of Dad's ports of call as a child when he rowed and sailed around Puget Sound.

He resumed searching for a job, and as fate would have it, this was an election year. He stopped by Republican campaign headquarters in Tacoma. William "Big Bill" Bantz, a Spokane, Washington, attorney, was running for the U.S. Senate at the time against the popular Henry "Scoop" Jackson. Bantz had a publicity director who wasn't working out, so his campaign manager, George Carlson, fired him. That day, Carlson received a call from Republican campaign headquarters saying a man had been in looking for a job, Frank Herbert. Carlson had never heard the name before, but met my father the following day, was impressed with him and hired him.

Dad was the best publicity man Carlson ever saw. Frank Herbert would put together six suggested publicity letters at a time and lay them in front of Carlson for review and approval. Carlson remembered approving, perhaps, four, rejecting one and specifying revisions on another. It was difficult to find people for jobs like that. The assignments were short-term and demanding, involving highly intensive work.

While Dad worked on the political campaign, his fourth, he dovetailed his schedule with Mom's, doing his publicity work in Tacoma while she was writing ads at the department store.

Unfortunately, William Bantz, like every other candidate my father worked for, lost! Scoop Jackson, an unbeatable foe in Washington State politics who ultimately went on to national prominence, garnered almost 70 percent of the vote.

Whenever my parents had friends over to the house, I sometimes tried to participate in adult conversations. Typically it was after dinner, with everyone sitting in the living room by a cozy fireplace. Too often my inadequate contributions irritated Dad, and he would send me out of the room. My status in the household, Howie told me later, was not dissimilar to that of a dog or a human subspecies. If I didn't please the master, I was dispatched from sight. After seeing my father do this to me more than once, Howie finally told him it was a big mistake, that he should let me participate, and Bruce as well. If he didn't, Howie cautioned, the boys would never bond with their father.

Dad listened attentively to his friend, but said he would raise the boys as he saw fit. We would grow up on our own, if need be, as he had. It would be good for us. He refused to change. And how ironic it was that this man, who one day would communicate effectively with millions of people through his writing, could not communicate with his own children.

One day I was beach-combing with Howie, and he said to me, "Your father cares about you more than you realize. If necessary, he would give up his life for you."

I was astounded to hear this, and didn't know what to believe.

My parents played cards frequently, the two-hand version of Hearts they had invented on their honeymoon. It was their private game. My mother, being what my father called a "white witch," enjoyed a certain advantage over him in these sessions.

When Mom was seated, Dad often went to her and leaned down to whisper in her ear, "I love you." She would smile and whisper the same back to him. There were many small acts between my parents that told us how deeply they felt for one another. The way they looked into each others' eyes and squeezed hands, their secret smiles, whispered words and lingering kisses. The help they gave one another.

Often when she came into the room he would exclaim, "Hi, beautiful!" and she would reply, "Oh, you're just saying that because you mean it."

They exchanged little gifts for no special occasion. He gave her red roses or her favorite perfume, Chanel No. 5, and she made him shirts and sweaters.

To a large extent we lived off the land. Dad maintained a pen of chickens, providing eggs and meat. We had a large, neat vegetable garden across the gravel driveway from the garage, and it provided us with the sweetest carrots I've ever tasted. Mom worked with an artist named Nancy Modahl, whose parents owned a waterfront cabin near us. I knew a spot in the woods near their place where huckleberries grew in abundance, so in the summer and fall I rode my bike over there and harvested them, for Mom's incredible pies. I also brought in blackberries by the bushelful from a field by our house.

To clean the berries, Mom dumped them in buckets of water. Most of the bugs, tiny worms and debris floated to the top, enabling her to remove them with a spoon or strainer.

In distributing her prize desserts to us, Dad employed a variation on Solomon's wisdom, thus preventing Bruce and me from arguing over who was going to get the largest piece. He ordered one of us to cut, and the other to select first.

At Thanksgiving that year, as always, Dad prepared what he called Stuffing Herbert, a concoction with chestnuts, celery and wild rice. Grandma and Grandpa Herbert joined us, and we gathered around our little table in the kitchen.

My mother always kept abreast of what Dad was writing, and she watched for newspaper or magazine articles or books that might be of interest to him. Frequently she guided him into areas he hadn't considered. Both of them read voraciously on every conceivable subject, and she constantly threw ideas at him that he subsequently incorporated into his stories.

Early in 1959 Mom was offered an important job as advertising manager for a new department store in Stockton, California, Smith & Lang. It was time for another move. Dad said we had to fit all of our things in a U-Haul trailer and on the top rack of our car. Much had to be sold or put in storage with friends.

Thinking our Studebaker wouldn't survive the trip, he sold it for only fifty dollars. It was leaking water and oil from the engine, and he thought it might have a blown head gasket. He told the buyer everything he knew that was wrong with the vehicle, and cautioned him, "Just run it until it stops. Whatever you do, don't take the engine apart!"

But the purchaser of the car, despite my father's honesty, didn't listen, and proceeded instead to take the engine apart piece by piece. Just before we left, he phoned to shout at Dad and call him names. Dad reminded him of what he had told him, and the man, unable to counter my father's debating skills, slammed the receiver down.

Almost a decade later, in his novel *The Santaroga Barrier* (1968), Dad wrote of a utopian town in which anyone advertising to sell a used car had to reveal all defects in advertisements. An ad for a $100 Buick described it as an oil-burner, while a $500 Rover had a cracked block. The town, Santaroga, refused all pork barrel government projects. The people were straightforward, honest, and didn't ask for special favors. They didn't smoke or watch television.

In one of the most memorable passages of *Dune* (1965), the Princess Irulan said her father once told her that "respect for the truth comes close to being the basis of all morality." This was Frank Herbert speaking through his characters.

By the end of February we were on the road south in a big black 1951 Nash, a car with a six-cylinder engine that only ran on four. The ugliest thing I had ever seen, it looked like a giant bloated potato bug. A U-Haul trailer with a tarp flapping in the wind rolled along behind us, and there were suitcases on the top rack of the car.

We had, as my father liked to say, packed with a shoehorn. In this process, known well to us, items were packed within items. Everything possible was nested, even if it meant mixing items from different parts of the house. This made for interesting adventures trying to locate things later, but was the most compact possible method of transport. We didn't have a wasted centimeter, or bring along a single unnecessary item.

So much for Tara, for the Washington State homeland where Dad could write. While he sold two short stories that were published early in 1959—"Missing Link" (*Astounding Science Fiction*, February) and "Operation Haystack" (*Astounding Science Fiction*, May)—they took him only a few weeks to write. He wasn't putting out very many words, though he continued to perform research for his desert book. Avenues of research were shooting out in all directions. Maybe with the economic stability of Mom's new job, he reasoned, he would have the time and resources to increase his output.

In Stockton we rented a modern ranch-style home, with an option to buy. It was a sturdily built one-story rambler with a painted concrete patio in the back yard and a big weedy field beyond that. Mom planted a small vegetable garden next to the garage, and I particularly recall how delicious the asparagus was.

Shortly after moving in, Dad pursued a wild scheme. He had heard about high altitude Air Force weather service ("Ptarmigan") flights over remote regions of Alaska, the Bering Sea and the North Pole. Ever curious, he wanted to go along on one of them in order to obtain material for a magazine article. So he contacted one of his old political buddies for help, Congressman Jack Westland, a member of the U.S. House of Representatives from Washington State.

Westland tried, but the Air Force rejected the request, citing extremely dangerous conditions encountered during the flights, and the unwillingness of authorities to expose civilians to such peril. In more recent times, with different technology, my father would have been trying to get a seat on the Space Shuttle . . . probably with similar results. He did not do well when it came to getting his ideas through bureaucratic channels. I don't think he ever figured out how to work through the decision-making processes of governmental and large private bureaucracies. Such endeavors apparently required more patience than he possessed.

Within two weeks of our arrival in Stockton, Dad was receiving child-support demands from Flora's attorney. Since we couldn't make the payments and Dad needed to balance the ledger, Penny came to live with us. The house was big enough for all of us to have our own bedrooms. Dad set his study up in the master bedroom, which was large.

Lurton Blassingame kept pressing my father for more material, and the agent made a number of inadvertent comments about the low output of stories, remarks that irritated Dad. Frank Herbert was finding it more and more difficult to send stories to New York, for reasons he couldn't quite define. The relationship with Lurton and science fiction publishers was becoming a rut, with increasingly negative connotations.

Frank Herbert wanted to write for magazines that paid well, not for science fiction pulps at four and five cents a word. "I was floundering," he confided to me years later, "not making a living. Bev was patient, but wanted to buy a house, ending our itinerant lifestyle. She didn't complain but I knew she wanted to settle down. I was nearly forty years old, with little to show for myself."

His book about the desert was almost becoming too massive to envision finishing. To do it right he wanted to create a universe and several cultures, a formidable, disheartening task that was bogging him down in the tedium of research.

Thus far he had committed very little to paper. Only disjointed plot ideas, descriptive passages and characterizations. His personal library was burgeoning. He had cardboard boxes full of notes.

To earn money more quickly he thought about writing television scripts, and purchased several books about the craft. He came up with a television show idea about a man-fish, a web-footed merman, and spent time writing a synopsis. MCA in Beverly Hills expressed an interest in the project, and he sent it off to them through his film agent, Ned Brown. It didn't sell.*

In ensuing years Dad would write other television treatments, all without success. Part of his problem, as paradoxical as it sounds, might have been that he rarely watched television. Our Hall Avenue house was the first home in which we had a set, and that one, an old Zenith portable, was given to us by a friend.**

---

*A later version, written in 1965, also didn't sell. In the second version, there were not only web-footed mermen, but shark goddesses as well.

**The "boob tube" or "Cyclops," as Dad called it at various times, arrived in our household amidst all sorts of dire warnings from him about how it would harm our bodies (by emitting X-rays within six feet of it) and our minds (through idiot programming and the devious, subliminal messages of advertisers). In *The Santaroga Barrier* (1968) he would make a scathing

Around this time, Dad became acquainted with the Zen writings of Alan W. Watts, particularly *The Wisdom of Insecurity*, which postulated the abandonment of safe courses of action in favor of uncertainty and insecurity. Watts spoke of a paradox in which the abandonment of safe courses of action opened a person to ineffable spiritual truths that could not otherwise be attained.

Frank Herbert held a similar belief, that the natural state of equilibrium in the universe was not a stable, fixed point or condition of being. It was instead a changing thing, always presenting new faces and new experiences. For an individual to be in harmony with the universe, my father believed, he needed to place himself in synchronization with the changing state of nature and human society. He needed to take risks. Thus in many of his stories he stressed the importance of adaptability, and his characters often had to adjust in order to survive.

So it was in our family, with the constant moving from place to place. I was always the new kid on the block, the new kid in school, having to fit into unfamiliar social and educational structures.

He told me that without change, without constant challenge, something in the human mind goes to sleep. "That's why I keep moving," he said, "why I keep looking for new experiences."

My mother wrote a series of advertisements for Smith & Lang that won national awards and became famous around the country. The first ad went something like this: "We're glad to be opening Smith & Lang again because our roots go deep here in the Valley of the San Joaquin." This was a brand-new store, replacing one that had burned down.

Subsequently, a number of stores on the East Coast picked up the advertising theme and began saying things like, "Our roots go deep in the Valley of Virginia," or "Our roots go deep in the hills of the Catskills."

Around New Year's, 1960, after less than a year in Stockton, Dad reached the emotional low point of his career. His writing income in

---

attack upon television, implying that people who watched too much of it had their mental faculties sucked away. In describing the town of Santaroga, which differed from normal American society, he wrote: "Dasein grew aware of an absence . . . about the houses he saw: No television flicker, no cathode living rooms, no walls washed to skim-milk gray by the omnipresent tube."

1959 had been only a few hundred dollars, from a pair of science fiction short stories and the trickle of earnings on *Dragon*. With the money he owed to bill collectors, including the Internal Revenue Service (who had levied a federal tax lien against him), his net worth was below zero. He even owed me back allowance.

While in Stockton, Dad wrote a mainstream story entitled "The Iron Maiden," an amusing yarn with strong sexual content. Approximately 4,500 words long, it was turned down by a number of publishers. Later, Dad would rewrite it under a pseudonym with an anagram surname, Ephraim Therber, but it would fare no better. Editors liked it, but for a variety of reasons, including length and a flat ending, it did not quite fit their needs.

Around this time, Dad also wrote a 12,000-word mainstream story entitled "The Little Window," about a Greek shoemaker and his young nephew, both of whom worked in a shop below street level. The store had a tiny window in the front, providing a view of the shoes and lower legs of passersby on the sidewalk outside. The shop workers saw everyone in terms of the shoes they wore, and in this story Frank Herbert made a number of interesting psychological comments about different types of people.

The action of the tale concerned a gang of thugs who commandeered the shop with the intention of using it as a base of operations to rob an armored car on its regular rounds in the neighborhood. Here my father was putting on paper a story about an armored car heist that his father had told him.

The protagonist of "The Little Window" was the shoemaker's young nephew, who bore the interesting name Paul—a name that would reappear one day as the protagonist of *Dune*. Earlier, he had also used the name in "Paul's Friend," the unpublished story of heroics in a South Pacific hurricane.

"The Little Window" was cleverly told, but had length problems. Lurton showed it to a number of magazines, including *Ellery Queen's Mystery Magazine* and *Alfred Hitchcock's Mystery Magazine*, since they were purchasing crime, detective and suspense stories. He tried mainstream publications as well, such as *Cosmopolitan*, but no one wanted the story.

I was struck by several scenes near the end of the story. In one, Paul overpowered a young hoodlum and took his rifle, which he then used to shoot the gang leader, who was running across the street. As he aimed at the gang leader, holding the rifle against his shoulder with the elbow out, Paul recalled the words of his army sergeant: *"Lead him a little! Lead him!"* This was from Dad's experiences as a young hunter, when his father and uncles taught him how to shoot running deer and fowl in flight.

After killing the gangster, an act of heroism that protected the lives of innocent people, Paul felt terrible remorse for having taken a life. This was Frank Herbert, speaking from his own heart. During the Depression when he had to hunt to put food on the table, he felt remorse each time he shot game.

It was a philosophy of non-violence that would ultimately lead to his involvement in the movement to stop the war in Vietnam. His anti-war beliefs were directly linked to his ecological writings, including the yet-to-be-written works *Dune* (1965), *The Green Brain* (1966) and *New World or No World* (1970). Wars were devastating not only to people, but in the harm they inflicted upon the environment.

The old shoemaker in "The Little Window," upon passing by his shop from the outside, looked through the window and saw for the first time how small and dirty the place was. He lamented having spent thirty-one years there with very little to show for it: just a squalid little shop with a little window.

This was a remarkable and poignant metaphor for the life of Frank Herbert up to that point. He was thirty-nine at the time he wrote the story . . . *thirty-one* years after declaring on his eighth birthday that he wanted to be "a author." The shoemaker's craft was a metaphor for the writing craft, and the shop window like the window my father had on the world, which he realized was very limited, indeed. The more he researched and studied, the more he realized how much he did not know, and it frustrated him.

He was a man in terrible fear that life was passing him by.

At his best, my father was a stream-of-consciousness writer, putting words on paper that emanated from emotions deep within his being . . . words that came almost automatically. I don't think he was fully aware

157

of the metaphorical, semi-autobiographical aspects of "The Little Window." This man made efforts to psychoanalyze other people, but very often failed to perceive his own motivations.

Dad had another short story in search of a publisher around this time. Entitled "A Thorn in the Bush," it bore surface similarities with *A Game of Authors*. Like *Authors*, it was set in a small Mexican village and involved a mysterious foreigner hiding from the past. This time it was an aging and infamous whorehouse madam from Alaska. The protagonist in "Thorn" was a young painter who fell in love with a beautiful but crippled Mexican girl, under the watchful, protective eye of the ex-madam. The story was seen by a number of publishers, most of whom considered it well-written. Unfortunately the length, at eighteen thousand words, was again cited as a problem. It didn't fit into available spaces.

With the failure to find publishers, my father was coming to believe that Lurton had lost faith in his ability to produce good, marketable manuscripts. Concerning the "Little Window" manuscript, Lurton saw immediately that it was a length that would be difficult to sell, but he wrote that he would "try" to market it nonetheless.

The use of this word, "try" sent my father through the roof. He said anyone using that word was presupposing failure, and in a letter he blasted Lurton. I had heard variations of this diatribe myself, in which Dad picked apart every word I used.

Lurton didn't take it lying down, and told my father he had no one to blame but himself for not adequately analyzing magazine and book markets.

Dad apologized. In his heart of hearts he knew the problem was of his own making, and could not be blamed on anyone else. He was a man in an artistic wilderness struggling to find his voice, struggling to find himself. He couldn't decide about subject matter, length or genre. He waffled between short stories, too-long short stories, too-short novelettes and novels, and between mainstream, crime stories, adventures, mysteries, and science fiction. Intermittently he came up with ideas for television programs. Most of his ideas went nowhere.

Frank Herbert wasn't focused, with one exception. In stops and starts he continued the monumental research for his big novel, the pie-in-the-sky book that might never be pulled together. He refused to copy other styles or formulas, even though they had proven successful to other writers. He wanted to write something entirely different, of uncommon intellectual complexity, in a new form.

In the spring of 1960, Mom used her contacts in the retail advertising field to find an even better job, in a glittering jewel of a city almost due west: San Francisco.

Bruce and I would have to leave school in the middle of the semester, but we were old troopers, having done this before. Penny married a truck driver named Ron Merritt, and they settled in Stockton to raise a family.

The move to the City by the Bay would prove to be very important for my father. It would place him in an oasis of intellectualism and culture, offering far more rewards for his investigative mind than Stockton.

CHAPTER
13

✴ Zen and the Working Class ✴

THE SAN Francisco Bay Area would ensnare my father with its charms for almost the entire decade of the 1960s. But as we navigated the highway west out of Stockton, I didn't know that, and was considering the benefits of keeping most of my things packed in cardboard boxes in my new room. That way I wouldn't have to continually pack and unpack. How many houses had I lived in now? I had lost count.

Our potato bug–shaped Nash pulled yet another U-Haul trailer. We didn't have everything we owned with us, since a lot of our stuff had been left in storage with Howie in Seattle a couple of years before, and other items had been stored with Ralph and Irene Slattery even longer.

On San Francisco's Potrero Hill, a working-class neighborhood of weathered Victorian row houses, we rented a flat, an entire level on the third floor of one of the houses. Within months we moved into a house that became available next door. Dad quipped that we moved "because we didn't like the neighborhood." It was a one-story white stucco house, built around 1930, with hardwood maple floors throughout and a red tile roof.

It was not a large house, so Dad set up his roll-top desk in the dining room. The old portable typewriters were getting "long in the tooth" (as he put it when something was past its prime), so he purchased a big Olympia electric typewriter, which was faster than the manual and made a smoother sound as he typed on it.

We had a black wicker couch in the living room, with a round, red-lacquered Chinese coffee table that featured a black dragon design in the center. The table had carved legs that curved outward. When Dad read his manuscripts to Mom in this room he sat on the couch, leaning over pages spread across the Chinese table, while she knitted or crocheted. Every few moments, she took a long drag on a cigarette, causing the tip to flare red-hot. When deep in conversation, she often didn't put the cigarette down, and kept working at it, tapping ashes meticulously into her ashtray.

Within a short time my parents made many intellectual friends in the Bay Area . . . artists, poets, psychologists, newspapermen, science fiction writers. They came for small dinner parties and retired afterward to the living room, where they talked and drank wine with Mom and Dad far into the night. Above all, my parents resumed their relationship with Jack and Norma Vance, who now lived just across the bay in the Oakland hills. Through the Vances, Dad met the well-known science fiction writer Poul Anderson and his wife, Karen, who lived nearby. The three couples became fast friends, and shared many fine dinners and outings together.

The Chinese coffee table in our living room was a reflection of my father's increasing interest in Eastern culture and thought. In his study and scattered all over the house were books reflecting the wide-ranging diversity of his mind, including philosophy, history, politics, mythology, mathematics, religion, foreign languages, deserts, ecology, mythology, science and technology.

In San Francisco, Mom learned how to make charts and predictions from the *Book of I'Ching* . . . Chinese astrology. Using this and her other means of prediction, she said to me one day, "Brian, you will marry a blonde" (which turned out to be correct). And after she showed me how the I'Ching worked, I had trouble putting the book down.

She also predicted that she would die one day in a distant land (which also turned out to be right). Afterward she was in the living room with knitting on her lap, lamenting to Dad about this, since she wanted to see so much of the world. It almost seemed amusing to her, but he perceived her fear, because of accurate predictions she had made in the past. During her entire life my mother tap danced with the paranormal.

It frightened her, but few other subjects intrigued her as much. So every once in a while, like an addict, she ventured into the dangerous realm of prediction.

Dad kissed her and told her not to worry. "After all, darling," he said, "Your predictions don't *always* come true!"

She returned to her knitting, but pensively. For my mother, predictions were always considered carefully, never disregarded.

"I don't know *where* I'll die," Dad said in a cheerful tone, "but I know what I'll be doing. I'll be at a keyboard, pounding out a story."

Around this time my father was teaching himself Kanji, the linguistic characters of China and Japan. He mixed his own black ink in a stone inkwell and with a fat brush made characters on large sheets of rice paper, true to the artistic technique of those cultures. The paper was thin, and shrank and wrinkled around the lettering.

Shortly after arriving in San Francisco, Dad got rid of the Nash. He negotiated a flat monthly taxi rate to transport Mom to and from the White House department store, where she wrote fashion advertisements. Thereafter at a set time every weekday morning, a green and red Veterans Cab Company car showed up outside. It was a twenty-five minute ride each way to her job at The White House department store. Now, at long last, Dad was free of having to drive her.

I played trumpet in the Everett Junior High School band. Mom liked my horn playing, but Dad had me under orders to practice only when he wasn't writing. Still he must have held some affection for my music (though he never told me so), since he wrote a humorous haiku poem about it. A seventeen-syllable Japanese form of poetry, it went like this:

> Number-one son play
> His horn better every day. Still—
> Neighbors move away. . . .

One day at school I got into a confrontation with a future Hall of Fame football player, the notorious O. J. Simpson. At the age of thirteen, I was in the habit of carrying cheap ball-point pens in my shirt pocket. Sort of a 1960s nerd look, but without a plastic pocket liner or slide rule. I was in the courtyard of the school, and a wiry black kid of around my height pulled the pens out of my pocket and threw them on the ground. I outweighed him, and to me he didn't look very tough. He had two friends with him.

"Pick 'em up," I said.

"Make me," the kid said, glaring.

I shoved him, and he shoved back.

"Get him, O. J.," one of his companions said. "Get that white boy."

The ensuing fight, which had no clear victor, was soon broken up by a gym teacher. O. J. and I never had another confrontation, and eventually became friendly. We often ran into one another on the 22 Fillmore bus, where we had a number of pleasant conversations.

In the summer of 1960, Dad accepted a position, once more, in the newspaper industry. He became night picture editor with the *San Francisco Examiner*, working the 4:00 P.M. to midnight shift. The steady old reliable news profession, a fall-back position, offered relative security. With Frank Herbert's tremendous qualifications and abilities in this field, jobs were almost always available to him for the asking—though he often went to great lengths to avoid asking.

The *Examiner*, which Dad and other employees referred to as "The Ex," was owned by the Hearst Corporation, and was the flagship of the chain, the very first newspaper owned and operated by William Randolph Hearst, Sr. The *Examiner* building was old, solid and colorful, and still a bustle of activity. In newspaper circles, it was considered hallowed ground.

Each weekday, Dad wrote or researched in the mornings and early afternoons. At shortly after 3:00 P.M., he would walk down to Third Street near Bethlehem Steel, where he caught a city bus. It took him downtown to the *Examiner* building at Third and Market.

"By writing in the mornings, I gave my best energies to myself," Dad recalled. "The Ex got what was left."

After he had been on the job a while, he went to the paper's book review editor and made an interesting proposition. In exchange for free books, Dad offered to write book review outlines in his spare time, which could then be fleshed out by the editor.

"I'm a fast reader," Frank Herbert said, "and when I'm at the typewriter it goes like a machine gun."

The offer was accepted, and Dad received his pick from carloads of books received by the book review staff. He outlined a wide range of fiction and non-fiction, but the books he wanted to keep were almost entirely non-fiction—works of history (especially Arab history), religion, psychology, ESP, dry land ecology, geology, linguistics, anthropology, botany, navigation . . .

William Randolph Hearst, Sr., a legendary figure, had worked in the *Examiner* building himself in years past. Traditionally, old newspaper files were kept in what was called the "Morgue." It wasn't called that on any Hearst paper, however, since "The Old Man" had an abhorrence for anything involving death. On his papers, it was called the "Library."

After working there six months, Dad was in the *Examiner* library one evening and saw several big photo album–size volumes stacked on a table. Ever-curious, he opened one of the books and was astounded to find original communications from Hearst, who had died in 1951.

Frank Herbert took a deep breath, and looked around. He didn't know where these albums were normally kept, but realized they should not have been left out. He was alone in the library.

If Hearst sent a note, a telegram or a cablegram, they were kept in the albums. These were his Orders, filed chronologically. Some were, in my father's words, "absolutely astounding." One telegram sent from the Hearst Castle at San Simeon said something like, "Who wrote the headline top of column three, page eight, First Edition Sunday? Fire that man."

Some telegrams from San Simeon told the city editor to assign a photographer and a reporter. The photographer was needed because he had a car. They were to assemble something like fifty-one halves of roast chicken, twenty-eight orders of coleslaw and sixteen cakes, and put them on the 3:00 P.M. train to San Simeon. Hearst was having a party.

Dad closed the albums and chuckled softly to himself.

A well-known Sausalito artist named Vargas was a sailing buddy of my father's. Vargas also knew Zen-master Alan Watts, as they were neighbors in Sausalito, just across the Golden Gate Bridge from San Francisco. When Dad expressed an interest in interviewing Watts for an *Examiner* story, Vargas arranged a meeting. This was no ordinary story for my father. He wanted to learn more about the most elusive of all religious philosophies he had encountered, Zen Buddhism. He had read every word Watts had ever written, and had made extensive notes from these and other Zen writings for his desert novel—a novel that still had not reached much beyond the file-building stage. Now Frank Herbert wanted to synthesize the information he had been reading, to hear what a master had to say personally.

Watts lived on the old ferryboat Sausalito, which had been retired and was moored in the picturesque town of that name. A passageway in which one had to bend over led from Watts' quarters to the quarters of another occupant of the ferry, Vargas. My father and Alan Watts were charmed by one another's company, and became friends. Watts used to invite Dad over for dinner and conversation, serving him Oriental food on black and white china in a black and white room.

"It was very Zen," my father recalled, "but our conversations were catholic, in the universal sense."

Watts was particularly taken by one of Dad's observations, that a person's personality could be compared with the impurities of a diamond. "A diamond's value is determined by its impurities," Dad told him.*

This was the height of Frank Herbert's oriental period. Aside from the meetings with Watts, the extensive research, the Oriental furniture in our house, the writing of Kanji characters, and fortune telling from the I'Ching, Dad called me "Number One Son," and Bruce "Number Two Son." We ate Chinese or Japanese food several times a week. Bruce and I received gifts of Chinese thinking caps and sets of origami paper. Dad hung a calendar from Chinatown on the wall of his study. And he gave Mom a beautiful red and black kimono, which she wore on special occasions.

My father was happy at the *Examiner*, and with the respectable com-

---

*Two decades later, Frank Herbert would write in *Chapterhouse: Dune*: "Some precious stones could be identified by their impurities. Experts mapped impurities within the stones. A secret fingerprint. People were like that. You often knew them by their defects. The glittering surface told you too little. Good identification required you to look deep inside and see the impurities. *There* was the gem quality of a total being. What would Van Gogh have been without impurities?"

bined income he and Mom were bringing in we were able to live a little better. We owed money to a lot of people, including Dad's Aunt Peg, Mom's Aunt Ruth, Jack Vance, Dad's former wife, Flora, businesses in the various towns in which we had lived, and last, but certainly not least, the IRS. Mom established a careful budget, and made regular monthly payments to repay our debts.

In 1961, Dad went on a health food binge, stocking the shelves and refrigerator with an array of foods that Bruce and I loathed, including oriental herbs, tofu and beef tongue. Convinced that beef tongue provided more nutrients and proteins than any other form of meat, he forced us to eat the foul substance in a variety of forms, including tongue sandwiches with mayonnaise on the bread and a tongue stew— both of which made me gag worse than green clam guts. I hated any form of tongue, especially the texture of the meat, which had sickening little bumps on it.

Our father also began consuming large quantities of vitamin pills (particularly vitamin C), and loaded up on brewer's yeast, which he sprinkled on many of the meals we ate. The latter had a rather strong flavor, but I got used to it and even grew to favor it. Dad said it gave us more energy. He extolled the virtues of honey as a natural source of energy, and kept several varieties of it in the kitchen. Bruce and I protested (to no avail) having to drink a nasty mixture of vinegar and honey, which Dad served to us at breakfast.

Every once in a while, Bruce or I didn't heed one of the oft-repeated rules of our father's house, and crumbs got into one of the honey jars.

"Who got crumbs in the honey?" Dad would shout, at the top of his lungs.

Uh oh, the guilty party would think.

The standard punishment for crumbs in the honey was a long lecture and yet another demonstration of the proper method. "Do it like this," Dad would say, in an irritated tone, dipping a clean butter knife in the jar. Withdrawing the knife, he then spun it slowly, using the motion to keep a gob of honey from dripping. He held the honey over a piece of whole wheat toast and let the golden syrup drip down.

"See? The blade never touches the toast. Now you can dip the knife back in and keep the honey clean."

166

"Okay, Dad," Bruce or I would say. And we would promise to do it right the next time. Anyway, our intentions were good. . . .

Before each lecture he would utter the familiar words, "I want your undivided attention." He was always repeating himself, which explains in part why Bruce and I frequently tuned him out. We knew it was risky to do so, but we just couldn't stand listening to him anymore. He saw too many details, expected perfection from us. Like many characters in his stories, he was hyper-aware. Our every action was viewed through a high-powered microscope. His attention to detail came from a perceived need to run our household with military precision, so that all would be orderly around him—an enforced environment that allowed him the serenity to create.

My parents thrived in San Francisco. Immersing themselves in the culture of one of the world's great regions, they were putting down roots. Mom even crocheted a large San Francisco map rug, with marks showing the location of our house, the *San Francisco Examiner*, and The White House department store. In our backyard, her roses were blooming, and Mom regularly placed vases of cut flowers on our dining room table.

Above all else in his life, my father was consumed with research for his big novel, set in the desert. In this effort he would eventually read more than two hundred books. He studied Oriental and Arabic languages and literature so extensively that he could think and write in those languages. He discovered the Japanese haiku and tonka poetry forms, and was fascinated by their pristine simplicity and beauty. They had a strange and alien power, he thought, in which they captured the essence of all life.

Dad sold six science fiction short stories in the three-year period of 1960–62: "The Priests of Psi" (*Fantastic,* February 1960), "Egg And Ashes" (*If,* November 1960), "A-W-F Unlimited" (*Galaxy,* June 1961), "Mating Call" (*Galaxy,* October 1961), "Try To Remember!" (*Amazing,* October 1961) and "Mindfield" (*Amazing,* March 1962).

His writing income during that period averaged only a few hundred dollars annually. Still, he remained in contact with the science fiction community, attending local science fiction conventions and other functions. He met science fiction writer Frederik Pohl at a party at Poul

Anderson's house. Science fiction writers Reginald Bretnor and Anthony Boucher lived in the area as well, and there were many get-togethers with them.

At a poker party, one of the writers, an elderly gentleman, tipped a beer over on his lap, drenching the crotch of his trousers. Upon seeing that, Reginald Bretnor quipped, neatly altering a line from Shakespeare: "Who would have thought the old man had so much beer in him?"

A number of famous and soon-to-be famous science fiction writers visited our homes in San Francisco, including Robert Heinlein, Poul Anderson, Jack Vance, and Isaac Asimov. Bruce, despite his youth, was developing an interest in science fiction and was eager to participate in conversations with these men. Unfortunately, whenever they arrived, Dad quickly dispatched my brother to his room.

Frank Herbert usually had many stories floating around looking for publishers, and, being an eternal optimist, he always expected good news to arrive in the mail. It rarely did, but there were occasional checks and letters of encouragement. Bruce and I were under strict orders not to touch the mail. Under no circumstances were we to collect it from the mailbox and bring it inside, because an important letter might fall from our hands and be lost.

With my father's lack of commercial success came a steady stream of suggestions from Lurton Blassingame as to how he might do better. The agent kept reminding Dad that he had tremendous talent, citing as an example *The Dragon in the Sea*. In every way possible, Lurton tried to steer his stubborn writer along a path that would produce more fine science fiction novels, since that was where his talent seemed to be.

Dad wanted to write a science fiction novel, the desert story he had been researching for too long. But he didn't think it would be anything like what Lurton wanted. This would be a big book—hundreds of thousands of words, perhaps. It would involve a new and dense style of writing, in which he would attempt to layer important messages beneath the text of an adventure, almost subconsciously. He didn't want to think about length or style or any other distraction from his work. He didn't want to worry about such things.

Frank Herbert burned with anger about ecology, religion and politics. He was furious at the publishing world for rejecting past stories he thought were good. And he had this troubling feeling that his agent was defending the publishing world too much, when he should have been fighting it for his client.

This impression my father had, as incorrect as it may have been, was blocking him creatively. It was late 1961, and he desperately wanted to begin the new novel. He'd written passages and thrown most of them out. A reason emerged: He couldn't stand the thought of sending any more stories into a New York system that didn't respect his efforts. In his troubled mind, Lurton seemed to represent that system.

On Dad's forty-first birthday, he released Lurton as his agent, attempting to do it as affably as possible. He asked Lurton to continue to handle royalties and future contracts on any works already in the agent's hands. But for anything written in the future they had no relationship. Lurton did not argue. He bowed out gracefully, wishing his friend every success. Lurton had no idea what Dad wanted to work on, the desert novel.

Afterward, his mind feeling more clear and relieved, Dad wrote a seventeen-syllable poem in the Japanese haiku style, a short poem that spoke to the essence of his new book. That afternoon he expanded the poem into prose, eventually setting the poem aside.

The haiku was selected for a number of reasons. First it was a mood setter, a sparse Zen statement about the direction he wanted to take with the story. Haikus frequently concerned subjects of nature, and this book was to have at its core a strong ecological theme. Subsequently he used other haiku poems for particular sections, or tonkas, or Western forms of poetry, most of which he expanded into prose. In this manner, he was able to create beautiful descriptive passages.

He considered setting the story on Mars but soon discarded this notion. Readers would have too many preconceived ideas about that planet, due to the number of stories that had been written about it. Frank Herbert needed something entirely new, totally of his imagination. He would have to construct a world and ecosystem on paper, set in a distant solar system.

One winter evening, I heard him read my mother a passage about a young man named Paul Atreides who was forced to place his hand into the blackness of a box while an old woman, the Reverend Mother Gaius Helen Mohiam, held a poison needle at his neck, the gom jabbar. Though I didn't realize it at the time, this was the opening chapter of *Dune*.

Paul's hand would feel intense pain, the wrinkled crone told him, but if he withdrew it from the box she would kill him with the poison needle. I was transfixed by the drama of the scene and by the strange words . . . gom jabbar, Muad'Dib, the Padishah Emperor, Kwisatz Haderach, Arrakis, Bene Gesserit, jihad, kull wahad . . . the throaty, mysterious resonance of words and names as they rolled off Dad's tongue, in his powerful voice. I was intrigued by the sounds. And by the way the Reverend Mother used "the Voice" on Paul to control him, similar to methods my father often employed against me.

"The language is beautiful," Mom said, after listening to the chapter. Frequently over the years she spoke of the poetry of his writing, and rarely made suggestions for improvement in that area. Her comments primarily concerned plot when she thought he was getting too convoluted, and characterization, particularly the motivational aspects of female characters.

I heard Dad speak passages aloud in his study as he wrote them, before presenting them to my mother. He understood the psychology of human society, the way stories had been told orally for centuries before anything was ever written down. The way troubadours and jongleurs traveled from castle to castle, telling tales and singing songs. He believed readers subconsciously heard the written text through their ears, receiving them as oral transmissions. As a consequence, he labored long hours to obtain just the right word selection and rhythm. The best writing, he believed, touched the subconscious.

He enjoyed relating his stories to my mother, a process that recalled times as a boy spent around scouting campfires when he captivated the attention of scouts and scoutmasters alike. It brought back as well darkened bedrooms Frank Herbert shared with his cousins, in which they hung on his every word. Mom enjoyed hearing his tales. She was an excellent listener, as she had been in her childhood when her Scottish father told her clever mystery stories about caves and secret panels.

CHAPTER 14

✳ The Worlds of *Dune* ✳

THE CREATION of a masterpiece like *Dune* was, for an author, the literary equivalent of a baseball player hitting the ball on the "sweet spot" of the bat and crunching one of the greatest, most memorable home runs ever hit. It not only soared out of the park, it kept going, and fans never tired of talking about it.

Dune ascended beyond the realm of science fiction, and has been called one of the greatest novels written by any author, and arguably the greatest novel of imagination ever conceived. It was a rare moment in literary history, the creation of a work that would be translated into dozens of languages and would sell tens of millions of copies.

It has been widely rumored that *Dune* was rejected by more than twenty publishers before one accepted it. This is not quite true, or at least it is not the whole story. Actually, it was accepted for one form of publication almost immediately.

Dad finished the first novel of an expected trilogy early in 1963, and named it *Dune World*, a segment of approximately eighty-five thousand words. After years of painstaking research, he produced a remarkable science fiction setting—an entire planet that had once been green and fertile but was now covered with sand. This was an obvious extrapolation of conditions on Earth, where sand dunes, if left unchecked, were encroaching upon arable land—inexorably marching over large surfaces of the planet, laying good soil to waste.

Many of my father's stories placed characters in difficult, challenging situations. The planet Dune, with its vast deserts, lack of water, and giant, dangerous worms, was the most challenging of all. In this harsh, unforgiving environment, special efforts and equipment were required to survive. Inhabitants wore stillsuits to recycle bodily fluids and dew precipitators on the desert set up to save every drop of moisture. Water was more precious there than gold—a basic truth of all life as well. The human body was, by weight and volume, predominantly water. And after all, he asked, what was life without water? He had a special perspective on the importance of the substance, from time spent in the outdoors and the safety precautions necessary in such environments.

Dune World set the stage for a drama that concerned, in large part, problems inherent with finite resources. In *The Dragon in the Sea* the finite resource was oil. In *Dune World* it was water and, of even more importance on a galactic scale, a precious natural commodity that was produced only on the planet Dune: the drug melange. In both novels, Frank Herbert wrote futuristic versions of "hydraulic despotism," an ancient political structure that originated in the Middle East. In that system, a small number of people exerted enormous influence by controlling water that was in short supply.

A work of stunning power and imagery, *Dune World* was not his first story with a desert setting. In 1961, while still researching his big novel, the science fiction short story "Try to Remember" was published, about an alien spacecraft that set down in a desert region of eastern Oregon and from there issued an ultimatum to the people of Earth that they must find a way to communicate with the aliens or face destruction of all sentient life on the planet.

He also had the unfinished magazine article based on the government research station at Florence, Oregon—a station set up to control the movement of sand dunes through the planting of special grasses. He had firsthand desert experiences as well. On our second Mexican trip, we stopped in an area of unusual geology, of interest to my father. He walked a short distance out on flint sands and scrambled down a steep embankment into a small arroyo. There he noticed that his footsteps on sand were echoing off the sides of the arroyo. Each step he took produced an eery, reverberating sound, which he theorized was caused by chain reactions in the crystalline interfaces of the sand. On the way back, we stopped in the same place, and he could not duplicate the phenomenon.

It became a key element in the science of the planet Dune:

> "When the worm has gone, one may try to walk out," Kynes said. "You must walk softly, avoid drum sands, tidal dust basins—head for the nearest rock zone . . ."
>
> "Drum sand?" Halleck asked.
>
> "A condition of sand compaction," Kynes said. "The slightest step sets it drumming. Worms always come to that."

Dad and Lurton Blassingame reestablished relations, and the agent agreed to handle the exciting new project. Along with *Dune World* (the first portion of what would ultimately be published in novel form as *Dune*), Dad completed and sent to Lurton an outline of intended sequel material, with some of the key passages that would go into the uncompleted sections. As in *The Dragon in the Sea*, where the basic science was psychology, the technology in this novel was essentially "soft," the science of ecology. These books were aimed at a wider audience than the core group of science fiction readers, who got regular fixes on the hard sciences of math, physics and chemistry.

Lurton submitted the material to legendary science fiction editor John W. Campbell at *Analog*, the successor to *Astounding Science Fiction*. Campbell, who had earlier serialized *Dragon*, made a quick offer on *Dune World* (which was accepted) of three cents a word for English language rights. The section *Analog* was publishing would run in three installments, between December 1963 and February 1964. For the second and third installments, Dad wrote synopses of prior events. After deducting Lurton's 10 percent commission, Dad received $2,295.00 from *Analog*.*

Having seen from an outline and excerpts where my father intended to go with the rest of his story, Campbell said the powers of Paul

---

*John Campbell favored stories that dealt with ESP. In the *Dune* material, Paul could see sporadically into the future, while his sister, Alia, could see into the past.

Atreides were excessive, and should be reduced. This was not merely a comment on characterization. If Paul's powers weren't reduced, Campbell insisted, no one could ever hope to oppose him, and there would be no decent plots for additional books in the series. He recommended a major rewrite.

The author disagreed, and fought for the version he wanted. After a number of lengthy discussions, Campbell agreed to proceed with the story, essentially as written. He and my father reached agreement on a number of minor changes not involving the powers of Paul.

In the summer and early fall of 1963, Dad set to work on completing the balance of the "trilogy." He considered the rather cryptic title of *C Oracle* for Book II, but wisely settled upon *Muad'Dib* instead. Book III was entitled *The Prophet*. In Books II and III, a major plot problem presented itself. Book I contained a strong environmental message, and initially in Books II and III, Dad wrote extensive passages involving Paul Atreides' involvement in the ecology of Dune—in which Paul and the Fremen natives of the planet attempted to reverse past damage inflicted upon the environment, restoring it to its former natural beauty. Dad also wrote passages in which the Imperial Planetologist, Liet-Kynes, was more central to the story.

Frank Herbert decided this was too much ado about a subtheme. The ecology of the planet, while important, was better suited as a backdrop for the primary story he wanted to tell, about a mythology-based future hero. He moved much of the ecological message to the epigrams preceding chapters, and to the first appendix of the work. In the process, between the second and final drafts, he cut forty thousand words from Books II and III, enabling him to focus more on political and religious events surrounding Paul Atreides—the mystical Muad'Dib.

Ironically, despite the direction in which the author attempted to point his story, ecology became the most famous and remembered theme of the book. The political and religious themes were often misunderstood by editors and readers. The ecological message was much easier to understand.

In the massive piles of books my father read to research *Dune*, he learned that ecology was the science of understanding consequences. This was not his original concept, but in the tradition of Ezra Pound he "made it new," and put it in a form that was palatable to millions of people. With a world view similar to that of an American Indian, Dad saw Western man inflicting himself on the environment, not living in harmony with it.

Doubleday, who published *The Dragon in the Sea* in book form, had the first option to look at *Dune World*, Frank Herbert's second novel. Based upon a difficult-to-read carbon copy, they expressed an initial interest in publishing it in hardcover, saying they *might* make an offer if it could be cut to seventy-five or eighty thousand words. Dad thought he could accomplish what they wanted. They indicated that the opening seemed too slow, with the philosophical content too high. A couple of months later, they changed their minds and declined the work.

Lurton liked the story very much, and never flagged in his enthusiasm for it. It reminded him in many ways of a personal favorite, *The Once and Future King* by T. H. White. He said *Dune World* would, at the very least, sell in pocket book form, and was likely to be snapped up by foreign publishers and filmmakers as well. Lurton was a "hands on" agent, part writing counselor and part salesman. He offered advice freely on story points and made suggestions for improvement—some of which my father followed.

With a gut feeling that his saga would be tremendously successful, Dad plowed ahead. Shortly before President Kennedy's assassination in November 1963, he completed books II and III of the "trilogy"— *Muad'Dib* and *The Prophet*—an additional 125,000 words.

When Lurton finished reading the material, he said that *Dune World, Muad'Dib* and *The Prophet* should not be published as separate books. True, he said, there were enough words for three novels, but to him it constituted a single story with no satisfactory points of division, carrying one character through events that occurred in a very short period of time.

Book publishers arrived at Lurton's opinion on their own. This was one story, they said, not three. But they felt it was far too long at 215,000 words and would require immense printing costs and a very high hardcover price for the time, in excess of five dollars. No science fiction novel had ever commanded a retail price that high. Years later, movie producers would express similar concerns about managing the incredible volume of material and producing it in a cost-effective manner that would leave room for profit.*

Book publishers also felt the story would confuse readers. It was too slow-moving and complex, filled with strange, difficult words. Rejections poured in. One editor said he was probably making the mistake of his lifetime in not publishing the work, but declined it anyway. Another said it could attract a cult following, but he didn't want it either.

Most editors couldn't get past the first hundred pages. But by design, the book started out slowly, with gentle internal rhythms that evolved through pace and crescendo to a grand climax. Dad said the rhythms were coital . . . sexual . . . starting slowly and gradually increasing pace. Calculated to touch something deep in the human psyche. An experiment in pacing, Dad called it, an experiment he knew was risky since publishers were rarely risk-takers. He said they preferred instead to purchase stories that were similar to previously published, successful works.

Twenty-three book publishers rejected Books I, II and III. They would not publish the material in any form, separate or combined.

Analog did snap up the serialization on the entire three-part work, but again Campbell had a number of suggestions about plotting, characterization, math and science. Dad's original version of Books I, II and III of *Dune* included a scene in which Alia was killed, and Campbell convinced him to revise this, letting her survive. She had an interesting talent, Campbell said (the power to see into the past), and he wanted to see a sequel that focused on her, as well as another story about the Spacing Guild.

Despite the closeness with which they worked, Frank Herbert and John Campbell never met one another in person. They had many long telephone conversations and exchanged letters and manuscript pages.

---

*Remarkably, Frank Herbert had an even bigger story in mind, and in the writing of *Dune World*, *Muad'Dib* and *The Prophet* he wrote large sections of material for two *additional* books, making a total of five. In fact he did have the makings of a trilogy, but the form it would take was substantially different from his initial proposal. The first three books would be combined into one novel, *Dune* (1965), while the latter two would ultimately form portions of the novels *Dune Messiah* (1969) and *Children of Dune* (1976).

My father once told me to put everything into a writing project. "Never hold anything back," he said. He put everything into Books I, II and III of *Dune*, so much so that by the time he completed the revisions for Campbell, he was wrung out—physically and mentally. All the years of research and intense writing effort left him so drained that for a week straight he slept twelve to fourteen hours a day.

For the cover of the December 1963 issue of *Analog*, Campbell selected the extraordinarily talented artist John Schoenherr. The result was spectacular, a haunting alien landscape with a pair of crescent moons on the horizon. The artist captured the essence of the story and the perilous, extreme desolation of the planet. It took him six attempts to arrive at a painting he felt was satisfactory.

Dad had been studying psychology in depth since meeting the Slatterys in Santa Rosa in the early 1950s. These studies had been instrumental in the characterizations in his excellent first novel, *The Dragon in the Sea*. Now, in *Dune*, he carried the psychological aspect to new dimensions, far beyond characterization.

With his understanding of subliminal messages, he used color coding in the text of his story. A color, such as yellow, was employed to indicate danger. Thus, when the reader reads yellow, he knows viscerally that danger is imminent. He may not be conscious of the realization, but it is a tugging force that keeps him turning the pages to see what will happen next. Dad also described the subtle body motions of characters—such as hand movements—to indicate more than their dialog or even their thoughts.

The women of the Sisterhood, the Bene Gesserit, are able to control people by Voice—the subtle use of intonation and precise word selection. Dad learned much of this in studies of semantics he made for the purpose of writing political speeches. Politicians had to be especially careful about word selection in order to avoid alienating large blocks of voters. And in order to appeal to them.

He read S. I. Hayakawa's seminal work on this subject, *Language in Thought & Action*, and the works of other writers in the field. Semanticists of the time recognized the existence of "metamessages" beneath actual spoken words—messages that would not be picked up if the words were merely displayed on paper. Something in the tone of voice revealed what was really meant. Perhaps the person didn't actually mean what was being said, or of two meanings, the normally secondary meaning was really primary. This was linked to my father's studies of the subconscious and to his analysis of subliminal advertising.

For the names of heroes, he selected from Greek mythology and other mythological bases. The Greek House Atreus, upon which House Atreides in *Dune* was based, was the family of kings Menelaus and Agamemnon. A heroic family, it was tragically beset by flaws and burdened with a curse pronounced on them by Thyestes. King Menelaus was the husband of Helen of Troy, whose abduction by Paris led to the ten-year Trojan war. Menelaus' brother, King Agamemnon, led the confederated Greek armies in the war. Upon returning from Troy, Agamemnon was murdered by his wife, Clytemnestra.

This suggested the troubles Frank Herbert had in mind for the Atreides family. The evil Harkonnens of *Dune* are related to the Atreides by blood, so when they kill Paul's father, Duke Leto, it is kinsmen killing kinsmen, just as occurred in the household of Agamemnon.

In Greek mythology, Leto was the mother of Apollo and Artemis. In *Dune*, Duke Leto is a man, the opposite sex of the mythological base. Dad said he did this in order to highlight a Janus-facing in the story. Janus was an ancient Roman god with two bearded faces, one looking forward and the other looking backward. One of the children of Duke Leto, Paul, can look far into the future, while the other child, Alia, can see far into the past. The Reverend Mother Gaius Helen Mohiam was in part named after Helen of Troy.

The characters fit classical archetypes from mythology. Paul is the hero prince on a quest, as described by Carl Gustav Jung, Joseph Campbell, and Lord Raglan. One of the books my father studied, Raglan's *The Hero* (published in 1936) outlined twenty-two steps followed by classic heroes. These included (all of which closely approximate the life of Paul Muad'Dib): (a) the hero's father is a king (a duke in Paul's case); (b) the circumstances of his conception are unusual; (c) he is reputed to be the son of a god (Paul is reputed to be a returning god, a messiah); (d) an attempt is made to kill him at birth (in Paul's case, the attempt occurred in his youth); (e) after a victory over the king and/or a giant, dragon, or wild beast, he (f) marries a princess (Irulan, his wife in name only, is the daughter of Emperor Shaddam Corrino. The mother of Paul's children, Chani, is the daughter of a kinglike figure to the Fremen, Liet-Kynes) and (g) becomes king.*

Other mythological archetypes were found in *Dune* as well, including a fool (Rabban), a witch mother (Reverend Mother Gaius Helen Mohiam), a virgin witch (Alia), and the wise old man of Dune mythology (Pardot Kynes).

The planet Caladan was named from Calydon, a town in ancient Greece where the Calydonian boar was hunted. This was one of the most famous stories of Greek mythology.

Dune is a modern-day conglomeration of familiar myths, a tale of heroism and great sandworms guarding a precious treasure of melange, the geriatric spice. The planet Dune features thousand-foot-long worms that live for untold years—ferocious dragonlike monsters who have "great teeth" and a "bellows breath of cinnamon." This is the Pearl of Great Price myth. In the Bible, a parable described a man who obtained a great treasure and then kept it hidden. This parable was linked to mythological stories of protected treasure, such as the golden fleece of the sacred ram sacrificed to Zeus, given by Phrixus to his wife's father and nailed to an oak tree, where it was guarded by a dragon that never slept.

In *Beowulf,* written by an unknown English poet, a ferocious fire dragon guarded a great treasure hoard in a lair under cliffs at the edge of the sea. A close reading of the epic poem reveals interesting detail, in which the dragon is described as a worm:

> . . . a foul worm, a dragon, took it upon itself to hold sway through the heavens at night . . . It seems there was a worm that slept upon a pile of treasure, which it had zealously heaped up under a stone bluff . . .

*In the sequel to *Dune, Dune Messiah*, Paul continues in the classic pattern of a hero, when: (h) for a time he reigns uneventfully, and (i) prescribes laws, but (j) later he loses favor and (k) he meets with a mysterious death and (l) his body is not buried.

... the worm took to the air, burning the houses of men, belching red fire in his anger. . . .

At a writing workshop recorded by his friend Bill Ransom, Dad said that the heroic warrior Duncan Idaho was named with a place in mind, the state of Idaho. Such a technique has traditionally produced solid-sounding appellations, such as "Dutch," "Scotty" and "Tex." For the antagonist family, he selected a harsh-sounding name, Vladimir Harkonnen, which to the Western ear sounded Soviet, a suggestion of the Communist enemy in existence at the time *Dune* was written. Dad found the name Harkonnen (which is actually Finnish) in a California telephone book. And, as he typically did in his stories, Frank Herbert included a friend's name in the novel. One was Holjance Vohnbrook, an anagram of Jack Vance's full legal name of John Holbrook Vance. Another was Poul Anderson, under the anagram Pander Oulson. (See *Dune*, Terminology of the Imperium—"krimskell fiber" and "Lady Alia Atreides.")

The planet commonly known as Dune is called Arrakis by the ruling nobles, a harsh-sounding name that is suggestive of an inhospitable place. And inhospitable it is, under the short-sighted, usurping control of the noblemen.

The very name "Dune" is like a great sigh, suggestive of a faraway, exotic land. The native Fremen have blue-within-blue eyes there, and they use an unauthorized planet name in defiance of authority. The name Fremen (pronounced Frem-men) sounds close to "free men," a suggestion that they are an independent, rebellious tribe who will never permit themselves to be dominated by outsiders.

According to edicts from the Imperial military-political powers holding this place, the desert world is named first Arrakis and later Rakis. But the Fremen of the desert, who have been there since time immemorial, understand the spirit of Dune and of the great Maker-worm, Shai-hulud. These are rebels, and the very name they use for their world, Dune, suggests this. No outside force, no foreign authority, can force them to alter their ways.

It was this spirit of rebellion, of human defiance against injustice and oppression, that Frank Herbert captured so magnificently when he set up his desert world and the empire encompassing it. He pitted Western culture against primitive culture, and gave the nod to the latter. In a later work, *Soul Catcher*, he would do something similar, and again he would favor old ways over modern ones.

In a tragic, ironic scene, Imperial Planetologist Liet-Kynes lies dying on the sands of Arrakis, left there by the Harkonnens without a stillsuit. They do this thinking it will be amusing for the planet to kill its ecologist, despite all his efforts, despite everything he knows about the environment. As my mother pointed out, this makes his death all the more terrible, knowing that his life could have been spared with a stillsuit, knowing that water is only a hundred meters beneath the surface of the sand.

Liet-Kynes is a metaphor for Western man, bearing all the adornments of scientific and cultural knowledge. But the rhythms of his life and Imperial society, like the rhythms of Western society, are out of synch with the rhythms of the planet. Intensifying the irony, Kynes sees desert hawks approaching, preparing to slash him, waiting to feed upon him when he dies—hawks that his father brought in from another planet to regenerate the ecosystem of Arrakis.

Like the nomadic Bedouins of the Arabian plateau, the Fremen live an isolated existence, separated from civilization by vast stretches of desert. And like the Bedouins, the Fremen feel their lifestyle is superior to that of more civilized people. The Fremen take psychedelic drugs during religious rites, like the Navajo Indians of North America. And like the Jews, the Fremen have been persecuted, driven to hide from authorities and survive away from their homeland. Both Jews and Fremen expect to be led to the promised land by a messiah.

The life and legend of Muad'Dib are rooted in the familiar religious concept of messianic impulse, along with the idea of a political and religious super hero. These themes are found in Islam, Judaism, Christianity, Buddhism and other faiths. Frank Herbert even used lore and bits of information from the people of the Gobi Desert in Asia, the Kalahari Desert in southwest Africa, and the aborigines of the Australian Outback. For centuries these people have survived on very small amounts of water, in environments where water is a more precious resource than gold.

The Fremen are also like any number of peoples who throughout history have concealed themselves in inhospitable mountain or desert regions, using them as bases of guerrilla warfare against more powerful occupying forces. The Turks did this after World War I when their country was occupied, while the Yemenese Arabs and Algerians did it after World War II. The tactic has been particularly effective against colonial powers, making occupation too expensive to continue. The Germans and Spanish resisted Napoleon's occupying armies in this manner. So did the North Vietnamese, driving American forces from Vietnam. The Fremen of Dune do this as well, resisting the occupation of the Imperial Empire and its franchise holder, the Harkonnens.

In creating the Fremen, Dad called upon personal memories of the Great Depression, in which the hardy, stubborn personality survived best against adverse conditions. The author understood the survivalist mentality, the ability of human character to overcome difficult circumstances.

Under his interpretation, the behavior of such people in extreme situations such as those found on Arrakis became inseparable from religion. It was ingrained in their group personality, in their ethics. And the religion of these people was in large part based upon the mystical practices of societies of people whose spiritual belief systems originated in desert regions—Muslim Sufis, Jewish Kabbalists, Navajo Indians, Kalahari and Gobi primitives, Australian bushmen . . . and more.

The Fremen religion spoke of "The Pillars of the Universe," a cosmology that derived in part from the four pillars of the Christian universe, the New Testament gospels of Matthew, Mark, Luke and John.

Master chef Frank Herbert concocted quite a banquet for the senses of his readers. His sprinklings of mysticism blend surprisingly well with portions of ancient mythology and handfuls of Jungian psychology about the workings of the subconscious. It all works because the reader, more visceral than he realizes, is a conglomeration of these things after millions of years of human history. The reader identifies with passages without consciously knowing why.

Dad studied and incorporated aspects of the life of "the Mahdi" (Mohammed Ahmed), who operated in the Egyptian Sudan in the 1880s and claimed to be a messiah. The Mahdi led rebellious Arab forces against the colonial British Empire.

Dad also studied the life and literature of T. E. Lawrence ("Lawrence of Arabia"), a British citizen who during World War I (with Feisal, son of the Sherif of Mecca) led Arab forces in a successful desert revolt against the Turks. Lawrence employed clever guerrilla tactics to destroy enemy forces and communication lines, and came close to becoming a messiah figure for the Arabs. This historical event led Frank Herbert to consider the possibility of an outsider leading native forces against the unlawful occupiers of a vast desert land, and in the process becoming a messiah to them.

He studied other historical military strategies and tactics as well. When Paul Muad'Dib attacked the Harkonnens under cover of a desert storm, this was an operation reminiscent of Eisenhower leading an allied invasion in 1944, aided by a storm that concealed much of the movement of his forces.

The Butlerian Jihad of Dune's history was a movement against machines, preventing them from ever exerting domination over men. This touched upon a natural fear humans have of machines. In recent years, this apprehension has focused largely upon computers, upon a fear that computers can be loaded with artificial consciousness and intelligence that will be superior to humans in important respects, eventually relegating men to subservient status.

The distrust of machines is actually, perhaps, a fear men tend to have of anything they do not understand—of things that are arcane and unpredictable from their perspective.

The roots of the Butlerian Jihad went back to individuals my parents knew, to my mother's beloved grandfather Cooper Landis and to our family friend Ralph Slattery, both of whom abhorred machines. Whenever Mom had trouble with a machine, she invoked Cooper's invective, well-known in our household: "Oh! The mindless malignancy of mechanical devices!"

In *Dune*, the Bene Gesserit sisterhood had a collective memory—a concept based largely upon the writings and teachings of Carl Gustav Jung, who spoke of a "collective unconscious," that supposedly inborn set of "contents and modes of behavior" possessed by all human beings. These were concepts my father discussed at length with the Slatterys in Santa Rosa.

The Bene Gesserit were in part based upon my father's maternal aunts, who attempted unsuccessfully to convert him to Irish Catholicism in his youth.

The three experiences my father had with drugs provided details that he wrote into the story of Paul Muad'Dib when the character took melange, the precious spice drug of Dune. Melange was irresistible, addictive, capable of transporting its user to alternate realms. It is interesting as well that at the bottom of a bottle of mescal (an intoxicating Mexican beverage) is a tiny worm which is said to contain so much "essence" that people have been known to hallucinate after consuming it. My father, of course, spent considerable time in Mexico.

I find pieces of our family history throughout my father's writings, and particularly in *Dune*. Lady Jessica, with her beauty, intelligence, loyalty and love, represented the way my father felt for my mother. She was perfection to him, all things that were right with his life. She was his strength and sustenance, nurturing all of us. Like the busy Duke Leto Atreides, my father was too wrapped up in his work to pay adequate attention to his offspring. Much of this responsibility was left for Lady Jessica, just as it was left for my mother in our family.

Lady Jessica's etiquette, like my mother's, was always impeccable. Such women knew how to behave in different, often challenging, situations—no matter the faces each situation presented. In Lady Jessica's case, if she needed help with a decision, she searched her Bene Gesserit past lives to determine the best course of action. It is interesting in this vein to note that "adab," the demanding and instant memory of the Bene Gesserit, is a word in Turkish Arabic for etiquette and politeness.

The Bene Gesserit genetic memory and the surrealistic effects of melange were occult phenomena, akin to the interests and powers of my "white witch" mother. These literary creations were linked with events in my father's life, including "Rhine consciousness" card predictions he made in the 1930s, his studies of Jung's collective unconscious theory, and personal experiences with hallucinogenic drugs.

Frank Herbert himself was in many of the characters in *Dune*, for they sprang from his mind. He was the dignified, honorable Duke Leto, and the heroic Paul as well. He was the swashbuckling risk-taker in Paul and in the loyal Duncan Idaho as well. Dad's religious and philosophical beliefs closely approximated those of Paul Atreides, combining the wordless, enigmatic elements of Zen with the self-determination of Existentialism.

My father once told me he felt he was most like the Fremen leader, Stilgar. This surprised me until I realized that Stilgar was the equivalent of a Native American leader in the story—a person who defended time-honored ways that did not harm the ecology of the planet. Stilgar was an outdoors man like my father, a person more comfortable in the wild reaches of the planet than in its more "civilized" enclaves. Such a strong name, Stilgar, combining the phonetic elements of "steel" and "guard." He was the stalwart and determined guardian of Dune, a position not dissimilar from the one my father placed himself in with respect to Earth.

Portions of the book were semi-autobiographical. Only a short while before, in 1961, Dad had been at the lowest point of his literary career, unable to write. He had been forty-one at the time, with a chronic sick feeling in the pit of his stomach, a fear that he had wasted his life. Recollections of that crisis come instantly to my mind whenever I read this excerpt from "Dirge for Jamis on the Funeral Plain" in *Dune*:

> Time has slipped away.
> Your life is stolen.
> You tarried with trifles,
> Victim of your folly.

I lived with my father during the years he worked on *Dune*, and I understand a great deal about the making of the work. Nonetheless, the creation of this magnificent piece remains to me almost beyond comprehension. I find something new and intriguing in it on nearly every pass through the pages. My father was a man who spoke to me often of the importance of detail, of density of writing. He understood the subconscious, wrote his books in vertical layers. He said a reader could enter *Dune* on any one of numerous layers, following that particular layer through the entire work. On rereading, the bibliophile might choose to follow an entirely different layer.

Despite all the work *Dune* required, my father said it was his favorite book to write. He used what he called a "technique of enormous detail," in the process of which he studied and prepared notes over a four-year period, between 1957 and 1961, then wrote and rewrote the book between 1961 and 1965. In all, it took the better part of a decade to complete the work with all the changes his editors wanted.

Dune is not a novel to be grasped entirely on first reading. There are important messages beneath the adventure, deftly intertwined with the action of the story. The layer of action is the most obvious one, the one most readers follow and remember best. It is an essential component, my father told me, for without structuring a book well, without remembering to entertain first, an author cannot hope to hold a reader's attention.

Frank Herbert said he was in love with language, particularly the English language. *Dune* is a marvelous tapestry of words, sounds and images. Sometimes he wrote passages in poetry first, which he expanded and converted to prose, forming sentences that included elements of the original poems. There are natural rhythms to life, to the desert, to forces of nature, and he wanted his book to echo such rhythms. This required careful word selection and sentence formation, with onomatopoetic words that imitated the sounds they were describing.

As he worked, he enjoyed listening to a wide variety of music, with the volume turned up. So it is not at all surprising that his best writing took on musical qualities. Writing was like a "jazz performance" for him, he said. He composed it as he went along. He could slow it down, speed it up, soften, intensify . . .

Some poetry in *Dune* was modeled after Provençal lyrics, the court poetry of troubadours in southwestern France and the Mediterranean between the late eleventh and mid-thirteenth centuries. To understand this style, Dad read the lyrics of poets of the period, including the work of Bernard de Ventadour, whose "courtly love" poetry is considered the finest surviving example of that style. He also enjoyed Japanese tanka verse, with thirty-one syllables.

He even studied and wrote Italian and Shakespearean sonnets. Like Provençal lyrics, much of this poetic form originally concerned the subject of love.

The subjects commonly found in these poetic forms are interesting, as they correspond with key subject matters in *Dune*: Nature (in haiku and tanka) and Love (in Provençal lyrics and in sonnets). Thus the atmosphere of a universe was constructed, with small and large pieces, layer upon layer, like a painter.

In interviews later, including one with his friend and collaborator, Bill Ransom, Dad said poetry was like a baseball player swinging three bats as he walked up to the plate. Frank Herbert was building the muscles required for prose writing, developing a powerful sense of rhythm and word selection.

The Japanese haiku is a Zen Buddhist art form. And the prana-bindu discipline of the Bene Gesserit was based upon Zen disciplines. Aware of a simmering women's liberation movement in the early 1960s and the desires of women in religious service for more recognition, Dad decided to postulate a "sisterhood" in control of an entire religious system. He thought readers would accept the premise of women with occult powers of memory, since females have traditionally been said to have "women's intuition."

St. Paul the Apostle was considered the greatest advocate of Christianity, so it seemed appropriate to Frank Herbert to name the messiah of his new desert religion Paul. The Christian thread in *Dune* is strong. An Orange Catholic Bible is in the book, suggesting a future merging of Protestantism and Catholicism, and there are numerous references to Christian ethics. Dad's early religious influence was Catholic, from his maternal aunts, which formed one of the bases of the Bene Gesserit. "Gesserit" was a name selected intentionally to sound like "Jesuit." Dad referred to the Bene Gesserit as "female Jesuits." My mother's early religious influence was strongly Protestant.

Many entries in the Orange Catholic Bible were Zen, speaking of sensing alternate worlds that were all around, and of great truths not easily expressible in words. Through his association with Irene Slattery, Dad knew of the studies of Professor Gilles Quispel of the Netherlands, a well-known religious historian. In the mid 1950s, Quispel became aware of an archaeological discovery near Naj Hammadi in Upper Egypt. An Arab found several ancient papyrus manuscripts in a large pottery jar there, many of which involved Gnostic Christian scripture that for political reasons had never been included in the Bible. At

Quispel's urging, the Jung Foundation in Zurich purchased one of the manuscripts, a leather-bound codex.

That codex contained *The Gospel According to Thomas*, which included a number of astonishing quotations ascribed to Jesus Christ—passages that sounded more like Eastern religious thought than Western. This was one: "Bring forth what is within you, and you will be saved." The Orange Catholic Bible of *Dune*, with its cryptic, mystical entries, had a strong basis in historical fact.

There were sandtrout in the deserts of Arrakis, and the fish was an early Christian symbol. When in a sequel to *Dune (Children of Dune*, 1976) a character allowed sandtrout to attach themselves to his body, this was based in part upon my father's own experiences as a boy growing up in Washington State, when he rolled up his trousers and waded into a stream or lake, permitting leeches to attach themselves to his legs.

There is much of the outdoors man Frank Herbert in *Dune*. The technique of "sandwalking," in which a person moves without producing a rhythm that might attract giant worms, is a technique my father learned in his childhood. The hunter moves silently and downwind from wild game, so as not to alert the prey of his presence. The fisherman does not make a disturbance in or near the water, for fear of frightening away the fish.

Frank Herbert knew from personal experience that living in harmony with nature was best, moving through it without disturbing it—taking from it, but only in ways that permitted renewal. One day he would become a leading proponent of wind and solar power, and would even propose obtaining methane from chicken droppings: "Use every part of the chicken except the squawk," he would quip.

On a philosophical level, living in the desert was not so different from the forest or the farm. Man had to pay close attention to resource preservation and recycling, to the preservation of systems. Nothing was wasted. The land was not to be stripped of its nutrients if it was expected to be usable in the future by our grandchildren and great-grandchildren. Dew precipitators were set up on the deserts of Arrakis to catch precious moisture, and humans traveling in desert regions wore stillsuits to recycle and preserve bodily fluids.

When Stilgar and Paul set hooks in giant worms and climbed up them to the top, it was like mountain climbing, driving metal pins into rock and ice for footholds. The hooks in worms were reminiscent of fishing as well, but an extrapolation beyond anything most people could ever imagine.

The Mentats of *Dune*, capable of supreme logic, were "human computers." In large part they were based upon my father's paternal grandmother, Mary Stanley, an illiterate Kentucky hill-woman who performed incredible mathematical calculations. Mentats were the precursors of Star Trek's Spock, first officer of the starship Enterprise.

Frank Herbert was an investigator who turned over rocks and made human creatures scurry out of hiding places. A modern-day Socrates, he tore into what he termed "unexamined linguistic and cultural assumptions," and in so doing he extrapolated words and traditions he thought might exist in the future. He observed that bits and pieces of the diversified past were entrenched in our own language and culture, and he saw no reason why this pattern of creation would not continue to hold course. He said there would be segments of the past . . . of today . . . nestled into words and customs thousands of years from now, like nearly forgotten detritus.

This accounts for the diversity of religious fragments encountered in *Dune*. It also accounts for Frank Herbert's exceedingly broad selection of words. Many of the words in *Dune* were rooted in Arabic and Hebrew, and in numerous cases he combined syllables from two languages, two cultures, or even two religions. He referred to Zensunni teachings, for instance, whereby Zen Buddhism and the mystical Islamic denomination Sunni were joined.

Such words suggest past historical events without detailing them. They also point to a fact of history: Languages change. They are in a constant state of flux, never static. Words appear and evolve.

The words and names in *Dune* are eclectic. The word "sihaya" is Navajo; "Bene Gesserit" is rooted in Latin; "sietch" is Chakobsa, a language found in the Caucasus; Tleilaxu is based upon a word for salamander in the Nahuatl dialect of the Aztecs. Atreides, as I have said, is based upon House Atreus, from Greek mythology. The "Padishah" Emperor ruling the universe of Dune is from Persian, East Indian, and

Turkish tradition. Jamis is an Old English name my father found when researching genealogical records.

"Jihad" is Islamic for holy war, and this word has the same meaning in Arabic as it does to the people of Dune. The Fremen language is based upon colloquial Arabic, in a form my father believed would be likely to survive for centuries in a desert environment. Alia is a name given to female descendants of the prophet Mohammed, a name that means "noble one" or "beloved of God."

His desert is a great sea with giant worms diving into the depths, Shai-Hulud's domain. Dune tops are like the crests of waves, and there are powerful storms out there, creating extreme danger. On Dune, life emanates from the Maker (Shai-Hulud) in the desert-sea; similarly all life on Earth is believed to have originated in our seas. Frank Herbert drew parallels, used metaphors, and extrapolated present conditions into world systems that seem entirely alien at first blush. But close examination reveals that they aren't so different from ordered assemblages we know . . . and the book-characters of his imagination aren't so different from people familiar to us.

If Frank Herbert could be categorized in a religious sense (and that is a very big "if"!) he came closest to Zen Buddhism. It was in that realm that he felt most comfortable, most certain of his footing. He did not participate in the dogma or rituals of any religion, though his deep commitment to ethics and the survival of humanity were apparent throughout his writings. He believed in quality of life, not merely in scraping by, and he spoke deftly (and at times didactically) about this through his characters. Sometimes in his characters, Frank Herbert spoke with Frank Herbert, exploring different avenues of his own belief systems, typically having to do with religion or the politics of power. At other times he spoke through people who represented, to him, anathematic types.

The mainstream of Buddhism is a highly ethical belief system, one that had great appeal to Frank Herbert. Of no little importance to him, Buddhists hold a spiritual reverence for nature and for the preservation of life on this planet. Dad also believed that Buddhists tend to be tolerant of the belief systems of others. Certainly there are exceptions, but for the most part he didn't see them in possession of the "holier than thou" missionary fervor of Western religions. It is interesting in this vein to note that the stated purpose of the C.E.T. (the Commission of Ecumenical Translators), as described in an appendix to *Dune*, was to eliminate arguments between religions, each of which claimed to have "the one and only revelation."

This is particularly revealing in light of the childhoods of my parents, when adults attempted to force-feed religious dogma to them.

Dune, the first novel in what would ultimately become a series, contained hints of the direction he intended to take with his superhero, Paul Muad'Dib, clues that many readers overlooked. It was a dark direction. When planetologist Liet-Kynes lay dying on the desert, he remembered these words of his father, spoken years before and relegated to the back reaches of memory: "No more terrible disaster could befall your people than for them to fall into the hands of a Hero." And at the end of an appendix it was written that the planet had been "afflicted by a Hero." These were sprinklings here and there, seeds of the direction Frank Herbert had in mind. The author felt that heroes made mistakes . . . mistakes that were amplified by the numbers of people who followed those heroes slavishly. By the second and third books in the series, *Dune Messiah* and *Children of Dune*, this message would become clear.

In another seed planted in *Dune*, he wrote, "It is said in the desert that possession of water in great amount can inflict a man with fatal carelessness." This was an important reference to Greek hubris. Very few readers realized that the story of Paul Atreides was not only a Greek tragedy on an individual and familial scale. There was another layer, larger than Paul, and in that layer Frank Herbert was warning that entire societies could be led to ruination by a hero. In *Dune* and *Dune Messiah* he was cautioning against pride and excessive confidence, the hubris of Greek tragedies that led to the great fall. But it was societal-scale hubris he was warning against . . . the potential demise of an entire society.

Among the dangerous leaders of human history, my father sometimes mentioned General George S. Patton, because of his charismatic qualities—but more often his example was President John F. Kennedy. Around Kennedy a myth of kingship formed, and of Camelot. His followers did not question him, and would have gone with him virtually anywhere. This danger seems obvious to us now in the case of such men as Adolf Hitler, who led his nation to ruination. It is less obvious, however, with men who are not deranged or evil in and of themselves. Such a man was Paul Muad'Dib, whose danger lay in the myth structure around him.

One of my father's most important messages was that governments lie to protect themselves. They make incredibly stupid decisions. Years after the publication of *Dune*, Richard Nixon provided proof. Dad said that Nixon did the American people an immense favor. By example, albeit unwittingly, Nixon taught people to distrust government.

Frank Herbert believed in importance of long-range planning, particularly with respect to the environment. He spoke of adaptation, of setting forces in motion to change the attitudes of men toward their own planet. In *Chapterhouse: Dune*, the sixth volume of the series, Reverend Mother Dortujla used an aphorism familiar long before the publication of *Dune*: "Never damage your own nest." That was Frank Herbert speaking, of course, since he believed we were doing precisely that to Earth.

One of the layers of *Dune* was an ecological handbook written by planetologist Pardot Kynes and his son, Liet-Kynes. Ahead of its time, it described the consequences of human actions. Environmental awareness was just awakening in the early 1960s, and Frank Herbert was one of the standard bearers. In 1962, Rachel Carson published *Silent Spring*, a monumental work that decried the killing of birds and harmless insects by toxic chemicals such as DDT. In 1963, shortly before the opening installments of *Dune* were published by *Analog*, the first clean-air act was passed in the United States. President Kennedy gave a couple of speeches that year about protecting the environment.

Analog readers liked *Dune World*, and fans nominated it for the 1963 Hugo Award for best novel—rather unusual, since the story hadn't yet been published in book form. While *Dune World* did not win the award, its popularity was in no small part responsible for the awarding of a Hugo for best science fiction magazine to *Analog* and its editor, John W. Campbell. At the awards ceremony, held at the Pacificon II science fiction convention in Oakland in 1964, Dad accepted the award as Campbell's proxy and shipped it to him.

During 1964, however, a steady stream of publishers rejected *Dune World* and its allied manuscripts in book form. Dad lost hope that it would ever be published in anything more than a magazine.

Trying to maintain his sense of humor, Dad came up with this:

Chinese Rejection Slip

Illustrious brother of the sun and moon! Look upon the slave who rolls at thy feet, who kisses the earth before thee, and demands of thy charity permission to speak and live. We have read the manuscript with delight. By the bones of our ancestors we swear that never before have we encountered such a masterpiece. Should we print it, his majesty the emperor would order us to take it as a criterion and never again print anything which was not equal to it. As that would not be possible before 10,000 years, all tremblingly we return the manuscript and beg thee 10,000 pardons. See—my head is at thy feet, and I am the slave of thy servant.

In the January 1965 issue, *Analog* began a new serialization of the 125,000-word completion of the story (Books II and III) under a single title Campbell preferred, *Prophet of Dune*. It would run in five monthly installments, ending in May.

Early in 1965, a few weeks after publication of the first installment of the new serial, Sterling E. Lanier, an editor with Chilton Book Company and a science fiction writer himself,* contacted Lurton Blassingame. Lanier had read the *Analog* installments, and when he finally got his hands on a complete copy of all three manuscripts, he wanted to publish them in a single edition.

In the buy of an editor's lifetime, the literary coup of coups, the farsighted Lanier offered a $7,500 advance (plus future royalties) for the right to publish *Dune World* (Book I) and *Prophet of Dune* (Books II & III) in hardcover. His offer was accepted.

Lanier said there were a number of loose ends in the story and rough

---

*Stirling Lanier wrote the novels *Hero's Journey* and *Under Marswood*.

transition points between Books I, II and III requiring more work. He wanted the entire work expanded. When he discovered my father had drawn a map of the planet Dune, he asked for a copy, to include it in the book.

Lanier proposed a simple title: *Dune*, which he liked for its power and mysticism. For the cover art, he wanted to use John Schoenherr, who had done such a fine job on the *Analog* covers.

Chilton was best known as the publisher of a series of automobile repair manuals, leading Dad to quip that they might rename his work *How to Repair Your Ornithopter.* (Ornithopters were the birdlike flying craft of the planet Dune). At least Chilton had experience printing large books. Their auto repair manuals were huge.

A short while after the Chilton agreement was reached, Ace Books, a well-known publisher of science fiction titles, made an offer to publish the book in paperback. That edition would appear in 1966, a year after release of the hardcover, in order to allow the higher-priced hardcover to run its course before receiving competition from the paperback.

15

✳ Number Two Son ✳

"What is the son but an extension of the father?"

—Frank Herbert, in *Dune*

DURING THE period when Mom was working in downtown San Francisco and Dad was writing the most difficult segments of *Dune*, he became increasingly irritable and more intolerant than ever of the slightest interruption to his concentration. It reached the extreme where he took the house keys away from Bruce and me and told us he was going to write inside a locked house. We were commanded to go elsewhere after school and he didn't seem to care where. Dad and Bruce got into a big row over this, and Dad yanked a string with a house key on it off Bruce's neck. Prior to that, my brother had been in the habit of coming into the house after school to make a sandwich.

Unhappy with the way Dad was treating him, Bruce ran away, walking more than twenty-five miles. Only eleven years old, he crossed the Golden Gate Bridge into Marin County and hid in a creek bed for several hours. The more he thought about his predicament, however, the more Bruce realized how cold, lonely and hungry he would be if he didn't return home. And he realized how angry Dad would be at him for yet another interruption to his writing process.

It must be understood that the son of a writer is not without creative energies of his own. To avoid Dad's wrath, my little brother came up with a wild, rather ingenious tale. He contacted the nearest police precinct in Marin County and reported in a state of feigned hysteria that he had been kidnapped by two men and thrown in the back of a laundry truck. It was only through good fortune, he said, that he was able to escape.

The police believed Bruce, and had him go through books of mug shots in an attempt to find the bad guys. Dad and Mom were contacted, and they drove to the police station. A detective there assured Mr. and Mrs. Herbert that he would investigate the case thoroughly, and would find whoever had done this terrible thing. Their son was fortunate to be alive, he said.

In our San Francisco house we had a number of large brown corduroy pillows, triangular in shape, which we used to lean against while reading, or while watching the little black-and-white television. They were foam-filled. Bruce had one on his bed. After coming home from the police station, he went in his room and lay on the bed, with his head on the big pillow. It was quiet in the house. Then he heard familiar footsteps on the hardwood of the hallway, and his pulse raced.

Dad opened the bedroom door, stared in at Bruce and said, "You were lying, weren't you?"

Under the piercing, see-it-all stare, Bruce coughed. He felt his eyes burning, expected to see his father pull off the wide leather belt and administer the usual. But Dad said, in a calm tone, "I'm not going to spank you this time, but you're grounded for two weeks. Come straight home after school every day and do extra chores."

In 1962, science fiction writers Frank Herbert, Jack Vance, and Poul Anderson went into partnership to construct a houseboat. I helped them, performing odd tasks such as painting the top white in blinding sunshine. The boat sank in a storm that year, and Dad lost every penny he had invested in it.

While working on the vessel, the men plotted a collaborative science fiction story. It was about a master thief whose specialty was underwater capers. They planned to publish it under the pseudonym "Noah Arkwright," so named in honor of their partnership.*

In the summer of 1963, when I had just turned sixteen, I decided I needed a real job. I had been washing cars and doing landscaping in the neighborhood, but I wasn't earning enough money to buy the car that I wanted. Dad suggested that I apply for part-time jobs at the three major San Francisco newspapers. In August the *Examiner* called and offered me a copyboy position, at $1.25 an hour.

Just before I reported to the "Ex," Dad took me aside and told me of a Mexican phrase, "la ñapa," meaning "the addition." It referred to something given as an extra, without remuneration, like the thirteenth item in a baker's dozen.** He told me to follow this principle in my work at the *Examiner* and in every job I held during my life. "Always produce more than they pay you for," he said. "That way they'll want to keep you around."

This was a credo he had been following all of his working life.

In *The Santaroga Barrier* (1968), his protagonist, Dasein, felt antipathy toward the society represented by his employers. But he also felt "a compulsion somewhere within him to make an honest report to those who'd hired him . . . His own remembered sense of duty urged it. To do anything else would be a form of dishonesty, an erosion of selfdom. He felt a jealous possessiveness about his self. No smallest part of it was cheap enough to discard."

Dad was the night picture editor, with responsibility for selecting photographs to be included in the paper and for writing captions beneath the photos. In this position, his experience as photographer, reporter, and freelance writer served him well. His desk was by a window, near the curved rim of the copy desk and the city desk. His 4:00 P.M. to midnight schedule usually differed from mine, so I only rarely worked when he was there.

In the fall of 1963, Dad bought a 1959 Volkswagen camper from

---

*Because of work pressures, Jack and Poul couldn't get to the project, and a few years later Dad wrote it himself under the title "The Primitives." (*Galaxy*, April 1966).

**There is a Creole French counterpart, "lagniappe," sounding very similar since both are from a Latin root. What a wonderful concept this is. Imagine what the world would be like if everyone followed it in all their relationships!

one of Jack Vance's musician friends, a car dealer named Earl Sheeler in Berkeley. It was orange and cream colored, with a sunroof, sink, refrigerator, small table, and bunks for two. Dad put a bumper sticker on the rear: "GIVE TO MENTAL HEALTH OR I'LL KILL YOU!"

He drove the camper to the *Examiner* every day. On his lunch or dinner breaks, depending upon his schedule, he wrote at the table of the camper with a ball-point pen, or set a timer and napped. A heavy sleeper, he could fall asleep in seconds, so the timer was a necessity. He said he didn't write that much in the van, that mostly he slept in it from the fatigue of getting up as early as he could each day to write before work.

In his spare time, Dad was always inventing things, much as his father had done before him. In Frank Herbert's case, most of his inventions consisted of descriptions of gadgets in his futuristic science fiction stories. Typically he conceived a world and the people to populate it, and then postulated the technology they might require. Thus he came up with an expandable underwater oil barge in *The Dragon in the Sea* to transport petroleum during dangerous wartime conditions, and, in *Dune*, stillsuits to recover precious wastewater from the body in the extreme desert conditions of the planet. These novels were filled with other inventions.

His 1965 short story "Committee of the Whole" described a home-made laser weapon, the secrets of which were released to the public by a "madman" who happened to think like Frank Herbert. Dad believed such technology should be made available to everyone, thus preventing dangerous people from monopolizing weapons and using them for their own ends. He wrote, "One man could destroy an aerial armada with it, knock down ICBMs before they touched atmosphere, sink a fleet, pulverize a city."

In the 1970s he would write a highly inventive film treatment, entitled initially "Jonathon Ley" and then "Asa West." It did not sell, but not for lack of imagination. Set on an alien planet, it described a Robo-Cop-type character, a man in an armored mask who was part human and part synthesized machine, with superhuman powers. Dad referred to his creation as "Supercop." A virtually unstoppable fighting machine, it had the power to detect lies and could not be poisoned or gassed. Its body had pockets "concealed by invisible skin flaps," compartments that contained many incredible weapons and tools. I found one device particularly interesting, in view of my father's passion for the outdoors. He called it a "caster," which, like a fishing pole, released a fine line and seeker-tip to retrieve whatever Supercop wanted.

In the early 1950s Dad invented a special type of slide rule that he never got around to patenting. With a lifelong interest in cooking and guns, he also came up with what he called a "spice gun." This was an ingenious device that looked like a target pistol, with a long sharp-pointed barrel on the end that was inserted into a roast. When the spice gun trigger was pulled, it injected spices into the meat. The tip was removable, with a second snap-on tip that had grating slots in it for injecting garlic juice.

Inspired by a conversation with Howie Hansen about the workings of a sextant, Frank Herbert also devised a navigation instrument that, in Howie Hansen's words, "used a beam of light to shine down into the inside of an arc to pinpoint a position."

During slow times at the *Examiner*, Dad developed his own one-panel cartoon series, which I named "Tingle" when I saw the characters. They were simple lines forming people who looked like bent coat hangers. The basic cartoon person was a long, slightly curved vertical line, bending out where the derriere would be—with a horizontal, connected line at the bottom representing feet. A not-quite-closed circle was attached on top, representing a head. The figure had no arms. He drew a witch's hat on one, with the caption, "Anyone call for a doctor?" Another figure had no hat, but the middle section was curved, as in a drainpipe under a kitchen sink. "Did you call for a plumber?" the caption read. He also drew what he called Zen cartoons. One was a horizontal line with an arrow on each end, with the caption, "a longer line than the other one." Another cartoon had an arrow pointing down, above the word "up"—and the caption, "up under some circumstances."

In addition to their own Hearts card game variation, my parents also came up with a silly parlor game called "Frog-It." To demonstrate, Dad would tell his dinner guests to talk in the tone of a frog croaking. "Like this," he said, "Frog-it, Frog-it, Frog-it."

After the guests practiced a bit, Dad would ask, "What's a nun frog?" And when no one came up with an answer, he said, "Hab-it, Hab-it, Hab-it."

Then Mom might ask, "What's a jeweler frog?" Another pause, and then, "Lock-et, Lock-et, Lock-et."

"And what are the four Safeway frogs?" Dad asked. "Why, Stack-it, Pack-it, Stock-it, and Bag-it."

And so on, they would improvise.

In another improvisation described by Howie, my father would begin by saying, in a creaking, aged hillbilly accent, "Uh, Ma?"

To which she would respond, in like accent, her voice also creaking, "Yes, Pa?"

After a long pause: "Ma, I got somepin' to say."

"Yes, Pa, what is it?"

"Ma, I'm a goin'. I'm a goin', Ma."

"Yes, Pa, and what is it you wanna say?"

Another pause: "I wanna say I'm a goin', Ma. But before I go, I've got somepin' to say."

"Yes, Pa?"

"I'm a goin', Ma."

It would go on like this for several minutes, to the amusement of all present.

Early in the 1960s, Dad learned that a British company had developed flexible underwater barges based upon his concept in *The Dragon in the Sea*. The company was marketing them under the trade name "Dracone," and, as this name suggested, they freely admitted the source of the idea. Science fiction authors Arthur C. Clarke and Fritz Leiber, friends of Dad, recommended that he take legal action to invalidate Dracone's patents. Dad consulted a number of people on this, including John W. Campbell, and learned from them, to his dismay, that he should have filed formal patent papers within two years of publication of his idea. The publication gave him "discovery rights" for that period, but his failure to file proper documents sent the idea into the public domain.

But an even bigger fish would be lost by my father as a result of this. Eventually *The Dragon in the Sea* would be published in Japan, where it would become very popular. The Japanese admitted creating overseas shipping containers as an adaptation of Dad's underwater barge concept!

Upon completion of the three segments of *Dune* (*Dune World*, *Muad'Dib* and *The Prophet*) in November 1963, Dad embarked upon a two-and-a-half-month leave of absence from the *Examiner*. He did some writing during that period, but mostly recuperated. He planned to take a vacation trip to the Pacific Northwest just before Christmas, and after that he intended to return to the newspaper.

Aside from the *Analog* serialization of *Dune World*, a very important sale, Dad sold only a couple of articles in 1963 to the San Francisco *Examiner*, for which he was paid small amounts in addition to his salary.

Mom left her job at The White House department store, and went to work in the advertising department of Macy's in San Francisco. She also wrote freelance for *Plan Ahead*, a national guide for advertising copywriters. She was working on a new mystery novel, too, entitled *Marked Down for Murder*. Her first novel, *Frighten the Mother*, which needed major rewriting, lay languishing in a file cabinet. She hadn't worked on it for several years.

At the age of sixteen I started drinking with friends, and experienced several near misses with death, invariably involving cars and alcohol. On occasion my parents had to bail me out of jail, where I had been placed in the drunk tank. The last time this happened, my mother said to me, "I've cried my last tear for you." As a result of a number of open confrontations between me and my father, she also told me that if she had to choose between us, she would choose him.

My little brother was in trouble with Dad on a constant basis, over picayune matters. Sometimes Bruce looked in the refrigerator a little too long and couldn't make up his mind what he wanted, keeping the door open and wasting electricity. This was a violation of one of Dad's many house rules. Or Bruce left the lid loose on the strawberry jelly, causing Dad to drop it and break it when he lifted it from the shelf by the lid. Or, from his fascination with things electrical and electronic, Bruce wore the batteries out on every flashlight in the house. Or he didn't get good enough grades, despite scholastic aptitude tests indicating an extremely high IQ.

Bruce's relationship with his father was, in its own way, worse than mine. I confronted Dad, venting my anger, but my brother never did. This proved to have devastating consequences for the young man, as his pent-up rage and frustration would lead him to make very bad, even dangerous decisions.

CHAPTER
16

✳ Honors ✳

JACK VANCE was a member of Mystery Writers of America, and earned considerable success in the field, winning an Edgar one year for the best novel. Through his encouragement, my mother and father made efforts to write and sell in that genre.

Early in 1964, Mom completed a new 65,000-word novel, *Marked Down for Murder*, and sent it off to Lurton for his efforts. She had not sold a piece of creative writing since the sale of "Corner Movie Girl" to *Modern Romances* in 1946, but had never given up hope that one day she might become a published author. For many years, she had been an avid reader of murder mysteries, so it was in this field that she felt most comfortable now. Unfortunately, Lurton had difficulty placing her novel and finally gave up. This book, like her earlier one, would need extensive rewriting, he said.

Dad, also interested in the genre, joined Mystery Writers of America. He was eligible for membership because of his publication credits in the science fiction genre, but my mother, without credits, could not join. In the spring of 1964, Dad sent a mystery novelette to Lurton, *The Heat's On*. The agent was unable to find a publisher for it. He praised it as an interesting story but said it was of a length that was no longer popular.

Worst of all, *Dune* in book form still had not found a publisher, as

Sterling E. Lanier and Chilton Book company were still a year down the road.

On their eighteenth wedding anniversary that June, Dad gave Mom a bouquet of eighteen red roses with a handwritten note on a card:

> Darling—
> Will you renew my option?
>   Love, Frank

Of course she did, and sometimes on special occasions she sent him singing telegrams, via Western Union.

Around this time, Mom increased her pressure on Dad to buy a house. They considered Santa Barbara to the south, where a number of Dad's uncles and aunts had settled, or the Santa Cruz Mountains, near the home of his author friend Robert Heinlein. But these were not practical locations. My father's writing income remained low, and for the near future he needed to stay tethered to the *Examiner.*

Beverly Herbert left Macy's, hoping to concentrate more on her creative writing and on freelance work for *Plan Ahead.* She was despondent, however, over *Marked Down for Murder*, and thought she might be better off starting a new yarn. Dad told her she should rewrite her two novels, that both were potentially publishable. Subsequently she tinkered with each, then tried an entirely new yarn, and finally gave up creative writing altogether, with the exception of a handful of Christmas stories that were published as department store advertising supplements.

Within weeks, my parents applied for and obtained two bank loans. With the first, they bought a house in Fairfax, twenty miles north of San Francisco, over the Golden Gate Bridge. With the second, they purchased a fifty-six acre unimproved parcel one hundred and forty miles north near Willits.

The Willits property was wooded with fir, cedar and pine trees, and had a long dirt road leading to a cleared building site where a previous owner had planned to construct a home. This remote property was Dad's ultimate destination. While living in Fairfax, he intended to spend weekends constructing a home in Willits, doing the work himself, along with volunteer labor from Jack Vance, me and anyone else willing to lend a hand. Dad intended to establish a small subsistence farm there, thus returning to the rural roots of his boyhood, a halcyon life that had been beckoning to him for years. He also intended to experiment on the farm with a number of alternative energy methods, such as solar and wind power, and power from methane obtained from chicken droppings. Years later, these experiments would become famous as Frank Herbert's "Ecological Demonstration Project."

One day that summer, Mom and Dad were at a laundromat in Fairfax. Our recently acquired tabby cat Punkin strolled in. Assuming he had followed them, they took him home in the car and carried him inside. There they were startled to find Punkin already asleep on the knit rug by the fireplace. Quickly, Dad returned the impostor to the laundromat.

This became the seed of a new short story, "The Wrong Cat," which Dad wrote in a few days. The story, while it featured a mix-up between two cats, involved quite a different situation. It was a 7,600-word mystery that Dad wrote under the pseudonym Stuart McCarthy. This name was a combination of my mother's Stuart family name on her father's side and Dad's McCarthy name on his mother's side. As a member of Mystery Writers of America, Frank Herbert planned to write a number of mysteries under the pseudonym.

Lurton was not favorably impressed with "The Wrong Cat," saying the solution to the story was too obvious. He also expressed concern over my father's recurring problem, story length. It was too long for a mystery short story, and too short for a novelette, the latter being a category of increasing interest to publishers. Still, Lurton did his best to sell it as written. He was unsuccessful.

That fall I went away to Berkeley in the East Bay, renting a little room just off campus, on the second floor of a turn-of-the-century house. I was barely seventeen years old. Due to real estate expenditures, our family finances were tight, but I was used to that. I worked for part of my tuition and room and board at the school cafeteria and at a book store run by a lively old woman in her nineties who still drove a car. It was an interesting, historical time to be at the University of California at Berkeley, a campus of twenty-seven thousand students. The Free-

Speech Movement was germinating there, a movement that would spread to college campuses all across the country. I majored in Sociology.

In addition to his picture editor duties, Dad wrote feature stories, some about the student unrest at Berkeley. The campus situation there reached such epidemic proportions of madness and chaos that Dad coined the name "Berserkley" for the university community. This had a certain ring to it, and soon the term came into common parlance around the Bay Area.

Dad had two short stories published in the fall of 1964, "The Mary Celeste Move" (*Analog*, October) and "The Tactful Saboteur" (*Galaxy*, October). "Celeste" was a science fiction mystery, expertly drawn, in which a peculiar phenomenon of human behavior was investigated. "Saboteur" originally had a working title of "What Did He Really Mean by That?", but Frederik Pohl of *Galaxy* renamed it "The Tactful Saboteur." This was the second story to feature Jorj X. McKie, following "A Matter of Traces" in 1958. McKie would later appear in the novels *Whipping Star* (1970) and *The Dosadi Experiment* (1977). He was a humorous, gnomelike character, sometimes involved with making governmental agencies look foolish.

Also in the fall of 1964, Dad completed his second science fiction ecology book, *The Green Brain*, a novel about insects that created a powerful artificial intelligence in reaction to human attempts to eradicate them. The story concept was an extrapolation of modern conditions on Earth, in which insects developed a resistance to insecticides, such as DDT. *Amazing* published a short story version ("Greenslaves") in its March 1965 issue. Ace Books purchased the soft-cover rights to the novel, for publication in 1966.*

Ecology was one of the recurring themes and subthemes of Frank Herbert stories. In a later novel, *Direct Descent* (1980), it would become a background detail. The central story thread concerned an ancient library, but mention was made of *Sequoia gigantica* trees (much loved

---

*The "Greenslaves" title had historical significance in our family, since our reputed ancestor King Henry VIII was said to have composed the classic song "Greensleeves."

by my father), trees said in the story to have only survived on a remote island of Earth.

It was shortly after the sales of "Greenslaves" and *The Green Brain* that Chilton Books made the offer to publish *Dune* in hardcover. Suddenly the name Frank Herbert was starting to mean something in the publishing world.

He completed a short story, "Do I Wake or Dream?", about artificial intelligence. *Galaxy* picked up the serialization rights for their August 1965 issue. Dad wrote an expanded version entitled *Destination: Void,* and Berkley Publishing Group purchased the paperback rights to it, also for publication in 1966.

Two more of his short stories were published in 1965, "Committee of the Whole" (*Galaxy,* April) and "The GM Effect" (*Analog,* June). In "Committee," one of many Frank Herbert stories with a political theme, politicians are made to look foolish. For the author, oft-frustrated by the conundrums of politics, this story was cathartic. "GM" touched upon a recurring Frank Herbert theme as well, genetic engineering—and in this case, as in *Dune,* he dealt with the issue of genetic memories that might be housed in the cells of all humans. In "GM," instead of a Bene Gesserit sisterhood bearing such memories, Dad explored the possibility of genetic imprints revealing unsavory information about some of the most heroic figures in history, including Abraham Lincoln and Jesus Christ.

During the next decade, Dad would explore other aspects of genetic engineering. In the novel *The Eyes of Heisenberg* (1966) humans were genetically individualized through processes known only to a select group of rulers. Just a chosen few were permitted to have children in the traditional manner, and then under strict laboratory conditions. In the short story "Come to the Party" (1978), written with F. M. Busby, the writers dealt with the questions of long-dormant technical abilities revealed when ancient racial memories were brought to the surface. In *The White Plague* (1982), Dad wrote of the catastrophic consequences of uncontrolled genetic engineering, in which a terrible plague was unleashed intentionally upon the women of the world.

Early in 1965, when Dad was forty-four, he quit his job at the *Examiner* in order to devote more energy to writing. In addition to

Mom's work for *Plan Ahead*, she freelanced, writing advertisements for a variety of department stores. Now both of my parents were free from the regimens of steady jobs. It was a good thing, too, because the commute from Marin County to San Francisco was getting crowded. Tens of thousands of people had recently moved to the Bay Area from all points of the globe.

When he wasn't writing, Dad began drawing up plans to remodel the Fairfax house. He wanted to expand the living room, enlarge the garage to accommodate two cars, and put on new exterior siding and interior paneling. A restless man who was never content with his surroundings, he was always looking ahead, always planning. His mind went in fifty directions at once.

On the strength of the *Dune* serializations in *Analog*, Dad was invited to be guest of honor at the 1965 Westercon science fiction convention, held in Long Beach, California. In his speech, he spoke of the haiku from which *Dune* sprang, and to demonstrate the concept he went on to reduce *War and Peace, Moby-Dick, The Grapes of Wrath* and other long, classic novels to haiku or tanka form—entire novels in only seventeen or thirty-one syllables. This was an example of his remarkable, cultured sense of humor. He brought the house down with laughter and applause.

My father was always impatient to achieve his plans. He had goals that were constantly eluding him. Now for the first time he could taste success, could feel it coming. But money was slow in arriving. He and Mom weren't earning enough, and they still owed back taxes to the IRS.

The Willits property had become an emotional and financial drain. The prior winter a storm had washed out the access road, requiring extensive bulldozer work. The property was more than a two-hour drive from Fairfax, too far away for a busy man to construct a home there part-time, especially with limited funds. Mom convinced Dad to sell it. Reluctantly, he agreed, and advertised it.

Shortly after the Westercon convention, Dad went back to work at the *Examiner*, four to five days a week. Abashedly, he told friends it was only on a short-term emergency basis, at the request of the paper. In reality he and the paper needed each other.

Chilton published *Dune* in August 1965. A thick hardcover with more than five hundred pages and a retail price of $5.95, it included a number of expanded passages, including stronger roles for some characters. A number of new epigrams were added as well, along with a glossary of terms and a map of the planet Dune, based upon my father's drawing. Four appendixes were included, too, providing important background information on the ecology, religion, history and politics of the planet.

For the book jacket, Chilton selected a John Schoenherr painting of Paul and Jessica crouching in a shadowy canyon. It was a dramatic scene with considerable sentimental appeal to my father. One day he would purchase the original art, along with other paintings by the same artist.

The first printing of *Dune* was only 3,500 copies, a typical hardcover run for the time. Of that amount, 1,300 were misprinted and had to be discarded. As a result, only 2,200 copies reached bookstores. Because of this small first printing and other factors, a first edition of *Dune* has become more valuable than any book in science fiction history. The first edition has a blue cover, with white lettering.*

Dad enlisted assistance from the DFPA advertising firm in Tacoma, and they did promotional work in the Pacific Northwest on the book, gratis. He arranged with a few local book stores to carry the book, and distributed twenty-five promotional copies to newspaper editors and columnists, as well as to radio and television commentators he knew in Los Angeles, San Francisco, Portland and Seattle. This was all he had the time or resources to do.

A month after publication, Chilton arranged to have a two-minute advertisement run on the "Inside Books" radio program, including an excerpt from the novel. This was broadcast to five hundred commercial and educational stations, and another one hundred seventy Veteran's Administration Hospital stations. Chilton also mailed a few copies of *Dune* to reviewers around the country.

All in all the book did not receive much promotion.

Dune came to the attention of only a few reviewers, and those who

---

*As noted by Levack and Willard in *Dune Master: A Frank Herbert Bibliography*, the first edition "States 'First Edition' on the copyright page. No date on the title page . . . The fifth and later printings all state 'First Edition' without further printing statements . . ."

cared to look at it wrote scathing commentaries. They hated the book, said it was too long and difficult to understand. Not surprisingly, my father became embittered against reviewers, referring to them privately as "poseurs" and "frustrated authors"—people who attempted to boost their own shaky egos by denigrating the works of others. He often said that the only valid critic was "time." If his work endured, he said, the comments of critics meant nothing.

From its eight-part serialization in *Analog*, which had a large circulation, science-fiction readers and writers were already quite familiar with the story and liked it. Arthur C. Clarke and Anne McCaffrey were among the first science fiction-fantasy writers to extol the virtues of the work. Clarke knew of nothing comparable to *Dune*, with the exception of J. R. R. Tolkien's *Lord of the Rings*. An epic story with larger-than-life, Machiavellian characters, *Dune* would soon become the standard against which other works were compared. It would be called the greatest novel of imagination of all time.

Science fiction writers voted *Dune* the 1965 Nebula Award for Best Novel, shared with Roger Zelazny's . . . *And Call Me Conrad*. The award was in the shape of a rectangular piece of clear Plexiglas on a square black pedestal, with a swirling, glittering three-dimensional nebula over a beautiful fragment of white, silver and lavender quartz. It measured nine inches high by four inches square around the base, and weighed six pounds.

Dad placed the award on the windowsill of his Fairfax study, so that it was visible against a backdrop of oak and bay trees that sloped down the hillside from the house. He described the award as a work of art, and with tongue in cheek suggested that there should be an "award for the award." Other science fiction awards, he said, often resembled "glistening phallic symbols."

Cal Berkeley was astir with political activity. The world-famous Free Speech Movement wasn't the only issue on campus. Most students were opposed to the war in Vietnam and the draft. They favored civil rights and women's rights and the allied free choice issue of abortion. They turned in or burned draft cards, held sit-ins at draft boards, burned brassieres in public, and generally railed against anything that smacked of "the establishment."

Long-haired, bearded protesters were out every day on campus with signs and bullhorns. They set up tables on the paved "commons" between the Administration Building and the Associated Student Union Building, from which they distributed political literature. One day they commandeered a police car on campus and took over the Administration Building.

Finding myself unable to identify with the protesters, I didn't participate in the vibrant intellectual atmosphere of the school, though history and hindsight indicate that their free speech and anti-war causes were justified. I didn't care for their methods. They taunted people trying to attend class and blocked entrances. They thrust flyers in front of us. The constant blare of their bullhorns outside class was a distraction from my studies.

As far as I was concerned, the political activists were dirty, smelly hippies. To a large extent they wanted a free and easy life, without obligations or responsibilities. Free love, flower-children, uptight, out of sight, groovy, like wow, the New Left. So many new phrases and concepts entered the lexicon in those days. They were bohemians, real and mock, straight out of Kerouac's *On the Road*. When they opposed something, they rarely offered alternatives.

My negative opinions about the protesters of the day were formed, in no small part, by the fact that my father was a bohemian who wore a beard. He spent a lot of time in the North Beach area of San Francisco and often showed up in City Lights book store, operated by Kerouac's friend, Lawrence Ferlinghetti. Ferlinghetti agreed to stock *Dune*, and featured it in a window display.

When I was at Berkeley between 1964 and 1968, I was in the college drinking crowd, a binge drinker. Perhaps this explains why I heard very little mentioned about *Dune* or Frank Herbert.* Besides, *Dune* was

---

*One evening I was hitchhiking near Carmel, California. A young couple in a Volkswagen bug gave me a ride. They asked me what my Dad did for a living, and I replied that he was a newspaperman and had also written a couple of science fiction books. "Oh?" the man said as he drove. "What has he written?" "Uh, a novel back in the nineteen fifties and another one more recently . . . *Dune*." "*Dune?*" the man exclaimed, causing the car to veer as he looked back at me in the shadows of the rear seat. "That's a great book!" "It is?" I said. Then—unfortunately—I forgot about this incident until years later.

slow to get going. Chilton would not go into a second hardcover printing until 1968, my last year at the university. Ace printed a relatively
small number of paperback copies in 1966, and they too went into a
second printing in 1968.

Just before Christmas, 1966, Dad sold the Willits property. "We'll
buy another piece when we can afford it," he said. By this he meant,
of course, another piece on which he could have his farm.

In 1966, science fiction readers voted *Dune* the Hugo Award as the
best science fiction novel of the year. This award was a futuristic stain-
less steel rocket, fourteen inches tall, atop a maple base six inches square
by four and a half inches high, with a total weight of four pounds. It
was presented to my father at the World Science Fiction Convention
in Cleveland, Ohio. He displayed it proudly on the windowsill of his
Fairfax study next to the Nebula Award.

A rumor made the rounds that *Dune* also won the International
Fantasy Award, but this, like similar rumors about *The Dragon in the
Sea*, was inaccurate. *Dune* was the first novel to win both the Nebula
and Hugo awards.

For years Dad kept copies of bad reviews, and as *Dune* became more
successful, he retaliated by reading the remarks of critics at science
fiction conventions and at writing conferences when he knew the authors of those pieces would be present. At one convention he confronted Harlan Ellison over an unfavorable review he had written years
before on *The Dragon in the Sea*, disputing every point Ellison had
made. These men, who had never met before, became fast friends.

Though revenues remained small, *Dune* was earning a little more
each year. "I feel a groundswell building," my father said. He was more
convinced than ever that he had an important literary property on his
hands. He was being told by respected people that he had elevated the
quality of science fiction and had written a new novel form, one with
complex layers that reached beyond science fiction to the heady realm
of "literature."

While Frank Herbert made many predictions that came true, including the eventual success of *Dune*, he was quite circumspect about
those he made. When he spoke of the future, he drew a distinction
between "the" future and "a" future. There were any number of possible

futures that might occur, he said, not just one, not just "the" future that any one of us might foresee. And there were no rules concerning the process of prediction.

To demonstrate the multiplicity of futures, which he said were as varied as the methods of developing a story, Dad often mentioned a 1970 Doubleday anthology he contributed to, *Five Fates*. This consisted of five stories written by different science fiction authors—Poul Anderson, Gordon Dickson, Harlan Ellison, Frank Herbert and Keith Laumer. The project creator, Ellison, wrote a first page, which he duplicated for each writer with instructions for them to go on from there independently, without consultation with the others. Five very different stories resulted from a common beginning, including Dad's, which he entitled "Murder Will In."

In *Dune*, Paul Atreides felt a "Terrible Purpose" building within, a sensation that both frightened and excited him. He was meant to do something important, but what? The young man had prescience, but it provided him with only fragmentary views of the future and his place in it. He, like Frank Herbert, saw a multiplicity of possible futures.

Three of Dad's novels were published in 1966. In addition to *The Green Brain* (Ace Books) and *Destination: Void* (Berkley Books), Berkley also published *The Eyes of Heisenberg*, shortly after its serialization in *Galaxy* as "Heisenberg's Eyes."

In June, *Analog* published the short story "Escape Felicity," and in August, "By the Book." 1966 also saw publication of "The Primitives" (*Galaxy*, April), the solo effort that had originally been plotted as a Herbert-Vance-Anderson collaboration.

The noted Ace editor and science-fiction writer Terry Carr was on the election committee that year for officers in SFWA (Science Fiction Writers of America), which had several hundred members. He asked Dad if he might be interested in running for either president or secretary-treasurer, but Dad declined the offer, saying he was too busy. He felt an urgency to survive as a *writer*, to break free of the financial shackles of a regular job. This had been a stated goal since his eighth birthday, and he couldn't divert from that course with volunteer activities.

Dad shifted to feature writing for *California Living* magazine, a joint publication of the *Examiner* and the other large newspaper in town, the *San Francisco Chronicle*. It was a position he called a "fur-lined cocoon," since his hours were flexible, permitting him time to write. After a few months he developed a schedule of working three long days a week on the magazine, one for doing interviews and feature writing, another for setting up photographs, and another for page makeup. Thus, he streamlined his schedule while drawing a full salary and still performing an excellent job for his employer.

The British publisher Gollancz purchased the right to publish *Dune* in the United Kingdom in hardcover, and stipulated that they wanted the glossary of terms at the end of the book instead of the beginning. New English Library purchased United Kingdom paperback rights, and the Paris publisher Laffont came onboard for French language rights, so *Dune* was beginning to pick up an international audience.

With the income from *California Living* and science fiction writing, money flowed into my parents' household more plentifully. At my father's insistence, he and Mom took out another real estate loan, purchasing an old farmhouse on ten acres near Cloverdale, ninety miles north of Fairfax. This property, slightly closer to Fairfax than Willits had been, was the new site of his dream farm.

My mother could only hold on to his coattails. Even when he appeared to be settled, he really wasn't. Things were constantly jumping around in his mind. He plotted out his life as if it were one of his stories, experimenting with this avenue, that one and yet another. At least now, at my mother's wise insistence, he was investing in real estate, with the prospect of appreciation in value, instead of collecting rent receipts.

Frank Herbert intended to remodel the farmhouse himself on weekends, with the help of volunteers such as Jack Vance and myself. The three of us tore the roof off the house and began framing a full second floor, where previously there had only been an attic. Dad scrounged around for doors, pieces of marble slab, frosted glass and brass ship's portholes, which he intended to install in the home. For safekeeping, he stored them with Ralph and Irene Slattery a few miles south in Sonoma County.

Sometimes I brought along my girlfriend, Jan Blanquie, and her younger brothers, Dan and Gary, who helped with cleanup. One day a big mongrel dog came onto the land and bit Dad's leg. Chronically at odds with unruly canines, my father chased it off, hurling 2 × 4 scraps at it.

The Cloverdale property was a lovely spot, overlooking an oak and maple dell where a brook ran. Dad thought this would be an ideal place to write, farm, and conduct his Ecological Demonstration Project experiments. Unfortunately, he was about to face another detour.

CHAPTER
17

✳ Tara ✳

IN 1966, Dad was working on a new novel, *The Santaroga Barrier*—about an unusual, insular northern California town. The book had a framework based upon the thinking of the German philosopher Martin Heidegger. In his classic 1927 work, *Sein und Zeit*, Heidegger presented a theory of man's existence in the world, which he called "dasein." The protagonist of *The Santaroga Barrier* was Gilbert Dasein. His girlfriend was Jenny Sorge, and in the Heideggerian view, "sorge" represented "care"—things that were within the care of mankind or dasein. Heidegger believed that man became disoriented and drowned himself in the vastness of the world and in the minutiae of following society's rules. Each man's experiences were too small, too parochial, for him to develop a proper philosophy of existence.

While working on *The Santaroga Barrier*, Dad contracted pneumonia, which laid him on his back for several weeks. He also suffered two back injuries in this period—one while lifting heavy building materials for the Cloverdale house and the other in a fall down the icy outside stairs between the Fairfax house and garage. His spinal injuries were so serious and so painful that at first his doctor thought he might have to undergo an operation to give him a stiff "ramrod spine." Before undergoing this irreversible procedure, my father asked for a second opinion. The second doctor thought swimming might benefit him, so Dad went regularly to a nearby public pool to exercise. This helped, but recuperation was slow. For several months his back hurt so much that he couldn't sit at his typewriter for more than two hours a day.

I think he had a black cloud over him. While at the laundromat one day, bleach that had been left on one of the washing machines got on his new clothes, ruining a new pair of slacks and a dress shirt.

It was no surprise, then, that the protagonist in *The Santaroga Barrier* suffered a succession of "accidents." In a series of near-misses he is almost drowned, poisoned, shot with an arrow, crushed by a car, and firebombed! Lurton thought the story had too many accidents, but from my father's point of view they were in there for a reason . . . based on his own personal experience. Similar to Alan Watts, Heidegger said man could only come to a full understanding of life and the mysteries of existence by placing himself in challenging, even dangerous situations. My father concurred with this philosophy.

In his life and writing, Dad constantly placed himself and his characters in demanding situations where they had to adapt in order to survive. In an essay for "Saving Worlds" (1973), he said that we are "surfboard riders on an infinite sea," and when the waves change we must adjust our balance. The single most important survival strength of mankind was adaptability, he said. It would prevent us from becoming extinct.

The influence of several great German thinkers could be seen in *The Santaroga Barrier*, harking back to studies my father made with the clinical psychologists Ralph and Irene Slattery in the early 1950s. The book was replete with concepts from Carl Gustav Jung, Sigmund Freud, Karl Jaspers, and others. In the town of Santaroga, the key industry was the Jaspers Cheese Cooperative, which produced a drug-laden cheese that bonded the members of the community within an alternate dimension. This, of course, bore more than a passing resemblance to the effects of the melange of *Dune*.

Santaroga bore another similarity with my father's most famous work. In the town of Santaroga, people attended the "Church of All Faiths"—a concept that bore a strong resemblance to the Commission of Ecumenical Translators of *Dune*, which attempted to eliminate a bone of contention between competing religions—"the claim to possession of the one and only revelation."

The Santaroga cheese cooperative concept was based upon a famous cheese business in California, the Marin French Cheese Company in Petaluma, near Santa Rosa. My parents went there often. It was out in the country in a valley, and Dad imagined a town built up around it. In the mid-1960s, bohemian cooperatives were springing up everywhere. Dad used to go to one in Berkeley that was a non-profit enterprise run out of a big warehouse, selling groceries and consumer goods to members. It is interesting as well to recall my father's childhood experiences in which he grew up in the town of Burley, Washington, once a socialist cooperative.

When Frank Herbert was a star debater for Lincoln High School in Tacoma, he learned how to take either side of an issue. This was necessary in order to prepare for a debate, thus anticipating the attacks an opponent might make. A similar line of reasoning was required of him when he wrote political speeches for Republican congressional and senatorial candidates.

Remembering such experiences, Frank Herbert presented arguments in *The Santaroga Barrier* of equal strength to support and condemn the Santarogan lifestyle—a lifestyle of strict conformity quite different from that of the outside world. The book was a utopian novel, but presented in such a manner that the reader went away wondering how the author really felt about Santaroga. Dad called this concept utopia/dystopia: "One man's utopia is another man's dystopia."

Around this time, the *Examiner* offered Frank Herbert the position of wine editor, in addition to his duties at *California Living*. Dad accepted the assignment, but told management he didn't feel entirely qualified for the position. Actually he knew quite a bit about wine, having spent some time in the Napa Valley studying vineyards and wine-making methods. Now, since he didn't want to appear inept, he took several days and stayed with a friend who owned a winery, receiving a crash course from him. To further Dad's education, the *Examiner* also agreed to purchase a number of expensive wine books for his personal library—one of the perks of the new job.

Before undertaking any writing task, Frank Herbert did his homework—a necessity, he joked, in order to avoid letters from readers that began, "Dear Jerk." He also began making his own wine, using the bar area of his Fairfax study, which was a converted family room. He favored the Cabernet Sauvignon variety, referring to it as "queen of the clarets." I recall seeing plastic wine vats and glass jugs on the floor of the study, with plastic tubes running between them in arrangements I didn't understand. On the counter nearby were black and gold stacks of his private wine labels bearing the face of Bacchus, the Greek wine god—an image from thousands of years before. He had five different labels: Cabernet Sauvignon, Rosé, Chenin Blanc, Semillon and a generic label, without a variety. Each said "Made by Frank Herbert." Next to the labels were piles of corks and packages of wine yeast, along with jars of enzyme tablets and sodium bisulfate. He had a brew tester, a hydrometer and a number of other gadgets, too. He also had beer-making equipment.

In 1967, John Campbell of *Analog* turned down *The Santaroga Barrier* for serialization, saying it wasn't truly science fiction. He also felt there were too many loose ends in the novel. Frederik Pohl of *Galaxy* rejected it, too, feeling the plot was thin, without enough narrative hooks for serialization. *Amazing* liked it very much and offered a contract. They published it in their October 1967 through February 1968 issues. Tom Dardis of Berkley Books liked it as well, and published it in paperback in 1968.

The loose ends cited by Campbell were placed in the story intentionally by Dad to reflect the realities and uncertainties of life. After turning the last page, the reader was left feeling disturbed and uneasy, with his mind going a mile a minute—like an engine that "diesels," refusing to shut off. This was done in *Dune*, too, as Dad intentionally sent his readers spinning out of the end of the book with fragments of it still clinging to them—fragments that would keep them thinking about the story. In large part this psychological element was why so many fans read my father's books over and over.

It was a storytelling technique he learned early in life, from reading such classics as *Tom Sawyer* and *Treasure Island*. After reading the books, he and playmates made up games and events based upon the stories. The stories had not ended with the conclusion of the printed texts.

Dad published a short story in 1967—"The Featherbedders" (*An-*

alog, August). He also sold a novel he had been working on for fifteen years, *The Heaven Makers*, serialized in *Amazing* in 1967 and then published in paperback the following year by Avon Books.*

In 1967, Dad's royalty income dropped slightly from the prior year, and would fall again in 1968. *Dune* still had not "cracked the nut" with either Chilton or Ace—that point where an author's royalties exceeded his advances, so that he received additional money.

The parents of my girlfriend, Jan Blanquie, did not approve of me because of my drinking habits, so that summer she and I eloped to Reno and were married. When we returned to Marin County, Mom and Dad let us live with them for a couple of weeks until we could find a place of our own, a cottage in nearby San Anselmo. At dinner the first night back, Mom took Jan aside and told her, "You'll never be bored married to a Herbert man."

Mom consulted astrology and found the intersection of my path with Jan's—where we met. She predicted we would remain together for the rest of our lives. Years before, she had predicted that I would marry a blonde, and this beautiful young woman was very blonde, with French-Scandinavian features.

The year 1968 started off with an announcement from Terry Carr, the *Dune* editor at Ace, that they were going back to press for an additional twenty-five thousand copies. Three months after this printing, Chilton printed more hardcovers. Still, Dad wasn't seeing more than a trickle of earnings from writing sales. He was at work on a sequel to *Dune*, with the working title of *Fool Saint* at first and then *Messiah*, before settling on *Dune Messiah*. He also considered and discarded the cryptic title *C Oracle*, representing a coracle floating on a sea of time.

He also conducted occasional writing seminars at local schools, including San Francisco State University, whose president was the noted semanticist and future U.S. senator, S. I. Hayakawa. The works of Hayakawa had been influential upon my father in researching *Dune*, and when the men met they liked one another instantly.

---

*This was the story that was based upon the sensational 1952 murder trial in Santa Rosa. It had been written and rewritten several times as we moved up and down the West Coast between the United States and Mexico, with the working titles *As Heaven Made Him* and *Storyship*.

Around this time, Mom came up with a promotional idea: a "Dune Tarot" deck, based upon descriptions in *Dune*. She thought it would go hand-in-hand with the book and its sequels, garnering additional attention and readership. Through her advertising contacts, she lined up a well-known San Francisco artist, who made several full-color prototype cards. Dad photographed the cards and tried to interest publishers and game manufacturers, without success.

Early in 1968, Dad again wanted to leave the *Examiner* and write full-time. He had in mind a book about American Indians on the Northwest Coast, a mainstream story he said had been boiling inside him since his childhood—about a modern-day clash between American Indian and white cultures. He had been told by government sources that he might obtain a federal grant from the National Foundation of the Arts to research and write such a book, because of the historical value of it.

Setting aside unpleasant memories of past attempts to penetrate the befuddling walls of bureaucracy, Dad contacted the agency. He requested a grant of fifteen thousand dollars for a project he estimated would take a year and a half to complete—nine months of research, and another nine months of writing. He wanted to hire his friend Howie Hansen as a research assistant, and planned to film and tape Indian rituals, along with many previously unrecorded legends and songs. After getting the run-around from a variety of departments in the agency, Dad was told he had contacted the wrong offices, that he should instead have gone through the National Endowment for the Humanities!

He was like a man who had waited in a long line, only to be told he had to go to the rear of another line and start all over again. Frank Herbert threw his hands in the air and gave up the effort, vowing to himself, "Never again!"

Jan was pregnant, and needed to learn how to drive a car to get back and forth to her doctor's appointments. My license had been suspended for a plethora of tickets and alcohol-related accidents, and I was hitch-hiking to my busboy job at a restaurant in San Rafael and to school in Berkeley. While I was at school one day, Dad and Mom stopped by our cottage to visit Jan. When Dad learned she needed a driver's license, he volunteered to give her driving lessons. She accepted before I could warn her that he might not be the most patient instructor.

In ensuing weeks, Dad took time off from his busy schedule to give Jan lessons in our little red 1955 Volkswagen. To my surprise, she reported to me that he was exquisitely patient with her, almost to a fault. With my wife's stomach nearly touching the steering wheel, they drove around Marin County, from Fairfax to Novato. When Dad told her how to slow the car down, he said, "Now apply the brakes gently, as if you had a little old grandma in the backseat with eggs on her lap."

Mom was as surprised at his patience as I was.

I don't recall thinking much in those days about the nice things my father did. I filtered that information out and from long experience living under his thumb, focused more on his bad side. What I was feeling about him was entrenched in my mind—little soldiers of hatred had bunkered in there, and would not surrender easily.

In April 1968, Jan had a nine-pound baby girl. We named her Julie, after Jan's paternal great-grandmother—and gave her the middle name Ann, the same as my mother's.

Just before our baby's birth, when we knew delivery was imminent, I got my license back and was driving Jan from Marin County to the hospital in San Francisco. At the exact same time, Dad was in an ambulance on the way to a different hospital. A short while before, he and Mom had been at the SFO Heliport in Sausalito, disembarking from a helicopter after a trip to Santa Barbara for one of Mom's *Plan Ahead* projects. On a pathway at the heliport, a speeding baggage cart ran into my father, knocking him down and reinjuring his back. He was in excruciating pain, and had to be transported on a stretcher.

It was an insane time in the United States and in our family. Only four days before, Martin Luther King, Jr., had been assassinated, and now race riots were sweeping the country. Soon Robert Kennedy would be gunned down, too. As Mom and Dad flew over San Francisco on their return from Santa Barbara, she looked down. Not seeing flames she thought, *Thank God it's okay.*

Dad began a new regimen of back therapy, with heavy doses of Valium for his pain. His back would never fully recover, and in bed each night he would have to arrange pillows in a special way, jamming them beneath the mattress to alleviate his pain.

Later in 1968, both of my grandfathers died—Frank Herbert, Sr., and Roscoe Stuart—and my mother broke her ankle. The year was incredibly bad, with two exceptions—the birth of our beautiful daughter and the increasing popularity of *Dune*. The book was growing by word of mouth, principally on college campuses, where it was being used as a textbook for many courses. Since *Dune* was an anti-establishment work, it was being referred to as an "underground" book.

Dad received word that *The Santaroga Barrier* was also being used as a textbook in a number of college-level classes—and that the sales of this book were increasing on the coattails of *Dune*.

The popularity of my father's work among bright college students pleased him. As a writer of science fiction, he wanted the leaders of tomorrow to receive his important messages, and his predictions. If they understood what he was talking about, he firmly believed the world would be a better place.

For a small amount of money, a German publisher purchased the right to publish *Dune* in that country, extending the international list to three—Great Britain, France and now Germany.

Favorable reviews began to trickle in on *Dune*. It was referred to as an environmental handbook in disguise, with intriguing characterizations and fantastic imagery.

Dad finished *Dune Messiah* in the summer of 1968, more than six months later than expected because of the injuries and deaths in our family. Despite the increasing international respect for *Dune*, John Campbell refused to serialize its sequel in *Analog*. His readers wanted stories about heroes accomplishing great feats, he said, not stories of protagonists spiraling into oblivion. He didn't like the strong anti-hero theme in the book, giving the protagonist "clay feet."

After I graduated from Cal Berkeley that year I went to work as an underwriter for Fireman's Fund American Insurance Co. in San Francisco. At the time my father was not a role model for me, and I had no thoughts of following in his footsteps. My creativity, which I had shown at an early age in artwork and in the writing of childish stories, was virtually non-existent at this point in my life. I felt that if a person had to be like my father to be creative, I didn't want that life. Writing was a profession for crazy people with out-of-control tempers. It was for flakes and penniless bohemians, living on the fringes of society.

My feelings of antipathy toward my father, justified or not, sent me reeling into an anti-intellectual, alcoholic period in which I opposed most of the things he represented. I would spend my first years in insurance as a "functioning alcoholic," reading little except insurance manuals and policies—a far cry from the intellectual world in which Frank Herbert lived. I held down steady jobs, showed up for work each day and performed what was expected of me—but on a regular basis I drank myself into comatose states. My marriage hung on, but only tenuously.

By the end of the 1960s, California was becoming too crowded for my father. Whenever he went fishing, he kept encountering rambunctious young people who were water skiing, throwing beer cans, and making love in the bushes. He began thinking about the Pacific Northwest again, and so did my mother, for she was a Northwesterner, too. Washington State was their Tara, glistening brightly in memory, and they realized they had to return.

Frank Herbert was a futurist who could see decades and millennia ahead, predicting the course of mankind and the planet Earth. Eventually, he would see many of his shorter-term predictions come to pass. But thus far, at the age of forty-eight, he had not done well in predicting the course of his own life. For years, he had been moving from city to city and state to state, making changes for the sake of change. Now he felt better than ever before about a move.

My parents listed their Fairfax and Cloverdale properties, which sold quickly, and sold other personal property as well. In order to give them time to wrap matters up in the Bay Area, they moved with my brother Bruce (who was seventeen) into a nice apartment on Post Street in downtown San Francisco.

While living there, Dad gave notice of his intent to leave the *Examiner*. The publisher, Ed Dooley, took him out for what Dad referred to as a "three-martini lunch" at a nice restaurant on Geary Boulevard in San Francisco. After ordering, Dooley said, "Frank, you shouldn't quit. I pulled your file this morning. Do you realize you'll lose all your retirement benefits—twenty-four thousand dollars?"

"I'm not even thinking about that."

My father went on to tell him he needed to leave the Bay Area for the sake of his sanity. "*Dune* sales keep increasing," he said. "The sequel is about to be published and I have the completion of the trilogy in the works. Ed, I think I can be writing full-time within a year. When I break free for good—and you need to understand *I will break free*—I want to live in the Northwest."

Dad wasn't telling him the whole story, that he still wasn't earning much money from his writing. In the last royalty year, 1968, he received less writing income than in any year since 1964. His last attempt to leave the paper, a short-lived one, had been in 1964.

Ed Dooley stirred his drink, looked up and said, sadly, "You've done an incredible job at the paper, Frank, and we all think the world of you. In five years, you could be sitting in my chair."

"Ed, I'm truly sorry. You've been wonderful to me, like a father. I'd like to stay, but honestly, I can't afford to."

They parted as friends.

Frank Herbert accepted the position of education editor at the *Seattle Post-Intelligencer*. This job, involving close contacts with the University of Washington, seemed perfect to my father. It was a stepping stone toward what he hoped to do soon—breaking away and writing full time. Mom would continue to write for *Plan Ahead* in the Pacific Northwest, and this income would help set up their new homestead.

When my parents and Bruce reached Seattle, they rented an apartment on Queen Anne Hill—in the same neighborhood in which my mother had spent much of her childhood.

My parents' large apartment was on the top floor of an elegant old mansion, a white structure with massive Greek columns. Perched on the edge of the hill, it provided a fabulous view of downtown Seattle, including the Space Needle and Elliott Bay. Referred to locally as "Cap Ballard's house," it had once been owned by a famous local personality, Captain William R. Ballard. It had a widow's walk on top, an architectural feature said to have been designed so that a wife could look out to sea, watching for the return of her husband.

The house was absolutely perfect, with the nautical atmosphere my father loved, in an area where my mother had been happy as a child. Soon they bought a thirty-foot cabin cruiser (which they named "Arrakis" after the Imperial name for the planet Dune), and they were taking trips all over the Puget Sound.

They were home, back to my father's Tara.

Another of Frank Herbert's dreams was coming to pass as well, the dream of being a successful author. There had been so many years of research and writing, of rejection, of anger and frustration, of not taking vacations, of burrowing deep into the confines of his study. But through it all, when he really got rolling, his typewriter sang. He made music on it, made love to it, with his fingers floating over the keys, faster and faster and faster. He focused his entire essence on each work, this man who knew so well how to work and only intermittently how to love.

In *Dune* he had his literary prize, and a glittering prize it was. Immense fame awaited him just around the corner. Tens of millions of copies would be sold all over the world, in many languages. Decades after its first publication, the book would remain in print, standing as the greatest work of science fiction imagination of all time—a classic novel in which an entire universe was described in tremendous detail. Not bad for a farm kid from Washington State.

Dune, a modern version of the ancient Pearl of Great Price myth, is a magnificent pearl of a novel with layers of luster running deep beneath its surface, all the way to its core. During the time that Dad took to create this pearl, a pearl that was nearly as complex as he was, he guarded his writing lair against interruptions, preventing harm to his treasure, his great book. He was like Shai-Hulud guarding the melange of the planet Dune.

In taking this course he lost the affection of his sons. We didn't bond with him. He wasn't our role model. I nearly killed myself with alcohol. My younger brother, believing his father disliked him, was experimenting with drugs and homosexuality. Of his children, only Penny did not have strong feelings of antipathy toward him.

But in a good novel, the kind my father wrote, the best and most interesting characters change. They evolve over the course of the story. Frank Herbert, a complex and unpredictable man, would change one day . . . forever to his credit.

BOOK II

✳ XANADU ✳

CHAPTER 18

✳ A New Relationship ✳

Somehow, inside yourself, your relationship with your father is something you need to come to terms with. Only then can you go on with your life.

—Actor Brandan Lee, son of Bruce Lee

MY FATHER was one of the most interesting men in the world. His writing was only part of that, a dimension of the man. He had other aspects, fascinating ones. Of all the complex characterizations he drew in his stories, including that of Paul-Muad'Dib, Frank Herbert was a more complicated person. He was not a man to be understood readily, not a man easily read.

By long-distance telephone from my apartment in San Francisco to Dad's in Seattle, he and I made something of a truce, without either of us apologizing. We didn't speak of our last confrontation, an argument over my drinking, and went on from there rather uneasily, talking instead about various family matters. How my brother Bruce was doing, and my sister Penny and her husband, Ron, who now had three sons, David, Byron and Robert. Dad said it was beautiful in Seattle, that he was glad to be home.

Then my father surprised me by asking if I might consider moving north.

"Maybe," I said.

The month Frank Herbert arrived in Seattle, astronaut Neil Armstrong became the first human to set foot on the moon. In a subsequent conversation I had with Dad, he told me of his tremendous excitement about that. And he added a bit of practicality: "We have to get off this planet. We can't have all our eggs in one basket."

In his position as education editor for the *Seattle Post-Intelligencer,* Dad met interesting people on the University of Washington beat, including the world's leading expert on land law and land reform, law professor Roy Prosterman. Prosterman invited his new friend to accompany him to South Vietnam to study land ownership, farming methods and problems of overpopulation—all areas of keen interest to my father.

Only six weeks after arriving in Seattle, Frank Herbert–the-adventurer had been inoculated against Third World diseases and was on his way to South Vietnam as a war correspondent for Hearst Headline Service—on the payroll of the *Post-Intelligencer.*

Shortly after his departure I called to see how Mom was doing. She sounded despondent, lonely. "I feel strange when your father's away," she said. "As if a light around me has dimmed." She said she missed his energy around her, his constant ebullience. When she arose in the morning she no longer heard his typewriter clacking rapidly from another room, a sound which for its comfort and familiarity had become music to her ears. She no longer felt his embrace or, when she was tired, the loving way he massaged her shoulders.

It was a time of heavy U.S. involvement in Vietnam, and more than thirty thousand Americans had already been killed in action. Many Americans were vocally opposed to U.S. participation in the conflict, and thousands had been taking to the streets in protest. Dad stayed at the USAID (U.S. Agency for International Development) VIP House in Saigon, where visiting U.S. senators and congressmen were housed. He was assigned a car and driver, and his Hearst press credentials permitted him access to the most important people in the country. He also received the assistance of American military pilots, who provided air taxi service, taking him almost anywhere he wanted to go.

Now for Hearst Headline Service he wrote of a bungled U.S. war effort in the region, asserting that our policy was poorly thought out and based upon faulty data and incorrect assumptions. As a result, he said, thousands of Americans were dying. His stories ran daily in the *Seattle Post-Intelligencer* for the two weeks he was on assignment. Each morning Mom read them and clipped them out.

Frank Herbert was, at various times, both a war protester and, almost paradoxically, a member of the National Rifle Association. It is important to understand that he was not opposed to all wars, although he could certainly see the folly of most of them. Wars had a tendency to destroy the habitat of mankind, he thought, the Earth-nest. One of his unpublished poems speaks to this point of view, and of the resilience of nature:

> Boots march past ruins—
> Then, one blade of grass springs
> Upright—and another. . . .

Just prior to the publication of *Dune Messiah* in hardcover by Putnam, it ran in five installments in the science fiction magazine *Galaxy*, from July through November, 1969. "The Mind Bomb," a Frank Herbert short story, also ran that year in the October issue of *If* magazine.

The serialized *Dune Messiah* was named "disappointment of the year" for 1969 by National Lampoon, Harvard University's satirical magazine. *Messiah* had earlier been rejected by legendary *Analog* editor John W. Campbell, who, like the Lampooners, loved the heroic aspects of *Dune* and hated the anti-heroic elements of the sequel. They did not understand that *Messiah* was a bridging work, connecting *Dune* with an as-yet-uncompleted third book in the trilogy. *Messiah* flipped *Dune* over, revealing the dark side of a messiah phenomenon that had appeared to be so glorious in *Dune*. Many readers didn't want this dose of reality; they couldn't stand the destruction of their beloved, charismatic hero, Paul Muad'Dib.

Dad was not entirely deaf to his readership. In *Dune* he had killed off the popular Swordmaster of the Ginaz, Duncan Idaho. This upset fans so much that he resurrected Idaho in *Dune Messiah* in an altered form—a "ghola" that was cloned from cells of the dead man, resulting in a creature that did not have the memories of the original.*

In *Messiah* my father wrote of the dangers of following any leader blindly. And during impassioned speeches on university campuses all across the country, he warned young people not to trust government, telling them that the American founding fathers understood this and attempted to establish safeguards in the constitution.

"Governments lie," my father said.

In the transition from *Dune* to *Dune Messiah*, Dad accomplished something of a sleight of hand. In the sequel, while emphasizing the actions of the heroic leader, Paul Muad'Dib, as he had done in *Dune*, the author was also orchestrating monumental background changes and dangers, involving machinations of the people surrounding that leader. These people would vie for position to become closest to Paul; they would secure for themselves as much power as possible, and would misuse that power.

Many critics didn't understand this subtle message and lambasted the book.

Through it all, *Dune* continued to increase its readership. Readers passed dog-eared copies back and forth, and word got around. They loved the novel so much that they read it over and over, discovering something new on each pass through. One fan claimed to have read the book forty-three times!

Four years after publication in novel form, *Dune* received what Dad considered to be its first "really perceptive" review, from Reyner Banham of New Society London. Banham loved the novel, and tabbed it as the next great cult book after Tolkien's *Lord of The Rings*. The first *Whole Earth Catalog* in 1969 included a big spread on *Dune*, presenting it as a revolutionary ecological handbook couched in a "rich and re-readable fantasy." The catalog sold paperback copies of *Dune* at ninety-five cents apiece, giving sales of the novel a sharp kick upward.

In January 1970, my insurance company transferred me to Seattle.

---

*As discussed in Chapter Fourteen, there are strong Greek influences in *Dune*. This is continued in the sequel. When the Tleilaxu give the gift of a ghola to Paul it is something of a Trojan horse, for hidden in that gift is the means of Paul's destruction, an implanted obsession to kill him.

This was at my request, for I had been born in Seattle. The move felt comfortable to me. Beyond that, I had been missing my parents, even Dad. The abuses of neglect and overzealous discipline that he had visited upon me in my childhood were fading in memory, and I was trying to be positive about him.

When we visited their home on a frosty, clear day, Dad was wearing a rust-red sweater that Mom had made for him. His full, slightly wavy beard was freshly trimmed, giving him a professorial appearance. His alert, youthful blue eyes had Santa Claus crinkles around them. His movements were energetic, belying his forty-nine years.

My mother's dark brown hair was cut stylishly short. Her eyes were a darker shade of blue than his, and with her nearly round, gentle face and quiet ways, she was the perfect complement to his dynamism. Each of them wore a simple gold wedding band. I always felt a sense of permanence about their relationship when I looked at those rings exchanged at their marriage in 1946—that no matter the vicissitudes of life, their rings would never change, would never be removed.

During dinner Dad told some of his favorite jokes and anecdotes. In the telling of a story, he often switched between characters, and if they were ethnic he mimicked their accents, usually quite well. His accents could range among various ethnicities, and this evening he told a rollicking tale of three retired British officers. At the conclusion of the story we all laughed heartily. When Dad laughed he invariably took a couple of extra gulps at the end, like an earthquake with ensuing tremors.

I sipped my red wine and gazed out upon Seattle, at the sparkling lights of the city. Beyond the Space Needle a harbor tour boat, brightly illuminated and filled with revelers, plied the waters of Elliott Bay, heading out toward Bainbridge Island. From an early age, I used to listen to my father's wondrous array of amusing and interesting stories as he regaled friends. He never told them directly to me or to my siblings, so whenever I heard them I felt like an eavesdropper, hanging around on the fringes. Now, for the first time, he was telling the stories to me. I was no longer a child, but was an adult with a wife and a child and all of the rights attached thereto.

As time passed I established a new relationship with my father. Both he and my mother became more than parents. They became friends to Jan and to me. But Dad was so busy, with public appearances and writing deadlines, that we had to make appointments to see him, fitting ourselves into available niches in his calendar. It wasn't a relationship where we could just pop over to their place unannounced.

As Dad's schedule permitted, we made occasional trips with them to the beach, to the woods, and out on boats. Above all, there were wonderful dinners, many of them prepared by my mother and father. Both had become, in recent years, gourmet chefs. At every sitting, Dad told marvelous stories in his rich, full-bodied voice, peppered frequently with his deep, contagious laughter. The voice that had once seemed so objectionable to me from the stern discipline it imparted was now quite the opposite, a source of delight.

At times, even when my father was being kind to me, I had difficulty shaking childhood memories of him towering over me with his hand upraised and voice thundering. I tried not to think of such things, but I needed to talk with him about them, to clear the air. But with someone as dominant as this man, that was not an easy task. Reluctantly, I set it aside.

On an adult level I began to see sides of my father I had not previously noticed. He dominated every conversation, even when a room was full of people, and sometimes I found his ego hard to bear. But that was his way, and he was, after all, the most interesting person any of us knew.

Whenever Jan or I had important announcements to make to my parents—something to do with our personal lives—such news would receive a few moments of polite, often excited reception from them. Then Jan and I would listen with rapt interest for hours to the thrilling events of their lives. At times this made us feel comparatively insignificant, but such thoughts were fleeting and of little concern to us.

Dad's criticisms of me were gentler than in earlier years, more considerate and better thought out. I came to realize that it had more than a little to do with my age, and that this man could relate better to adults than to children. He had little patience for the activities of the young, for their hyperactivity, for their loud and importunate behavior.

Also I was no longer living with him, which must have helped immensely. The plethora of personal habits that can irritate a housemate weren't occurring. With breathing room our relationship was beginning to look as if it might stand a chance.

Conversely, there were large sparks flying between Dad and Bruce, almost every time I saw them together. Bruce was eighteen, of an age when he instinctively wanted to break away. Around 5'10" and slender, with long brown hair, he was speaking his mind more freely to Dad, venting previously pent-up hostilities. Bruce had also developed an intelligent procedure of minimizing confrontations with Dad by coming in the back door and heading straight for his room.

My brother's feelings of attraction toward other males were mixed with feelings that he should be attracted to women, that he should behave in socially accepted ways. He took girls to high school proms and other dates and had one particular girlfriend for a time, an intelligent young woman with round eyeglasses.

But Bruce was experimenting with amphetamines, getting "high" on a regular basis. He told me of a dinner one evening with my parents when he was so high that he laughed at everything they said. They didn't comment on his behavior, perhaps thinking it was only the wine that was served with the meal. Or perhaps, as Bruce suspected, our mother "turned her head" on this occasion and others, not wanting to see, not wanting to face the possibility that her second son was on a destructive path.

When University of Washington students gathered in opposition to the Cambodian War, my father the *Post-Intelligencer* education editor was in their midst, as supporter and reporter. The protesters commandeered the I-5 freeway through Seattle, preventing cars from using it while they marched on the federal courthouse, an army without arms.

Some months earlier, a Los Angeles community group concerned about air pollution had paid for Dad's services as an expert consultant. At one of their meetings, the conversation kept returning to the internal combustion engine as the primary cause of dirty air.

Frank Herbert told them that for every new car placed on the road, a hundred new trees would have to be planted to make up for the oxygen consumed by the vehicle. Then he discussed a personal pledge he had taken to drive his present car into the ground and never buy another one with an internal combustion engine. He qualified the pledge now and added that he wouldn't buy such a vehicle until government and industry took drastic steps to clean up the air. Dad said he had once driven a Packard powered by a Dobel steam engine in Santa Rosa, and he was intrigued by another steam engine built in Ohio. Such power plants could burn a variety of combustibles with an efficient system of external combustion that left no unconsumed hydrocarbons.

"The Packard has five hundred thousand miles on it," he said, with anger rising in his voice. "Detroit is wedded to planned obsolescence, to bringing out new styles each year. It's no wonder they aren't interested in steam power."

Upon hearing this, a man and a woman stood up and took the pledge. Word about the incident spread around Los Angeles, and converts began joining a new cause.

In April 1970, Dad was one of the principal speakers at Earth Day ceremonies, held in Philadelphia.* He told a crowd of thirty thousand people: "I refuse to be put in the position of telling my grandchildren, 'Sorry, there's no more world for you. We used it up.' " He asked the attendees to begin a love affair with Planet Earth, and they applauded wildly.

Frank Herbert spoke of his internal combustion engine pledge and asked if anyone in the audience would join him. Enthusiastic cheers rang out. All thirty thousand stood to repeat what became known as "The Frank Herbert Pledge."

Book sales accelerated.

Certainly my father, being a former political publicist and married as he was to an advertising copywriter, understood the basics of promotion. But he wasn't being phony or hypocritical. Innately honest, he believed wholeheartedly in the causes he espoused, and his audiences knew it.

In conjunction with Earth Day, Dad wrote entries for and edited

---

*The organizer of Earth Day was Ira Einhorn, a charismatic hippie guru who later became the international fugitive and convicted murderer known as "the Unicorn Killer." Frank Herbert and Einhorn wrote a number of letters to each other.

New World or No World, a book about the importance of protecting the environment. Published in paperback in 1970 by Ace Books, it included entries by Senator Edmund Muskie and Secretary of the Interior Walter J. Hickel. The book also contained transcripts of interviews by Hugh Downs of NBC's *Today Show*, in which he spoke with environmental experts such as Margaret Mead, Rene Dubos, Paul Ehrlich, Barry Commoner and Ralph Nader.

Unlike many authors who could not speak in public, Frank Herbert was a natural at the podium. Universities all over the country invited him to lecture and conduct writing conferences. His beard was an entree to college campuses—distinguishing him from establishment types who could not be trusted. He smiled often, was at ease and funny on stage. When he built up a head of steam about abusive political practices or the lack of environmental planning, he was absolutely captivating, as fascinating in person as he was in print.

After his performances, students mobbed around him. He received telephone calls from people who seemed to be on drugs, telling him they had been reading *Dune* aloud to acid-rock music. In an interview conducted by Bill Ransom, Dad said a stoned fan woke him at 3:00 A.M. and exclaimed, "I just had to call and tell ya, man, what a trip!"

Of course Dad intended his book to be lyrical, but not in the sense he was discovering. Too many unsolicited telephone calls were coming in day and night, taking precious time from his writing and disturbing his serenity. My parents changed to an unlisted telephone number under my mother's initials, "B. A. Herbert," so that their many personal friends could still contact them.

A drug element in *Dune*, along with its ecological messages, made the book particularly attractive to college students in the late 1960s and early 1970s. Melange, the spice drug guarded by the great and ancient sandworm Shai-Hulud, was the most precious commodity in the universe described in *Dune*.

University intellectuals had been among the first to embrace *Dune*, and such connections were a continuing source of comfort for my father. With his long history of rejections from publishers, a number of political campaign failures and his inability to deal with the labyrinthine passageways of bureaucracies, he had not always been on the inside during his life.

The status he had earned in Mexico for a brief time in the 1950s, where he had been an unofficial farm adviser to villagers, had been an exception. Now through hard work and perseverance he had earned a much higher standing. He was the talk of the younger generation on campuses from coast to coast. With this group he was developing a strong base of support—a platform from which he could fight for his political beliefs, particularly environmental protection and the control of abusive political power.

Despite the accolades he was receiving on campuses, he was discovering, to his dismay, that most book stores still were not carrying his novels. This was proving to be very embarrassing to him, as well as financially unrewarding.

Dad and his literary agent complained to Chilton, publisher of the hardcover edition of *Dune*. But the publisher pointed its finger at bookstores, saying book vendors were more interested in newer titles, not in a book first published five years before.

CHAPTER

19

Soul Catcher:
❋ The Story That Had to Be Written ❋

WITH THE growing popularity of *Dune*, several book editors were soliciting new Frank Herbert stories. One was Norbert Slepyan, trade editor of Charles Scribner's Sons in New York City. Dad was working on an important book at the time, a story he said had been stirring inside him since his childhood—about a modern-day clash between American Indian and white cultures. Back in 1968, he had tried, unsuccessfully, to obtain a government grant to write the book. Now Slepyan expressed interest, and Dad agreed to show it to him first.

To research this story, Dad immersed himself in the Indian cultures of several of the Northwest Salish tribes, picking up where he had left off in his youth. As a boy some four decades before, he had spent a lot of time with an outcast Hoh Indian who was living alone on an island near his home. The outcast had taught him many of the ways of the Indians—how they survived in the wild, what their customs were, how they felt about white society.

In 1969 and 1970, my father visited a number of Pacific Northwest Indian tribes. In the process he recorded legends told by the elders as well as chants and songs that were used to call spirits or to make women fall in love with men. There were power songs about the feats and abilities of braves, and love songs about the gentler side of Native American life. One love song in particular, called "How She Looks When

She Walks," was beautiful. Known as a "walking rhythm song," Dad memorized portions of it and sang it for my mother.*

On this occasion and others, Dad would look upon her with a gentle glow in his eyes, almost misting over from the tenderness he felt. And when she gazed back, it was with her eyes bright and full of pride. She had always looked upon him in this way . . . long before he became famous.

Despite the demands of his writing and the lack of attention he paid to his children when we were growing up, he was constant in his devotion to her. Each wedding anniversary he presented her with a bouquet of red roses, one rose for every year of their marriage, with a handwritten, endearing message.

In the fall of 1970, he completed a 65,000-word novel entitled *The Soul Catcher* but delayed sending it out. This was not unusual, because sometimes he liked to let a story sit for a month or so and then get back to it with fresh eyes.

One evening he attended a seminar conducted by Native Americans, at which they expressed their anger toward white society in a way that deeply disturbed him. For the first time in his life Frank Herbert became fully aware of the extent of Indian outrage. Oh, he had expressed Indian anger in *The Soul Catcher*, but intellectually, as if he were a "great white expert" talking about the problems of another culture without ever having experienced them personally, without ever having lived them.

He'd always told himself that the experiences he'd had with Indians as a child, and later through his friend Howie Hansen and others, provided him with a unique insight into the condition of Native Americans, enabling him to write accurately about what it meant to be one. But a sinking sensation told him the book he had labored over for the better part of a year was hogwash, written from the wrong point of view. He faced an ethical decision.

After further consultation with Howie, he burned the manuscript and then started over from scratch. In the rewritten version he removed

---

*The Herbert family later placed all copies of these recordings into the custody of one of the tribes for spiritual safekeeping.

the definite article from the title, making it *Soul Catcher*. He wrote of a university-educated Indian living in white society who seeks revenge for the rape-murder of his sister by white men. This scenario was based upon an actual event, in which a Native American woman was raped and beaten by white men near Port Angeles, Washington. Afterward the victim's brother sexually mutilated the attackers, preventing them from committing the same crime again.

In his fictionalized version, Frank Herbert has the university-educated Indian kidnap the young son of a high U.S. government official, taking the boy deep into the woods. The two become friends, leading the reader to think the boy will be spared. But the story takes a startling direction, and in the end the Indian kills the boy anyway. In Dad's view it was the murder of an innocent, a killing that should never have been necessary. But it *was* necessary, he said, because it had happened so many times to Indian innocents. This hard truth, he insisted, really made the story.

Soul Catcher became a variation on one of the key *Dune* themes, of Western man inflicting himself upon his environment, failing to live in harmony with it. In *Dune*, the consequence of Western man inflicting himself on the planet was a world denuded of its soils, left in an inhospitable desert state. And the Fremen natives of the planet, once its masters, now lived in hiding, having been driven for cover by Western-like conquerors.

Similarly, in *Soul Catcher* Frank Herbert asked the question, "What is the consequence of Western man imposing himself upon a primitive culture?" Instead of Fremen primitives, this time he was talking about real, not imagined people, the American Indians.

He saw these natives as noble creatures, superior to white men in countless ways. For the most part they lived in harmony with their environment, while white men did not. Tribal beaches, once unspoiled, were fouled by the plastic containers and other garbage of outside civilization. Indian languages and stories had been lost, subdued by an oppressive culture that did not tolerate old ways, different ways.

American Indians, like the Fremen people of planet Dune, were part of their environment, one with it. As part of the environment, my father believed, Indians and their cultures should be preserved.

Dad finished *Soul Catcher* in late February 1971. Slepyan liked the book and wanted to publish it but was overridden by Scribner's management. He said it might have been different if Dad could promise him the as-yet uncompleted third *Dune* book, but the author was noncommittal on that. He didn't tell Slepyan so, but he wanted the Berkley Putnam Group to take over the entire *Dune* series, so that it could be promoted more efficiently.

Subsequently John Dodds, executive vice-president of G. P. Putnam's Sons, made an offer on *Soul Catcher*, to publish it the following year in hardcover. The offer was accepted.

The manuscript was only 214 typed pages, fifty-three thousand words, and Dodds wanted to promote the story as a "major novel." He asked Frank Herbert to expand as many scenes as he could, and recommended an alternate title, *The Omen Tree*, since *Soul Catcher* sounded too much like science fiction to him.

Within a few days, Dad lengthened the story as much as he could, getting it up to 243 pages of manuscript, around sixty thousand words. He held his ground on the title, however, insisting that it was an action title with Indian connotations, and that it didn't sound at all like science fiction to him. Dodds went along with this.

Soul Catcher was published in hardcover in April 1972, the same month Jan and I had our second baby daughter, Kim. Early reviews on the novel were excellent, including one from a writer my father admired, Dee Brown, author of *Bury My Heart at Wounded Knee*. In appreciation, Dad sent a signed copy of the book to him, with thanks. Some Native Americans told Dad the ending was perfect, that he had written it the way an Indian would have.

Others disagreed. One of the naysayers was my father's best friend Howie Hansen, the Quileute Indian who had given him the seeds of the story during the many years of their relationship. Howie felt strongly that Katsuk should not have killed the boy, that this was not the way of the Pacific Northwest Indians my father was depicting. He said Katsuk would have performed a ceremony at the end in which he might have danced and frightened the boy with the knife, but he then would have turned the knife on himself instead. Howie said he tried to convince Dad to change the ending and other aspects of the story, including an incorrect depiction of the Indian spirit world, but Dad wouldn't bend.*

Even with its controversial ending, the book was nominated for the National Book Award. It did not win.

Back in December 1970, Chilton went into a small third printing of *Dune*, an additional three thousand copies. In the five years after publication, 6,500 hardcover copies had been sold. The book was short of being a national hardcover bestseller, but sales were increasing each month—an anomaly for a five-year-old book.

On the paperback side with Ace Books, sales of *Dune* were exploding, and in the early 1970s the book became their top-selling science fiction title of all time.

Dad and his agent were developing a good relationship with Berkley Books, the paperback publisher of a number of Frank Herbert titles, including *Destination: Void, The Eyes of Heisenberg, The Santaroga Barrier* and *Dune Messiah*. At the first opportunity Dad and Lurton wanted to make arrangements for Berkley and their allied hardcover publisher, Putnam, to pick up *Dune* . . . and eventually this was accomplished.

Newsweek and *Time* ran flattering stories on Frank Herbert and his desert saga. *Dune* became the subject of numerous Ph.D. theses, in multiple languages. It was made a textbook in such classes as English, writing, psychology, philosophy, comparative religion, earth studies— even architecture and human living space analysis. Book stores in college towns sold *Dune* out so fast that they couldn't keep it on the shelves. Customers, including professors needing textbooks for their classes, put their names on waiting lists. Readers formed *Dune* discus-

---

*In two years, Frank Herbert would meet the poet Bill Ransom, and they would collaborate to write a series of novels. Bill, who had extensive knowledge of Native American myths and customs, disagreed with Howie. "I think it's a gutsy ending," Bill told me in an interview. He went on to say that Katsuk didn't follow the Quileute way throughout the story anyway, and had in fact become an abomination who was making a mess of Indian rituals. "It's a tough ending that Americans can't handle," Bill said, ". . . it's not a Quileute ending but it's . . . proper . . . for what Frank set up. There is no other way out of the (story dilemma) except melodrama."

sion groups, in which they read sections and got together regularly to go over the material in depth.

Since there were only 2,200 first edition copies of the hardcover *Dune*, it began to have value in the rare book market. Copies were being stolen from libraries all over the United States.

Sales increased on all of Dad's old titles, including his first novel, *The Dragon in the Sea*, and publishers reprinted to keep up with demand. Foreign publishers began competing for Frank Herbert titles, and his books were printed in Great Britain, France, Germany, Spain, Japan and the Netherlands. Reports even came in that *Dune* was printed without authorization in Urdu (a Pakistani language) and in the languages of a number of Communist countries, although we never saw copies. The Science Fiction Book Club also picked up the title.

In the summer of 1971, the Apollo 15 astronauts David Scott, James Irwin and Alfred Worden unofficially named one of the craters on the moon "Dune." A NASA press release said this was "for the classic science fiction novel by Frank Herbert and for the dune-like structure on the southeast rim of the crater." It was near the Hadley Appendine landing site.

Movie mogul Arthur P. Jacobs, producer of *Planet of the Apes* and its sequels, purchased an option to film *Dune*. The advance was not large, but Dad was slated to receive a substantial amount if Jacobs exercised his option. Jacobs, who projected a fifteen-million-dollar budget, planned to begin filming after completing the *Apes* films.

Early in 1971, Dad had made enough money from *Dune* to quit the *Seattle Post-Intelligencer*. He did this with the intent of devoting more of his energies to writing and speaking engagements, as well as to publicity work for the World Without War Council, a group he'd become involved with in the Earth Day activities and in the preparation work for *New World or No World*.

Dad reached agreement with the University of Washington to conduct a political science class, "Utopia/Dystopia," for them as a visiting professor. The class, about utopian societies and myth structures, was tremendously popular, and he conducted it in the spring quarter of 1971 and the fall quarter of 1972. To explore what he called "the myth of the better life," he used as textbooks his own novel *The Santaroga*

Barrier and a number of classic utopian novels, including Aldous Huxley's *Brave New World*, Sir Thomas More's *Utopia*, and other works.

At the beginning of each class he asked the students to define "human." After receiving a variety of medical and anthropological answers, he offered his own psychological definition: "It means 'just like me.'" He said people had difficulty relating to people who were different from their own psychological myths, and that this was a major contributor to misunderstandings between ethnic, religious and cultural groups. Each person was surrounded by countless myths he wasn't even remotely aware of, involving the selection of clothing, food, homes, cars, political leaders, and all sorts of other pieces that went into the construction of human society and human psyches. In class, Professor Herbert discussed the reasons for such world views.

His professorship was more than a little ironic, since Dad had never graduated from college, and had in fact dropped out of this very university some twenty-five years earlier in a dispute over the courses the registrar wanted him to take for a major. Frank Herbert's teaching methods, not surprisingly, were somewhat unorthodox.

Since everyone had different abilities, he said he didn't feel grades were fair. He developed a variant of pass/fail, in which everyone who passed received an "A." When a student asked if he could write one term paper for Utopia/Dystopia and for another class instead of separate papers, Dad told him to go ahead, as far as he was concerned.

My father also used what he called a "looped feedback system," in which he did not stand in a power position at a podium higher than the level of the class, lecturing down to them. Instead he sat on the same level as everyone else and conducted discussions in the round like King Arthur, where no one occupied a position of relative strength. His utopian, "leaderless" classroom was an idealistic state of affairs. In reality he was in total control at all times.

Frank Herbert told his university students that we live in a "light-switch society," in which we flip a toggle and the light goes on, without any awareness of the mechanics producing the end result. To demonstrate his point, he invited an entire Utopia/Dystopia class to hike and camp with him in the Olympic National Forest northwest of Seattle, a rain forest. It was March, with a high likelihood of precipitation. He

245

told them only that they would camp for two days in a rain forest, and that they would need survival gear and supplies. He didn't specify exactly what they should bring, except a mention of warm clothing and sleeping bags, along with paper and pens for taking notes.

Incredibly, a young woman arrived in a fur coat, toting a leather suitcase! At the trailhead, Dad used his knot-tying expertise (from many years spent sailing in his youth) to rig up a rope sling so that she could carry the suitcase on her back. Most of the students had never been in the woods before, and brought along an odd assortment of heavy equipment. They had cast-iron skillets, china plates, cans of chili and bottles of soda pop.

At my father's brisk pace, they hiked several miles to an area called the Flats. Dad dug a drainage trench around his own pup tent to keep rain water away from it, but seeing blue sky and no rain, most of the students didn't bother. Within hours a deluge came down, and many of the students spent a miserable night. Early the next morning, as everyone gathered around a campfire, Frank Herbert told them, "We're the only survivors of a nuclear war and this is where we're going to live."

They discussed which technologies might continue—how people would eat, clothe themselves, build shelters, and travel. What sorts of social groups would form? And he spoke of new utopias unimagined by his students, utopias known to Native Americans and other "primitive" peoples. He taught them methods of finding food in the woods, how red ants could be mashed and spread on crackers or bread for sweet topping, or eaten straight. He said they were even sweeter if the heads were cut off. With a pocket knife, he obtained grub worms from the undersides of logs, which he said, like leeches, could be mashed up for high protein stews. When one of the students asked how leeches were caught, Dad said, "There's a pond up ahead. I'll show you." He rolled his trousers up and waded into the water. When he came out, leeches were clinging to his calves. He laughed and knocked them free.

In 1971 Dad began organizing files he had been building for several years on a third book in the *Dune* series, a novel he planned to name *Arrakis*. It would be the completion of a trilogy he had envisioned when *Dune* was written a decade earlier. In response to the desires of his fans and editors, this book would carry a stronger ecological theme than the previous book in the series, *Dune Messiah.*

For several months he had also been negotiating with Bantam Books to write a novel based upon the Oscar-winning documentary film *The Hellstrom Chronicles,* but didn't want to start it without a written agreement. When he finally had the contract, he only had a short time to complete the book before leaving for Europe on a scheduled trip.

He set *Arrakis* aside and in seven weeks completed an 85,000-word novel, which he entitled *Hellstrom's Hive.* Bantam was very pleased with it, and scheduled publication for 1973. Prior to publication in book form it was serialized as "Project 40" (*Galaxy,* November 1972 through March 1973). When the French edition was published by Editions Robert Laffont in 1978, it won the Prix Apollo award, considered the most coveted science fiction award in Europe.

In *Hellstrom's Hive,* Dad presented two conflicting world views (human versus insect) in such a way that half of his readers identified with human society and half with the social structure found among humans living secretly in a massive underground hive. In doing this he used the technique of "utopia/dystopia" that had been explored in the classes he taught at the University of Washington. It was also employed in his 1968 novel, *The Santaroga Barrier,* in which the world views of an insular California town and outside society were compared.

The mythology of the hero, so central to *Dune* and its sequels, is written from a different angle in this story. Dr. Hellstrom, the key individual in the hive, can be viewed as hero or villain, depending upon which world view the reader finds most compelling.

After returning from Europe in the summer of 1971, Dad tried to resume work on *Arrakis,* hoping to complete it by the following spring. After only a few days he experienced problems with plotting, and set the manuscript aside, intending to look at it again in a few weeks with fresh eyes.

But other projects soon filled his time, diverting him from this schedule. He signed a number of contracts for books, articles, and short stories, including contributions to anthologies. One of these projects was with G. P. Putnam's Sons for the novelization of a Frank Herbert short story that had been published in 1960, "The Priests of Psi." Dad set to work on the novel, and it became *The God Makers*, published in hardcover in 1972.

In the summer of 1972, with funding from the Lincoln Foundation, Dad and his friend Roy Prosterman visited Pakistan, India, Bengal, Thailand, Indonesia and Vietnam to study land reform, overpopulation and ecology problems. My mother accompanied them, at considerable danger because of the ongoing war in Vietnam.

The *Dune* movie project had been stalled for a while, as Arthur P. Jacobs was too involved in producing sequels to *Planet of the Apes,* as well as a musical version of *Tom Sawyer.* There were rumors that he might not proceed with *Dune,* and his option was about to expire.

While my parents were in Pakistan, however, good news arrived from Dad's film agent in Hollywood, Ned Brown. Mr. Jacobs, through his production company Apjac International in Beverly Hills, was exercising his option, and was contracting with David Lean (of "Lawrence of Arabia") to direct. Robert Bolt would write the screenplay. Filming would begin in 1974, with story boarding, set design and other preparatory work beginning right away.

Dad was elated, for he felt Jacobs and Lean, with science fiction and desert movie experience, respectively, would do a fine job of translating his novel into film. This was no small task, in view of the length of the book, the complexity of the characters, and the layers of ecology, philosophy, psychology, history, mythology, religion, and politics it contained.

My mother kept a journal on this trip, the first time she had done so in almost two decades. It was a simple account, with brief daily entries made on binder paper. In one entry she described a romantic side trip that she took with my father to Hong Kong, where they celebrated their twenty-sixth wedding anniversary.

In the early 1970s Frank Herbert sold a number of short stories: "Seed Stock" (*Analog,* April 1970), "Murder Will In" (*Five Fates* anthology, 1971), and "Death of a City," (*Future City* anthology, 1973). Two collections of his short stories and articles were published at that time: *The Worlds of Frank Herbert* (Ace Books, 1971) and *The Book of Frank Herbert* (Daw Books, 1973). Three previously unpublished short stories appeared in *The Book of Frank Herbert*: "Gambling Device,"

"Passage for Piano," and "Encounter in a Lonely Place." A complex non-fiction article, "Listening to the Left Hand," appeared first in *The Book of Frank Herbert* and later in the December 1973 issue of *Harper's* magazine.

Just as *Soul Catcher* addressed a theme found in *Dune*, the clash between primitive and Western cultures, Dad found new avenues to explore other themes found in *Dune* and its sequels. In *Whipping Star* (G. P. Putnam's Sons, 1970), the dangers to human freedom caused by big government were described satirically, offsetting the seriousness of anti-government themes found in the *Dune* series, particularly in the sequels. In this setting he promoted one of his earlier short story characters, Jorj X. McKie of the Bureau of Sabotage, to the status of protagonist in a novel.

Religion, a subtheme of *Dune* and its sequels, was also the theme of his 1972 novel, *The God Makers*. In this story, a human god was created by the mentally induced "psi-forces" of worshipers. Dad liked to refer to *The God Makers* as a "semi-caricature" describing how religions and myths developed.

In the early 1970s, a Seattle film company, Gardner-Marlow-Maes, purchased the rights to *Soul Catcher*. The project failed, primarily because my father insisted upon maintaining his controversial ending, in which the Indian protagonist kills the innocent white child.

While the *Soul Catcher* film project was still alive, Gardner-Marlow-Maes produced a film about the Blue Angels precision flying team. In conjunction with that production (which was a film festival winner), Dad wrote *Threshold: The Blue Angels Experience* (Ballantine Books, 1973). This involved the writing of an introduction and script narrative, used in the film and book, to accompany photographs of the planes and the men who flew them. In the script narrative, comprising some seventy-eight pages, much of it was similar to caption writing he had done in the 1960s as picture editor for the San Francisco *Examiner*. Dad was fascinated with the hero mythology of the pilots, the symbiosis of man and machinery, and the way men, with all of their frailties, responded to high-pressure situations. All were themes found elsewhere in my father's writing.

He wrote *Threshold* in three days.

Around this time, while Dad was working on *Arrakis*, he and Bruce found it impossible to live together any longer, and, according to Bruce, Dad kicked him out of the house. My father didn't remember it that way, asserting instead that "Bruce needed to test his wings," and made the move on his own. The relationship between father and "Number Two Son," while tenuous, was not severed entirely. My brother remained close to his mother, and for her sake went to visit his parents regularly.

Unbeknownst to me or to my parents, Bruce was living in a "drug house" with people who injected themselves with amphetamines. The favored drugs were little pills called "criss-crosses" that looked like aspirins with crosses on them. Also known as "CCs" or "beans," they were ground into powder on a spoon with the end of another spoon or a pocket knife. A little distilled water was mixed with the powder on the spoon, then cotton was laid on top and liquid was drawn through the cotton with a syringe. The mixture was, in turn, injected by the addict. My brother didn't take criss-crosses that way, because he hated needles and didn't want track marks on his arms. Instead he "dropped" the pills, swallowing up to thirty-five a day. Eventually Bruce moved out of the drug house and returned to the San Francisco Bay Area.

By now my younger brother wasn't dating girls anymore. In the new relationships he was forming, he was becoming a gay man, expressing feelings that had previously been latent or which had surfaced and been suppressed. Thus he was entering two worlds that were at once dangerous and socially unacceptable—those of hallucinogenic drugs and homosexuality. I had no idea these metamorphoses were occurring in him.

In part it was a reaction to our macho father, who spoke of homosexuality as if it were an immature, unseemly activity. I recall him saying to me that "repressed homosexual energy" could be employed for killing purposes by armies. In *God Emperor of Dune* and *Heretics of Dune* he described homosexual, lesbian and adolescent forces at work in armies. And, in an unpublished version of his epic poem, "Carthage," Frank Herbert wrote:

Homosexuals,
Bureaucrats
And bullyboys
Increase before
Each fall into darkness.

All the while Mom, unaware of Bruce's sexual inclination, or turning her head away so as not to see the indications, was longing for a baby boy Herbert to carry on the family name. Thus far Jan and I had two daughters. Penny bore three sons, David, Byron and Robert Merritt, but through marriage had lost the Herbert name. My mother hoped Bruce would marry soon, to improve the odds.

CHAPTER

20

✳ Xanadu ✳

IN *DUNE*, Frank Herbert wrote, "Polish comes from the cities; wisdom from the desert." In his view, the rural and desert lifestyles bore certain similarities, and were superior to circumstances found in urban centers.

Shortly after Christmas 1972, Dad and Mom moved again—this time north, to the Olympic Peninsula of Washington State, near the northwest corner of the "lower-48" United States. They purchased a house and farm on six wooded acres on the outskirts of the mill town of Port Townsend, Washington, population five thousand. Employing bargaining skills learned when we lived in Mexican villages in the 1950s, Dad dickered the price down by several thousand dollars.

There was a symmetry to my father's life. In his childhood some of his fondest memories had been spent living on a small subsistence farm in Washington State. He never forgot the experience and always longed for a return to it, to his roots. This man of letters could be urbane and sophisticated, desiring the comforts of the good life. But he was not truly happy unless he was living in the country, with a rural base of operations. City life, with its crowds and noise and pollution, did not suit him.

On the National Historic Register, Port Townsend had many turn-of-the-century Victorian homes, giving it architectural similarities with San Francisco—an area my parents missed for its beauty. Like San

Francisco this was also a port, but on a smaller scale and in a much different setting, situated as it was between the Strait of Juan de Fuca and Puget Sound. It had a small airport, Jefferson County International Airport—the subject of much amusement among locals for the name. It was dubbed "international" only because of regular small plane flights in and out of nearby Canada, necessitating a U.S. customs facility at the airport.

With six acres, Dad had room for the farming he wanted to do and for certain ecological demonstration projects he had in mind. Above all, he needed an isolated, quiet location where he could write without interruption. The phenomenal success of *Dune* had been bringing people out of the woodwork looking for Frank Herbert, and too many of them had his address and telephone number when he lived in Seattle.

Dad loved to ride his bicycle, and frequently ran errands on it around Port Townsend. The sight of a burly, bearded author leaning down over the handlebars of a Schwinn ten-speed became a familiar sight to locals. He and Mom fit in well and made many friends on all rungs of the social scale.

Their new house, comprising five thousand square feet, was a three-level cedar A-frame with two bedroom wings, located at the end of a rough, one-third-mile-long gravel road, just off a paved country road. In reality this was just inside the city limits, but it was a pastoral setting, with numerous farms and ranches nearby.

In the fall, each side of the gravel road and the nearby woods were full of edible mushrooms—primarily shaggy manes (*coprinus comatus*) and meadow mushrooms (*agaricus campestris*). Every time we visited during mushroom season my father organized family mushroom hunts, and we would go traipsing through the woods with him, filling plastic bags with delicacies. On such treks he quoted Latin names for the fungi he saw, edible and inedible, along with more commonly known references. He examined each plant closely to be certain it wasn't poisonous, often slicing it open with a pocket knife before throwing it away or tossing it in one of our bags. Back at the house, after we cleaned the mushrooms, Mom or Dad would slice them and sauté them in butter as a side dish, or would pour them over T-bone steaks or filet mignon.

It was always warm and cozy inside their home, a welcome shelter from cool Northwest weather. A heavy sliding glass door led from the front porch into the main level of the house, onto a Zen-like floor of black and white squares that extended into the kitchen. The kitchen was to the right of the entry, separated from the entry by a black countertop eating area with stools pulled up to it. Copper pans and utensils hung from beamed ceilings in the kitchen. Large white globes hung from the peak of the high-pitched ceiling—light fixtures that ran from the entry straight into an expansive, red-carpeted living room.

On the top level of the modified A-frame, beneath slanted ceilings, was a large loft for Dad's study. The study had a long desk (shop-built by my father) beneath gable windows that looked out on cedars and firs and a private driveway that led uphill to the gravel road at the top. To the right of the desk was an Olympia-65 electric typewriter on a typewriter stand. A large bookcase divided the room in two, with a sling chair reading area on the other side, by a camera tripod and stereo equipment. A weathered white and green Forest Service sign lay on the window sill:

KELLY BUTTE TRAIL
LESTER GUARD STA.—5
KELLY BUTTE RD.—1

This memento came from the trail to Kelly Butte, the Forest Service lookout where my parents had honeymooned in 1946. The sign had been retrieved by Dad on a recent hike when he found the path abandoned and overgrown.

On a large portion of the lower level of the house he had rows of bookcases built, for an extensive personal library that he intended to organize one day according to the Dewey decimal system used in public and university libraries. The house was only two years old when he purchased it, and some portions of it were not quite finished.

Mom's office was in one of the bedroom wings of the main level, with a view in the same direction as Dad's. She had a tall fir tree by the window nearest her desk, with a bird feeder that Dad had mounted for her on the trunk so that she could watch wrens, robins and other feathered visitors as they fed.

In the Port Townsend telephone directory my parents listed themselves under Mom's name, "B. A. Herbert," with the address "Xanadu."

Samuel Taylor Coleridge's unfinished poem, "Kubla Khan," which he wrote about a wondrous place called "Xanadu" while experiencing a dream-vision, was my mother's favorite poem. She could quote every word of it and delivered it thespian-style, as if she were on a theater stage. Dad particularly enjoyed listening to her, and said it reminded him of acting performances she gave in 1946 when my parents attended the University of Washington.

Most often she quoted the first paragraph, closing her eyes as she did so, and raising her voice dramatically:

> In Xanadu did Kubla Khan
>   A stately pleasure-dome decree:
> Where Alph, the sacred river, ran
> Through caverns measureless to man
>   Down to a sunless sea
> So twice five miles of fertile ground
> With walls and towers were girdled round:
> And here were gardens bright with sinuous rills,
> Where blossomed many an incense-bearing tree,
> And here were forests ancient as the hills,
> Enfolding sunny spots of greenery.

So like my parents' Xanadu were these words, for all around them were fertile grounds, gardens bright, ancient forests and sunny spots of greenery. And one day, if my father's construction dreams came to pass, there would even be a tower with a windmill on it, for his Ecological Demonstration Project.

The Port Townsend house was not a palace in the physical sense. It was unpretentious, comfortable and rather simple, without excess. It had little view, except of woods, an orchard and a duck pond. But under the influence of my father and mother it became a palace of intellect, of conversation and of love. We had many remarkable and memorable conversations at the dinner table and in the living room beside bookcases filled with books that Dad had written. Ten original

255

Dune paintings by the Hugo award–winning artist John Schoenherr made a dramatic and colorful backdrop on the south wall of the living room.

Dad designed two large stained-glass windows to go high on the western gable wall over the living room, one a rooster and the other a writer's quill. I often thought, as I sat in the living room and looked up at these delicate, graceful windows, that they represented two key facets of my father's life—his love of working the land and his love of writing.

From the beginning, he had grand construction projects in mind to radically alter the character of the property. He wanted to build a large workshop with a windmill tower on top, a solar-heated swimming pool, and a poultry house heated by methane generated from bird droppings. This was with the intent of turning the property into his "Ecological Demonstration Project" ("EDP"), where he could establish a nearly self-sufficient farm and test the practicality of alternative energy sources, such as power from wind, sun, hydrogen and methane. The U.S. Department of Energy, he said, had never done a very good job of investigating alternative energy sources, and he especially wanted to reduce the dependency of society on petroleum products and nuclear energy.

Through his writings, Dad liked to explore different aspects of issues in separate works. Thus *The Dragon in the Sea, Dune, The Green Brain* and *Hellstrom's Hive** dealt with various environmental issues, shedding new light on our world in ways that were not possible within the story limitations of one work. In like manner, his "EDP" was yet another

---

*(A) *The Dragon in the Sea* (Doubleday, 1956): Accurately predicted the worldwide petroleum shortage that would occur two decades later.

(B) *Dune* (Chilton Books, 1965): Considered an environmental handbook by many, the novel extrapolated existing world conditions in which deserts were encroaching upon arable land, and envisioned an entire planet covered by sand.

(C) *The Green Brain* (Ace Books, 1966): Based upon insects that actually developed a resistance to insecticides, such as DDT, Frank Herbert extrapolated and described a society that created a massive and powerful insect intelligence in reaction to human attempts to exterminate them.

(D) *Hellstrom's Hive* (Doubleday, 1973): Extols the benefits of insect society as opposed to human society, including the way insects co-exist better with their environment than humans do.

environmental story, one in which he would learn and teach by doing, by rolling up his sleeves in the innovative American way he so admired.

Fans, editors and his literary agent were after Frank Herbert for the third book in the trilogy, but he had to do it at his own pace, in his own way. There were too many uncertainties in the unfolding story, too many potential directions that were not set firmly in his mind, so he kept putting off the writing of the work or only pecking away at it in the midst of a very busy schedule. He wasn't focused on *Arrakis* as he needed to be. It wasn't flowing, wasn't coming together, so in the spring of 1973 he set it aside again.

Dad felt the American Indian movement was just beginning, and that despite slow initial sales *Soul Catcher* would, like *Dune*, ultimately find a huge audience. Certainly *Soul Catcher* deserved such an audience, for it was a powerful, finely crafted novel, filled with poetic beauty and suspense. After the film project on this book failed he became involved in another Indian project, the writing of four closely linked stories based upon actual historical events in the Pacific Northwest. He entitled the work *Circle Times*, and it was most intriguing, about the cyclical Indian view of the universe. It was an involved work, making up a thick manuscript, but Dad was not able to obtain a publisher for it. He did sell it as a television screenplay to Wolper Pictures, Ltd., of California— but ultimately the project fell apart when the producers felt Dad was trying to remain too true to historical facts, at the expense of drama.

Yet another movie project began to unravel around this time. *Dune* had reached the storyboard phase, in which scenes were depicted by artists, according to instructions from the director and producer. But in the spring of 1973 producer Arthur P. Jacobs died unexpectedly, and since it had been his pet project, indications were that his company, Apjac International, intended to abandon it. Under terms of the contract, they had until 1974 to make their decision.

While this was up in the air, Dad devoted several months to completion of a half-hour documentary film based upon field work he had done with Roy Prosterman in Pakistan, Vietnam and other Third World countries. Entitled *The Tillers,* it was written, filmed and directed by Frank Herbert. Produced in cooperation with the Lincoln Foundation, the World Without War Council, and King Broadcasting

Company, it appeared on King Television in Seattle and on the Public Broadcasting System.

By early 1974, my father was champing at the bit to get *Arrakis* underway, a novel he expected to be longer than *Dune Messiah* and perhaps as long as *Dune*. Finally he set other projects aside and made it his all-consuming priority.

He wanted ecology to be stronger in this climactic novel than it had been in the bridging work *Dune Messiah*, but he didn't want to overdo it, didn't want to curry favor with powerful environmental groups for the sake of sales. It was a balancing act. Throughout much of the 1950s he had been unable to sell many of his stories because they hadn't been written with particular markets in mind. They weren't the right subject matter for certain publishers, weren't the right length, didn't fit what was popular at the time. Maybe with a little of this and a little of that, editors told him, or if the market ever changed, they *might* sell. . . .

In the 1950s his stories had been rejected by editor after editor. Now he was in demand, an unaccustomed circumstance for him. Readers and editors were clamoring for more *Dune* stories, and he realized he had to give them what they wanted, what they expected, to a certain extent. He had to write for a particular market, after all. But he had important messages he wanted to convey, and there had been so much misunderstanding over *Dune Messiah*.

Bernard Zakheim, my father's artist friend, invariably included anti-holocaust political messages and religious quotations with his paintings and sculptures. Similarly, Dad wanted his own important messages to be contained within every novel he wrote and included them in *The Dragon in the Sea*, *The Santaroga Barrier* and *Dune*—all books that had experienced good to excellent sales. The success, he came to understand, lay in keeping the adventure first, the excitement of the story—and fitting the lessons, the messages, underneath. He could not be pedantic, could not preach to his readers.

"While writing the third *Dune* book," Dad recalled, "I first realized consciously that I had to be an entertainer above all, that I was in the entertainment business. Everything else had to be secondary, if I wanted readers to keep turning the pages."

He began to find the proper balance.

When we went to visit Xanadu we were four—Jan, me and our daughters, Julie (age four) and baby Kim. We made regular trips to Port Townsend, going up on alternate weekends and staying with my parents for one or two nights. If Dad had a book signing in Seattle or other business there, we got together for dinner at restaurants or at our house.

My mother, uncomfortable with "Grandma" or "Grandmother" because of the antiquity such references implied, taught the children to call her "Nona" instead, as her maternal grandmother had been known to her. She said Dad should be referred to by his grandchildren as "Panona." Neither nickname stuck, although the children did develop the habit of calling my mother "Nanna," as I had earlier referred to my own maternal grandmother, Marguerite. Mom accepted this without complaint, as well as "Grandpa" for my father.

Mom had been taking Szechuan Chinese cooking lessons in a class sponsored by a restaurant in Bellevue, a Seattle suburb. One evening my parents held a dinner party there for friends and family. We sat at a long table with a huge salmon on a platter in the center, prepared Szechuan style. Dad sat at one end of the table, and regaled all present with his stories. In the middle of one convoluted yarn, he rose and went around to the salmon in the center of the table. Using his fingers, he dug an eyeball out of the fish, popped it in his mouth and swallowed it whole as we looked on, aghast. "A real delicacy," he said, with a boyish smirk.

Now each time I saw Dad I enjoyed his fun-loving, playful side, a facet of his personality that had been revealed to me only intermittently when I had lived with him.

Since his father died in 1968, his mother, Babe, now seventy-one, had been living alone in a trailer home in Vader, Washington, one hundred miles south of Seattle. Dad and Mom visited her often and so did we. Sometimes I drove Grandma to and from family gatherings. But she was getting up in years, and Dad worried about her. So early in 1973 he brought her to live with him in Port Townsend, setting up an apartment for her downstairs with her own kitchen and bathroom. In doing this he displayed his generous, loving nature toward a mother who had been an alcoholic during much of her life, and often an inattentive parent.

Babe kept Mom company when Dad was writing and helped organize the household. But at times my grandmother could be domineer-
ing and troublesome when it came to matters of household cleanliness.
Mom came home one day and found the old woman up on a ladder
against the side of the house, cleaning the second floor windows!

"I just don't know what I'm going to do with her," Mom confided
to Penny.

Dad had a talk with his mother, but came away shaking his head.
"She's so stubborn!" he exclaimed. All he could think to do was to
chain and padlock the ladder, which he did.

George Carlson, formerly a Republican campaign manager who had
hired my father to do publicity work in the 1950s, now had a local
travel program on television, called *Northwest Traveler*. Carlson purchased 16mm footage from the trip and did a story highlighting Dad's
latest novels. Subsequently he became my father's agent for speaking
engagements.

When making connections with airliners, Dad and Mom regularly
chartered a small plane and pilot from Jefferson County International
Airport. They flew to Seattle, where Jan and I picked them up, or they
took cabs. Carlson regularly expressed concern about the safety of little
"puddle-jumper" airplanes that his friend and prized speaker flew so
often, and tried to talk him out of using them. Dad listened, but didn't
change his habits. And, despite his scientific mind that extolled logic
and discounted superstition, he often relied upon my mother's astrological and other predictive methods concerning the safest times to
travel.

CHAPTER
21

✳ A New Struggle ✳

I NOW worked for Insurance Company of North America as a commercial property underwriter. On a typical Friday evening after work I would pick up Jan and the kids and drive to the ferry dock in downtown Seattle. Following a brief wait, surrounded by a sea of cars and passengers waiting to board, we would catch the ferry to Bainbridge Island. From there it was about an hour's drive north, over the famous Hood Canal floating bridge to Port Townsend.

At the bottom of a long gravel driveway stood my parents' modified A-frame home, with a pair of bedroom wings jutting left and right. A two-car garage was beneath the right wing, which on the main level was the master bedroom. We pulled to the left onto a parking area, our tires slipping a little on loose gravel. Usually we could see Mom working in the kitchen, and as we were getting out of the car, my burly-chested, bearded father would bound down the stairs, smiling and calling out to us.

Behind him, a large wooden circle with a writer's quill was mounted over the entry doors. A gargoyle statue with a terrifying, ancient face sat on the ground by the base of the stairs, in the midst of rhododendron and azalea shrubs. Dad claimed, with a twinkle, that it warded off evil spirits.

Invariably the house would be filled with mouth-watering cooking and coffee aromas, and sometimes Mom or Babe had apple, berry or

261

pumpkin pies lined up in the kitchen on cooling racks. I'd give the women big hugs and kisses on the cheeks, feeling the softness of my mother's skin and the creased toughness of my grandmother's. Sometimes Mom would ask me to taste a sauce, as I had done for her as a child. And then Dad would take me outside and show me around the property, discussing all the things he and Mom had added since our last visit, along with the grand construction plans he had for the future.

Occasionally he'd have a copy of his latest book for me on the black Formica countertop between the kitchen and the dining room, and he would sign it with a personal message for me and my girls. But, since I still harbored feelings of rebelliousness and resentment toward him, I didn't read his books. They accumulated on a bookcase at home.

It was early 1974 before I made any attempt to read *Dune*. After forty pages I gave up. I couldn't get into the book. It seemed convoluted, opaque and full of strange language. Instead I opened my copy of *The Dragon in the Sea*, and paused at the flyleaf, where Dad had written a personal message to "Number One Son" nearly two decades before. In all that time, I had only glanced through the first few pages, but now I read the book straight through and enjoyed it.

The next time I saw Dad in Port Townsend, I complimented him on the story. He beamed in response, and brought forth a copy of *Dune Messiah* from the kitchen countertop. He opened to the title page, and with several bold strokes of a gold Cross pen wrote a brief message of love to me, Jan, and our girls, then crossed out his printed name and signed below it.

I asked him why he signed that way.

In an erudite voice he told me the practice was "as old as English letters," that it dated back to when books were first printed in the late fifteenth and early sixteenth centuries. He said authors of the time were used to seeing their books handwritten, in the ornate script of scribes. When they saw their names printed they thought it lacked a personal touch, without the closeness they wanted when they communicated with a reader. So they began crossing off their printed names and signing each copy. My father started doing this himself sometime in the 1960s, and it became his cachet.

Now I made another attempt to read *Dune*, using a library copy since I had loaned mine to a friend and it had been lost. On second reading, the opening pages became more clear, and I found myself hooked. I read it all the way through, finishing it early one morning, when I had to go to work in only a few hours. While lying in bed I couldn't go to sleep. The story still churned in full color in my mind. I thought it was the greatest book I had ever read.

I was thrilled with the way my father had captured, on such a grand scale, the human spirit of defiance and rebellion against injustice and oppression. The very name the Fremen desert people called their planet, "Dune," was unauthorized, in defiance of the military-political rulers, whose edicts proclaimed the world was called Arrakis. How well I understood this spirit of rebellion, because for a number of years I had been in revolt against the book's author.

In my mother's office one day I saw a file marked "Story Ideas." I asked if they were for her stories, and she said, "No. Frank's." She went on to say she was more of a commercial ad writer, without my father's talent for creativity.

Near her desk stood a bank of file cabinets. Several drawers were marked "Opus," and she explained this was a filing system shared with them by science fiction author Robert Heinlein and his wife, Ginny. Under the system, each literary work of the author was assigned an "opus number," in the order of creation date. Into an opus folder or folders went the manuscript, contracts, royalty statements, reviews and correspondence pertaining to a particular work. She found it easiest to use separate folders for each of these categories, all bearing the same opus number. Each story, even if its title was changed, kept the same opus number.

Since Dad wanted to forget his pulp Western that was published in 1937, Opus Number 1 for Frank Herbert went to "Survival of the Cunning," published in 1945. *The Dragon in the Sea* (1956) was number eleven, and *Dune* (1965) was number twenty-five. There were some errors in the numbering, because the system was set up late and Dad had many unpublished stories that pre-dated the system.

As part of the system she maintained a loose-leaf binder, with separate sheets on each work arranged by opus number. On those sheets she wrote the title or titles, copyright dates, advances, royalties, foreign translations and other important information. She said that this binder served as a "tickler file," reminding her of money that was due from each publisher, when to renew copyrights and the publishing history of the work. With the help of an alphabetical master list that she constantly updated, she could locate important files quickly and keep documents in order.

Based upon another Heinlein system she also set up an annual correspondence section, in which all non-opus letters for a particular year were filed in sections from A to Z, according to the last name or company name of the other party. A 1972 letter from Jack Vance, for example, went into the "V" section for 1972. There were many other files maintained.

Dad depended upon Mom entirely to keep his business affairs organized. In addition to editing his stories and handling all of his paperwork (including the answering of fan letters), she coordinated his speaking and other travel arrangements, wrote publicity for him, and kept careful accounting ledgers. When interviewed my father frequently could not remember when a particular story was published, or some other detail requested by the interviewer. "I'll check with Bev," he would say. "She's always right about details like that."

Business and monetary affairs hardly entered Dad's mind at all, and soon slipped away entirely, to be fielded by Mom. This despite the fact that his study was a model of efficiency and organization, as were the stories he wrote in there. He was also highly organized when it came to affairs of the kitchen, since he so loved to cook. He kept kitchen pans and utensils clean, and, of utmost importance to him, kept them in exacting locations in cupboards and drawers, near where they would be used. Baking dishes were by the oven, pans by the range, and so on. He called it "point-of-use" storage.

Because of his inattention to financial details he had a tendency to overspend, and to buy impulsively. Mom was constantly reining him in, reminding him of stark economic realities.

Frank and Beverly Herbert were more content in Port Townsend than anyplace they'd ever lived before, and in large measure their happiness came from the beauty of the land itself, and from their attention to improving it. With my grandmother's help they planted roses, rhododendrons, hydrangeas, bougainvillea, poinsettia, and geraniums along the driveway and around the front of the house. Mom poured coffee grounds around roses and other plants, saying that something in the chemistry was good for the plants. The results bore this out.

By mail order they obtained seeds for trees and seedlings, and they planted giant sequoias, redwoods, firs, sugar maples and dogwoods. Based upon research my father did, they kept the giant sequoia seedlings in a refrigerator for two months before planting them, simulating winter temperatures at a young age in order to improve the odds of their surviving through the first real winter.

Above the duck pond stood an old apple, pear and plum orchard, where they added young apricot, crabapple and filbert trees. They researched wine grapes carefully, hoping to find varieties that would do well in the cool northern latitudes. It was a risky proposition, but near the orchard they planted a small experimental vineyard of Merlot, Sauvignon Blanc, and Cabernet Sauvignon. At the top of a hill overlooking the orchard, vineyard and duck pond they constructed three large stone-walled vegetable (and low-growing fruit) garden areas, with drainage holes in the walls to keep excess moisture from damaging the plants.

In Frank Herbert's studies of Native American planting methods, he discovered that they often planted corn in circles. Supposedly this was for religious reasons, since the circle had spiritual significance to them, but after several seasons Dad discovered a practical reason as well: higher yields were produced. Subsequently he employed a variation on circles—spirals—and obtained even higher yields.

Dad had a poultry house built, connected to a wire-screened enclosure, and filled it with nearly a hundred Rhode Island Reds (prolific brown egg–layers) and other breeds of chickens, and thirty ducks. Turkeys became occasional, if short-term visitors before they were relocated onto a dinner table or into one of the freezers in the main house. And there were a pair of geese living in the yard, a working couple who earned their keep by weeding the garden.

Some of the ducks were Rouens from France, examples of genetic engineering that looked like dark-feathered mallards but grew much faster and didn't fly well. A meat breed, they laid green, blue or tinted white eggs. They were allowed to forage around the pond, an unfenced area, and in this way were able to come up with most of their own food—supplemented by small amounts of grain left around the shores of the pond by Dad. He also stocked the pond with tubers and salamanders (for the ducks), fresh water clams, pond snails, and bass. Always thinking of the interrelationships of an ecosystem, my father said that duck droppings sealed the bottom of the pond better than concrete.

In his travels to Third World countries, Frank Herbert learned about high-yield hybrid rice, which he wanted to plant on the shores of the pond. He set up bird feeders on trees all around the main house, including on a fir outside Mom's office, so that she could watch activity at the feeder from her desk. Dad referred to birds as "feathered insect killers," and said they kept insect levels down on his patio and decks during summer months when insect populations were highest.

My parents were amateur bird watchers and frequently went for long walks in the woods together, taking binoculars and Audubon bird callers.

Doing most of the construction work by himself, Dad put together a fancy Lord and Burnham greenhouse adjacent to the house. When the structure was complete they used it in the winter to "get an edge on the growing season," keeping plants inside during the cold months and then planting them at the first opportunity in the springtime. They kept warm-weather fruit trees in the greenhouse year 'round, providing their table with fresh lemons, limes, oranges and figs. They also grew strawberries in there.

Dad arose early each day to write, before Mom or Babe were up. After a small breakfast of unbuttered whole wheat toast with jam or honey and freshly squeezed orange juice, he was at work on *Arrakis* by 5:30 or 6:00. He continued without interruption until noon or early afternoon, depending upon where he was in the story. Friends and family were instructed never to call him before noon.

After lunch, Dad did farm work, often involving heavy manual labor. To compensate for the sedentary life of a writer, he liked getting his hands dirty and exercising in fresh air. He and Mom often said the earth calmed them as they gardened, when they immersed their hands in the soil. One day when my daughter Julie was upset they suggested that she go outside and do this. It worked for her, and the farm benefitted as well from the weeds that they suggested she pull.

My father designed and built a number of farm gadgets, including an enclosure for the garbage cans (with a lid that propped itself open), a brush (nailed bristles-up to the deck by the front door) for cleaning mud from shoes, and a funnel arrangement (nailed to a tree by the chicken house), for draining fowl he had slaughtered. It was an efficient farm, producing the fresh makings of fabulous gourmet meals, which we shared with them often. Each morning, awakening with our stomachs pleasantly full from the evening before, we heard the crowing of roosters.

Frank Herbert was the most famous person in town and liked by every level of the social strata, from contractors to professors. They helped him guard his privacy. Whenever an outsider came to town looking for Frank Herbert, no one seemed to know where he lived.

When Howie Hansen's best friend became famous, for a time Howie didn't know how to relate. It wasn't the same to him, no matter how he tried to achieve the closeness they had known in the past. Finally Howie initiated a heart-to-heart conversation. Dad told him he was very skittish of people who wanted to know him only after they found out he wrote a book. "You're different, Howie," he said. "You know me as a guy who runs a typewriter, and I know you as a guy who runs a fishing boat. There isn't a lot of difference from one person to another when you look at it that way."

After this, Howie was more relaxed.

Another time, Dad showed Howie a manuscript he was about to mail to New York. Dad noticed an error and said, laughing, "Look at that. I haven't even got this word spelled right." He left it misspelled, and quipped, "I'm not proving myself as a typist, Howie. I'm proving myself as a writer."

Actually, Dad was just having a little fun with Howie—enjoying his success. My father was an excellent speller, and always prided himself on clean manuscripts sent to publishers. He was such a perfectionist, in fact, that he sometimes reopened envelopes in the post office before mailing them out, just to change a few words.

267

✳ ✳ ✳

For sixteen months my parents led a busy but idyllic life at Xanadu, their Port Townsend property. In the middle of April 1974, they were scheduled to fly to New York City for an important meeting with one of Dad's publishers. Then the world fell out from under them.

For several weeks, Beverly Herbert had been experiencing congestion in her lungs, and after taking antibiotics prescribed by her family doctor, the condition wasn't getting better. In the middle of the night, her condition worsened, and she couldn't stop coughing.

At 2:30 A.M., Dad telephoned a friend who owned a small plane and asked if he could fly them to Seattle right away, to get Mom to Group Health Hospital. The answer was yes, so Dad bundled Mom up and helped her downstairs to their 1966 Volvo sedan, then drove to the small county airport just outside Port Townsend. On the way he reached speeds in excess of one hundred miles an hour.

In the air, the pilot radioed ahead to Seattle and arranged for an ambulance to meet them at Boeing Field. In the ambulance half an hour later, with red lights flashing, Dad was at my mother's side holding her hand and telling her she was going to be all right. A paramedic assured him he wasn't in the way and worked around him, taking Mom's vital signs and radioing them to emergency room personnel waiting at the hospital.

On the way she kept saying, "I can't go to the hospital. We have to be in New York."

"Don't worry about it," Dad said.

From the hospital, Dad telephoned me. It was dawn, and I was just getting up for work. He said Mom had a collapsed lung, and there were ominous indications of even more serious problems. Jan and I bundled up the children (Julie was six, and Kim, two) and rushed to the hospital.

Mom was in intensive care, and the children weren't allowed in her room. I went to see her first, leaving Jan in the waiting room with the kids.

My mother appeared pale, but smiled weakly when she saw me. Her eyes looked pained and murky. She had an intravenous line connected to one arm, with a plastic bottle hanging from a portable metal frame nearby. Clear liquid in the bottle bubbled as it fed through the line into her body. A book of Emily Dickinson poems and a *Vogue* magazine sat on a rolling cart to her left. Dad was slumped in a straight-backed chair on her other side, looking very tired.

"Did you shave this morning?" she asked, looking at me closely.

Sheepishly, I admitted I hadn't. I felt like a little boy under scrutiny for dirt behind the ears.

She smiled gently.

I waited while doctors tended to her. She said she had a collapsed lung from pneumonia, but assured me everything was fine. It was being taken care of well, she said. And I recalled but did not mention the fact that pneumonia had killed her mother, Marguerite, at the age of fifty-one. As I stood looking down on my mother I thought of her age: forty-seven.

The doctors wanted each visit kept short, so I had to leave after a few minutes. Dad walked out in the hall with me, saying he needed to stop at the cafeteria to get a cup of coffee. He said he would check into a hotel near the hospital that evening to be near Mom.

"You can stay with us," I offered.

But he declined, saying our house was small, and besides, he wanted to remain closer to Mom.

Jan went in to see Mom afterward, and I didn't learn until the following year what transpired during their conversation. Mom told her she didn't have pneumonia at all, that what she had told me had not been true. From X-rays the doctors strongly suspected lung cancer, and further tests were being conducted. She said if it was cancer she didn't think I was strong enough to hear the news.

"You're stronger than Brian," my mother said. "I don't want him to know yet. He's like me. He'll be up worrying all night."

Mom said she'd known for several weeks something was seriously wrong, but she'd been afraid to see a doctor about it. On a number of occasions she had repeated to herself the Litany Against Fear, written so beautifully in *Dune* by her loving husband:

I must not fear. Fear is the mind-killer. Fear is the little-death that brings total obliteration. I will face my fear. I will permit it to pass

269

over me and through me. And when it has gone past I will turn the inner eye to see its path. Where the fear has gone there will be nothing. Only I will remain.

She had been lying awake at night, depressed and worrying over her condition and how she would pay bills. Dad had been writing checks and transferring funds between accounts, without leaving a clear paper trail that she could follow.

Inside, Jan didn't feel strong at all, but she tried not to show this. She was falling apart herself, fighting back tears. Unable to speak, she hugged the woman who had become a mother figure to her.

After a long while, Jan pulled away and said, "I love you, Bev. I'll pray for you."

"I love you, too." Mom's eyes were moist, filled with pain at the thought of separation. "I'm getting the best care. The doctors are doing everything possible."

In a short time, without my knowledge, my mother was diagnosed with inoperable, terminal lung cancer, apparently caused by having been a heavy smoker during most of her life. Two daily packs of Lucky Strikes, a brand having extremely high quantities of tar, nicotine and carbon monoxide, had taken their toll. They called it "squamous cell carcinoma," and it was in the region of the left upper lobe.

Mom was especially despondent upon hearing a doctor tell a nurse, "Let her have whatever she wants." It meant that they were giving up on her, that as far as they were concerned it didn't matter what pain-killer drugs she took, or what she ate.

She obtained opinions from two physicians, and the most optimistic prognosis gave her only a five percent chance of surviving beyond six months. Thereafter she began a rigorous program of chemotherapy and cobalt radiation treatments.

Dad canceled his New York City appointments. He also slowed his work on *Arrakis*, writing only a few hours a day or not at all, so that he could concentrate upon his new priority—helping Mom find the best medical attention possible. While she was undergoing treatment, he was burning up the telephone wires, asking everyone he could think of for advice. He wanted the best technology available for Mom, even if he had to take her out of the country to get it. Radiation and che-motherapy were attacking the disease from two directions, and he was zeroing in on a third, the possibility of a trip to Mexico for laetrile, also known as the "vitamin B17" treatment, derived from apricot pits. Her odds were low, and he wanted to give her every extra fraction of a percentage point that he could.

As a result of his investigation, Dad decided that Mom's best op-portunity lay with chemotherapy and radiation in the United States followed by laetrile treatments in Mexico, since they were not legal in the U.S.*

Dad's mother, Babe, sent a Catholic nun—Sister M. Jeanne of Saint Leo Convent—all the way from Tacoma to see her. The nun gave her a set of rosary beads, along with a scapular. When Sister M. Jeanne returned to the convent, she supervised twenty nuns in prayer sessions for my mother. Despite a lifelong aversion to organized religion,** Mom graciously accepted the attention. Over the years she had come to regret the lack of a relationship with God in her life, and at the brink she was trying to make up for lost time.

Five weeks after the awful diagnosis, during a time when my mother was undergoing chemotherapy and radiation treatments in Seattle, Jan telephoned her. Mom said the treatments were hard on her, and she was sick to her stomach. She asked if Jan had told me.

"No," Jan replied.

"Don't. It's for the best. I'm fighting this thing, Jan, and I'll be damned if it's going to get me, not when Frank and I have reached the point where we can begin enjoying our accomplishments."

---

*Laetrile was developed in France in 1840, and by the 1970s it was a fad cancer cure, replacing another fad cure of the 1960s, krebiozen. By the 1980s, most medical authorities felt there was no evidence of any anti-cancer properties in laetrile.

**My mother and father rarely spoke to me of religion when I was living with them. Mom explained this was because religion had been shoved down their throats when they were chil-dren, and they did not want to inflict anything like that upon Bruce, Penny, or me. They wanted us to make our own decisions about God, with all choices open to us. Later in her life, Mom would have a change of heart, saying our lack of religious experience gave us nothing to fall back upon during times of extreme difficulty. In her own way, she would one day form a strong relationship with God.

A month later she received good news. Her body was responding to treatment, and the cancer was in remission. The doctors said it was a miracle, that she had developed a "warrior spirit" in order to survive. My parents still planned to go to Mexico for laetrile later in the year just to play it safe, to employ every possible cure.

While receiving radiation treatment, however, Mom's heart had sustained irreparable and serious damage, destroying one-fourth of the muscle. The medical process, which left quite a bit to be desired but was the state of the art at the time, involved the administration of more than five thousand rads of irradiation to her left mainstem bronchus (lung) through a single anterior port, with no shielding of the heart. Now, while she was much improved overall, her heart condition caused her to tire easily. Doctors prescribed an exercise program that involved swimming.

Dad refinanced the house to obtain funds, and arranged for the rush construction of a swimming pool on the property and a cedar pool building. He had a custom weather vane installed on the roof of the new structure—with a writer's quill for a wind direction arrow. The pool water was kept pleasantly warm for Mom, and Dad made sure that she completed the swimming exercises she needed. If she ever had trouble finishing a lap, he was right there to help her to the edge.

With Arthur P. Jacobs deceased, his company, Apjac International, was still uncertain if they would exercise their option to film *Dune*. The option was about to come due, and with a higher mortgage payment and the extra (uninsured) medical treatments that Dad wanted Mom to receive in Mexico, they were in need of the money this would bring in.

Marvel Comics made an offer to print a *Dune* comic book, but Dad was not enthusiastic about the idea. He delayed responding.

For the first time in two and a half months, he had *Arrakis* rolling again. A gut feeling told him this book would be tremendously successful, but his hardcover publisher, Putnam, was cautious. They paid a small advance and were talking about a limited print run.

While awaiting word from Apjac, Dad taught a writing workshop at the Symposium in Creative Print, conducted in Fort Worden State

Park, Port Townsend.* His uncle, Ken Rowntree, Sr., had commanded this U.S. Army fort in the 1940s, before it was decommissioned and turned into a state park. A young Port Townsend poet, Bill Ransom, was director of the workshop. In a short time they would become fast friends, and then collaborators on a number of book projects.

When Mom finally returned to her desk, she found it overflowing with unpaid bills, unread contracts and unanswered letters. By the fall, she was feeling much better, and could swim three laps of the pool. I was told only that she was recovering from the lung condition that had been described to me earlier, pneumonia—and I had no idea of the suffering she had experienced. I did hear her complaining about cold, damp weather, so typical of the Pacific Northwest—and I later learned that the radiation treatment had contributed to this condition. Her radiation-damaged heart wasn't pumping as much oxygen as before, so that her circulatory system wasn't working well. Her weight loss undoubtedly made her feel colder, too.

She told me she had stopped smoking, and I had to get used to seeing her in the new way, without the customary cigarette in her hand or in an ashtray nearby. In a few months she could do forty laps of the pool nonstop—around five hundred meters in all. She had been a strong swimmer before her illness, had even placed first in an all-city swim meet in her youth.

Apjac did not renew their option to film *Dune,* which came as a financial blow to my parents. In October, however, they received substantial royalties from still burgeoning *Dune* sales, more than enough to pay their bills, including a Mexico "vacation" by car. Or so I was told. The Marvel Comics offer for a *Dune* comic book was not accepted.

Reflecting good sales of *The Dragon in the Sea* and a poorly named paperback version, *21st Century Sub,* Ballantine came out with a new "Classics" edition using yet another title for the same story. This was the original "Under Pressure" title from a magazine serialization (*Astounding Science Fiction,* November 1955–January 1956). The sales of all Frank Herbert novels increased with the amazing success of

---

*The 1982 movie *An Officer and a Gentleman* was filmed there.

Dune, and his publishers, domestic and foreign, scrambled to reissue the old material.

In a readers' poll conducted by *Locus,* the newspaper of the science fiction field, *Dune* was voted the greatest science fiction novel of all time.

Just before departing for Mexico in mid-October, Dad completed the second draft of *Arrakis*, the long-awaited climax of the *Dune* trilogy. He renamed it *Children of Dune*, and planned to write the final draft upon his return.

Upon returning from their trip in early December 1974, good news awaited them. A French production company led by Michel Seydoux was making a substantial offer for the right to film *Dune*. The offer was accepted, and their advance provided welcome financial breathing room.

Seydoux, a millionaire Parisian, obtained the Chilean director Alejandro Jodorowsky for the project. Jodorowsky, director of the controversial cult films *El Topo* and *The Holy Mountain,* was a brilliant eccentric with left-wing political views. The budget was set at $9,500,000, substantially lower than Arthur P. Jacob's $15,000,000, especially considering inflation in the intervening years. But Jodorowsky planned to film in Spain and the deserts of Algeria, where costs were not excessive. He was confident he could come in under budget.

Jodorowsky wrote the screenplay and proceeded with storyboarding, the creation of special effects, set construction, and costume-making. He also reached tentative casting agreements with an interesting group of actors. Jodorowsky intended to play Duke Leto Atreides himself, while Orson Welles would be Baron Vladimir Harkonnen. The Surrealistic artist and filmmaker Salvador Dali would be the Padishah Emperor (Shaddam IV), David Carradine would be Imperial ecologist Dr. Kynes, and Charlotte Rampling would be Lady Jessica. Jodorowsky hoped to reach agreement with either Mick Jagger or Pink Floyd to do the soundtrack.

Dad was slated to be technical adviser, but quipped in an interview with Bill Ransom that this meant "Third Assistant Flunky."

Now he was on the home stretch of *Children of Dune* (*Arrakis*), and expected to finish the book in five or six weeks.

CHAPTER

22

✳ *Children of Dune* ✳

ONE SNOWY winter day in early 1975, Jan took me aside and told me how ill my mother had been. I was stunned, and immensely proud of my father when I learned all the wonderful things he had done for Mom, setting his important work aside and taking her to Mexico to improve her odds at life.

As this new and very human side of my father revealed itself to me, I began inquiring about him. I asked my mother about their early years together and other times when I hadn't been around.

For years my mother's dependency upon him had been obvious. She didn't even have a driver's license, and for much of her life had yielded to his decisions, to his changing whims. Her method of influence had been one of unflagging love and constancy, of enduring his mood swings and pushing him gradually toward settling into a property of their own. Now this was the Port Townsend house. Xanadu. Skillfully, she had brought him around not only by asserting that it would make her happy, but by showing him it was the only way he could have a farm and the ecological demonstration projects he wanted.

Much of her life had been spent waiting for him to complete a story so that they could do things together. This was a micro and macro pattern of relationship. She waited to see him each day until he emerged from his study, when they could share private times together: romantic dinners and walks in the woods, boat trips, times shared in the garden and swimming pool. And she waited even longer for him, months and years, to take trips after Dad finally finished each book. Everything they did revolved around his writing schedule. He was dominant, the one in charge.

But he was vulnerable, I came to realize. Vulnerable without her. They were a remarkable writing team. If my mother was ill, he couldn't write, not until she felt better. They flowed together as one organism.

Howie Hansen put it this way: "There are two Frank Herberts—the one I knew prior to Bev and the one that you know who was created by Bev. Frank Herbert the author would not exist had there not been a Beverly Forbes to marry him and . . . coalesce him mentally . . ."

Over the years I had been mailing items from my office joke file to my mother. With her illness, it occurred to me that my light fare might be therapeutic, might perk her up. So I increased my schedule of mailings to her. She posted her favorites on bulletin boards in the kitchen and in her office.

Mom and Dad made their second trip to Europe in late 1975. Just before leaving, Mom took me into her office in one of the bedroom wings and said, almost matter-of-factly, "If we fall out of the sky, Brian, I want you to take care of things."

I hated hearing her talk like that, particularly with the way I felt about flying. In 1968, I had an unfortunate experience while taking a flying lesson in a single-engine Piper Colt, an incident where, due to the error of my instructor, we nearly collided with an airliner. Since that time I had not flown, and had vowed I would never do so again, in any sort of aircraft.

Mom went on to give me the combination to their home safe and to a padlock on a file box. She had me stand beside the desk while she opened the third drawer down and showed me where keys to the desk and file cabinets were kept, under a book of zip codes. The safe deposit box key was on a separate key chain. More keys on a big brass ring were hidden in the master bathroom—keys to the various locks around the property. She showed me a list of Dad's publications, kept in an orange notebook, and the location of the contract files.

"Be sure to renew the copyrights every twenty-eight years," Mom said. She told me which ones were coming up soon, and mentioned a recent renewal on the first published work in his opus files, "Survival of the Cunning," published in *Esquire* in March 1945.

As we came out of the office, my seven-year-old daughter Julie was seated on a kitchen stool next to her grandfather, sharing ice cream with him. His hair was thinning on top, and she asked him, wondering about the origin of his beard, "Grandpa, did the hair from the top of your head slip onto your face?"

He let out a loud guffaw.

A four-part *Analog* serialization of *Children of Dune* in early 1976 was a resounding success, causing issues to sell out on newsstands. Letters poured in from excited fans who loved the story.

But at 3:00 A.M. on a holiday, President's Day, 1976, Beverly Herbert became extremely ill. Dad rushed her to Jefferson General Hospital in Port Townsend. It was a medication problem, from post-cancer-treatment medicines she had been taking, causing dangerous changes in her vital signs. Medical personnel arranged to fly her to Group Health Hospital in Seattle for more specialized attention. At Group Health she was kept overnight and her medications were adjusted. The Group Health doctor told her the emergency room technician at Jefferson General had saved her life by making a difficult diagnosis and then obtaining the proper care for her.

For months, David Hartwell, Dad's astute editor at Putnam, had been trying to convince company management that they weren't printing enough copies, that when *Children of Dune* was printed soon in hardcover it was going to be a national bestseller, purchased by more than science fiction fans. Like *Dune*, it would be a genre buster, he said.

Dune itself had not made it onto very many bestseller lists, since its sales had been a gradual ground swell. Its sales since publication were impressive, and *Dune Messiah* had sold relatively well. But *Dune Messiah* hadn't been favorably received by the critics, and consensus held that its sales came on the coattails of *Dune*. Would *Children of Dune* be an even bigger critical disappointment than *Dune Messiah*?

There had never been a hardcover science fiction bestseller, so Putnam management proceeded with extreme caution. Suddenly the *Analog* results provided David Hartwell with the necessary ammunition.

Putnam increased the first printing to seventy-five thousand copies (instead of seventy-five hundred), more than any science fiction hardcover printing in history. Publication was scheduled for later in the year, after completion of the magazine serialization.

At Jan's encouragement, in the midst of the 1976 serialization, I began creative writing. I had in mind a satire about the workplace, based upon my experiences at insurance companies. When Dad discovered this he became very excited and wanted to help. Thereafter whenever we were in Port Townsend Dad would say to me, "Let's talk story." And on his desk or a coffee table I would spread my precious manuscript pages for his perusal.

When *Children of Dune* came out in hardback in 1976, it was an instant bestseller. True to the predictions of David Hartwell and the gut feelings of my father, it became the top-selling hardback in science fiction history up to that time . . . more than one hundred thousand copies in a few months.

"It's a runaway bestseller," Dad told me in a telephone conversation. He enjoyed this phrase, and I heard it often in ensuing years, for much larger print runs.

Children of Dune was nominated for the 1976 Hugo Award for the best novel of the year, as determined by science fiction fans, but lost to *The Forever War* by Joe Haldeman.

At the age of fifty-five, Dad went on his first book tour, and it was a big one—twenty-one cities in thirty days, including an appearance on *The Today Show* in New York City with fellow science fiction writers Frederik Pohl and Lester Del Rey. The Literary Guild made arrangements to offer all three books of the *Dune* trilogy in a boxed hardbound set.

When *Children* came out in paperback the following year, Berkley Books initially printed 750,000 copies. This wasn't half enough, and they went back to press. Six months after release of the paperback, Dad said paperback sales were approaching two million copies. By the end of 1977, *Dune* alone had sold more than five million copies in nine languages, while trilogy sales totaled nearly eight million copies.

At the vanguard of an explosive growth of sales in science fiction, Frank Herbert blazed the trail for other writers in his genre. After his phenomenal success, Isaac Asimov, Arthur C. Clarke, Robert Heinlein, Ray Bradbury, and other science fiction writers had national bestsellers.

In October 1976, Mom and Dad made their third trip to Europe, largely to see what was going on with Alejandro Jodorowsky's *Dune* movie project. They had been receiving secondhand information that the production was not going well. As was usual with trips my mother went on, she first underwent a battery of tests at Group Health Hospital and received her doctor's blessing.

In Paris, Dad and Mom met with representatives of the French film consortium holding the rights to film *Dune*, and received bad news. Jodorowsky's script was too complex, and would result in a mind-boggling fourteen-hour film. He had spent two million dollars getting the project under way, and it was becoming increasingly clear that the film could not be produced for anywhere near the $9,500,000 budget.

To make matters worse, Jodorowsky (a left-winger politically) and Salvador Dali (a right-winger) were refusing to work with one another, having had a vociferous argument in front of others involved in the project. Investors were getting wind of the production and personality problems, and funds were drying up.

When my parents returned to the United States they learned that Italian movie producer Dino De Laurentiis wanted to purchase the *Dune* film option from the French consortium. Dad had no objection, and as part of the new deal, he was retained as technical adviser and paid to write the screenplay. De Laurentiis had recently produced the twenty-five-million-dollar special-effects extravaganza *King Kong,* and my father quipped, "Anyone who can make a giant ape should have no trouble with sandworms."

Early in his career De Laurentiis had produced the critically acclaimed film, *Bitter Rice,* starring the Italian bombshell Silvana Mangano, whom he married. He also backed two classic films directed by Federico Fellini, *La Strada* and *Nights of Cabiria,* much loved by critics and movie-goers. Subsequently he became involved with big-budget spectaculars, such as *The Bible, War and Peace,* and a number of other films. While these and others were not well received by critics, they were money-makers.

Though he didn't say so publicly, Dad was concerned that the movie mogul might turn his book into a "worm that ate the desert" movie—a horror film about monster sandworms. Consequently he insisted upon being technical adviser and screenplay writer for the film. Still, he was pleased that De Laurentiis had the financial resources necessary for the complexities of his epic desert saga, which seemed to require a long movie. De Laurentiis promised a film to compare with *Gone With the Wind.*

With part of the movie advance, Dad purchased a new sailboat, which he christened "Ghanima," after Paul Muad'Dib's daughter. Ghanima also meant, according to the "Terminology of the Imperium" in *Dune,* "Something acquired in battle or single combat." My father's field of combat, for nearly four arduous decades, had been writing.

Through 1976 and 1977 I used every moment of spare time to work on two humor books. After mailing each manuscript out in search of a publisher, I had a tendency to worry about its fate. Dad counseled me not to do that, and that he always went right to work on another project immediately after mailing out a story.

My humor books didn't sell. The writing was hard work for me, did not come naturally. I wrote and rewrote and rewrote again. In the process, I began to understand what my father had been through in all the years he spent sequestered from this world, creating other worlds. I didn't forgive him, but I understood his life and motivations a little better. I gained new respect for what he had accomplished. This was an important step toward reconciliation with him. There would be others.

Around this time I had a conversation with Dad about my difficult childhood. It was a dry, crisp day late in the fall, and we were on a walk in the woods on the Olympic Peninsula, at the crest of a hill where the trees thinned out and a broad grassy field opened up before us. Dad was bundled up in a puffy down coat, bright orange in color, while I wore a nylon jacket, open at the front.

Craggy, snowy mountains and a ridge of clouds were visible beyond, profiled against a pale blue ice-beautiful sky. A cool breeze sent leaves scuttling across our path and rattled dry leaves that still clung to a nearby aspen.

We took shelter in a stand of cottonwood trees, where I told him my feelings and he listened. I told him it was wonderful what he had done for Mom to save her life and that I appreciated the interest he had recently taken in me. But I told him that Bruce and I had been in a lot of pain for a long time. I asked him rhetorically why he had used a lie detector on us when we were little. There were other questions as well, in a similar vein.

I had practiced what I would say to him a hundred times, running over the exact words as I drove to and from work, as I sat at my desk, and as I lay awake agonizing in the middle of the night. Now they didn't come out as I wanted them to; they needed editing, polishing, reworking. They were too harsh, too direct, too emotional. As I spoke I felt a shortness of breath from the outpouring, and I expected him to explode at any moment with an all-too-familiar burst of temper.

Without protestation he listened to my diatribe. His arms were folded across his chest, and he shifted on his tennis-shoed feet, uneasily. His eyes were filled with pain, and as I glared at him he looked beyond me or at the sky or at the ground, rarely meeting my gaze. When I finished, he looked up and said, in an unsteady voice, "They were difficult times. My work. I had to do my work." His lips quivered, and words caught in his throat, not making their way out. This man of many stories, this master of words, could not speak.

He gazed toward the mountains, and I saw tears welling in his blue eyes, rimming the lower lids. I took a deep breath, and after a long moment I hugged him.

He was shaking, and when he hugged me back he was like a clumsy bear, powerful but gentle. As we pulled apart he wiped his eyes quickly and wouldn't meet my gaze.

I felt like a parent who had scolded a naughty child, and said to him gently, "Dad, I love you. I'm sorry I had to say those things. But . . ." My voice trailed off.

Now he met my gaze, and his eyes flashed intensely. "I love you, Number One Son," he said. He smiled reassuringly, then started toward the path. "We'd better get back, Brian. Your mother is fixing pot roast and wild blackberry pie."

As we returned along a narrow path, pushing brush aside to get through, I knew he had apologized in his own way, and that I had forgiven him. I knew as well, but did not say to him, that my siblings and I had competed with other children for his attention—the stories that were the offspring of his creative mind. When we lived with him, the story-children had been easier to control than their human counterparts, and received more love than we did.

As weeks passed, my father and I went on fishing, oyster-digging, and crabbing trips together and enjoyed many fine feasts afterward. We began kidding one another and laughing a lot . . . the way people do when they like one another and the relationship is new and fresh. If I said, "How you Dune?" or something of equivalent silliness he would point off in the distance and say in a mock-gruff tone, "Go to your room!"

These were not welcome words to me when I was a child, not in the least, and he knew that. Now, in using them with a different tone and a wide smile on his bearded face and little laugh crinkles under his eyes, he was softening my harsh memories.

This is not to say that Frank Herbert became perfect. He remained an incessant nit-picker about the smallest and most insignificant of details, disagreeable and impatient too often with children, and a grouchy bear before dinner. He drove his car too fast, frightening the passengers, pedestrians, and other drivers. He didn't like to admit weakness or fault.

But I was crossing things off my list, replacing old bitterness with new, fond memories. For the first time in my life, I could say with pride that I had a loving, attentive father.

CHAPTER 23

✳ Caretakers of the Earth ✳

DURING ONE of our walks at Xanadu, my father told me that none of us own real estate. "We are only stewards," he said, "charged with taking care of the planet for our grandchildren." This philosophy became, in *Chapterhouse: Dune*, a tenet of the Bene Gesserit Sisterhood. Similarly, he wrote in his short story "Death of a City" (1973): "Only the species owned land, owned cities."

On his six-acre Port Townsend farm, Frank Herbert finally established his "Ecological Demonstration Project" (EDP) to explore the application of alternative energy sources, such as wind, solar and methane gas. From *Dune* to *New World or No World* to the *Green Brain*, he wrote frequently about the environment, presenting frightening images of world ecological systems in trouble. His famous EDP was a Frank Herbert story in and of itself, one in which he "learned by doing," as he liked to say—the best way of learning anything.

He started it largely because he wanted to practice what he had been preaching. For years he had been crisscrossing the United States talking about environmental issues, and for a long time he had wanted to get his hands dirty, performing experiments that would bring the discussion out of the realm of theory and into the realm of application.

When he began the EDP shortly before the Arab oil crisis of 1973–1974, he spoke of a five-year plan. In that time frame he hoped to prove it was possible to live in comfort while only drawing small amounts of resources from the public energy system. However, my mother's illness and other factors prevented him from meeting this deadline, one of the few times in the life of this journalist that he did not meet a deadline.

Xanadu was one of his visions for mankind's future, in which he was developing methods by which modern man might utilize the resources of the planet efficiently, with minimal harm to the environment. As he spoke, I thought of Leto II in *Children of Dune*, receiving the visions from his father, Paul Atreides, when the elder's time was past.

A great deal of misinformation about Frank Herbert's EDP has circulated in the science fiction and environmental communities—principally that my father intended to become entirely self-sufficient, producing one hundred percent of his food and energy needs. Dad said that was like the myth of the perpetual motion machine, a machine that could operate without external influence.

"We're all part of society," he said. "We can't stop interacting with it."

During his entire life, Frank Herbert shopped in food markets, and never disconnected his homes from public utility systems. Through experimentation, he just utilized these facilities less than most people . . . and espoused that others follow his lead.

Dad coined an interesting word for self-sufficiency, no matter the degree of application. He called it "technopeasantry," almost an oxymoron, and spoke of the particular adaptability of Americans to such systems. He always said we were a nation of "screwdriver mechanics," with a lot of people who didn't mind getting their hands dirty.

My parents' modified A-frame house featured vaulted ceilings and large windows, with large sheets of glass in each gable—all the way to the eaves. The glass was single pane—so it was not the most efficient home to heat. They had an oil furnace with a two-hundred-gallon tank, but were considering the installation of a forced-air wood-burning system.

Before doing that Dad wanted to try solar power, which he believed held great promise for solving his heating problems. With the assistance of an environmental housing expert he designed a passive solar collection system that he hoped would reduce his dependence upon heating oil by around fifty percent. The results were slightly better than that.

Even on fifty-degree days when the sun was partially or completely behind clouds, the system produced seventy-two-degree heat. In fact, heat even came out of the system in the middle of the night, despite the absence of a heat storage facility in the design. Dad was amused by this, and found it baffling.

The solar energy system, built on the south roof of the house just above the greenhouse, had simple panels made of plywood, large sheets of thermopane glass, and, remarkably, aluminum beer cans. It had Fiberglas insulation. To keep the cost down, thermopane seconds were used, which had small scratches on them. A control panel with a cedar cover was installed on one wall of the living room.

For solar heat collectors, a few inches behind the thermopane, they set up banks of aluminum beer cans cut in half horizontally with a power saw and attached so that their cupped insides faced the sun. The solar collector system comprised an area of one hundred forty-five square feet, set in six panels. In one of the panels, the cans were painted entirely flat black, with high-temperature paint. In another panel, the cans were left unpainted, in a plain aluminum color. And in the remaining four panels, the cans were only painted black on their interior bottoms, leaving the rest in their natural aluminum reflective state.

Through experimentation Dad found that the completely black cans absorbed slightly more infrared heat, making them more desirable for this application. It was a convection heat redistribution system, in which he used the furnace fan to circulate the air into the solar collectors and back into the house.

He used approximately one thousand, seven hundred and fifty aluminum beer cans, most of which were purchased from a recycling center. Still, he liked to imply other sources, quipping, "I received a lot of help from my friends putting the system together."

While Dad got this passive-solar system going, he still believed solar technology was too expensive for the average household. He wanted to develop a low-cost alternative energy system for homeowners, something that could be sold in Sears or Wards catalogs for five hundred dollars or less. Until the prices for solar collection technology came down, he thought wind power might be the best answer to produce electricity, which would in turn be converted to heat.

Dad found that buildings used more energy for heating when the wind blew because of the wind-chill factor, and came up with an ingenious solution. If a building had a windmill for generating electricity, it could offset the cooling effect of the wind, flattening out the heat-loss curve by turning a generator and warming a house electrically whenever the wind blew. The harder the wind blew, the more it would heat.

He built a sturdy concrete-walled shop on the hill above his house, intending to construct a second-level conference center with guest bunks sometime in the future. In this scenario he had dreams of teaching writing classes and of conducting courses on environmental issues for corporate and political leaders. All electrical and heating needs for the conference center would be provided by on-site systems. Above the conference center there would be, someday, a thirty-foot concrete tower with a windmill on top. In studying wind technology, he found there had been very few advances since the invention of the horizontal-axis Dutch windmill in the sixteenth century. He envisioned developing something that focused wind power and employed modern aerodynamic principles.

Working with an architect he designed and patented a cylindrical, vertical-axis windmill with a horn on top that focused and concentrated the wind. Air passing through the horn spun a vertical shaft by pushing vanes on it, and this in turn activated an automobile alternator, producing AC electricity. The device had no gears or belts, and was very simple, with relatively few parts.

Dad had a four-foot-high, four-foot-diameter prototype built, which was mounted on a truck chassis and connected to a calibrated speedometer for testing. The unit, self-propelled and drivable on public roadways, enabled them to estimate that a ten-inch-tall unit having a three-foot diameter could produce one horsepower in a fifty-mile-per-hour wind.

Frank Herbert also developed a rather unusual methane gas generating system by slitting a large truck-tire inner tube, filling it with chicken and duck manure and straw, and then patching the tube. A piece of flexible rubber tubing was attached to the tube at the unsealed valve stem, with a spigot on the other end of the tubing. As the manure and straw decomposed, it produced pressurized methane gas, which Dad used to singe the feathers off chickens and ducks he had slaughtered. He also connected the apparatus to a gas heater, and heated the poultry house.*

He believed that methane had potential large-scale applications for cities, which could convert sewage into methane gas for the operation of city vehicles, including buses. The byproduct would be fertilizer, useful in gardens and farms. On his own farm, my father shoveled poultry manure into buckets and spread it on the vegetable gardens.

Frank Herbert always had plans to improve his solar, wind and methane systems, but the development, maintenance and promotion of his ecological experiments were taking too much of his valuable time. He decided to reorder his priorities, and as the 1970s drew to a close his Ecological Demonstration Project took a back burner. There were novels to write, book tours, and above all my mother's health, which required constant monitoring.

---

*Due to the danger of methane explosion, the reader should not attempt to replicate this system.

CHAPTER 24

✳ Miracles ✳

IN 1977, my father's novel *The Dosadi Experiment* was published in hardcover by Putnam, after its serialization in *Galaxy* (May through August issues). Like the earlier novel *Whipping Star* and a number of earlier short stories, *Dosadi* featured Jorj X. McKie and the Bureau of Sabotage. *Dosadi* sold well, and when Berkley released the paperback the following year it became a national bestseller, one of their top-selling science fiction titles of all time.

That year, Babe passed away of a stroke while visiting her favorite sister Peggy Rowntree in Tacoma. She was seventy-six. Her services were held at a Catholic church in Tacoma, an old building downtown. As the priest spoke, I sat behind Mom and Dad, and I recall seeing his head shaking back and forth constantly, an involuntary condition whenever he was very tired or feeling too much stress.

Though my father was not a formally religious man, he could, like my mother, be spiritual at times. In the limousine as we rode to the cemetery, he said, "There is a place for ceremony." He also said drivers kept their vehicle lights on in a funeral procession to light the darkness for the one who had passed on.

George Lucas's hit movie *Star Wars* came out the same year. The film was shocking to me, for all the similarities between it and my father's book, *Dune*. Both featured an evil galactic empire, a desolate desert planet, hooded natives, strong religious elements, and a messianic hero with an aged mentor. *Star Wars'* Princess Leia had a name with a haunting similarity to *Dune's* Lady Alia of the noble house Atreides. The movie also had spice mines and a Dune Sea.

I phoned my father and said, "You'd better see it. The similarities are unbelievable."

When Dad saw the movie, he picked out sixteen points of what he called "absolute identity" between his book and the movie, enough to make him livid. He thought he saw the ideas of other science fiction writers on the screen as well, including those of Isaac Asimov, Larry Niven, Ted Sturgeon, Barry Malzberg, and Jerry Pournelle.

Still, Frank Herbert tried to be upbeat. He and the other science fiction writers who thought they saw their work in Lucas's movie formed a loose organization that my father called, with his tongue firmly placed in his cheek, the We're Too Big to Sue George Lucas Society. Through humor, Dad tried to mask the pain.

One of his biggest concerns: *Star Wars* made the filming of *Dune* an even bigger challenge than before, even more insurmountable, because of the important concepts that had now been pre-empted on the screen. Not the least of these was the young hero of *Star Wars*, Luke Skywalker, who, like Paul Atreides of *Dune* had messianic qualities, with a link to a mystical religious force.

That year my sister Penny and brother Bruce were visiting for the Thanksgiving holiday, staying in Port Townsend. During his visit, Bruce confided to me for the first time that he was gay, and said one of the reasons he felt he had taken this course was because of the terrible example his own father had been for him. "After seeing how Dad treated children," Bruce said, "I didn't want to have any." He asked me not to discuss it with Mom or Dad yet, since he wasn't sure how he wanted to break it to them.

I thought of, but did not comment on, Mom's desire for a boy grandchild to carry on the Herbert family name. I didn't know anything about the gay community, didn't know what to say to him. I told him I loved him anyway, that his sexual preference would never change how I felt for him. But I felt awkward discussing the subject. Words did not come easily.

Bruce was a studious young eccentric, a genius in electronics who built and maintained sound systems and other equipment for San Francisco rock-and-roll groups and for celebrities, such as the actor Stuart Whitman. My brother always carried little pen-shaped television adjustment tools in his shirt pocket, which he used to keep all sets in the Herbert family operating at their optimum. He made a steady stream of unlucky business decisions and investments, however, and seemed unable to keep his financial house in order.*

In June 1978, Dad interrupted his writing schedule to travel to Metz, France, with Mom, where he was guest of honor at an immense science fiction convention. My mother kept one of her rare journals on this trip.

That year the *Dune* movie project had fallen apart for the third time. Producer Dino De Laurentiis decided Dad's screenplay was unworkable, and based upon further research thought the book might be too complicated to ever be reproduced on film. He did this despite feeling drawn to *Dune*, and thinking that it might be a big hit.

Upon hearing that my father would be in Europe, Dino De Laurentiis asked Dad if he could lend a hand with the screenplay for a science fiction movie that was being filmed in England and was in trouble, his thirty-five-million-dollar production of *Flash Gordon*. Dad agreed to help, and spent a month in London working on the project. To do the patch-up job, Dad purchased an ultra-lightweight manual typewriter, much lighter and more compact than his old Olympia portable. In the hotel suite he shared with Mom at the Grosvenor House on Park Lane, he set the typewriter keys in motion. Dad and De Laurentiis enjoyed working with one another, and the popular movie that resulted was given high marks by a number of critics.

My parents took a side trip by air shuttle to Edinburgh, Scotland, the country of my mother's paternal ancestry. They took a drive along the coast, and like characters in *Wuthering Heights*, one of my mother's favorite novels, they had a romantic walk across the heather-covered moors and climbed a hill for a magnificent view of a white sand beach.

---

*But Bruce was brilliant. In the 1960s, he invented the "karaoke" music system. Without naming it or attempting to exploit it commercially, he simply set it up for personal use in his own household.

One day in Edinburgh they opted to ride a double-decker city bus. They sat on the upper deck at the rear, on a wide seat with other people. A man next to my father pulled out a pack of cigarettes and a lighter, and as he was lighting up inquired of those around him, "Does anyone mind if I smoke?"

He had the cigarette lit before the question was completed.

In a tense voice, Dad told him to put it out. Nervously, the man dropped the lighted cigarette on the floor and crushed it out under his shoe. Ever since Mom's brush with death, Dad had become fanatical against anyone smoking in his or my mother's presence.

Returning from Europe, Dad found himself under pressure to complete a number of projects at once. One day he showed up at the door of his friend Bill Ransom and inquired, "Can you write like me?" He needed help with a short story for a project inspired by Harlan Ellison called *Medea: Harlan's World*. My father's story was slated for publication in *Analog* prior to the Ellison collection. Bill, a Pulitzer Prize nominee for poetry three years before, said he would try to help. He proceeded to write the first draft of the story, which they entitled "Songs of a Sentient Flute." Dad edited the manuscript and typed the final draft, making additional changes as he did so.

Dad was also being pressed by Putnam to come up with a new science fiction novel, so he and Bill brainstormed and came up with a way of using the same concept for the short story and for the novel. They laid out "Songs of a Sentient Flute" with the idea of expanding it into a novel entitled *The Jesus Incident*, which would be a sequel to *Destination: Void*.

So, on the same day that they mailed "Songs of a Sentient Flute" to *Analog,* they also sent it to their agent Lurton Blassingame, in the form of a book proposal for *The Jesus Incident*. Putnam offered a substantial contract to publish the novel in hardcover, and Dad and Bill set to work on it.

Bill, who had many shared interests with my father, was only a couple of years older than I was. He had an intelligent, oval face and long black hair combed straight back. In the novel, he and my father alternated chapters, using a "leapfrogging" technique, after which they edited one another's work. Their styles meshed so closely that even my mother, who knew her husband's style better than anyone, could not identify the writer of particular sections. Despite strong egos the men did not clash, because of the high regard they held for one another. Mom often heard them laughing uproariously in the loft study as one or the other came up with a *bon mot* for the developing tale.

To a great extent the collaboration was a *quid pro quo*. Frank Herbert received assistance with a short story and a novel from an energetic, talented young writer, and in return Bill Ransom was given a rare opportunity to learn at the elbow of a master. Bill told me, "The key thing that I wanted to learn from Frank was how to maintain a story for a novel length, because working in poetry I'd always been focused on making things smaller." Bill also felt he needed to learn a lot more about literary description, which was one of Dad's strengths. One day upon looking at a passage written by his young collaborator, my father told him to rewrite it with more sensory detail. "Look, Bill," he said, "we need to smell this guy, right in the armpits."

Bill worked hard and learned quickly, but when *The Jesus Incident* was nearly complete a major crisis occurred. Ellison learned they were using the same planet and characters as in "Songs of a Sentient Flute," and he got his book publisher (Phantasia Press) and the publisher of *Analog* involved. They told Dad and Bill to cease and desist, that they were using material they didn't own. Dad made an emergency trip to New York City, where he met with his agent and the publishers involved. When he returned to Port Townsend, he was extremely upset and nervous. "We can't use the planet, the characters or any of that," he told Bill. "Harlan Ellison owns the rights to them."

Thereafter they rewrote *The Jesus Incident*, changing the names of characters, locales, and other details. The racial background of one character was altered, but aside from that the basic characterizations were not changed. They rewrote problematical passages and tried to make the plot that they had already written fit. It took two weeks of nonstop rewriting, and they kept a professional typist working into the wee hours. The collaboration had ceased to be fun, and instead of heady, joking sessions, long periods went by without laughter. When at last they finished, little gaps were apparent in the story, and they weren't particularly happy with it, especially with the way they had to end it. Nonetheless the book was accepted for publication, and sales were brisk.

While working with my father, Bill Ransom had an opportunity to watch the interaction between my parents over an extended period of time. They were physically passionate toward one another, he said, and often took breaks alone during the day. To Bill's amusement they were open about the reason for this, and laughed about it. He enjoyed teasing them on the subject.

Bill also observed my parents as a writing team, in which Beverly, for a long time Frank's reader, became the reader for the product of the Herbert-Ransom collaboration. "That was where she really shined," Bill said, adding that her comments contained detailed reasons and suggestions, not just general statements. He saw the mountains of other work she did as well, including the financial management that she performed and the handling of voluminous correspondence that came in from fans, agents, publishers, and other writers. He noticed, too, how she screened calls and inquiries and kept people away from Dad, so that he could create, and how she coordinated all interviews and public appearances.

In a very real sense I was struggling to know my father, just as he was struggling to know me. We were trying to make up for lost time. We went on long walks together and I helped him around the farm, feeding poultry, tending to plantings, working in the shop. It had been a long and difficult road to this point in my father's life—a road from tattered rental houses and unpaid bills to worldwide fame.

In the Old Testament it was said that the skin of Moses "shone" when he came down from Mt. Sinai with the Ten Commandments. This phenomenon has been noticed as well about successful people at the heights of their careers. They glow. And so it was with my father at the pinnacle of his success.

Through it all, I still had dimensions of this man to discover. There were nooks and crannies in his marvelous mind and in his emotional makeup that I didn't know existed. He was not as strong as I had always imagined. Dad was more vulnerable to comments from me than I thought he would be.

I told him I had been reading his books, and that I thought *Dune* was more smoothly written, more polished, than *The Dragon in the Sea*, a book written a decade before *Dune*. I was talking about style, having noticed a certain choppiness in the earlier work when it was laid down beside the later one, with its beautiful, poetic prose. He was obviously hurt at my remark, for he said, simply, "*Dragon* is one of my favorite stories." Of course he would feel this way, for it had been his first book sale. And it was a fine book, a well-told story.

Another time we were outside on the patio, preparing the fire pit for a pig we were going to roast. It was a cool day, and he wore a sheepskin vest to cut the chill. As I looked at my bearded father in his vest I was struck with the similarities between him and Ernest Hemingway. Beyond beards and sheepskin vests, both were great writers and outdoorsmen. Both had more than a little machismo. I kidded Dad about his vest, asking him if he was "playing Hemingway." He seemed displeased by the observation, and didn't laugh.

Rather awkwardly, rather late, I was learning how not to hurt my father's feelings. I also received advice from my mother, who was pleased with the improving relationship. "It's not too late for you to be close," she told me.

In 1978, Berkley published a trade paperback, *The Illustrated Dune*, with a dozen illustrations by John Schoenherr, the artist who had done such a wonderful job on *Dune* subjects. A *Dune* calendar was printed with the same artwork.

Dad had intended to end the *Dune* series with *Children of Dune*, which he saw as the completion of a cycle. But the characters and settings he had created would not die. His trilogy became so popular that requests for more *Dune* books poured in from fans, and all the editors involved, domestic and foreign, were asking for more as well. In considering the prospect of a fourth book, it occurred to Frank Herbert that the universe of Dune was a canvas and that he might resume the series on the planet Dune three thousand five hundred years later. This would require a new set of characters, but they would be linked genetically with people in the past. . . .

He began reviewing the first three books in the series, making notes as thoughts occurred to him. New file folders sprang up around him like mushrooms, and he started writing more about a most unusual character from *Children of Dune*, Leto II, a noble human of the Atreides family who was evolving into a sandworm . . .

That year I began collecting wine labels from the dinners with my parents, soaking labels off bottles at home and drying them out. On the backs of the labels, I made brief notations of the events in the family—a few highlights. When we ate at my parents' home, we invariably had Dad's special Caesar salad dressing, which he prepared with great care and divided among the hungry diners. It was so good that no matter how much he prepared there never seemed to be enough.

After many years of being dependent upon Dad and taxis for transportation, Mom obtained a driver's license and her own car—a sporty new light green BMW. At the age of fifty-one. She loved the independence it gave her, but Dad wasn't nearly as enthusiastic. He worried about her constantly and missed her terribly whenever she was away.

When Jan's father, Ray Blanquie, died that year, my mother came from Port Townsend to drive Jan to the airport for a flight to the funeral in California. Entering our kitchen, Mom found Jan at the table going through photographs of her father.

"Oh no," Mom said, "don't look at those." Gently, she put the pictures away.

At the airport, Mom took Jan to a restaurant, where they shared a meal. Mom said not to worry about anything on this end, that she would stay with me and the kids.

Jan was looking out on the tarmac, thinking of her father, and my mother remarked gently, "When you lose somebody, you have to gather your skirts and go on."

In February 1979, Dino De Laurentiis made his second deal with my father for the rights to film *Dune*, after having let the first option lapse. Dad said it was the second-highest price ever paid for the screen rights to a book, behind only the amount paid to Peter Benchley for *The Deep*. Again, Dad was retained to write the screenplay.

That month a ferocious storm with hundred-mile-per-hour winds hit the Hood Canal Floating Bridge, causing half of it to sink. Because of this we had to ride substitute ferries, and it took us at least three-and-a-half to four hours to get to Port Townsend, almost twice as long as previously. A new bridge was in the planning stages, but would take time to complete.

Shortly after the bridge went down, my parents caught a flight to New York City, where they met with some of the top figures in the New York publishing world. They were excited to hear that Dad was working on a fourth book in the *Dune* series, a book he thought he would name *Sandworm of Dune*. Then my parents flew to Paris and afterward to London, where they met with Dino De Laurentiis to discuss the *Dune* movie production.

Upon returning from Europe, Mom prepared a Mexican dinner for us, served with a Chateau Beychevelle red Bordeaux wine. They had a new *Dune* painting on the wall, recently purchased from the artist John Schoenherr. Now they owned ten of these paintings and were negotiating to purchase three more.

In my mother's post-cancer treatment program she was continuing to swim laps of the pool and was taking half-mile walks two or three times a week. She was trying to lose weight so that her heart, damaged by radiation treatments, would not have to work so hard. For some time, however, Mom had been suffering in the cold, damp climate of the Pacific Northwest. She had been talking with Dad about finding a second home in a warmer climate where they could spend the winters. With the millions of dollars received from the movie (if it met revenue projections) Dad hoped to buy that second home for her.

He was receiving huge book royalties every April and October for past book sales, and higher advances for each book he wrote. But too frequently he received an advance on a book and then spent it before actually completing the writing. Despite my mother's counseling, Dad was always spending money impulsively, putting them behind in their cash flow. One of the expense outlays involved a forty-four-foot sailboat, which Dad named "Caladan," after the planet in the *Dune* universe where Paul Muad'Dib was born. The *Ghanima,* his smaller sailboat, was sold.

Dad was also putting money into the design and construction of a new 10.5-million-byte computer system, tailored to his needs by a young Port Townsend computer expert, Max Barnard. Dad and Max were talking about patenting the system and writing a computer book together.

Around this time I was feeling pretty discouraged about my own writing. I'd written two humor books and a novel, none of which were accepted by publishers. I was considering writing short stories, but one day I mentioned to Dad that I had a number of "funny files" that might be worked into humor books. One was a collection of classic comeback lines from history, and the other was a folder full of amusing insurance claims. Dad, with his interest in history, suggested that I proceed with the comeback lines book. I did so.

I was also beginning to keep a full-fledged journal. Previously, my documentation of family events had involved only sketchy notations made on the backs of wine labels. Now I began asking my mother about genealogical matters, which I combined with current events and personal observations. As these notes accumulated I had too much information to fit on the backs of small pieces of paper.

My creative writing was not selling, but I began to notice an interesting phenomenon. Where once I had been the life of the party, the drunkest, funniest one present, I wasn't drinking much at all anymore. The more I wrote, especially in my journal, the less I drank—and the less I blamed my father for any of the woes of my life.

With the assistance of journal entries, I was coming to the realization that no matter our backgrounds, no matter the troubles we endure, each of us has to grow up one day, accepting responsibility for our own lives, not blaming others. When we attempt to transfer fault to others it frequently amounts to making excuses for our failures, thus creating the likelihood of future failures. Thus if we do not succeed, we can always say it wasn't our fault.

✳   ✳   ✳

That fall my father and I regularly sailed the *Caladan* on the cold blue waters of Port Townsend Bay. Frequently we brought along my daughters, eleven-year-old Julie and seven-year-old Kim. With his competitive nature, Dad often raced other boats, and usually won. After sailing, we would go to nearby wooded areas in search of chanterelle mushrooms. For our evening meal, Mom would brown the mushrooms in butter with a dash of nutmeg and would serve them with pork roast or other dishes.

297

Dad was completing the *Dune* screenplay, and liked to read it to us in the evenings. Jan and I would sit in deep leather armchairs by a glass-fronted bookcase containing copies of his books, while he sat on a black leather couch, leaning forward over script pages spread across a glass coffee table. Mom sat in her favorite orange naugahyde chair nearby, clicking her knitting needles as she listened to him. Occasionally she would make comments or offer suggestions.

On Sunday mornings, Mom prepared sumptuous breakfasts of blueberry pancakes for us. They were served with real Vermont maple syrup, one of many items my parents purchased by mail order.

Located as they were in a rather remote area, they had mail order catalogs from all over the world, and were constantly ordering things—kitchen items, seeds, gourmet foods, clothing, and much more. They kept the catalogs stacked on a bookshelf and on the bottom shelf of a table—in a reading area just off the kitchen. Mom enjoyed shopping by mail, but Dad was a fanatic about it, to the extent that he would never throw away old catalogs out of for fear he might need them one day. The only time Mom could ever throw away catalogs was when Dad wasn't around.

Some weeks before, I had mailed a manuscript about comeback lines to Price/Stern/Sloan, a publisher in Los Angeles. I didn't know how they would feel about it, but I wasn't sitting around waiting for an answer. My attentions were focused on a new science fiction novel, which I entitled *Sidney's Comet*. It was about a society of overindulgence, a new angle on a previous unpublished novel I had written. In the new version I was postulating a world that had no more room for garbage, nuclear wastes or even the burial of human bodies. I'd been reading about a new technology of electromagnetic mass drivers, through which capsules of material might be launched from a planet into space. A wild scenario was forming in my mind, as I envisioned all the garbage coming back at earth like an avenging angel, in a fiery garbage comet that threatened to wipe out the planet.

In October, Chuck Gates of Price/Stern/Sloan called to say he wanted to publish my humor manuscript under the title *Classic Comebacks*. It was my first book sale! Dad told me he would look over the contract when it came in. We made arrangements to celebrate my book sale and his fifty-ninth birthday at the same time.

He went on to say that we had other reasons for celebration. Mom had received a checkup which produced good news. Through her exercise program and diet she had lost ten pounds, while substantially increasing her heart and lung functions. They still weren't what they had been before the onset of cancer and never would be, but Mom had survived the disease for more than five years, defying odds that were 95 percent against her.

"She's a miracle cure," Dad said.

"Thank God!" I said.

Dad said he always asked doctors for their first names, and afterward he refused to refer to them as "doctor," using the first name instead. It prevented them from being condescending, he thought, and was a psychological method of making the doctors reveal medical details they might not otherwise tell a patient.

"Call your doctor Jim," my father said. He thought this might be a good title for something, and I agreed it did have a certain ring to it.

They left for Europe a week later. In London, they met Dino De Laurentiis and the new *Dune* director, Ridley Scott, whose suspense-filled science fiction/horror movie, *Alien,* had recently been released. Scott said he liked eight of the scenes from Dad's screenplay, and said that a number of new scenes would be needed.

My parents returned to Port Townsend in mid-November. At long last, Dad was working nonstop on *Sandworm of Dune,* his working title for the long-awaited fourth book in the series. He was in an intense creative phase where he wouldn't answer letters with the exception of the most important until the project was complete.

CHAPTER
25

✳ Old Dreams, New Dreams ✳

ON THE first Saturday in 1980 in the icy month of January, Jan and I delivered a case of Beaujolais Nouveau wine to Dad, having picked it up for him at a wine shop in Seattle.

At dinner that evening, Dad said that he and Mom had decided to buy a vacation cottage in Hawaii to winter there, on one of the small outer islands along the sixteen-hundred-mile chain. "Something simple on the water," he said. "Bev can't stand the cold here in the winter."

My mother's preference for warm weather had been mentioned before, especially since losing weight and the insulation of her fatty tissue. She kept saying she felt much better when the weather was warm. I was worried about the availability of medical services for her in remote regions, but said nothing of this since the subject of her health was so uncomfortable to me. And inside I felt a gnawing terror of a different nature, a feeling I'd experienced on occasion that forces were at work trying to make me fly, against my will. I hadn't flown in more than ten years. Now it was a deep-seated fear ingrained in my psyche, and my parents were talking about living at least part of each year on a remote Pacific island. What if they decided to live there year-round?

I asked if all the islands had electricity so that Dad could operate his electric typewriter and the custom computer he was having built, or if he intended to go back to using a small manual typewriter. He wasn't certain about the availability of electricity, but went on to talk about setting up solar panels and windmills to generate power, and maybe even a simple system of extracting hydrogen from sea water.

It didn't sound very simple to me.

On Monday, January 14, 1980, Jan and I met my parents at Hugo's Rotisserie, a fine Seattle restaurant in the Hyatt House Hotel near SeaTac Airport. Both of them looked elegant and manicured—Mom in a beautiful new green blouse (one of her best colors, according to a color consultant) and Dad with his salt-and-pepper beard freshly trimmed.

They were scheduled to fly to Hawaii the next morning to spend two weeks looking for property. Terrible storms had been ravaging the islands the past week, and Dad quipped, "This is always the best time to look at a piece of property—when it's at its worst."

He had selected a rather unusual title for the computer book he was writing with Max Barnard, an idea that was indicative of my father's sense of humor: *Without Me You're Nothing*. This was Frank Herbert's philosophical comment about the secondary importance of the computer in relation to the human, and brought to mind the Butlerian Jihad of *Dune* that opposed computers and certain other thinking machines, under the commandment, "Thou shalt not make a machine in the likeness of a human mind."

The Hawaii-bound travelers seemed a little nervous. At the salad bar, Dad was passing out plates to all of us in line, and I guess he lost count, because he tried to hand one to a stranger. Later he knocked over my Creme de Menthe. Mom tried to rest her arms on a chair that had no armrests.

They returned in two weeks. On the first Sunday in February, Dad delivered a speech at Tacoma Community College. He spoke to a packed auditorium about ecology and a wide variety of subjects, and told the audience about my first book sale. He was mobbed afterward by people wanting to talk with him. In a reversal of the usual roles they played, Mom drove him to Tacoma in her BMW.

That evening my parents told us they had made a $425,000 offer on a piece of unimproved Maui waterfront—five acres in the beautiful, remote area of Hana. This was a region of cattle ranches and tropical jungle, separated from the more populated side of Maui by a fifty-mile long chuckhole-infested stretch of the notorious Hana Highway, with more than six hundred turns! Most of the locals did not want the road improved, to keep developers and tourists out. The narrow route ran along cliff faces with sheer drop-offs to the ocean hundreds of feet below, crossing more than fifty bridges and many waterfalls.

The property owner had been asking for $550,000, but the piece had been on the market a while and the realtor thought they were making a good offer.

"I always dicker," Dad said, a carryover from the times we lived in Mexico in the 1950s. He went on to say that the property was too nice for a simple cottage. They had decided to live in Hawaii full-time and sell their Port Townsend home.

The words I hadn't wanted to hear.

But the place sounded incredible. As we sipped my mother's favorite Puligny-Montrachet wine, we talked about selling our Mercer Island home and moving to Hawaii ourselves, and about the education available there for Julie and Kim. Maybe Bruce and Penny and the rest of the family could move there, too. Jan and Mom were ready to go even before the property deal closed!

Dad said they had consulted a number of doctors, and with the impairment of Mom's lung capacity from radiation treatment they were sure that a tropical climate would be more beneficial to her than the colder Northwest weather.

"My lungs feel clear when it's warm," she said.

I showed Dad my new book contract on *Classic Comebacks*. He suggested several changes, including the addition of a clause stipulating Price/Stern/Sloan had to publish the book no later than October 31, 1981. Otherwise, he said, they could just hold on to the rights and delay publication indefinitely. He also had me cross off a sentence that enabled the publisher to copyright the book in their name, requiring instead that they copyright in my name. That gave me more control, he explained, and made it easier for me to go to a different publisher in the future if the book went out of print. They weren't paying an advance, and I would receive royalties based upon actual sales. But Dad said the contract wasn't bad for a first book.

Two weeks after our dinner my parents announced that they had reached agreement to purchase the Hawaii land for $500,000, a sub-stantial sum for that year and for the extremely remote location of the property. At my house, Dad unrolled a set of plans for the new house that they wanted to build.

"I researched old records," Mom said, "and found a map showing our property. It's five miles from Hana town, in an area that used to be called 'Kawaloa.' That means 'a nice long time' in Hawaiian. Isn't that nice? I think we'll spend a nice long time there. It's a magical place, unlike anything I've ever seen!"

I nodded, and thought how mysterious it all sounded. I studied the house plans, and a grand production it was, with a huge sunken living room and custom-made, curved couches forming a conversation ring around a round coffee table—all looking out on the sea and the "Big Island" of Hawaii, with the volcano Mauna Kea visible. There would be a large writing wing for my father, with an extensive library adjacent, a wine cellar and a darkroom. A Japanese motif would be evident throughout, with shoji screens and artwork. Electricity would be gen-erated with rooftop solar panels and a separate windmill structure.

Botanical gardens would surround the home, with covered decks, a swimming pool, coconut and lauhala trees, stone walkways, lava walls, Polynesian sculptures and a carp pond with a fountain. One area would be designated as a vegetable garden, and there would be a potting shed.

Kawaloa was not only a perfect spot for Mom, he said, but an ideal place for him to hide from the legions of people clamoring to reach him. He'd gone to Port Townsend in 1973 for much the same reason, with fame pursuing him. But now he was far more famous—and as before, too many people knew where he lived. He had millions of fans, and many of them had placed him on a godlike pedestal, a myth-status that troubled my father.

They said they were listing the Port Townsend house for sale soon. I felt energy and excitement around them, from the changes they were setting in motion. It was romantic, charming, and heartwarming, with joy and sadness intermingled. They were off on a South Seas adventure such as my father might have written, or perhaps my mother, given the inclination.

303

In large part, of course, he was repaying Mom for the sacrifices she had made for him when she gave up her own promising career as a creative writer in order to work and support him while he wrote. Despite this and their excitement, I was deeply troubled. With my fear of flying, their move to an island in the Pacific would effectively isolate them from me. Unfortunately this was occurring not long after I had become close to my complex, enigmatic father—after I had begun to understand him better.

In Port Townsend in early March 1980, Mom and Dad showed us revised plans of their Hawaii dream house, and color slides Dad had taken of the land and the nearby Hawaiian scenery. The property was situated at the edge of a lush tropical jungle, and there were breathtaking vistas of aquamarine water, framed in black lava along the island shores.

Many Hollywood personalities owned property at Hana, including Carol Burnett, Richard Pryor, Jim Nabors, George Harrison and Bill Dana ("Jose Jimenez"). Hana was also the secluded paradise where aviator Charles Lindbergh chose to spend the last days of his life, when he knew he was dying. Lindbergh, a man obsessed with privacy since the tragic kidnapping and murder of his baby son, owned a beautiful, isolated piece of property several miles past my parents' place, toward Kaupo Gap. During his final days, he needed to stay close to medical personnel, and rented a small house at Pu'uiki between Hana town and Kawaloa. There he worked on his memoirs.

So my father was not the first famous person to seek refuge from fame in the Hana area. But this, of course, was not his primary purpose in going there.

Later that month, Dad opened a bottle of 1973 Piper Heidsieck champagne with us and toasted Victor Temkin, the Berkley Publishing Company president who had been instrumental in paying Dad a huge advance for "Dune 4," *Sandworm of Dune*. Dad said it was a package deal with a future non-*Dune* science fiction book, and said he had to work fast. "Victor's nervous about paying all that money up front."

During our second bottle of champagne, a Taittinger, I told him *Sandworm of Dune* sounded "Ozzie," and he said he'd been told by publishers and editors that he had an Oz situation in hand, where the reading public was clamoring for the next book before it was written. He had plans for even more *Dune* novels in the works. This book sale made it possible for them to begin construction on the Hawaii house without first selling the Port Townsend place.

By the spring of 1980, construction of a caretaker's house at Kawaloa was underway on the upper side of the property, which sloped down from the Hana Highway toward the sea. This was Phase I. Under the next phase to be begun later that year they would live in the caretaker's house while the main house was built a little lower on the land, but still well away from the water.

Each time we got together with my parents I recorded the events of our lives in my journal, and committed to paper a plethora of details they were relating to me about their early years together, their childhoods and our ancestors. This chronicle was becoming a growing, living force, demanding my undivided attention. I became obsessed with it, and before retiring to bed in the evening, I would scribble rough notes on odd sheets of paper, for fleshing out when I had the time. The sooner I got it all written down the better, I realized, when memories were fresh.

As I lay in bed trying to fall asleep, the events of the day kept flowing through my mind, scrabbling to remain. I found myself unable to drift off until I had converted them to detailed notes. In a sense, I was becoming a prisoner of my journal, and in ensuing days when I was finally able to convert my notes to narrative I felt wrung out. Oftentimes this was as much from the emotion of the events as from the writing chore. But I was driven to keep up, fascinated by what I was learning about the esoteric world in which my parents lived, a world I shared at times and heard stories about at other times.

I was intrigued by something else as well, by the insights my journal gave me to my inner being. It helped me to understand myself as I never had before. It became a tool for relieving stress and depression, for better analyzing situations, for removing the emotional component from decision-making and replacing it with reason. Written words, if carefully laid down, represented the civilized ideal of reason. They were instruments of analytical, organized thought.

I told my journal my innermost secrets. It became a living entity, a comforting presence in times of need, someone to talk to who wouldn't laugh at me and wouldn't tell others what a fool I was. My journal did not begin at the beginning; it grew from the inside-out. I had a love-hate relationship with it.

On the morning of Sunday, March 2, 1980, I saw Mom in a long white robe, standing in the living room by the sliding glass doors on the west side of the house, gazing out at the duck pond. Sunlight glinted off the water, and she said, "It's beautiful here. I'm going to miss it."

In the middle of April, Mom and Dad made a quick four-day trip to Hawaii to check the progress of construction on the caretaker's house. They stayed in the elegant Hotel Hana Maui, and met my brother, Bruce, there.

Around that time, I sold a second humor book to Chuck Gates at Price/Stern/Sloan, a collection of authentic and bizarre insurance claims entitled *Incredible Insurance Claims*. The book would be published in late 1981 or early 1982, while my other book, *Classic Comebacks*, would be published in the spring of 1981.

On April 26, 1980, a Saturday, we arrived in Port Townsend at 7: 15 P.M. Dad barbecued filet mignon in the kamado Japanese cooker and made an exquisite Caesar salad—served with a Clos Duval Cabernet Sauvignon. We celebrated my second book sale. They said they traded Mom's BMW (and a Volkswagen that we had given to them) for a small 1980 Mercedes coupe, which they were going to ship to Hawaii.

Mom spoke again of her hopes for a boy Herbert baby to carry on the family name, and of her long-standing desire for Bruce to get married. She was losing hope that he ever would, and commented, "I'm afraid he's running with the boys from San Francisco." This was a suspicion only and a reference to the gay community there, one of the most politically active in the world. I said nothing.

Shortly after the eruption of Mt. St. Helens in May 1980, we spent the weekend with my parents. At the conclusion of a Friday evening dinner, Dad said to me, "Let's talk story." Dutifully I followed him up to his writing loft, carrying my *Sidney's Comet* manuscript in a gray-and-white box under my arm. He reviewed my work, which I hoped was now complete at almost 250 typed pages. He read and scanned rapidly, pausing occasionally to speak about certain sections, making numerous suggestions.

As he spoke, I scribbled notes on sheets of newsprint. Since Dad worked in the newspaper business during many of the years when I grew up, newsprint was a common sight in our household. Many of Dad's manuscripts, typed on newsprint, bore further evidence of his journalism career—the number "-30-" on the bottom of the last page. This was a coded instruction from copy editors to typesetters, confirming that a news story had ended at that point.

The following day, a Saturday, was drizzly in Port Townsend. In the living room, Dad and I worked on my novel. He said it was good through the first hundred pages, but after that it lapsed too frequently into narrative, somewhat like an expanded outline. He thought I should expand the book, fleshing out many of the narrative passages into action and conflict among the characters.

Just past lunch, an architect brought the Hana house plans over and we reviewed them. They were for the main house, not yet under construction. Dad wanted to change the graceful shape of the living room, but Mom and Jan convinced him otherwise.

When the architect left we continued the writing session, and Dad spoke about plot—the importance of keeping a story rolling so that the reader wants to turn the next page. Then he took me upstairs to his writing loft and went over two hundred pages of *Sandworm of Dune* with me in detail to show how a plot and suspense should be set up.

Afterward Jan and I treated Mom and Dad to dinner at Lido by the Sea, a restaurant near the city marina. I was rather depressed after the writing session. After so much work on my book, I thought it was close to being done. It would take me three days to recover, during which time I didn't work on the manuscript at all. Then, determined, I set to work on it again, in every spare moment of time I had.

CHAPTER 26

✳ The Apprenticeship of Number One Son ✳

WHEN MY father began to discuss my writing with me, he took great pains to say that no one could teach another person how to write. It was a craft best learned in the performance, he said, by placing the seat of one's pants on a chair for long periods of time with some sort of writing instrument before him. It wasn't as glamorous a profession as people believed.

A writer was similar to a carpenter in his estimation; they were just different jobs. The writer even had a toolbox, except his was full of words. "A carpenter carps and an author auths," he quipped.

He thought he might counsel me, working with my basic writing style to make it more clear, more organized. And then he intended to get out of my way. "I can't write for you," he said. "You must put in the long hours yourself."

Frank Herbert could write at tremendous speed. *Hellstrom's Hive*, an eighty-five-thousand-word novel, was written in seven weeks, and during that period he corrected two sets of proofs on other novels of his that were about to be published. On one of his *Dune* sequels, he produced six hundred single-spaced pages of scenes, notes and characterizations in just a month and a half! He let it flow, overwriting, knowing he would cut the material way back later. To produce a one-hundred-thousand-word novel, he said he often wrote two hundred thousand words.

Once when I said I was going to leave some items out of a story, saving them for another work, my father shook his head and cautioned, "Never hold anything back. Put it all into your story. Don't worry that you won't have enough left for next time. It'll be there when you need it."

The time he spent writing was not always productive. He recalled staying up into the wee hours one night working on a novel, writing what he thought at the time was some of the best material he had ever produced. But when he looked at it the next day, it was so bad he had to throw it all away.

Dad didn't talk about his secret worlds while they were in development, except to my mother and occasionally to other members of the family. This was a piece of advice given to him in the 1950s by the noted western writer Tommy Thompson, the favorite author of President Eisenhower. "Save your energy for putting words on paper," Thompson counseled. "You use the same energies talking about a story as you use writing it." He said young writers often talked their stories to death and never actually wrote them.

My father took this advice to heart, and as he adopted it he rather enjoyed playing a little game with anyone questioning him, rarely letting out the secrets he was conjuring until they were printed. His conservation of energy was an interesting example of the man . . . almost mirroring a facet of his most famous story, *Dune*. In his writing he conserved energy as if it were precious water in the desert.

This technique was also an effective psychological ploy used by the writer on himself, as the energies of his story became pent up, needing release. Ultimately ideas exploded through his fingertips to the typing keys to the page.

Frank Herbert believed his creative processes were partly in his fingers, the result of natural processes enhanced by years of training at a typing keyboard. He described it as a kinesthetic link, in which thoughts flowed from his brain through his body to his fingers and onto the paper. He tapped into something in that process, a powerful creative vein, and stories emerged.

Some of his favorite ideas came from examining what he called "our dearly beloved assumptions." One set of assumptions, found in the Jorj

X. McKie stories (*The Dosadi Experiment, Whipping Star,* and other tales) was that big centralized government structures helped people cope with rapidly growing, bewildering technology and that justice could always be achieved through perfected systems of laws.

His fervent political views provided an endless source of story ideas. He was particularly intrigued by the myths in which we live, by the "unconscious assumptions" we make regularly—assumptions that cause us to behave in predictable ways.

In *Children of Dune,* he wrote:

> These are illusions of popular history which a successful religion must promote: Evil men never prosper; only the brave deserve the fair; honesty is the best policy; actions speak louder than words; virtue always triumphs; a good deed is its own reward; any bad human can be reformed; religious talismans protect one from demon possession; only females understand the ancient mysteries; the rich are doomed to unhappiness. . . .

Myths are not always old, he taught. Mankind is constantly in the process of creating its own. The Camelot of John F. Kennedy was the myth of a better society, in which leisure was king and everything man could desire was obtained effortlessly. It was linked with the long familiar, ever-recurring myth of a heroic young leader, fulfilled in the minds of millions of Americans by the youthful President Kennedy.

Other story ideas of my father's were extrapolations of present world conditions, a common source for science fiction writers. In the industry, the process is known as "What if?" What if a new form of humans could be created, whose members could pass unnoticed in our society? (*Hellstrom's Hive.*) What if mankind could travel instantaneously from one side of the universe to the other? (*Whipping Star, Man of Two Worlds, Dune.*) What if women dominated a political and/or religious hierarchy? (*The God Makers, Dune.*)

The setting of *Dune* was my father's best-known extrapolation, in which a historical pattern of desert encroachment upon arable land was taken to the extreme, creating a world entirely covered by sand. In his 1959 short story "Missing Link," which later became part of *The God Makers,* he described "planet-buster" bombs, which were an extrapolation of city-buster atomic weapons then available. In *The Dragon in the Sea,* historical oil shortages were extrapolated, and he postulated technology that might exist in a world where oil was far more precious than it was today.

There are many themes in the stories of Frank Herbert. Frequently he wrote about politics, religion, philosophy, water and water worlds, ecology, machines, genetics and myths. I found a number of sub-themes or motifs particularly interesting as well, since he employed them as plot vehicles.

He went to the well many times with stories of investigators traveling to far-off lands or strange places to unravel mysterious events, not un-like an investigative reporter going out to do a story. His variations were highly creative and interesting, and show how he successfully ac-complished the Ezra Pound adage, "Make it new."

Dad's first novel, *The Dragon in the Sea,* employs this motif. Ensign John Ramsey is assigned to the subtug Fenian Ram on a dangerous wartime mission to determine why crews on prior missions have not been able to endure psychological stresses. It is suspected that an enemy "sleeper agent" may be aboard as a saboteur, and it is Ramsey's duty to find out for certain.

Perhaps my father's most memorable use of the investigator tech-nique in a novel occurred in *The Santaroga Barrier.* A supermarket chain has not been successful in expanding to the insular town of San-taroga, and sends a university psychologist, Gilbert Dasein, to find out why. Prior investigators sent to the town have met with unfortunate "accidents." Dasein becomes immersed in the affairs of the town and comes to empathize with the reasons the townspeople don't want his company's supermarkets. Still, he feels a strong obligation to his em-ployer—and thus we have the seeds of conflict within the protagonist.

In *The God Makers,* a galactic empire is trying to reassemble itself after a series of terrible "Rim Wars." The story's protagonist, Lewis Orne, is charged with investigating various planets to ensure that all is peaceful and that no seeds of warfare are germinating anywhere. One of his investigative missions, the climactic one, involves a trip he must take for his own sake, to the priest planet of Amel.

Hellstrom's Hive concerns a mysterious underground hive of humans that is being investigated by a government agent. The hive, it turns out, is secretly a staging ground for humans who are adapting insect methods to improve the odds of survival of the species. An earlier agent has disappeared on this dangerous assignment.

In *The Dosadi Experiment,* Jorj X. McKie is sent to investigate a secret psychological experiment in which the population of an entire planet is confined—an experiment that threatens to harm the whole galaxy.

Other Frank Herbert short stories and novels involve the investigator motif, sometimes involving colonization, exploration and experiments away from Earth—all used as plot vehicles. In *Destination: Void,* scientists are trying to develop an artificial intelligence, but due to failures and deaths in prior experiments they plan to perform future experiments away from Earth, on the distant planet Tau Ceti. The experiments are highly secret, and are concealed in an apparent colonization mission to Tau Ceti.

The colonization plot is closely allied with another recurring motif in my father's work—survival and adaptation to difficult circumstances. This is the subject of his early short stories, "Survival of the Cunning" and "The Jonah and the Jap," as well as of the novel *Dune,* where the planet is covered with sand and the most precious commodities are water and a mysterious spice-drug, melange, found only on Dune. Expressing his philosophy about the necessity for adaptation, Dad wrote that this drug is "like life—it presents a different face each time you take it."

In *The Dragon in the Sea,* Captain Sparrow's definition of sanity is "The ability to swim . . . the sane person has to understand *currents,* has to know what's required in different waters . . . Insanity is something like drowning. You go under, you flounder without direction . . ." In *Dune,* this variation appears as a Bene Gesserit axiom: "Survival is the ability to swim in strange water."

Hellstrom's Hive is about species adaptation and survival—about whether mankind might survive longer on Earth by utilizing insect methods.

In *Destination: Void,* a complex ship's computer (Organic Mental Core) fails entirely while the ship is in deep space, stranding three thousand passengers. To avoid certain death, the occupants must come up with a method of performing mind-boggling calculations previously done by the computer.

There are inhospitable planets in a number of stories, where characters must adapt to new and dangerous conditions. These include the desert planet Arrakis (Dune) of the *Dune* series, the water world Pandora of *The Jesus Incident* and two sequels, and the overcrowded war-torn world Dosadi of *The Dosadi Experiment.*

He wrote often of beings with godlike powers, entities that took on differing forms. In *God Emperor of Dune,* the entity was part sandworm, part human, with a Frank Herbertlike mind containing a vast storehouse of knowledge. In *Destination: Void* and *The Jesus Incident,* the entity was a supercomputer. In *Whipping Star,* it was a celestial body, a star. In *The God Makers* and *Dune,* the gods were in human form.

Sometimes story ideas came to my father in dreams, or as he lay in bed half-awake. These would be scribbled on a notepad by his bed. He called them his "dream notes." One night he came up with the most remarkable story idea of his entire life, even better than *Dune.* Upon awaking in darkness, he flipped on the lamp by his bed and scribbled the story idea down, intending to work on it the following day. When he awoke the next morning, he read the notepad. It said only, "Great idea for a story!"

When I began writing novels, my father told me rather ominously that editors made decisions about stories based upon the first three pages. "If you don't hook them by that time, they'll probably toss it." A powerful narrative hook is essential in the beginning of the story, he said. Sometimes Dad placed his narrative hook in an epigram preceding the text of the story, and sometimes it was enmeshed into the early action of the tale. But always it was there.

He taught me how to ground a reader quickly and solidly, much in the fashion of a newspaper story, and how to coax the reader to delve further into the tale. As with so many facets of writing, it was a balancing act, he said, as the writer doesn't want to overwhelm his reader with too much information too soon . . . like turning on a fire hose.

Dad liked to end scenes and chapters on a note of suspense, and did this to keep the reader turning the pages, to maintain his interest. This was Frank Herbert's definition of plot: "Stringing words together to make a reader want to read the next line." He put his characters under mounting tension in a story, pressure situations where they had to improvise and adapt in order to survive. Mirroring real life, his story-people were constantly presented with surprise situations, wild-card events. In *Destination: Void,* each leading character had what he called "a dominant psychological role" to perform, based upon Jungian archetypes. This squared the characters off against one another, and made the predicaments in which they were placed more challenging and suspenseful than they might normally have been.

After examining one of my early attempts at novel-writing, Dad looked at me and said, "I can't see what you're trying to describe. It's not coming alive for me." The answer lay in providing more details, he said, but only the right kind of details. During a writing session on *Sidney's Comet,* he was wading through a number of my passages in which I described characters getting up, sitting down, walking around, moving their heads and the like. "Too much business here," he said, using a ballpoint pen to line things out. Another time he said, "Cut, cut and cut again."

While working on *Sidney's Comet,* I had a scene that wasn't going anywhere, and I telephoned Dad to ask for advice. After describing the situation to him, he said I had a plot problem, and that I should go back and examine closely the motivations of my characters. "That's how I always free a story," he said. I tried it, and to my excitement it worked.

Another time I was having trouble making my dialogue sound realistic. Dad said it would help me to listen in on conversations in restaurants and other public places. "I've always been a shameless eavesdropper," he confided, a phrase that he repeated at writing workshops. He also suggested that writers speak their dialogue aloud, to make it flow more smoothly.

My father taught me a great deal about his craft, and sometimes as I write now, many years after our earliest and most basic writing sessions, I hear him speaking to me, counseling me in ways that I might improve my work.

CHAPTER
27

✴ We Used to Visit Them All the Time ✴

AT XANADU in July of 1980, Dad sat in the living room with Jan and me, drinking coffee and talking about art. Jan had recently been accepted into the interior design program at the prestigious Cornish Institute in Seattle, and I had just received my second book contract, for *Incredible Insurance Claims.* He said if I kept working at it, I would eventually be a published novelist.

"Now that you're both getting into artistic endeavors," my father said, "you'll experience more exaggerated highs and lows than most people have. You'll need to lean on one another for support during the low times, and when you succeed, the good times will be all the sweeter."

He gave us other advice, and said that Jan and I would become best friends through an understanding of one another's work. Then he looked over at Mom, who was needlepointing a pillow. "There's *my* best friend," he said.

Director Ridley Scott was in the early production phases on the *Dune* movie, operating from an office at Pinewood Studios in London. He had retained the services of the noted production designer H. R. Giger (who had worked with him on the 1979 science fiction film *Alien*), to make drawings and storyboards. Scott had also conducted an exhaustive search for a screenplay writer capable of handling *Dune,* and after many interviews had settled upon Rudolph Wurlitzer.

315

Other movie people were interested in *Soul Catcher,* with two rival groups looking at the screenplay. One production company was headed by Robert Redford, the other by Marlon Brando and Henry Fonda. Dad expected a call at any moment from Redford.

My mother and I stayed up talking that evening after Dad went to bed, and she told me that Hana, the town nearest their new home, was named after a Japanese word for flower. A very spiritual place, it was inhabited by native Hawaiians who seemed locked into a bygone time, with a slower, less hectic pace of life. I understood this, but expressed a great deal of sadness to her about the move.

The following day Dad called me at home. He said he'd been talking with Mom, and they had decided to keep the Port Townsend house now, with the place at Kawaloa and a third home—an apartment in Paris or London.

In ensuing weeks, Robert Redford called my father to ask about acquiring the option to film *Soul Catcher.* Dad referred him to Ned Brown in Beverly Hills, his movie agent. "Redford is the buyer," my father said, "and I make it a practice never to negotiate directly with buyers. That's what I hire agents for."

On a Saturday later that month Jan and I pulled onto the gravel driveway in front of my parents' house at shortly before 6:00 P.M. The children were not with us. I noticed an ominous presence on one side of the parking area—a large trans-ocean shipping container. From telephone conversations, I knew it was almost full and would be picked up in a few days.

In the house later that evening, we spoke of many things. I noticed the final draft of *Sandworm of Dune* open to page 516 beside my mother's chair, near the conclusion of the just-completed manuscript. Dad said it was a totally new type of love story, unlike anything ever written before.

Just before ten o'clock Dad bid us good night at his usual time, so that he could rise early the next morning and write. He kissed Mom and whispered something in her ear, which caused her to smile. As he shuffled off to bed he yawned, simultaneously making a drawn-out, mid-range tone that was punctuated with a high pitched "yow" at the end. He entered the master bedroom and closed the door behind him.

316

On Sunday morning Jan and I were intending to leave after breakfast, because of long ferry lines in the summer. The worst times were Sunday evenings, when many people returned to Seattle from weekends on the Olympic Peninsula. When I got up, Jan told me she'd been out on the deck with my parents, looking over the pond and the trees, and Dad said he wanted us to stay for dinner. It might be our last moments together in Xanadu for a long time.

We told them we would stay, and my father generously set out a very special bottle of 1970 Chateau Mouton Baron Philippe Pauillac, a Bordeaux red.

Robert Redford would be in Port Townsend on July 21, Dad said, for a "very secret" meeting with him. He didn't elaborate and seemed hesitant to discuss whatever was in the wind. I only knew it had something to do with a potential *Soul Catcher* movie.

Dad had just reached agreement with Berkley Books for a huge advance on the paperback rights for the fifth *Dune* book, to be entitled *Heretics of Dune*. It was scheduled for completion in 1981. The title of the fourth, soon-to-be released book was now *God Emperor of Dune* instead of *Sandworm of Dune*.

Under the terms of the *Heretics* sale, payments were to be stretched over a number of years. Mom was feeling the financial pinch of everything they were trying to do, and she mentioned a much-needed royalty check that arrived ahead of its due date in recent days, for French sales of *Dune*. "Just when we need money, it seems to arrive," she said.

It was a warm day, and we all went swimming in the pool. Mom did two-thirds of a lap underwater, while Dad remained alert, ready to help her at any moment. When it was nearly time for dinner, he got the kamado (a Japanese barbecue) going, and cooked steaks, which we enjoyed with the Pauillac wine at a picnic table on the patio.

Dad told a funny story about two Irishmen who met two Mexican girls in Scandinavia. Then he asked me how I was coming on the rewrite of *Sidney's Comet*. I told him I was around 190 pages into it, and I didn't think I could complete it before they left for Hawaii later in the month.

"Use the mails," he said. "Maybe you can send it to Lurton Blassingame after I look it over. He's still active and involved with young writers."

The ferry lines were terrible that evening, and it took us five hours to get home.

✳　✳　✳

By late August 1980, the first draft of the *Dune* screenplay written by Rudolph Wurlitzer was in front of my father. Dad was not at all pleased with it and said Wurlitzer had oversimplified the story, almost turning it into a "juvenile." Too many key scenes were missing, he said. It rubbed him too that the screenplay omitted Dune's baliset, the stringed instrument used by Gurney Halleck, the troubadour-warrior. My father wanted the film to be the first to introduce an entirely new musical instrument.

Two more drafts would follow.

Just before their departure for Hawaii, my parents visited us at our Mercer Island home. They mentioned two going-away parties given for them recently in Port Townsend, one a highbrow affair at the Farm House Restaurant and the other a chili feed at a friend's house. It amused Mom to have close friends on both ends of the social scale, from gourmets to chili-eaters. Dad said that the computer book written with Max Barnard, *Without Me You're Nothing*, was essentially complete, just one of many projects he had taken care of before leaving Port Townsend. "I've been running around like a chicken with my head cut off," he said.

My parents kept changing their minds about whether or not they would sell Xanadu, the Port Townsend house. Initially it was to be six months in Xanadu and six in Kawaloa. A short while later they thought full-time in Hawaii might be better. Then, when *Dune* series royalties and a big movie advance poured in they came up with the three-residence idea—Hawaii, Port Townsend and London or Paris. Now they told us they had changed their minds once more and decided to sell the Port Townsend house after all. This was a blow to me, though I couldn't say it was entirely unexpected.

It made the move seem so final.

Dad also said the *Caladan*, only a year old, wouldn't be a suitable sailboat for Hawaii, with its fin keel and large expanses of glass. Consequently he was listing it for sale with a Seattle yacht broker.

Mom was pretty worried about whether we were going to be able to visit them in Hawaii, since I couldn't fly, and she emphasized how much she wanted us to live there. She checked with three cruise ship lines about trips between the mainland and Hawaii and found that all were either unsafe or no longer operating.

Dad gave me a floppy Hawaiian hat, and with misty eyes said he wanted us to get together for Christmas in Hawaii, maybe around January 6. That was Twelfth Night, the date we had celebrated Christmas several times in my childhood. I reminded him I couldn't fly.

"You'll have to bite the bullet and do it," he said. And he spoke of how safe flying in Hawaii was, how Royal Hawaiian Air Service, which flew between the islands, had never experienced a fatal accident.

My mother spoke of the beauty of Hawaii, made more breathtaking when seen from the air. She described Royal Hawaiian flights over cliff faces with waterfalls pouring down them, vast stretches of water between the islands and spectacular sunrises. Hana Airport was a swath of runway at the edge of a jungle.

A week went by before I was able to continue my journal entries, since I was too upset to write. I finally made the entries on Sunday, September 6, while we sat in the car in yet another ferry line. This time Jan, the kids and I were coming back from the Port Townsend house. We had picked up some vegetables and a couple of boxes of canned goods my mother and father had left for us. We slept in the house Saturday in sleeping bags. Xanadu was not entirely empty, but may as well have been for the lack of life in it. They left some basic furniture groupings in the main rooms so that it would look better for realtors to show to buyers.

They also arranged for a caretaker for the property, a friend named Doug Sandau, and while we were there he was getting moved into the apartment downstairs. He slept on a mattress on the floor during our visit. Nice fellow, and conscientious about details.

All the wonderful *Dune* paintings that had been on the south wall of the living room were gone, having been placed in storage. They were in a top-secret facility on Elliot Avenue West in Seattle, an unobtrusive,

319

rather rundown-appearing building with no sign, used by local art museums to house the works of renowned painters.

Dad's loft study was almost bare except for an electric typewriter, so that he could write if he came back to visit before the property was sold. The pool was drained. Xanadu seemed so dark and cold. It was still special in and of itself, but it was the people who had illuminated it. I couldn't hold back the tears.

Jan wanted to see the wine room, where Dad and I had always gone to make the wine selections. It was empty except for a few bottles of ordinary wine.

Saturday night we ate at the Sea Galley Restaurant on the bay in Port Townsend, and had to wait more than an hour for a table because crowds were in town to visit Port Townsend's third annual Wooden Boat Show. When the public address system announced, "Herbert, table of four," many people we didn't know turned their heads to look at us.

We left early Sunday morning because it was too difficult remaining in the empty house. Cartoons and notes were still on the kitchen bulletin board, and there was a note under the door from a couple who visited on August 31, unaware my parents had flown to Hawaii two days before that.

As we rode the ferry across Hood Canal that Sunday morning, I looked east at the half-missing Hood Canal floating bridge. When that was closed by a storm in February 1979, it hastened my parents' feelings of isolation in Port Townsend. Thereafter a three- to five-hour multiple ferry and driving trip to Seattle was required—twice the normal length of time.

Julie piped up from the backseat, "I wanna see Nanna and Grandpa again. We used to visit them all the time."

And Kim said, "When I go to Hawaii, I'm gonna wear my 'mula' (she meant muumuu) dress. Julie, are you gonna wear Nanna's mula dress that she gave you? She'd like that."

Julie grew very quiet.

A week later I spoke with my parents by telephone and learned they were living in a rented house midway between Hana town and their property, and would stay there until January, when the contractors

Frank in a friend's sailboat off
Raft Island near Tacoma, 1932.

Washington State Highway Patrolman
Frank Herbert, Sr., ("F. H."), 1929.

Frank's high school
yearbook picture, 1938.

Frank, Penny, and
Flora, 1942.

Frank, 1943.

Frank Herbert, 1945.

Photograph by Alfred A. Monner.
Oregon Journal © 1945, Oregonian Publishing Co.

Raising the flag at Kelly Butte, 1946.

Wedding day in Seattle, June 23, 1946: Howie, Frank, Beverly, and Frankie.

Frank (holding Brian) with Bev surveying our Vashon Island house
under construction, 1948.

1943   1944

Beverly at the University of Washington:
a dramatic change in just one year.

Beverly in Santa Rosa, 1951.

Penny, Frank, and Brian,
Santa Rosa, California, 1950.

Patricia Herbert, 1952.

Photograph courtesy of

Patricia Herbert.

En route to
Mexico in a
hearse, 1955.

Beverly and Bruce, 1957.

One of Dad's glamour shots of Mom,
Stockton, 1959.

The house in San Francisco where Dad wrote most of *Dune*. My room was downstairs behind the garage.

Dad's study in San Francisco. Unanswered correspondence went on the copy spike to the right. Above that are school pictures of Brian and Bruce taken three years before.

Poul Anderson and Jack Vance going to work on the houseboat.

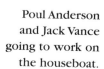

Babe—You could tell by her expression and her laugh that she was full of the dickens.

Study at Cap Ballard's house, 1972.

(Promotional photograph used for speaking engagments arranged by George Carlson & Associates) Photograph by Phil H. Webber.

Bruce in the library at Xanadu, 1973.

With legendary
science fiction editor
Judy Lynn Del-Rey
at Xanadu.

At the controls of the
windmill prototype
mounted on a truck
chassis.

Frank reading
at Xanadu.

Photograph by
Phil H. Webber.

Thanksgiving, 1977.
Front row: Babe, Byron, Julie, Robert, Bev, Jan, Penny. *Back row:* Bruce, David, Brian (holding Kim), Gary, Ron. (Byron, David, and Robert are the sons of Penny and Ron Merritt; Gary Blanquie is one of Jan's brothers.)

Beginning work on *The Lazarus Effect*, 1979. "Sic 'Em Huskies" (University of Washington Huskies) button behind them.

Frank Herbert and William Ransom, authors of *The Jesus Incident*.
G. P. Putnam's Sons/200 Madison Avenue/NYC 10016/212-576-8900.
Photograph by Constance B. Wieneke. Reprinted with permission.

Kim and her Grandpa, 1980. The bookcases are filled with writing awards
and first editions of his books.

With Julie at the helm of the *Caladan*, 1979.

Ron Merritt and Margaux, 1986.

Brian getting trimmed at Xanadu, February, 1984.
Standing: Jan, Frank, Julie, Kim, and Penny (holding Margaux).

My mother's resting place in Kawaloa beneath the kimani tree, 1985.

Frank Herbert and Theresa Shackelford, 1985.

Brian and Frank, 1985.

Photograph courtesy of
Theresa Shackelford.

Seattle University
Commencement Address,
1980.

Photograph courtesy of
Seattle University.

Newsman's identity card,
Seattle Post-Intelligencer.

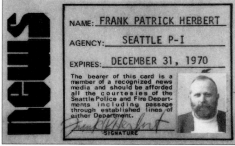

NAME: FRANK PATRICK HERBERT

AGENCY: SEATTLE P-I

EXPIRES: DECEMBER 31, 1970

The bearer of this card is a member of a recognized news media and should be afforded all the courtesies of the Seattle Police and Fire Departments including passage through established lines of either Department.

SIGNATURE

expected to complete their twenty-four-hundred-square-foot caretaker's house. The plan was that they would move into the caretaker's house, and from there supervise construction of the main house.

Dad said his new Mercedes coupe wasn't working out in Hana, because of extremely rough road conditions. Each day they had to drive over ruts, potholes and washboard areas that would probably never be repaired, since the locals liked the road that way. He wished he had brought a four-wheel-drive Jeep instead, and asked if I could locate a new one for him and have it shipped. I agreed to do so.

The worst bumps and sections of road around Hana had names for them, and he spoke of the most notorious stretch of roadway, known as the "Molokai Washboard," which had a surface like an old washboard. It was between his house and town. "It'll shake your eyeballs out," he said.

On the first of October, I mailed my just-completed three-hundred-page manuscript of *Sidney's Comet* to Dad, with this note: "I'm very tired, but I have a feeling I'm not finished yet! It seems there's no end to pages that need correcting . . ."

Later that month my father returned the manuscript with a note written on a yellow sheet of paper that had been wrinkled by typing strikes from other sheets on top of it. I recognized this as a sheet placed beneath another to prevent striking the platen too hard, thus avoiding indentations on the platen. His note said, "These pages . . . 22–27 . . . show how editing tightens the story. Go now and do likewise."* These six pages were closely edited, while others had fewer notations on them.

I spoke with Mom shortly before the November 1980 presidential election. She said that she and Dad had been arguing about politics, since she held a high opinion of Ronald Reagan, while Dad loathed him. Recently my father had purchased what he called a "voice stress analyzer," a little handheld device that when activated could supposedly tell when a person was lying. He had been pointing it at the television during Reagan's speeches, and periodically Dad would exclaim, "Rea-

---

*Frank Herbert, while not formally religious, knew scripture. In Luke 10:37 of the New Testament, Jesus told his followers the story of the good Samaritan, and then said, "Go, and do thou likewise."

gan's lying again! Bev, come in here and look at this meter!"

A while later, Mom wrote to me on her new stationery, with "Kawaloa" printed on it in large letters beside a drawing of the house.

While my parents were in Hawaii, the *Dune* movie project came unraveled again. As Harlan Ellison reported in the June 1985 issue of *Fantasy & Science Fiction,* the third draft of Rudolph Wurlitzer's screenplay included an incestuous relationship between Paul and Jessica. As Ellison put it, "Have you ever heard Frank Herbert bellow with rage?"

I heard it on a number of occasions, including this one. Dad said that he wasn't interested in any variation of this theme, including one in which Alia—Paul's sister, as Dad wrote *Dune*—becomes his daughter as well.

Appalled, Frank Herbert told Dino De Laurentiis that *Dune* fans would never tolerate an incestuous relationship between their beloved characters, and De Laurentiis agreed. To make matters worse, director Ridley Scott, who had spent months in the early stages of production, now had to leave for another film he was under contract to direct, *Blade Runner.* Once again, the long-awaited film version of the greatest science fiction novel of all time, *Dune,* had no director and no screenplay.

In mid-December, I mailed a satirical science fiction short story to my father for his opinion. Called "Earth Games," it was about an alien world where Earth people were kept prisoner and forced to perform games with hot-rod automobiles. Those games strongly resembled rush-hour commute times in any major city, when drivers competed for lane space and made unfriendly gestures at one another. A slight difference: these cars had machine guns on the fenders and cannons on the rooftops.

As before, I could not telephone my parents before noon, since Dad wrote in the mornings. Now I had to calculate the difference in time zones, since it was three hours earlier in Hawaii than in Seattle. During phone conversations with my mother, at all hours of the afternoon or evening, she invariably said Dad was writing in another room—and she could hear the rapid machine rhythm of his electric typewriter. This time, however, I heard Dad playing his harmonica in the background, a happy sound I hadn't heard in a long while.

She said Dad was setting aside the custom computer system he had been designing and building with Max Barnard. The technology was changing too rapidly, Dad thought, and he was considering the purchase of a stock computer and printer. He planned to study available systems upon returning to the mainland.

In those conversations across the Pacific, I realized how much the Hana area reminded my parents of rural Mexico. They described tropical, verdant colors, and the relaxed work ethic of the dark-skinned natives, in which tasks were often put off for another day.

And I realized something else as well. My father, a most imperfect man, had done an absolutely perfect thing for the woman he loved. The construction he undertook at Kawaloa was his gallant effort to save her life, or at the very least to make what remained of it pleasurable.

BOOK III

✳ KAWALOA ✳

CHAPTER
28

※ First Class ※

From this cup I drank as deeply as any man should do, and was
sated with it.

—T. E. Lawrence

In mid-January 1981, Dad and Mom called, one on each line
from Kawaloa. Because of the underwater telephone cable between Hawaii and the mainland, their voices sounded as if they were coming
from the insides of coffee cans, and I heard static. They spoke sadly of
my first cousin Matt Larson and a hiking companion, who had lost
their lives on Mount Hood in Oregon that winter.

Recently my parents had shipped their '80 Mercedes coupe to me
from Hawaii, for safekeeping. They wanted me to take care of a number
of maintenance items on it. Several boxes were also being sent to us
"for baby-sitting," as my mother put it. They had packed the transocean container hastily in Port Townsend, and had things they would
never use in the tropics, including tire chains, snowshoes, ski poles,
wool-lined boots and even a goodly amount of fishing equipment they
couldn't use since fishing was done differently in Hawaii, using long
poles or spear guns. Brass and metal items were coming back as well,
including rifles, to protect them from the moist, corrosive salt air of
Kawaloa. In addition, they were experiencing problems with some ar-

ticles of wood furniture that were warping from moisture in the air. The jeep I had shipped to them was running well, but was too drafty for Mom. They were thinking of trading it in on a more enclosed vehicle, such as a Chevrolet Blazer or Ford Bronco.

Then they said something heartening. Xanadu had been listed for sale for several months without offers, largely because of a depressed economy in the area. They had decided not to sell the property after all. It would be one of their "bases of operation," as my father put it. He had also decided to keep the sailboat *Caladan*.

Judging from all of this, taking the wrong car and other things to Hawaii, as well as their indecision about keeping Xanadu and the sailboat, it was clear they were making decisions emotionally, without adequate planning. It made me wonder if my mother might be even more ill than they were letting on, if she had received bad medical news that we hadn't been told about yet. Everything they did was in a big rush, a desperate surging this way and that.

But every time I asked how Mom was feeling, she or my father said, "fine" or "great" or "much improved." She had survived inoperable lung cancer since 1974. This was nothing less than a triumph of human spirit. She had fought the disease, refusing to succumb to it. My parents spoke of wanting a swimming pool for her at Kawaloa, so that she could resume her exercise regime. She missed the laps in the pool in Port Townsend.

They were living in the caretaker's house, though it was not quite complete, and mentioned difficulties with the main house plans. Dad had obtained bids based upon his architect's drawings, and found construction would cost millions more than he wanted to spend. Beyond that he felt the house was more suited to the Pacific Northwest, where the architect lived.

In researching homes that were best suited to the Hana area, he contacted entertainers Jim Nabors and Richard Pryor and a number of other locals, all of whom were kind enough to show my father through their homes. He determined that the best and most cost-effective dwelling to build was a pole-house, where the structure sits up off the ground on a heavy piling foundation. The house would have a manually operated louver system in the walls, a feature that would permit outside air to circulate inside, cooling the home. In outward appearance it would most resemble the Nabors' home.

Dad drew up his own plans, and had them transformed to blueprint form by a structural engineer. The site was on a hillside, which presented difficulties in making the home accessible to a heart patient. He tried to place most of the areas Mom needed to reach every day on one level, including the swimming pool, the main living areas and the master bedroom. He didn't want her to have to climb stairs. Additionally, since Dad was acquainted with marine architecture, he would incorporate a number of boat features into the design.

The main house had to go in before the pool could be begun. At first Dad wanted to utilize wind power from constant trade winds to heat the pool, but he opted instead to heat it with solar panels. These panels would be factory-built, and not the unique beer-can variety he had designed for Port Townsend.

While he was explaining this to me, something came up with the contractors and he had to leave the telephone. Mom stayed on and told me about Hana. It was the most beautiful place she had ever seen.

In ensuing weeks we had numerous telephone conversations, discussing family business and personal matters that they wanted me to handle for them, and the other day-to-day activities of our lives. In one conversation, Mom said a neighbor gave a party and she won a Smithfield ham. As she spoke to me she was gazing out upon three palm trees below the house, and said a lovely, warm breeze had been blowing all day. "I've been painting," she said. "Flowers, the sea, cattle in the fields . . . This is an artist's paradise. I only wish I had more talent."

Early in the morning of April 11, 1981, a Saturday, we brought boxes and packages of my parents' things to them in Port Townsend, stuff shipped back from Hawaii. A number of fishing poles were in aluminum tubes, and some of the boxes were quite heavy, being full of brass and steel items. The weather was brisk, in the forties but feeling colder from the wind.

Mom and Dad looked tan but tired. They had been back only a few days, and still hadn't adjusted to the change of climate. He had been trying to write, but didn't have the energy to go full steam.

After lunch my father and I played Hearts at the dining room table, while Mom and Jan sat in the living room, talking.

"One thing was sent back here that should have remained in Hawaii," my mother said. "*Me*." She wore a heavy sweater, and was curled up in a lounge chair with an orange and brown Afghan blanket over her. "Look outside," she said.

Dad and I glanced up from our card game. Hail was coming down!

She spoke about how much warmer it was at Kawaloa, with warm trade winds blowing. They planned to return to Port Townsend a little later the following year, in May, staying through October or November. Dad needed two hundred days of residency on the mainland because of extremely high state income taxes in Hawaii, yet another detail he had overlooked in the rush to move there. By spending that amount of time away from Hawaii, his income would not be taxed under Hawaiian law.

They said the caretaker's house was finished on their property and was very comfortable. Ground was just being broken for the main house.

We spoke of Penny, who was doing well. Then the matter of Bruce came up. My parents said he had revealed to them what they had long suspected, that he was a homosexual man. Furthermore, he was participating in "Act Up" gay political marches and other events in San Francisco. Mom and Dad were not at all pleased by this information.

On the heels of this we told my parents exciting news: Jan was going to have a baby that fall. Suddenly they were ecstatic. Dad took me to the wine cellar and located a special wine to celebrate the occasion, a Château Prieuré-Lichine Margaux. Before anything else was done we opened it and shared a toast to the newest Herbert.

I helped Dad put a desk together in his study. Since his roll-top was now in Hawaii, this was a makeshift plywood unit he had built himself. It was stained black, matching the color of the Port Townsend house trim.

When we finished, he said the familiar and welcome, "Let's talk story." Dad went downstairs and brought back a cup of freshly brewed coffee for himself. I didn't want any, fearing I might tip it over in my nervousness. We were about to look at a novel I had labored over for many months. *Sidney's Comet* was now more than 350 pages long.

After a couple of hours, Dad complimented me on my work but said he felt I needed to get my main character, a handicapped government office worker named Sidney Malloy, more centrally involved in the story.

I was given a signed hardcover copy of *God Emperor of Dune*, and my father said that in addition to his other writing projects he was just beginning work on a sequel to *The Jesus Incident*, with Bill Ransom. A substantial hardcover advance had been paid by Putnam for the new work.

On a Saturday two weeks later Dad and I took the kids on a hike in the woods while Mom and Jan fixed dinner. On the trek we were accompanied by a new addition to their household, a big gray and white cat who had a curious habit of running alongside us like a dog. It was a foundling they discovered upon returning from Hawaii, and Dad originally named it Caterwaul, for the commotion it made at night. They had it neutered to quiet it down, and renamed it Baron, from Baron Vladimir Harkonnen of *Dune*. They also enjoyed a certain play on words with that name, a nice double entendre actually, as the cat was now "barren" and unable to produce offspring. He was house-trained, and his only fault seemed to be that he nuzzled in from behind under his mistress's arm when she was trying to type. Mom had always been fond of cats.

At dinner that evening we learned that my parents had found care-takers for Kawaloa who would eventually live in the separate residence that had already been built for them. They were a couple in their thirties. We had been offered the caretaker's position some months earlier and had turned it down, because of the isolation of Hana.

God Emperor of Dune had just been released in hardcover and was already a national bestseller. Even before publication, Putnam had been deluged with thousands of advance orders from bookstores anxious to carry it.

"It's hot," Dad said.

Special editions of the book had been run—750 boxed and signed copies in addition to the regular printing—and Dad had a number of these stacked on a table in the lower level library, where he was signing them. The hardcover volumes were black, with gold lettering on the spines, and would be sold by the publisher for $45.00 apiece.

We talked at length about our family tree, and I took a lot of notes. Mom said she was proud of me for being so interested in chronicling our family, that we had a lot of interesting things going on that should not be forgotten.

Afterward Jan and my mother occupied themselves with projects in the living room, while Dad and I were in the loft study just above them, going over *Sidney's Comet* again, including the rewrites I had done since our last conversation. He said it was very close. It just needed one additional scene and some syntax modifications.

My father praised my writing more than he ever had before. He said I had learned a great deal through hard work and persistence, that my plot was clever and well laid out, with good dialogue and narrative passages. He said I had written a first-rate satire and that it was something of a "pastiche," a melding of motifs and techniques.

On May Day, 1981, my mother called from Port Townsend and said something was happening on the *Dune* movie project again. I heard excitement in her voice. They had a number of meetings scheduled with movie people, and producer Dino De Laurentiis was getting a new director, breathing new life into the project.

Three days later, Dad left with Mom on a thirteen-day *God Emperor of Dune* book tour, with scheduled appearances in Seattle, San Francisco, Berkeley, Los Angeles, Chicago, New York and Boston.

On this and other book tours, my parents developed a routine. Arriving at the airport of a city, Mom would take a taxi to the hotel to register them, while Dad would go off in a taxi or limousine on promotional activities. She liked to bring along a portable Sony radio and miniature Sony television as well, to listen to Dad or watch him during interviews. Mom didn't want to miss anything no matter where she was. She also made certain he had all of the books or promotional materials he needed for public appearances, and she coordinated his appointments, making certain he didn't miss one. During the hectic activities of a tour, with thousands of people clamoring for his attention, Dad relied heavily on Mom's organizational skills. Some of their days were filled with twenty to twenty-four hours of promotional activity, so they got pretty "bleary-eyed," as Dad said.

When his appearances involved speeches, she wrote promotional flyers and made up press kits, including news articles, photos and other literature about Dad and his writings. She sent these to newspapers, magazines, radio stations and television stations all over the country, a month or two ahead of Dad's appearances for speeches or autograph parties—to make certain that stories were run on him.

That month Dino De Laurentiis, now in concert with Universal Studios, announced a new director for the *Dune* project—thirty-five-year-old David Lynch, director of the highly acclaimed films *Eraserhead* and *The Elephant Man*. An avid fan of the book, he would write the screenplay himself, and promised a production that would be true to the author's original. Lynch's creative talents were not confined to writing and filmmaking. He was a painter, which excited my father for the special visual perspective this art form could bring to the story.

Lynch had come a long way in a short period of time. Only three years before, he had produced and directed *Eraserhead* for around thirty thousand dollars—a film that went on to become a cult classic. His budget for *Dune* was initially set at thirty million dollars and would soon go much higher.

✳　✳　✳

In the midst of Frank Herbert's worldwide fame, his son-in-law, Ron Merritt, asked of him, "Frank, what do you want out of life?"

The response, without equivocation: "First class."

Dad was never made of patience, and with his success he was required to travel more and more, on book tours, to conventions, to meet with agents and publishers. This took him away from his study, where he really wanted to be, creating new stories. He decided that if he couldn't write he would demand the best services while he was on the road. In part this was from having experienced the finest hotels and restaurants in the world, so he was using them as standards of comparison. But increasingly he came to demand excellence for the sake of my mother's comfort and for her dietary requirements. He was extremely protective of her and attentive to her needs.

Thursday, May 28, 1981, was a beautiful seventy-degree day in Seattle, with blue skies and lazy, drifting clouds. My father had been on a local television show for half an hour the previous evening. This morning he was on *The Today Show,* taped earlier and broadcast nationally from New York. At the office of Stanley T. Scott & Company—the insurance agency where I worked—we watched him on the lunchroom television set. Later in the morning Dad was interviewed by a Seattle radio station.

The radio interview concluded at noon, after which my celebrity father was driven by limousine to a downtown delicatessen for a sandwich. Then he hurried to afternoon autograph parties at two Seattle bookstores, lasting until 5:30 P.M. We made arrangements to meet at a restaurant that evening.

At dinner, Dad was a bit demanding, which he had a tendency to be at restaurants when he was hungry. Initially we were seated at a table where surrounding conversation was too noisy for us to converse comfortably. Dad went to the maître d' and demanded another table, which he received, but only after telling the maître d', "This is a disgusting way to treat a regular customer." On other occasions Dad would stand at the front counter waiting for a table, positioning himself so that he interfered with the normal flow of patrons and employees. In this manner he was able to get seated sooner, as the restaurant wanted to get him out of the way. It was a trick he had learned from another science fiction writer.

Once we had our table, Dad was in fine form. He told such an amazing array of interesting stories and jokes that people at nearby tables were eavesdropping, even laughing at Dad's punch lines. Howie Hansen and his new wife, Joanne, were with us this evening, and on one occasion Howie said something about computers. Dad disagreed with the comment, and became very authoritative.

It was characteristic of my father that he never admitted he was wrong about anything. He was "super-knowledgeable," as my mother put it. Everything he said came out as if it was supported by the entire research facility of the *Encyclopedia Britannica.*

This evening I found it all very amusing.

Dad filled us in for several minutes on *God Emperor of Dune.* It was number four on the *New York Times* bestseller list for hardcovers, number one on other lists, and even hotter than his biggest previous bestseller, *Children of Dune*. Berkley Books would come out with the paperback after the hardcover had run its course at around two hundred thousand copies, with one million first-edition paperback copies planned.

He gave me a colorful stand-up cardboard cutout with a spaceship on it, bearing the words "FRANK HERBERT *IS* SCIENCE FICTION." It had been printed and distributed by B. Dalton Bookseller and used for promotion of his books.

He said the *Dune* movie looked like a "go" once more in its long and checkered history. Dino De Laurentiis was talking about a forty-million-dollar production, including a ten million dollar cost overrun guarantee from Universal Studios. Dad said with luck the movie might be completed in a year and a half, but added quickly that he would be surprised if it happened that soon.

"I'll believe it when I'm sitting in the theater with a box of popcorn," he quipped.

My father and his longtime best friend, Howie, talked a lot about old times, and in the process told a number of great stories, some of which I had heard previously. Howie told some amusing jokes from the 1950s.

Howie also said when he heard his buddy was going to be on Seattle's KIRO Radio that morning, he called the show's producer and asked him to be certain that the moderator, Jim French, didn't ask the usual stupid questions my father had faced on other programs. "This man has something important to say," Howie said. "Ask him something intelligent." He went on to tell the producer that Frank Herbert was a member of a writing team when he created his great novels. My mother, Howie said, was the other member of that team.

"Tell French to ask about Bev," Howie said.

And French did exactly that, eliciting an emotion-filled expression of gratitude from Dad for her contributions to his life and career.

When Dad felt it was time to leave the dinner table, he rose first, and the rest of us followed. I had seen this interesting phenomenon in my business career as well—the boss rising first and the rest following. The dominant person who knew he was in control.

On the way back to the room, I walked with Dad and noticed, for the first time, that he always walked half a shoulder ahead, never content to relax and fall in beside or behind another person. He was a man with an incredible energy source. A dynamo.

I realized as I got to know my father that he wanted it all. He wanted strong family ties, and he tried hard in that direction. But he wanted celebrity status, too, which left him less time to be with his family. Ironically, he had become a hero to millions of readers, despite his professed aversion to heroes—a key point of his most famous series of books. If he was ever asked whether he considered himself a guru, he invariably quipped that he was planning to open Herbertville in Guyana to house the inner circle of his cult, and he needed someone to handle the Kool-Aid concession for him. Or he might say, with disarming humility, "I'm nobody."

The following morning, Mom and Dad caught a plane to Hawaii, where they checked on the progress of construction. After that they flew on to Australia, where Dad was guest of honor at a big science fiction convention. From Australia, Mom sent postcards to Julie and Kim with pictures of baby kangaroos in the pouches of their mothers.

They flew to Singapore, where they stayed at the famous Raffles Hotel, but for only one night. "The service has gone to pot," Dad told me later. A new Raffles Convention Center was being built near the hotel, and they felt the area was becoming too tourist-oriented. They found another hotel.

Then on to Zurich, where they stayed in a second-floor suite in the elegant Dolder Grand Hotel. After that they spent a couple of days in Scotland touring castles and a week in Ireland, where Dad researched the setting of his new novel, *The White Plague*. He had contracted with Putnam to write this book under a package arrangement with *God Emperor of Dune*. In Ireland he obtained maps, coastline charts and other documents, and took hundreds of photographs, tracing the entire path he had in mind for characters in his book.

"When we were in Ireland," Mom would report to me later, "I saw you everywhere." This was in reference to my facial features, which she said were very Irish.

Ireland was followed by London, where Dad called upon his favorite tailor, Anderson & Sheppard, from whom he ordered a suit. He and Mom then took a one-day side trip to Birmingham for an autograph party, where hundreds of English fans queued around the block to purchase his books and obtain autographs.

Early in July, I completed *Sidney's Comet* and mailed it to an agent in New York City. His name was Clyde Taylor, and he had been recommended by my father after I'd experienced difficulty finding an agent. Following Dad's advice I set immediately to work on another novel, a sequel about a magical universe in which comets were sentient life forms. My new novel, *The Garbage Chronicles,* would resume the satirical ecology theme from *Sidney's Comet,* about garbage catapulted into deep space.

CHAPTER
29

✳ Some Things My Father Did Well ✳

IN THE summer of 1981, Frank Herbert received the biggest science
fiction book contract in history for *Heretics of Dune* ("*Dune* 5"). Part
of the deal was a high-limit accident insurance policy, to be paid for
by the publisher. To reduce income taxes, he was receiving the funds
over several years.

Mom kept saying she couldn't believe the size of the contract, but
there was good reason for it. *God Emperor of Dune* was a phenomenal
bestseller, and the sales of the entire *Dune* series, now at four books,
were exploding. A full-page *Washington Post* article ran that year about
the tremendous success of *God Emperor*. Putnam's hardcover edition
of the book had a sphinx on the cover, but in the newspaper article the
artist drew Frank Herbert's bearded face on the sphinx!

Soon, Dad's literary agent was in London negotiating for the book
rights to *Dune* 6," as yet untitled. Dad expected to receive more than
twice as much for it as he had received for *Heretics*.

During the next writing session with my father at Xanadu, I saw
maps of Ireland displayed in the study—and Dad showed me several
slides of Dublin and of the completed Kawaloa caretaker's house. His
upcoming novel based in Ireland, *The White Plague*, would begin with
a man's family being killed by a bomb explosion in Dublin. On the
maps, Dad showed me the path of the story in detail, across the Re-
public of Ireland. He pointed out a place they visited in County Clare

338

on the west coast—Spanish Point—where a large portion of Philip II's Spanish Armada ended up on the rocks in September 1588. He also showed me a burgee from the Royal Cork Yacht Club in Ireland that he intended to fly on his own sailboat. It was a triangular red banner with a harp maiden and a crown on it, based upon the burgee design of the first yacht club in the world, established there in 1720.

Dad and I played Hearts that evening, and he beat me soundly.

The next morning, Sunday, he was preparing hot chocolate and toast for us, with Hawaiian guava jelly, and I said to him in a mock-pitiful tone, "You didn't have to win every game of cards, did you? Couldn't you have lost just one to make me feel better?"

He smiled impishly and replied, "There are some things I don't do well."

When we left to return home, Dad gave me a ball-point pen on a leather neck strap, a pen that he had used for autograph parties. I liked the gift very much, not only for its utility but for its symbolism. The writing instrument clicked in and out of a clip on a necklace that remained around the neck. He said he had a number of them in a variety of colors, purchased at a stationery store in London.

I was busy with my writing during this time. In addition to the novel, I was collaborating with an elderly friend, Walt Green. We were putting together a collection of aphorisms that had grown quickly to five books. A number of local stores were carrying my *Classic Comebacks* book, which buoyed my spirits—and Jan helped even more by asking other stores to order the book.

In mid-July, I learned that Mom had been coughing a little. She said it had begun some weeks before, after touring a damp and drafty Scottish castle. It was nothing, she assured us, and had been improved with medication prescribed by a Port Townsend doctor.

But on July 27, Dad called from Port Townsend and said in an unsteady voice that Mom had been diagnosed by a local doctor as having pericarditis, meaning the pericardium (the membranous sac containing her heart) had been filling with fluid, placing a strain on the heart. She was tiring easily, and was short of breath. Her lungs were congested. Dad said he would be taking her into Group Health Hospital in Redmond in two days. He assured me that it was a correctable condition, and that the recovery period on pericarditis was dramatic. "The prognosis is good for a full recovery," he said. Still, I heard the strain in his voice.

The following day Mom telephoned Jan, and expressed concern that now she wouldn't feel well enough to help with our baby, which was due in October or November. There had been plans for my thirteen-year-old daughter Julie to stay in Port Townsend that summer as well, and now they would have to be canceled. Mom had been knitting a tiny white sweater for the baby, and doubted if she would have the energy to complete it.

On her first day in the hospital, Mom looked good, and told us she was feeling better than the night before, when she had been congested. I sat by the bed and held her hand for a moment. Her hand was warm, and she squeezed mine reassuringly.

In ensuing days I took a bag lunch and ate with her in her room, while she complained about the steamed hospital fare and picked at it. One day I brought along a file folder of cartoons from my office funny files, since Mom so enjoyed ones I had mailed to her in the past. Sometimes Jan and I brought her treats for her sweet tooth, such as a fluffy raspberry mousse in a glass dish. On other occasions we brought her balloons and boxes of Frango Mints, her favorite chocolate candy, and a chocolate milkshake. Mom drank the milkshake too quickly, and it caused a coughing spell that worried us. Maybe it was the temperature of the drink, or the milk. Dad sent the nurse to get Cepacol throat lozenges, but the coughing subsided before the lozenges arrived.

Mom was sent by cabulance to Seattle for tests at another facility, and then back to Redmond. After three days she was released from the hospital, but would have to return the following week for pericardial surgery, at which time surgeons would open the chest cavity and determine whether portions of the pericardium needed to be removed.

Back in 1974, Mom had received four thousand rads of radiation to her left lung, without shielding of the heart. The treatment had been administered through a single anterior port, according to the best technology of the day. Subsequent studies determined, however, that patients undergoing such a procedure had a high chance of sustaining damage to the pericardium such as pericardial effusion (the leaking of fluids into a body cavity). It would have been safer to have administered lower doses of radiation through multiple anterior and posterior ports, with shielding of the heart.

On Sunday, August 9, 1981, Dad checked Mom into Group Health Hospital in Redmond. She seemed to be much better, and we were told that the doctors planned to operate Monday or Tuesday. But late that afternoon her condition worsened. She was diagnosed with cardiac tamponade, a condition in which her heart was compressed due to an accumulation of fluids in the pericardium. Doctors were using pericardiocentesis to remove the excess fluids and stabilize her. We soon learned that she would need to have most of her pericardium removed surgically at University Hospital in Seattle, where they could give her more specialized heart treatment. She was taken to Seattle and placed in a Critical Care Unit.

Two days later, Mom underwent surgery. They removed approximately two-thirds of her pericardium, in what was called a pericardiectomy. I did not learn until later that she experienced cardiopulmonary arrest just as she was being transferred from the operating room. Her trauma involved an excessively rapid heartbeat and uncontrolled twitching and quivering of the heart ventricles, with low blood pressure. Medical personnel administered nearly twenty minutes of CPR on her, with the aid of drugs, and finally her vital signs improved.

She was in a glassed-in room, and over the next couple of days, Jan and I were not permitted inside. We could only look in, while she slept for much of the time. It was difficult for me to write anything about it. I scrawled some rough, often unintelligible notes on scraps of paper. We brought her cheerful balloons and a big pink rose. Mom had catheter tubes in her upper chest to drain fluids that might remain after the surgery. She was uncomfortable from the tubes, but reportedly was recovering well. She looked weak and thin, and had a tender, wan smile as she gazed at us. When we were finally able to squeeze her hand she squeezed back feebly, but there wasn't much said.

It wasn't a time for words. It was a time for prayers.

During most of the period that Mom was hospitalized, Dad stayed with us. He slept in the carriage house over our garage, on a Japanese futon. I recall seeing him in our bathroom in boxer shorts one morning,

341

flossing his teeth. He had always taken care of his teeth. They were perfect, without a cavity. He said he didn't sleep well the night before, and that when he drifted off he snored more than usual, and it kept waking him up. His back was bothering him a little, too, though he propped a big pillow under the head of the mattress as he normally did. We offered him some aspirin for the pain, but he said he was all right.

Most mornings, by the time I got up, Dad had already gone to the hospital. Sometimes he was so tired when he got home that he climbed the separate stairway to the carriage house and went directly to bed. On other days he insisted upon cooking a gourmet meal for us. He even bought cooking utensils and left them for us, since he didn't like to cook with our comparatively primitive equipment. One evening when we arrived home we found a note from Dad. He had misplaced his key to our house, but got in by climbing through an unlocked laundry room window. He did his laundry and ours and then returned to the hospital. The note said he would make dinner for all of us when he returned.

Dad spent entire days in the hospital with Mom, except for errands, such as an hour and a half to get a haircut. One day he had to return to Xanadu for things they had forgotten, clothes, books and other articles that Mom wanted. It was no small task going back and forth to Port Townsend, with the main bridge being out of commission, but when it came to doing things for my mother, Dad knew no bounds.

In her hospital room they talked, read and played the two-hand version of Hearts that they had made up during their honeymoon. It seemed fitting to me that these people who loved one another so fiercely played a game called Hearts, and a special version of it no one else in the world knew.

When we visited Mom one evening, Dad was seated in his usual place beside her bed eating Cha Shu Bao—steamed Cantonese barbecued pork that he had picked up at a delicatessen near the hospital and heated in the nursing station's microwave. Another day when he went to a friend's house for dinner, he called the hospital every hour to check on Mom. Some nights he stayed with her in her room, sleeping in the chair by her bed. It was exhausting for him, and he wasn't able to write at all.

Late one evening Dad returned to our house with a *Dune* movie treatment under his arm. He said it arrived that morning, delivered to him at the hospital. It had been written by director and screenplay writer David Lynch. He was a third of the way through it, and I asked him his reaction. He made a circular "perfect" sign with his fingers, and said, "Beautiful. They've got it toned into shape and are saving the original."

By the middle of August, Mom looked considerably stronger. She smiled a lot and said she was looking forward to returning home, and was worried about whether a pretty red-breasted nuthatch would ever return to the bird feeder outside her office window. It had been coming by for weeks, and had been a delight for her to watch. Now, with no seed in the feeder, it might not.

She was so much better and receiving such excellent care that Dad told us not to worry, and that we should go ahead and take a short trip out of town we had been planning. In our absence he stayed in our home, where he entertained David Lynch and a team of Hollywood writers, all working on the *Dune* movie script. They played volleyball in our backyard and created quite a stir among neighborhood children, who somehow got the idea that Lynch was George Lucas.

Soon Mom was released from the hospital, and she continued to improve. Within a month it was as doctors had hoped, and her tests showed rapid recovery from pericardial surgery, with improving check-ups every week. Still, the doctor told her he wanted her to be more active. She was getting tired too easily.

We had dinner with my parents at a Seattle restaurant, and my mother had to ask the hostess to slow down as she led us to our table. That evening, Mom and Dad stayed in a nearby hotel, where we visited them. She sat on the bed with pillows propped behind her and a blanket over her lap, knitting a little white baby sweater. She said she really messed it up in the hospital while on medication, and now she was redoing much of it. Jan was due to deliver in two months.

When we were leaving I commented to Dad, "Congratulations on your book contract, and on the most important thing of all—Mom."

"Doesn't she look great?" Dad said, looking at her as she sat on the bed with her knitting.

And she did look better to me, with good color in her face. She smiled at me, in a gentle way.

As we drove home, however, Jan and I agreed that Mom was acting as if she were on heavy medication—a little foggy and forgetful. Somewhat like an old person, breaking off in midsentence to speak about silly matters and not always returning to her original thought. We thought she might still be depressed. It was her second major health crisis.

We fell silent as we crossed the old Mercer Island floating bridge that spanned Lake Washington, with the lights of oncoming cars and houses along the shoreline ahead. Lately I had been having second thoughts about the Boswell role in which I had placed myself, chronicling the life of Frank Herbert and the people around him. It hadn't started out that way in September 1978, a halcyon time when I only jotted brief notes on the backs of wine labels. By 1980, however, the information gathering process had grown out of control, to the point where I was obsessed with a full-fledged journal.

Gradually the journal became a looking glass into the goodness of my father, which far and away was his most significant character trait. The things he did for my mother in her hours of need were beyond anything I could have imagined him capable of. Day after day he sat with her in hospital rooms, lifting her spirits, telling her he loved her, obtaining anything she needed or wanted.

But it was excruciatingly difficult for me to write about the sufferings of my mother, and this had become a terrible weight upon my mind. I was more than a man writing in a journal. These were people I loved, my own flesh and blood. I wasn't just a reporter; I was a participant, drawn like those around me along a powerful, uncontrollable current, not knowing what lay ahead.

Another week passed, and during a telephone conversation with my father he said he was in the midst of a lot of tax work that Mom was too tired to do. She hadn't been eating well, didn't seem to have much of an appetite, and was suffering from nausea and indigestion. Some of the medicines she had been taking, particularly the systemic diuretic Lasix, seemed to disagree with her, and he was talking with the doctors to get the medications adjusted. In the meantime, she was refusing to take the Lasix.

Dad wanted to get up to his study and work on his book, *The White Plague*, but couldn't.

✳   ✳   ✳

On October 2, 1981, while I was at work in my insurance office, my agent Clyde Taylor called from New York City to say that Berkley Books had made an offer to publish *Sidney's Comet* . . . including the payment of a modest advance.

I called Jan first, but she already knew, from talking with Clyde. "Great, honey!" she said. I had Mom and Dad on the phone seconds later, congratulating me. He was in his study, back at work on *The White Plague*, while she was at the phone in the greenhouse. Mom had been taking a new combination of medication, making her feel much better.

Still, whenever we got together to share a meal, Mom said she couldn't entirely enjoy it yet, as something funny had been happening with her sense of taste, something to do with her continuing recovery from the heart operation. Her breathing and cardiovascular strength were improving to the point where she could swim two and a half lengths of the swimming pool now—around thirty-five meters—before Dad had to jump in and help her. She could also climb two flights of stairs at a time, whereas before surgery she'd had to rest after each half flight. So she was improving—but she lamented times only a few years before when she could swim forty lengths nonstop. Mom looked good, but complained of bothersome itches from the surgery.

A fine toast was raised to my novel sale, and more toasts followed, to Mom's improving health, to my parents' birthdays coming up that month, and to Dad's tremendous success. After we toasted Mom's health, Dad put his arm around her and with a sweet smile said, "I don't know why I love this woman so much."

She nuzzled against his chest.

Finally the *Dune* movie was under way. David Lynch had created a fine screenplay, in Dad's opinion, very close to the novel. Lynch and the film producers were thinking of filming the desert scenes in Mexico's Sonora Desert, a picturesque region that would have the added benefit of cost-effectiveness, from the devalued Mexican peso. They were talking with, of all people, George Lucas to do the special effects. This bit of irony was of some concern to my father, considering alleged "borrowings" in *Star Wars* from *Dune*, but he decided to stay out of the matter.

From various projects Dad was scheduled to receive an astronomical sum of money in the next ninety days—a much-needed infusion of cash to pay the contractors in Hawaii and Mom's medical expenses, which were not all covered by insurance.

Mom said he was often writing before dawn on his Irish story, *The White Plague*. He hadn't started until mid-August, and now—less than two months later—he was already on page 233.

Before beginning the book, extensive DNA research had been required, since Dad had in mind a story about a DNA experiment gone bad, in which a dangerous virus was released into the populace. He read as many books as he could get his hands on about recombinant DNA, spoke with scientists and doctors, and went a step beyond. To see how easy it might be for an unbalanced, dangerous person to obtain the ingredients and materials necessary for recombinant DNA research, he impersonated a doctor and telephoned medical suppliers.

"This is Dr. Herbert," Dad said. "What does my purchasing department need to do to obtain boxes of XR-27 and enzyme applicators?"

Because of the potential for misuse of such items, Dad expected to encounter difficulty. Instead, to his amazement, he was told that he only had to send in a check for the proper amount. When the check cleared, the items would be shipped, no questions asked.

He developed what he thought could be an actual deadly plague, and considered including details of it in the book. Mom and I told him we didn't think he should do that, since the wrong people might obtain the "recipe." After consideration, he said he would follow our advice and only specify fragments of information—too little for anyone to put together.

Several days later a friend of my father's told me, "Frank doesn't look well." I responded that I assumed Dad was just short of sleep. I

346

dropped a humorous card in the mail to my father, telling him I loved him.

Two days later Mom called me at work. She said Dad had been up since 3:00 A.M. typing, and he hadn't eaten a regular meal in all that time or said much to her. I repeated the friend's comment to her, and she insisted Dad was fine, just tired. He was on page 450 of *The White Plague*. He was trying to meet an October 31 deadline—only three days away—but it had been made nigh impossible because of the time he'd taken off for her illness.

She said G. P. Putnam's Sons had already arranged for the book's publicity, and a special boxed edition of signed copies at fifty dollars apiece had been promised, in addition to the regular printing. It was like a newspaper deadline for him, she said, a reminder of years he had spent working as a newsman while writing in his spare time. He was obsessed with meeting the deadline.

They planned to leave for Hawaii on November 27, waiting until after Thanksgiving so that we could spend the holiday together. I knew they were delaying departure for another reason as well. They wanted to meet the newest Herbert, due to emerge from a private world into a more populated one around November 13.

On Tuesday, November 3, Dad came out of his cocoon and phoned me. He was on page 491 out of a projected 550. Some of it was first draft, he said, but most was second. I marveled at his incredible pace. He could really put it in high gear when he wanted to.

I told him I was having trouble getting going on my new novel, *The Garbage Chronicles*. I had a general plot in mind and some of the characterizations, but little more. He said not to bother too much with small details at this point, syntax and the like, that I should try to write through to the end of the story—even if it was sketchy—and then go back and fill in the details. I took his advice, and it helped speed my progress.

While he usually did not discuss particulars of his works in progress, preferring to save his energy for writing, he said *The White Plague* was about a man whose wife and children have been killed in Ireland in a terrorist bomb attack. The man, a molecular biologist, decides to avenge himself by setting loose a terrible plague. After Dad selected the title for the book, he learned it had been used previously, for a book in the 1930s about tuberculosis. It didn't matter, he said, since titles normally couldn't be copyrighted anyway.

He spoke of his schedule. Later that month, on the day before Thanksgiving, he had a date at a recording studio in Seattle to read from *God Emperor of Dune* for a phonograph album being produced by Caedmon Records. He also mentioned that around December 15 he was going to meet Bill Ransom in Hawaii to begin their sequel to *The Jesus Incident*. The collaboration was expected to take three or four months.

The following week I called him regarding our upcoming Thanksgiving dinner, saying I had made reservations at a nice restaurant. "Great," he said, but he went on to say he was having trouble with his Kawaloa house plans. He had included a number of features to make the structure accessible to a heart patient, but the Maui Land Use and Codes Department was giving him trouble, citing nonconforming construction. They were making him jump through hoops, and he had to modify the plans to comply with their requirements. He was also obtaining a letter from a doctor concerning Mom's medical condition, which he would send to the planning department.

On Thanksgiving morning my parents and I accompanied Jan on an appointment with her doctor in Bellevue. The doctor wanted to examine her before he went away for the holiday, as she was two weeks past due and was getting rather large. While Jan was with the doctor, I sat in the waiting room with my parents. We thumbed through magazines without reading much and conversed in nervous tones, hoping the baby might, miraculously, be ready for delivery that day.

Presently a long-faced doctor came out with Jan. He told my parents he was afraid to face them, because he knew how badly they wanted to see the baby before leaving, but he had nothing encouraging to report. She was only dilated two centimeters, as she had been for a couple of weeks. It had been more than nine years since the birth of Kim, and with only a hint of a smile the doctor asked Jan if she had forgotten how to have babies.

Mom and Dad were scheduled to board a plane to Hawaii the next morning. Due to the rash of Christmas flights to the islands, it was the last flight they could get on. Otherwise, they would have had to wait until January—and they had to get there before then to supervise house construction. A number of important jobsite decisions had to be made. They planned to return to Seattle in June, and perhaps for a short while in March to see the baby.

Back at our house, we visited for a while before dinner. Mom had lost a lot of weight, and couldn't seem to stay warm in the cold weather, no matter how much she wore. She kept on a heavy, fur-lined coat indoors and sat by the wood stove in the family room. We also had the thermostat turned way up, and a curtain drawn over a large sliding glass door behind the couch, to retain heat and reduce drafts.

The next day, Dad called from Hawaii to say they had arrived safely, and that the main house was turning out better than expected. The walls and roof were up. The caretakers, a young couple, were living in the residence that had been built for them, so my parents were staying with a friend, Mary Moore, the mother of race-car driver and ABC sportscaster Sam Posey. She owned an elegant waterfront home a mile down the road toward Hana town, and was providing my parents with what she called "the stateroom," for guests.

Mom was happy and breathing easier in the warm air, but Dad still hadn't finished *The White Plague*. He was spending long hours on it.

On Saturday, November 28, 1981, I worked on *The Garbage Chronicles* until 2:00 A.M. At 5:45 A.M., Jan woke me up, saying she was experiencing labor pains. Margaux Beverly Herbert was born at 10:36 A.M., with no medication. Nine pounds, six ounces! In the past few days we had decided on the French name Margaux (pronounced "Margo") for a girl, in honor of my maternal grandmother, Marguerite, who went by the name of Margo. With my mother in mind we selected the middle name of Beverly. Of course, Jan and I also had in mind the wonderful bottles of Margaux wine that we had shared with my parents.

CHAPTER
30

* Kawaloa by the Sea *

As Xanadu was my father's place, so Kawaloa was my mother's place.

—Entry in my journal

ON NEW Year's Day 1982, my mother telephoned from Hawaii. After static on the line cleared, she said she loved a packet of baby pictures we had sent to her, along with a bag that had the design of a green cat on it. "It's the most elegant cat I've ever seen," she said. "But can we give it to Mary Moore? She's been letting us stay with her for a month and a half's without charging any rent. Bill Ransom is staying here, too."

"Sure," I responded.

She said she didn't want to hurt our feelings.

My solution: "You give Mary the bag. Our gift to you is a month and a half's room and board in her house."

Mom laughed. Dad came on the line. He said Bill Ransom had done a lot of the work on their sequel to *The Jesus Incident*, and that it shouldn't be too difficult to finish. They didn't have a title for it yet.

I needed my parents to sign several forms for their property and liability insurance, forms I had mailed to them some weeks before. But neither Dad nor Mom recalled seeing my request. "You have to imagine the confusion here," Dad said. "Your mother has a little office space in

Mary Moore's house . . . There are papers all over hell . . . We've lost several pieces of mail." He asked me to send another copy of everything.

I told him that a friend from Port Townsend called and wanted to know if they had received the smoked salmon she sent.

"What salmon?" Dad asked.

Mom said the house was almost finished, the ocean was blue and it was 82 degrees. "Ain't it hell?" she quipped.

Dad planned to be in Seattle in April for a second big book tour on *God Emperor of Dune*, this time for Berkley's paperback edition. My mother probably wouldn't accompany him, as it would still be too cold in the Pacific Northwest.

The hardcover edition of *God Emperor of Dune* was still on national and international bestseller lists, where it had been firmly entrenched for most of the previous year. This was Mom's favorite story in the series, and apparently she was not alone in her feelings. Because of stronger than anticipated hardcover sales, the mass market paperback would not be issued until 1983.

Dad said they might be in England in a few months, where they were scheduled to begin filming *Dune*. The producers had decided against filming in Mexico's Sonora Desert, in favor of Tunisia in North Africa. The base of operations would be in London, with a number of sets built at Pinewood Studios near London, the same location favored by the previous *Dune* director, Ridley Scott.

At Mary Moore's house, Bill Ransom worked alone on the sequel to *The Jesus Incident*, while my father continued to struggle on *The White Plague*. Shortly after the first of the year, Dad gave the manuscript to Mom and Bill to read, since he valued both of their opinions.

After reading it, the two readers discussed the book privately, and agreed that it was too long, with excessive detail about the Irish countryside. At coffee, they worried about how to tell Dad. Finally it was decided that Mom would do it.

At the appointed time, Bill made himself scarce.

Upon hearing the bad news from my mother, Dad stormed out of the house and asked Bill if he agreed. The answer was yes. Dad's shoulders slumped in disappointment, as he realized they were right. He had been attempting to work through too many distractions, and in the process had lost the focus of his story.

He set about a major rewrite.

Later that month Mom called with questions about her insurance policies. She had an agent in Hawaii handling matters over there, while I was taking care of their insurance in Washington State. She was confused about things that she'd always understood before, and this concerned me. I wondered if she was taking on too much for her condition, trying to keep up with the demands of Dad's very busy and often complex activities.

They had moved into the new main house, where construction was still in progress. At Dad's request, Bill, a former fireman and CPR instructor, trained each of the workers in CPR, for my mother's safety. Bill also made up emergency instruction cards for each of the men to carry with them at all times.

As I spoke with my mother, I heard carpenters hammering and sawing in the background. She said she was gazing out at the aquamarine sea, with palm trees swaying in the wind on the lower portion of the property, and could hear the duet of Dad and Bill Ransom typing in the upstairs study. Already the salt air had destroyed two rental typewriters, and they'd rented two more.

Dad's study was smaller than the one in Port Townsend, Mom said, but with a similar low-slanted ceiling. It had a skylight, and built-in bookcases lined the walls, with shelves even over the doorways. One doorway led to her office and out to an upper mezzanine that looked out on the main level of the house, while the other doorway led to a private bath.

Mom said the weather had been nice, but a "bit chilly" at night.

"What's your definition of 'chilly?'" I asked.

"Sixty-nine degrees!"

The house my father designed for my mother in Hawaii had a number of nautical features. Its floors were of rare and expensive reddish-brown koa wood, known as "Hawaiian mahogany." A beautiful and durable acacia variety native to Hawaii, it was the wood ancient islanders utilized to construct canoes. The kitchen pantry door had a bright brass ship's porthole, with heavy glass. A pair of great split posts rose through the center of the home alongside the living room, like pilings by the seashore. A graceful spiral stairway led from the main level to the upper, and in every nook and cranny, as on a boat, storage compartments had been built. It was a graceful, serene home, and with wall louvers open all day, the air from trade winds circulated inside. This was a palace in paradise, built by an emperor for his empress.

In this exotic locale there existed ancient legends and superstitions concerning a vengeful volcano-goddess, Pele, and menehunes—little fairy creatures who played tricks on people or became "night marchers" walking over rooftops in the darkness. Legend said that pieces of volcanic rock could not be removed from the islands, at the risk of incurring terrible bad fortune brought on by Pele, commonly referred to as "Madame Pele." It was considered bad luck to sleep with your feet toward a doorway, as spirits could force you to walk away from your body. And geckos, little lizards that crawled along the ceilings and rafters, could not be killed except by accident.

My mother learned about malevolent spirits, and how best to remain in their good graces. In this and other ways Kawaloa became a spiritual place for her where she could touch her inner being, as she had not done since she was a little girl and fantasy creatures roamed through her mind.

The sea calmed her, and she remembered the tranquilizing effect of water upon her when she was a child living in the Pacific Northwest. Whenever little Beverly became rambunctious, her mother frequently sent her into the bathroom to stand in front of a sink of water and splash in it, or to sit in a tub of water and let warm moisture soak into her pores.

The new home was right for her and comfortingly warm, so that she could breathe easily. She felt secure here and unafraid, within the protective envelope her husband had designed and built for her. Beverly and Frank became *"kama'aina"* here, accepted as natives by the local people.

Back home, February 4, 1982, was an off day. It was a Thursday, and at work I commented to people how I felt "out of sync," but didn't know why. I was not able to write over the noon hour, even though *The Garbage Chronicles* had been going fairly well. I didn't feel like eating my bag lunch, either, and worked on insurance straight through the hour. Gradually I felt worse and worse as the day progressed. At low points, I considered packing everything up and moving my family to Hawaii. Mom had not sounded well the last time I talked with her. Maybe Jan and I could do some of the work that was burdening her.

At 6:00 P.M., I was showering after jogging when Julie ran upstairs to tell me, "Grandpa's on the phone—from Hawaii!"

I threw on a jogging suit and ran downstairs. Over a static-filled telephone line, Dad related bad news: Mom was in the hospital again, this time Kaiser Foundation Hospital in Honolulu. He was calling me from the nearby Alamoana Hotel, room 1919.

Mom had been feeling very tired lately. Following surgery the prior August, she had developed a number of symptoms, including distention of her jugular vein, increased abdominal girth and liver congestion. A series of medical tests had been run, and her case had been discussed at a special cardiology session involving surgeons from Kaiser Hospital and the University of Hawaii. She had, among other conditions, paroxysmal nocturnal dyspnea, which was an inability to sleep well at night caused by shortness of breath when lying down.

Doctors were working to remove fluid from her liver, and she would have to go on a strict low-salt diet that also involved water management and the use of diuretics to remove excess fluid from her system. He mentioned what I already knew, that she had heart muscle damage, but added a new and disturbing twist. Her diminished heart condition was not holding. She was suffering from degenerative heart disease, and if her life was to be saved this condition had to be stabilized. They wanted to keep her weight down in order to take a load off her heart, so it wouldn't have to work so hard.

She would have to follow a new routine. In addition to a low-salt and fluid-management diet, for every two or three hours of activity for the rest of her life she would need to rest an hour. She would weigh herself several times each day, and if she gained two pounds one day she would have to lose it within twenty-four hours.

I asked how long she could be expected to live, and Dad said the doctors were not giving estimates. "She could live five or ten years," Dad said, "or she could go tomorrow."

My father was exhausted, and asked me to call Bruce and Penny, but to tell them not to call and not to rush over to Hawaii for a "big deathbed scene." He said Mom was strictly against that, and so was he. Everything was under control, he assured me. He expected to be back at Kawaloa with her by Tuesday.

I told him my thoughts about Hawaii, that perhaps we should come now and help Mom with her work. He said we should wait a year, that Hana was not a metropolis and not a good place for kids. He liked the idea of us helping—but Mom didn't like to delegate it. He felt her work sustained her, gave her a reason for going on.

Dad said it was difficult living in such a remote location for more than a month or two a year. In recent weeks he had been considering replacing the Port Townsend base with one in San Diego or Santa Barbara, California, where the weather was warmer and Mom wouldn't feel such a pressing need for the warmth of Hawaii.

Whatever she wanted, whatever she needed, he would be her superman, obtaining it for her, comforting her. He would set his writing aside entirely if necessary, sacrificing his hard-earned career—just as she had set aside her own creative writing efforts in the 1950s and 1960s and took jobs in retail advertising while he wrote. In effect she had put him through writing school, loaning him the better part of her life. Now he was repaying the debt.

"Please don't tell your mother I called," he said. "I don't want her to think I'm worried." And he concocted a subterfuge, asking me to say I had phoned Bill Ransom in Hana and learned about Dad being at the Alamoana, and about Mom being in the hospital.

As we closed our conversation, my father asked me to fly to Hawaii in April while he was away on a book tour. I mentioned the possibility of Jan going instead, since Jan had become like a daughter to Mom.

"That or get some psychological help for your fear of flying," he said.

I knew he hated leaving Mom, and I wondered if he would even make the book tour. I was nervous after the call. Despite being a couple of pounds heavy, I went in the kitchen and gorged myself on oatmeal-raisin cookies until I felt an odd swooning sensation from excessive sugar.

In my youth I had felt certain extrasensory powers of my own. Little occurrences, nowhere near those experienced by my mother. Frequently

I sensed things about people, almost read their thoughts and concerns—and they were accurate readings, from indefinable sources. After meeting and talking with a person for only a short while, I picked up things about their nature, took readings on them, and understood their motivations. My ability came and went, but at times its accuracy astounded me.

I used to think my intermittent ESP was inherited from my mother, but after I was married it seemed to lapse and I thought anything I had perceived in the past might have been coincidence. But now as I considered the events of the day a chill coursed my spine, and I shivered. Could my feelings of depression all day have been a sympathetic reaction? Did I sense my mother's anguish from thousands of miles away, across the Pacific Ocean? I so hoped she would live to be at least seventy. She was fifty-five, and deserved time to enjoy Hawaii.

When my parents returned to the Hana house, there were huge changes. Dad went into a tirade in the kitchen and ransacked the cupboards, throwing out every can and package of food that wasn't low in salt. "This is the enemy!" Dad said angrily. "We've brought the enemy into our house!"

It saddened Bill Ransom, almost to tears, that my father felt betrayed by food, something he and my mother loved so much. Bill thought back to happier times in Port Townsend only a short while before, when they picked fresh vegetables and combined them with clams and oysters from nearby beaches to make elegant, simple meals.

During this period I made a number of calls to Hawaii, checking on Mom. Under the new regimen her condition improved. She was a survivor, a fighter, and bounced back yet another time. And my father, ever her protector, continued to guard her so closely that he didn't allow her to ascend or descend stairs alone, not even when she was feeling better.

In one conversation, she and I talked about Margaux, Kim, and Julie, and she said she wished she had the opportunity to know them better. I said she was doing fine as their "Nanna" and told her how much Julie and Kim appreciated receiving postcards and notes from her whenever she traveled. She sounded pretty good, all things considered, and nothing was mentioned about her trip to the hospital in Honolulu. She said she was sitting on the couch with a pair of binoculars on her lap, looking for whales.

"I saw two yesterday!" she exclaimed happily.

On a Sunday later in the month, Dad called, and as usual there was a moment of fuzzy static, followed by his voice: He said that *The White Plague* had finally been dispatched to New York after two rewrites, one of which was major, cutting more than a hundred pages from the manuscript. The hardcover edition was due out in September, and a paperback would be published the following year. "This one will make waves," my father told me. "It's a real shocker."

The book with Bill Ransom was also going well, and they would call it *The Lazarus Effect*. Dad told me he had been derailed from the work by the close attention he had to pay to Mom, and he still was not back on track. But Bill had been picking up the slack.

Early in March my father called very late at night to tell me that he and Mom were arriving in Seattle on March 26, and she was going to Group Health Hospital on the 29 for the correction of a faulty heart valve. Unaware of this specific condition until now, I'd been laboring under a general picture of degenerative heart disease stemming from radiation treatment, without understanding much about the details. It was unclear why such a serious-sounding procedure could be delayed for a month, but I hoped it would help her.

Dad asked me to make reservations at the Westin Hotel for the night of the 26. He specified a warm room on a lower floor, deluxe. In the past they had been in cold rooms on the upper floor of the tower, where "the wind blows right through." Sixty-five degrees was cold for Mom.

CHAPTER

31

✳ Brave Heart ✳

ON A windy Sunday in March 1982, Mom called to make certain
we had requested a warm room at the Westin. Nervously, she spoke of
her upcoming hospital appointments here: "I don't know what's going
to happen when they look me over."

The following Friday, Jan called my office to say my author's copies
of *Incredible Insurance Claims* had arrived. After work I saw my nine-
year-old daughter Kim on the front porch of our house, excitedly waving a copy of the book. I signed copies for my family, using the
autograph pen on a leather cord that my father had given me.

At 10:15 P.M., we picked up Mom and Dad at SeaTac Airport. To
my shock, she was in a wheelchair with him pushing her. The chair
had a high aluminum bar overhead which must have been for intravenous fluids and other life support equipment, if they were needed.

"Don't let the wheelchair frighten you," Mom said, smiling nervously. "I don't need it, really."

They were bound for Port Townsend for the weekend, and Mom
would go to the hospital in Seattle on Monday. She looked tan and
cheerful, but too thin at 119 pounds on a 5'7" frame. In a little over
a month she had lost 17 pounds on her new low-salt diet and had been
feeling much more energetic—the weight loss reduced the workload
on her heart and lungs. But she looked startlingly older to me, far
beyond her fifty-five years. The skin of her face had always been full

358

and rather smooth, and now it was much looser, with many more wrinkles.

Her doctor in Hawaii, Milton Howell,* had thought oxygen might be necessary during the flight, so Dad had wanted to bring his own aboard. He discovered this was a violation of FAA regulations, however, so for an extra charge United Airlines provided the tank. Mom had sat in an area designated "Handicapped," with her feet over an oxygen tank. Fortunately, she did not need to use it.

While Dad wheeled her to the elevator, I handed her a bouquet of red roses and a copy of my second book.

Mom and Dad were seeing Margaux, now almost four months old, for the first time, and we talked about the French spelling of her name. Mom enjoyed holding the baby, but only for a short while since in her weakened condition a sixteen-pound chunker was too heavy.

My father told of standing at the island in his kitchen and watching a humpback whale jump just offshore like a huge salmon. Whales did this to clear the barnacles off, and for other reasons. His manuscript of *The White Plague* had been well received by Putnam in New York City. Their editors had gone over it carefully, and it was, in my father's words, "ready to go." I asked him how the *Dune* movie was going, and he looked a little blank, but said it was still on track as far as he knew.

The next day, a Saturday, we arrived in Port Townsend around 7:00 P.M. It was fifty degrees, overcast. The bullfrogs in the pond below my parents' house were croaking loudly.

"Quite a crop this year," Dad said. "How you doin', Number One Son?" He patted me on the back.

They were cooking a spaghetti dinner, with a big pot of outrageously good-smelling tomato sauce bubbling on the stove. After I kissed Mom on the soft skin of her cheek, she asked me to prepare one of my specialties, the garlic bread. As I worked she said she had read *Incredible*

---

*Milton Howell had been the attending physician for aviator Charles Lindbergh when Lindbergh died at Hana in 1974. Lindbergh loved this tropical paradise, and it was where he chose to live during the final months of his life.

Insurance Claims the night before and thought it was much funnier than my first book.

Dad opened a bottle of white wine (1977 Gundlach-Bundschu Kleinberger) before dinner, and we sipped while talking in the living room. The south wall of the room looked bare, as the *Dune* paintings were still in storage. The three overhead skylights had been covered on the outside with Styrofoam to reduce heat loss, and looking out at the pool building I noticed some strips of tarpaper had been torn from the roof, probably by wind. It was nice to be with them in Port Townsend again, but things were not the same.

My father was suffering from jet lag,* a recurring problem, and it would probably take him two days to recover. He seemed more tired than Mom, and looked haggard. As he was leaving the room for a moment, Mom called out something to him, but he kept walking. She explained what I already knew, that there were sounds in the upper ranges he could not hear, especially when tired.

At dinner, we had a rich red 1976 Hermitage with the pasta. Dad spoke of jongleurs, medieval entertainers who sang songs and told stories, traveling from castle to castle. Before the time of the Gutenberg Bible, when there were no efficient means of printing, people had to remember stories as they were passed down. Only the most essential elements of each tale continued.

Mom complained about the cold a couple of times, even though it must have been eighty degrees in the house. We closed all the drapes and kept turning the heat up. Everyone except my mother had their shoes and socks off, trying to cool down. Kim kept saying how hot it was, so I had to take her aside and tell her not to make Nanna feel bad.

Julie and Kim asked their grandfather for autographed books from the glass display case in the living room, so he presented each of them with a signed book—*Direct Descent* for Kim and a Del Rey gold seal edition of *Under Pressure* for Julie. A large and impressive cardboard poster of the Del Rey book jacket was leaning against one living room

---

*Dad had read a medical report to the effect that complex carbohydrates could reduce the effects of jet lag. For that reason, he and Mom invariably ate pasta after returning home from trips.

wall. Looking at it, I pointed out how much larger Dad's name was printed than the title. "That's when I knew I had really made it," he said, beaming.

Dad said there had been competition and minor friction between the Kawaloa caretaker and the supervising contractor, both of whom wanted to be, in my father's words, "Frank Herbert's main man." Both men were doing excellent jobs, Dad said, and he expected things to smooth out. He ordered some corned beef for each of them that day (in equal amounts!) and ordered it shipped back to Hawaii.

Surrounding my father there had been other similar tensions, involving friends and even family. Such competitions, I learned, were not uncommon around famous people, including those around President Reagan and certain religious leaders. It occurred as well among the associates of Oscar Wilde, and led to personal animosities that simmered for years after his death. Typically, subordinates jockey for position and attempt to undermine the positions of competitors, real or perceived. In Dad's case, much of it had to do with the force of his personality. He was extremely cordial with people he liked, to the point where each of them thought they were closest to him and found it difficult to believe anyone else could have any part of him that was comparable to what they had.

On Sunday, March 28, 1982, I was the first to rise, and jogged four miles. Shortly after I returned, Dad wandered out of the master bedroom in a striped blue and yellow caftan. With his long, neatly trimmed beard, he looked like a distinguished Muslim. Or a guru, which he often told his fans he didn't want to be, though they tried to build him into one.

He sat in one of four high wicker chairs at the kitchen counter, with a cup of coffee. Still perspiring, I sat by him with a glass of water and a banana.

Dad spoke of his love for snorkeling. He described many "dog pools" (tidal pools) on Maui, next to jungle and deserted stretches of beach. If he didn't take a spear gun in the water, parrot fish, flatfish and other sea creatures swam up to him and looked in his goggles. Since the Hawaiian fish had been hunted for centuries with spears and spear guns, Dad said they seemed to have developed an inbred fear of such weapons. He said the only danger in the dog pools was from moray eels, if he stuck his hand into a hole or stepped into one.

"Wear flippers," he said with a smile. "Let 'em bite the hell out of your flipper."

He said the eels fed on lobsters, so you could get bitten reaching into a hole for a lobster. If one of the lobster's antennae was pointing at you and the other was pointing back in the hole, you could bet a moray eel was in there. (A lobster's antennae are covered with sensory hairs that detect food and enemies, beyond what the eyes can see).

He wanted to get a cat-rigged Cape Cod dory for sailing in Hawaii, with an inboard/outboard motor and a centerboard keel that raised and lowered to get in and out of shallow areas where the most interesting dog pools were. Too often the best places could only be reached from the land after traversing treacherous cliff trails. Such a spot was within walking distance of the house, toward Kaupo village (away from Hana town).

Dad went up to his loft, and soon I heard the rhythmic pumping of his rowing machine. I thought of what he had told me that morning about Hawaii. He seemed to be adjusting well to life there, but was he, really? For years he had been attracted by the tropics, and now, ironically, he'd been forced to go there by my mother's medical condition, leaving family and friends on the mainland, isolating himself from other science fiction writers he had known.

I have never heard of a finer friend than my father. He loaned money to some and even bailed an advertising artist out of jail in the middle of the night, where he had been taken for unpaid parking tickets. Dad provided advice about writing, edited his friends' manuscripts, and arranged for publishers to see their writings.* He had many good friends with a variety of backgrounds. They included the merchant seaman Howie Hansen, the authors Jack Vance and Poul Anderson, the artist Bernard Zakheim, the photographer Johnny Bickel, and our companion in Mexico, Mike Cunningham. One of Dad's closest

---

*One of the people he helped, Mom's friend Frankie Goodwin, said that he taught her to never use the word "very" in anything she wrote. If she ever had the urge to use it, he told her to substitute the word "damn" instead.

friends was Russ Ladde, a California highway department employee who introduced him to the Zen writings of Alan Watts. Another who had appeared in recent years was the poet and author Bill Ransom. There were many more. My mother's close female friends were equally numerous, and all were strong, intellectual women, as she was. Sadly, with all the changes in the lives of my parents they lost track of some people over the years. The move to a distant tropical island put up one more barrier, and they would not see many of their dearest friends ever again.

Still, in the *Dune* series my father wrote of the importance of change and adaptation, and asserted that those who didn't do so grew stagnant. Frank Herbert was anything but stagnant. He decided to make the best out of the move to Hawaii, turning it into an adventure and filling his ever-curious mind with new, exciting information that one day would find its way into his stories.

Early that afternoon Dad and I were alone in the living room, and we talked about what it took for a marriage to work. He said it was a sharing experience, and that one party should be careful not to make all of the decisions, or the mate would stop growing and become dull in comparison. Or resentful. Even with his apparent dominance over Mom in many respects, she had her methods of persuasion, more subtle than his, less obvious. He didn't always dominate her. They had their niches. Mom managed to grow despite him, and had turned into a very interesting person in her own right. My father had become, to his credit, something of a benign dictator when it came to people he loved.

Jack Vance called just before we left, and I spoke with him, his wife Norma and Dad on an extension phone. Dad said he was going to do a fifth *Dune* book, and Jack quipped, "Did the publisher ask you to call it *Rebecca of Sunnybrook Dune?*"

"No," Dad said without missing a beat, *"Gunga Dune."*

Jack congratulated Dad on his success. A few moments later, Mom came on the line and mentioned my three book sales. Jack congratulated me as well, and spoke a little about his own career. A modest, self-effacing man, Jack didn't boast. But I knew he was a science fiction superstar in Europe, where people lined up for blocks to obtain his autograph.

After the call, Mom said Dad was always telling publishers how excellent Jack's work was. Frank Herbert was like that about other writers, very generous with his compliments if he felt they were deserved. I never knew him to harbor any professional jealousy.

He looked at me and said, "I've praised you in New York, too."

On the drive home with Jan and the kids, we encountered rain mixed with snow.

On the evening of the sixth of April, 1982, I received a telephone call. "This is Robert Heinlein," a deep, distinguished voice said.

At first I thought it was a practical joke, and I darn near made a flippant remark. I had several friends and a father who had been known to do such things. But it really *was* Heinlein, and he proceeded to ask how my mother was doing. I told the science fiction author that she seemed better, but that she was going in for tests the following day. He sounded formal, but likable. I thanked him for showing concern.

"Bev is a very special person," he said. He asked me to call and tell him how Mom was doing, and provided his unlisted telephone number. Heinlein also mentioned wanting to see Dad at the Science Fiction Writers of America convention later that month at the Claremont Hotel in Oakland.

I told Heinlein that Mom and Dad were in Port Townsend, but he did not seem to want to bother them. "Oh, they're stateside now," he said. "I mean mainland . . . now that Hawaii's a state."

After the call, I put two and two together. Heinlein was going through the back door to find out how my mother was doing. He'd had a falling out with my father, but still had feelings of affection for my parents. I picked up the distinct impression he was sad about what had happened to the friendship they once enjoyed. (They had gotten into a heated argument over a controversial literary agent, with the Heinleins and Herberts taking opposite sides of the issue).

The following day, Wednesday, was pleasant in the Pacific Northwest, with blue sky, few clouds, and temperatures in the low fifties. Late in the afternoon, I picked up my mother at Group Health Hospital in Redmond to take her to a family dinner engagement. She was in good spirits and said she felt pretty well, but she got a little winded going up a small hill in the parking lot. I helped her into the car, then gave her a large photograph of Margaux.

On the way to an elegant Japanese restaurant where we were to meet the others, I told her Robert Heinlein had called, and his purpose. She mentioned how close they had been once, with pleasant visits to the Heinleins at their place in Santa Cruz, California. She said so many fans discovered where the Heinleins lived that they had to put a high wall around the property for privacy.

At dinner that evening, Dad asked me to call Heinlein and pass along his regrets that he could not meet him at the Claremont Hotel because of a book tour that conflicted. I wondered aloud if my father shouldn't make the call so that Heinlein would not feel snubbed, but Dad insisted that I do it. He looked tired, and Mom said he had been doing a lot of her work—bookkeeping, issuing checks, coordinating public appearances, promotional coordination, answering huge piles of mail and the like.

Soon my father turned his attention to Margaux, who was being held by Jan on his immediate left. We were at a low table with our shoes off. He touched Margaux's hand and began talking with her. For a moment the four-month-old child stared at her grandfather wide-eyed. Then she let out a little squeal of displeasure.

"It's probably Frank's beard," Mom said. "A lot of babies are afraid of beards."

Later, as Margaux was crawling around on the straw mat and Jan called her, my mother said, "It seems funny to hear the name 'Margo' around the family after so long." More than thirty years had passed since the death of her mother, Marguerite, also known as Margo.

We got to talking about hands, looking at one other's lifelines on our palms. Mom was expert in the subject, said she used to read a lot of people's futures from looking at their hands. "But I was too good at it," she said, "and had to give it up." She spoke of some frightening predictions of hers that had come to pass, all of which she had determined by sensing "vibrations" while holding another person's hand. In one case, she warned the person, a close female friend, of an impending accident and counseled extreme caution. A short time later the woman was seriously injured in an automobile accident, with severe brain damage.

Dad said the filming of *Dune* was still scheduled for England, with the desert scenes slated for Tunisia. He was waiting to be called on location as the technical advisor.

We drove my parents to the Westin Hotel in downtown Seattle. On the way, Mom talked about needing to have her gold wedding band cut down. It was too loose on her finger, from all the weight she had lost.

Dad suggested that they find the same justice of the peace who had married them in Seattle in 1946. "Then I'll marry you again," he said.

The following Thursday, my father flew off alone to start his second *God Emperor of Dune* book tour, across the U.S. and Canada. Mom had to remain in Seattle for more medical tests, and planned to leave the next day to join him. After the tests, she and Jan had lunch together at an East Indian restaurant in Seattle, and went clothes shopping for Julie's fourteenth birthday. Because of Mom's limited energy, they had to take cabs on three occasions for short distances.

At the restaurant, which was on the second floor of a building across the street from Pike Place Market (a farmer's market with fresh produce), Mom told Jan she had been given bad news by the doctor that morning, and she hadn't told Dad yet. Her heart function was disturbingly less than it had been on her previous test, and the doctors seemed unable to arrest her degenerative condition.

Fighting back tears, Jan asked, "How bad is it?"

"The doctor told me, 'You won't survive this one.' " Following a long pause, she added, "I'm afraid to tell Frank."

Jan looked away at people bustling around the market. She regained her composure. "You can beat this, Bev," she said, gazing back across the table at the frail, impeccably dressed woman with her. "You have before and you'll do it again."

The doctor my mother had seen that morning said her heart had been strong or she wouldn't have survived so long, nearly eight years after the diagnosis of terminal lung cancer. But, he went on to say, it was only a matter of time before her heart gave out on her altogether. He could not predict how long she might live.

"I worry most about Frank," Mom said, with a brave smile. "We've always been like one person. When I go, what will happen to him?"

366

CHAPTER
32

✳ I'll Take Your Worries If You Take Mine ✳

ON THE evening of April 17, 1982, we met my parents at Trader Vic's Restaurant in the Westin Hotel. My father was in the midst of a big book tour, with another week to go. He had signed thousands of books in Toronto alone, so many that he'd been forced to wear a wrist brace. This was a custom appliance that wrapped tightly around his wrist and the heel of his hand, looping around the thumb. It kept the wrist straight and stable so that it didn't constantly flex with each signature he made, tiring it out. Even so, he said he could hardly move his right hand after the signings.

A limousine met them in every city. "I'm not playing B.T.O. (Big Time Operator)," he said. "The limo is a matter of survival."

In Philadelphia, the vehicle was a fabulous 1926 Rolls Royce Landau, with an open area for the driver. It had a cigar lighter in the back, and little snippers on chains to cut off cigar tips. The driver was always using "No Parking" zones, and never got a ticket. They parked illegally and went to see the Liberty Bell. When they came out, a policeman was standing by the car. Dad thought, *Uh oh!* But the policeman was just admiring the car.

For the Los Angeles segment, Dino De Laurentiis sent an immense private limousine to pick them up at the airport. The chauffeur gave Mrs. Herbert an exquisite red rose and served champagne in the car.

Dad caught a cold in Texas and was still hacking from it. He had to take lozenges during many interviews. He also had a skin split on his right eyelid, and Mom had a sore on her upper lip—conditions from the dry, windy cold on the East Coast.

They didn't talk about Mom's medical condition, and she looked much the same as the last time I had seen her—rather thin and drawn, but courageously cheerful. She wore a lovely Hawaiian shell necklace outside her blouse. Dad's beard was freshly trimmed, and he and Mom looked manicured. Dad was giggly and in a good mood, and he spoke cheerily of Mom walking off the plane this time, instead of being pushed in a wheelchair—as if she were doing better. This didn't track with what Jan had told me, and as I gazed into his eyes and into my mother's I detected new sadness there. He was in denial, desperately looking for the slightest encouraging things, while overlooking the negative.

Dad told us that the *Dune* movie director, David Lynch, wanted to leave theater-goers with the same feeling after seeing the movie as they would have after reading the novel. Lynch was going to extra efforts to remain true to the novel.

We learned that their first caretakers in Hana, the young couple, were quitting to return to the mainland. "They got island fever," Dad said, "couldn't take the confinement of the island." New caretakers were on the job, Bart and Sheila Hrast.

We all had quite a bit of wine, and were getting pretty silly. Dad was telling some hilarious jokes, when Mom touched his arm gently and asked, "Did you tell the one about the two Mexicans?"

He then proceeded to tell the story, and got it so fouled up that Mom interrupted him and said, "You've got it all wrong, you know. I hope you can get out of this."

"Oh I will," Dad said with his eyes twinkling. "That's my business!"

A week later Jan, Kim and I met my parents at Seattle Tacoma International Airport. They were just in from San Diego, last city on the book tour. Mom was standing straight as she walked, and holding onto my father's arm. Weary, they took their car and drove straight to the ferry terminal in Seattle.

On the first Friday in May, Mom cooked an entire dinner for us in Port Townsend, a delicious roast rack of lamb served with mint jelly, corn on the cob and roasted potatoes. She said she was feeling a lot better, with her energy returning. She had been swimming laps of the pool in recent days, an essential part of her rehabilitation program. The water temperature was set at ninety-one degrees for her, which resulted in substantial electric bills.

Margaux sat on the living room floor atop a blanket while we ate. Looking down at her, Mom recalled how cute Julie and Kim had been as babies, and how Margaux resembled them. Dad played a lot with the baby during the evening, pushing his beard in her face and making her giggle.

That weekend, Dad, Jan and I went sailing on the *Caladan*. It was a beautiful day, but a little too cool for my mother. So she stayed home with the kids. Jan and I did really well, as the boat was easier to sail than the ones on which we took lessons. Standing at the helm, Dad said he determined wind direction by feeling it on his face, and that he had learned to do this as a boy. This seemed an extraordinary ability for anyone to have, and I was doubly impressed because he didn't have a heck of a lot of his face exposed around his beard.

I thought of Paul Muad'Dib in a burnoose on the desert planet Dune, with most of his face obscured by the tucks of the robe. Sniffing at the air, Paul could sense the approach of a storm, and could tell wind direction just as my father did.

In ensuing weeks my book *Incredible Insurance Claims* received quite a bit of publicity, and I was interviewed by radio stations in the United States and Canada. Dad said a number of people had seen notices of the upcoming publication of my first novel, *Sidney's Comet*, and they were asking if we were related.

Early in June, my mother called me at work and said excitedly that she had received a letter from an astrologer friend in New York, a letter mentioning her "firstborn"—me. I was supposed to have great success in the future, involving a door opening for me that had previously been closed. Apparently the woman had been very accurate with her predictions in the past.

I never paid much heed to such matters, and was more concerned with finishing my second novel, *The Garbage Chronicles*, which was near completion. I wanted to show it to my father that weekend, and had worked long hours, including a marathon Thursday night until 3:30 A.M., allowing only three hours before going to the office. There had been more work remaining in the book than I had anticipated, but I pushed all the way through to the end . . . 402 pages. In the process I created some pretty unusual characters, including one I really liked, a young magical comet named Wizzy. One of the chapters was based upon an unpublished short story I had written the year before, "Earth Games."

I was a zombie at work the next day.

When I next saw my father in Port Townsend, he said everything was progressing on the *Dune* movie, although he had no idea who would star in it. Apparently the desert scenes would not be filmed in either of the most frequently rumored locations, Tunisia or China's Gobi Desert. The latest plan called for using a giant World War II blimp hangar in England, the interior of which would be converted into a desert. My parents were flying to Universal Studios in Los Angeles in a few days to talk with director David Lynch and Raffaella De Laurentiis, Dino De Laurentiis's daughter. She had been put in charge of the film by her father.

Dad was looking forward to a ten-day fishing trip in Alaska with his first cousin Ken Rowntree, Jr., and a friend, Jim McCarren. They planned to leave at the end of June—my father's first real vacation in ten years. He went to bed at 8:30 P.M., taking my just-completed manuscript with him.

In the morning he cooked blueberry pancakes and prepared fresh juice, a tasty mixture of orange and grapefruit. We were talking about vitamins and nutrients, and Dad said that British seamen ("limeys") discovered they could avoid scurvy by drinking lime juice. "They used to drink it with rum," he said.

"Sounds like a daiquiri," Mom quipped.

After breakfast Dad said, "Let's talk story."

The two of us took my manuscript in the living room and spread it out on the coffee table. "I didn't get very far last night," Dad said, while my heart hammered in trepidation, "but far enough to see that you've really improved." He had read the first chapter.

We worked all day, both of us sitting on the black vinyl couch. He made corrections here and there and passed the pages on to me. At times as he read he would take deep breaths and pick at his ear, and I tried to determine whether these were signs of boredom or fatigue. Five or six times, he laughed boisterously, once at a passage that was *not* intended to be funny. At other times, he would slouch back on the couch and drop his right arm to his side, in apparent disbelief. Sometimes he would stack pages neatly after reading them on the cushion between us. Other times, he would slam them down or hand them to me one at a time. He didn't say anything, just kept reading, and most of the signs seemed bad.

It was hot in the house, and as the session proceeded, I became sticky with perspiration. Partly from nervousness, no doubt. We could hear the excited squeals of the children as they swam with Jan and Mom.

By 6:00 P.M., Dad had read 328 of the 402 pages, with a couple of breaks. Once he sat back and closed his eyes. Within seconds, he was asleep—an enviable ability of his to nap anywhere.

We drove to the Harbormaster Restaurant in Port Ludlow. Fortunately, we got a nice corner window table with a view of the yacht harbor. Dad was not familiar with a particular selection on the wine list, a 1978 Mount Veeder Cabernet Sauvignon. He was afraid it might be too young, but decided it was probably okay since it was from California. It turned out to be very good.

Dad said a British publisher had made an unprecedented offer for United Kingdom book rights on *The White Plague*, higher even than he had received for any *Dune* book. Knowing he was hard at work on a book with Bill Ransom and had "*Dune 5*" to do after that, I asked him if he couldn't take life a little easier. He said Mom's illness had cut five and a half months out of his writing time, and they had some huge bills to pay for the construction in Hawaii.

"He's always worked hard," Mom said.

Jan toasted my new novel, *The Garbage Chronicles*, and to my relief Dad commented, "It's very good."

Mom mentioned that Bill Ransom and my father were writing alternate chapters in a "leapfrog" method, and that she never had been able to tell who wrote which chapter. "Bill has a smooth writing style," she said.

They were going better than anticipated, and now expected to complete *The Lazarus Effect* in August.

Keeping his voice from carrying to other tables, Dad told me how much he expected to earn the coming year, a seven-figure income that was equal to his entire net worth. In one year he would earn the equivalent of what it had taken him an entire lifetime to accumulate.

Three days later they flew to Los Angeles to visit Universal Studios and see how the *Dune* movie was going. In the process, my father lost another week from his writing schedule.

While they were gone, I finished *The Garbage Chronicles* and mailed it to Clyde Taylor in New York City.

After my parents returned, Dad was anxious to get back to his study, but Mom needed still another checkup with a heart specialist at Group Health Hospital. With all the ferry rides this would cost him yet another day. But my mother arranged with a pilot friend, Graham Newell, to fly her in a small plane from Port Townsend to the Bellevue Airfield, near our house. Jan picked Mom up in Bellevue and took her to the hospital, and then back to our house afterward.

I arrived home at shortly past 5:00 P.M., just in time to take Mom to the airport for her return flight to Port Townsend. Kim went with us and gave her Nanna a heart pendant necklace that she bought with her allowance. Kim, now ten, had lost a molar tooth that day, and for the first time said she no longer believed in the Tooth Fairy.

Tremendously excited about the movie, Mom described meetings at Universal Studios with David Lynch and Raffaella De Laurentiis, discussing cuts that might be needed in the film to keep it under budget. Lynch was having trouble with cuts to his "baby," so my father (after praising the work he had done) offered to help. One evening Dad worked at the studio editing the script, after which he and my mother went to a late dinner with Raffaella and David.

Frank Herbert's changes were incorporated into the screenplay, which would ultimately go into a sixth draft. In all he cut fourteen pages of material, resulting in a savings of fourteen million dollars in the budget. A million dollars a page. They had discussions about giving my father a share of the screenplay credit, but he wouldn't hear of it, saying he felt David and his associates deserved it for doing such a masterful job. He would accept a consulting fee only.

Raffaella De Laurentiis showed my parents a series of storyboards that had been prepared by the art department—pictorial instructions for the positioning of actors in key scenes. It was an intriguing process to Beverly Herbert. All of the castle scenes, for example, would be filmed at once, no matter where they appeared in the story. Then they would tear the castle set down and build another one. It would be extremely costly if they forgot to shoot a scene and had to rebuild a set. After all the filming, the scenes were pieced together where needed, in the film editing process.

An air of secrecy surrounded the production. Lynch, who referred to his scriptwriting team of Eric Bergren and Christopher DeVore as "The Great Team," wrote regular memos to them. During the first three days of June 1982, his transmittals included this: "Any leaks concerning what we are doing on this project will decrease the curiosity factor and cause us to lose power. I beg you to keep this in mind."

My mother found it all fascinating, but beneath her excitement I heard layered sadness and concern. She was wondering if she would live long enough to see the film. I prayed that she would.

Much later I ran across an entry in her travel journal from that Los Angeles trip, on binder paper. It comprised less than one page and revealed all the excitement of a schoolgirl confiding in her diary: "I can't believe it's really going to happen!"

She didn't have the energy to write more.

A few days later I spoke with Dad about his upcoming fishing trip to Alaska. "I don't know if I'm going," he said, and refused to discuss it further.

I knew he felt run down by what he'd been through—all the writing deadlines, the movie, the nonstop work, and the care he'd given to my mother. He needed that vacation desperately, had been looking forward to it for months. But Mom's latest medical tests had been so bad, showing a continuing downhill slide, that he thought he shouldn't go after all.

To save the fishing trip, Mom wondered if Jan could come to Port Townsend and stay with her. But Jan was having her difficulties at

Cornish Institute, where she was hanging on by a thread. These troubles had been caused in part by her concern over Mom, and in part by the demands of taking care of the baby. Her grades had been falling, and she couldn't afford to miss any more classes.

In a telephone conversation my father revealed to Jan that Mom wanted only her there in his absence—no one else who lived nearby would do.

Without approval from the school, Jan promised she would be in Port Townsend the next day. After catching the first ferry, from Seattle to Bainbridge Island, she called the school. The director said he understood, that he realized she had to take her chances and go. But he made no promises.

Dad waited until Jan arrived before leaving on his trip. He told her he felt bad for her having to leave school, but said he needed to get away. Jan told him not to worry, that it was all worked out at school. This was not true, of course.

Their first evening together, Mom did needlepoint while she and Jan talked in the living room about what was going on in their lives. Dad had found a new high-carbohydrate diet that was supposed to stop his chronic jet lag, and he was going to test it during the Alaska trip. Mom spoke as well about her best friend in high school and college, Frankie Goodwin, how they would exchange worries to relieve the burden of them. "I'll take your worries if you take mine," one girl would say to the other. And then they would trade. They called it the "Worry Game."

"Why don't we do that now?" Jan suggested.

Mom smiled, and said softly: "All right."

Jan did not mention her concerns about school, and spoke instead of worries about how our daughters would grow up, and who they might marry. And her hope that I might do well enough in my writing to leave the insurance business, since it seemed to her that I was wearing myself out writing and working full-time to support a family.

Mom spoke of her illness, and again of her concern over what might happen to Dad if she passed away. She said she'd been staying awake worrying about bills again, how they would be paid, and how she would get the energy to make sure the checks were sent out, and all the filing

374

and letter writing she had to do. She said while she was in the hospital or at doctor's appointments, Dad moved funds between their various accounts, leaving a bewildering trail she couldn't follow. He told her that he had issued important checks, paying mortgages, construction bills and other things. But she couldn't figure out which accounts had been used for what, and if they were the correct accounts. Now there were piles of unpaid bills, bills that Dad hadn't gotten around to paying because he was preparing for his trip and meeting writing deadlines.

He kept assuring her the money she needed for bills was available, and there was nothing to worry about. But to her their cash flow and cash on hand positions were not clear, and she didn't have the energy to figure it all out. Bills flowed in constantly. Big ones.

"Why don't you hire an accountant?" Jan suggested.

"Then what would I do? This is my job."

The next day Jan pulled two chairs up to Mom's desk and said, "We'll just sit here and figure it out together." Jan looked over the ledgers and made a telephone call (with Mom) to a banker, obtaining current bank balances. Jan couldn't quite figure it all out, and needed to ask Dad questions. But plenty of money seemed to be in the accounts and she said to Mom, "You tell me who to write the checks to, and out of what account." And every day with my mother, Jan helped her organize and pay the bills.

In this process, Jan felt frustrated that she could not do nearly enough, that she was like the little Dutch boy holding a finger in a massive dike—and anything she did was just stopgap, didn't really solve anything. So much more needed to be done for Mom, and Jan realized her own frustration must be minor compared with Dad's feelings.

Mom was too weak to cook, so Jan did it all, as Dad had done in recent months. Jan put her mother-in-law to bed, laid an electric blanket over her and set it up, brought her glasses of water and books—all the things Dad had been doing.

Some days they painted together—landscapes of the gardens, the duck pond, the tall, graceful trees around the property, the flowers. Or they went to the beach and took their paints and a picnic lunch along. On large sheets of newsprint, my mother showed Jan how her mother, a professional artist, had taught her to draw large scale without looking

375

at the page, keeping her eyes glued on whatever she was painting.

While Dad was in Alaska, Mom received a dramatic cover art poster from New York for *The White Plague*, which was soon to be released. It depicted a lush green Irish countryside, a dark, stormy sky and a giant double helix in the foreground. Dad had hoped to see the cover art before he left, but it hadn't arrived in time. Mom said she was putting it up in a prominent position on the kitchen bulletin board, so Dad would be sure to see it the minute he came in the door.

Mom gave me a phone number so that I could reach my father in Alaska at his fish camp near Lake Creek, which actually was a river. She said it was a radio telephone connection, in which only one person could talk at a time. When one spoke, it cut the line off for the other. Dad told her he was catching a lot of king salmon and rainbow trout and throwing them back, for the sport of it. He quipped that mosquitoes there were so big that four of them marked one fisherman with pheromones (external hormones) and carried him off. They dropped him when they saw a bigger, juicier fisherman. To thwart this danger, Dad claimed he wore a scuba diver's weight belt while fishing.

On the morning of the July day that Dad was due back from Alaska, Mom said she hadn't slept well, worrying if everything would be just right for him when he returned. She and Jan were sitting in dark yellow recliner chairs in a reading and television area just off the kitchen, with a table full of books and mail order catalogs between them.

"Could you make Frank a special meal?" Mom asked. "He really likes the barbecued sparerib recipe you gave me."

Jan went through two big boxes of recipe cards and found one in her own handwriting, from which she made the ribs. As soon as Dad phoned from the airport to say he would be home in a couple of hours, Jan left, so that my parents could share the meal in private.

When Dad arrived, he was so engrossed with having missed Mom that he didn't notice the giant, bright green poster for *The White Plague*—it was clearly visible, just inside the entry. Not until hours later, after he had savored the spareribs and was cleaning up in the kitchen, did he see it.

When I think of how my parents felt for one another, about the depth of their love, this incident comes quickly to mind. No matter the glory my father achieved from writing, no matter how many millions of people read his books, it all meant nothing to him without her.

CHAPTER
33

✳ *The White Plague* Is Taking Off! ✳

EARLY IN July 1982, my parents announced that they were leaving
for a month in Hawaii the following day, a decision they had made on
the spur of the moment.

At a hastily arranged dinner in Seattle just before their departure,
Dad told us in a sharp, angry voice about the difficulties they were
having finding low-salt foods for my mother in restaurants and grocery
stores, and how frustrating it was. Salt was everywhere in the American
diet, he said, and much of the blame had to do with the ignorance of
the medical profession. Doctors knew too little about diet, and not
enough meaningful research was being conducted about the benefits
and dangers of particular foods and diets.

While Dad was taking care of Mom, Penny was trying to keep
Bruce—now thirty-one years old—out of trouble. An incurable disease
had recently been discovered that was killing homosexual men—AIDS.
From her home in Stockton, California, Penny telephoned Bruce in
San Rafael near San Francisco. The most thoughtful and generous person in our family, Penny was always sending us notes and little gifts.
Now, with her stepmother seriously ill and weakened, Penny tried to
be a mother figure to Bruce, providing him with important advice. She
warned him about the dangers in the homosexual community from the
new disease and cautioned him against having unprotected sex and
relationships with multiple partners. Like the rest of us in the family,

378

she wished he wasn't homosexual at all. We were all worried about him.

Bruce promised to be careful.

Later that summer after my parents returned, Jan, Julie and I borrowed the *Caladan* and took it on a week-long sailing trip to the San Juan Islands, along with one of Jan's brothers, Ron Blanquie, and his wife. It was a great trip, with beautiful weather and excellent winds. When we returned to the Port Townsend Yacht Club, however, I didn't back the boat in the way Dad wanted it done. Backing confused me, so I took it in bow-first. Dad was on the dock watching, shaking his head in disapproval. After we disembarked he boarded the sailboat and restarted the engine. "Release the lines!" he shouted.

This was done, and he pulled the *Caladan* out, then turned it around quickly and backed it toward the slip. But he came in at the wrong angle, and too fast. The dock and boat were about to merge when Julie saved the day with quick thinking. At the last possible opportunity the 14-year-old threw a line from the boat around a cleat on the dock and heaved on it as hard as she could.

Subsequently all of us, especially my father, acted as if nothing had happened.

At Xanadu, Mom said her fingernails had been flaking lately, and she was not sure why. I said nothing about it, but worried that it might be an indication of her condition. When she tried to swim the length of the pool, she only made it three-fourths of the way on her own. Dad walked alongside the pool by her as she swam, and dove in quickly to help her finish.

The following Thursday I telephoned to see how she was doing, and she said, "I'm bearing up. Frank took me swimming this morning."

My mother went on to talk about her jewelry insurance, which I was handling for her. She had a valuable Cortina quartz watch with a gold band, a gift from Dad during one of their European trips, and she told me what amount to use in insuring it. Recently she took the watch to a jeweler and had one of the links in the band taken out so that it would fit better. Her wrist was much smaller from all the weight she had lost.

My mother had bookkeeping ledgers spread before her as she talked, and gave me a couple of tips about looking for errors in the books: how to tell if a figure had been transposed, and if an amount had been moved from debit to credit by mistake.

Sometime that summer my father and mother stopped by our house for a short visit. I recall standing in bright sunlight with him in the backyard. He spoke about the beauty of Kawaloa, and the perfect Hawaiian weather. "There's a certain kind of warmth you get from the sun that you don't get anywhere else," he said.

These words conveyed another message, that the paradise he had provided for Mom in Hawaii had become his as well. It more or less sealed what I already knew and feared, that one day they would finally decide to sell the Port Townsend property and live year-round in Hawaii.

In September, Dad went on a big book tour to promote the hardcover edition of *The White Plague*. Chauffeured limousines picked up my parents in every city on the tour, and huge crowds greeted Dad at every public appearance.

By the twenty-seventh of the month, the tour was wrapping up and he was scheduled to appear in Seattle. Jan and I met my parents at the *Seattle Times* at 11:30 A.M., where Dad had just been interviewed by the newspaper's book editor. A limousine provided by Putnam took us to a posh restaurant in downtown Seattle. I brought along their insurance files, to review at the table.

"*The White Plague* is taking off!" Dad said, as he broke open a French roll.

I said I hoped he meant the book, and not the plague germ that would wipe out all womankind on the planet. This elicited a hearty guffaw from him. Dad's beard was neatly trimmed, shorter than usual, and he was ebullient. He was having the absolute best time of his life, at the height of his success. To crown it, Mom had been strong all through the tour, and said she was feeling good.

The novel had gotten rave reviews from a number of prestigious publications, Dad said, including *The New York Times*.

It was his sixth national bestseller. *Children of Dune, The Dosadi Experiment, God Emperor of Dune* and *The White Plague* had all appeared on weekly bestseller lists. *Dune* and *Dune Messiah* were bestsellers as well, from a ground swell that built up over years. Each title in the *Dune* series sold millions of copies, and the canvas of his imagination kept getting bigger. All Frank Herbert books were selling exceptionally well, with so many reprints of old titles all over the world that it was difficult to keep up with sales figures.

At one of the stores on the tour, a frail old woman in her nineties brought Dad a hardcover first-edition copy of *Dune*, a collector's edition. She placed it before him, and leaning close by his ear, whispered in a crackling voice, "Write something dirty in the book for me, please." Dad's eyes twinkled as he caught her gaze, and he thought for a moment. Then he wrote, "Something Dirty," and signed his name.

Another time, Dad actually did write a profanity alongside his signature, in a book he gave to a friend. It had been an impulsive prank, but subsequently he felt guilty for it and sent the friend a substitute copy, more properly autographed.

Occasionally, very rarely, readers would come to Dad with criticisms—some involving major plot points. Dad always smiled pleasantly and said, "Why don't you go write your own book?"

Despite brisk book sales, my parents were still having trouble keeping up with ongoing construction expenses at Kawaloa. They were drawing up plans for an apartment wing to be built next, and a swimming pool was planned soon after that. A number of the estimates they had received for construction were proving to be woefully low, and they didn't have a written contract to keep costs down. Even if they'd had a contract, Dad said, it wouldn't mean much, because of the number of changes he kept making in the design during construction.

In early October, Mom prepared a special birthday meal for Dad—oysters from nearby Quilcene Bay and wild blackberry pie. She said the oysters, as she prepared them, were a favorite of his, and I made notes on how to do it.

After work the following Monday I worked at the public library on a new nonfiction book I was writing about how to deal with dishonest businessmen, which I entitled *The Client's Survival Manual*. When I arrived home, Julie said there was an article on her grandfather pinned to a library wall at her high school. It was next to a large paper fish.

Proudly, Julie told a friend, "That's my Grandpa on the wall there."

"That fish?" the friend exclaimed.

Margaux, now ten months old, could stand without holding on, but was pretty shaky.

On the eighteenth of October, Mom received good news at her Group Health checkup. Her heart function had improved slightly, undoubtedly from the strict diet and careful exercise regimen she followed. Her potassium level was on the low side, however, so her doctor prescribed Slow-K to keep the level up. To further improve the condition, she was told to eat bananas and drink orange juice daily.

In Seattle that day, however, Mom and Jan rode with an insane taxi cab driver who drove too fast and cornered over the edges of sidewalks, causing pedestrians to jump clear. Another matter unsettled my mother as well, since she was taking her wedding ring to a jeweler that day to have it reduced. Her fingers had become extremely thin from weight loss. It was the first time in thirty-six years she'd had to leave it anywhere.

When we saw Dad that evening, he said that the casting call had gone out on the *Dune* movie, and that all parts were set with the exception of the three leading roles of Paul Atreides, Lady Jessica and the Reverend Mother Gaius Helen Mohiam. The base of operations was uncertain, but the desert scenes would be filmed in the Samalayucca Desert in Mexico, since Mexican peso devaluations made it economically attractive.

Dad said that *The Lazarus Effect* was finished, and that it was a substantial improvement over *The Jesus Incident*, where he and Bill Ransom had experienced plot and characterization difficulties.

The next morning my parents left for Hawaii, planning to remain until spring. On their second day there, Dad called to say that he had forgotten their passports in Port Townsend, which they needed for a romantic Christmas trip to Samoa and Bora Bora. I promised to retrieve them, along with other items that Mom wanted sent to her. He said he was in tennis shorts looking out at two mountain peaks on the "Big Island" of Hawaii, Mauna Kea and Mauna Loa. It was eighty-four degrees, and they were about to leave for dinner at the elegant Hotel Hana Maui.

A month later, by the seventeenth of November, I had typed 170 pages of *The Client's Survival Manual.* That evening, Margaux took her first steps—five of them. Her steps were extremely hesitant and uncertain, with no bending of the knees at all. In the manner of a tightrope walker, she had her arms extended at her sides for balance.

Dad called when we were getting ready for bed. It was three hours earlier in Hawaii. He was eighty pages into a new manuscript, *Heretics of Dune*, fifth in the *Dune* series. They had decided not to go to Samoa or Bora Bora after all, as he was in the middle of a book and did not want to leave it.

I heard Segovia classical guitar music in the background, from his extensive reel-to-reel collection. Mom came on the line and said she hoped he would change his mind about the South Seas trip. They never did go, and later I learned it was really because of the constant cash flow problems. The trip was on the frivolous side.

Early in December I spoke with Mom by telephone, about Christmas gifts for the children. She said Honolulu was a "two-bit town" for shopping. "It's not like the places I've seen," she said. "Oh! The places I've seen!" The way she said this brought to mind exotic, colorful marketplaces all over the world. It also made me think of an entry in Leto II's journal in *God Emperor of Dune*: "Oh, the landscapes I have seen! And the people!"

She was depressed about spending the holidays away from family and said, "Give the girls a big hug for me."

"I can see your arms stretching across the Pacific to us," I said.

"Well they are," she responded.

Four days before Christmas, my father called. He said their Christmas tree was a five- or six-inch-high Hawaiian bush with ornaments on it.

The De Laurentiis people were building sets now, with a $56,000,000 projected film budget, substantially more than earlier estimates. After changing their minds a number of times, the producers had decided to film the entire motion picture in Mexico, because of Mexican peso devaluations. They hoped to release it in the spring or summer of 1984.

I asked Dad how many pesos there were in fifty-six million dollars. His answer: "Muchisimo." ("Very many.")

CHAPTER

34

✳ Her Warrior Spirit ✳

EARLY IN January 1983, I finished *The Client's Survival Manual*, nearly five hundred pages, and dispatched it to Clyde Taylor in New York. I had heard my father speak of needing to get a manuscript out the door, getting it finished and out of sight for the sake of sanity, and now I knew what he meant.

I set to work on a new science fiction novel, *Sudanna, Sudanna*, about an alien planetoid where music was outlawed.

Around this time I spoke with Dad by telephone. He and Mom had just returned from a tiring trip to Carmel and San Francisco. Mom had gone in for medical checkups before and after the trip, and the deterioration of her heart muscle had slowed. This was bittersweet news, since it was still deteriorating.

While in San Francisco, my father wandered into a Market Street bookstore, as a customer. And, as he did occasionally, he began removing copies of his books from the racks and signing them. Suddenly the clerk, a huffy young man, rushed over and said, "Now see here! What do you think you're doing?"

"I'm autographing these books, of course," came the response, in an erudite tone. And Dad pulled another book down from the shelf, a hardcover edition of *Children of Dune*. On the title page he drew a line through his name and scrawled his signature, with practiced strokes.

"You'll have to stop, sir!" the clerk exclaimed, believing him to be a pretender, perhaps even a megalomaniac.

"But I'm Frank Herbert."

The clerk didn't believe him, not even when Dad held the photograph of himself on the back cover of *Children of Dune* next his face. It wasn't until the bearded man produced identification, including a raft of credit cards, that he was finally believed. Then the poor fellow became the most embarrassed, apologetic person on the face of the earth.

Dad told me he was ninety pages into the first draft of *Heretics of Dune*. He referred to it as "the one all the money's riding on," since he was being paid so much for it.

He said Mom and one of the caretakers, Sheila, were planting poinsettias for Jan on the hillside just outside the kitchen window. Poinsettias had been important to my wife since childhood, when she placed them at the base of a statue of the Virgin Mary and prayed for her mother to recover from an illness. Reportedly a miracle had occurred. Over the years, my mother had given Jan poinsettia gifts in a variety of forms, from tablecloths and napkins bearing the design to live plants. Now Beverly Herbert wanted to present her daughter-in-law with fresh flowers when we went to visit. Mom had also been looking for information on cruise ships for me, and had found a couple that she was anxious to tell me about.

On Sunday, January 9, 1983, Dad called and told me angrily about an attempt by Chilton Books to assert an interest in the *Dune* movie, despite having waived all such rights when Putnam became the hardcover publisher of *Dune*. I asked him if there might be loopholes in the waiver, and he said there were none to his knowledge. "I'm going to put a Philadelphia lawyer in his place," he said, referring to the attorney representing Chilton.

My father said he was putting in long hours on the new novel, pressing to complete it as soon as possible. That morning, as usual, he rose before dawn and worked out on a rowing machine and exercycle. Then a quick shower and a light breakfast of toast and guava juice, which he took to his study. He took a large number of vitamins each day.*

After writing for three hours, he helped Mom get ready for the day. He made her hot Cream of Wheat with sliced bananas on top, found books and knitting materials and art supplies and whatever else she needed, and by 9:30 he was back at his desk. He was using a Compaq word processor now instead of a typewriter, since it was much faster. Each night he put the computer away in a dry room, to prevent it from being damaged so quickly by salt air.

My mother was sitting outside in the sun as he spoke, with a sketch pad on her lap, painting lush flowers from their garden.

During this time, I performed the usual chores for my parents, involving insurance, maintaining their car, straightening out bank accounts and tracking down items that they could not locate in Hawaii. A number of telephone calls came in as well, from people looking for them. I played "moat dragon" by screening the inquiries, so that Mom and Dad would not be disturbed unnecessarily.

In mid-January I spoke with my parents, with each of them on an extension phone. After listening to Dad for several minutes, I asked my mother what she had been doing to keep busy.

"Checking up on your father," she said with a chuckle. "It used to be easier when he wrote with a typewriter, but now he has a word processor and I have to listen carefully for the keys."

Dad laughed.

"How are you feeling, Mom?" I asked.

---

*For years Dad had been on a regimen of twelve to fifteen vitamins daily. Bottles of them were lined up on the bathroom counter. Since vitamin A was retained in the body and he could overdose on it, he took it every other day. And, since vitamin D came from the sun, he took it on alternate days while in Hawaii and daily on the mainland. He said that every person should take a different quantity of vitamin C, and that it had to be taken with vitamin B for best assimilation. He based this on the fact that some people needed sixty milligrams a day to avoid scurvy, while others only needed five milligrams. He said each person could determine his proper amount by loading up on the vitamin until the stool started to loosen—and then backing off a little on the dosage. When vitamin E became popular in the early 1980s, ostensibly for its ability to inhibit the aging process, both of my parents took it. They found an additional property for it as well, which my mother described for me. A gelatin capsule of vitamin E could be opened and spread on a cut, she said, in order to make it heal faster.

386

"Oh fine, fine." She sounded cheerful, with a hint of the giggly little-girl cuteness she could exude at times.

Dad spoke of a party they had been to, and how easy it was in Hawaii to eat and drink to excess and get too much sun. He suggested a book we might write together, in a year or so. It would be non-fiction, with a working title of *Looking for America*. The book would examine American myths, including reminiscences and comparisons . . . discussing how far off course we had drifted. I expressed interest, keeping in mind occasional discussions we'd had to do a humor book or cookbook together. Such discussions had petered out, but in retrospect I hadn't pressed them, and my father had to be the busiest man on the planet.

I learned later that Mom had been encouraging him to write a book with me. I discovered as well that she wanted to sell Xanadu, the Port Townsend house, and purchase a waterfront place on Mercer Island, near us. At her urging, they planned to begin looking for the house upon returning to the mainland. "I love the water," she said.

It was all part of a secret and well-thought-out plan she had, one that would become increasingly evident to all of us.

In mid-February, after experiencing plot problems on my new novel, I was beginning to build up a head of steam. I was sitting at the typewriter when Mom called.

"I called for nothing," she said. "I was thinking about you guys, missing you."

We discussed *Sidney's Comet*. She was anxious to see it in book form. I told her I received a color proof of the cover art several days earlier, and would make a copy for her. Publication was scheduled for June.

Dad came on the line for a few moments, and said he was on page 366 of *Heretics of Dune* out of a projected five hundred. This was only forty-six pages better than a month earlier, and he said he had run into plot problems, slowing him down. I learned later that Mom had not been feeling well in recent weeks, with nausea and loss of appetite, as well as abdominal pains from serious fluid accumulation in the peritoneal cavity. Dad had been required take her to the Hana Medical Clinic almost every day, and Dr. Howell, thinking her medications might be causing her discomfiture, reduced her medications. This, however, resulted in a severe loss of energy, and the medications were reinstituted. Dad didn't tell me these things with Mom nearby, as she didn't like him sharing too much detail about her condition, fearing it would make us worry.

But the next day, a Monday, Dad phoned me at work and said, "I don't want you to think this is a big medical emergency, Brian, but we may be back in three days."

Dr. Howell wanted Group Health Hospital in Redmond (near Seattle) to monitor her blood condition and other vital signs to see how her body chemistry was reacting to medication. They had to balance it carefully. The doctor was checking with his mainland counterparts on this, and a flight was being arranged.

My father wanted me to pick them up at SeaTac Airport on Thursday, February twenty-fourth, and said they needed to stay with us. But he was rattled, and called me before knowing the flight schedule. I was worried about him, knowing how difficult it was for him to be pulled out of the middle of a book.

I heard my mother's voice in the background, rather a high tone, and Dad paused to listen to her. "I'll be right back," he said to me. The receiver thumped as he set it down.

Presently Dad returned, saying Mom got a shot from Dr. Howell and was complaining that her thigh hurt. I heard her say something about not wanting to climb the stairs to the bedrooms in our house. She might stay in the hospital, Dad said, and he would stay with us. My mother was unhappy, too, about having to leave Kawaloa.

Afterward Jan and I spoke about how unfortunate it was that they had chosen to live in such a remote part of the world, with Mom needing so much medical care. Hana was good for my mother's soul, but the decision to live there had been emotional, not thought out well.

I didn't sleep well that night, and learned in the morning that Jan and I had said separate prayers for Mom.

On the evening of the twenty-fourth, we drove Mom straight to Group Health Hospital in Redmond. I had a color proof of the *Sidney's Comet* cover in the car, and showed it to them. It depicted a fiery orange and yellow comet against a starry backdrop of space. It was a comet composed of Earth's own jettisoned garbage, coming back to destroy the planet.

We checked Mom into the hospital. She had been experiencing abdominal pains, and according to tests performed in Hawaii had minor fluid accumulations in her abdomen and liver. One of the nurses asked her to list all the medications she was on, and Mom rattled off four or five.

Dad went with her to X-ray, made sure the phone in her room was hooked up, and explained details of her condition to the nurses and a doctor. It took over two hours, and we did not arrive home until nearly 1:30 A.M.

On the drive to our house, Dad said the *Dune* movie should be completed by 1984, but perhaps not until late in the year. He said the dispute with Chilton over movie rights had been settled out of court, with Dad paying 37.5 percent and Putnam the balance. The problem was a clause in the contract that gave Chilton "three-dimensional reproduction rights." Dad asked what it meant at the time and recalled being told that it referred to movie promotional items, such as pop-up books and tee-shirts. The Chilton lawyers used this clause, in my father's words, "to harass the movie production," and he thought they might have to be paid around seventy-five thousand dollars under the settlement agreement.

We discussed the *America* book we were going to do. He spoke passionately about the blunders of existing governmental systems. Whenever he started talking about politics, he had a lot to say. Millions of readers knew this from the *Dune* sequels in particular, where the characters spoke at length about power and politics, didactically at times. Frank Herbert was, after all, a teacher.

He was a staunch believer in America and in democracy, but his active mind envisioned any number of improvements that might be made to the system. One of them involved what he called a "national jury democracy" or "national town meeting," in which governmental power would be taken away from politicians and bureaucrats, in favor of the citizenry. The U.S. House and Senate, and similar state institutions, would be eliminated entirely, with their veto power transferred to the electorate. Under a nationwide "jury" system linked by computer, the electorate would be given the power to veto any decision, any policy made by their leaders. It didn't matter what governors or even the president of the United States said. The people would have a direct voice in everything.

My father went on to say that he wanted to remove entrenched functionaries, that the American bureaucracy needed to be radically overhauled. In an incredulous tone he told the story of a Washington, D.C., bureaucrat who had been ensconced in his position for more than four decades. Like many others, he could not be fired. Incredibly, the bureaucrat referred to members of the U.S. House and Senate as "transients."

The morning after our brainstorming session, a Friday, Dad was up at dawn, on his way to the hospital to see Mom. She spent the day traveling between Redmond and Seattle by cabulance, for the various tests she needed. Her abdomen had flattened out, and she was feeling better. He'd gone to a department store at noon, skipping lunch, and bought her a warm robe.

At our house that evening Dad talked about his childhood and what he knew of Mom's, and frequently his eyes misted over. But he kept on, as if trying to recapture halcyon, simpler times.

Dad, Julie and I visited Mom that evening. She looked nice in the new light blue robe he had given her. On the way home, Dad gave us ominous news. He said she had "cardiomyopathy" and "pneumonitis," linked to the radiation treatments of 1974, with only 60 to 65 percent of her normal heart and lung functions remaining. Most of the right side of her heart had collapsed. She would be checking out of the hospital soon, and he was arranging for her to have oxygen at home when she slept. A home-unit would convert ambient air to 95 percent pure oxygen. Since the heart produces oxygen for the body, he explained, Mom needed more oxygen to supplement the loss of function. He thought the best they could hope for was for the heart to remain stable, or eventually the condition would kill her.

"There are no guarantees in this life," he told me.

"At least Mom has had a better life than many people," I said.

He thought for a moment, then said, in a determined voice, "It's not over yet."

On Saturday, February 26, 1983, Frank Herbert woke up at around

4:00 in the morning and telephoned the hospital to check on his wife. She'd had a good night's sleep, according to the nurse on duty.

When I saw him later that morning, he had a one inch gash on top of his forehead. He had been sleeping in our carriage house room under a low overhang, and whacked his head when he sat up too quickly.

Dad and I went to see Mom at around 11:00 A.M. On the way, he said Mom's best hope might lie in ongoing research into the body's immune system. If certain problems could be resolved, she might be able to receive a heart transplant. Up to that time, only a few hundred transplants had taken place in the entire world, and many of the patients had died when their immune systems did not accept the new organ or when other complications set in, such as pneumonia.

Dad said he had to do all of the cooking now, as Mom did not have the energy. He was feeling pretty tired himself, suffering his usual jet lag on top of everything else. He brought his manuscript along, but hadn't been able to touch it. "I'm too wrung out to write," he said.

At our house that evening, Dad was showing Kim and me how to prepare one of his favorite meals, Oyster Sauce Beef. He took a call from his film agent, Ned Brown, in the midst of this and told him how Mom was doing. In some detail, they discussed a complete waiver that was being signed by Chilton Books, at the conclusion of which my father said, "Righto. They'll hold me blameless for everything and will never sue me, even if I urinate on them."

Later at the hospital, Mom asked about the cut on Dad's head, which she hadn't noticed previously because of the effects of her medication.

"It's not serious," he responded. "Just a little hole."

Dad sat with Mom on the bed. He was a little too clumsy for her this time, however, with his arm around her shoulder so that it hurt her neck, and leaning against her so that she had trouble breathing. With a girlish giggle, she dispatched him to his chair.

When we were about to leave, Dad leaned close to Mom and held her hand, telling her he loved her and adding, "I wish you were with me."

"Why?" she asked, looking at the cut on his forehead. "Then I'd have a hole in my head, too!"

On the drive home Dad said his income had doubled in a short period of time, but mentioned what I had heard before, that they were still having a great deal of trouble keeping up with expenses. I offered to loan him thirty or forty thousand dollars, if that would help, but he said that would hardly touch his financial obligations.

"I'll keep your offer in mind," he said, "but I think I can pry something loose from my publishers."

During the next week, Dad stayed with us most nights, but at least half the time he slept at the hospital near Mom, in a waiting room or on a cot they set up for him.

Jan and I visited Mom every day. To outward appearances she seemed too healthy to be in the hospital, and I was hopeful for her. She told me Dad was always making sure she had everything, and if anything was lacking or slow in arriving, he went in search of a nurse. He even monitored the medications she was receiving, and asked doctors and nurses to explain the purpose of each one, and the dosages. "Sometimes he orders the nurses around," Mom said with a smile, "as if he were a doctor."

Just before we checked Mom out of the hospital in early March, Dad told me the doctors only gave her two years to live. "I think she'll live longer," he added in a resolute tone. "She's fooled the experts before."

I was shaking, and he comforted me.

A few days later the telephone rang at my office, and I answered with my name.

To this she replied, "Hello, Brian Herbert." She sounded surprisingly good, and it comforted me. She was in Port Townsend, and said Dad had been interviewed that morning by *The New York Times*. She had been to her doctor in Port Townsend, giving blood for a sample he needed.

I asked what else she had been doing during the week.

"Just giving blood," she said. "I've been paying bills."

"Are you swimming?" I inquired.

"Starting again," she said. "Your father is helping me."

Among Dad's many ideas in recent years he had mentioned the possibility of setting up a family compound near Issaquah, just east of Seattle. But Mom had her own input, which differed. They spent a day in the middle of March with a realtor, looking at houses on Mercer Island and in nearby Bellevue. They wanted a rambler due to Mom's exertion problem. No stairs. Jan went with them, and told me afterward that Mom had trouble breathing under the slightest exertion. They didn't find a house that they liked.

That evening, we went to dinner at a gourmet restaurant on Mercer Island, and I noticed the breathing noises my mother was making, too. I held her arm and walked with her from the car to the table. She seemed so delicate and small, but she was cheerful and smiled at me frequently. At the table, I helped her out of her elegant, long black coat. She wore a lavender Missoni dress and a pearl necklace with matching earrings. A gold Swiss watch adorned her left wrist.

I told Dad that for a couple of weeks I had been worrying about books I had in New York in search of publishers, *The Garbage Chronicles* and *The Client's Survival Manual*. I was quick to add that I was at work on a new novel, *Sudanna, Sudanna*, and this pleased him.

On Monday, March 28, 1983, Dad was scheduled to fly to Mexico City to operate the clapboard for the first scene of the *Dune* movie. Mom had planned to go, but her doctors felt that the altitude there (7,350 feet) and severe air pollution could make it difficult for her to breathe. Consequently, she would remain home. Deeply disappointed at not being able to be with him on such a momentous occasion, she was grouchy the whole week that he was gone.

Jan shifted her school schedule around to be with Mom, and arrived in Port Townsend just before Dad left. He explained my mother's dietary needs to Jan, and her exercise program, with this caution, "You have to stay with her every second in the pool."

A strong swimmer, Jan told him not to worry.

Max Von Sydow, José Ferrer, Jurgen Prochnow, Linda Hunt and Sting would be in the cast, and they had a new actor for the leading role of Paul Atreides, Kyle MacLachlan, a recent graduate of the University of Washington acting school. He had played Shakespearean parts, including Octavius Caesar and Romeo, and when discovered by a *Dune* casting agent was playing in The Empty Space Theatre's production of *Tartuffe* in Seattle. MacLachlan, signed to a multi-picture deal for more stories in the *Dune* series, had been a fan of *Dune* since reading it at the age of twelve or thirteen. Remarkably, he had sometimes fantasized about playing the part of Paul. Two screen tests were required before he won the coveted role—one in Los Angeles and the second in Mexico City.

I spoke with Dad on the telephone early in April after he arrived home. He was not feeling well, having contracted what he termed *"mal de la pais,"* meaning "the ill of the country." He was euphoric nonetheless, saying that the movie production was going extremely well. He said he had dined with Sian Phillips, Richard Jordan, José Ferrer and other members of the cast.

The filming was taking place at Churubusco Studios, near the site of the 1968 Olympic Games. Dad got to keep the clapboard from the very first take of the first scene, after he clicked it to start the cameras rolling. Later the film crew would shoot desert scenes in the Samalayucca Desert of northern Mexico.

"I shot off the starting pistol," my father said.

Frank Herbert was pleased with the way that David Lynch was directing the project. "David understands the essence of my book," Dad said. "He's translated my swashbuckler to the language of film."

He said that half a dozen people recognized him on the plane coming home, and he suspected it would get worse after the movie came out. This comment was based not only on the general publicity but on the fact that he might do an Alfred Hitchcock–style cameo appearance in the movie. Some people were suggesting that he shave off his beard to protect his privacy. To this he replied, steadfastly, "No way. It's my trademark."

He also said there was continued strong interest from Paramount Pictures about doing *The White Plague* as a movie, and that he'd been on the telephone with his film agent, Ned Brown, about that recently.

On Monday, April 11, Clyde Taylor called from New York with fantastic news. He said Berkley Books wanted to publish *The Garbage Chronicles*. After listening to an account of their offer, which he thought was satisfactory, I told him to accept.

The following Saturday we arrived in Port Townsend just before noon. The new Hood Canal floating bridge was completed and open, making the trip a lot easier and saving at least an hour of travel time.

That afternoon my father and I discussed our collaboration, the book about America. He had some intriguing ideas, and showed enthusiasm for a number of my suggestions. He also said to me, "You'll establish your name as a novelist. In fact, from what I've been hearing out of New York, you already have."

Margaux ran around getting into things all day, with my mother and the rest of us saying, constantly, "No, no!" Finally, Mom quipped, "I've always wanted the kids to call me Nanna, but I'm afraid this one is going to think my name is Nono."

The following morning I arose before dawn and went up to Dad's loft study, where I typed a couple of pages of *America* notes from the previous day's discussion. He had a big Olympia typewriter on a side table, in addition to the computer and printer, which were set up on the desk.

Dad came upstairs just as I was finishing. He wore a blue terrycloth robe, with the script initials "F H" embroidered in gold on the pocket. His blond hair was wet and slicked back, from swimming. "I *thought* I heard my typewriter going," he said.

My father scanned the notes, then slapped them down on the desk and said, "Good. I'll add to them later. You want some orange juice?"

"Sure."

We squeezed half a dozen oranges in his big manual press on the kitchen counter, poured the juice in glasses and drank quickly, before the vitamin C dissipated.

"I did forty laps this morning," he said. "About average."

For him, perhaps, but not for most sixty-two-year-old men.

He gave me a cast list for the movie, showing a number of names we hadn't discussed before, including Dean Stockwell, Francesca Annis and Dino De Laurentiis' wife, Silvana Mangano, who had been a re-nowned beauty in her youth. Dad said he and Mom were getting a percentage on sales of movie tickets, and a different percentage on toys, dolls, coloring books and other products.

Emerging from the master bedroom, Mom joined the conversation. She had ideas for a fuzzy stuffed worm and a breakfast cereal called Melange. (After the precious spice of *Dune*.)

"I'm taking your mother to the movies next year," Dad added. "Our movie."

She beamed.

We were getting ready to leave for home, when Margaux slipped into Mom's office and flipped on her electric typewriter. Dad got pretty mad about this, and yelled at Julie and Kim for not keeping a better watch on their little sister.

Later that month my mother telephoned me at work while I was assembling a vegetarian sandwich on my desktop. She said excitedly that *Sidney's Comet* had just received a rave review from *Publishers Weekly*, a prestigious literary publication.

This was a total surprise to me, as my book hadn't been published yet. Scheduled for June, I had been told it might be out as early as May. Mom said they must have reviewed an advanced reading copy of the book and said it was a significant step in my new career.

"We're very proud of you," she said.

Dad got on the line and said something kind of corny, that I liked anyway. "That's my boy."

Clyde Taylor called from New York that afternoon, and read the review to me. Then he mailed me a copy. It read, in part:

The son of Frank Herbert has produced a fine first work, a carefully crafted social satire written with maturity, empathy and a dark wit . . . Herbert's work is unusually inventive and original. He displays real talent.

Two weeks later I received copies of the book in the mail, and began distributing signed copies to my family. On the title page, I crossed off my name and signed next to it, just as my father did. It had become a family tradition.

My mother was driving the Mercedes coupe now, giving her a degree of independence. She did pretty well, except for one day toward the end of May 1983, when she hit a garden stake with a nail on it that gouged paint along the bottom of one of the car doors. I took information on the claim from her.

On Thursday, June 2, Dad called to say a local bookstore wanted him to sign several boxes of his books for a special Frank Herbert display. He asked me to pick up the books and bring them to him. After work I picked up eleven boxes containing a mixture of his titles.

The next day we arrived in Port Townsend at 5:30 P.M. It was cooler than it had been, around sixty degrees, and overcast. Only a few days before, the Pacific Northwest experienced record temperatures in the high eighties and low nineties.

Mom was reading Dad's just completed fifth *Dune* novel when we walked in. She was seated in one of the dark yellow recliner chairs in the sitting area adjacent to the kitchen, with manuscript pages spread out on the table beside her. She said it was great, that she couldn't put it down. She felt each book in the series was better than the one before, with plots and characterizations that were even better than *Dune*.

Dad said his newest, *Heretics of Dune*, was at least two hundred thousand words, and had gone beyond his earlier five-hundred-page manuscript projections. The words would probably be trimmed to 180,000 by Victoria Schochet, the freelance editor working on the project for Berkley/Putnam.*

I went outside and brought the boxes of books into the basement, through the garage. Dad sat at a table and signed half the books, while I unpacked and repacked them. He signed each title page with a flourish, after first crossing out his printed name.

During our meal, my mother said it was unusual that I was selling novels without first having sold short stories. I told her I had incorporated one of my short stories, "Earth Games," into *The Garbage Chronicles* as a chapter.

After dinner, I was pouring Grand Marnier for the adults, while Jan was helping Mom and Dad in the kitchen with the dinner dishes. Suddenly all hell broke loose. Margaux, a year and a half old, was in the living room, and had gotten into some *Dune* movie slides that Dad had brought back from Mexico City. She made finger marks on many of them, and Dad said these marks had acid in them and would never come out. He was furious, though he probably should not have left the slides on a coffee table with a toddler running around. He tried

---

*Victoria Schochet—the wife of noted author Eric Van Lustbader.

to blame Kim for not watching Margaux, when suddenly Jan erupted in tears and told my father it was as much his fault as anyone's. She said it would be impossible to keep the baby out of their other things and that perhaps it would be better if we left right then and went home.

Mom calmed Jan down, and Dad said he was sorry for blowing up.

Several times afterward, though, he muttered, "She was *walking* on them! I can't believe she was *walking* on them!" But gradually things settled down and we stayed.

Children, my father's *bête noire.*

Dad put the Mexico slides in a projector, set up a screen and showed them to us. The pictures showed the *Dune* movie sets along with many of the production people. De Laurentiis and Lynch were assembling a crew of nine hundred, along with thirty-nine principal actors and a cast of twenty thousand extras. There would be seventy-five sets and eight sound stages—and four exotic planets would be depicted. Some of the scenes would be filmed in one-hundred-and-twenty-degree desert heat. Dad said they would not be doing the famous banquet scene from his book due to time and budgetary constraints. He disagreed with this decision, but did not seem visibly upset by it.

In a determined tone, Mom said she would go with him on the next movie trip, "come hell or high water," as she felt she was missing out on all the fun. She swam almost an entire pool length before we arrived—the best she had done since returning to the mainland earlier in the year. I got the feeling she was highly motivated, the way she'd been when she first discovered she had lung cancer back in 1974. She had a warrior's spirit.

All of us had seen *Sidney's Comet* next to Dad's books in bookstores. Both Mom and Jan were always rearranging our books, making sure they were neat and moving them up to eye level . . . displaying them more prominently. Jan mentioned receiving a telephone call in January, from a science fiction writer wanting to reach Dad. She said the fellow was rude, couldn't wait to get past her. "He was abrupt with me," Jan said, "treated me like a bump. So the next time I saw his books in a store, I moved them to the back and put Herbert books in front of them."

"Revenge of the Bump," I said.

"What a title!" Dad exclaimed.

While I was running an errand with my mother the next day, she quipped that she was married to Imhotep the Pyramid Builder, with all of the construction projects he had going on all the time. I thought back on my father's life. His Vashon Island, Washington, house hadn't been completed. Neither had a home remodel in Cloverdale, California. A houseboat project turned into a near disaster, financially and otherwise, as it strained relations with two of his closest friends. Then Dad purchased the Port Townsend place, and building activity reached new heights for him. He was forever giving me tours of the property and pointing out the changes he had in mind. Frank Herbert enjoyed showing visitors around, be they friends, family members or interviewers. He was always looking toward the future, toward what he hoped to build soon. No matter how much he completed, there was always more to come. And this was appropriate, I imagine, since he was a man of the future.

Now Kawaloa on far-off Maui was in a category of its own, way beyond anything he had attempted previously. And once it was built, what then? He wasn't only like Imhotep, I told Mom. He was like William Randolph Hearst, another powerful man who always had construction projects going on around him. My father liked the ongoing activity as a creative outlet when he had finished writing for the day.

"I hadn't thought of it quite that way," she said, "but I think you're absolutely right." As I turned onto the gravel road, I saw her nodding her head. She glanced at me, said, "You've become very observant, Brian."

"I figured him out with my journal."

"Good," she said. "And I suppose you've figured me out that way, too?"

"I'm still working on you," I replied, with a laugh.

My parents planned to spend their thirty-seventh wedding anniversary together in Mexico City, and were flying there on June 17. We got together with them the night before in Seattle.

Mom had been working hard on her conditioning program, improving her cardiovascular system to the maximum it could be. Doctors were concerned about the altitude of Mexico City and the terrible air pollution there, but she pressed to go. Finally they relented. They were absolutely amazed at how well she was doing, considering the damage they knew had been done to her heart from radiation treatment to cure lung cancer. She could swim two laps of the pool now, and almost half a lap underwater.

Universal Pictures was paying for the trip and for visits to the movie set by leading film distributors. The studio was spending hundreds of thousands of dollars, Dad said, for all the people they were bringing to Mexico City.

My parents' trip to Mexico this time differed markedly from an earlier excursion in 1955–56, when we were poor and had to return to the U.S. nearly penniless in a hearse with bald tires, our family car.

✳　✳　✳

After the return of my parents from Mexico in early July 1983, we picked them up at the Red Lion Inn in the Seattle suburb of Bellevue and took them to dinner at a French restaurant. Mom looked good but admitted feeling a little tired. Dad said she was continuing to improve. He put his arm around her at the table and said, "She swam laps at our hotel, at eight thousand feet!"

Mexico City was at 7,350 feet, but I said nothing. I knew what he was saying, that she had done well with her exercises at altitude, where the air was thinner and exertion more difficult. Not to mention the pollution.

"And she's up to four laps at home now!" he said.

"Four and a half," Mom said, proudly.

Two big parties had been given while they were in Mexico City, and they met many cast members. My parents sensed charisma in the handsome young actor playing Paul Atreides (Kyle MacLachlan), and thought he'd have to be on the alert for groupies. They saw three and a half hours of the first prints of film, called "rushes." Filming was 60 percent done, and should be completed around September. The editing, scoring, special effects and other finishing touches would take quite a bit of time after that, and the production staff thought it might be released to the public no earlier than June 1984.

Dad tossed around some staggering eight-figure numbers in terms of income he expected to receive from the film, and said he wanted to use a small portion of it, "a few million" to set up a foundation for the "study of social systems," with the goal of setting the American bureaucracy on a new course.

He said he had been plotting the sixth book in the *Dune* series for several days, while I was around 60 percent through my new novel, *Sudanna, Sudanna.* I had been working on it since February.

At least once a week, Mom and Dad came south from Port Townsend to look for a house in the Seattle area, hoping to find that waterfront piece on Mercer Island. They found a house that my mother loved, only a few blocks from our place on Mercer Island. A sprawling single-level home with Japanese architecture and landscaping, it featured a fine view of Lake Washington, but was not waterfront. They submitted an offer, and on the day it went in, Mom told Jan how much she hoped they could get that house. But my father had his own price in mind, substantially lower than the asking price. He "lowballed" the place, making such a bargain basement offer that it angered the sellers and the deal fell apart.

When Jan told me about this, about how much my mother wanted that house, I blew up. Jan had been going around with them looking for real estate for weeks, helping in every way possible. Now, after all the trouble, Dad had blown the deal. I called him and expressed my displeasure in no uncertain terms.

He didn't have much to say, but somehow after I hung up it resulted in Mom crying about the whole thing. I don't know how much I contributed to the upset, and how much of her unhappiness was from losing the house. In any event Dad called me back and we had a less emotional conversation.

"I'm not totally lost in a maze," he said to me.

I found this comment somewhat perplexing, and thought about it afterward without coming up with an answer. Only later, much later, would I realize what was truly going on. Mom was convinced she was dying, and wanted to be certain Dad had a home near Jan and me, so that we could care for him. The year before she had expressed concern to Jan so poignantly: "I worry most about Frank. We've always been like one person. When I go, what will happen to him?"

After her poor medical diagnosis she began formulating a plan, as-suring herself that the members of her family would be taken care of if she was not around. The Mercer Island house was part of it. In a related part of the plan, she was encouraging him to write a book with me, perhaps more than one, so he would be kept busy and wouldn't have time to get depressed.

A place to live near loved ones and work to keep him busy. Other pieces of her plan would emerge soon.

Dad's comment about not being "totally lost in a maze" came be-cause he knew exactly what she was doing. If he purchased property near us, it seemed tantamount to an admission on his part that Mom was not going to make it. So he lowballed the place and lost it. I think Dad would have found something wrong with any house on Mercer Island.

He was also extremely hesitant to sell the Port Townsend farm. He had put too much work into Xanadu, too much love. It fulfilled some of his most closely held lifelong dreams. Frank Herbert could not have a farm on a Mercer Island lot—it was a highly suburbanized area, with comparatively small pieces of property and neighbors that would not understand ducks running around and roosters crowing at the break of dawn.

✳ My Mother's Plan ✳

IN LATE July 1983, Frank Herbert told me that he typed one hundred rough-draft pages on *"Dune 6"* (as yet unnamed) in just four days. (I didn't dare ask, but I had seen some of his rough drafts done *single space*.) In contrast, it had taken me six months to write 152 rough-draft pages of *Sudanna, Sudanna*, double-spaced. He said he normally spent six hundred to eight hundred hours on a completed novel.

His contract on *"Dune 6"* was in the stratosphere, providing him with even more money than the astounding figure he had received for *"Dune 5," Heretics of Dune*.

Around this time Jan and I went to a dinner dance with my parents, where the entertainment was a small combo that played music ranging from the 1940s to modern, popular selections. Mom and I had one slow dance together. While a little short of breath, she was laughing like a schoolgirl when I led her back to the table.

The following month, Mom decided she wanted to start a newsletter, reviewing Seattle restaurants as well as restaurants from their travels. She planned to call it "BAH," using her own initials, and wanted Jan and me to eat at restaurants and provide her with reports. I suggested the use of a form for the criticisms, an idea she liked. Dad and I offered to help edit the newsletter, while Jan said she would be the "Chief Eater." Mom said we were the only people, along with Dad, that she was telling about the idea.

Late that evening after Dad had gone to bed, Mom told me that if the newsletter got off the ground it would be the first time she ever got her name on a publication. I asked her about a romance story she had sold in the 1940s, a "plan ahead" book she worked on for the Retail Reporting Bureau, and a number of Christmas stories she had written for department store promotions, all of which were published.

"My romance story was published anonymously," she said. "And the other writings, well, they weren't very significant. They were part of my job, part of structures I didn't create. This newsletter would be a big step for me. I plan to have fun with it."

Our first foray for BAH was the elegant Mirabeau Restaurant, a few days later. This gourmet dining establishment, on the forty-sixth floor of the SeaFirst Building in downtown Seattle, provided a spectacular, panoramic view of Elliott Bay and the Olympic Mountains. There were flat mirror surfaces on pillars by the windows, reflecting the views from a variety of directions.

When the conversation grew too serious, Mom touched Dad's arm and asked him to tell a favorite joke of hers, one I hadn't heard in years. Dad told it like this: There were these old friends, and one of them finally turned to the other and said, "Alfie, we've been friends for a long time, and I can barely tolerate you putting down my stories, and the way you're always late to my parties. Most of all, I've just now decided I absolutely cannot tolerate the fact that you've become so pretentious."

To this, Alfie responded, "Pretentious? *Moi?*"

Dad provided a brief history lesson about the use of the French word "*moi*," meaning "I," or "me." He traced it back to Louis XIV, king of France longer than any other monarch, who said, *L'etat c'est moi*—"I am the state."

All of us gave our opinions of the meal, while Mom scribbled "BAH" notes on a notepad from her purse. The waiter seemed a little nervous, and I saw him watching her.

On August 31, 1983, we drove my parents to Rosellini's Other Place Restaurant in Seattle, for a 6:30 dinner reservation. Walking in from the car, Mom had to stop and catch her breath twice. "It's nothing," she said. "I've just been a little tired lately."

We ordered a bottle of Richebourg before eating. With only two bottles remaining on the premises, a 1979 and a 1966, Dad said, "We'll have the '79 now and the '66 with dinner." He wanted to build up to the better, richer wine.

The waiter removed the cork from the '79 and set it on our table. With a very serious, intense expression, Dad smelled the cork. Then a smile broke across his mouth, and his blue eyes sparkled. "Grind this up, will you," he said, "and put it in our salad."

Our waiter, a cheery, portly fellow, laughed so hard that he nearly popped his cummerbund.

It was a favored Frank Herbert line in elegant restaurant settings, delivered with a sense of comic timing at an ostensibly serious moment. It deflated any semblance of pretentiousness, which he abhorred, and never failed to elicit hearty laughter.*

Soon we were immersed in our dinner and in conversation about my parents' upcoming trip to Hawaii. Mom said she always enjoyed the flight across the ocean, and that a wonderful feeling came over her when the Hawaiian Islands came into view through the windows of the plane. She described the islands as green and brown jewels on a shimmering aquamarine sea.

Mom said she was glad she'd gone to Mexico City to see the *Dune* filming, that for her it had been the trip of a lifetime. "A Channel 5 (Seattle) news team was with us," she said, "but they won't run a story until the movie is ready for release."

To build up public interest, Universal and De Laurentiis were keeping the cast list secret. I saw a television story on the movie, run by Channel 7 in Seattle, in which they interviewed the mysterious and unnamed leading man, with his back to the camera. It was Kyle MacLachlin, I knew. But not too many other people did.

---

*One evening we were enjoying a sparerib dinner, along with a big bottle of Chianti. Dad told a story about a group of literati gathered in New York City, discussing which foods went with certain wines. Science fiction writer Ben Bova was talking about Chianti, and a pretentious woman asked, aghast, "What food could possibly go with a wine like that?" To this, Bova responded, "Peanut butter." When the diners thought about it, they realized he was absolutely right. Only one wine, Chianti, had a strong enough flavor to keep from being drowned out by the flavor of peanut butter! My father found the discussion highly amusing.

Two days afterward, on September 2, Clyde Taylor called, and told me that W. H. Allen, a large publishing house in London, wanted to publish *Sidney's Comet* and *The Garbage Chronicles* in the United Kingdom, in hardcover and paperback. I told him to accept their proposed terms.

Later in the week I called Mom in Port Townsend and discussed the "BAH" newsletter with her. We went over the format and specific language that might be included in every issue. She wanted it to look elegant.

She and Jan spoke on the telephone for a long while, after which Jan told me my parents wanted us to visit them in Hawaii that winter. If I wouldn't fly, Jan wondered, would I mind if she went alone? Mom said she was afraid Dad would steamroll her on the interior decorating at Kawaloa, and she wanted Jan there to prevent that.

I assented. Details were worked out, but because of school Jan couldn't go until after Christmas. Mom expressed disappointment, and said, "Come as soon as you can."

After discussing this with my mother by telephone, Jan sat silently for a long while and then asked me if she should interrupt her classes and go earlier. Knowing the difficulties she had been through at school, I suppose I didn't answer very well. I left the decision to her.

The following week, I mailed my mother four restaurant reviews I had written, using a form I had developed for the purpose. I also edited a sample "BAH" letter she wanted to mail to a selected list of people and offered my suggestions for improvement. We were establishing a tone with the letter, appealing to a discriminating class of diners. Mom had decided not to show her name anywhere in the publication, to guarantee the integrity of calls she made upon restaurants. She was afraid that restaurateurs, upon learning a food critic was on the premises, would roll out a red carpet.

So, despite her earlier excitement about receiving credit in the publication for her operation of it, she was now slipping, once again, into anonymity. Her point seemed well taken, however.

On the sixteenth of September, 1983, Dad called. He said Warner Brothers and Paul Newman were making a bid for the movie rights to *Soul Catcher*, my father's 1972 novel about a clash between American

Indian and white cultures. Previously there had been interest from a Seattle production company, Gardner-Marlow-Maes, as well as from Robert Redford, Marlon Brando, and Henry Fonda. I found myself unable to keep up with the history of these film rights. It was turning out to be almost as complex and ill-starred as the early history of the *Dune* movie project.

My father said he had a possible ulcer from tension over all the things he and Mom had been trying to do. The construction at Kawaloa was on the very top of their stress list, and below that their struggle over selling the Port Townsend house and purchasing something closer to me. Temporarily they had stopped looking for property in the Seattle area but would resume the search in the spring, upon returning from Hawaii. His stomach didn't feel good, and to compound matters, he was battling the flu. He was grumpy from flu shots, said his muscles were so sore that he could hardly walk up the stairs to his writing loft.

Despite this, Dad rode his ten-speed Schwinn bicycle to a market in Port Townsend the following day—a distance of six miles round trip—and purchased fetuccini for the evening meal.

On September 23 I called Mom, and she said Dad was feeling a little better, but she wasn't. Only two months before she had been up to four and a half laps of the swimming pool, and now she could barely do one. As she spoke to me, I realized this was an unusual conversation. Previously, Mom didn't like to talk about her condition, and we had to receive information on it from Dad. I was worried.

She said both of them had doctor's appointments in Seattle on the twenty-ninth. She also wanted to take her gold wristwatch to C. Rhyne & Associates to have the band shortened so that she could wear the watch again. "I want to buy a gold maple leaf coin at Rhyne Precious Metals, too," she said. "In the same building. I've just begun collecting coins."

She asked if I would take her, and I said I would be glad to.

I told her I was just finishing my novel, *Sudanna, Sudanna*, which was coming in at around 310 pages, double-spaced, or seventy-five thousand words.

She said Dad had three hundred single-spaced pages done on the first draft of "*Dune 6*," and that she had gone over the plot with him,

407

offering comments. "I also suggested a title to him," she said. "*Chapterhouse: Dune*. He likes it. That's the title now."

Mom cleared her throat and said the newsletter idea was dead, because of a rival publication already in existence.

We discussed business matters I'd been helping them with, and then I had to listen to one of the things I hated to hear, that she and Dad were executing "living wills," giving one another the authority to "pull the plug" if either of them slipped into a vegetable state.

My mother paused, as if awaiting comment. I didn't say anything. What could I say to *that*? She added that if both of them were being kept alive by machines, they wanted to give me the authority to pull the plug, and she asked if I would do that for them. I said I would do as they wished.

It was a quality-of-life issue, she said, of particular concern to her. Dad once told me she used the term frequently, that she wanted the right to die in dignity, without the interference of unnatural and uncomfortable medical equipment. It was why she wanted to live at Kawaloa when she was so ill, despite its great distance from hospitals and modern medical equipment. She didn't want to die in a cold, sterile hospital, connected to machines, and Kawaloa was as far from that environment as she could possibly get.

Late that month, Dad had an autograph session in Seattle. While he was there, I had lunch with my mother in the Garden Room of the Four Seasons Olympic Hotel. They conducted a fashion show as we ate, with models strolling between tables in expensive Paris gowns. Afterward I drove Mom over to a jewelry store in an old building in downtown Seattle, where they would measure her wrist and remove gold links from her watch, since she had lost so much weight. The building didn't have an elevator, so I helped her up a long flight of stairs to the second floor. She was weak and frail, and had to rest on almost every step. My heart went out to her. I was confused and concerned by her physical downturn, because only a short while before she had been doing well with her exercise program, improving steadily. I hoped it was only a temporary setback and that Hawaii would make her stronger. She seemed so much older than her fifty-six years.

Two days later I drove Jan and the kids to Port Townsend, and we arrived at midmorning. There were five deer in the yard. Dad came out to greet us in his customary fashion, and gave us warm hugs. "Did you bring your manuscript?" he asked.

I had completed *Sudanna, Sudanna* only a couple of days before. Opening a back door of the car, I reached in and pulled a manuscript box off the ledge above the backseat.

He took the story that I had sweated over these many months to the living room, and set himself up on the couch. He seemed anxious to read it.

Mom wanted to go over a number of business matters with me, and we went in her office. At her desk I pulled up a chair to sit beside her. She gazed through a tall window that overlooked her garden and a little wooden bird feeder attached to a cedar tree. A brown-and-white wren was eating seeds, and she watched it for a moment. Her desk was more cluttered than usual, and she had a large green ledger book open on it, with a Cross pencil lying on the exposed page.

She was breathing hard, taking deep, erratic gulps of air, and I thought she was going to sneeze. Then I realized her breathing was labored from the exertion of walking into her office, only thirty feet from the kitchen. I wanted to help her, but didn't know how. Touching her hand, I asked, "Mom, are you okay?"

She smiled, looked at me and said, "I'll be all right in just a moment." I saw pain in her dark blue eyes.

To the left of her desk, on the side where I sat, stood a light teak filing cabinet, with a miniature black and white Sony television on it. Above that, on the wall, a bookshelf held reference books, including a zip code directory, a Roget's thesaurus, and a big black hardcover volume, the new Cassell's German dictionary.

Between her desk and the doorway to the kitchen, a photocopy machine sat on a small oak library table that had belonged to her father, with manuscript pages stacked neatly beside the machine. A bulletin board by the doorway had little snips of paper and cartoons on it, including a number of cartoons Jan and I had sent. There were two large and significant items on the board: A smiling, black and white photograph of Dad, much favored by my mother, in which he looked happy and regal in his full beard. And a complete list of the cast in the *Dune* movie, printed in large type.

We talked about a number of accounting matters that she had been handling, and she showed me the incredible volume of bills she had to handle. Some of the entries in the ledger were in Dad's handwriting.

I asked why she didn't hire an accountant or a bookkeeper to help her, not knowing at the time that Jan had asked her the same question during an earlier visit.

"This is my work," she told me. "Frank has his work, and I have mine."

I learned that foreign royalties went directly from foreign publishers to a bank in Zurich, Switzerland, with documentation then forwarded to Mom from the bank and from their literary agents. Mom made careful accounting entries for each deposit. They had a precious metals account in that bank as well, for gold and other metals in which they had invested. She said she had to be extremely careful not to release the account numbers to anyone, not even to their accountants, since anyone with those numbers could withdraw the funds. My mother took great pains to delete the account numbers on any document copies she distributed.

She maintained four separate ledgers—Port Townsend (personal), Hana (personal and construction), Herbert Limited Partnership (for domestic royalties and expenses) and Swiss (foreign royalties and investments). In addition, Dad kept separate check registers of his own, issuing drafts for everything imaginable. As part of her job with the partnership, for which she received a six-figure income of her own, Mom re-entered every check that Dad had issued onto the main ledgers, lining out the entries in his personal registers as she did so.

She needed to go to the bank that morning in downtown Port Townsend, and asked if I would take her. So, without realizing what she was doing—her secret plan—I helped her to the car and drove her downtown. At Seattle First National Bank, she placed some Canadian gold coins in a safety deposit box and then introduced me to the bank employees she knew, including the vice president.

We went into the office of an account executive, a middle-aged woman, and sat in front of her. There Mom described a number of accounting problems she had been experiencing. Mom left her business and personal bank records with the woman, for help in figuring them out.

I didn't realize until months later how these events fit neatly into a plan Beverly Herbert had in mind, one she never revealed to her husband, though I know now that he had guessed some of it. She had worked it out meticulously, and, unawares, I was part of it. Showing me the records in detail for the first time . . . introducing me to bank employees . . . It was all for transition. She wanted me to handle the financial affairs of my father if she didn't return from Hawaii.

It was gray and drizzly as we drove back to the house, and Mom said, "I really hate this weather."

Dad served lunch for all of us. It was a delicious chicken broth, thickened by puréed potatoes and pumpkin from their garden. No solids. He poured crème fraîche in the bottom of each soup bowl, sprinkled nutmeg on top of that, and poured the soup over it all.

He made an entertaining production out of it, and told us not to dump croutons in the soup. Instead, he had us place two of them in our bowls at a time (just enough for a spoonful) to keep them crisp.

I sat in the living room with Dad the rest of the afternoon while he read my novel. High on the gable wall beside us were the stained-glass windows my father had designed—a rooster and a writer's quill—and through windows below I could see another writer's quill, this one a weather vane on top of the pool building.

When he finished reading, he pronounced my story fit but thought I might add more descriptive language in a couple of places. "You've come a long way," he told me. He said the novel had many "marvelous passages" and a good plot. I loved the way "marvelous" rolled across his tongue, as if you could taste the excellence of what the word was describing.

That evening, all of us were standing in the living room looking out on the pond. We saw a small family of deer cut into the woods, one trailing after the other.

The following Wednesday, October, 5, 1983, Dad drove Mom into Group Health Hospital in Redmond to run her through a battery of tests before they left for Hawaii. They hoped to leave by the tenth of the month.

When I spoke with Dad at my house later that day, he said Mom had been afraid to see the doctor. Aside from increasing fatigue and shortness of breath she had been experiencing backaches, and was worried that her cancer had spread. Sometimes she awoke in the middle of the night and suffered silently, without disturbing him. She didn't want to make him tired, detracting from his ability to write. Dad found out about this, and told her to wake him up at any time for a back rub. "What good am I if I can't do that?" he told her.

So each night after that he brought her warm milk in the middle of the night and massaged her back. "I tell her I love her when I do these things," he said, his voice full of emotion. "My hands tell her I love her too, as I massage her back."

During Dad's stay with us, he ordered four live Maine lobsters from the Village Fish Market in New Canaan, Connecticut, sent by express and packed in seaweed and blue ice. Each lobster weighed at least two and a half pounds, and they were sent directly from Connecticut to the Mirabeau Restaurant in Seattle, where they would be prepared for a gala dinner the four of us were scheduled to have that evening.

But after all the medical tests, Mom wasn't feeling well enough to join us. The doctors said she had been experiencing a problem with her potassium medication that had been making her ill, leading to the fatigue she had been feeling. It had to do with "Slow-K," Dad said, a medicine to keep her potassium level up. So Dad, Jan and I went to the restaurant. It wasn't the same without Mom, but we enjoyed my father's company nonetheless.

With the lobster, we had a 1979 bottle of Puligny-Montrachet, Mom's favorite white wine. "And mine, too," Dad said.

We discussed special effects in the *Dune* movie, which he said were impressive, particularly with respect to the "weirding" machine, the sandworms, the Guild fish-creature Edric in a transparent tank,* and the hunter-seeker units. He said that he had been writing "*Dune 6*"

---

*While my father admired the special effects, he had a contractual reason for disputing the use of Edric in the *Dune* movie, as noted in Chapter 44.

under the working title *Hunters of Dune* until Mom suggested the title he liked better, *Chapterhouse: Dune*.

Warner Brothers and Paul Newman were still after the film rights to *Soul Catcher*, and Dad was insisting upon doing the screenplay himself. He thought he might receive a six-figure fee for the task, in addition to funds from the sale of movie rights.

"There are two juicy parts for Newman," he said. "The boy's father or the sheriff."

In our usual wide-ranging conversation, we entered into the subject of pheromones, external hormones. Dad said people had them and so did lower life forms, such as mosquitoes. He suspected that pheromones were responsible for mob hysteria and crowd activity in general, and for two women living together going onto the same menstrual schedule. He planned to investigate this.

That week I took my lunch to the hospital several times, to be with my mother. On the way to her room on Friday I saw Dad in a downstairs nurse's office, and stopped to talk with him. He had his own test results in, and didn't have an ulcer or the flu. No medical problems showed up in any of his tests. The doctors were correcting the problem with Mom's potassium medication, and she was feeling better. He said that no reason had been found for her backaches.

In the hallway, he told me he was making arrangements for a special showing of *Dune* in Seattle, with the proceeds going to Group Health Cooperative, which he felt had been largely responsible for prolonging Beverly Herbert's life. It had been more than nine years since she had been diagnosed with terminal lung cancer. With the hospital's assistance she had proved the statisticians wrong.

On Dad's birthday, Saturday, October 8, he checked Mom out of the hospital and took her to her hairdresser in the Westin Hotel. She looked trim and elegant when she and Dad stopped by the house for a short while. She said she was feeling better, and smiled readily.

They had hoped to leave for Hawaii by Monday, but that was delayed by my mother's *bête noire*—constant tests the doctors wanted to perform. She could hardly wait to return to Kawaloa.

Saturday, the fifteenth of October, 1983, was the last time I ever saw my mother. I was thirty-six years old. It was a rainy day, around sixty degrees. I worked on *Sudanna, Sudanna* in the afternoon, primarily moving key items forward in the story.

We had dinner with Mom and Dad at Hugo's Rotisserie, in the Hyatt Hotel near SeaTac Airport. Mom was in a wheelchair that squeaked because it had a bent wheel. As Dad pushed her through the long corridors of the hotel, from their room to the restaurant, I thought of the countless times I had been with them in similar places. For years it had been an endless maze of hotel corridors, it seemed.

We crossed the lobby, and I helped Dad carry Mom in her chair down a short flight of stairs, three steps. She wasn't very heavy. He pushed her to our table, a booth at the back of the restaurant, and she slid off the chair onto the seat.

Mom didn't look well at all. She was tiny and terribly fragile, and I wondered why she had to be taken so far from modern hospitals and technology. Of course she wasn't being "taken," I realized. She was the prime mover in the drama, and wanted to be at Kawaloa.

Frank Herbert would do anything for her, in return for the love she had given him, and for supporting the other love in his life, writing. Many women wouldn't have done the things for my father that she did. They would have told him to get a real job and support his family properly. Writing was, after all, a tremendous gamble.

But she was a white witch, my father said. A good witch. Mom could predict events with frightening accuracy. In her heart she had always known her husband would be successful one day.

And now, as she prepared to leave for her beloved Kawaloa, she sensed her own future.

She didn't eat a meal with us, had only a dish of vanilla ice cream. She was in obvious discomfort of some sort. I couldn't tell exactly what, didn't feel I should ask. She was quiet, suffering inwardly. Still she put on a gallant face, and was intermittently cheerful.

Mom was on my immediate left, and I placed my hand on hers. Her skin was cold and without fat, and I felt the bones and sinews of her hand. Such an inadequate covering for my mother, for this important person. I could only hope that she knew what was best for her, that her Kawaloa would regenerate her.

414

She gripped my hand in hers, squeezed. We exchanged smiles, and I had to look away so that I wouldn't cry.

Dad was telling a true story about a professor he knew at the University of Washington. The professor pulled his car into a gas station that was within view of Western Washington State Hospital near Tacoma, a large institution for the mentally infirm. His car needed water, but in error he grabbed an air hose and stuck it inside the radiator. The gas station attendant took one look at this and nodded toward the hospital. "Wait right here, sir," he said. "They'll be right over to help you."

My father told other stories, one about a resident of the mental health facility in Napa, California. Something about wheel nuts and a tire being repaired. From my concern over my mother, I wasn't paying attention, and in a fog I heard the punch line: "I may be nuts, but I'm not stupid."

I remembered other punch lines from other days, going back to when I was six years old at a tiny beach house we lived in near Tacoma, listening from the mezzanine while Dad told long, convoluted "shaggy dog" stories. I was supposed to be in bed then, not eavesdropping. Now I was supposed to be listening, but wasn't.

Kawaloa became my mother's dream, her paradise on this planet. We all have dreams, but to some of us they are only vague mental images or plans drawn on paper and never implemented. Some people only see the dreams of others, and never realize their own.

Beverly Ann Herbert obtained her dream house, and a magnificent palace it was, fit for any queen! She called it Kawaloa, meaning "a nice long time," but only spent a small portion of her life there.

When she was away from her paradise, she longed to be back. She would be there the following day, where it was warm and comfortable. Kawaloa beckoned. And I kissed her on her cheek for the last time.

415

CHAPTER
36

✳ There Are Flowers Everywhere ✳

ON A Sunday in mid-October, 1983, I was working on the final
draft of *Sudanna, Sudanna.* A phone call came in from my brother
Bruce. He was in California, said he had seen *Sidney's Comet* in bookstores, that it was selling and being restocked. Other friends called to
tell me the same thing.

A few days later, on my mother's fifty-seventh birthday, I telephoned
Hawaii to give her our love. She said she was tired but better. "It's
warm here," she said, "and there are flowers everywhere."

They were planning to have dinner at home, and Dad was preparing
a special low-salt recipe of Oyster Sauce Beef for her, one of her favorite
meals.

In ensuing weeks, I spoke with my parents often but made few
journal entries. I needed a respite from the demands of the word-eating
monster that sometimes threatened to consume me if I didn't feed it.
And through the middle of November I got my fill of writing, anyway,
finishing *Sudanna, Sudanna* and mailing it to Clyde Taylor. I then set
to work on a light project, a science fiction humor book in collaboration
with an artist friend, Dick Swift.

It wasn't easy working as an insurance agent and writing on the side,
and I longed to write full-time. I understood now what my father must
have been thinking during his own monumental struggle to make a
living as a writer. There were many dimensions of him that I under-

stood now only because I became, like him, a writer. "The best way to learn a thing is by doing it," he often said. And so it was in learning about this enigmatic genius, Frank Herbert. The process of becoming a writer myself helped me to forgive him.

In phone conversations across the Pacific, I usually spoke with Mom, for Dad was almost always working, trying to get out of a financial straitjacket. Mom carried a cordless telephone around with her, and usually sat with it in her favorite spot on a large gray sectional couch, where she could do her knitting and gaze out upon the sea. She didn't sound noticeably different to me, and never complained to me of discomfort. I was to learn later that Dad was dressing and bathing her, and that her condition had so deteriorated that she needed oxygen to sleep. I was to learn as well that Mom was being attended constantly by Dr. Howell, who lived a short distance down the road toward Kaupo Gap. I wasn't told how bad it was getting—or maybe there were things I should have heard, but didn't.

I knew the swimming pool was under construction at Kawaloa, for example, but I didn't fully understand the desperation my father felt to get it completed, so that Mom could resume the exercise program that had worked so well for her in the past. Work seemed to drag along on the pool, going at the special slow pace reserved for the tropics. The process took forever, he told me later.

In every telephone conversation, I was told that Mom was doing better, that she was happy and warm.

That November they felt a strong earthquake at Kawaloa, centered at Hilo on the "Big Island" of Hawaii. Dad said it lasted forty-five seconds to a minute, and "felt like someone running across the deck."

Months later, Dad told me he woke up once during the night and my mother was blue, a condition known as cyanosis, from inadequately oxygenated blood. He noticed that the oxygen tube had fallen from her mouth, so with trembling hands he reconnected it, and her color returned. After that he slept only lightly, listening for changes in her breathing pattern. He said he had been averaging just three hours of sleep a night.

In the middle of December we received a letter from my father:

417

Dear Brian, Jan and kids:

This letter is being composed on the word processor that I am readying for Bev to use in writing all of our correspondence. It works much faster than ordinary typewriting and saves the letter on a disk that is much easier to store. One disk 5 ½ inches in diameter can store hundreds of letters and find them when required (provided you label the disks correctly).

As I write this letter, I can hear the workmen outside finishing the swimming pool. Bev really needs it desperately. Her muscle tone has gone down dangerously since our arrival, although she still is stronger than she was when we arrived. Dr. and Mrs. Howell were here for dinner last night and brought good news about Bev's latest blood test. She is managing to keep up her potassium level without taking the slow-K that made her so ill just before we left Port Townsend.

For Jan's information, the guest house* is coming along rapidly, as well. [The contractor] put in the steel supports for the corner tables yesterday and we decided to surface them with the same blue tile we are using in the bathrooms. We are overflowing with that tile because, on learning that they no longer are making it, we bought out the store's supply. We had visions of needed repairs sometime in the future and no source for the tiles.

We're really looking forward to Jan's visit and only wish Brian would be with her . . . Too much activity around here to do much else except watch the work. I always say I love work. I could watch it forever.

Love,
Frank

---

*New apartment wing, attached to the main house by a covered walkway.

CHAPTER
37

✳ The Race to Finish Kawaloa ✳

AT THIS point in writing *Dreamer of Dune*, I found myself unable to continue. For many weeks, the manuscript languished, untouched, while I busied myself with other things, with "make work projects" that were without substance. Ultimately a great depression set in over me, for I was not writing, and beyond that, far beyond that, I was not telling the story that had burned in my heart for so long.

One evening I sat down at my computer to resume work on the book. But my fingers were numb on the keyboard, moving sluggishly, stumbling over keys and producing misspellings. My brain and fingers refused to cooperate in the telling of something so terrible. Fatigue overwhelmed me, and I wanted nothing more than to sit in the soft side chair by my desk and nap. It was the large orange Naugahyde chair that had been my mother's favorite, one she said "leaped out and grabbed" her as she tried to walk by it in a department store. Maybe tomorrow I would be able to proceed. But not this evening. Not now. I settled into the chair and fell asleep.

Tomorrow arrived, but again I put the work aside. Three more days passed, and eventually I looked through the old notes again. . . .

In December 1983, I set to work on an outline and some of the scenes for a new science fiction book that I hoped Dad and I might write together—a novelization that would include some of the *America* concepts we had been discussing. This was a book my mother very much wanted us to do, as she felt we might become like Irving Wallace and his son, David Wallechinsky. But as I got into the outline, many of the *America* concepts didn't seem to fit.

Instead, I envisioned a universe that was entirely dependent for its existence upon the imaginations of an alien race, called Dreens. They lived on the planet Dreenor and created entire worlds with the power of their imagination. Out of their imaginings, worlds came into existence. Earth was one of those worlds, and a situation would come to pass where the people of Earth would perceive a threat from aliens living on a distant planet, Dreenor, and a military mission would be sent to destroy that far off planet. Of course, such an act could destroy Earth as well if all the Dreens were killed, since our planet only existed by virtue of the imaginations of these beings. But the military people on Earth would have no knowledge of such an impending catastrophe.

The key character in our story would be a newspaperman, a young publisher who operated a paper owned by his business-mogul father, a number-cruncher who cared little about the newspaper industry and was more interested in his widespread, diversified enterprises, which were far more profitable than publishing. In many respects, our young protagonist would be modeled after William Randolph Hearst, who, like the character in our story, was left a newspaper by his wealthy father. The real-life newspaper owned by Hearst, the San Francisco *Examiner*, had been employer to both Frank Herbert and me in the 1960s—he as picture editor and me as a copyboy. And of course, I had in recent years been intrigued with the life story of Hearst, for the similarity he bore with my father when it came to ongoing construction projects.

Dad liked the concept when I described it to him over the telephone. He liked my title, too, *A Man of Two Worlds*—a reference to the character becoming split in his obligations between the worlds of Dreenor and Earth. Dad told me to go ahead and set the story up as much as I could.

Shortly after Christmas 1983, Jan flew to the international airport at Honolulu on the island of Oahu. From there she caught a Royal Hawaiian Air Service Cessna to the island of Maui. As she flew over the water, it was the most incredible aqua blue color she had ever seen, breathtaking in its beauty and brilliance. The plane skirted Maui and headed for its eastern shore, where she beheld spectacular vistas of waterfalls, cliffs, and jungle. Tiny settlements and ranches were carved out of the jungle that ran up the slopes of the massive inactive volcano Haleakala, the dominant topographical feature of the island.

It had been a cold winter in Seattle, with rain and snow and temperatures dropping into the teens. But when Jan stepped out of the plane at the Hana Airport, it was eighty degrees with trade winds blowing gently. Darkness was just beginning to blanket the island. The airfield was a strip of pavement between the jungle and the sea.

Dad greeted her at a little gate between the tarmac and a small terminal building, and helped her load luggage and Christmas gifts into his white Chevrolet Blazer. Jan hadn't known about this vehicle, and when she commented on it he said it was perfectly suited to their lifestyle in Hawaii. It was large, permitting them to fill it with groceries and other items during all-day shopping trips to the other side of the island, necessary because Hana had only two small general stores. The Blazer had four-wheel drive, enabling it to traverse rough roadways and off-road terrain.

In the gathering dusk, Jan saw tropical beauty she had never imagined, with lush jungle vegetation and bright flowers pressing in all around the highway, threatening to overwhelm civilization. Dad drove as if he didn't own the vehicle, too rapidly and with little respect for rough spots in the road. The Blazer wasn't that old, but already the shock absorbers were shot and it rocked crazily on every bump. He spoke of construction work at the house, and said, with great concern, "If we could only get the pool done, Bev could do her strokes. She'd be stronger then. Her heart would get better."

Jan knew the unspoken, that he meant improvement of her whole cardiovascular system, including her lungs.

They passed the luxurious Hotel Hana Maui and the quaint, busy Hasegawa's General Store, about which a popular Hawaiian song had been recorded. Outside town were large green pastures, most of them the property of the Hana Ranch (owners of the hotel), with black lava rock, tumble-down fences and cattle grazing. There were outstanding vistas of the sea.

The road became worse on this side of town and seemed to have been paved in a prior century, so filled with potholes and washboards was it. The natives liked it that way, Dad said with a chuckle as they went over the eyeball-rattling, bumpy stretch known as the Molokai Washboard. It kept visitors to a minimum.

"I'm one of the natives now," he said, proudly. "A *kama'aina*. We've been very well accepted by the community."

Five miles down a road that seemed like much farther, by the second fruit stand out of town, Dad slowed and wheeled sharply left, rolling over a metal cattle guard that kept hoofed intruders off his property. The cattle guard, which rattled when they crossed it, had been installed after a Hana Ranch bull chased my mother around the yard.

From the parking area as Jan got out of the car she saw the hip roof of the main house just downhill and palm trees along the shoreline, swaying gently in trade winds. The sea, a darker shade of blue in receding daylight, stretched far into the distance. On the far right she could barely make out the outline of the island of Hawaii and its nearest volcano, Mauna Kea. A flower-lined walkway curved downhill to the entrance of the main house.

When Jan walked in the door, with Dad just ahead of her toting luggage, he called out, "Bev, I brought your sunshine!"

Mom rose from the gray sectional couch in the living room and walked slowly toward her eagerly awaited visitor, smiling broadly. My mother was thin, only 110 pounds on a 5'7" frame, and her skin was ivory, in striking contrast with her dark brown hair. A delicate whisper f a woman, she wore an exquisite red Polynesian muumuu, red with nk and white flowers.

'Oh finally!" she exclaimed, "Our breath of fresh air! Frank, every-
· will be all right now. Jan's here."

one of my parents, Jan was sunshine, and to the other fresh air.
ι took Jan outside, and on the hill facing the kitchen showed
e she had planted poinsettias. "I planted them for you," she
she expressed worry that the caretakers might not water them
ι didn't ask about this, but wondered why anything in Ha-
extra watering. Maybe it had to do with how young the
he thought, or the time of year.

An apartment wing had been completed, on the other side of the pool that was still under construction. But the apartments (two of them) were a good distance from the main house and only reachable by going outside and traversing a long, covered walkway. My mother thought Jan might be lonely out there, so they set her up on a Japanese futon folding mattress on the mezzanine of the main house.

"You'll be cozier here," Mom said. Her voice was weak, filled with sickness.

The following morning, Jan saw beauty she had never imagined possible. Kawaloa, a five-acre piece of paradise, brimmed with flowers, breadfruit trees, palms, papaya trees and banana fronds—at the edge of an aquamarine sea with dancing whitecaps.

A few days later the poinsettias were not doing well and my mother became displeased with the caretakers, Bart and Sheila Hrast, saying they weren't watering the plants enough. Mom's displeasure reached the ears of her enforcer, my father, and he became very angry. He wanted everything to be perfect for her, didn't want her upset in the least, because of her precarious medical condition. Dad got on the phone to the caretakers, who were in a separate house on the upper level of the property (by the Hana Road), and said, "Get down here and water the poinsettias! We don't want them to die!"

Jan and Sheila became friends, and Jan learned that Sheila loved my mother dearly, and tried to do everything she could to please her. The poinsettias had been watered, she insisted. They just weren't adapting well. She showed Jan around the land, which was nearly five acres, with three hundred and thirty feet of oceanfront. The grounds were exquisitely kept.

After visiting Sheila one day, Jan returned by herself to the main house, where Mom made a surprising remark. "Don't ever get too close to the help," she said. "It's best to keep your distance."

Jan found this pretentious but didn't argue. It was one of my mother's few flaws that she had a tendency toward snobbishness, even when we had been poor. Subsequently Jan was more discreet when she visited Sheila, waiting until Mom was taking a nap.

My wife spent two weeks there, and in that time noticed that Dad hardly ever went anywhere, so worried was he about my mother. Any time he went to town without her, he couldn't stand to be away, and drove even faster than usual. The locals were learning to watch out for him on the road. On one occasion, he became impatient trying to get around another car and went up a shortcut by the Pu'uiki cliff, blew a stop sign and roared back onto the Hana Road just ahead of the other vehicle.

Each day, Dad spent time in his study, but when Jan passed his open door and looked inside, she could see he wasn't writing much. He would sit at his computer and stare at it, or move his fingers listlessly over the keyboard, where once they had danced across the keys with furious energy.

Dad was forever listening for Mom to be sure she was all right. If she so much as whimpered his name, he bolted out of the study to help her. He was overly attentive at times, to the point where Mom grew irritated with him and would say, "Jan's here. You can go back to work."

Because of the heat in his upper-level study, a tropics-related design problem he hadn't contemplated, he regularly wrote with his shirt off. He looked so sad to Jan, rarely smiling or breaking into laughter, making her suspect he cried in private and that he was pretending to write or trying to write through tears. Whenever he came downstairs, he invariably looked sweaty and upset.

My mother tried not to disturb him, except when she had to. She liked him upstairs working. She wanted everything to be normal, the way it used to be. But she must have sensed that he was not writing wholeheartedly, and that he was way behind schedule on *Chapterhouse: Dune*.

With all the diuretics she had to take and her lack of energy, little accidents were inevitable, and embarrassing for Mom. She would try to make it to the bathroom, but after only four steps would be out of breath, leaning on the wall. One day Dad was away briefly and Jan tried to help her, but she wouldn't allow it, saying she only allowed Frank to help her. My mother could be stubbornly independent.

But Jan said to her, "After all the years you've helped me, won't you let me do this for you?"

The woman she knew as Bev, the woman who had become a mother to her, smiled gently at this and said, "All right."

424

Mom relied on her more after that. At bedtime Dad normally came down from his study to help her. But this evening, while Dad worked in his study, Mom allowed Jan to assist her to bed, and told her how the oxygen was to be hooked up. This was a shock. Jan had seen two tanks in the bedroom, but hadn't known they were in constant use, thinking they were only there "just in case."

Jan eased her into bed and connected the oxygen. Just before shutting out the light, Jan kissed her on the cheek, as I had done so many times. Her face felt cold.

On her night stand, my mother kept a Catholic rosary, given to her by the nuns from Tacoma when she had been close to death almost a decade before. Simple black beads and a brass cross bearing Jesus. She also had a scapular—two tiny pieces of rectangular woolen cloth connected by a string. The scapular bore pictures of Catholic saints, with the words "Have pity on us" and "Be our aid." Each night before she went to sleep she held the religious artifacts and prayed.

My mother attributed her extra years of life in large part to a newfound faith in God. Not particularly in the Catholic version of God, or in anyone else's version of a deity. Instead, Beverly Herbert was a free thinker who did not easily accept the constructs of others.

Each morning Jan prepared breakfast, usually serving Mom in bed on a tray according to strict dietary requirements: a bowl of Cream of Wheat and banana slices, with fresh guava or papaya juice. Alongside, Jan placed a fresh hibiscus flower in a little crystal vase—a vase I had given my mother some years before.

During the day, Mom liked to sit in the "vee" of the sectional couch, which gave her commanding views of the home's interior and the ocean. Jan helped set her up each day, providing pillows, bringing books and knitting materials, and placing the cordless telephone nearby.

Jan prepared all the meals and performed other tasks my father normally did, making her realize the full extent of the time-consuming chores he performed out of love. Prior to Jan's visit Mom hadn't allowed anyone but him to help her, so he was her medical attendant, masseur and personal chef. He cleaned the house, did her laundry, made and changed her bed, performed her bookkeeping chores, wrote

425

letters for her, and bathed her. In caring for a person this ill, he was forced to reach deep for the strength he needed.

The fatigue showed on his drawn face, with dark circles under his eyes. He had gained a lot of weight, more than fifty pounds at one point from nervous eating, from the stresses of building the house at Kawaloa and not knowing from day to day if the woman he was building it for would survive to see it completed. He had more wrinkles, more gray hairs. His beard and hair, usually neatly trimmed, were long and unkempt.

In recent weeks he had begun losing weight, having lost his appetite and enthusiasm for food. Ten of the fifty pounds had fallen off. Jan tried to make certain he ate a balanced diet each day, but often he wouldn't finish what she put in front of him and she would have to remove it. At times he seemed listless.

Each morning, Mom had to take her medicine, but once while Jan was there, she resisted, saying it didn't taste good. She was seated in her usual place on the couch, with the medicine on the black slate table in front of her.

Dad came up behind Mom and started rubbing her neck and shoulders. He pushed his hand inside the back of her sweater to massage her upper back, and as he did so, said, "I'm not getting fresh."

"I wish you were," she said, with a winsome smile.

Jan wanted to paint the glorious Hawaiian countryside around her. One very special afternoon, with warm, gentle trade winds blowing in from the sea, Mom followed Jan out on the deck. Barely able to walk, Mom went six feet, held on to something, and then struggled another six feet. They sat by the pool, where Jan sketched and painted. Adding to what she had taught Jan before, Mom described more of the techniques her mother had used, this time in the mixing and matching of watercolors and in brush strokes. And, while she did not have the energy to paint, she enjoyed watching Jan spread colors and shapes on paper.

"Yes, that's it," Mom would say. "You're very talented."

Inside the house, my mother showed Jan a number of sketches and paintings she had done when they first moved to Kawaloa, when all the excitement of the tropical scenery was new and fresh in her mind.

One painting was of the house and garden, a happy production full of bright flowers. Another was a potted flower drawn in black ink.

Mom gave Jan a set of Japanese watercolor paints, with colors in little porcelain dishes. While Mom was napping one day, Jan went out on the deck by the stairway that led up to the caretaker's house and painted a picture of a lacy Coral Hibiscus and a bright red Ostrich Plume Ginger. Looking around the side of the main house, she had a glimpse of the water, but most of that view was blocked by the house.

Mom awoke and saw her out there. Slowly, painstakingly, she worked her way outside, and came up behind Jan to admire her work.

Jan set up a chair for her, and ran back inside to get my mother's favorite wool shawl for her shoulders. In one of their conversations, Mom told Jan she was sorry she hadn't spent more time with her grandchildren but that if she kept her distance it wouldn't hurt them so deeply when she passed away. Jan had suspected as much. Sadly, she thought of how much Kim resembled her grandmother as a teenager, with baby fat that would soon melt away, revealing hidden beauty. They shared an interest in astrology, in sewing and knitting, and had many other similarities of personality, especially in the subtle ways of obtaining what they wanted.

Still, Jan held out hope for future closeness between Bev and the girls, and found it hard to accept that my mother was dying.

Dad also spent time with Jan. He alternated between depression and optimism, refusing to believe his wife of nearly four decades might not be able to continue. Proudly, he showed Jan his computer system. From his nonstop nursing duties and trying to meet a writing deadline, he had let his personal appearance slip. So he asked Jan to neaten him up, with a haircut and beard trim.

While cutting his hair, Jan noticed a large mole on his back and said, "Frank, this looks like it needs taking care of."

"I'll have it looked at," he assured her, "when I get back to the mainland."

During Jan's visit the swimming pool was finally completed and filled with water. The solar heating unit was not functioning yet, so the water was too cold for Mom. Dad and Jan swam, however. The pool was large and beautiful, just off the master bedroom. Partially completed redwood decks surrounded it, and on one section, in a chair beneath the shade of an Italian umbrella, Jan often gazed out over the magical, shimmering sea.

To pay for the remaining construction he wanted for Mom, Dad took out a large bank loan. "I'm expecting movie money soon," he told Jan. He then sought interior design advice from her as to how they might decorate the main house and the apartment wing.

At 3:30 one morning Jan awoke to noises. From her futon bed on the mezzanine floor, she heard someone walking around, and a sliding door opening and closing. She went in Dad's study, and through an open skylight heard a splash and someone swimming in the pool. It was my father taking a wake-up dip before going to work in his study. This was his daily routine, rising earlier than ever so that he could have precious writing time alone while Mom slept. After swimming his "lengths," he squeezed fresh orange juice and prepared a light breakfast for himself.

Jan discovered that Dad was taking No-Doz tablets to stay awake . . . to work through intense fatigue as he sought to keep the writing deadlines that were so important to him.

At times Jan needed to get away alone. Sensing this, Mom told her to take the Blazer and drive to nearby Hamoa Beach, owned by the Hotel Hana Maui. From dues they paid, my parents had the right to use the recreational area, described by Dad as the most beautiful stretch of white sand beach he had ever seen.

Jan sat on one of the lounge chairs provided by the hotel and cried for Bev, hardly noticing a famous actress who was seated nearby, Julie Newmar. A man in his forties approached Jan and introduced himself as "Smitty." Friendly and compassionate, he said he was a preacher and that he lived in a cave nearby. He wore boxer shorts and a faded Hawaiian shirt.

Jan told him about my mother.

"Let's say a prayer for her," Smitty suggested.

And for long minutes they prayed together, silently.

Later Jan learned he was quite a well-known personality in those parts, known as "Born Again Smitty," a man who had saved many swimmers from the dangerous surf and undertow just offshore. Tragically, Smitty died a short while later when the cave in which he lived collapsed on him. He was one of many people living off the land around there, in shacks or caves, fishing and picking fruit from the jungle. No one starved, not even people who didn't fish, because of the abundance of bananas, papaya, guava, breadfruit and other fruit that grew readily in that climate.

When Jan arrived home from Hamoa Beach, she came in late, having lost track of time.

"Where the hell were you?" Dad demanded. "I was just about to call the police! I had people driving around looking for you!"

She apologized for causing concern, and hurried in to prepare dinner. Later, during one of her visits to Hamoa Beach, Jan made these notes:

When I think of Bev and how she must feel inside, I hurt for her. She has always been so strong, but now I think she would welcome death from all the hurt and sorrow she has suffered. I will miss her so very much that I hope she will hold on for us all. Today I feel so sad inside for all of us who love her. I wish to leave this beautiful place only because I cannot watch her hurt, and I miss my babies and Brian. . . .

A short while afterward, Jan asked my father if she could leave a few days earlier than expected, so that she could get back to Margaux, who was only two, and take care of other obligations. She said nothing about her real reason. If my father sensed anything else he didn't comment, though his eyes were filled with pain. Jan knew as well that my sister, Penny, would arrive soon to help out. Bruce had wanted to come afterward, but Dad was delaying in giving him a time that would be convenient. My brother wondered, but did not say so to Dad, if this had anything to do with his homosexuality, which our father had never accepted.

A couple of days later when it was time to leave, Jan said good-bye to Mom, who was too weak and fatigued to rise from the gray sectional couch. Mom wore her colorful Missoni shawl and her favorite red cotton muumuu with pink and white flowers. Jan had ironed the dress for her that morning.

429

"Thank you, dear." Beverly's face was a mask of sadness and pain. "You've been a big help."

Jan leaned over, kissed the frail woman on her cheek and hugged her. Then she turned quickly to leave, because she didn't want my mother to see her crying. From the front entry, she looked back at the woman who had become a mother figure to her. A mounting fear filled Jan, a terror that it was the last time she would ever see her, and she saw in Mom's face that she sensed this as well.

The leaving process was like slow motion to Jan, a terrible pulling and wrenching. She didn't want to go, wanted to look upon Bev just a little longer, wanted to be with her for just a few moments more.

On the way to the Hana airport, Dad said, "You know she's dying."

Jan couldn't respond. It was why she needed to leave. She didn't feel she had the strength my mother saw in her, and was torn between wanting to help and fearing the imminence of death.

My father was torn as well, in different ways.

One moment he believed Mom might die, and the next moment he didn't believe it. Whenever the terrible reality of her fragility hit him, he tried to overcome it with his powerful sense of optimism—his knowledge of what the human spirit, particularly my mother's, could accomplish. She had survived so many close calls that it seemed to many of us that she would continue to beat the dread disease that afflicted her body. Like my father, we always held out hope.

His optimism was contagious, and I hung on the slender thread of hope that he spun, without realizing how tenuous it was. Or how fragile he was himself. Of course I was spinning my own threads as well, my own illusions.

Shortly after Jan left, he wrote to me on Kawaloa stationery:

Dear Brian:

Here are the two . . . insurance checks we discussed on the phone. Let me know if I committed a goof. Bev always took care of these things for us and I'm sometimes not as careful with them as I should be. (Mind off somewhere in current book).

She's very slightly improved today but, as the doctor says, she is walking a very fine line with her medication. We keep our spirits up, though, and Hana is good for both of us. Bill Dana said the other day that "This is a very spiritual place." I think maybe he's right.

The saws are buzzing outside as they complete the deck around the pool. Looking beautiful, and Bev is showing signs of impatience to get into warm water. Soon!

We enjoyed Jan's visit and she was a great help to us both. By the way, tell her we received a letter from Kim to her and sent it back "Return to Sender." It should arrive in a day or so.

Love from your papa—
Frank

Mom had my father's fighting abilities and his sense of determination, and he had hers. They were, as each of them often said, "one"— different parts of the same organism. At times Dad tried to intellectualize her condition, and these were the worst times for him, when he had to face stark, cold medical facts. He was the most optimistic when he permitted his heart full rein, when he *believed* she would pull through and convinced himself she would.

He convinced her of this, I am sure.

Curiously, though he, like my mother, never accepted any formal religion, he was basically a man of faith, and this made him good and true and strong. It made him capable of writing books that inspired millions of readers. It enabled him to become, at long last, a father to me.

Over the decade that the precious human cargo known as Beverly Herbert had been fighting for her life—first against cancer and then against heart disease brought on by radiation treatment, all of us grieved for her. We expected the worst at any moment, but hoped for the best.

When Jan arrived home from Kawaloa, she couldn't talk about all of the sadness. She didn't show me what she had written at the beach or fill me in on all the details, such as the oxygen my mother had to take to get through each night. Jan looked numb, lower than I had ever seen her, and just said, "Your mother is dying."

I couldn't believe it, didn't want to believe it, didn't want to talk about it. I didn't ask probing questions, things hindsight tells me I

431

should have asked. But I had a terrible, ominous feeling. For weeks I had been battling a bad case of the flu; I was tired and really depressed.

For the first time in my life, I called the airport and made a reservation for a flight on an airliner—to Hawaii.

Then I reread Dad's recent letter, in which he said Mom was slightly improved, and I deluded myself. The swimming pool was almost ready, and soon she would be in the water, resuming the exercise program that had worked so well for her in the past. My terrible fear of flying returned and overwhelmed me. I couldn't go through with the flight after all and canceled it, without ever having told my parents I'd made it.

The poinsettias my mother planted on the hillside did not survive.

CHAPTER 38

✳ A Woman of Grace ✳

Love . . . always protects,
Always trusts,
Always hopes,
Always perseveres.
Love never fails.

—I Corinthians 13:7–8

RESUMING HER interior design classes early in 1984, Jan was given
an opportunity to study at an extension class that summer at the University of Paris at the Sorbonne. We discussed it but were wavering
because of the high cost of the trip, including lodging at a *pension*
(boarding house) in Paris, near Luxembourg Palace. We had the problem of child care, too. Julie was going through a rebellious stage at
fifteen, and was quite a handful. Margaux was quite young, only a
toddler.

So Jan telephoned my mother and told her about the situation,
expressing concern about leaving little Margaux and her sisters in my
care for an entire summer.

"My God, Jan," Mom exclaimed. "An opportunity like that doesn't
come along every day!" And making a reference to Jan's ancestry she
said, "You're French, aren't you? You have to go!"

Jan had a feeling she would disappoint my mother if she didn't go, and beyond that, Mom was right. Opportunities like that weren't likely to come along again soon. We talked about it more, decided in favor of it, and made the reservations. She would leave in late May.

On January 25, 1984, I wrote to Mom, enclosing my usual light fare, and among other things said to her, "I'm working hard on an outline of a science fiction story to present to Dad for possible collaboration. Working title: *A Man of Two Worlds.*"

I spoke with her a couple of days later, and she said Dad had given her the sweetest, most intriguing note. It said, "There is no 'real' or 'unreal,' only what we create together."

I found a similar entry in *Chapterhouse: Dune*, just one of many passages indicating he was thinking of her when he wrote the book:

I stand in the sacred human presence. As I do now, so should you stand some day. I pray to your presence that this be so. Let the future remain uncertain for that is the canvas to receive our desires. Thus the human condition faces its perpetual *tabula rasa.* We possess no more than this moment where we dedicate ourselves to the sacred presence we share and create.*

One morning my mother awoke earlier than usual and sat up in bed. The long vertical blinds over the windows were open, and she gazed through them at a golden sunrise. The sun was rising on another perfect day in paradise, but she felt her life setting. She heard my father pass her door and called out to him.

"Good morning, darling," he said in response, then nuzzled his bearded face against her cheek and kissed her. "Would you like breakfast now?"

"Maybe later. I just want to sit here for a while. Look at that glorious sunrise!"

Dad felt a surge of hope, because she was smiling and her voice

*In *Frank Herbert*, William Touponce said that "many strong independent women's voices" could be heard in *Chapterhouse: Dune*. This is an indication not only of my father's grief concerning my mother, who died during the writing of the book, but of his recognition of the contribution she made to the *Dune* series and to his other writings.

sounded strong. Beverly Herbert gazed out on the water, as if hypnotized by it.

"Call if you need me," he said. And he went back to his book, the one she had named, *Chapterhouse: Dune*.

On January 30, Dad called and spoke with Jan while I was out. He was in tears, said Mom refused to eat. "She wants to die," he said. "She's slipping away." Penny was there with him, helping. He was having a cardiac specialist fly in from Honolulu.

I wasn't home when he called because I had lost my wallet, something I never did, and I was searching for it in the woods where I had been gathering kindling. I didn't find it, and when I returned, Jan told me of the call.

Somehow I seemed to be feeling my mother's anguish, as before, from far across the ocean. It was sending scattered signals through my brain, leaving me in dazed confusion.

I reached Dad by telephone, and he sounded dismal. He said Mom refused to go to a hospital, where they could hook her to life-support equipment. "She doesn't want to die in a hospital," he said. There were long periods of silence and broken sentences, when he couldn't talk. I told him I loved him.

He canceled a scheduled book tour.

The following day I called him again. He said the specialist had given Mom medicine that was working well, and that she was starting to eat once more. Dad was planning to hire a private jet with medical equipment to bring her back to Seattle in March or April. That was two or three months off, so I thought the emergency had passed.

He said things were better, under control.

That evening I wrote a letter to my parents:

Dear Mom and Dad:

I know these have been hard times for both of you. Each of you have always drawn strength from the other over the years, and now we worry about both of you. Dad, I know you're tired and I know Mom is, too—so it may be hard for each of you to give and take the strength that is needed to go on. I wanted you to know that we are here to draw upon for whatever extra measure of support you need.

In the past years we have enjoyed many fine dinners and good conversations together. During the last five or six years in particular, I think, Jan and I began to think of both of you as friends as well as my parents. There is a bond there which goes beyond love, I suppose, if that's possible. Maybe it's a special kind of love, or a special kind of friendship.

Somehow, Mom, you have to reach for that intangible extra. You are a strong person, and I hope you know the depth of what we feel for you.

Margaux is showing some of the Herbert artistic talent. She loves to dance, and last night was spinning to the music to the point of dizziness—she just kept going around in circles, getting giddy as she did so. She also likes to rub Daddy's shoulders to relax the tight muscles after a hard day at the office. She's smart, having seen Jan do that for me only once. Margaux is trying to be good, too. If she spills something, she often tries to clean it up. And she's carrying a lot of stuff around with her all the time— her new Christmas doll, a blanket, a bottle and a little pillow. It makes me think of Linus in the *Peanuts* cartoons. Her vocabulary is increasing by leaps and bounds, but she has trouble with the "L" sound. Pillow, for example, comes out "piddow."

I am enclosing cards that Kim and Julie made up for you. They miss both of you, as we all do.

Love,
Brian

On February 3, I spoke with Dad, and he said Mom was doing a little better. We discussed *A Man of Two Worlds*, and it looked like we would definitely write the book together. He suggested the title *Man of Two Worlds* instead, which he thought would be stronger, and I agreed. The newspaper element in the story would concern a high-technology communications empire, with a strong lead character. Dad had spoken with his literary agent about it, who felt we might obtain a large advance for the book. We spoke of sending him a short outline of our proposed plot, perhaps two pages.

When Mom woke up the next morning she said to Dad, in a faraway voice, "You will fall in love with a younger woman."

Oh no, he insisted, that would never happen. And besides, he told her, he didn't want her talking that way, as if she weren't going to be around.

On February 5, Dad called and said Mom had taken a sudden turn for the worse. The doctor only gave her three days to live. There was nothing to be done for her now, he said. His voice wavered, and he couldn't talk for several moments.

"I'm sorry for breaking down," he said, finally.

I felt numb. "You don't need to apologize, Dad. I love you. Tell Mom I love her."

He mentioned an unusual incident that occurred several days before, when Mom sat up suddenly in bed and said, "I just saw Federico [De Laurentiis, son of the *Dune* movie producer]. He was talking to me." She had been especially fond of young Federico, who had died some years earlier in an Alaskan plane crash. This was a common experience, my father told me, in which dying people had visions of those already gone.

I also spoke with Penny, who was still with him. She was in tears.

For several hours after talking with my father and sister, I again struggled with my terror of flying. That evening I made my second reservation to fly to Hawaii, leaving the afternoon of the sixth. Again, I didn't tell Dad I was coming. Events lay before me in a haze. I would go to the airport and get on the plane, entirely sober. Drunkenness would only make it worse, would intensify my fear, I thought. With any luck at all I would arrive in Hawaii, where I would telephone my parents and surprise them. It didn't make a lot of sense, wasn't thought out at all.

But Jan told Dad about my plans, and he said for me not to come, that there was nothing I could do, and besides Mom was adamant that she didn't want a "big deathbed scene." Dad said he had just read Mom a letter from a friend of hers, but she had trouble concentrating on the words, only picking up bits and pieces. Mom gave Dad a list of things she wanted him to do after she was gone, and made him promise to do them. It was a long list, he said, and involved us.

I spoke to Bruce, who said he had been told by Dad (pursuant to Mom's wishes) not to rush to Hawaii for a big ending scene. Mom didn't want drama. She just wanted peace.

I tried to sleep that night, but couldn't. I got up and tried to write, then tried to read, then tried to watch a late movie on television. I couldn't remain in bed either. Finally I dozed off on the family room couch, holding a letter she had written to me.

On the morning of the seventh, I called Dad early, afraid of what I might hear. Mom had slipped into a coma and was not expected to survive the night. He said it was her last wish to be cremated, with her ashes scattered on the land she loved, Kawaloa. He said he would come back to Seattle after it was all over. And he spoke of one of the items on her long list.

"She made me promise to finish *Chapterhouse* and get it off to New York, but I can't do it here." He said it was a little over half completed, and that he had read many of the passages to Mom, receiving her comments and suggestions on them.

In a failing voice I asked if she might possibly pull through, but he said no. It was beyond that. I broke down and couldn't talk any more. Since she was in a coma, she wasn't going to fight back again, as she had so many times before. This was finality. I went in the family room and hugged Margaux while I cried. I asked Julie and Kim to pray for their Nanna.

I hadn't given them any details yet, feeling my daughters were too young to sense the immensity of what was going on.

Early that evening, Dad called. My mother, Beverly Ann Herbert, passed away at 5:05 P.M. at the age of fifty-seven, while he was holding her hand. Dr. Milton Howell was in attendance, and he said, when she was gone, "She had grace."

My father told me that after my call that morning he held Mom's hand and told her I said I loved her. She was in a coma, but he told her, "If you understand, darling, nod your head."

She nodded her head.

I was only a little heartened when Dad assured me she was not in pain at the end.

They weren't going to spread her ashes yet, as it was Mom's wish that the ceremony, a simple one, be held at a future date at Kawaloa when the entire family could be there.

After the call, I told the girls, and we all cried.

I learned later that in her last days my mother had remarked, "I wish Brian were here." It is a tragedy that I was not there, and I think I shall always suffer for it. What an astounding woman my mother was. What a terrible loss to me, and to everyone who knew and loved her. She had a valiant, strong heart.

And I recalled some two decades earlier, when we were living in San Francisco before the phenomenal success of *Dune*, when Mom predicted that she would die in a distant land.

A story on Mom's passing ran in Retail Ad Week, describing her career in retail advertising, and featuring Dr. Howell's description of her as a woman with grace.

Dad wrote a poignant poem about their life together, which he entitled, with the simple elegance that represented my mother, "Bev." It spoke of their honeymoon on a mountaintop and little details about their life together, spanning nearly thirty-eight years. In reference to the cause of her lung cancer, he wrote, "Smoke buys your life."

In the closing lines of the poem my father described their final moments together, when he held her hand.

BEV

My God! There's a bear!
Black nose in fireweed,
Silver forest in your eyes,
Cold ground beneath our bed.

Making love on a mountain top,
A good place to begin.
You fear the hum of bees,
A packrat's beady eyes.

Saliva smell on your cheek,
Stain of huckleberry there,
Black as a lover's night,
The color of your hair.

White witch knows her man,
"You will fall in love
With a younger woman."
Soft and hard and eager.

Our bed smells of aloe vera,
Sweetness in the spines.
Your shape in the pillow
Moans of the summer dark.

One puff kills a bird,
Smoke buys your life.
It rushes over the brink,
Waterfall of blinding light.

Eyelids flicker twice,
Your hand in mine
Trembles when you die.
Nothing is ever lost.

CHAPTER
39

✳ Her Plan, Revealed ✳

ON SATURDAY, February 11, 1984, I jogged in the morning, running from my house up a hill to the top of Mercer Island. It was windy and rainy, but the cover of woods at the top of the hill offered some shelter.

That afternoon, Jan, Kim, and I met Dad and Penny at Boeing Field in Seattle. They came in on a long, sleek Israeli Westwind private jet that Dad said cost almost $20,000 to charter.* He couldn't bear to ride a commercial jet back from Hawaii with all the cheerful, talkative vacationers. (Another option he considered but rejected would have been to reserve the entire first-class section of a commercial airliner.) Jan thought he looked thinner than he had been only a few weeks before, and Dad said he had lost nearly twenty pounds in a short period of time.

His face appeared flushed, especially the top of his forehead—a shade of red that looked like high blood pressure but actually was from overexposure to the intense Hawaiian sun. His eyes were deeply set in their sockets and filled with pain. He looked devastated, as if he had been shot through the heart. Nothing in his life had ever hit him that hard.

---

*I learned later that this plane—a twelve-seat, twin-engine turbojet—had originally been reserved for by Dad in order to fly Mom back to the mainland to see their children and grandchildren. Unfortunately she never felt up to such a trip.

We had two cars, as Dad had five hundred pounds of luggage, files, and other items to go to Port Townsend. I had made arrangements to accompany Dad and Penny to the house, having taken two weeks off work to help them. Jan couldn't take the time off from school. We filled the cars, then headed for Port Townsend.

We ate dinner at Lido's Restaurant in Port Townsend, which served good Mexican food. Dad talked a little about Mom, and said before falling silent about her, "Bev was fey." It was a reference to her supernatural and spiritual powers, including her ability to see into the future.

He had a Carta Blanca beer with the meal, and as he finished the beer he said there were many things Mom wanted taken care of after she was gone. His gaze was remote, as if he still imagined himself at Kawaloa with her, and he said, "I have all these things I've made promises to her about, promises I have to keep." She had mapped out his entire year of 1984 and beyond, with lists of things to keep him busy, to pull him through.

Her first wish: She didn't want any of us to cry for her, though she must have known we would. This was an impossible request, it seemed to me. We weren't tough enough to comply. As Frank Herbert wrote in the *Chapterhouse: Dune* tribute to her: "She recognized tears as part of our animal origins. The dog howls at the loss of its master."

Her second request was just as difficult for me to hear. She wanted Dad to remarry, didn't want him to spend the rest of his life alone.

Third, he was supposed to talk with the children, Penny, Bruce and me, about our futures, helping us wherever possible. In this category, Dad promised Mom he would write a book with me. And, since my mother had grown so close to Jan, Dad said he would help her with her interior design career.

Fourth, Dad was supposed to talk privately with all the grandchildren about their futures, providing them with advice and financial assistance as needed.

Next, she wanted him to ask family members for assistance with all the support work involved in his writing—keeping accounts in order, answering fan letters, maintaining his schedule, and the like. It was her hope, my father told me, that I might be able to perform many of the tasks she had done, and that Bruce and Penny might assist. I assured him that we would do whatever we could.

As her sixth request, she wanted Dad to purchase a house near Jan and me on Mercer Island. Sensing her plan when she was still alive, he had resisted this previously, but now he was committed to do it.

Her seventh request: Finish *Chapterhouse: Dune*. This was proving difficult for him, since she had been so involved in the creation of the book, but he would do his best.

Number eight, she did not want a funeral with her body on display. Instead she desired cremation and a modest ceremony held at Kawaloa, with family members present. Her ashes were to be spread by the shore beneath a large, sweeping kamani tree. It was a species considered sacred by Hawaiians, one that produced small, round fruit, from which oil could be obtained. At the ceremony the Simon and Garfunkel song "Bridge Over Troubled Water" would be sung by a Hana friend and professional musician with a beautiful voice, Danny Estacada. This song represented what my father and mother had become for one another—bridges over troubled waters.

Ninth, because she felt Group Health Hospital had extended her life by nearly a decade, she wanted Dad to coordinate a special benefit showing of the *Dune* movie when it came out, with the proceeds going to Group Health. Mom also wanted him to telephone some of the doctors who had been most instrumental in her survival, including the radiologist who had cured her cancer while inadvertently damaging her heart with radiation. She wanted this doctor in particular to know she felt he had done his best with the medical technology available at the time.

Lastly, it was her hope that the Kawaloa property might be kept in the family and used by her children and grandchildren for many years. Toward this end, she and Dad had taken certain steps in setting up their estates.

After Dad went to bed at around 7:30 that night, Penny stayed up to talk with me. We sat on the recliner chairs in the reading area by the kitchen, and she told me how difficult it had been at Kawaloa, and how worried she was about Dad. He had been getting up in the middle

443

of the night for months, unable to sleep. In her final days, Mom stopped eating. Dad tried with only limited success to force-feed her. I learned later that dying people often stopped eating, the almost unconscious act of a body that knew it was going to pass on.

Penny also said Mom was extremely worried about how Bruce would fare in the future. She felt Penny and I were set up better financially than our little brother, and that we were stronger than he was. Mom and Dad had discussed hiring a business manager for him, to give him financial planning advice. It troubled Mom as well that Bruce had not found a lifelong companion, and that he was exposing himself to grave dangers in the gay community. The rest of us, especially Penny, had also been concerned about this.

That evening I slept in the living room, on an inflatable mattress. This was the room at Xanadu where I had spent so many enjoyable hours with my parents, discussing all manner of fascinating subjects. I was beneath the high gable with stained glass windows that my father had designed, the rooster and writer's quill, and had my mattress pulled up next to the couch that he and I had sat upon while working on my manuscripts.

It was quiet. I wept for my mother and prayed for my father. And it seemed to me that there could be no greater love story than the way my parents felt for one another—no greater story of sacrifices each made for the other. I was proud to be their son.

At 4:30 Sunday morning, I was awakened by clattering noises in the next room, the master bedroom. The door was partially open, with a light visible. I went inside, where I found Dad going through Mom's things. He said he had to clear everything out, that he was too upset when he encountered items that had been precious to her, and he wanted to get the pain over with. He had a dresser drawer open, and was putting her clothing and jewelry in boxes and large white plastic bags.

Dad showed me a long letter from his accountant, Marilyn Niwao of Hawaii, with all sorts of information she needed to prepare the 1983 tax return. A short while later, I started on the paperwork in Mom's office. I found nearly three years of backlog in there, with tax records in disarray, unanswered fan, business and personal letters, and a dizzying assortment of bank statements, undocumented deposits and with-drawals, and receipts. Only a few had Dad's notations on them con-cerning what they had been for. I set to organizing everything into existing file folders, and created new folders where necessary.

Mom had been very organized before becoming too ill to keep up, and I'd had no idea that she had been forced to let so much go. When I saw the state of the records, I told my father I would return to Port Townsend on weekends to help, until he could find a secretary.

At mid-morning the three of us decided to go for a walk. Dad wore a heavy sweater and a blue Gore-Tex coat, and when he stepped outside, even though it wasn't that cold (in the high forties), he zipped and tied the coat, with the collar tight around his bearded mouth.

"My blood is still thin from Hawaii," he said.

On farm roads and forest trails near the house, Dad talked more about Mom, saying he averaged only three hours of sleep a night during the last months of her life. With a chuckle he spoke of her skill with comeback lines, and suggested that I might have inherited her talent. He referred to my book *Classic Comebacks*, and to an incident he had been told about at the Norwescon science fiction convention the prior year, when I dispatched a rude panelist in front of hundreds of people. The audience had cheered me.

The following day, Penny and I did more paperwork in Mom's office, and ran several errands for Dad. Since Penny offered to under-take the task of answering all fan mail from then on, I separated out all such unanswered correspondence for her.

That afternoon, Dad and I sat in his study loft, where I described my *Man of Two Worlds* plot ideas for him. He liked them. It had taken me two months to work them up, and I was heartened by his reception. He said I was now a professional writer, and that I had made excellent progress in a relatively short period of time.

Later that evening I heard my father crying in his loft. When I went up there and put my arm on his shoulder he showed me something Mom had left in his desk, a tiny white slip from a Chinese fortune cookie. It said, "With patience, you will find happiness."

"It hurts so bad," he said, "and I can't do anything about it."

I remembered helping my mother up a long stairway the previous

445

September, to the Seattle shops where she left her watch and bought two Canadian gold coins, so I knew she hadn't climbed easily to Dad's writing loft. It must have taken her an excruciatingly long time, probably in the middle of the night when she couldn't sleep. She must have paused to catch her breath after each step.

When my brave mother sensed that she would never return to Port Townsend, she left things for Dad.

Here and there in his study over the next few days, on the tops of books, on the windowsill, or in a box of computer paper, he found other fortune cookie messages. And he found other things she left, including a shiny lucky penny in a tiny red envelope with Chinese characters on it.

The next day, Valentine's Day, Penny helped me with some of the paperwork. The filing and searching seemed endless. At low tide that evening, Dad, Bill Ransom and I took buckets, shovels and flashlights and went clam and oyster digging at Marrowstone Island. We brought back a nice haul, which we planned to share later in the week when Jan arrived with Bruce and the kids.

The next morning, I jogged at sunrise. Then more filing and searching for tax records. Dad and I typed a two-page outline on *Man of Two Worlds* and sent it off to our agents in New York. When he was typing the outline, he typed "By Frank Herbert and Brian Herbert." Then he looked at me and asked, "Is that all right?" He was referring to the placement of his name first. I nodded.

Dad wrote Mom's birth and death dates in her Bible, which had been passed on to her by her father. The cover was coming apart, so I repaired it.

Penny, Dad and I took walks each day. We made plans to meet at Kawaloa in February 1985, to conduct a service for Mom. I would take a ship, while the others would fly. Dad wanted to be certain that I could be there, since it was one of my mother's specific wishes.

Dad's face, particularly his forehead, was scaly and blotchy, which he said was caused in large part by medication a doctor had given him for his Hawaiian sunburn. Tests indicated that he did not have melanoma, but that was an ever-present concern since he was fair-skinned, and he would need close monitoring. "It's better than skin cancer," he said.

Frank Herbert was beginning work again on *Chapterhouse: Dune*, and hoped to have it completed by the middle of March. He said it was difficult going, like fighting a head wind, but he was doing his best. At the end of each day's work, he printed the hard copy. The printer made squawking and clicking noises.

Friday morning I found one of Mom's messages in the top drawer of her desk, where I was doing bookkeeping. It was on a Chinese restaurant's matchbook and read, "A long life to you."

I showed it to Dad. He smiled gently and said, without hesitation, "That was left for you, Brian."

I knew he was right, and recalled so many little things she had said to me in our final months together, her tones of voice, her gestures with her hands and arms. The way she turned her head and looked at me, and smiled. All were clues to deciphering the puzzle my mother had left. My mother's plan, as it became clear, had been laid out with the meticulous care and attention to detail of a mystery writer setting up a plot. Her plan was selfless.

It was difficult working where she had worked, constantly seeing her handwriting, her thoughts, her wishes. It was especially hard seeing old records so carefully organized with meticulous, loving care, contrasting with recent records in such disarray. She hadn't complained about her workload, hadn't wanted to give up her work.

Dad was extremely thoughtful in his time of greatest grief. When Jan arrived with Bruce, Dad gave her a book about Monet that my mother had ordered before her death. For Bruce, Penny and me, he had an *Omni* magazine photograph of him and Mom enlarged, reproduced in three copies and framed. In the color photograph, my parents looked very happy, with Dad in his full beard and she nuzzling against his neck.

He also gave each of us a signed 1,100-word piece he had written about their life together, written at Kawaloa the day after Mom's

death.* It roughly paralleled the poem he had written, "Bev." True to
the way he wrote much of his prose, the tribute to my mother seemed
in some respects to be an expanded version of the original poem.

Two of the passages in the dedication, in particular, reveal what my
father did for my mother, and what they meant to one another:

> . . . In her final days, she did not want anyone but me to touch
> her. But our married life had created such a bond of love and
> trust she often said the things I did for her were as though she
> did them. Though I had to provide the most intimate care, the
> care you would give an infant, she did not feel offended nor that
> her dignity had been assaulted. When I picked her up in my arms
> to make her more comfortable or bathe her, Bev's arms always
> went around my shoulders and her face nestled as it often had in
> the hollow of my neck.
>
> . . . Is it any wonder that I look back on our years together
> with a happiness transcending anything words can describe? Is it
> any wonder I do not want or need to forget one moment of it?
> Most others merely touched her life at the periphery. I shared it
> in the most intimate ways and everything she did strengthened
> me. It would not have been possible for me to do what necessity
> demanded of me during the final ten years of her life, strength-
> ening her in return, had she not given of herself in the preceding
> years, holding back nothing. I consider that to be my great good
> fortune and most miraculous privilege.

I spent all day Sunday working on the accounts in Mom's office.
Late in the evening, after Dad had gone to bed, I emerged and told
Bruce, Penny and Jan that the list from the accountant, when added
to the dismal paperwork involving my mother's death, was over-
whelming. I could envision an impossible workload in the future, in
addition to my responsibilities as an insurance agent, writer, husband
and father. I could do the filing for Dad and write checks, but it was

---

*In 1985 the prose piece would appear as a testimonial in *Chapterhouse: Dune*, eliciting an
outpouring of supportive letters from fans.

clear that he needed a bookkeeper in Port Townsend to help out. We all agreed to talk with him about it in the morning.

I didn't sleep well that night. At one point, around 5:30 A.M., totally exhausted and nearly forgetting how much my father needed my help, I almost got in my car to drive home alone. Jan stopped me. Later we discussed the situation with Dad, and he agreed to bring in a bookkeeper to help me.

One day while working in his loft-study, Dad heard me downstairs and came down. "Did I hear footprints down here?" he said with a smile.

So that we might spend more time together, Dad and I went to a bicycle shop in Seattle one day, and each of us purchased new mountain bikes with fat tires. His was silver, a fifteen-speed with every gizmo the store could cram on the bike. Mine was bright red, a more practical twelve-speed. We broke the bikes in on a sunny day in Port Townsend at the end of February.

We cycled around North Beach—a six-and-a-half-mile trip from the house, over hilly roads. Dad walked up some of the hills, while I pedaled up and then waited for him each time at the top. On the first downhill stretch, he took off like a Kamikaze, going at a speed that left me far behind and apprehensive for his safety. He didn't touch the brakes at all, and said he thought he reached forty miles an hour. It looked like a lot more to me. Perhaps he was being competitive, showing me the old man still had it. But even more it revealed the risk-taker in him, and his youthful enthusiasm for life.

Before Penny returned to California, she asked several of his friends to be sure and spend a lot of time with him after we left. She was concerned about how he would feel being alone in the house for the first time.

I stayed with Dad until February 27, and as I loaded my luggage into my car, he thanked me for the help. He placed his right hand on top of my open car door, and I touched his hand. Then, when he pulled his hand free and extended it to shake mine, we couldn't get coordinated, and a clumsy, slapstick maneuver took place until finally we grasped hands in the manner of modern school kids . . . sort of a "hip" handshake achieved accidentally.

Dad gave me a slender briefcase during my stay, which I opened on the ferry while crossing from Bainbridge Island to Seattle. Inside I found a note in Dad's handwriting, probably forgotten by him there. It was the last stanza of "The Waking," a poem by Theodore Roethke, one of the poets he most admired. The final lines read:

> I wake to sleep, and take my waking slow.
> I learn by going where I have to go.

On the other side of the paper, my father had written the last line of another Roethke poem ("Four for Sir John Davies"), a work he had quoted more completely in *Heretics of Dune*. This last line was, I knew, one of his favorites in all of poetry:

> The word outleaps the world and light is all.

CHAPTER
40

✳ Live Your Life! ✳

The greatest hell one can know is to be separated from
the one you love.

—Bill Moyers

PROCEEDING WITH loving care, my father complied with each of
the wishes on my mother's list. While doing so, he often said, as if she
were still alive, "Bev is a white witch. I'm in big trouble if I don't do
what I'm supposed to do."

He gave advice to all of us, and told us to trust our instincts, our
gut feelings. "If you feel sick to your stomach about something," he
said, "your body is talking to you. Listen to it." This advice was similar
to his writings, to the inner awareness of the Bene Gesserit of *Dune*
and to the statements of Leto II in *Children of Dune*, when he said,
"You have felt thoughts in your head; your descendants will feel
thoughts in their bellies," and, "It is time humans learned once more
to live in their instincts."

Dad developed a special relationship with Julie, who turned sixteen
in April 1984. He took her to the American Booksellers Association
Convention in Washington, D.C., where she was thrilled to meet entertainers Raquel Welch and Mr. T. She also watched my father deliver
a speech at a big breakfast banquet. When Julie returned from the East

451

Coast, she said her grandfather was referred to as "The Big Ragu" by New York publishing people.

Frank Herbert spent quality time with his other grandchildren, including a writing session with Kim, then twelve, critiquing stories she had written on a word processor at school. Margaux, only two, was too young for a heart-to-heart conversation, but she and her grandfather developed a close mutual affection. Initially he asked her to call him Panona, which had been my mother's request of Julie and Kim in the 1970s. Just as that name had not stuck in the earlier attempt, it failed again, as Margaux misunderstood and referred to him as "Banana."

"No!" we would all exclaim, breaking up with laughter. "Panona!" She couldn't quite get it, and finally we encouraged her to call him "Grandpa." This evolved in her young mind, and Margaux settled on calling him "Pop Pop," which he loved. Every time we went to see Pop Pop, she became very excited and often took him drawings and colorings she had done. He particularly liked her depiction of a spaceship filled with aliens, which he put up on the kitchen bulletin board.

Based on our outline for *Man of Two Worlds*, G. P. Putnam's Sons made a substantial offer, which we accepted and split evenly. With this, another of the promises my father made to my mother was on track. However, since Dad was busy providing technical advice and promotional assistance on the *Dune* movie (scheduled for release in December 1984), and on the writing of screenplays for two of his other works in which producers had expressed recent interest (*The Santaroga Barrier* and *Soul Catcher*), I was left with the task of doing most of the work on our book during 1984. Dad thought we might be able to begin work on the project without distractions in the spring of 1985, with completion expected by the end of that summer.

On the same day that our Putnam offer came in, I received an offer from another publisher, Arbor House, to publish *Sudanna, Sudanna* in hardcover. A third publisher, Berkley Books, was making an offer on the paperback rights for this book. My agent, Clyde Taylor, said, in an understatement, "This is your day." He also said my first United States hardcover contract was a breakthrough for me, a real boost to my career. I told Clyde to go ahead and accept the offers.

A few weeks later, I received and accepted offers from W. H. Allen to publish *Sudanna, Sudanna* in the United Kingdom, in hardcover and paperback.

In the spring of 1984, Jan and I spent every other weekend in Port Townsend, and she helped me with the accounts. A local bookkeeper had been selected, but her duties were limited to balancing the books monthly. Plenty of other work remained. Sometimes we handled things without asking Dad. On other occasions we accumulated items and asked him if he wanted to attend such and such a conference, or if he wanted to donate to particular causes, or if he wanted to deliver a speech in San Francisco, and the like. Occasionally he asked me to send signed copies of *Dune* or other Frank Herbert titles to people unsolicited, as a way of thanking them for favors.

Much of the time, if I asked him for financial information or the location of certain needed documentation, his eyes would glaze over and he would stiffen, unable to respond. He seemed to be wishing he were somewhere far away, or that I would just take care of it for him without asking. One weekend before leaving Port Townsend I told him it was necessary to transfer $100,000 between his accounts the following week. He made the withdrawals correctly, but two months later I found two cashier's checks for $50,000 apiece in a pile of papers he had delayed giving me. In his grief, other important documents were constantly misplaced as well, papers that had been sent to him by publishers, accountants, lawyers, and banks.

I also found a large Alaskan gold nugget in the bottom of a file drawer, which I made sure he put into his safety deposit box. In the glove box of his car, he had an envelope containing thousands of dollars in cash. And visiting the safety deposit box with him, I found thousands more in cash. I suggested that he deposit a lot of that cash to one of his bank accounts, which he did.

Prior to my involvement in my father's financial affairs, he had incurred a heavy debt load, with many items purchased on an installment basis, including motor vehicles, computer equipment, clothing and other articles. His credit cards were all at or near their limits. He owed a substantial amount of money on the Hana property and had refinanced the Port Townsend place in order to pay for construction at Hana. He had lines of credit at banks, which he dipped into frequently whenever he got in the hole and needed cash. He owed money to the Internal Revenue Service.

Frequently we heard him make insulting remarks about the IRS, which had hounded him throughout his writing career. My father had only paid lip service to financial planning without ever really understanding it, and now his tax problems were bigger than ever. As fast as money came in, he spent it on the heavy debt load, especially for ongoing construction at Hana. This left him behind on tax payments to the IRS, and caused him to write the sixth *Dune* book—*Chapterhouse: Dune*—at least two years sooner than he would have done otherwise.

While it is true that these books were the most lucrative of any that he wrote, it is not true that he didn't want to write *Dune* sequels, and that he only did so because he was forced to do so. He loved the *Dune* universe, and enjoyed exploring the many dimensions of the fantastic realm he had created. The classic first novel in the series had been complex and multi-layered, and in the sequels—particularly *God Emperor of Dune, Heretics of Dune*, and *Chapterhouse: Dune*—he went on intellectual excursions through some of the layers, particularly those of religion, history, politics, and philosophy.

But he wanted to complete other projects in between the *Dune* books, other science fiction stories and novels in other genres. In 1972 he had published a mainstream novel, *Soul Catcher*. It was a story that touched a special chord in his heart, and he had been intending to write more about the Native American's mystical view of the universe. He told Bill Ransom he was looking for another "*Soul Catcher*-like story."

Back in the late 1950s, Frank Herbert had attempted to depart from science fiction so that he could write mainstream stories. He did this despite the success of *Dragon in the Sea*, but could not accomplish the shift. Now, despite the phenomenal success of *Dune* and its sequels—and even of *The White Plague*—he longed for other pastures. It wasn't that he didn't enjoy science fiction. In fact, he often said he loved the "elbow room for the imagination" that the genre provided, and the *Dune* universe was the most challenging of all. But he wanted to stretch, longed to try new things. Frank Herbert was a risk-taker, an adventurer at heart.

On a visit to Port Townsend several weeks later, at the end of March,

I found my father still working on *Chapterhouse: Dune*. It was taking longer than expected. "I've been polishing it," he said, "making it primo." He paused, and his eyes misted over. "For Bev."

Around that time, I was reading a book about Alexander the Great. Dad mentioned a number of interesting facts about him, including a unique method Alexander had for timing the charges of his troops. Apparently Alexander learned of a chemical that could change a red rag to blue in thirty minutes, and he ordered that such chemically treated rags be placed on certain spear tops.

"Really?" I said. "I never heard about that."

"Yeah. It was the beginning of Alexander's Ragtime Band!" He turned as deep a shade of purple as I've ever seen on him, and exploded into gleeful laughter. He got me pretty good on that one.

A short while later he completed *Chapterhouse: Dune* and mailed it to New York. A twelve-day, eight-city national book tour followed, for the new hardcover edition of *Heretics of Dune*. This book, like others before it, would rocket onto bestseller lists. A hardcover reissue of *Dune* appeared on bookshelves at the same time, and enjoyed brisk sales.

Dad took a copy of the work I had done on *Man of Two Worlds* with him on the tour and reviewed it in hotel rooms, making pencil notations in the margins. During the tour, his forehead was still scaly and blotchy from sunburn and medication, and he had to wear heavy makeup during interviews.

When he asked a mainland doctor to check this condition, shortly after returning to Port Townsend, he neglected to ask about the big mole on his back, first noticed by Jan. He'd had them before, and wasn't overly concerned about this one. It's "probably benign," he assured us. But he was procrastinating on a biopsy, which would determine for certain how dangerous it was. Disturbed by this, Penny, Jan and I pressed him to get it taken care of quickly. No one could force my father to do anything however, except my mother. Dad said medical attention for the mole, or "benign tumor" as he called it, would have to wait until after the book tour.

Los Angeles was one of the cities on the tour, where he was met at the airport by a limousine and driver, and escorted to public appearances by a young woman who was the Putnam book representative for the area.

In mid-April, Dad saw a three-and-a-half-hour rough-cut version of the *Dune* movie at Universal Studios in Universal City, California. It was a private showing in Screening Room #1. This was part of a four-hour, fifty-minute film David Lynch had made, and the producers were ordering more cuts, to get it down to a little over two hours. Dad was not overly concerned about this, and when he returned home told me he was pleased with the production, that director David Lynch had created a "visual feast," capturing the book remarkably well. Even more vividly than Dad had imagined when he wrote it. "I hear my dialogue all through it," he said.

Dad also said Putnam wanted us to do a joint book tour on *Man of Two Worlds* sometime in late 1985 or early 1986, when the book was published.

While I was still grieving for my mother, I had lunch with Dad in an Italian restaurant in Seattle late in April 1984. He was just back from a triumphant *Heretics of Dune* book tour, and I was happy for him. He had worked hard to achieve such success. We were at a small window table, in the Capitol Hill district of the city. A street wound up the hillside outside our window, with cars rolling by. Dad's forehead was raw and scaly, worse in appearance than before, and he said he expected to be taking the skin medication for another two weeks.

We spoke of religion, and agreed that it seemed ridiculous for so many religious systems to contend that they had the "one and only" path to God. This was, of course, one of the subjects covered in an appendix of *Dune*, where the C.E.T. (Commission of Ecumenical Translators) was said to have held a meeting among representatives of the major religions, at which they set a common goal: "We are here to remove a primary weapon from the hands of disputant religions. That weapon—the claim to possession of the one and only revelation."

Without a title yet, I had in mind a story about the terrible things religions could make people do to one another, purportedly in the name of God. In the beginning of the tale, God would announce his location on a planet far across the universe and would invite people to come and visit him—for an unexplained purpose. The competing religions would then race for God, stopping at nothing, including murder, to get there first.

456

"There's your title!" he exclaimed. *"The Race for God!"*

He was right. It was a good title. I added it to a file full of notes that I hoped to work on soon. We discussed two other story ideas, one of mine and one of his, with thoughts about collaborating on them some day, after the completion of *Man of Two Worlds*.

He said he was impressed with the work I had done on our collaboration, especially descriptive passages of the alien planet Dreenor and its people, through whose imagination the entire universe was sustained. He wanted to include those passages as I had written them, without revision.

Dad fell silent for a long while, then cleared his throat. Nervously, he told me he had fallen in love with the Putnam book representative he had met in Los Angeles while on his *Heretics* tour. "I hope you aren't going to be upset about this," he said, "but she's only twenty-seven. She's an old twenty-seven, though." He added that this was in reference to her maturity, not to the way she looked, and didn't reveal her name.

From across the table, I noticed my father's eyes gave him the appearance of a guilt-consumed child looking painfully at an adult, fearful of impending punishment. He seemed to be waiting for my criticism.

Dad was sixty-three years old. He was approximately thirty-six years older than she was, which happened to be my age. I was, to say the least, shocked.

Trying to hide my feelings for his sake, I said, "You're not really that far apart in age, Dad. If we accept the fact of genetic memory that you've written about in *Dune*, you're five million and sixty-three years old, while she's five million and twenty-seven."

This pleased him exceedingly, and he beamed from ear to ear. Soon I heard the story repeated back to me by other members of the family.

He admitted that the young woman was not responding to his advances, though she seemed to like him. He thought it might take time, and then added that there were two other women of interest in his life, both of whom were in their mid-forties. Until now, I had not given much thought to the idea of him remarrying.

My father described an unusual experience during his last flight from Los Angeles to Seattle. On the plane, he was recalling the young book representative, thinking of the way she moved her hands and touched his arm. Somehow he was convinced he was picking these memories up as bits of data from her brain, what metaphysical philosophers called "petite perception." Simultaneously, he received messages from my mother in which she told him, "It's all right. She's the one. You're still alive, Frank! Live your life!"*

I looked away as he spoke, trying to keep my composure. Presently I looked back at him and smiled, reassuringly. "Then it's all right," I said.

As days passed, however, I became angry with my father about his love interests, and so did Jan. We said nothing to him about it, but it seemed to us that he hadn't waited long enough, hadn't spent enough time grieving. But when my mother passed away, we were beginning to realize, a terrible feeling of loneliness came over Frank Herbert. He had lost his lifelong companion, his reason for living, his true best friend. We tried to empathize, but it was not easy, for a lot of reasons.

Dad seemed terribly fragile, helpless and lonely. He was vulnerable. He telephoned me constantly, and it seemed that he needed to hear someone's voice all the time. This wasn't at all like a writer, perhaps, who should have been accustomed to cloistering himself in his study. In becoming a writer myself, however, I began to realize what he must have been feeling. When my mother lived with him, he could confine himself for hours without speaking to her, feeling great serenity because he knew she was there, just outside his door. It became quite different when someone was not physically nearby, not waiting to give him love and reassurance.

I knew he had been dependent upon my mother, so I expected him to be very low about her death. Since he always kept guns around we

---

*Frank Herbert was not the only one of us to report the paranormal influence of my mother after her death. When Margaux was eight years old, she was about to step in front of a truck on a busy street. Suddenly she felt "a gasp of air" that pushed her back onto the sidewalk to safety. No one was near her. Thinking back, however, she recalled seeing a dark-haired woman beside her, just before the incident. Years later, as I was completing this biography, I was contacted by Frankie Goodwin, who had been Mom's best friend back in the 1940s. Frankie filled in details on the courtship of my parents. Then she added, "I don't know what made me write to you after all these years." I smiled and said, "My mother had a hand in this." As proof, I described a number of events to Frankie, many of which are detailed later in this biography.

worried about suicide, and about a serious disease overtaking him, brought on by stress. Medical studies showed that losing a spouse was the number-one creator of stress. But Dad had always been a strong man, and I expected him to bounce back. I thought his writing would carry him far into old age, but it wasn't working out the way I had expected. He didn't seem to have his heart in it any more.

Howie Hansen, with his Native American perspective, later said, "Frank was a genius, and Bev was equal to but different from him. She had more power than he had. He was only a shell after she died."

At times, Dad's telephoning drove me crazy. He called me at all hours for minor things, pulling me out of my writing, shattering my concentration. He had a speed dialer on his telephone, with my name on it. While I considered this a compliment, since he depended on me so much, there was a definite downside. If someone in my household was on the line, and my two oldest daughters did talk on the phone a lot, he contacted the operator and put through an emergency call. ("Call waiting" service was not available from the phone company at the time.) None of his calls were emergencies, not even close. He needed paper products from a store in Seattle. Would we pick them up and bring them to Port Townsend? Or, had we seen a certain politician talking on television? That guy was dangerous, and we shouldn't think of voting for him in November.

An ingenious man, my father developed a habit of calling me at 5:30 A.M., when he knew no one would be on the line. One morning, Jan answered the phone, then woke me up. I stumbled downstairs in my bathrobe, half asleep.

"Hullo," I said.

A dial tone greeted me. When I finally got through to Dad forty-five minutes later, he told me he hung up to take a call on his other line from an East Coast reporter who wanted to interview him.

When I asked him what he was calling me about, he went into a plot point about *Man of Two Worlds*, and asked my opinion. I wasn't sure why this conversation couldn't have occurred at a more civil hour, but I gave him my thoughts about the story question, not mentioning something else that was on my mind. Afterward, I returned to bed, but couldn't go back to sleep. All that day I was too tired to write, and could only muddle through my insurance agency tasks.

Since Dad gave me very little story copy that he had written during the year, I could only presume that he wrote material and subsequently threw it away. He probably rose early to work on *Man of Two Worlds*, ran into distractions and then could not proceed. At one point, he told me that I might have to write the entire book myself, with him adding "finishing touches."

Dad still hadn't gone in to get the mole on his back removed, and the skin condition on his face could be more serious than he was letting on. It was becoming obvious that he had neglected his own health while caring for Mom's. Whenever we visited him, we brought along homemade soups, pasta dishes, desserts and other foods that we knew he liked. We stocked his freezer with them, so whenever he was alone he could at least know people who loved him had prepared something for his table. Gradually the scaliness on his face cleared, and he began to look much better. But he was more nervous than ever, constantly in a state of hyperactivity.

With Mom gone, much of his behavior became erratic. He had lost her steadying influence. Many of his discussions about new women in his life seemed immature, as if he were a teenager involved in the dating game. Once, unable to find a bag of unsalted potato chips for me in the Port Townsend Safeway, he went into a tirade at the checkstand, announcing that he would "shut Safeway down" if they didn't pay attention to what he wanted. And his habit of nit-picking, which so bedeviled me when I lived with him, actually worsened.

It was all odd, the behavior of a man whose mental health was on the edge, in danger of plunging over a precipice from which he might not return. And understandably so, considering the magnitude of his loss.

He was a great and loving man, and his flaws were infinitesimal. If I ever raised my voice to him, only slightly, he nearly fell apart, so I went overboard to avoid hurting his feelings. Jan and I told the children he was going through a difficult time, and that they should try to do whatever he wanted, being as understanding as possible.

One weekend Dad raved about my children constantly leaving his kitchen drawers open and about me leaving a cereal bowl in Mom's office where I had been working on his accounts. Holding the bowl in my hands, I asked him humbly if he might find it somewhere in his heart to forgive me. Suddenly he laughed heartily.

Thank goodness he retained his sense of humor. On a beautiful, clear day he and I went sailing on the *Caladan*. We didn't encounter a lot of wind, but got the boat up to six knots on the jib alone, without the mainsail. Afterward I joked in the car that I couldn't have done anything wrong, as Dad had not yelled at me once.

"I overlooked a lot of things," he said, with a wry smile.

For much of 1984 he was not writing productively. The screenplays on *The Santaroga Barrier* and *Soul Catcher* remained in his "To Do" file, as did much of our collaboration. While Jan was in Paris at the Sorbonne that summer, he wrote to her:

Dear Jan:

Your card from the Monet home makes me want to go there at once. I intend to see it in 1985 because I still have this dream of spending most of a year in Paris. . . .

I'm getting back into the book Brian and I are doing. I went through my first writer's block* recently (I should say semi-block, because I could still do some things). It was partly due to all the pressure I went through doing that sixth *Dune* book, six months' work in two months. I got burned out. And then my love life got rocky for a time but is now back on track.

It's an odd thing to have this many beautiful women interested in me. I wonder, of course, how much of it is the glamor and affluence? With one of them I'm sure it's me. With one I'm sure it's the glamor, etc. One question mark.

Publishers and movie people are yo-yoing me around on promotion gigs. I go to Vancouver, BC, next month for a hectic day of radio, TV and autograph parties.

Brian will be up here this evening and we will get back into the swing of things after he does his usual economic chores. Saturday night, I'm going to a flamenco dance benefit at Fort Wor-

---

*Actually he had experienced writer's blocks before, but not since the late 1950s and early 1960s.

den and then it's once more into this word processor to make the new book do what it should.

The telephone keeps ringing and interrupting. Important stuff, too. I can't ignore it. That was *Psychology Today* wanting to send a photographer up here. They have the cover of the magazine in mind. I suppose you already know that *People* magazine, *Washington* magazine and *Pacific Northwest*—all of them on the covers. *Publishers Weekly* with a nice article and picture. *New York Times* with a wonderful review. Have to build the fence higher and get in a secretary.

Have to go back to work now. Stick in there on your Paris Project. It will be extremely important to you for the rest of your life. Brian and I are holding down the fort here. Miss you and are looking forward to your return in August.

Love,
Frank

Since his personal life was up in the air, he spent a great deal of time thinking about it, trying to decide among the three women, only two of whom were showing overt interest in him. The third, the Putnam book representative, was not responding as he would have liked. He said that she liked him for himself, not for the glamor or luxury surrounding a famous author, and that he wanted to be more than friends with her. This was the young woman he had met on his *Heretics of Dune* book tour. Her name was Theresa Shackelford.

As for business, it was much the way it had always been. Many times when I asked him about this or that involving his finances—important questions—he threw his hands up and I had to solve whatever it was. His head was in outer space, but not in the productive manner it had been there in the past, not in a manner that would permit him to write the greatest science fiction anyone had ever read. Dad indicated to me that he was having trouble disciplining and motivating himself, and I received the distinct impression that he couldn't write on his own. His collaborator for more than three decades, in a very real sense, had been my mother, Beverly Herbert. Now I was the collaborator, thus attempting to pick up yet another of the important functions of my mother.

But a son-collaborator–business manager can never fulfill the functions of a wife, can never be the source of inspiration and intimate tenderness that my father so desperately needed in his life. He was empty inside, a man with a terrible ache.

To make matters worse, all the *Dune* movie publicity was generating a steady stream of telephone calls and letters from movie people, reporters, agents and publishers. Mom used to screen his calls and correspondence for him, coordinating appointments, allowing him to continue writing without interruption. But now he found himself constantly scattered in his thoughts, unable to concentrate. My mother had been ten people for him at once.

Despite all of his distractions, during our collaboration the most remarkable transformations would take place in Dad. Only a short while after he had behaved unusually or immaturely or distractedly, he would become, quite suddenly, coherent and brilliant in talking about a story scene, teaching me something with almost every sentence. His writing, when he could immerse himself in it, was a refuge from the cares and tribulations of life, from the pain and upset he was enduring in the aftermath of the shelling of his life. As I wrote with this man who had been impatient for much of our relationship, he surprised me by listening patiently to every suggestion I made and agreeing with many of them.

Early in our collaboration Dad spoke of chapter lengths and story cohesion. He wanted to make Chapter One medium length, Chapter Two short, Chapter Three very short and Chapter Four long. Thus a rhythm was established in the story, a rhythm he said we could repeat at various points in the book to reflect back to the beginning.

One time when I was spending the weekend with him, I was so bothered by a direction he wanted to take at the beginning of our story that when I went to bed I slept only fitfully. I awoke at 3:30 A.M. and wrote him a long note with my objections and reasons, which I left on the carpet outside his bedroom door. In my opinion, we needed something fast-moving at the start, and too much background information would be required to establish the scene he wanted to do. Later he said he spent two hours thinking over my note, and that I triggered his thinking to the correct starting point—a starting point we agreed to use.

41

✳ This Is for Bev ✳

DURING 1984, we had a number of conferences about *Man of Two Worlds*. After making an outline we agreed upon a division of labor in which Dad would write some chapters and I would write others. In the end, however, he couldn't find the time to do the writing that year, so eventually I went back and wrote his chapters as well.

On my lunch hour at work one day, I wrote around eight hundred words longhand. That evening Dad came to my house, and he wanted to see what I had produced. It was too rough to give him, so I sat on the family room couch with his old Olympia portable typewriter atop a drawing board on my lap, while he sat to my left, waiting and reading each page as I completed it. I had carbon paper in the machine (so that we each could have a copy) and pecked at the keys. I knew my typing speed was nowhere near his, but it didn't bother me. Once Kim interrupted me, and Dad told her to leave me alone while I was writing.

A few days passed. One day in May, Dad was in a limousine, and on impulse he told the driver to stop at a drug store. Dad went inside and got shaving equipment and shaved off his beard in the car. Jan and I did not know about it yet and were scheduled to meet him at the Ajax Cafe in Hadlock, near Port Townsend. At first we didn't recognize him as he sat at the table, giggling to himself. Then I noticed something familiar about "that man over there"—the eyes and hair, and the shape of the face. He had a belly laugh over this, and it *was* pretty funny.

But without his luxuriant, distinguished beard he looked older, and smaller. More like a man and less like the myth he had created around himself.

When he went on the road without his beard, to conventions and the like, he had fun playing tricks on people he had known for years. Often they didn't recognize him at all, until they heard his deep, resonant voice, or until he laughed in the wonderful way only my father could laugh. Arthur C. Clarke mailed him two tickets to the world premiere of *2010*, held at a theater in Westwood, near Los Angeles. In the restroom, Dad saw Ray Bradbury, and said, "Hi, Ray." Bradbury responded dispassionately, "Oh, hello."

"You don't recognize me, do you?" Dad said, with an impish smile.

Bradbury leaned close, then closer. He looked at the eyes, combining them with the characteristic timbre and cadence of the voice. "Frank?" he said. "Are you Frank Herbert?"

Early in June, Dad caught a morning flight from Port Townsend to Seattle. I picked him up and drove him across the Evergreen Point floating bridge to Group Health Hospital in Redmond, where he checked in for surgery on the mole on his back. Then I returned to work.

At noon I brought him grilled chicken breasts, pasta salad and Italian fish and chips from Osteria Mitchelli in Seattle, a restaurant he liked. As I did this I thought of all the times he had gone out and obtained goodies for Mom while she was in hospital. Now I was doing for him what he had done for her—setting things up with the nurses, having them refrigerate what was left and warming it in the microwave when he wanted it.

Dad made the nurse give him each of his vital signs, and this seemed to irritate her. Most patients were content to let the medical staff do their thing, but not my father! He wanted to know what they were doing each step of the way.

When I arrived at the hospital at noon the following day to help him check out, he was pacing the hallway by his room, champing at the bit to get going. He said the growth on his back, now removed, had been a tumor, but thankfully it was benign, confirmed by a biopsy. Dad was elated. "Benign is the most beautiful word in the English language," he said. My father was right, and I thought of the ugly sound of its antonym, malignant.

He underwent a complete medical checkup, and the results were good. I had been noticing, however, that his head frequently shook from side to side. It was involuntary and almost imperceptible, a condition I first began to notice in 1977 at his mother's funeral. I assumed it was just fatigue.

One Thursday when Jan was still in Paris, Dad needed me to come up to Port Townsend to help him with a number of banking tasks that could only be done when the bank was open. It was on short notice, but after making arrangements at work, I picked up my daughters and we all drove to Port Townsend for a long weekend.

The next morning, Dad went into Port Townsend with me, and we did the banking and ran a number of errands. He was cheerful and obviously well-liked by shop owners and people he saw on the street. He even held a door open for two teetering old ladies. On the way home, however, he drove the city streets like a madman, passing one car at the crest of a hill and then tailgating a pickup truck while beeping his horn at the driver for going too slowly.

On a cool, rainy afternoon that year, Dad was driving his Mercedes coupe through Port Townsend, when he saw an old woman pulling a heavy cart of groceries up a hill. He stopped and assisted her, loading her things into the trunk and helping her into the front seat. She was wet and shivering. While carrying her groceries into her tiny, cluttered house, he asked why she didn't ride the bus, since it ran close to where she lived. She said she barely had enough money for groceries. It was cold in her house, and he learned that her heating oil tank was empty. The next day, Dad put money into a bank account for her, so that she could always afford to ride the bus. He also made arrangements with the local heating oil company to pay the bills for her and for other needy people in the area, so that they would not freeze during the winters. He did it all anonymously.

One Sunday morning in July, after I had been working on Dad's accounts far into the night, he popped his head into the guest bedroom where I was sleeping and woke me. It was early, and I was groggy.

"Do you want to go to breakfast with me and Kyle MacLachlan?" he asked.

I knew he was referring to the young actor who was playing the lead role of Paul Atreides in the *Dune* movie.

"No," I said, and I rolled over and went back to sleep.

Julie did accompany her grandfather, and it was thrilling for her. They ate at a pancake restaurant in Port Townsend, and she returned with a movie poster signed by both the actor and her grandfather. Dad gave other signed posters to the rest of us.

We were scheduled to hold the service for Mom in Hawaii on the first anniversary of her death, the following February. The delay was primarily due to my inability to fly, making it necessary for me to find a ship for the passage. This was not an easy task, due to a downturn in the number of cruise ships that were operating. When Dad heard about my difficulties he said he would have a doctor fill me with tranquilizers and pour me on a plane. He tried to encourage me to take a fear of flying course, but I declined. In an attempt to avoid a discussion of the subject, I said I didn't feel like hurrying from one place to another. I said Isaac Asimov and Ray Bradbury did not like to fly either, but were pretty good science fiction writers.

"I fly, and I'm a better writer than both of them," Dad said.

After trying many travel agents unsuccessfully, Jan found a cruise line with a ship that could take me, and she made reservations.

Toward the end of the summer, I left my lucrative insurance agency job to work for my father, receiving a salary from him for the first time. Dad also made arrangements with Penny and Ron to make them caretakers of the Port Townsend property, which Dad planned to keep. They would wrap up affairs in California and move north early in 1985. Frank Herbert was drawing his family close around him, as Beverly wanted.

Around this time, he was in close contact with the renowned mountain climber Jim Whittaker, who lived in Port Townsend and had been the first American to climb Mount Everest, back in 1963. Dad wanted to go on an expedition to the Himalayas in the spring of 1986 before the monsoon season, doing a documentary film on the trip. He intended to fly to Kathmandu, capital of Nepal. In Kathmandu he would visit the Old Royal Palace and a number of nearby Buddhist temples, including the spectacular Taleju temple. The Gurkha regiments of the British Indian Army came from that part of the world, he said, troops that had been of special interest to him for years.

Dad fixed dinner in Port Townsend for Whittaker, and together they drafted a letter to Nawang Gombu in India, a man only five feet tall who had been Whittaker's sherpa guide in the 1963 Everest assault. On the very first ascent of Everest, by Sir Edmund Hillary of Great Britain in 1953, Gombu had been a seventeen-year-old porter. In 1955, Gombu reached the top of the mountain for the second time, the first person to accomplish the ascent twice. He was also a nephew of Tenzing Norgay, the famous sherpa guide who reached the top of the mountain at the same time as Hillary.

For my father's purposes, Gombu, now forty-eight, appeared to be a fine choice. Gombu responded positively, and they made plans to make a nineteen-day, two-hundred-mile trek in the Everest Base Camp region on the Nepal side of the mountain. From Kathmandu they would fly to the town of Namche Bazaar, at an elevation of 11,300 feet. From there, accompanied by porters, they would hike to the lakeside village of Gokyo at 15,720 feet and then up to the top of Gokyo Ridge at 18,000 feet, for a 360 degree panoramic view of the upper Gokyo Valley, the massive Ngozumpa Glacier and three mountain peaks rising between 25,990 and 27,826 feet. They would ascend afterward to Gokyo. A climb to Chola Pass at 17,783 feet would follow, and then across the high, scenic pasture of Dzonglha. Toward the end of the trek they would climb to the highest point, the top of upper Kala Pattar at 18,450 feet, from which point they would be able to see the South Col of Everest.

Dad invited me to participate in the trek, with a caveat because of the altitude at which we would be climbing, "Get yourself in shape for this one." He went on to talk about the dangers of altitude sickness— and of the many trekkers in the Himalayas who had died of this. It was especially important to acclimatize yourself to altitude, he said— and to ascend gradually and go back down at the first symptoms of illness. Many people disregarded warning signs, he said, and died as a result.

I wanted to go on the trip, and began thinking about how I might travel by surface to Asia. Even if I managed to get to Kathmandu by surface, and I wasn't sure if I could do that, Dad planned to fly from there to Namche Bazaar, and there might be other connections by small plane. It all sounded perilous, but tremendously exciting. Late in 1985, just before the trip, he intended to live at an altitude of eight thousand feet in Switzerland for a month, to build up the hemoglobins in his blood.

And following the Everest Base Camp trek, perhaps a year later, Dad hoped to return to the Himalayas, becoming the oldest man to ever climb Mount Everest, at 29,028 feet.

Around this time my father, almost sixty-four years old, began talking about buying a new Porsche. I vowed to myself I would never get in such a vehicle with him, for obvious reasons. Recently he had gotten a ticket for going more than sixty miles an hour on city streets.

He also made arrangements to rent a nice apartment near the Strand in the Los Angeles area (Manhattan Beach), so that he could work on the two screenplays near Hollywood and be around many of the people who were putting the finishing touches on the *Dune* movie. He had the Hollywood bug, and even spoke of directing a film one day.

But above all, he had fallen completely in love with the Putnam book representative, Theresa Shackelford, who lived in the Los Angeles area. He wanted to spend more time with her, with the object of marriage. She was now twenty-eight years old.

My father was emerging into his second youth, desperately attempting to grab another chance at life. He fell in love with a young woman, wanted to drive fast cars and climb mountains. He and Theresa took skin diving lessons and Dad developed a liking for popular music, especially the songs of Engelbert Humperdinck.

One day my father asked Penny, "When you were so in love with Ron after meeting him, did you have butterflies in your stomach and hear bells ringing?"

"That was a long time ago," Penny said. "I don't remember."

"Well that's the way I feel now," Dad said.

In early September 1984, I helped Dad move some of his things out of Xanadu into a big yellow Ryder rental truck, which he was having driven to California. He would accompany the truck, driving his Mercedes coupe. It was an interesting scene, watching this famous man do once more what we had done so many times in my youth when we were poor, packing boxes "with a shoehorn" and moving. He still had his remarkable strength and endurance, and hardly broke a sweat as he ran in and out of the house carrying heavy boxes and other articles. He was planning to keep both the Port Townsend and Hawaii houses. While he was in California he wanted me to go to Port Townsend once a week to pick up his mail, handling what I could myself and sending the rest to him.

All during 1984, the *Dune* movie was advertised as the greatest film production of all time, and perhaps the most expensive. Comparisons were drawn between it and *Gone with the Wind*, and there was a great deal of secrecy about who was playing the lead role of Paul Atreides—Kyle MacLachlan. When the actor was interviewed on television, his back was to the camera. It was one of the most coveted screen roles in years. His Seattle phone number, known only to a few people, was 547-DUNE.

It may have been the most heavily promoted movie in history. Months before the film came out, toys and other novelty items were made available, in addition to Avalon Hill's *Dune* board game, which had been out for years. There were toy sandworms and Paul Atreides dolls, *Dune* weapons, obsidian paperweights with House Atreides gold hawks on them, tee-shirts, posters, games, soundtrack record albums and tapes, calendars, puzzles and mazes. Merchandisers had to pay Universal Studios as much as $100,000 apiece for the rights to produce spinoff products.

A mind-boggling assortment of spinoff books appeared as well, plus reissued Frank Herbert books. Almost everything he had ever published went back into print or had its press run increased. Most of the books were published by Berkley/Putnam. In addition to reprints and special boxed sets of all the books in the *Dune* series they came out with *The Art of Dune, The Dune Storybook, Dune Activity Book, Dune Coloring Book, Dune Coloring & Activity Book, Dune Cut-Out Activity Book, Dune Pop-Up Panorama Book*, a book about the movie production entitled *The Making of Dune*, and a speculative compendium about the

470

worlds of Dune, entitled *The Dune Encyclopedia*. Every envelope and parcel mailed by Berkley/Putnam during the year was stamped, in red letters, *The Year of Dune*.

Universal Studios established a *Dune* fan club, and in only a few weeks had several thousand members. Under arrangement with Lifetime Learning Systems, Universal also developed *The World of Dune* teaching kit, which was given to four thousand middle and high school teachers in the United States and Canada. Waldenbooks came out with a contest, "The World of Dune Sweepstakes." The winner received a trip to Los Angeles and a dinner with Frank Herbert. Waldenbooks also produced and distributed interviews of Frank Herbert and David Lynch on cassette tape.

The film's budget was variously quoted between forty and sixty million dollars, production numbers that were, at the time, astronomical. Universal Studios had a promotional budget of an additional eight million dollars. They announced the movie would be released just before Christmas 1984, timed to obtain the most attention for Academy Award nominations.

Promoters, eager to take advantage of Christmas shoppers and follow in the footsteps of *Star Wars* merchandising (which had brought in three billion dollars in revenues in addition to movie ticket sales), tried to promote *Dune* in the same manner, with toys, coloring books and the like aimed at children and teenagers. Frank Herbert did not object to the merchandising, saying the investors needed to do it in order to maximize their profits, and the movie might never have been made without the prospect of such additional earnings.

But from the beginning I had my doubts about this approach. I knew from fan mail that young people read the *Dune* books, but they were a decided minority. The books were far too intellectual for most people in that age group. As weeks passed many fans were put off by glitzy, misdirected promotions, and sales on the novelty items were slow.

In the midst of all this, Dad signed on to do a Pacific Bell television commercial, which would run during prime time and special events, including the Super Bowl. In the commercial, Frank Herbert stood in front of an alien backdrop, looking rather different without his beard from the way his fans were accustomed to seeing him. He spoke of a subject he knew very well—the future.

Around September, when Dad was leaving for California, he was telling people he liked what he had seen of the film. When asked about it, he frequently kissed his fingertips and exclaimed, "They're capturing the essence of my book, doing it just right!"

His contract with Dino De Laurentiis didn't allow him to publicly criticize the film, but Dad always said if he didn't like it he would remain silent. He really did like it and was extremely excited. He predicted that it would be a cult movie, and in the innovative hands of David Lynch felt it would be a breakthrough film as well, exploring ground that had never before been covered on film.

In early December, Dad took his new love, Theresa Shackelford, to a world premiere of the movie at The John F. Kennedy Center for the Performing Arts in Washington, D.C. President and Mrs. Reagan were among more than one thousand in attendance. Also present were stars of the movie, including Kyle MacLachlan, Dean Stockwell, and Francesca Annis. The building had been decorated to look like the Palace of Arrakeen on the planet Dune, and it housed an enthusiastic audience. After the movie one woman kept saying, "Wow! Wow! Oh, wow!" A state dinner at the White House followed, at which the President and Mrs. Reagan told Dad they had enjoyed the movie.

The Group Health premiere would be held the following week in Seattle. Dad would come up by himself from Los Angeles and would escort his favorite aunt, Peggy Rowntree, to the event.

Dad was given fifty tickets for his friends and family, and I coordinated the guest list, making doubly certain that each invitee would attend before mailing out tickets. This was on top of all the *Man of Two Worlds* work, our Hawaii trip preparations, the handling of Dad's voluminous paperwork (including the accumulation of data needed for his 1984 taxes) and the preparation of my own taxes—all of which had to be done before we could leave in early January.

On the afternoon of Tuesday, December 11, 1984, Jan and I picked up Penny and her husband Ron at the airport, then met Dad in his hotel suite at the Four Seasons Olympic Hotel in Seattle. My brother and his gay lover were already there when we arrived. Dad looked natty in his thirty-five-year-old tuxedo, with a ruffled white shirt and a black bow tie. Gold cufflinks glimmered at the sleeves.

I took him aside and we discussed a number of his pressing income tax and legal matters. We spoke of *Man of Two Worlds* as well, and Dad said we might create a "mushy" monster in the story, perhaps a "dragon that runs away when kids throw rocks at it."

At 5:00 P.M., all of us walked across the street to a *Dune* reception at the Rainier Bank Tower. The reception was held on the fortieth floor, which afforded a panoramic view of Seattle and Elliott Bay. Guests were dressed in tuxedos and jewel-bedecked evening gowns. The hors d'oeuvres and wines were first-class. Mayor Royer of Seattle was present, along with a number of other notables, including mountain climber Jim Whittaker.

At 7:00, the family members and V.I.P.s were taken in three limousines to the King Cinema a mile away. Powerful spotlights stood in front of the theater, crisscrossing beams of light through the night sky. We filed into a reserved loge area and sat in big, soft seats. A murmuring air of anticipation filled the theater, as everyone wondered how close the movie would come to Frank Herbert's masterpiece.

At 7:30, Dad walked down to the stage in front of the curtained screen and spoke to a full house, introducing the movie. He said it had been a long time in the making, and gave a brief history of earlier attempts, including mention of Jodorowsky's plan for a fourteen-hour epic and a subsequent screenplay that would have made an incest movie about Paul and his mother. Upon learning of the incest concept, the audience gasped. All along, Dad had been correct in asserting that his fans would never tolerate anything like that.

When he spoke poignantly about Mom and the reasons for the Group Health benefit, including her initial efforts in setting it up shortly before her death, his voice broke and he could hardly speak. He closed by saying, "This is for Bev," then stood there looking very lonely and sad. The audience gave him a standing ovation, and then, head down to conceal his tears, he walked back to his seat.

The curtain went up, the lights dimmed, and Toto's magnificent soundtrack filled our ears. It was a wide screen, best for this particular film, and soon I found myself immersed into the story. The desert scenes were spectacular, bringing to mind an alien *Lawrence of Arabia*. The atmosphere in the Palace of Arrakeen was Shakespearean, with dark, mysterious rooms and corridors and scheming, plotting characters. When Paul rode the giant sandworm, chills ran down my spine. The audience clapped and cheered when Alia stabbed the Baron Harkonnen with a gom jabbar needle and thrust him into the jaws of a sandworm—a slight variation from the book, in which he slumped over in his suspensors, dead from the gom jabbar.

When the film finished and the lights went back on, I looked at my father, who was in my row two seats away. He was staring at the screen, transfixed, eyes open wide and face almost expressionless. An empty box of popcorn lay at his feet.

For nearly an hour, Dad signed movie programs and books until his hand ached and he could do no more. He said he had forgotten to bring along the wristband that gave him additional strength for marathon signings.

A short while later, in an interview on national television, Dad mentioned the novel we were writing together. The interviewer asked him if I was really a good writer or if Frank Herbert was only doing something to help his son. Dad's eyebrows arched at the rude inquiry, and he responded, "The acorn didn't fall far from the oak tree."

Forbes magazine said *Dune* might become the first billion-dollar movie, far surpassing the revenues of any other motion picture in history. Dad thought this was entirely possible. Based upon book sales, he said the movie had a built-in audience of fifty million people, and many of them would want to see it over and over, just as they read and reread the book. In the opening weeks, as expected, crowds lined up to purchase tickets.

Going along with the movie, book sales skyrocketed, and the paperback edition of *Dune* reached number one on *The New York Times* bestseller list. "It's highly unusual for this to happen nearly twenty years after publication," Dad told me. In honor of the occasion, his publisher had the list from the newspaper enlarged and framed for him. For the week of January 6, 1985, it showed *Dune* number one, ahead of novels by Danielle Steel and Stephen King.

CHAPTER
42

✳ Bridge Over Troubled Water ✳

MOM'S CEREMONY would be held at Kawaloa on February 7, 1985, the first anniversary of her passing. While we found a cruise ship to take us there late in January, there were no return voyages until June. As a consequence, Jan and I made arrangements to live in the house at Kawaloa through June, taking our children with us and putting them in public school for that time. We had high hopes of making an adventure out of it and that it would be an alternate cultural encounter for my children—somewhat like experiences I'd had in Mexico in the 1950s.

In mid-January 1985, before boarding the ship in San Francisco, Jan and I drove further south to Manhattan Beach near Los Angeles to visit my father. He had asked me to bring a typewriter to him, and I assumed he meant his vintage 1970 Olympia electric. It turned out to be the wrong one. He wanted the tiny portable he had used in London to work on the screenplay of "Flash Gordon" for Dino De Laurentiis.

This time, after a moment's displeasure, he forgot about my perceived failure and nothing more was said about it. But it reminded me of a plethora of other small failings that I, my siblings or my children had committed before his eyes, not performing according to his exacting standards. It was frustrating for me, trying to please this man. I was thirty-seven, but around him I often felt like a small child, unable to meet my father's expectations.

It made me think about something that hadn't occurred to me, and I made new notes for my journal, notes that would help me to better understand myself. In recent years, as I strove to become a writer, I had been asking my father questions not only about writing but about science and math and history and any number of things, much as a curious child might do. I hadn't asked nearly as many questions when I had been small, since he had not been available for me. Now that he was available and we had dramatically improved our relationship, I was doing a lot of catching up.

For a brief time, we met his auburn-haired girlfriend, Theresa. Shy and intellectual, she seemed quite nice and paid special attention to Margaux. Then she left for an appointment.

Bookshelves lined many walls of the apartment, and it had a large, cheerful kitchen, filled with state-of-the-art cooking devices. In his loft office, a little nook reached by climbing a separate stairway, Dad proudly showed me an extensive assortment of new camera gear he had purchased for the Himalayas trip the following year. We spoke again of making the trip together, and looked forward to it.

Having gone as far as I could on *Man of Two Worlds*, I gave him a complete copy of the manuscript, as much as I had written thus far. He said he would get busy on it after completing a screenplay for "The Santaroga Barrier."

"I have a Harold Lloyd chase scene in the screenplay," he said, "where the person chased doesn't know he's being chased."

I also had with me his uncompleted manuscript of *Circle Times*, a historically accurate story about Northwest Salish Indians, a project he had abandoned in the 1970s. Having read it carefully, I had a number of suggestions I thought might improve the pacing and organization of the story, and he liked my ideas. We made plans to collaborate on the book when time allowed.

"First I'm going to write '*Dune* 7,' " he said.

"Another one?"

He smiled and said, "I can't seem to let go of the series."

I asked him how the *Dune* movie was doing, and he said it was setting box office records overseas. The results were not as clear in the

United States, he added. I asked him what he meant, but he didn't seem anxious to talk about it.

On a file cabinet in his office were the framed list of bestsellers and the *Dune* movie clapboard he had used ceremoniously to begin the filming in March 1983. The board had written on it:

DUNE . . . Slate 1, Take 1

I gave him an autographed copy of my latest paperback novel, *The Garbage Chronicles*. Just as he often wrote messages from father to son in the books he gave me, I now reversed it, with a message from the son to the father.

On January 20, 1985, Jan, Margaux and I boarded the S.S. *Independence* in San Francisco. Julie and Kim were flying to Hawaii separately, because of conflicting schedules. In the ship's lounge we saw Dad in the Pacific Bell commercial, during a break in the Superbowl game.

"Pop-Pop!" Margaux squealed.

Upon arriving in Honolulu, Jan and Margaux flew a Royal Hawaiian Air Service Cessna to Maui, while I chartered a thirty-two-foot sailboat. It was more than thirty miles to Molokai, the first landfall. We sailed in moderate winds at first but the wind died down and we had to motor. Unfortunately the boat motored at only two or two and a half knots. It was painfully slow! We proceeded in this way all night, and instead of anchoring at Molokai as planned we made directly for Lahaina on the island of Maui. I alternated at the helm with the skipper, and we slept in shifts.

When we were out in the Big Water, I asked the skipper where the lifeboat was, thinking he must have an inflatable raft stowed somewhere. To my surprise, he said rather casually, "I thought about it, but never got around to it."

"Oh," I said, in a small voice. How ironic my situation was, taking this route because I thought it was safer! The boat had a ship-to-shore radio, flares and lifejackets, but on the radio I heard a Coast Guard report of another boat taking on water in its number-one hold.

It was a clear night and the blackest sky I had ever seen. Stars glimmered along the horizon to the south, and to the west where the sun had set was a bright star or planet. There were shooting stars and luminous, iridescent flying fish.

As morning broke, we passed the island of Lanai and the vast Dole pineapple fields. A porpoise swam alongside the starboard bow, and in the Auau Channel approaching the Maui town of Lahaina we saw a dozen humpback whales. It was impressive watching them flop their monstrous black tails and blow water through their spouts.

Jan was supposed to pick me up in Lahaina with Dad's Chevrolet Blazer, but it was out of commission in a repair shop with a rusted-out fuel pump. We borrowed an old pickup truck from the mechanic.

The Hana Road, that legendary and foreboding passage between a tourist civilization on one side of Maui and an old Hawaiian way of life carved out of the jungle on the other, passed more than fifty waterfalls. The road was bumpy, and we had to drive it in a light rain, with night fast approaching. There were crumbling turn-of-the-century bridges and cliffs dropping off to the sea. We passed ferny jungles of bamboo, breadfruit, papaya and mango trees, and a most interesting tree called the hala or lauhala (*Pandanus odoratissimus*). Known as "the walking tree," the hala had large, finger-like aerial roots above the ground that seemed to prop the tree up and were said to "walk" across the land, shifting the tree's position slightly as the roots extended.

It was a treacherous stretch of road—requiring more than three hours to drive fifty-three miles—but it wasn't nearly as bad as I had heard. The tropical smells and verdant greens were reminiscent of Mexico, as were the simple huts and fruit stands we passed, and the old, rattling pickup in which we rode. Dented, rusted, rattly old vehicles were a way of life in such places. Front end alignment? Forget it!

At a gravel parking area adjacent to the apartment wing on Dad's property, caretakers Bart and Sheila Hrast helped us unload the truck— groceries, office supplies and luggage. A blond man in his thirties, Bart stood around six feet tall, with a pleasant, weathered face. Sheila was dark-haired and pretty. Both were well-tanned. They shared an interest in flowers and cats.

In centuries past this eastern shore of Maui had been a favored area for Hawaiian royalty. They had summer homes, court baths (down the road at Seven Pools), and royal coconut groves, which according to legend were groves of palm trees planted by powerful chiefs.

On the afternoon of our first full day in this magical place, Jan and I walked down to the craggy black lava rocks that rimmed the property, where we saw waves crashing against the shore some twenty or thirty feet below us, foaming white around the rocks and throwing spray high in the air. The water all around the white foam was turquoise and aquamarine, in subtle variations of color. It was as Jan had described, unlike any water I had seen before.

Behind us, not far from the shore, stood the wide-boughed, graceful kamani tree where my mother's ashes would be spread.

We saw a humpback whale a hundred yards offshore, indicating deep water a short distance out. In one of the tidal pools (framed in black rock beneath our perch), Jan spotted a fish, and if I'd had a net handy I would have gone down there and tried to catch it. We found a cave secreted in the rocks as well, with a small amount of debris to indicate that fishermen had camped there recently.

On the grassy expanse between the house and shore were rustic rock walls only a couple of feet high, property lines from centuries past when the Hawaiian royal family issued land grants that extended from the top of the volcano Haleakala all the way down to the sea. Some of the walls were the remnants of a Filipino village that had once been on the site.

Kawaloa . . . A nice long time. I wished my mother had been able to live here longer.

We went to a big luau that evening, a Hawaiian feast where much beer and good food was consumed. It was in honor of a baby's first birthday—and in ensuing weeks we would learn that luaus were given to celebrate a wide variety of events.

At shortly past 2:00 P.M. on February 3, 1985, I picked up Dad at Hana Airport in the old pickup, since his Blazer still had not been repaired. A strong wind blew as he got off the two-engine prop plane, causing the gate between the tiny terminal building and the landing strip to swing and creak. In the truck, Dad told me that both *Dune* and *Dune Messiah* were now on *The New York Times* paperback best-seller list.

479

I showed him the new cover for Arbor House's upcoming hardcover edition of my third novel, *Sudanna, Sudanna*, along with two excellent national reviews on the book. "I told you it was a good story," Dad said.

My father and I walked around the property, and in familiar fashion he told me about all the future construction ideas he had for Kawaloa. Dad said he planned another apartment beneath the house for a maid or gardener, plus a concrete parking area under the house and a screened-in dining room on what was now an outside deck, by the present dining room. He had run short on funds the year before, but eventually he intended to have blue Italian tile installed in a gazebo already built by the swimming pool. Adjacent to the gazebo, cut out of the steep, flower-covered hillside that ran up to the caretaker's house, would be a waterfall and a carp pond.

At dinner that evening, we heard the smacking click-click-click of a gecko (tiny lizard) coming from somewhere on the exposed beams over our head. Dad said he welcomed them in the house, as they ate insects and were considered good luck by the natives.

Dad said he planned to do a screenplay for a pilot film after our collaboration was completed. The pilot film (for what he hoped would be a television series) was to be entitled *Nashville*, about power, politics, and love in the deep South. When that was completed, he would write "*Dune 7*," followed by his trip to Nepal in the spring of 1986, then a documentary film and a book on that. A third book with Bill Ransom would follow, set in the same universe as their prior collaborations, *The Jesus Incident* and *The Lazarus Effect*. Sometime in 1987, he hoped to be able to start the new book with me about Northwest Salish Indians, based upon his *Circle Times* manuscript.

Frank Herbert would not sleep on the king-size bed in the master bedroom, since his beloved wife had passed away on it. He wanted to sleep in his study. So beneath the skylight, by a bookcase-lined wall where he had many poetry books, we set up a lounge chair that was folded open into a cot, and placed a Japanese futon mattress on top. It couldn't have been very comfortable, but he didn't complain.

His roll-top desk stood against the wall opposite the cot, with a makeshift table between. The table was a flat door stained black, set on top of a pair of two-drawer black file cabinets. Three manuscript boxes were stacked on top, by a small pile of my father's business cards. His card was white and simple, with "Frank Herbert" in the upper left corner and a line beneath that extended the width of the card. In the lower left corner, it said, simply, "Hana, Hawaii—USA 96713."

We had all of Dad's mail forwarded to us in Hawaii, and I worked on his paperwork the following day. That afternoon, Margaux was riding a tricycle on the deck at Kawaloa, yelling and screaming with exuberance. At around 4:30, Dad, who was preparing dinner, emerged from the kitchen to announce that he couldn't work while Margaux was screaming. "It just does something to my head." He stood in the living room, staring at Margaux through the screen door, refusing to work on dinner anymore until we did something about her. It made me think of times as a child when our house had to be absolutely quiet, to the point where I wasn't able to bring my friends over.

Julie, now sixteen, was watching television when Dad went into his routine, and she thought his behavior was so out of line that she left the room without comment. Later she told Jan that Grandpa had not been treating her very well, either. "He used to be nice," Julie said. Actually, my eldest daughter was just beginning to see a more complete picture of a complex man. We explained to her that this was a terrible time for him, coming back to Kawaloa for the ceremony—and stress seemed to bring out the most difficult side of his personality. Besides that he seemed tired, undoubtedly from not sleeping well.

I was frustrated by the situation, because I probably knew better than anyone how important strong family ties were to my father. Over the years, he had often expressed an interest in setting up a family business, since he believed in strong family ties. Now a number of us—Penny, Ron, Jan, and me—had pulled together and were working for him. Penny and Ron were living in Port Townsend now, as caretakers, and Penny was handling fan letters. Jan was helping me with the astounding piles of paperwork generated around the phenomenon known as Frank Herbert, and besides that she was working on the interior design of a new caretaker's house that Dad wanted to build in Port Townsend for Penny and Ron.

Around 8:00 that evening, Dad said he wasn't feeling well and went to bed, saying he thought he was coming down with something. In the middle of the night, he was awakened by Julie's stereo. First he went out to the guest apartment and asked her to turn it down. When she didn't turn it down far enough, he went out a second time, got into an argument with her, and took the stereo away from her.

The following day, a Tuesday, Dad awoke, perhaps not surprisingly, in a foul mood. I found aspirin for him. A few minutes later he was scolding me for allegedly leaving two kitchen utensils in the left sink, where they could fall into the garbage disposal. I had not done it, and told him so. But he kept raving about it, on and on.

He was also on an uncompromising mission to make certain that all the closet doors in the house were kept closed in order to ward off moist sea air that might get in, and about keeping drawers shut for the same reason and about keeping plastic over certain things. Moisture was a big problem here, especially on metal objects, so he had set up "dry rooms" in all of the closets and in a large pantry off the kitchen, using electric heat rods that I had purchased for him in Seattle. The pantry was the largest dry room. When the house was shut down, and each night, he stuffed these special rooms with everything he thought might be subject to damage. Now, with us in the house, he was nervous about maintaining his carefully designed system.

I said I understood his concerns, and promised to monitor the dry rooms for him.

Julie and Kim, now enrolled in the local public school, were on holiday due to teacher's conferences, and Jan took them to Hamoa Beach to escape their grandfather's constant haranguing. For the same reason, I jogged three miles on the Hana Road in the direction of Kaupo Gap, away from Hana town, running up long, steep Drummond Hill. When Jan returned later in the afternoon, I gave Margaux a swimming lesson.

By then, Dad was feeling better, and on the mezzanine he went through a box of his mother's family pictures with me, marking the backs of photos to show who people were. He had photos of himself as a two- year-old with his head bandaged from a severe dog bite, and for the first time I saw pictures of colorful small-town characters he had described, and of his favorite grandmother, Mary Stanley Herbert. It was exhilarating for me, matching faces with stories that I had been hearing him tell for years. He gave me a number of pictures and asked me to ship the rest to him on the mainland.

At 5:00 P.M., Jan and I went with Dad to visit Dr. Milton Howell, my mother's doctor, sharing hors d'oeuvres with him and his wife, Roselle, at their house. Dr. Howell was tanned, curly-haired and relaxed. He wore shoes and socks, and I wondered how he kept from getting sweaty feet in the Hawaiian climate. His wife was stocky and peppery, an affable, generous woman. She loaned me two autographed books that had been given to her by her close friend, Anne Morrow Lindbergh, wife of Charles Lindbergh. They were *Gift from the Sea*, written by AML herself, and *Autobiography of Values*, by her late husband. I felt honored, and took extra care with the treasures.

Dad told the Howells we were doing a book together, "one that would knock down a lot of the conventions in science fiction." This had never been mentioned to me before, and I remained silent. I was shocked. What did he mean? And I'd already written my part!*

That evening we went to Frayn Utley's place for dinner. A large woman in her eighties, she was the mother of NBC television news correspondent Garrick Utley and a radio personality in her own right back in the 1940s and 1950s in Chicago (with her late husband, Clifton). Frayn wore a red muumuu with white flowers on it. She was jovial, alert and talkative. While cooking dinner, she scolded her two black cats repeatedly and chased them out of the house. They kept sneaking back in, so perhaps this was a little game played by master and pet. The dinner conversation was largely political.

As we were leaving, Frayn invited Jan and me to monthly "concerts" held at her house. This would involve listening to music from her extensive recording collection. She said she started the concerts a dozen years before with her husband, and it became a popular event in the Hana area, attended regularly by forty or more guests. We promised to attend.

---

*In *Frank Herbert*, William Touponce postulated that *Man of Two Worlds* "is obviously a send-up of many science-fiction themes—creator figures and races, their responsibilities, and the chance that humankind may be a casual toy."

My mother's ceremony would be in two days. Whenever Dad spoke of it to friends he explained that it wasn't going to be a formal service and that there would be no holy man. "Bev made me promise to keep it simple," he said, "and I don't want her coming back to haunt me."

The next day I read *Gift from the Sea* from cover to cover. It was the perfect book to read on this paradise island, and spoke a great deal about the need people have to be alone. I had that need, and Jan spoke of requiring it for herself as well. It wasn't that we wanted to be apart, but we needed our individual quiet times, times that improved our relationship. Personal space.

My father had always demanded his own personal space, but paradoxically he often didn't allow people close to him the same privilege. He had a tendency to smother people with his dominance. Not intentionally, of course. Not even selfishly. He simply didn't realize he was doing it.

A contractor stopped by, and Dad told him to build gates for the swimming pool to keep Margaux from getting in without supervision. Dad was very concerned about her safety.

Two more excellent reviews came in on *Sudanna, Sudanna*, and I recall standing on the mezzanine by the stairway telling Dad about them. He was below me in the living room reading, on the big gray sectional couch. He looked up at me, and after congratulating me he said, "Even bad reviews sell books, Brian. Best of all is a bad review from *The New York Times*. That sells at least ten thousand copies for me." He went on to say emphatically that he cared more about sales than about critics, because if his works were selling the fans were telling him they liked his work. Fans were the only reviewers who mattered to him.

When Jan brought Margaux home from preschool at around 4:00 that afternoon, our daughter had a new plastic lunch pail from Hasegawa's General Store. She ran into the kitchen with it to show her grandfather. But Dad was already talking with Jan, and he told Margaux to be quiet. She went away dejected, and he never did ask her what she wanted.

Dad loved Margaux dearly, but didn't always have the patience for her. She had boundless energy, much as he'd had as a child. The adult

Frank Herbert, I am certain, would have booted the child Frank Herbert out of the house!

Ron, Penny and their youngest son, Robert, fifteen, arrived shortly after that, having rented a car in Kahului and driven the tortuous Hana Road. My sister had gotten sick along the way from all the curves. Bill Ransom and Dr. William and Zee Scheyer arrived, too, from Port Townsend. We shared dinner.

It was one of Dad's specialties, sukiyaki, with the added ingredients shrimp and nenue (pilot fish) caught the day before by Julie. She said she caught three of them, having been shown how to fish with a bamboo pole by her new Hawaiian girlfriends. They used shrimp for bait.

At dinner, Bill Ransom said there had been some confusion about the completion date on their new collaboration, which they were going to call *The Swimmers*. It had been my father's understanding that it had to be completed by November 1987, but the actual date required by the contract was a year earlier: November 1986. Bill had recently begun work on the project, and said he had to complete his portion prior to September 1986, when he would begin classes in nursing.

Bill also mentioned a British publisher of one of the earlier collaborations, who printed the name "FRANK HERBERT" in huge letters on the cover, with "Bill Ransom" in small print on the back cover, as if he were a reviewer. The publisher received a heated letter from the "reviewer," and deservedly so, considering all the work that Bill had contributed.

On the day we looked forward to and dreaded, I arose early and ran three miles, toward Kaupo Gap. It was overcast, and in the breezes I smelled thick sea air and dew-moistened earth, redolent with pungent, decaying vegetation that had soaked into it.

Later, after breakfast, I went to my upstairs office to write in my journal. Ron and Jan joined me, and we talked about Dad's reputation around Hana as an aggressive driver, and about a number of incidents that had occurred over the years with him at the wheel. When he wanted to get from Point A to Point B, he was so goal-oriented (as he was in the rest of his life), that he sometimes made dangerous passing maneuvers—even on the right shoulder of the road. Now, on top of Dad's luggage in his study was a book entitled *Expert Driving*, and he had plans to pick up a new Porsche turbo (top speed 180 m.p.h.) on his next trip to Europe.

At shortly before 2:00 in the afternoon, many friends of Mom and Dad, mostly locals, started arriving. Dad took me aside and said, "We're going to use the past to make the future more pleasant. Bev wanted it that way, and I do, too."

He told all of us to wait on the deck on the water side of the main house, and at a little before 2:30 he went off alone to the kamani tree several hundred feet below us, just above the craggy shoreline. He wore dark blue pants and a blue Hawaiian shirt with white flowers on it, and in his right hand he carried a bag that bore the urn containing my mother's remains. He stood below the large, spreading tree and motioned to one of the guests, Danny Estacada, a local musician. Danny was too choked up to play and sing the song that Mom wanted, so he had a cassette player, which he turned on.

We heard "Bridge Over Troubled Water," by Simon & Garfunkel, representing what my parents had become for one another in their times of need. As the music played, Dad opened the bag and removed the urn. I saw him spread a thick dusting of ashes beneath the tree. Tears blurred my vision. I watched Dad moving around the tree, and then I looked down to the expanse of grass and old lava rock Hawaiian walls between the house and the tree. Jan cried softly at my side, and we held each other tightly. Jan pulled Kim close to her on the other side.

> Like a bridge over troubled water
> I will ease your mind. . . .

Water . . . I thought of *Dune*, of the most precious commodity on the planet—water—and the saying of the people when a person passed away. The water of my mother's life was gone.

With the music still playing, I watched Dad walk back up a tire-tracked area of the grass. As he reached the edge of his landscaped yard, a huge wave hit the rocks behind him, just beyond the kamani tree,

486

sending white spray high in the air. It was spectacularly beautiful, this place my mother had chosen. I understood why she wanted to die here, refusing to go to a hospital.

After scattering the ashes, Dad remained alone under the deck somewhere—undoubtedly crying and trying to compose himself. I never saw him cry that day, although he looked near it a number of times. That evening he was in a pretty good mood considering the circumstances, undoubtedly relieved at getting the service behind him.

At a luau the next evening, I spent a lot of time talking with one of Dad's contractors. He was a likable fellow, with dark skin and a quick smile. Beneath the charming exterior I detected glimpses of a tough businessman, and I let him know that I could be just as tough in negotiating the final tasks to be done on Dad's property, a responsibility that had been given to me.

The following day I had a lunch appointment with Bill Ransom. He telephoned late in the morning and moved the time back, to 1:30. When I subsequently met him at the Hana Ranch Coffee Shop, he said Dad showed up that morning at his door at the Aloha Cottage in Hana, saying he wanted to "talk story," and that this was the only time he could do it. After they talked for a while, Dad dragged Bill off to lunch, and Bill ate lightly, saving room for a second lunch with me.

Bill spoke of a number of contractual matters on the books he and Dad had written together, and about the newest project. At my father's instruction, the contract for the latest collaboration had been drawn up under the title, *The Swimmers*. Upon seeing this, Peter Israel, president of G.P. Putnam's Sons, called Bill to say he didn't like the title at all. Bill agreed, and offered a better one that ultimately was accepted by all concerned, *The Ascension Factor*.

Our table overlooked the Hana Road and a sweeping stretch of pasture that extended to the sea. Bill expressed gratitude toward Frank Herbert for the opportunities given to him. He also told me of fond feelings he held for my mother, and of his compassion for her. When he stayed at Kawaloa for four months in 1982, he would jog along the road and then come back to the house, perspiring. On one such occasion, Mom said to him, "I hate you when you run." Thereafter, Bill did his running elsewhere. Her remark hit him hard, and he felt it reflected her terrible frustration at her own weakened body.

That afternoon I worked in the office at Kawaloa. An hour before we were scheduled to go to Mary Moore's for dinner, Dad came upstairs and stood in the doorway between my office and his study. On the wall beside him was a massive built-in bookcase filled with his titles, many of them rare first editions. But now this phenomenal man did not speak about matters of great note, about philosophy or religion or history or science or any of the other wondrous things he knew. He simply said, in an irritated tone, "Would you help me keep the pantry door closed? They just left it open again."

"I've already spoken with them," I said, seething. I slammed my pen down on the ledger, tried every method I knew to calm down. But this was the proverbial last straw, and I blew. The door of Mom's office was open, and Dr. and Mrs. Scheyer (from Port Townsend) were sitting just below us in the living room, waiting to go to dinner. Penny and Ron were with them. At the top of my voice, I told my father I was sick of the nit-picking, and that I had tried to help him with everything he wanted. "You want the dishwasher loaded just so. The forks have to be tines down, the spoons can't be together, the closet doors have to be left shut at all times, and the pantry door has to be kept shut. Well, the pantry door is set to stay open when pushed all the way open, by the hinges on it. Change the hinges! All of us are mourning Mom, not just you. Can't you understand that?"

In a sense I had been egged on, because almost everyone in the family had been complaining to me about his nit-picking, about his moods. But I was unkind, I'm afraid, and my father looked crushed. Without a word he went into his study and closed the door softly behind him. Presently, Penny came up and called through the door, telling him it was time to leave for dinner. Dad said he wasn't going. I felt angry and dejected, and told Penny I was in no mood to go, either. I asked Jan to stay, too, to mediate in case I got into another argument with Dad.

Shortly after the others left, Jan and I heard Dad sobbing. I was still angry, and closed down my office to go outside and sit on the deck. Jan pleaded with me to go upstairs and make up with him. She said his tears were his way of apologizing, that he wasn't a man who could say he was sorry in so many words. "I can't go up there for you," she said. "It wouldn't be the same. Please, Brian. I can't stand to hear him crying."

I took a deep breath, went inside and climbed the circular staircase to the second floor. The sobbing coming from the other side of the door was unbearable, and I hurried into his study. Dad was lying on his back on the futon cot we had set up for him. He had a blanket pulled up to his waist and wore no shirt, revealing blond hairs on his chest. He held one arm over his eyes and forehead.

"Dad," I said, "I'm sorry."

He wiped his eyes and looked at me in the saddest, most doleful manner. His head was propped up by a small pillow.

All my anger washed away. I told him I loved him and that he was a wonderful, sensitive man. He looked more pitiful than anyone I had ever seen in my life, with tears all over his face and pained, red-streaked eyes. I knelt on the hardwood floor by him, and he said he loved me, too. I hugged him and he held me tightly, while still crying. The skin and hair on his chest were moist with perspiration, and his face was wet against mine, from tears and from the heat of the hottest room in the house.

"I didn't mean to nit-pick," he said, in a voice choked with emotion. Then he said something that devastated me. "I built this house for your mother. I was just trying to maintain it the way she would have wanted."

He put on a fresh Hawaiian shirt and came down to join Jan and me for white wine and a light meal.

It had surprised me how readily my father, this once powerful and aggressive man, had folded in the face of my onslaught. I worried about his vulnerability. It had been a year since my mother's death, but he didn't seem to be getting over it, didn't seem to be coping well, as she had so desperately wanted him to do. It had been the essence of her plan.

My dispute with Dad came only hours after a less vociferous argument he'd had with Penny. She and Ron had rented a car for the week, and he virtually commandeered it that day, without telling her where he was or when the car would be returned.

When Jan checked Dad's horoscope, she discovered that he was forecast to have trouble with his children, but not until Sunday, the next day. His trouble came a few hours early.

CHAPTER
43

✳ Ho-Hum, Another Day in Paradise ✳

IN THE four additional months we spent in Hawaii after my mother's services, Jan placed fresh flowers under the kamani tree each time she jogged or took long walks.

One afternoon I gathered mango and passion fruit that lay on the ground, then went for a jog along the rut-filled Hana Road. The air was moist from a recent rain. After coming down Drummond Hill on the way back, my approach flushed a ring-necked pheasant out of nearby bushes. It flew hurriedly across my path, giving off a rattling, loose-throated cry. Reaching the boundary of Kawaloa, I turned right onto the gravel driveway used by fishermen to reach the shore and ran downhill past the caretaker's vegetable garden and the apartments, nearly to the kamani tree. A gust of wind swirled around the base of the tree, carrying particles from the ground into the air and out over the waves of the sea.

I stood, transfixed by the scene before me. Some of the flowers Jan had left for Mom lofted on the wind and were carried out to sea. A childhood memory flickered back to me, from the time I was four or five, of a plaintive, beautiful song my mother used to sing for me— Redwing—a song that always made me cry. In that song, an Indian brave who has died in battle lies beneath a tree in a distant land.

While living at Kawaloa, I began work on a new novel, *Prisoners of Arionn*. Following my thirteen months of work on *Man of Two Worlds*,

Dad was working on it in California. He telephoned me regularly with questions and comments to tell me how it was going, but I wasn't left with enough writing to do. Hence, a new project.

Prisoners of Arionn was to be about an eleven-year-old girl whose mother was generally thought to be psychotic and dangerous. The girl would refuse to believe this, seeing wonderful things in her mother that no one else seemed able to see. It would be set against a highly unusual science fiction backdrop, but the story would in reality be mainstream. I realized this was a big risk, since the story didn't hinge upon any aspect of science, which traditionally was a requirement of science fiction. In my story, the characters would be the main focus.

In one of my conversations with Dad about *Man of Two Worlds*, he reported, "It's going well. I've got Prosik in deep fecal matter."*

"It sounds like you're having an immensely good time," I said.

"I'm enjoying it," he said.

Reports on *Dune* movie revenues in the United States were coming in, and were not good. Facts began to filter in, some of which were provided by Harlan Ellison in his *Fantasy & Science Fiction* articles. During the production of the movie, Universal Studios underwent a change in management. After the new president saw the film for the first time at a private screening, he stood up and said the movie was a dog and was going to bomb.

Shock waves went out. Advance screenings had been scheduled for the fall of 1984 with movie reviewers all over the country, and most were now canceled. Only reviewers the company thought would write favorably about the film were permitted to see it. This built a large pool of resentment in those who had been excluded, as might be expected.

In early November 1984, a story surfaced in *Variety* that Dino De Laurentiis was offering a large portion of the movie to investors through a securities dealer in New York City. Was this to spread his risk? Had he lost faith in the film? There were no clear answers.

---

*One of our characters in the story, a Dreen alien named Prosik, had changed the shape of his body for security purposes, taking the form of a snake. Dad wrote a passage in which Prosik, while in that shape, was caught in a sliding door and then run over by a power mower.

Initially Dino De Laurentiis promised a movie to compare with *Gone with the Wind*. In the midst of production it was said to be the most expensive film ever produced. It had the most elaborate and costly special effects ever attempted, and was one of the most heavily promoted films in history, with secrecy about the cast and a variety of attendant merchandising schemes. Now, with everyone running scared, people began to wonder if it would be the biggest flop in Hollywood history.

After all the hype, the over-merchandising, the manipulation and secrecy, and now the canceling of advance showings, many American reviewers were ready to pick the movie apart the moment they saw it. A film critic for *The New York Times* said the actors in desert stillsuits resembled Groucho Marx, while another said the sets in the movie were suggestive of the "interior of the old Roxy theater." Another reviewer said the movie had "the feel of a seventh-grade science project run amok." Roger Ebert said the sandworms looked "as if they came out of the same factory that produced Kermit the Frog," having "the same mouths." The movie was called "a total mess," "a failed attempt," "a gigantic turkey," "ponderous," "tedious," "confusing," "incomprehensible," "witless" and "overblown."

Like carrion, they piled on, and many of the criticisms were unfair to David Lynch, a man who had attempted to film a faithful interpretation of the book.* His effort resulted, unfortunately, in a film that was nearly five hours long. Too long for commercial success, movie moguls thought. They began cutting it up, paring it down to barely more than 40 percent of Lynch's work—a little over two hours. As a

---

*Director David Lynch and director of photography Freddie Francis did put their trademark on the film, bringing a somber darkness to the screen. According to *The Making of Dune*, a promotional book written by Ed Naha for the Dino De Laurentiis Corporation, the art director Tony Masters said, "Dino visited the set one day when it was being built and he was very worried about the film being too gloomy and black-looking. He wanted everything lightened up. More color. As I was lightening things up and putting more color around, David showed up. He wanted things darker. So, I was struck between the two of them. Eventually we compromised . . . a little. Dino has accepted everything now. I don't know if he gave up on us or what." (Considering this with 20/20 hindsight it does seem to me that the film might have benefited by more light, emphasizing the blinding brilliance of the desert planet *à la* the film *Lawrence of Arabia* instead of cave-dark sietches and gloomy castles.)

result, too many scenes from the book were missing, left lying on the cutting-room floor. On screen, some of the characters and events came out of nowhere, without proper background. But even with the cuts, the movie was not nearly as bad as U.S. reviewers wanted the public to believe.

People who had not even seen the movie began talking about how awful it was, and how dismally it compared with the book. They saw no point in actually going to see the film and forming their own opinions. A pack mentality set in, and anger surged through the science fiction community over what Hollywood had done to the book they all treasured, *Dune*.

There were excellent reviews, but only a few, not nearly enough to turn the tide. *The Washington Post, Newsweek* and *USA Today* gave it rave notices. The *Seattle Times* called it "spellbinding" and a "miraculous transformation of a difficult classic." Comparisons were drawn between the work of David Lynch and Federico Fellini. The *Seattle Post-Intelligencer* said it was "the single most audacious space extravaganza to come along since Kubrick's *2001*.

Dune received only one Academy Award nomination, for Best Sound Recording, but lost to *Amadeus*. The lack of recognition from the Academy was a great disappointment to my father and to the film-makers. When I discussed it with Dad in late March 1985, he said he felt that as a very minimum the picture should have won Best Sound, as well as Best Visual Effects, and perhaps Best Costumes.* It should have been nominated for Best Picture, he said. But he added quickly, "Don't worry about it. The movie's doing beautifully in Europe." He said that U.S. and worldwide revenues were around eighty million dollars so far, and that Dino De Laurentiis was considering a sequel. We heard that the film was breaking box office records in Europe, Japan, Australia, South Africa and Indonesia. In the United States, it was showing in more than seven hundred theaters.

There was a lot of confusion about how much revenue the film was

---

*If singer Michael Jackson had been a member of the Academy, he might have voted for *Dune*. After seeing the costumes in the movie, he had similar clothing designed for himself, which he wore on stage.

generating, and about how much it needed to make before it would show a profit. Since Dad's future share, if any, was based upon a percentage of profit, this was of prime concern to him. At one point he said the film needed to generate forty-five million dollars in revenues to show a profit. Another time he thought it needed eight-five million dollars.

After completing its theater run in the United States, the film did become one of the top U.S. video rentals. This was not enough, and the producers disseminated earnings statements to us showing a wash of red ink.

Based upon early rough cuts my father saw (with more scenes than were included in the finished product), he had spoken of how much he liked the film, of how it was a "visual feast," and a testament to David Lynch's genius. Now he joined the grumblers, and spoke angrily about the cuts that had been made, including the missing "banquet scene," and about the missing character developments on Stilgar and others. "They cut the hell out of it," Dad said. He also disputed the characterization of Baron Vladimir Harkonnen, who was depicted in a somewhat laughable, cartoonish fashion, when he should have been a terrifying presence.

The ending disturbed him as well. He had never given the protagonist Paul-Muad'Dib the omnipotent power to make rain, as depicted in the end of the movie. The conclusion of the book was much better, he thought, leaving Paul with less godlike, more human qualities. In the book, the emphasis was on Jessica's last line, reflecting human, female concerns: "While we, Chani, we who carry the name of concubine—history will call us wives."

Living at Kawaloa for five months allowed me to understand what my parents had experienced there. I found a sameness to life on this side of Maui. Weeks and days flowed by, meshing into one long moment. The surf pounded against the shore incessantly and timelessly, to the point where I often didn't notice it. And I remembered something my father used to say about Mexico, when we lived there: "Days blend softly casual into one another." It was very similar here.

Each morning Jan looked out upon the incredible beauty of Kawaloa and said, in a bemused tone, "Ho-hum, another day in paradise."

495

The native Hawaiians were deeply superstitious, in constant fear of incurring the anger of malevolent spirits. When this belief system was combined with Christianity, the resulting amalgam produced interesting practices, such as one described for us by Dad's friends Ed and Jeannie Pechin. Shortly after the construction of their house in the early 1970s, a native Hawaiian man and a Catholic priest came by to perform a ceremony that would rid the home of bad spirits. The Hawaiian uttered a traditional blessing, and in a merging of religious ceremonies, the priest sprinkled holy water in every room. Ed asked the good father where he got his holy water, and received this response: "Oh, I just get it out of the creek. Then I boil the hell out of it."

During a time of reflection I felt like a tiny cell in an infinitely larger cosmic scheme. The rocky shoreline was being worn away by the surf, melting island fragments into the sea, making the land one with the water. I thought of the erosion of the island, of its entropy as it merged with the ocean, and of the entropy of cells within my own body. The amniotic fluid in which I spent my initial months on this planet had the approximate chemical composition of sea water.

I heard the surf now, a sudden roar. It filled my mind, washing away all thoughts.

One afternoon while reading in a corner of the living room, I heard the wind picking up in intensity. The pole house creaked and popped around me. A stand of banana fronds outside the dining room moved to the left in unison, curling their leafy fingers away from the wind-force that came from the sea. Suddenly, in a powerful blast of air, the fronds went all the way over, flat against the hillside. Rain began pattering on the roof.

"Here it comes," I said to Jan. I hadn't been in a tropical downpour since my last trip to the interior of Mexico, in 1968, but I knew the signs.

The rain intensified, jackhammering the roof and slanting from right to left across my line of sight. I felt the house move beneath me and shudder, as from a moderate earthquake. Then the rain and wind subsided, as quickly as they had appeared. This weather was of a hard-edged variety, with definition to it. It didn't tiptoe around. It shouted at you, demanded your attention.

496

Sometimes I rose quite early, and on such occasions I saw what used to greet my father at the start of each work day in Kawaloa. One glorious dawn, the water seen from the house was deep blue with white, lacy foam along the shore's black, volcanic edge. The horizon was pastel orange, streaked in gray. Above that hovered a horizontal cloud layer, dark gray and foreboding. Atop that, a pastel blue sky stretched into infinity.

The residents of the area had a "*mañana* mentality," my phrase based upon the Spanish word for tomorrow—*mañana*. Nothing was hurried in Hana, and any *haole* (white person) from outside who tried to get anything done on a schedule became an object of derision. My father understood this from attempts to have his home constructed on schedule and from trying to get his car repaired expeditiously.

One day in Hasegawa's General Store, I overheard a tourist woman asking one of the clerks for a copy of the *Honolulu Star-Bulletin*.

"Do you want today's paper or yesterday's?" inquired the clerk, a plump Hawaiian woman.

"I'd like today's, please."

"Then come back tomorrow," the clerk said, in her pigeon English.

Of all the Hawaiian Islands, Hana had the second-highest concentration of the pure Hawaiian ethnic group, second only to the small island of Niihau. An incredible number of locals were related to one another. I spoke with one woman, a waitress at the Hotel Hana Maui, who told me she had more than a hundred cousins, most of them living along the Hana Road. And I met an elderly Hawaiian gentleman who said he had two thousand members in his extended family, living all through the Hawaiian Islands. His great-grandfather had maintained seven wives simultaneously. Everywhere I turned, it seemed, someone was saying, "That's my cousin."

When *Chapterhouse: Dune* came out in hardcover in the spring of 1985, it immediately hit national and international bestseller lists. Fan letters poured in, especially prompted by the stirring tribute to my mother.

Dad's personal life came together while we were in Hawaii. He asked Theresa Shackelford to marry him, and she accepted. They talked about getting married in the same Reno chapel where Jan and I had taken our vows in 1967. Dad felt that if our marriage had lasted so long from such unpretentious beginnings, his might be similarly blessed. But in Reno they had difficulty locating our chapel and were married instead in a different chapel near the courthouse on May 18, 1985.

Now he had completed nearly all of the wishes on my mother's list. But he still had not purchased a house on Mercer Island, near me. With this in mind, he asked permission to stay in our Mercer Island home while we were in Hawaii, and from that base of operations he began to look for his own place nearby. Since we were living in his place at Kawaloa, this seemed like an appropriate *quid pro quo*.

One morning while I was writing, Sheila Hrast telephoned from the caretaker's house to tell me that a beautiful blue lily, one of my mother's favorite flowers, was in bloom in the upper garden. She said it was a rare occasion, and that the delicate petals, now full in the coolness of morning, would soon wilt in direct sunlight.

I hurried up the hill with a camera.

CHAPTER
44

✳ And a Snowy Good Morning to You! ✳

UPON RETURNING from Hawaii in late June, Jan and I lunched with my father at a small sandwich shop. He and Theresa were living in an apartment now, but were in the process of purchasing a house on Mercer Island. He was fighting an apparent case of stomach flu, and had visited the doctor that morning. Whatever he had was hanging on tenaciously, though he was feeling better than the week before.

The following weekend, Dad stopped by my house with the *Man of Two Worlds* manuscript, prepared on his word processor system. We spent two hours going over 319 pages that he had completed.* Then he left them with me for editing and rewriting. The title *Man of Two Lives* kept going through his mind, he said, but I wasn't enthusiastic about it. I suggested *Man of Two Visions* as an alternative, mentioning, however, that one of the characters in his unpublished *Circle Times* manuscript was an Indian named Two Visions. He rejected that title, saying he tried to avoid Latin-rooted words, especially in titles. Given a choice between Latin- and Germanic-based words, he said to choose Germanic, since it was more closely allied with English.

He complimented me on two passages I had written in *Man of Two*

---

*Many fans, upon reading *Man of Two Worlds*, assume that I wrote the humorous passages . . . because of my earlier satirical novels. To a large extent, this is not the case. In the first draft, I wrote it as a serious novel, and Dad later added most of the funny, wacky stuff.

Worlds, one involving the headquarters of the French Foreign Legion and the other about a character dying and melting into the superheated soil of Venus. Another passage I had written, involving a giant spider, had technical problems. Dad said a spider wouldn't scale up, since it couldn't support great weight without a skeleton. We would rewrite the scene with this in mind.

My father had been working on *Man of Two Worlds* in my old office at the insurance agency, by arrangement with my former boss, Hal Cook. Hal's fiancée, Jeanne Ringgenberg, was a realtor, and she was handling the purchase of the Mercer Island house. Because of all their help, Dad wanted to dedicate the book to them. I concurred.

As I reviewed the first 210 pages of the *Man of Two Worlds* material my father had given me, I found it fairly clean and surprisingly in line with what I had already written. In a number of places, however, Dad inserted words I either didn't understand or had never seen before. When reading his work I always kept a dictionary handy.

On June 30, 1985, the day after my birthday, Dad and I worked on *Man of Two Worlds* at my house for two hours. It was going well, and he concurred with most of the changes I suggested. The major bone of contention surrounded our feminine protagonist, Nishi D'Amato. In Dad's rewrite, he had her aggressively pursuing our protagonist, Lutt Hanson, Jr., to the point where I felt it was out of her character. She was, I told him, a virgin, and would know of Lutt's reputation as a womanizer. In the end, Dad came around to my way of thinking, except he still wanted Nishi to be highly interested in Lutt's money.

We also argued over a wild scene he wrote involving the French Foreign Legion going from Venus to Earth in order to protect the honor of a solitary woman, Nishi. I thought it was too far-fetched, and said this would deplete forces the Legion needed for military engagements on Venus. But Dad said the Legion would do this for honor. He mentioned an actual historical incident involving besieged Legionnaires in the desert. A hundred men were trapped, but for honor they still sent out a squad of ten men to retrieve the bodies of six fallen comrades. We reached a compromise. In our story, Legionnaires would perform the mission, but with only a small force.

Dad said he had to delay his Himalayan expedition for a year, until the spring of 1987. The Nepal government was edgy about having foreign journalists in the country, and he didn't want to go in under false colors. "I've enlisted the aid of Sir Edmund Hillary," he said.

Around this time, Bill Ransom told me he wrote three chapters of *The Ascension Factor*, didn't feel good about them and rewrote them almost entirely. He also said this collaboration would be the first of the three in which neither he nor my father were experiencing a personal crisis. Bill had been in the throes of a marital breakup during the writing of *The Jesus Incident*, and Mom had been seriously ill when *The Lazarus Effect* was written.

Unfortunately, Bill spoke too soon.

The Mercer Island house transaction closed in the second week of July 1985, and Dad and Theresa were able to move in. We made the move a family affair. It was an unusual one-story home, with metal siding and a huge vaulted dome in the middle of the structure that gave it, perhaps appropriately, the appearance of a flying saucer. My father, true to form, had extensive remodeling plans, and enlisted the help of Jan to do the interior decorating. In this endeavor, Jan would meet with him and Theresa regularly to determine what would best suit their needs and tastes.

It was a hot day, and toward the end of it when the moving was nearly complete, we saw Dad sitting on a chair in his study, staring blankly at unopened boxes all around him. I thought he was just tired, but he said he was still having trouble with his stomach, and thought it was either an enzyme problem involving milk products or chemical poisoning from a tainted California watermelon he had eaten. (There had been a recent watermelon recall.)

Two days later I was visiting my father, standing with him beneath a carport in front of his house. He had a Band-Aid on the vein of one arm and said he had been in for a complete medical checkup. "They gave me an EKG," he said cheerily, "a blood test, everything. The doctor even held two fingers up next to one of my ears, looked through the other ear and saw the fingers!"

A short while afterward he held both hands in front of himself, palms open, and exclaimed, "Don't touch me, nurse! I'm sterile!" And he laughed boisterously.

On the morning of Friday, July 12, 1985, Dad dropped off pages he had printed through number 432, for my review. He wore white tennis shoes, blue jeans and a dark blue Gore-Tex coat, open at the front to reveal a gray and blue Ralph Lauren polo shirt. Today, as he often did recently, he wore a dark gray Irish cap with a brim all the way around. Without his luxuriant beard, he looked old. His skin seemed thinner and more wrinkled, with age spots on his hands. I recalled a time only a dozen years earlier when he was fifty-two and a woman had commented that he looked young enough to be my brother.

I never thought of him as old before my mother died, but afterward he seemed to age with frightening rapidity. His short-term memory became increasingly bad, although typically he could recall events vividly from half a century before. Despite the recent travails of his life and the diminishment of the familiar burly man in the beard, he still walked briskly wherever he went, with a youthful spring in his step.

As we sat in my family room, Dad estimated our book would reach six hundred typed pages, leaving us around a third to go. We discussed what he called "seeds" or "loaded guns" in the story. These were dispersed throughout the early pages to be used later. A character trait, for example, that might come in handy later to solve a crisis. Or the beginnings of a problem that would ultimately have to be resolved.

Overall, despite occasional mild disagreements over the course of the story, we worked smoothly together. We shared many fine and memorable times, when his study or mine was filled with laughter. In the process we put together some wildly hilarious scenes.

In the midst of all the activity around Dad and the book we were writing, I never really got to know his new wife. She and I acknowledged one another politely—but then one or the other of us rushed off alone with Dad to do this or that. I knew Theresa had an interest in popular music, because I heard it on the stereo system as I came in the door. And she showed special attention to Margaux, giving her several children's books. Theresa had a passion for books, though she had been forced to leave her job in that industry in order to be with Dad. He said she spoke of wanting to collect rare books.

Most of the *Man of Two Worlds* sessions were at my father's house, in a study he set up in a small room at the rear. He had a rustic black desk on one wall, with a single bookshelf holding books about Nepal and mountain climbing, along with the *Dune* movie clapboard. Along the opposite wall were his word processor and printer, and to the left of that was a closet with an immense fire safe inside. A brass lamp stood on a shelf over the word processor. On the floor by the window sat the framed list of national bestsellers from earlier in the year, showing *Dune* as number one.

He would sit in front of his Compaq computer, with its black lettering on a light green screen, and I, not knowing how to use a computer at the time, sat in a chair to his left with notes on my lap. The dot-matrix printer was set up in front of me, with a large box of tractor-feed computer paper beneath it on the floor.

He couldn't seem to beat the stomach problem. I heard it making noises as we sat together—a growling, squeezing sound—and sometimes he complained about it.

We were frequently interrupted by telephone calls. One came in from comedian Tommy Smothers, calling from Petaluma, California. The men had met in the past year, and while I waited, they spoke of getting together in Hawaii or in Australia, both destinations on a trip Dad was planning to take after our book was completed. The conversation was witty and jovial.

Another call came in from Warner Recordings, who wanted to do a six-hour cassette covering, in abbreviated form, the stories in all six *Dune* books. Dad was interested, but said he didn't have time to do the script. They spoke of hiring another writer for that task. Dad's literary agent was suggesting the creation of a special book to go along with the recordings—presenting shorter versions of the stories—and Dad and I kicked around the possibility of doing it together. Other calls came in from foreign literary and film agents, and from reporters wanting to interview him, and always he took time out to handle whatever they wanted with great patience.

In one of the telephone interviews, with a Salt Lake City newspaper reporter, my father said, "I always feel a little funny during these interviews. I was on the other side of them for so many years, asking the questions." Dad mentioned our collaboration to the reporter, saying he thought it would be published in the spring of 1986.

Many of the interruptions involved construction work that was going on around us—questions from contractors or from Jan, who was re-decorating the entire interior of the house, section by section, with new carpet, marble, tile, countertops, window treatments, appliances and fixtures. Electrically operated shades were being installed over the insides of the glass dome, at great expense.

The home had many roof leaks when Dad bought it, so reroofing was one of the first priorities. Still, after the new roof was finished he worried, and during the first heavy rainfall he checked every room, luckily finding no problems. "That night," he told me later, "it rained cats . . ." He thought for moment, and his eyes twinkled. ". . . and *cats*. A dog wouldn't go out on a night like that."

By the third week of July, we were on a roll with *Man of Two Worlds*. Dad agreed to delete a number of his passages that I didn't like, and he went along with my suggested substitutions. He concurred with almost all of my recommendations, but said I was too expository on occasion, that I should leave more to the imagination of the reader. We went over characterizations carefully, fine-combing each scene to make certain our people acted within their motivations, with actions that advanced the plot. Much of the material we reviewed was his first-draft work, and I was impressed by the quality—especially considering the rapid pace at which he wrote and the fact that he wasn't feeling well.

Incorporating his material, I typed an outline of all the scenes, which I kept handy. Dad was impressed at the way I used it to access scenes we needed to find. Very often my supposedly primitive method was faster than the search function on the computer.

Sometimes Dad and I did role-playing games to draw out characters, seeing how they might react to the situations in which we placed them. The dialogue went back and forth, and when we liked the way it was going, we wrote it down.

At the end of July 1985, when we were not quite finished, he had to go to a writing seminar in Brianhead, Utah, where he and Bill Ransom were teaching. We planned to finish the book upon their return, before Dad and Theresa left on August 12 for a month-long trip to Hawaii, Australia and Hong Kong.

On August 6, the day after Dad returned from Utah, we resumed work on *Man of Two Worlds*. His stomach continued to make growling noises, and he took occasional drinks of a thick, chalky liquid to settle it, complaining about the bad taste. He admitted he was in considerable intestinal pain and was taking high-potency painkiller medication, which worried me.

Thursday, August 8, 1985, was our longest day. We tended the printer and made corrections through the end of the book on page 565. During a break, he shared a hard-to-find Echt Paulaner beer with me, his last bottle. He wore a navy blue pullover shirt and blue jeans, but in the evening changed into a regal red velvet robe. His glasses had black rims, and as he looked through their lenses that night at the green-illuminated computer screen his head shook a little from side to side . . . the constant, apparently involuntary motion I had noticed previously, perhaps from fatigue.

When we were still at it past midnight, I reflected on how wonderful it was to be working beside my father, this great and learned man. I watched him leaning over the computer screen, punching buttons to cut words from a paragraph. Whenever we added material, he tried to find somewhere on the page where he could cut, so that the page numbering would not be altered. I was amazed at the way virtually any paragraph could be cut, without harming the quality of the writing. He felt this process actually improved the writing.

This man, whom I had once disliked, had been so generous in recent years, helping immeasurably with my writing and entrusting me with the management of his financial affairs. Considering the bad start in our relationship, I have never heard of anyone who tried harder to get to know his eldest son, or who changed more than he did. The effort was late, but at least he made it.

Now he was working in pain, and I was growing increasingly worried about him. Others in the family were equally concerned.

As we finished up in the wee hours of the morning (except for some minor corrections remaining), Dad asked, "What day is this, Wednesday?"

"It's Friday."

"Friday?" He rubbed his eyes, mentioned something about having to run some important errands later in the day, and that we could get together again afterward.

We said our good nights, and he trudged off to bed. As I drove home on the empty dark streets, a light mist fell.

The next afternoon I helped him with the final corrections. When it was done and we had a ready-to-mail manuscript, Dad walked out of his study, while I collected my notes. In the hallway, he let out a relieved and exuberant "Whooey!"

As we chatted in the kitchen he said the book "might hit," meaning the bestseller lists. He spoke of a sequel, and we tossed around a couple of ideas, mentioning the characters we hadn't killed off yet. We agreed to celebrate the book's completion after his overseas trip. "We'll have reaction from the publisher by then," he said.

We were both exhausted.

Shortly before leaving on his trip, Dad gave Jan and me long lists of tasks he wanted us to complete in his absence, involving the ongoing interior decorating work and a number of other matters.

When Dad and Theresa returned on September 10, he looked jaunty in a wide-brimmed Australian outback hat. He was tired but in good spirits and shared many funny jokes he had heard in recent weeks. I told him the feedback I had received from the people in New York who were publishing our book, that two out of three editors loved it, while a third thought we had begun extremely well and then lost course a bit. The editors had suggestions for changes, which we set to work on. These were relatively minor, but would take several weeks.

On the second day back, my father went to Group Health Hospital for tests, saying his stomach was still bothering him, and he had lost weight and energy. When I looked at him closely, I noticed that he was pale and drawn. Still, he was in a good mood, with his sense of humor unbowed. When Jan said something to him at dinner about economy air fares, he quipped, "I took a budget flight once. I had to bring my own folding chair!"

On his sixty-fifth birthday, October 8, 1985, Dad showed me the cover proof for *Man of Two Worlds*, which Putnam had just sent to him. We agreed that it was well done, though privately I noticed a *Dune* feel to it. I commented that my name was in lettering of equal size to his, and Dad said, "That's right. I arranged to have it this way."

We spent the morning working on *Man of Two Worlds* revisions. My shoulder and neck were bothering me, and Dad's stomach was really acting up. He said he wasn't processing fats, that they made him ill, and he was having to eat extremely lean foods. He had to watch what he ate at his birthday dinner.

A few days later we completed our novel and mailed it to New York. Thereupon I set to work on *Prisoners of Arionn*, my uncompleted science fiction novel.

Later in the month Dad and I were in my car on an errand, and he said his film agent, Ned Brown, was going to seek a large amount of additional money from Dino De Laurentiis, since De Laurentiis had allegedly used portions of two books (*Dune* and *Dune Messiah*) in the movie, but only paid for the rights to use one.* Dad said Universal had lost money on the movie, but De Laurentiis had made a "bundle" on the venture—a profit of thirty to forty million dollars.** I didn't see how that could be possible.

My father began to refer to his medical condition as an intestinal malady. It might be one of half a dozen parasites, he thought, possibly acquired in Mexico in 1983 during the filming of the opening scenes of the movie. Just to play it safe, Group Health was going to perform a biopsy, inserting a long fiber optic tube down his throat and taking "a bite" out of his small intestine. His weight was down twenty pounds in recent months to 150, and he looked thin.

By Wednesday, October 30, 1985, I had developed a bad case of flu and congestion, in addition to my continuing shoulder and neck problems, which I thought might have something to do with stress. In fact, I couldn't recall the last time I hadn't felt high stress. Slowly, without

---

*This involved the use of a key *Dune Messiah* character in the film version of *Dune*, Edric the Spacing Guild Steersman. Because of Frank Herbert's poor health, the issue was dropped, without ever having been resolved.

**Dino De Laurentiis does not agree with this statement. A few years ago, he indicated to Mary Alice Kier, the literary and film agent for the Herbert Limited Partnership, that he, like Universal, had lost money on *Dune*. I am only reporting what Frank Herbert said, and cannot comment one way or another on details of the accounting.

warning, it seemed to have crept up on me. A lot of it had to do with my concern over Dad.

He spent the day going back and forth to Group Health facilities in Seattle and Redmond with specimens, along the same highways and roads my mother had traveled when she was so ill. That afternoon he telephoned with good news on *Man of Two Worlds*. In addition to our sale to Berkley/Putnam, a big foreign publisher, Victor Gollancz, wanted to publish it in the United Kingdom.

At preschool the next day, Margaux, just shy of her fourth birthday, became terrified of the costumes other children were wearing. It was Halloween. She had to sit in the headmistress's office during a party, eating cookies and drinking milk. That afternoon we stopped by Dad's and gave him a plate of cookies. He gave us a pumpkin he had carved for Margaux and some pumpkin seeds he had roasted in the oven, referring to them by the Mexican name, *semillas*. It brought back old memories. That evening I dialed the phone for Margaux, and she thanked "Pop-Pop" for the special pumpkin.

Margaux felt very close to her grandfather. Even when he didn't have the patience to be around her for long periods, he tried to be sweet and invariably gave her a hug and a kiss. He got a big kick out of her nickname for him.

By the first week of November, doctors were telling Dad they thought he had Crohn's disease, a chronic intestinal disorder that sometimes involved inflammation and sometimes other problems. If he did have one of the forms of this malady, it looked as if it had been caught early, which was good. It was treatable with sulfa-drugs, and doctors were speculating that the condition might have lain dormant in him, surfacing after the stresses of Mom's death.

On Saturday, November 9, I visited Dad, and he looked very weak and fragile. He said he was down to 140 pounds, and I noticed with alarm that his handwriting was shaky. The house, with construction activity still going full tilt, was noisy, dusty and depressing. Scaffolds had been set up inside the high dome area, and as I looked around it seemed to me that Dad had taken on too much for his age and condition. Normally he liked to have things under construction as a creative outlet when he had finished writing for the day, or when he took breaks from his study. But now, with everything torn apart, he was too sick to keep up with what he had begun.

That evening he was watching *Dune* on cable television but fell asleep during it. We teased him about this. His own movie!

Two days later, he was feeling a little better and started working seriously on "*Dune 7*," as yet unnamed. To begin, this involved carefully reviewing the other six books in the series for the threads he wanted to continue in the new work. He used a yellow highlighter pen, with which he marked key passages in the books.

After a few days, Dad told me he didn't have Crohn's disease. Now the doctors thought it was diverticulitis, a colon inflammation treatable with the same medicine he had been taking. He sounded ill at ease, and I could tell that the continuing uncertainty was bothering him. Penny had been trying to obtain information from Dad in order to help him, but he wasn't always forthright. Finally he admitted to her that there was a "CAT scan problem," something that had turned up, and so he had to undergo more tests, involving needle biopsies.

On the twenty-second of November, 1985, Dad called in the morning while I was writing, and told Jan that Group Health had discovered two "small spots of cancer" in his liver, each approximately half an inch wide. He said they were recommending chemotherapy, and added that they still had not figured the intestinal problem out. Jan said she would bring me to the phone, but he did not want to disturb me.

Ten inches of snow had fallen the night before, and when I called my father back a short while later he answered with surprising cheer, saying, "And a snowy good morning to you!"

He possessed, among other attributes, tremendous courage, not unlike that of my mother. "I've been leading an interesting life," he said, in reference to an ancient Chinese curse that no longer seemed funny to me. ("May you lead an interesting life.")

The following Monday afternoon Dad reported that his liver problem was adenocarcinoma, which alarmed me. "I'll have to undergo chemotherapy," he said, "which means nausea and hair loss. After Bev went through the suffering of her initial treatments, she told me, 'The mind has a marvelous capacity to forget.' I'm going to keep that in

509

mind." He paused, and added, "It's funny, Brian, but I don't feel too bad about this. They caught it early."

I recommended that he obtain a second opinion before undergoing chemotherapy, because of side effects, but he didn't feel that was necessary.

Dr. Bill Scheyer, his friend from Port Townsend, called that evening. Jan got on the line with us and the doctor said, "Don't listen to what he's saying about catching it early. Once it's in the liver, a person's in big trouble. It's going to get worse before it gets better. He's in tough, and I thought you should know what's going on." He said chemotherapy had not been successful in the past in treating adenocarcinoma of the liver, so he had convinced Dad to obtain a second opinion from an oncologist at Swedish Hospital in Seattle, which had an excellent department for the treatment of cancer. They had computer hookups to other facilities around the world, permitting them to determine state-of-the-art treatments for each disease type. He said the emphasis in diagnosis now would be in determining the primary source of the cancer, which at this point was unknown. If the primary source was in the liver, that would be very bad, so he hoped it was in a more treatable place, such as the colon.

In a dismal mood, I responded that each time we got news on Dad it seemed to grow worse and worse. We thanked Dr. Scheyer for his concern and honesty, and especially for the invaluable counseling he was giving my father.

On Tuesday, November 26, Jan and I were snowbound, since Dad had borrowed our tire chains several months before without telling us. Now he wanted me to drive him back and forth to the clinics for tests, but I couldn't get out to do it. I telephoned every dealer in the Seattle area looking for chains, thinking I could have a taxi deliver them. But all the chains were sold out. Penny and Ron came to his aid all the way from Port Townsend with their four-wheel-drive truck and chains.

By the first of December, after the snowiest November on record in the region, the weather was beginning to warm. The roads were clearing, and we were able to get over to Dad's place, where Jan and I lunched with him and Theresa. We had soup and sandwiches. In a surprisingly good mood, Dad said Penny called from Port Townsend to say she was having trouble with a skunk that got into the greenhouse through the cat's pet door. The whole house was acquiring an aroma. Desperate, she asked Dad if he had an old-fashioned skunk remedy. To this he quipped, "I think you can still find some old-fashioned clothespins for sale in Port Townsend."

He told me his intestinal disorder was dramatically improved, and that he was eating regular food again. Doctors were still performing tests, however, trying to locate the source of the cancer spots in his liver.

We discussed traction devices for the snow, and I mentioned a bucket of kitty litter I was keeping in the car, to get in and out of difficult parking areas. He mentioned a trick of his own father's from the 1930s: pour Clorox on the tire treads, thus softening the rubber and providing improved traction.

On Wednesday, December 4, temperatures were warmer, into the mid-forties, and most of the snow had thawed. I struggled in the morning to build up a head of steam on *Prisoners of Arionn*, and finally pulled seven typewritten pages out of the air—1,750 words. That was pretty good for me, as my usual day of first-draft typing produced around four pages, one thousand words. Often when I felt the worst in the morning I had a good day of writing—starting out slowly and then getting on a roll. As if I was able to tap a deep reservoir of strength in the struggle to produce.

I went to visit Dad at 1:30 that afternoon. When I entered his study at the rear of the house, he smiled at me and closed a paperback copy of *Chapterhouse: Dune* that he had been highlighting in yellow. He wore a red plaid Pendleton shirt and said he was feeling pretty good, that his weight was up to 152 pounds. Doctors had completed their tests, he said, and had pinpointed the pancreas as the primary source of his cancer.

At the time I had no idea what I was hearing, how serious it was. But I didn't like the sound of it.

He described a new hyperthermic cancer treatment at the University of Wisconsin Medical Center in Madison, Wisconsin, learned about through the computer network at Swedish Hospital. He said it involved using radiant heat and water vapor to induce fevers of up to 108 degrees

Fahrenheit, heating the blood. Dad and Theresa would be leaving the following Sunday.

The doctors wanted him to be physically strong before undergoing treatment, so in Madison they would give him treadmill and other tests before proceeding. He expected to remain there for ten days or so if they accepted him for treatment and added that he would have to go back once a month for the next six months.

This treatment would be administered in conjunction with a type of chemotherapy that didn't result in hair loss or other undesirable side effects. "I'd rather not get sick to get well," he said.

The out-of-state procedure was extremely expensive, and he said his Group Health medical insurance would not cover it, due to its experimental nature. He was investigating his Medicare coverage, since he had just turned sixty-five, but didn't think that would apply either. He said the hyperthermic treatment was "frontier medicine," but that results for his type of cancer in other people had been encouraging. He emphasized that his cancer had been discovered early, and his tone was upbeat. "When we come into this world we're given a death sentence anyway," he added, with an impish wink.

Considering his suffering in recent months I was concerned that the disease had not been discovered all that early, but I said nothing. At least he seemed optimistic, and I thought this would carry him through the difficult times ahead. He had a strong will to fight, to survive.

He also had a sweetness about him in this difficult time, and a quieter, more pensive way. Most of the time he wasn't his old blustery, exuberant self, but occasional flashes of it gave us hope.

The day after Dad arrived in Wisconsin, he told me by telephone that doctors in Seattle had only given him a 25 percent chance of survival, but his doctor at the University of Wisconsin said, "Oh, you have a much better chance than that."

The University of Wisconsin had only treated twenty-five or thirty patients under the experimental program, and only one with similar pancreatic and liver conditions. That particular patient responded well and survived the treatment, but did suffer a side effect—a nervous system problem. They felt they could avoid such side effects with Dad through a once-weekly treatment for four successive weeks and other modifications. Indications from the medical team were that Dad appeared to be strong enough for the rigors of the program, but he would be in the hospital for a couple of days undergoing a battery of tests.

On Friday, December 13, 1985, an editorial assistant telephoned from G. P. Putnam's Sons, saying she was mailing the *Man of Two Worlds* galleys out for authors' corrections and that she needed them back by the first week of January. She said she would mail Dad's copy to him in Wisconsin, and that publication was scheduled for April 1986.

When I spoke with Dad the next day, he said he was starting hyperthermia on Monday, with chemotherapy beginning two days after that. There would be four weeks of treatment through January 4, 1986 (four hyperthermias and four chemotherapies). Then, from January 19 through February 2, they had three more of each scheduled.

My father went into his first hyperthermia session on December 16, and did extremely well, with his heart rate only accelerating to one hundred and twenty beats per minute—better than a thirty-one-year-old jogger who underwent the same procedure. Frank Herbert surprised the doctors with a number of quips, causing them to laugh. One, while his head was sticking out of a heating chamber, was, "What you see is what you get!"

I often sent him humorous messages, including cartoons, jokes, and funny or cute things the children said, items that simultaneously went up on our bulletin board. As with my mother, I hoped humor would be therapeutic, knowing that Norman Cousins credited laughter with curing him from cancer. We also sent Christmas poinsettias.

In subsequent telephone conversations, Dad said Theresa was very supportive and always at his side. She'd only known my father a short while, and already their life together had taken an unfortunate turn with the onset of his illness.

He sounded tired, wrung out from the treatments. The processes were draining his strength, and he had difficulty sleeping well, even with medication. And I heard more than fatigue in his voice. No matter how he tried to get around it, depression was weighing him down. It tugged at my heart to hear this terrible, debilitating emotion in his voice, and I knew it was from more than the physical rigors of hyperthermia and chemotherapy. For some time he had not been able to write, and this was a man whose psychological well-being depended upon his ability to create.

But I heard something else in his voice as well, and this gave me pause for hope. No matter how tired my father sounded, no matter how slowly his words came, he was always struggling to be upbeat, fighting to sound cheerful. A constant air of excitement surrounded him. There were new directions Frank Herbert wanted to explore, new worlds to conquer and write about. I sensed that he was reaching for something deep inside, this man who was no stranger to working long hours—reaching for something to keep alive the book that was his own remarkable life.

CHAPTER

45

✳ How Bare the Pathway Down
This Mountain ✳

*As I look back on it, I think there may have been some prescience in
my father, too. . . .*

—Frank Herbert, in *Dune*

I SPOKE with my father in the morning and again in the afternoon
on December 28, 1985. He said he was under 140 pounds and feeling
weak. After reading the galleys on *Man of Two Worlds*, I wanted to
insert more material into a war scene on Venus, and we discussed what
I would include.

He returned to Seattle from Wisconsin on January 5, 1986, having
completed four hyperthermia treatments and the same number of chemotherapy treatments. On the flight back, he and his young wife happened to be on the same plane with science fiction author and editor
Frederik Pohl. I met Mr. Pohl at the airport for a brief time, before he
hurried off in one direction and I went with my father and Theresa in
another.

The doctors reported that he was doing well, but he looked very
thin, down to 132 pounds. He had his coat off for a while, and I noticed
around the short sleeves of his navy blue pullover shirt that his arms
were still muscular, though much less bulky than before. Able to carry
heavy luggage without difficulty, he stood erectly and walked briskly,

515

with astonishing energy. His eyes were the familiar eyes, but older and sadder. His smile, like my mother's when she was so sick, was wan and distant.

Dad said he would be checking into Swedish Hospital in Seattle for two weeks, where they would monitor his condition and build up his weight and strength for the next round of treatments in Wisconsin, scheduled to begin January 19.

He spoke of his aversion to hospital food, as my mother had done before him. It saddened me to think of my father, the gourmet and raconteur who had so captivated dinner table audiences over the years, unable to truly enjoy his meals. I thought of his deep, rolling laugh that used to fill every corner of a room, and wished I could hear it again. But now his laughter returned only intermittently, in bursts that were caught short by the grim reality of his struggle for survival.

He no longer had his heart in the writing process. His life was too cluttered with bleak hospital corridors and little rooms and infernal machines, and men and women in white smocks with clipboard-charts. These were, as well, constant and painful reminders of Beverly and her monumental suffering.

I visited Dad regularly at Swedish Hospital, where I found him sitting up or lying in bed, with a catheter attached to his chest and tubes at his arms. He wore a pale green gown that emphasized how thin he had become. He had a birdlike appearance now, and this made me think of character descriptions in his stories, particularly in *Dune*, where the features were compared with those of hawks. I saw little of the hawk in him, however. This was a less aggressive bird, with a sweetness and gentleness of disposition.

Of course there was the one time I appeared in the doorway of his hospital room with Kim. She had brought him a gift, but Dad went into an alarmed microphobia posture, dispatching her without even looking at what she had brought for him. Children carried too many germs, he said, and he couldn't risk having her near him. Kim, only thirteen, went to the waiting room, her feelings hurt. She got over it when Jan, Theresa and I explained to her that her grandfather loved her very much, and that he may even have been correct from a medical standpoint.

Now he was as thoughtful as anyone could be, asking about us and about his grandchildren, inquiring how they were doing in school, what their special interests were. I wanted the laughter to return to his heart and voice, wanted him back to his normal self, driving everybody crazy around him. I hated seeing him so subdued and devoid of his former spirit.

In what had become a family tradition, albeit one I wished had never been necessary, I took him jokes and humor bits from my "funny files." There were also handmade cards from Jan and Julie, short stories from Kim and drawings from Margaux to her "Pop-Pop."

At Swedish Hospital, Dad was at first quite pale, but as days passed and he received care the color returned to his features and he put on a few pounds. Like his old self, he monitored his vital signs constantly, and the medical personnel were quite open with him about everything. The signs were good, especially considering his age and what he had been through. Dad spoke of how well the first round of treatments had gone in Wisconsin, and of how much he looked forward to returning to work on *Dune 7*." The new book was barely under way when he had to leave it. He said we might work on a *Dune* book together one day—perhaps a *Dune* "prequel" idea I had suggested to him, set in the mythical time of the Butlerian Jihad. He said my writing had come a long way.

He had his up and down days, and seemed to want me to stay longer when he was feeling good. Perhaps this was the opposite of the way it should have been, for I might have lifted his spirits on down days given enough time. Overall he was upbeat, far more cheerful than the rest of us. Theresa was almost always there, either in the room or in a nearby waiting room, and I knew it was difficult for her. She and my father had made many plans, and had only been married for a few months.

On January 10, 1986, a Friday, I parked my car near Swedish Hospital and walked a couple of blocks, leaning into a cold, wind-driven drizzle. Moments later, in the warmth of my father's private hospital room, he was sitting up and alert. He recounted a number of Zen parables, some of which I recalled hearing before, emanating from his conversations in the 1960s with Zen master Alan Watts.

One was the tale of a Zen priest and a young proselyte in his tutelage, both celibate. Walking alongside a river in India they encountered a beautiful young woman in a white gown, moaning that she couldn't get across the water to her wedding without spoiling her dress. Upon hearing this, the priest carried her across, while she lifted her skirts above the water. Then the holy man and his young associate continued on their way.

Soon it became clear to the priest that something was troubling his companion, so he asked what it might be.

"We've taken vows of celibacy," the youth answered, "but that beautiful woman, I must confess . . . she tempted me sorely."

"Oh, you're still carrying that young woman? I left her back at the river."

As if to sum up the folly of existence, including his own, Dad told another Zen parable: "Before I achieved satori (sudden enlightenment) a mountain was a mountain, a river was a river, and a tree was a tree. After I achieved satori, a mountain was still a mountain, a river was still a river, and a tree was still a tree."

He seemed at ease with himself this day, full of smiles and good cheer, and I left with a powerful thought: *Dad's going to beat this!*

His laughter was returning. He was upbeat, felt he was winning the battle. Dad knew that the power of the mind could defeat the ills of the body. In his domain, the mind ruled supreme.

On January 15, 1986, I wrote in my journal that I had been experiencing excruciating pain, radiating from my neck to my shoulders. I couldn't turn my head to the side, and when working on *Prisoners of Arionn* I had to set up a music stand behind my typewriter for the material I was retyping, so that I could look straight ahead. It was difficult jogging as well, but I ran in pain. A physical therapist wasn't of much help to me at all.

On January 17, one of Dad's last days at Swedish Hospital before leaving for Wisconsin, I visited him and showed him the cover art for my soon-to-be-released Berkley paperback, *Sudanna, Sudanna*. It depicted a Picasso-like man on an alien world, with a powerful wind blowing his cape. My father showed great enthusiasm for it, said it was very striking and different from most science fiction covers.

He returned to Madison on the nineteenth, ready to strike a final blow against the illness. Theresa accompanied him. I spoke with my father by telephone that day, and two days later. In the second conversation he filled me in on his medical condition and treatments. He spoke of cancer in his pancreas, colon and liver, and his words were a blur to me. It was hard for me to discuss this, and he detected my depressed mood. "I don't want people around me to prepare for the worst, Brian," he said. "It's under control, really it is."

I said I knew he was strong and that I was fine—that it was only the long-distance telephone wires making me sound that way.

Just before midnight on Friday, January 24, Penny telephoned, crying. She said Dad had taken a sudden turn for the worse. During surgery the doctors had found extensive cancer, much more than expected. She was catching the first plane to Wisconsin to be with him. I telephoned Madison, but couldn't get any more information. I didn't know why my father had suddenly gone into surgery, but it sounded very bad.

My mind went numb. I decided to get there the only way I could, by driving. How many miles was it? Around two thousand, I thought. It was the middle of the night in the dead of winter, during one of the worst cold snaps on record, with snow, ice and record-low temperatures across the heart of the country. Wisconsin, my destination, had subfreezing temperatures and icy roads. I packed hurriedly, throwing things into a small travel bag, and, of all things, a cardboard box. I couldn't find any other luggage, didn't have time to look for it.

By 1:30 A.M. I was driving north on Mercer Island, heading for the interstate. As I reached Interstate 90 and headed east I fought back tears, vowing I would be with my father in his time of need—that there would be no repetition of what had happened with my mother. I cursed myself for not being able to fly. A full moon was out, casting a cold glow on snowy mountain peaks ahead of me in the rugged Cascades. The mountain where my parents had honeymooned as forest service lookouts was in that range, to the south. The highway was slick, and I had to keep my speed under fifty miles per hour.

I made several stops along the way to telephone Jan and check on Dad's condition, but didn't obtain any new information. At 11:00 A.M. the next day, without sleep, I reached Missoula, Montana, nearly five hundred miles from home. Now I learned from a phone call to Jan that Dad was fine, that he had undergone surgery and was in satisfactory condition. Apparently the earlier reports from his doctor had been incorrect. He was sitting up in bed in good spirits, wondering what all the fuss was about. Penny and Theresa were with him, and Dad wanted me to turn around and go home.

Jan said Bruce was on a trip, and she could not reach him. Bill Ransom, however, had been in touch with her, and he was offering to fly ahead and meet me in Billings, Montana, to help with the driving. Our earlier plan had been for Jan to do this.

I felt somewhat foolish, with fifteen hundred miles still to drive in some really treacherous weather and terrible road conditions. I was developing a cough and checked into a motel to sleep the rest of the day and await further developments. By the following morning, I received confirmation that Dad was doing extremely well. Through Jan I passed word to Penny and Bill Ransom that I was heading home. It was eleven degrees in Montana that morning, with a pale blue sky and sunlight sparkling on ice alongside the roadway. It was so cold that the ice didn't melt from the hood of my car for a hundred miles.

By Monday the twenty-seventh, I was back on Mercer Island, still behind on my sleep, with a hacking cough. Penny telephoned from Madison to say that Dad was up and walking around. Doctors were shaking their heads in disbelief, saying no one else recovering from that surgery had ever walked before five days. He was up in three.

When I spoke with my father that evening, he sounded chipper. In all the confusion I didn't understand what his surgery had been all about, but assumed it must have been exploratory in nature, or perhaps to cut away some of the cancer cells, as an additional treatment. In the process of this surgery, Dad said he had received a vertical incision from his chest to his midsection. He said it rather matter-of-factly, leaving me impressed by his courage.

I was doubly impressed when I learned that before going into surgery, Dad asked his doctors and nurses how long it took other patients to recover. He wanted to know what the record was, and earlier he had asked similar questions with respect to the chemotherapy and hyperthermia treatments. With each answer he received, he tried to beat what other patients had done. He insisted on having his morphine dosage cut in half, was out of bed in half the time it took other patients. He was using his competitive nature in a new way.

The following morning, January 28, 1986, Dad was watching the launch of the space shuttle *Challenger* on television, broadcast from Cape Canaveral, Florida. When the shuttle exploded in the sky, killing all aboard, Dad was terribly upset and started shaking. His doctor made him turn the TV off.

Still, as days passed, Dad sounded better each time I talked with him. He was sweet and appreciative of my calls. He assured me that the cancer was in remission, that he was completing the round of treatments that had already been scheduled in order to play it safe.

When she was sure Dad was all right, Penny flew back to Port Townsend. This provided the rest of us with additional reassurance, and we looked forward to seeing him in February.

In my household and in telephone conversations with my brother and sister, we commented that his recovery was absolutely amazing. He needed to complete his treatments, but the indications were clear. He had the cancer on the run.

At 7:00 in the evening on Friday, February 7, 1986, I telephoned Dad and asked how he was doing. He said great, that he had a new laptop computer and tape recorder in his room, and he was writing a short story about his dream experiences while under anesthesia. It was, I would learn later from Bill Ransom, the beginnings of the "*Soul Catcher*-like story" that my father had been seeking for several years. His dreaming mind had come up with something the conscious mind could not produce. He also composed an essay for *Writers of the Future*, an anthology of short stories by talented new writers. He was always willing to share his knowledge with others, even when he was fighting for his life. In that essay, he wrote, "Remember how you learned, and when your turn comes, teach."

My father and I talked about a new movie contract that had been sent to him for one of his novels, *The Green Brain*. Then he paused for a moment and said, in the gentlest of tones, "We were in Hawaii a year ago, weren't we?"

"Yes," I said. "I'll bet it's beautiful there. And warm."

521

"I wish I were in the tropics right now, Brian. It's too cold here for my blood."

We didn't specifically mention what day it was, the second anniversary of my mother's death and the first anniversary of her ceremony at Kawaloa, but I knew it was on his mind, and that he had never, despite all the changes in his life, forgotten the love he felt for my mother.

At the close of the conversation, I said, "I love you, Dad."

"I love you, too," he said.

They would be the last words we would ever exchange.

Four days later I was taking care of Margaux, who was playing in her room upstairs. I was at the dining room table with my *Prisoners of Arionn* manuscript spread out in front of me, writing a chapter in longhand.

Shortly before noon, the Mercer Island Police knocked at my door. A uniformed officer told me my sister had been trying to reach me, and that something was wrong with my telephone. He said it was urgent, and left. From the telephone in my study I was able to dial Port Townsend. My heart was pounding through my chest.

She was crying, and gave me the shocking news that Dad had died of a pulmonary embolism . . . a blood clot that lodged in his lung, blocking the flow of blood. We spoke of his many attributes.

I learned later that Dad had been working on a story with the new computer on his lap, when suddenly he called for a nurse and said he wasn't feeling well. He had been in a cheerful mood, happy to be writing again. It was shortly before 11:30 A.M.

Like my mother, who accurately predicted many years earlier that she would die in a distant land, Dad had predicted—back in the 1960s—that he would pass away at a keyboard, typing out a story.

It is clear that Frank Herbert leaned toward the scientific and away from the occult, and that he wanted to believe in a universe that was based upon analytically provable premises. He was not one to have faith in the existence of a Supreme Creator. This is not to say that he ruled out the possibility of paranormal events. He had experimented with Rhine consciousness in the 1930s, and had shown intense interest in Jung's theory of the collective unconscious. My father relied upon gut feelings, and depended upon the abilities of a "white witch," my mother.

Some people assume that the remarkably accurate predictions in Frank Herbert's stories were made purely on the basis of reason and genius, linked with a process of intensive research and analysis. After all, it doesn't require occult talents to accurately predict shortages of finite resources on this planet and fallen heroes. It is significant to note, however, that he never argued with my mother when she prepared astrological charts before making important decisions. In fact, he walked the fence when it came to astrology, as can be seen in the dedication he wrote for the book *Eclipse* by Brian Brewer (1978):

. . . It is well to remember that more than half the Earth's human population still uses astrology as a guide in the making of decisions. There is a possibility that a kernel of truth remains at the core of this ancient belief. We are Earth creatures. It would be remarkable if the rhythms that influence this planet where we evolved produced no effects on our flesh comparable to the influences upon our religions and philosophies. When we look at the heavens, we look at a cosmic clock that has marked every evolutionary development upon this mundane surface. That clock is still ticking. . . .

After talking with Penny, I sat in my study in stunned disbelief. Margaux wandered in and looked at me quizzically. Intending to tell her that Pop-Pop had died, I held my arms out and asked her to come to me. But she held back, as if sensing I was going to tell her something terrible.

She approached eventually and stood close.

I couldn't put the awful event into words. "I really love you, honey," I said. "You're so sweet. I'm glad you're here with me, do you know that?"

She smiled, the toothy grin of a four-year-old, and rested a small hand on my knee.

A reviewer for *The New York Times* once quipped that Frank Herbert's head was so overloaded with ideas that it was likely to fall off. In

God Emperor of Dune, my father described Leto II, who through genetic processes had acquired all human information. In "Pack Rat Planet" and *Direct Descent*, Dad wrote of a vast Galactic Library, a storehouse containing the written wisdom of humankind. Frank Herbert, like Leto II and the Galactic Library, was a repository of incredible, wondrous information. His words captivated millions of people all over the world. He had worked so hard, but suddenly, in the ugly retch of a pulmonary embolism, it was all taken from him, and from us. I was struck with the utter, horrible waste of it, and I was angry.

I thought as well of the poignant passage written by his friend Ray Bradbury in *Fahrenheit 451*, concerning an old sculptor who died:

> He was part of us and when he died, all the actions stopped dead and there was no one to do them just the way he did. He was an individual. He was an important man. I've never gotten over his death. Often I think, what wonderful carvings never came to birth because he died.

During my mother's final years, Dad had been frustrated by the primitive level of medical knowledge about dietary matters, and by the scarcity of low-salt foods for her. He had taken her to Mexico for laetrile, seeking what he thought was the latest, most effective cure for her. In his own eleventh hour, he had searched a computer network for the technology needed to save his life, and had gone across the country to participate in an experimental program.

If only my mother had been able to receive a heart transplant, a technology Dad wasn't confident about at the time. And if only he had been able to secure a cancer cure for himself. In another, future time, both of them might have lived many years beyond the onset of their illnesses. So many things I wished for them.

My parents were fighters. Mom beat her cancer and ultimately succumbed to heart disease. Dad had his cancer in remission, only to be struck down by an embolism.

I wished I had done more for them, a feeling that haunted and paralyzed me. It's been said that we all have 20/20 hindsight. It's only natural to wish, to regret, to want to revisit old pathways, doing better the second time around. I wish I had been with my mother and father when they died, to offer comfort. But in this life you can't totally prepare for anything. Events rarely occur the same way twice. I didn't expect my mother to die. She was too much of a fighter, and Dad told me she was improving. I didn't expect my father to die, either. He was too strong and vibrant, too optimistic to lose his life prematurely. He was like a mountain climber going up the tough side of a peak and then falling off the easy side. It wasn't expected. We thought he would climb other mountains.

I didn't cry when I first heard about Dad, though in my anger and disbelief I trembled and felt glassy-eyed. In a daze, I made a number of telephone calls, including one to Jack and Norma Vance. "I'll raise an empty glass for him," Jack said, his voice breaking as he referred to an Irish tradition, saluting the warrior who has not returned from battle.

Very few of Dad's friends and business associates knew about the nature and severity of his illness, so for them, too, his passing came as a shock.

While running an errand later that afternoon I saw Jan in our other car, and motioned her over into a school parking lot. There we stood outside and I told her what had happened. Like me, she was in shock, but unlike me, she burst immediately into tears, to the point where she had trouble driving home.

Later that day I returned to the table in the dining room, where my manuscript pages were still spread. I don't know why I sat there with the thought of going back to work, but I did. Maybe I thought my father would have wanted me to keep writing. It was the craft he had taught me. My thoughts were fuzzy. I lifted pen to paper, but all I could write was, "My father died today."

I still had not cried for him.

The next day, Jan and I were in line at the post office. We reached the counter, and by that time a long line of people had gathered behind us. The clerk, a sweet woman named Agnes, had heard about the tragedy on the news and was telling me how sorry she was. Without warning, the terrible immensity of it overcame me, and I broke down in tears.

Outside in the car I asked Jan, "Why in the post office? Why?"

Then it dawned on me. The mails had been our lifeline, our instrument of survival when I lived with Dad. He mailed manuscripts to his agent and watched mail deliveries carefully, because checks, contracts and important letters arrived that way. For him, especially during the early years of creative struggle, the postal system represented hope more than anything else, his hope for the arrival of good news about a story.

Bruce's homosexuality had never been fully accepted by my father, and they had never reached full rapprochement. Still, when my brother came to Seattle he broke into tears while riding in the backseat of my car. Penny and Jan consoled him. My brother told me later that he didn't cry from love, because he didn't feel he loved the man. He said he cried from what he had never experienced in the relationship with his father.

"I missed almost everything," Bruce said. "I never saw the good side he showed to you. He wasn't there for me."

He went on to say that he couldn't watch movies or television programs having to do with father-son relationships, because they upset him so much. I told him that Dad loved him, that he spoke of him often and fondly, and that he just didn't know how to show it. I reminded Bruce of all the ways that he emulated our father, and of the many interests that they shared . . . electronics, computers, science fiction, photography, flamenco guitar . . . and I asked if that could possibly mean that he loved Dad after all. My brother fell silent.

I told him that love is a complicated equation, fraught with countless different motives and angles of interpretation. One person's definition does not correspond with another's. Everyone would agree, however, that it is a strong bond of affection.

I am convinced that Bruce felt this for his father.

My telephone rang off the hook—reporters from all over the country—but I refused all interview requests. I found myself unable to talk with any of them. I had images in my mind of grief-stricken family members on the 5:00 news, sitting on a couch under the hot glare of TV lights, fielding insensitive questions from intruders. Instead I suggested that anyone wishing to do so could send donations to the "Frank

Herbert Cancer Research Fund" at the University of Wisconsin Medical Center.

Frank Herbert was brilliant, loving, honest, loyal, generous and thoughtful. His deficiencies were more interesting than significant. In the days and months after my father's passing, I experienced more apparent grief for him than for my mother. I felt a terrible emptiness. In moments of privacy and silence or during conversation I would suddenly be overwhelmed with emotion, and it confounded me. Perhaps it was because we grieved for Mom over a long ten-year period, during her illness. We were conditioned to expect her death. But with Dad it had been so nightmarishly sudden and shocking. He was such a survivor, such a larger-than-life figure. I thought he could beat anything.

> All say his day had ended . . . How bare
> the pathway down this mountain.
>
> Frank Herbert, in *Dune Messiah*

EPILOGUE

✳

We say of Muad'Dib that he has gone on a journey into that land
where we walk without footprints.

—Frank Herbert, in *Dune Messiah*

MY FATHER made a mere sixty five trips around the sun with this
planet. Still, he crammed a thousand years of living into his life.

I was not there when he died, but I was there when he lived. And
perhaps this is better, for I can remember him as he was, a remarkably
alive person with such boundless energy and enthusiasm for life. Only
one thing could stop this giant of a man prematurely, this creator of
magnificent worlds—and that was losing my mother. Though none of
us knew it, as she faded away, he was fading, too. His own suffering
was obvious to us, particularly after she was gone, but still we hoped.
There was always hope.

After Mom died, several people including myself tried to fill in the
gaping holes left in his life by her departure, but it wasn't enough to
keep him whole. The sum total of all of us did not equal my mother.
His heart had been shot away.

Following Beverly Herbert's death, the only productive writing Dad did involved the fulfillment of promises made to her. He completed *Chapterhouse: Dune* and the collaboration with me, *Man of Two Worlds*. Additional projects either didn't come to fruition (screenplays on *The Santaroga Barrier* and *Soul Catcher*) or were left for others to finish (*The Ascension Factor* and other books in the *Dune* series). He also left undone a new collection of science fiction stories, which was to include a 20,000-word novella set in the *Dune* universe.*

Without his companion of nearly four decades, my father could not go on. I did not discover one of the terrible pieces of the puzzle until months after my father's death, when it was too late. For years there had been stories of surviving spouses dying shortly after the death of their loving companion. I always thought of it as a vague phenomenon, something nebulous . . . dying of a broken heart. But it was more than that, much more. It was tangible, with ugly teeth. Even the onset of a serious illness in a spouse could be dangerous to the mate, as in the case of Buckminster Fuller. Fuller was in good health, though elderly at eighty-seven. He suffered a fatal heart attack at the hospital bedside of his wife, Anne, while she was in a coma. She died two days afterward, reportedly without learning of his death. But I think she knew. After nearly sixty-six years of marriage, with the tremendously close bond the Fullers had, she knew.

According to a Harvard Medical School article published in October 1986, entitled "Depression and Immunity," bereavement, depression, and loneliness in the surviving spouse can cause the immune system to break down, making the survivor more susceptible to illness.

In one of the obituaries on Dad, the writer said that Frank Herbert "was condemned to sequelizing himself . . ." I was furious upon reading it and shouted at the page that it wasn't true, that the needs of my mother forced him to write the sequels. There were astronomical costs for the construction of Kawaloa and for medical expenses that were not covered by insurance.

After I calmed down, I realized the press could not be expected to

---

*The new short story collection was a contractual obligation to G. P. Putnam's Sons, as part of a package deal that included the "*Dune 7*" novel.

understand my father's motivations. Even if they read the touching dedication to my mother in *Chapterhouse: Dune*, they could not know the pain of this complex man, could not possibly know his innermost thoughts.

A week after my father's death, we held a simple ceremony for him on the Olympic Peninsula, in a forest he loved, attended by family and friends. On a high spot of ground, in a small clearing with evergreen trees towering overhead, we dug a small hole and scattered his ashes in it. Pursuant to his wishes, we planted a young dwarf McIntosh apple tree there and suddenly realized no one had watered the hole. At that moment, to our amazement, rain began to fall, not unlike the rain at the end of the David Lynch film version of *Dune* that watered the parched planet.

It was just enough water for the tree.

In the mist, Bill Ransom read one of our favorite passages from *Soul Catcher*:

> Our brothers will sing of this. I will cover your body with white feathers from the breasts of ducks. Our maidens will sing your beauty. This is what you have prayed for from one end of the world to the other every day of your life. I . . . give you your wish because I have become Soul Catcher.

And I remembered one of the Zen parables my father had told me shortly before his death: "Before I achieved satori a mountain was a mountain, a river was a river, and a tree was a tree. After I achieved satori, a mountain was still a mountain, a river was still a river, and a tree was still a tree." Now it seemed to me that the satori he had been speaking of was the burst of enlightenment that he had been on this planet—a brief and brilliant flare of energy, a miniature sun with human frailties. Despite his achievements, he was tied inextricably to the human group, and its fate became his fate. As in American Indian thought, he had come full circle, and the end was like the beginning.

A quarter century before, Frank Herbert wrote this unpublished poem:

I am a Human of Earth!
My kind ebb and flow like the tide—
Whipped on by an unseen master:
Myself, a prisoner.

My other side calls out from its prison:
"Logic binds me in chains of flesh!"
And, with part of me chained,
There is fear!

I am a Human of Earth!
The sense comes out behind my words
Like a deer startled in the forest:
Fearing movement.

Only one avenue remains open to flotsam,
Driven before the wild currents of time
With part submerged:
To lift my eyes and look ahead.

But bound down and weighted by the chained side,
By the other side that I sought to deny,
I must flounder,
I must sink!

I am a Human of Earth!
In despair, I seek the farther shore,
And the dark
Drags me down into terror.

In *The Good Earth*, Pearl S. Buck wrote, "Men when old awake to a brief youth." So like my father, those words. He married a young woman, ordered a new Porsche, grew fond of popular music, took skin diving lessons, and made plans to climb magnificent peaks in the Himalayas. Late in life, Dad wanted to spend a year in Paris, wanted to direct a movie. There were unfinished story ideas, including more

books with me and with Bill Ransom. He left loose ends, dreams un-
completed. Like the painter Jean Géricault at the end of his life, Frank
Herbert spoke of all the things he would do when he was well again.
And like Géricault, he never got well.

In many ways my father never grew up, and this was part of the
charm of the man. Like a small boy, he always looked forward to his
birthday, and to my mother bringing him back little gifts on the few
occasions when she took *Plan Ahead* business trips without him. In his
youth, he had gone on a daring adventure all the way to Alaska in a
small sailing canoe. Later, just before meeting my mother, he and his
best friend, Howie Hansen, spoke of vagabonding around the world.
He was an explorer at heart, an adventurer. He was forever curious.

As fate would have it, the very last novel my father wrote was with
me, the book my mother wanted us to do together, *Man of Two
Worlds*.* He never saw the completed first edition, though he did see
the cover proof and typeset galleys. It was an emotional moment when
I received copies of our book from the publisher shortly after Dad's
death, especially when I saw the photograph of us together on the back.
Theresa took the picture on his sixty-fifth birthday, his last.

A lifelong workaholic, he wrote with me on that day. More than half
a century earlier, on his eighth birthday, he had written as well, after
announcing to his family at breakfast that he wanted to be "a author."
In the final scene of *Man of Two Worlds*, written by Dad, the characters
are planning a vacation in the Himalayas. Each time I read this I think
of my adventurous father and of his uncompleted trip to those mountains, the highest on earth. He wanted to become the oldest man to
climb Mt. Everest.

In June, a single green McIntosh apple appeared on the tree. I know
my father, who always wanted to beat the odds and do better than the
next guy, had something to do with this. The young tree, you see, was
not supposed to bear fruit until the following year!

On the cold February day that we scattered Dad's ashes, we held a
wake for him in the Port Townsend house, at which we played Irish

---

*Frank Herbert and Bill Ransom worked on plotting and characterization for *The Ascension
Factor*, but the writing had to be done by Bill, after the death of his collaborator.

music and celebrated the remarkable life he had led. His friends and family were there from points near and far, and we drank the wines in his wine cellar—grand crus, premiere crus, and even ordinary vintages. We drank all of the bottles of Château Prieuré-Lichire Margaux.

The following month, I was asked on very short notice to speak at two events in my father's behalf, both at the Norwescon science fiction convention in Seattle. One was an awards ceremony for the Writers of the Future contest, where Dad had judged stories written by aspiring writers. The contest organizers wanted me to address four hundred people at a banquet. I had always been petrified at the thought of public speaking, but I got up and managed it. I felt my father's spirit there with me. He told me that the people in the audience were our friends.

The other occasion was a showing of film clips on Frank Herbert and the making of the *Dune* movie. At first I told them I didn't think I could talk to all of the people who were gathered. Then I reconsidered, feeling strongly it was something I needed to do. I spoke about the film clips and about my father, and fielded questions from the audience. I was overwhelmed with a feeling of love and sorrow from his fans, and this gave me strength.

Later in the year, a most remarkable event occurred. For many years my mother had tried to reestablish contact with her childhood playmate and first cousin, Marie Landis. During all those years, Marie was also trying to reach my mother. But each was married, and in the process their maiden names had been lost. They could not find one another. Then, after Dad died, Marie read in a science fiction magazine that Frank Herbert had been married to Beverly Stuart.

Marie wondered if this could possibly be the same Beverly Stuart she had last seen in the 1930s when they were children in Seattle, before an unfortunate argument created a rift between Marie's father and his sister, Beverly's mother.* Marie began bird-dogging, and finally made contact with me several months after Dad's death. It turned out that she lived on my street on Mercer Island. It was a rather long street, more than five miles, and we were only three miles apart. Every week-

---

*See Chapter 4. My mother was born Beverly Stuart but changed her maiden name to Forbes later after her mother remarried.

day for seven years, I had driven by her house commuting to my job at the insurance agency. My parents passed her house many times as well, while coming to visit me or looking for real estate on the island.

Marie was an accomplished painter, as my maternal grandmother Marguerite had been. Marie was also a potter and interior designer, like Jan. And, of great interest to me, she was an excellent writer, having won several awards for her short stories. We began collaborating, and sold a science fiction novel, *Memorymakers* (1991). Numerous short story collaborations followed, and another novel, *Blood on the Sun* (1996).

Through Marie I met many cousins I had been totally unaware of, including her siblings and children. Following such tremendous losses, when I was grieving terribly, a whole new loving family opened up for me. . . .

Then, eleven years after the death of my father I began to consider the possibility of writing new *Dune* novels, in collaboration with the noted science fiction author Kevin J. Anderson.* We were trying to figure out what Dad had in mind for "*Dune 7*," the book he was just beginning to think about when he passed away. That novel would have been a direct sequel to *Heretics of Dune* and *Chapterhouse: Dune.*** In *Chapterhouse: Dune*, the Honored Matres—the dark side of the Bene Gesserit—were laying waste to much of the galaxy, destroying planets, killing our Bene Gesserit heroines, driving them back. But something else was out there in the galaxy as well, something terrible that was chasing the Honored Matres . . . and Frank Herbert did not reveal what it was.

He left us with a tantalizing mystery.

A short while after beginning my discussions with Kevin, I was contacted by an estate attorney and informed of the existence of two safety deposit boxes that had belonged to my father. For years they had

---

*For more details on our collaboration, refer to the Afterword of *Dune: House Atreides* by Brian Herbert and Kevin J. Anderson.

**Dune, Dune Messiah,* and *Children of Dune* formed a trilogy. *God Emperor of Dune* was a bridging work to a new trilogy that included *Heretics of Dune* and *Chapterhouse: Dune.* "*Dune 7*"—only a working title that would eventually be changed—was to be the third book of that trilogy.

slipped under the proverbial radar screen, and had been languishing in a bank vault in Bellevue, Washington. An attorney inventoried the contents of the boxes, and found old-style computer disks and comprehensive notes on "*Dune 7*"—the grand finale of the series. This was a tremendous surprise to all of us, since we didn't know that my father had made any notes at all. As if this was not enough, we subsequently located more than fifteen hundred pages of working notes that Dad had been using to write the entire series—notes that were in manuscript boxes inside a storage room.

With all of the events unfolding around me I recognized the handiwork of my mother, Beverly Herbert. The white witch who gave me life, who loved and nurtured my entire family, was continuing to do so. I felt comforted in her presence.

SOURCES AND
BIBLIOGRAPHY

✳

The Published Writings of Frank Herbert

Note: A number of entries show the phrases "publication details not shown," or "publication date not shown." Nonetheless, these are presumed to have been published since they were found in Frank Herbert's working files from his newspaper career.

"A-W-F Unlimited," in *Galaxy,* June 1961.
"Adventures in Movement," in *San Francisco Examiner & Chronicle*, California Living, 8/11/68.
"Archaeological Find at Cape Alava," in *Seattle Post-Intelligencer*, 8/30/70.
"Arctic," publication details not shown.
The Ascension Factor (with Bill Ransom). New York: Ace/Putnam, 1988.
"BYU," (Brigham Young University), publication details not shown.
"Baker," (Rev. Kenneth Baker), publication details not shown.
"Banks," marked "P-I file," publication details not shown.
"Bass," marked "Sunday," publication details not shown.
"Bay" (San Francisco Bay), (marked "California Living, 1/19/69").
"Beard," marked "California Living," publication details not shown.

The Best of Frank Herbert 1952–1964, Angus Wells, ed. London: Sphere Books Limited, 1976.

The Best of Frank Herbert 1965–1970, Angus Wells, ed. London: Sphere Books Limited, 1977.

"A Better Taste with Chopsticks," in *San Francisco Examiner*, 2/6/63.

"Bike," marked "for Sunday/illus. available," publication details not shown.

"Bio," marked "Sunday," publication details not shown.

"Blanks," marked "rew/blanks—precede," publication details not shown.

The Book of Frank Herbert, DAW, New York: 1973.

"Budget," publication details not shown.

"Bufano," (sulptor Berry Bufano), in *San Francisco Examiner & Chronicle*, California Living, 7/13/69.

"By the Book," in *Analog*, August, 1966.

"California—Notes," publication details not shown.

"California: Land of the Instant Native," in *San Francisco Examiner & Chronicle*, California Living, 12/8/68.

"Campus," marked "Sunday," publication details not shown.

"Campus Moratorium Events Planned," in *Seattle Post-Intelligencer*, 11/12/69.

"Care," publication details not shown.

"Carthage: Reflections of a Martian," in *Mars, We Love You*, Jane Hipolito and Willis E. McNelly, eds., New York: Doubleday, 1971.

"Cast of Zakheim Work Shown in Santa Rosa," in *Santa Rosa Press Democrat*, 3/1/53.

"Cease Fire," in *The Best of Frank Herbert 1952–1964*, Angus Wells, ed. London: Sphere Books Limited, 1976.

"Ceramics," marked "Sunday—*Seattle Post-Intelligencer*, 9/20/70."

Chapterhouse: Dune, New York: Putnam, 1985.

"Chemical Food Additives Described as Dangerous," in *Seattle Post-Intelligencer*, 10/25/69.

Children of Dune, New York: Berkley, 1976.

"Children of Dune," in *Analog*, January–April, 1976.

"Chinatown: A Changing World," in *San Francisco Examiner*, 2/6/63.

"Clarke" (Interview with Arthur C. Clarke), publication details not shown.

"Class" (marked "for Sunday"), publication details not shown.

"Clinic" publication details not shown.

"Come to the Party" (with F. M. Busby), in *Analog*, December, 1978.

"Committee of the Whole," in *Galaxy*, April, 1965.

"Commune Folk Stress Love, Not Sex," in *Seattle Post-Intelligencer*, 1/16/70.

"Communes: Are They Worse than Panty Raids?", in *Seattle Post-Intelligencer*, publication date not shown.

"(Communes): Behind the Commune Curtain," in *Seattle Post-Intelligencer*, 1/15/70.

"(Communes):—New Communities Shun Religion," in *Seattle Post-Intelligencer*, 1/20/70.

"(Communes):—Outside Reaction to Communes Is Widely Varied," in *Seattle Post-Intelligencer*, 1/19/70.

"Computers: For Better or for Worse," in *Seattle Post-Intelligencer*, 11/29/69.

"Conflict," publication details not shown.

"Confrontation in the Streets," in *Seattle Post-Intelligencer*, 3/1/70.

"Confrontation: UW Black Turmoil Echoes Mad Dance of SF State," in *Seattle Post-Intelligencer*, 3/15/70.

"The Consentiency and How It Got That Way," in *Galaxy*, May, 1977.

"Cristo" (marked "illustrated"), publication details not shown.

"Daily," in *Seattle Post-Intelligencer*, 7/10/70.

"Danz," publication details not shown.

"Death of a City," in *Future City*, ed. by Roger Elwood, New York: Trident, 1973.

"Defoliation, Heavy Rains Peril Vietnam Rice Crop," in *Seattle Post-Intelligencer*, 9/9/69.

"Democracy at Dos Rios," in *San Francisco Examiner & Chronicle*, California Living, 6/29/69.

Destination: Void, New York: Berkley, 1966.

"Dialogue: Forum," in *Omni* (magazine), August, 1983.

Direct Descent, New York: Ace, 1980.

"Do I Wake or Dream?", in *Galaxy*, August, 1965. (Expanded to novel form in *Destination: Void*.)

"Dog," publication details not shown.

"Doll Factory, Gun Factory," in *The Maker of Dune*, ed. by Tim O'Reilly, New York: Berkley, 1987.

"Don't Buy Death!!!" in *The Stranger*, June, 1970.

The Dosadi Experiment, New York: Putnam, 1977.

"The Dosadi Experiment," in *Galaxy*, May–August, 1977.

The Dragon in the Sea, Garden City: Doubleday, 1956.

Dune, Philadelphia: Chilton, 1965.

Dune. Norwalk, Conn.: Easton Press, 1987. (Includes "Remembrances" by friends and associates of Frank Herbert.)

"Dune"—unpublished—see The Unpublished Writings of Frank Herbert.

Dune (young adult version), adapted by Rosemary Border, London: Oxford University Press, 1980.

Dune Messiah, New York: Putnam, 1969.

"Dune Messiah," in *Galaxy*, July–November, 1969.

"Dune World," in *Analog*, December, 1963–February, 1964.

"Dune" (brief article), publication details not shown.

"Dune—For Family Weekly," publication details not shown.

"Dune Genesis," in *Omni*, July, 1980.

"Dune—Introduction," in *Eye*, Byron Preiss Visual Publications, New York: Berkley, 1985.

"Dune—States/The Bene Gesserit View/All States are an Abstraction," publication details not shown.

"Egg and Ashes," in *If*, November, 1960.

"Election" (marked "with art"), publication details not shown.

"The Encounter Group," in *Seattle Post-Intelligencer*, date not shown.

"Encounter in a Lonely Place," in *The Book of Frank Herbert*, New York: DAW, 1973.

"Escape Felicity," in *Analog*, June, 1966.

Eye, Byron Preiss Visual Publications, New York: Berkley, 1985.

The Eyes of Heisenberg, New York: Berkley, 1966.

"Fancy Feathers," in *San Francisco Examiner & Chronicle*, California Living, 11/10/68.

"The Featherbedders," in *The Worlds of Frank Herbert*, New York: Ace, 1971.

"Feathered Pigs," in *Destinies*, October–December 1979, New York: Ace Books.

"Featuring: The City of San Francisco," in *San Francisco Examiner & Chronicle*, California Living, 6/2/68.

"Fiction Writer 'Saucer' Expert," in *Santa Rosa Press Democrat*, 2/15/53.

"Fire," (marked "California Living"), publication details not shown.

"A First Look at our Galaxy," in *San Francisco Examiner & Chronicle*, California Living, 7/14/68.

"Flying: Opens a New World for Californians," in *San Francisco Examiner & Chronicle*, California Living, 12/10/67.

"Flying Saucers: Facts or Farce?" in *The Maker of Dune*, ed. by Tim O'Reilly, New York: Berkley, 1987.

"Forward," in *Eclipse*, by Brian Brewer, Seattle: Earth View, 1978.

"Fourteen-Year-Old Bride Misses Death by Hair's Breadth!", in *Santa Rosa Press Democrat*, publication date not shown.

"Frank Herbert," in *The Faces of Science Fiction*, by photographer Patti Perret, New York: Blue Jay, 1984.

"Frank Herbert Gives His Name to Turkey Stuffing, and Kitchen Posterity," in *Santa Rosa Press Democrat* (marked "1949").

"Freeway Signal Arrangement Is Confusing to Drivers," in *Santa Rosa Press Democrat*, 7/20/49.

"Frogs and Scientists," in *Destinies*, August–September, 1979, New York: Ace Books.

"G. McNamee Has Dynamic Personality, Says Writer," in *The Lincoln News*, 9/23/38.

"GIs on Vietnam Crime Carousel," in *Seattle Post-Intelligencer*, 10/8/69.

"The GM Effect," in *Analog*, June, 1965.

"Gambling Device," in *The Book of Frank Herbert*, New York: DAW, 1973.

"Of Ginsburg, Vishnu and a Sea of Grass," in *Seattle Post-Intelligencer*, 3/31/70.

"A Glance at Areas of Campus Conflict," in *Seattle Post-Intelligencer*, 9/13/70.

God Emperor of Dune, New York: Putnam, 1981.

"God Emperor of Dune," excerpt in *Playboy*, January, 1981.

The God Makers, New York: Putnam, 1972.

"Goldwater" (marked "Barry"), publication details not shown.

"The Gone Dogs," in *The Book of Frank Herbert*, New York: DAW, 1973.

The Green Brain, New York: Ace, 1966.

"Greenslaves," in *Amazing*, March, 1965. (Expanded to novel form in *The Green Brain*.)

"Gulick" (Bill Gulick), in *Seattle Post-Intelligencer*, publication date not shown.

"Have We Left the Woods Too Far Behind . . . Or, Where in the Environment Are We?", in *Seattle Post-Intelligencer*, Northwest Today, 7/26/70.

"Hearing," publication details not shown.

"Hearing Insider," publication details not shown.

The Heaven Makers, New York: Avon, 1968.

"The Heaven Makers," in *Amazing*, April and May, 1967.

"Heisenberg's Eyes," in *Galaxy*, June and August, 1966. (Published in novel form as *The Eyes of Heisenberg*.)

Hellstrom's Hive, Garden City (NY): Doubleday, 1973.

Heretics of Dune, New York: Putnam, 1984.

"Highest UW Grad Merely 'Played Game,' " in *Seattle Post-Intelligencer*, 6/14/70.

"His Bag Is Being a Gentle Savage," in *San Francisco Examiner & Chronicle*, California Living, 7/21/68. (feature on the artist Vargas).

"Ho's Death Could Advance War's End, Says U.S. Aide," in *Seattle Post-Intelligencer*, marked "September 4th."

"Home Again," in *San Francisco Examiner & Chronicle*, California Living, 3/29/70. Also published as "You Can Go Home Again," in *The Maker of Dune*, ed. by Tim O'Reilly, New York: Berkley, 1987.

"How Indians Would Use Fort," in *Seattle Post-Intelligencer*, 3/22/70.

"Ice" (marked "ecology file"), publication details not shown.

"Ice/Insider" (marked "ecology file"), publication details not shown.

The Illustrated Dune, New York: Berkley Windhover, 1978.

"Indian Rights to Alaska Land Emphasized at Land Law Meet," in *Seattle Post-Intelligencer*, 12/8/70.

"Inside/Editor," publication details not shown.

"Institute" (marked "with illustration/Kash—Don E. Kash"), publication details not shown.

"Into V.C. Land," in *Seattle Post-Intelligencer*, 9/30/69.

"Intro/Herbert Collection," pre-publication manuscript.

"Introduction," in *Nebula Winners Fifteen*, Frank Herbert, ed. New York: Harper & Row, 1981.

"Introduction," in *Saving Worlds*, Roger Elwood and Virginia Kidd, eds., New York: Doubleday, 1973.

"Introduction—Tomorrow's Alternatives?" in *Frontiers I: Tomorrow's Alternatives*, Roger Elwood, ed., New York: Macmillan, 1973.

"Introduction," in *Tomorrow and Tomorrow and Tomorrow*, New York: Holt, Rinehart & Winston, 1973.

The Jesus Incident (with Bill Ransom), New York: Berkley, 1979.

"The Jonah and the Jap," in *Doc Savage*, April, 1946.

"Knighthood Re-Flowers in Medieval Marin," in *San Francisco Examiner & Chronicle*, California Living, 9/8/68.

"Land," publication details not shown.

"Land" (marked "with art"), publication details not shown.

"Land of the Instant Native," in *San Francisco Examiner & Chronicle*, California Living, 12/8/68.

"Land Reform" (marked "Memo to Lou Guzzo 8/20/70—*Seattle Post-Intelligencer*), publication details not shown.

"Land Reform Crisis in South Vietnam," in *Seattle Post-Intelligencer*, 8/31/69.

"Land Reform or Civil War (Philippines)," in *Seattle Post-Intelligencer*, publication date not shown.

"Land Reform Enters Week of Decision," in *Seattle Post-Intelligencer*, 10/9/69.

"Land Reform: Vietnam's 'Other War' Can't Wait," in *Seattle Post-Intelligencer*, 9/3/69.

The Lazarus Effect (with Bill Ransom), New York: Putnam, 1983.

"Letter" (marked "Precede/Letter"), publication details not shown.

"Listening to the Left Hand," in *The Book of Frank Herbert*, New York: DAW, 1973.

"The Little Green Car That Could," in *Seattle Post-Intelligencer*, 8/6/70.

"Location of Freeway Signs Confuses Many Motorists," in *Santa Rosa Press Democrat*, 7/19/49.

"Lodge's Goal to Shake Hanoi's Hopes of Victory," in *Seattle Post-Intelligencer*, 10/10/69.

"Looking for Something," in *Startling Stories*, April, 1952.

"Lying to Ourselves About Air," in *San Francisco Examiner & Chronicle*, California Living, 12/8/68.

"Mah-Jong and Changing Chinatown," in *San Francisco Examiner*, 2/21/62.

Man of Two Worlds (with Brian Herbert), New York: Putnam, 1986.

"Market Day; Mexico's Vanishing Bargain Game," in *San Francisco Examiner & Chronicle*, California Living, 11/3/68.

"The Mary Celeste Move," in *Analog*, October, 1964.

"Mating Call," in *Galaxy*, October, 1961.

"A Matter of Traces," in *Fantastic Universe*, November, 1958.

"Medalist" (marked "Sunday—with art"), publication details not shown.

"Men on Other Planets," in *The Craft of Science Fiction*, ed. by Reginald Bretnor, New York: Barnes & Noble, 1976.

"Mendocino" (marked "California Living"), publication details not shown.

"Merry-Go-Round at South End Is a Tough Problem," in *Santa Rosa Press Democrat*, 7/21/49.

"The Mind Bomb," in *If*, October, 1969.

"Mindfield," in *Amazing*, March, 1962.

"Missing Link," in *Astounding Science Fiction*, February, 1959.

"Moratorium," publication details not shown.

"Murder Will In," in *Five Fates*, New York: Warner, 1971.

" 'National Interest' Declining In Youths," in *Seattle Post-Intelligencer*, 6/28/70.

"New Lincoln Bowl Would Aid Girls', Boys' Sports—Goold," in *The Lincoln News*, 9/16/38.

New World or No World, editing and commentary by Frank Herbert, New York: Ace, 1970.

"The Next 100 Years; Overview," in *San Francisco Examiner & Chronicle*, 7/4/76. Also published as "The Sky Is Going to Fall," in *The Maker of Dune*, ed. by Tim O'Reilly, New York: Berkley, 1987.

The Notebooks of Frank Herbert's Dune, ed. by Brian Herbert, New York: Putnam, 1988.

"The Nothing," in *The Book of Frank Herbert*, New York: DAW, 1973.

"Occupation Force," in *Fantastic*, August, 1955.

"Oh, Doctor! Lincoln Has Quintuplets! Williamses, Not Dionnes Baffle Beal," in *The Lincoln News*, 2/14/38.

"Old Automobiles, a Human Skull, Money, Silverware All in Day's Work at the Dump," in *Santa Rosa Press Democrat*, 5/22/49.

"Old Rambling House," in *The Worlds of Frank Herbert*, New York: Ace, 1971.

"Old Volcanoes Can Be Vicious," in *Seattle Post-Intelligencer*, 10/23/69.

"Olson," publication details not shown.

"One of Those Days," published as newspaper article, with publication details not shown. (Published under title, "Frank Herbert: To One Part Verne, Add Galley of Zomb, Drop in Heathcliffe and Expect Occidental.")

"Operation Haystack," in *Astounding Science Fiction*, May, 1979.

"Operation Syndrome," in *Astounding Science Fiction*, June, 1954.

"Opposition Promised On Smelter," in *Seattle Post-Intelligencer* 11/19/69.

"Oregon: Where the Crowds Aren't," in *San Francisco Examiner & Chronicle*, California Living, 4/28/68.

"Origami" (marked "California Living"), publication details not shown.

"Pack Rat Planet," in *Astounding Science Fiction*, December, 1954.

"Panel Explores 'Theology of Earth,' " in *Seattle Post-Intelligencer*, 12/9/70.

"Passage For Piano," in *The Book of Frank Herbert*, New York: DAW, 1973.

"Phone Company Statements of Improvement Expenditures Difficult to Break Down," in *Santa Rosa Press Democrat*, 7/5/49.

"Piaget" (marked "Psycholinguistics; The art of relative thinking; art—not science"), publication details not shown.

"Plywood for Boats," in *Fisherman*, June 1955.

"Poetry," in *The Maker of Dune*, ed. by Tim O'Reilly, New York: Berkley, 1987.

"The Policeman's Cry For Help," in *San Francisco Examiner & Chronicle*, California Living, 1/5/69.

"Poll," publication details not shown.

Preface to *The Dune Encyclopedia*, Dr. Willis E. McNelly, Compiler, New York: Berkley, 1984. (Note: See the website dunenovels.com for a joint statement to fans from Brian Herbert, Kevin J. Anderson, and Dr. Willis E. McNelly concerning the alternate *Dune* universe presented in *The Dune Encyclopedia*, which does not represent the "canon" created by Frank Herbert, or the canon that is continuing to be developed by Brian Herbert and Kevin J. Anderson).

"The Priests of Psi," in *Fantastic*, February, 1960.

The Priests of Psi (anthology), London: Gollancz, 1980.

"The Primatives" (plotted with Jack Vance and Poul Anderson, written by Frank Herbert), in *Galaxy*, April, 1966. (Story also spelled as "The Primitives.")

"Project 40," in *Galaxy*, November 1972 through January 1973. (Published in novel form as *Hellstrom's Hive*.)

"Prophet of Dune," in *Analog*, January, 1965–May, 1965.

"Proposals for Pakistan Social and Economic Justice," in *Seattle Post-Intelligencer*, publication date not shown.

"Pub," publication details not shown.

"Pulse," publication details not shown.

"Put Logical End In Transit Plans, Says U.S. Expert," in *Seattle Post-Intelligencer*, 10/12/69.

"Rah-Rah Declines In College," in *Seattle Post-Intelligencer*, 11/15/69.

"Rain," publication details not shown.

"Rat Race," in *Astounding Science Fiction*, July 1955.

"Realism in the Movie Bullitt," in *San Francisco Examiner & Chronicle*, California Living, 6/2/68.

"Renewed Hope for a Desperate Pakistan," in *Seattle Post-Intelligencer*, publication date not shown.

"Report," publication details not shown.

"Research Headed by Prosterman," in *Seattle Post-Intelligencer*, 8/22/70.

"Riding the Rail: Black Shirt Benito Wins by Final Burst of Speed," in *The Lincoln News*, 9/30/38.

"Riding the Rail: Black Beauty," in *The Lincoln News*, 10/7/38.

"Riding the Rail: Nut Housers Hold Series; Corrigon Runs Wrong Way," in *The Lincoln News*, 10/14/38.

"Riding the Rail: Li'l Abe Says," in *The Lincoln News*, 10/21/38.

"Riot," (marked "memo/insert"), publication details not shown.

"The Rise and Fall of English," in *San Francisco Examiner & Chronicle*, California Living, publication date not shown.

"The Road to Dune," in *Eye*, Byron Preiss Visual Publications, New York: Berkley, 1985.

"Role" (marked "precede/Role"), publication details not shown.

"Rossellini" (Roberto Rossellini), publication details not shown.

"Rules," publication details not shown.

"Rules Hearing on Conduct Opens at UW," in *Seattle Post-Intelligencer*, 6/2/70.

"SST" (Supersonic Transport), publication details not shown.

"SU" (Seattle University), publication details not shown.

"Saigon Forces Earn Low Rating," in *Seattle Post-Intelligencer*, 10/7/69.

"Saigon Worries About Land Reform Future," in *Seattle Post-Intelligencer*, 9/8/69.

"Same Old Music—4,000 Years Old," in *San Francisco Examiner*, 2/6/63.

"A San Franciscan Remakes Texas," in *San Francisco Examiner & Chronicle*, California Living, 5/12/68.

The Santaroga Barrier, New York: Berkley, 1968.

"The Santaroga Barrier," in *Amazing*, October–December, 1967.

"Science Fiction and a World in Crisis," in *The Maker of Dune*, ed. by Tim O'Reilly, New York: Berkley, 1987.

"A Sci-Fi Superstar Says, Play It Again, Sam," in *Pacific Sun*, Week of May 15–21, 1975.

"Security" (marked "California Living"), publication date not shown.

"Seed Stock," in *Analog*, April, 1970.

"Sex: Like Handball, Or Like Pushups?", in *Seattle Post-Intelligencer*, 4/5/70.

"Shooting a TV Ad," in *San Francisco Examiner & Chronicle*, California Living, 8/3/69.

"The Single Most Important Piece of Advice," in *Writers of the Future*, Vol. II, Los Angeles: Bridge Publications, 1986.

"The Small Worlds of UC Santa Cruz," in *San Francisco Examiner & Chronicle*, California Living, 9/22/68.

"Smog" (marked "California Living"), publication date not shown.

"Snoopery," in *San Francisco Examiner & Chronicle*, California Living, 6/8/69.

"Sober Tones At UW Graduation," in *Seattle Post-Intelligencer*, 6/14/70.

"Some Arthur, Some Tolkien," in *The New York Times Book Review*, 4/10/77. (review of *The Sword of Shannara* by Terry Brooks.)

"Songs of a Sentient Flute" (with Bill Ransom), in *Analog*, February, 1979 and in *Medea: Harlan's World*, ed. by Harlan Ellison, Huntington Woods (MI): Phantasia, 1985.

Songs of Muad'Dib—Poems and Songs from Frank Herbert's "Dune" Series and His Other Writings, ed. by Brian Herbert, New York: Ace, 1992. Includes two poems quoted in *Dreamer of Dune:* (a) Untitled Haiku (About Brian), originally published in *San Francisco Star*, Issue 5, November 9–December 2, 1960, p. 4 and (b) "Bev" (previously unpublished). (Note: After publication of this book, Penny Merritt located an additional file of unpublished poems written by our father. Some of the newly discovered poems are quoted in this biography.)

Soul Catcher, Putnam, New York, 1972.

"Speech" (marked "with grads"), publication details not shown.

"Stamps" (marked "Sunday"), publication details not shown.

"Strike," publication details not shown.

"Suicide Prevention Lagging Here, Says National Expert," in *Seattle Post-Intelligencer*, 10/21/69.

"Survival and the Atom," *Santa Rosa Press Democrat*, 1952.

"Survival of the Cunning," in *Esquire*, March 1945.

"The Tactful Saboteur," in *Galaxy*, October 1964. (Also titled, "What Did He Really Mean By That?")

"Taking the Big Mini-Plunge," in *Seattle Post-Intelligencer*, 2/17/70.

"Telephone Company Endeavoring to Improve Service," in *Santa Rosa Press Democrat*, 7/3/49.

"Thieu," (president of South Vietnam) publication details not shown.

"This . . . Or This . . . ," in *San Francisco Examiner & Chronicle*, California Living, 6/8/69.

Threshold: The Blue Angels Experience, New York: Ballantine, 1973.

"Today's Playground Is Tomorrow's World," in *San Francisco Examiner & Chronicle*, California Living, 7/21/68.

"A Tough Look at Viet Land Reform," in *Seattle Post-Intelligencer*, 9/19/69.

"Transcript: Mercury Program," in *The Planets*, Byron Preiss, ed., New York: Bantam Spectra, 1985.

"Transit," publication details not shown.

"Trip" (marked "Northwest Today"), publication details not shown.

"Trip" (marked "precede" and "with art"), publication details not shown.

"Try to Remember!" in *Amazing*, October, 1961.

"Turmoil, Tradition Theme At UW Commencement," *Seattle Post-Intelligencer*, 6/14/70.

21st Century Sub, New York: Avon, 1957.

"2068 A.D.; A Bold Look 100 Years Into an Exciting Future," in *San Francisco Examiner & Chronicle*, California Living, 7/28/68.

"U. Faculty Refuses to Condemn War," in *Seattle Post-Intelligencer*, 11/19/69. (U.: University of Washington.)

"U.S. Aid Set as Viet Flood Threat Eases," in *Seattle Post-Intelligencer*, 9/11/69.

"U.S. May 'Blunder' Into Total Abandonment of S. Vietnam," in *Seattle Post-Intelligencer*, 10/5/69.

"UW Asks Bids on $27-Million Expansion of Medical Complex," in *Seattle Post-Intelligencer*, 12/20/69. (UW: University of Washington.)

"UW Decision on Scott Rankles Many," in *Seattle Post-Intelligencer*, 6/9/70.

"UW Minority Students Given Special Orientation Program," in *Seattle Post-Intelligencer*, 9/24/70.

"UW Notes" (marked "March memo"), publication details not shown.

"(UW) Regents," publication details not shown.

"(UW) Regents Insider" (marked "with art"), publication details not shown.

"UW Regents Approve Stiff Conduct Rules," in *Seattle Post-Intelligencer*, 9/19/70.

"UW Regents, Blacks Talk," in *Seattle Post-Intelligencer*, 3/28/70.

"UW Student Group Disavows Support of Violent Protest," in *Seattle Post-Intelligencer*, 12/4/69.

"UW/Sunday," publication date not shown.

"UW to Spend $160 Million," in *Seattle Post-Intelligencer*, 7/5/70.

"UW—'Wrong University?'", in *Seattle Post-Intelligencer*, 12/2/69.

"Under Pressure," in *Astounding Science Fiction*, November, 1955—January, 1956. (Published in hardcover as *The Dragon in the Sea* and in paperback as *21st Century Sub*.)

"Undersea Riches for Everybody," in *The Maker of Dune*, ed. by Tim O'Reilly, New York: Berkley, 1987.

"Universities Gird for Fall Classes," in *Seattle Post-Intelligencer*, 9/13/70.

"Viet Bird-Dog Flights Eerie, Perilous," in *Seattle Post-Intelligencer*, 9/12/69.

"Viet Cease-Fire: Letter from U.S. Senators" (marked "rewrite/Letter"), publication details not shown.

"Viet Cease-Fire Plan: Disaster," in *Seattle Post-Intelligencer*, 10/4/69.

"Vietnam 'Land Reform Bill' Could Dispossess Thousands," in *Seattle Post-Intelligencer*, 9/10/69.

"Vietnam—Pullout Will Hurt," in *Seattle Post-Intelligencer*, 9/29/69.

"Voting Today on Autonomy," in *Seattle Post-Intelligencer*, 11/25/69.

"Weekend's Search for Church," in *Seattle Post-Intelligencer*, 2/16/70.

"We're Losing the Smog War," in *San Francisco Examiner & Chronicle*, California Living, 12/1/68.

"When Is a Noise a Noise That Annoys?" in *Seattle Post-Intelligencer*, Northwest Today, 8/30/70.

"When Lynch Law Was Invoked: A Story of Sudden Death and Mob Violence in 1920," in *Santa Rosa Press Democrat*, 7/17/49.

"Where Does White House Authority Start and Finish?" in *Seattle Post-Intelligencer*, 9/28/69.

Whipping Star, New York: Putnam, 1970.

"Whipping Star," in *If*, January–April, 1970.

The White Plague, Putnam, New York: 1982.

"Who Runs That Place?: The UW in Focus," in *Seattle Post-Intelligencer*, 5/31/70.

"Who's Left? Right?" in *Seattle Post-Intelligencer*, 3/19/70.

"Wine," publication details not shown.

Without Me You're Nothing (with Max Barnard), New York: Simon & Schuster, 1980.

"Women," publication details not shown.

"Workshop—Group and Individual Dynamics," publication details not shown.

The Worlds of Frank Herbert, New York: Ace, 1971.

"Yellow Fire," in *Alaska Life*, June 1947.

"You Don't Have to Know the Language," in *San Francisco Examiner & Chronicle*, California Living, 9/29/68.

"You Take the High Road," in *Astounding Science Fiction*, May 1958.

The Speeches of Frank Herbert

ABA (American Booksellers Association)

Artificial Intelligence

Change

Don't Buy Death!—(two versions of speech)

Earth Day (1970)

Ecology Solution: Recycle Your Body

Ecology Talk, with Jim Tate (recording—April 11, 1969)

Government

How to Live and Create in a Dune World

Librarian's Association

MIT Paper—Technology
Non-Violence
Prediction and Social Criticism in Science Fiction
Seattle University (1980)
The Tragic Feast: A Symposium on Population (recording of October 27, 1970, talk at Western Washington State College, Bellingham, Washington)
The Universe of Magic

The Herbert Papers (Unpublished)

Includes the correspondence files of Frank and Beverly Herbert, records of construction and plantings at Xanadu, records of construction at Kawaloa, windmill and solar designs, patent and other drawings of Frank Herbert, records from the Kelly Butte honeymoon, travel itineraries, the travel journals of Beverly Herbert, genealogical records, manuscripts, screenplays, photographs, and other files.

The Unpublished Writings of Frank Herbert

"The Abortionist and the Paperhanger"
"The Accidental Ferosslk," publication pending in *The Last Dangerous Visions*, Harlan Ellison, ed.
Angels' Fall (*We Are the Hounds*, working title)
"The Cage"
Circle Times (originally a film treatment, but written like a novel)
"The Curate's Thumb"
The Dune Concordance, compiled by Brian Herbert
Dune 7 (outline and notes)
"Dune" series notes (Frank Herbert's working notes for writing the series)
"The Ferry Godmother" (third in series with published stories "Frogs and Scientists" and "Feathered Pigs")
"Finding Things" (Alternate title: "Oh Say Can You See")
A Game of Authors
"God's 'Helping Hand' Gave Us 5,000 *Amigos*"
The Heat's On
High-Opp
"The Invisible Car"
"The Illegitimate Stage"

"The Iron Maiden"
"A Lesson in History"
"Life with Animalitos"
"The Little Window"
"Look Out!" Also: "Lookout" (with Beverly Herbert)
"Movietown Number Two"
"Paul's Friend"
"The Piñata That Talked"
Poetry of Frank Herbert
"Public Hearing"
Recipes of Frank and Beverly Herbert
"A Stitch in Time"
"Story Ideas of Frank Herbert"
"Survival Is Their Business"
"They Stopped the Moving Sands"
"A Thorn in the Bush"
"The Trial of Renee Truant"
"The Waters of Kan-E"
"Wilfred"
"The Wrong Cat"
"The Yellow Coat"

Screenplays, Film Treatments, and Scripts

Asa West
Dune (by David Lynch, with suggestions from Frank Herbert)
Dune screenplay (by Frank Herbert—not filmed)
Dune Messiah Film Treatment
Dynasty, by Frank Herbert and James Goldstone
Jonathon Ley
More Than Gold, by Frank Herbert and James Goldstone
North Sea to Irish Sea (captions of photos taken on Ireland trip)
Soul Catcher
The White Plague

Films Involving the Works of Frank Herbert

The Hellstrom Chronicle, directed by Walon Green, 1971.

North Sea to Irish Sea, television script by Frank Herbert for c. 1971 Northwest Traveler television episode, hosted by George Carlson.

Threshold: The Blue Angels Experience, directed by Paul Marlow, 1973.

The Tillers television program, produced and directed by Frank Herbert, 1974.

Dune, directed by David Lynch, 1984. (Some versions show the generic director "Alan Smithee," produced by Dino De Laurentiis.)

Frank Herbert's Dune, six-hour television mini-series produced by Richard P. Rubinstein and Mitchell Galin, 2000. (Brian Herbert served as creative consultant, directed by John Harrison.)

Frank Herbert's Children of Dune, six-hour television mini-series produced by Richard Rubinstein and Mitchell Galin, 2003. (Brian Herbert served as creative consultant, directed by Greg Yaitanes.)

Recorded Interviews of Frank Herbert
(Audio, unless nothed otherwise)

Bray, Faustin and Wallace, Brian, "At Home with Bev and Frank Herbert," Dolphin Tapes, August, 1983.

Entertainment Tonight, undated video. King Television, Seattle, "Freedom at the Grass Roots," February 11, 1977.

Ransom, W. M. (Bill), "It's like Swinging Three Bats: Poetry and the Fiction of Frank Herbert"—transcript of 3/3/76 interview.

Today Show, July 29, 1976.

Today Show, undated video.

Other Recordings
(Audio, unless noted otherwise)

Herbert, Brian, Frank Herbert's anecdotes and jokes, May and June 1976.

Herbert, Brian, Frank Herbert's anecdotes and jokes, Thanksgiving 1977.

Herbert, Brian, Interview of Bill Ransom, 3/22/96.

Herbert, Brian, Interview of Howard Hansen, 3/23/95.

Herbert, Frank, "*The Battles of Dune*," Caedmon, 1979.

Herbert, Frank, "*Dune:* The Banquet Scene," Caedmon, 1977.

Herbert, Frank, First wind machine run, May 2, 1978.

Herbert, Frank, "*God Emperor of Dune*," Caedmon, 1981

Herbert, Frank, "*Heretics of Dune*," Caedmon, 1984.

Herbert, Frank, Miscellaneous: Obituary; On *Dune* set; On fishing trip (1984–86 videos).

Herbert, Frank, Pacific Bell commercial, 1985 video.

Herbert, Frank, "*Sandworms of Dune*," Caedmon, 1978.

Herbert, Frank, "The Truths of *Dune* Fear Is the Mind Killer," Caedmon, 1979.

Herbert, Frank, and Bill Ransom, "The Great Secret of Writing"—Bill Ransom's transcript of August 1985 panel discussion.

Herbert, Julie, Christmas 1978.

Simon, Paul (words and music), "Bridge Over Troubled Water," in *Sheet Music Magazine*, November, 1984.

Toto, *Dune* motion picture soundtrack, PolyGram Records, Inc., New York: 1984.

The Published Writings of Beverly Herbert

"Corner Movie Girl," in *Modern Romances*, 1946. Working title: "My Free Lance Date."

Popcorn for Christmas, Montgomery Ward booklet, Phillips & Van Orden, undated.

The Tree from Magic Mountain, Montgomery Ward booklet, Phillips & Van Orden, 1966.

Where Did Mrs. Santa Go?, booklet for The White House store and for Carson Pierie Scott & Co., Phillips & Van Orden, 1962.

The Unpublished Writings of Beverly Herbert

Astrological records

BAH restaurant reviews, 1983.

"Creativity by the Numbers"—1976 article about opus filing system. Alternate title: "The Paper Explosion."

Frighten the Mother, 1955.

"Look Out!" Also:"Lookout" (with Frank Herbert)—1946.

Marked Down for Murder, 1964.

Poetry of Beverly Herbert

Recipes of Frank and Beverly Herbert
Travel Journal, Mexico, 9/17/55–1/11/56.
Travel Journal, Japan, Hong Kong, Pakistan, India, Thailand, Vietnam, Malaysia, Indonesia, 6/23/72–8/11/72.
Travel Journal, Universal Studios, June 1982.
Travel Journal, Germany, France, England, Scotland, 5/28/78–7/17/78.
Travel Journal, Boston, New York: Paris, 2/6/79–2/25/79.

The Published Writings of Brian Herbert

"Afterword" to *Dune: House Atreides,* by Brian Herbert and Kevin J. Anderson, New York: Bantam-Spectra, 1999.
Dune: The Battle of Corrin, by Brian Herbert and Kevin J. Anderson, New York: Tor Books, forthcoming (2004).
Dune: The Butlerian Jihad, by Brian Herbert and Kevin J. Anderson, New York: Tor Books, 2002.
Dune: House Atreides, by Brian Herbert and Kevin J. Anderson, New York: Bantam-Spectra, 1999.
Dune: House Corrino, by Brian Herbert and Kevin J. Anderson, New York: Bantam-Spectra, 2000.
Dune: The Machine Crusade, by Brian Herbert and Kevin J. Anderson, New York: Tor Books, forthcoming (2003).
The Forgotten Heroes, by Brian Herbert, New York: Tor Books, forthcoming (2004).

The Unpublished Writings and Edited Works of Brian Herbert

Banquets on Dune
"Brian's Mexico Book," 1953.
The Client's Survival Manual
The Dune Concordance, compiled by Brian Herbert.
Family Journal, 1978–1986.
The Frank Herbert Companion, ed. (with Penny Merritt). Alternate title: *The Frank Herbert Fan Letter Book.*
On Company Time

Public Records

Burley (WA) Cemetery records.
Criminal Case: The People of the State of California v. Joseph A. Daugherty, Crim. No. 5366, Case #3008.
Daugherty Case—Also described in *Santa Rosa Press Democrat*, 5/15/52, 5/23/52, 5/30/52, 6/2/52, 6/5/52, 6/6/52, 6/20/52, 8/3/52, 10/17/52, 12/2/52, 12/19/52.
Kitsap County (WA) Historical Society records, including:
    Anderson, Cathryn, "Burley, Peninsula Gateway, 10/13/50."
    Anderson, Margaret Kay, ed., "The Co-operative Colony at Burley, Kitsap County."
    Carlson, Larry A., "A Short History of the Cooperative Brotherhood—Burley, Washington."
    "From the Account Book."
    Granger, Patricia, "The Co-operative Colony at Burley, Kitsap County, Wash."
    Interviews of H. W. Stein, Mrs. Mary Corporan and Mr. L. M. Fenton.
    Legal records of Burley Colony.
    Stein, Katherine and Son, "Burley."
    Marriage Records, Birth and Death Certificates, Military Records, School Records.
U.S. Census—1900, Seattle and Tacoma, WA.
U.S. Census—1910, Ollala Precinct, Kitsap County, WA.

Other Published Sources

Albright, Thomas, *Art in the San Francisco Bay Area 1945–1980*, Berkeley: University of California Press, 1985.
Allen, L. David, *Herbert's Dune & Other Works*, Lincoln (Nebraska): Cliff's Notes, 1975.
Andersen, Soren, "Dune," in *The News Tribune* (Tacoma, WA), 12/7/84.
Andrews, Paul, "Sand Dollars," in *The Seattle Times*, 12/18/84.
Anonymous, "1984—The Year of Dune," in Berkley/Putnam catalog-brochure, 1984.
Anonymous, "Sidelights" on Frank Herbert for a *Who's Who* publication, undated.
Arnold, William, "Dune," in *Seattle Post-Intelligencer*, 12/14/84–12/20/84.
Banham, Rayner, "Dunesaga," in *New Society London*, 8/28/69.
Baumgart, Don, "It Has No Name," *Earth Times*, July 1970.

Furry, Eric, "Frank Herbert—The Real Emperor of Dune," in *Sweet Potato*, 6/16/81.

Godley, A. D., ed., *The Poetical Works of Thomas Moore*, London and New York: H. Frowde, 1910.

Goodrich, Norma Lorre, *The Medieval Myths*, New York: Mentor, 1961.

Gorman, John, "Sherpas Keep on Trekking Across the Roof of the World," in *The Seattle Times*, 9/22/84.

Granberg, Bill, "Burley," in *Seattle Post-Intelligencer* Pictorial Review, 1/26/64.

Gregg, Rodman, ed., *Who's Who in the Motion Picture Industry*, Beverly Hills (CA): Packard House Books, 1989.

Griffin, Nancy, "Raffaella," in *Life*, November 1984.

Gunn, James, *Alternate Worlds*, Englewood Cliffs (NJ): Prentice-Hall, 1975.

Gunn, James, "Inner Concerns in Outer Space: The Real and the Surreal," in *Fantasy Newsletter*, January, 1982.

Guthman, Edwin, "Correspondent Got Bum's Rush," in *The Seattle Times*, 5/23/84.

Guthrie, Jim, "A Way of Asking Questions," in *The Daily News*, Port Angeles (WA), 3/4/80.

Hamilton, Edith, *Mythology*, New York: Mentor, 1953.

Hansen, Keith, "Neuberger Serene as Belated Returns Change Defeat to Victory," in *The Oregonian* (Portland), 11/7/54.

Hartl, John, "New chapter in 'Dune' film saga," in *The Seattle Times*, 2/3/79.

Hartl, John, " 'Dune,' " in *The Seattle Times*, 5/29/83.

Hartl, John, " 'Dune'—Hit or Miss?", in *The Seattle Times*, 12/2/84.

Hartl, John, "Spell-binding 'Dune' Is Like No Other Sci-Fi," in *The Seattle Times Tempo*, 12/14/84.

Hartl, John, "Movies of '84: Best to Worst," in *The Seattle Times*, 12/30/84.

Hayakawa, S. I. (with Pillard, Basil H.), *Language in Thought & Action*, New York: Harcourt Brace, 1949.

Heward, Bert, "Messiah, 'System' Fight for Future in Herbert World," in *The Citizen* (Ottawa), 3/3/78.

The Holy Bible (New International Version), Grand Rapids (MI): Zondervan, 1985.

Hunt, Sir John, *The Conquest of Everest*, New York: Dutton, 1954.

Jakubowski, Maxim and Edwards, Malcolm, *The SF Book of Lists*, New York: Berkley, 1983.

Kelley, Dennis, "Frank Herbert: A Science Fiction Messiah," in *View of Puget Sound*, May, 1979.

Kitsap County Historical Society Book Committee, *Kitsap County History*, Seattle: Dinner & Klein, 1977.

Kyle, David, *A Pictorial History of Science Fiction*, London: Hamlyn, 1976.

Landgraf, Susan, "Worlds Apart" and "The Road to Disaster," in *Journal American* (Bellevue, WA), 7/1/80.

Lash, Joseph P., Eleanor and Franklin, New York: Signet, 1971.

Leimbacher, Ed, "Frank Herbert: The Ecology of Survival," in *Fusion*, 5/29/70.

Letteier, Carolyn, "Frank Herbert: Science Fiction Author Dies, 'Dune' Series Ends," in *Port Townsend Leader*, 2/19/86.

Levack, Daniel J. H. (compiler) and Willard, Mark (annotatator), *Dune Master— A Frank Herbert Bibliography*, Westport (CT): Meckler, 1988.

Levine, Paul G., "The Worm Turns for Sci-Fi Writer," in *Los Angeles Times*, 5/11/79.

LeWarne, Charles Pierce, *Utopias on Puget Sound 1885–1915*, Seattle: University of Washington Press, 1978.

The Lincoln News, Lincoln High School (Tacoma, WA), 2/4/38, 2/18/38, 3/4/38, 3/18/38, 3/25/38, 5/13/38, 5/27/38, 9/16/38, 9/23/38, 9/30/38, 10/7/38, 10/14/38, 10/21/38, 11/4/38, 12/2/38.

Lincolnian yearbooks—1936, 1937, 1938, Lincoln High School (Tacoma, WA.)

Lowe, Robert K., "Loneliness," in *Thanatos,* Spring, 1987. (Quotes from "Depression and Immunity," in *The Harvard Medical School Mental Health Letter*, October 1986.)

Lucia, Ellis, ed. and commentator, *This Land Around Us: A Treasury of Pacific Northwest Writing*, New York: Doubleday, 1969.

MacGougan, Denny (column), in *The News Tribune* (Tacoma, WA), 5/6/77.

MacKenzie, Pete, "Science Fiction Master Frank Herbert," in *View Northwest*, July 1977.

Maltin, Leonard, ed., *TV Movies*, New York: Signet, 1982.

Marshall, John, "Lessons Learned From Teacher's 'Show and Tell,' " in *Seattle Post-Intelligencer*, 4/11/84.

Martin, D. R., "Frank Herbert & *Dune*: Giving Readers Their Money's Worth," in *Twin Cities Reader* (Minneapolis, MN), 4/22/77.

McCready, Al, "Greater Flair for Publicity . . . ," in *The Oregonian* (Portland), 11/7/54.

McDowell, Edwin, "Behind the Best Sellers," undated newspaper clipping, c. 1981.

Mead, Eileen, "Science Fiction Writer Herbert Concerned Environmentalist," in *Port Townsend Leader*, Summer 1974.

Miller, Ron, " 'Environment' Messages Via Fiction Works," in *San Jose Mercury News*, 8/2/70.

Naha, Ed, *The Making of* Dune, New York: Berkley, 1984.

The New York Times Film Reviews (1983–1984), New York: Times Books & Garland Publishing, 1988.

Nicastre, Michael, *Dune Coloring Book*, New York: Grosset & Dunlap, 1984.

Ognibene, Peter J., *Scoop: The Life and Politics of Henry M. Jackson*, New York: Stein and Day,1975.

O'Hanlon, Tom, "The First Billion Dollar Flick?", in *Forbes*, 11/5/84.

O'Reilly, Tim (ed. and writer), *The Maker of* Dune, New York: Berkley, 1987.

O'Reilly, Timothy, *Frank Herbert*, New York: Frederick Ungar, 1981.

Pagels, Elaine, *The Gnostic Gospels*, New York: Random House, 1979.

Pement, Jack, "Top Sci-Fi Writer Started at Journal," in *Oregon Journal*, 6/12/77.

Petersen, Clarence, "Herbert's solution: Get Out of this World," in *Chicago Tribune*, 5/4/82.

Pintarich, Paul, "Dune Creator's Sci-Fi Story Almost Made Paper's Page 1," in *The Oregonian* (Portland), 2/19/86.

Pyle, Jack, "Did 'Star Wars' Steal Plot from 'Dune'?", in *The News Tribune* (Tacoma, WA), 8/7/77.

Pyle, Jack, "Sci-fi Author Hits Jackpot," in *The News Tribune* (Tacoma, WA), 2/2/79.

R. L. Polk & Co. city and county directories for various years, Seattle, Tacoma, Bremerton and Kitsap County (WA), Portland (OR).

Raglan, Fitzroy (Lord Raglan), *The Hero*, Westport (CT): Greenwood, 1975.

Randall, Katherine, *Dune Puzzles-Games-Mazes-Activities*, New York: Grosset & Dunlap, 1984.

Reuven, Ben, "The Dunes Sayer: Turning a Prophet," in *Los Angeles Times*, 4/25/76.

Rigdon, Walter, ed., *The Biographical Encyclopaedia & Who's Who of the American Theatre*, New York: James H. Heineman, 1966.

Robertson, Ian, ed., *Blue Guide—Ireland*, London: Ernest Benn, 1979.

Robertson, Michael, "How Science Fiction Changes the Future," in *San Francisco Chronicle*, 4/28/82.

Roethke, Theodore, *Words for the Wind*, Seattle: University of Washington Press, 1981.

Ronck, Ronn, "It's the End of the World—and the Beginning of a Novel," in *The Sunday Star-Bulletin & Advertiser* (Honolulu), 9/5/82.

Rovner, Sandy, "The Myth-Master of Dune," in *The Washington Post* Style section, undated newspaper clipping, c. 1981.

Rozen, Leah, "Pages," in *People Weekly*, 6/25/84.

Rumley, Larry, " 'Dune' Author Says He Writes Future History," in *The Seattle Times*, 5/29/81.

Rumley, Larry, "The Author of 'Dune' Writes Science Thriller," in *The Seattle Times*, 9/29/82.

Rumley, Larry, "Heretics of Dune," in *The Seattle Times*, 4/11/84.

Sammon, Paul M. (writer and editor), *The Dune Reader*, Volume One, Number One, c. 1983.

Sammon, Paul M., "David Lynch's *Dune*," in *Cinefantastique*, September, 1984.

Sanborn Insurance Maps (for Tacoma, WA, 1912–1930), New York: The Sanborn Map Co.

Schulman, J. Neil, "Creator of 'Dune' Ecstatic with Film Version," in *San Antonio Light*, 9/22/84.

Shakespeare, William, *Macbeth*, Chicago: Henry Regnery, 1949.

Shakespeare, William, *Richard II*, quoted in *Bartlett's Familiar Quotations*.

Shoemaker, Mervin, "Battle for Senate Seat Tightens as Campaign Nears Finish," in *The Oregonian* (Portland), 11/1/54.

Shoemaker, Mervin, "GOP Holds Post-Mortem on Reasons for Defeats," in *The Oregonian* (Portland), 11/7/54.

Silver, Diane, "Author Foresees Change," in *Michigan State News* (East Lansing, MI), 4/11/75.

Silverman, Maida, *Dune Activity Book*, New York: Grosset & Dunlap, 1984.

Silverman, Maida, *Dune Cut-Out Activity Book*, New York: Grosset & Dunlap, 1984.

Solow, Michael, "Frank Herbert: 'Dune' to Eugene and Back," in *Livingwell* (Eugene, OR), 12/2/77.

Sowa, Tom (column), *The Spokesman-Review* (Spokane, WA), 9/11/77.

Staff Correspondents:

"A Woman of Grace," in *Retail Advertising Week*, 7/9/84.

"Author's Wife Finds Life a Partnership," in *Port Townsend Leader*, 4/21/77.

"Ballot Boxes Put Under Guard," in *The Oregonian* (Portland), 11/4/54.

"Big Colony Comes In," in *The Tacoma Daily Ledger*, 11/18/1898.

"The Bomb Killer," in *The Shipbuilder*, Los Angeles Shipbuilding & Drydock Corp., March, 1942.

"Buys Hearse for Journey to Old Mexico," in *The News Tribune* (Tacoma, WA), 9/4/55.

"Crater Honors Writer," in *Seattle Post-Intelligencer*, 9/18/71.

"De Laurentiis Floats Big 'Dune' Offering," *Variety*, 11/7/84.

"Dune Author Herbert Writes Sci-Fi for Earth Lovers," in *Berkeley Barb*, 7/30/76–8/5/76.

" 'Dune' Premiere Dec. 11 to benefit GHC Foundation," in *Group Health Cooperative View*, GHC of Puget Sound, Seattle, November 1984.

"E. T., Phone 'Dune,' " in *Newsweek*, 12/24/84.

"Early Count Finds Winner Almost Ready to Concede," in *The Oregonian* (Portland), 11/4/54.

"For a United Colony," in *The Tacoma Daily Ledger*, 3/8/1899.

"Frank Herbert, Creator of Worlds," in *The News Tribune* (Tacoma, WA), 2/13/86.

"Frank Herbert Part II," in *Northwest Passage*, 2/4/74–2/18/74.

560

"Frank Herbert Revealed," in *Locus*, July, 1984.

"Future Grok," *Time*, 3/29/71.

"Highway to Open Rich Territory" and "Highway to Touch Historic Ground," in *The News Tribune* (Tacoma), 6/25/25.

"How Socialism and Co-Operation Are Progressing at Burley Colony," in *The Tacoma Sunday Ledger*, 5/20/1900.

"Libraries—Atmosphere for Spirited Imagination," in *Port Townsend Leader*, 1/27/77.

" 'Looking Backward', at Burley 'Dream' Colony," in *The Tacoma Sunday Ledger*, 8/5/40.

"Massive 'Dune' Promo Includes Book & Department Store Tie-Ins," in *Variety*, 11/21/84.

The New York Times, 2/13/83.

"On the Co-Operative Plan," in *The Tacoma Daily Ledger*, 12/14/1898.

"Pleasure in Quilting," in *The Bremerton Sun*, 12/23/35.

"Putnam Launches Promo for Dune-Related Titles," in *Publishers Weekly*, 5/4/84.

The Salt Lake Tribune, 8/4/85.

"Science-Fiction Author Wants 'Future Shock' Not Historical Cliches," in *Port Townsend Leader*, 12/25/75.

"Sidney's Comet," review in *Publishers Weekly*, 4/29/83.

"Star Chamber—Frank Herbert," in *Galileo—Magazine of Science Fiction*, 1978.

Stardate, October 1985.

" 'Star Wars' Taken from Him?" in *The Spokesman-Review* (Spokane, WA), 9/4/77.

Sundancer, October 1977.

"30,000 Hear Performers, Politicians in Earth Day Rally in the Park," in *The Philadelphia Inquirer*, 4/23/70.

This Week at K&B, 5/29/81.

"Time Capsule Recounts Life at Burley Colony," in *The North Peninsula News*, Kitsap County, WA, 5/17/89.

"Under Uncle Sam's Eye," in *The Tacoma Daily Ledger*, 11/29/1898.

"Visit to the Colony," in *The Tacoma Daily Ledger*, 5/22/1899.

"Votes Cast on 'Class,' Economic Lines Credited for Election of Neuberger," in *The Oregonian* (Portland) 11/7/54.

Stanley, Don, "Me and History," in *Sacramento Bee*, 12/15/84.

Stanley, Susan, "Science Fiction Seer Hunts 'Possible Future History,' " in *Oregon Journal*, 3/16/77.

Stone, Pat, "The Plowboy Interview—Frank Herbert," in *The Mother Earth News*, May/June 1981)

Tewkesbury, Don, " 'Dune' Author Strikes It Rich," in *Seattle Post-Intelligencer*, 2/2/79.

Thouless, Robert H., *Experimental Psychical Research*, Baltimore: Penguin, 1963.

Touponce, William F., *Frank Herbert*, Boston: Twayne, 1988.

Turner, Paul, "Vertex Interviews Frank Herbert," in *Vertex*, August, 1973.

Tyson, Virginia, "Frank Herbert: Man in the Dunes," in *Los Angeles Times*, 8/31/84.

Unger, Jeffrey S., "Frank Herbert—'Dune' Author a Busy Man," in *Dallas Times Herald*, 6/29/84.

United States Navy, *The Bluejackets' Manual*, Annapolis: U.S. Naval Institute, 1940.

Untermeyer, Louis, *A Concise Treasury of Great Poems*, Ontario: Pocket, 1968.

Van Hise, *The Secrets of Frank Herbert's Dune,* New York: Simon & Schuster, 2000. (includes DVD produced by Michael D. Messina).

Velasco, Dorothy, "What Does the Future Hold? Some Thoughts . . . ," in *Northwest*, 1/15/78.

Vinge, Joan D., *The Dune Storybook*, New York: Putnam, 1984.

Wakeman, John, ed., *World Film Directors, Vol. II, 1945–1985*, New York: H. W. Wilson, 1988.

Wallace, Irving, Amy and Sylvia and Wallechinsky, David, *The Book of Lists # 2*, New York: Morrow, 1980.

Washington State Patrol, *Washington State Patrol, 1921–1981*, Marceline (MO): Walsworth, 1983.

Watson, Emmett (column), in *Seattle Post-Intelligencer*, 10/3/72, 9/18/73, and 6/12/74.

Weiner, Ellis, *National Lampoon's Doon*, New York: Pocket, 1984.

Weiner, Steve, "Science Fiction 'Invades' Business Minds," in *The Seattle Times*, 5/31/78.

West, D. J., *Psychical Research Today*, Penguin Books, 1962.

Westbeau, Georges H., *Little Tyke*, Pacific Press, 1956.

Westervelt, William D., *Hawaiian Legends of Ghosts and Ghost-Gods*, Rutland (VT): Charles E. Tuttle, 1963.

Westervelt, William D., *Hawaiian Legends of Volcanoes*, Rutland (VT): Charles E. Tuttle, 1963.

Whole Earth Catalog—Spring, 1969, Berkeley (CA): Portola Institute.

Wieneke, Constance, "Science Fiction Author Testing New Wind Machine," in *Port Townsend Leader*, 11/9/78.

Williams, Paul, "A Visit with Frank Herbert," in *Ariel, The Book of Fantasy*, Vol. 3, ed. by Thomas Durwood, Kansas City: *Ariel Books, 1978.*

Wingrove, David, "Frank Herbert," Vector 88, July–August 1978.

"Wings Interview: Frank Herbert," in *Better Wings and Gardens*, Jan.–Feb. 1979.

Winokur, Scott, "Looking at Earth Cyclically," in *Oakland Tribune*, 3/22/77.

Wirsing, Dale, "Sci-fi Writer Set for Movies," in *The News Tribune* (Tacoma, WA), 10/24/75.

Index